THE KING'S WAR
1641-1647

THE
GREAT REBELLION

THE
KING'S
WAR

1641-1647

C. V. WEDGWOOD

COLLINS
ST JAMES'S PLACE, LONDON

FIRST IMPRESSION 1958
SECOND IMPRESSION 1959
THIRD IMPRESSION 1964
FOURTH IMPRESSION 1967
FIFTH IMPRESSION 1974
SIXTH IMPRESSION 1978

ISBN 0 00 211404 6

© C. V. WEDGWOOD 1958

Made and printed in Great Britain by
William Collins Sons & Co Ltd, Glasgow

CONTENTS

CONTENTS

BOOK THREE
BETWEEN WAR AND PEACE
OCTOBER 1645–JANUARY 1647

LIST OF ILLUSTRATIONS

ILLUSTRATIONS

LIST OF MAPS

MAPS IN APPENDIX

MAPS IN THE TEXT

FOR JAQUELINE

INTRODUCTION

The King's War covers five years in the reign of King Charles I, from the attempt on the Five Members in January, 1642, to the handing over of the captive King by the Scots to the English in January, 1647. I have tried to do justice to the many interlocking events and themes of these years—the strife in Scotland between Covenanters and Royalists, the national and religious revolt of Ireland, as well as the English war, and the emergence out of religious speculation and social disorder of a new and powerful popular movement.

This book, like its predecessor *The King's Peace*, is a narrative history, a description of what happened, and *how* it happened, which often by implication answers the question of *why* it happened. Thus the demand for greater freedom of religion, for a wider distribution of political power, for more equal justice and greater opportunities for all men grew naturally out of the physical experiences of war. Theory and doctrine are more often the explanation of actions already envisaged or performed than their initial inspiration.

Not all the developments of this epoch are so clear to the observer as this theme of social revolution. The story of the war is immensely complicated and, as in *The King's Peace*, I have tried to tell it in such a way as to bring out the hourly urgency and confusion through which contemporaries lived. This is not the clearest way of telling the story. But a lucid simplification of the Civil War with significant incidents dramatically lighted would not, to my mind, add anything to our understanding of it. It would also be false to the facts for there was very little either simple or lucid in the developments of these troubled years, and the historians' choice of significant incidents is often different from that of contemporaries. The siege of Gloucester for instance is seen by historians and was also felt by contemporaries to be a turning point; but the creation of the New Model Army and the passing of the Self Denying Ordinance, on the other hand, were moves which might or might not have been successful, were paralleled at the time by the reorganisation of the King's army, were greeted by contemporaries with mixed attention and could only be seen in their full significance as the years went by.

In the Civil War political, military and economic events reacted constantly upon each other, so that to simplify and to separate them is essentially to falsify. The fighting was often unco-ordinated and incoherent, owing to the difficulties of communication and the local interests of commanders and their men. Events in one part of the country repeatedly influenced events in another, so that the war cannot be imaginatively understood without some idea of its infinite territorial ramifications. I have deliberately included many lesser local incidents that Gardiner, in his longer book, passed over. The intention is not to burden the reader with hundreds of details that he cannot possibly remember; much that I have included here (as also in *The King's Peace*) is not in itself memorable and is not meant to be precisely remembered. A painter covering a gigantic canvas does not expect the spectator to register and identify accurately all the secondary figures and background details, but they may none the less enhance the general impression that he is trying to convey. So in this book, as also in its predecessor, I have tried by the inclusion of many incidents and many people to recapture the variety of a vanished epoch and, in this book more especially, to indicate the strain of conflicting ideas, demands and personalities, the anxieties, surprises, fluctuating hopes, and continual confusions of war. I have purposely postponed a summing up of the economic and social effects of the war to the beginning of the next volume which will be devoted to the struggle between Army and Parliament, and within the Army itself.

Several great historians have already told this story, and no one who has worked seriously in the seventeenth century can fail to respect the perception of Leopold von Ranke, the steadfast industry of Gardiner, and the vision of Dr. G. M. Trevelyan— to whose encouragement I owe so much. But there would be no point in re-telling the story on lines laid down by these great predecessors. My account is essentially my own and was constructed in its earlier stages out of the numerous collections of public and private documents in which the seventeenth century is so rich, and out of the vivid and voluminous pamphlet literature of the war. As the book took shape it became apparent from my notes as they stood that I was describing the war rather as the defeat of the King than as the victory of Parliament. I did not struggle much against this tendency. For one thing the military story has been more often told from the Parliamentary angle and there was a certain novelty in treating it more fully from the other point of view; furthermore this way of telling seemed to me to bring out much more clearly the tension and expectancy of a conflict whose outcome was for long uncertain. To follow Cromwell is, so to speak, to ask the reader to bet on a certainty: neither writer nor reader can easily forget his ultimate achievement or put themselves in a position to doubt the coming victory of Parliament's forces. To follow Rupert is to catch at the excitement and despair of near victory and final defeat. I believe also that Cromwell did not, even at the end of the first Civil War, loom quite so large in the eyes of contemporaries as our *ex post facto* knowledge has made him do. I am aware that his stature at the end of this book will seem to many less impressive than might have been expected, but it was not until the crisis between Army and Parliament in 1647 that his formidable powers became fully apparent, and of that I hope to write in my next volume.

Once again I would like to express my gratitude to the

Institute for Advanced Studies at Princeton where much of this book was written. I am by this time indebted to so many friends and colleagues that I have tried to express my thanks for help and enlightenment at the relevant places in the " Notes and References" rather than in general terms here. I would however like to indicate my special indebtedness to the late Mr. G. M. Young for suggestions and ideas on many subjects, going back over many years; to Professor J. H. Hexter for his elucidation in *The Reign of King Pym* of the management of Parliament during the first critical eighteen months of the war, and to Professor William Haller who in his *Liberty and Reformation in the Puritan Revolution* has mapped as no one else has done the highways and byways of the immense Puritan religious and political literature of the sixteen forties.

BOOK ONE

FROM PEACE TO WAR

November 1641—April 1643

CHAPTER ONE

LONDON LOST

November 1641—January 1642

WHEN King Charles came home from Scotland in the autumn of 1641, London was bright with hangings and the fountains ran wine. The November day was overcast and the highway beyond Moorgate was ankle deep in mud, but planks had been laid down to prevent the Royal coach from sticking and to save the shoes of the eminent citizens who had come to welcome their sovereign on his return from Scotland. The Queen and her children met him at Theobalds, and Charles reached the city limits at ten in the morning of November 25th with his wife, his three eldest children, his nephew and the Duchess of Richmond in one cheerful coach load.

The Recorder of London made a speech of welcome to which the King cordially replied. He affirmed his resolution to maintain the liberties and the true Protestant religion of his people, and he assured the Londoners that he would restrict the privileges which protected his courtiers against arrest for debts owed to tradesmen, and would restore to the City their forfeited estates in Ulster as soon as the present rebellion in Ireland should be put down. He concluded by knighting the Lord Mayor and the Recorder; then, mounting his horse, he rode on with his eldest son into the City. The Queen and the rest of the party followed by coach.

Guards of honour provided by the City Companies lined

the streets; the citizens, heartened by the claret which was running from the fountains, leaned over the railings which had been put up " for the advantage of the show " and cheered loud and long. After banqueting at Guildhall, the King and his family continued the homeward journey, past the south door of St. Paul's, where the choir hailed them with an anthem, down the Strand to Whitehall, the citizens lighting them all the way with flaming torches.

Such difficulties as the Lord Mayor had experienced from those who resented the expenditure and disapproved of junketing —from John Venn, for instance, one of the members of Parliament for the City—did not appear on the surface. The welcome confirmed the King in his belief that, when it came to a trial of strength between him and his Parliament, the City would support him. Convinced that he had won over the Scots and no less sure that he could command London, he did not doubt that the time had come to outwit and overthrow that " juggling junto " of his enemies at Westminster, led by John Pym.[1]

He was right at least in this: the crisis of his reign had come. In essence it was very simple: a straightforward contest for power between him and his opponents in Parliament. Logically his seventeen years of action and aspiration as a reigning King had carried him to this moment. He had ruled always in the assured belief that God had chosen him for his high and holy office. He knew it his duty to ensure to his realm justice, peace, civil order and true religion, and he earnestly believed that he, and he alone, was the God-directed judge of the acts and policies by which these benefits could be secured. In this he was not original, but held only with supreme faith to doctrines evolved by the political writers of his time. " The King is the head of the Commonwealth, immediate under God, and therefore carrying God's stamp and mark among men, and being as one may say, a God upon earth, as God is a King in Heaven."[2]

Finding his first three Parliaments obstructive and critical he had resolved to call no more. He had been deceived—for he was easily deceived—into thinking himself successful because of the tranquillity which for several years lapped his Kingdoms. But his enforcement of uniformity in religious worship offended some of his subjects and his intervention in the regulation of commerce interfered with the material interests of others. He increased his revenues by an agreement with Spain to transport bullion for the payment of their troops in English vessels, and by this bound his country to the Spanish-Imperial party in Europe, who in the earlier years of his reign had been remarkably successful in restoring great parts of Germany to the Roman Catholic faith, and had dispossessed the King's own brother-in-law and driven him to die in exile. This foreign policy distressed the Protestant subjects of King Charles and hampered their colonial expansion in regions dominated by the Spaniard. At home, too, the King's Government fell short of the ideals which inspired it. He lacked the ability and the industry to bring his practice into recognisable relationship with his theory. He made too little use of his ablest ministers—the Archbishop of Canterbury and the Earl of Strafford—and his council degenerated from the centre of government to the centre of intrigue for profit and place.

In 1638 the Scots rebelled rather than accept the new order of church worship which he designed for them. The revolt took him by surprise. His English Parliament, briefly called to vote money for a Scots war, refused to do so: this also surprised him. The Scots utterly defeated him, and had to be paid to go away; to raise the money he was compelled to call Parliament again in November 1640. This new Parliament was led by John Pym, a man already in his fifties, born and bred in the Elizabethan age, strong in his Protestant religion and in the conviction that England could and should challenge the mastery of Spain and invade her colonial empire. Pym and his following in the Commons attacked the King at every vulnerable point. He had at first no choice but to retreat before the onslaught. He abandoned his two ablest and least popular ministers—

Archbishop Laud to the Tower, Strafford to the block. He agreed never to dissolve this dangerous Parliament except by its own consent. He passed legislation which destroyed the prerogative courts, the Crown's chief instrument for enforcing policy.

In those first months of what was later to be called the Long Parliament the King had been generally unpopular. But as he still made concessions and the Commons still made demands, many of his subjects experienced a revulsion of feeling. They saw the King harried as no King within their memory had been harried, and they doubted the wisdom and good faith of his opponents. There was, for one thing, too much persecution of those who had served the King in his days of power, persecution undertaken—so it began to be rumoured—not from the cleanest motives. Thus Sir Roger Twysden, once a critic of the royal policy, now complained that Parliament " did not so much seek to redress things amiss as to spend time in setting out the miseries we lay under, or quarrelling at offenders, or indeed at any man almost that had gotten an estate in these times."[3]

If the King had exercised too much power in the past, Parliament exercised too much in the present. The House of Commons sent out orders to Justices of the Peace, and empowered them to imprison those who refused to give information which Parliament required. These innovations troubled the conservative, while the studied mildness of the King convinced even some who were most bitterly opposed to his views that he had recognised the errors of his past career and would henceforward prove a judicious and generous ruler. A Puritan divine, Calybute Downing, after frankly comparing the persecution recently endured by the Puritans to that which had caused the Protestant Low Countries to revolt against Philip II, predicted that all would end in peace and amity because of " the universal Love of his Majesty's royal person, the confidence of his absolute justice " and the desire of all to serve him " upon new endearing obligations."[4]

By the late summer of 1641 the King had once more a certain popularity on which to build, while his opponents faced a growing distrust. The time was ripe for Charles to make his counter-attack. He believed in the holy character of his Kingly office, and could not therefore permit the curtailment of his power by Parliament to become permanent. He had made no concession (except the irretrievable sacrifice of Strafford) that he did not intend to withdraw. He worked out his future strategy not only to prevent fresh encroachment on his rights, but to outflank the Parliamentary position and recapture all that he had lost. With this end in view (and he was bound in faith and honour to want no less) he took steps to make for himself a party within Parliament, and to gain, or regain, the support of Scotland and of the City of London.

In the late summer and early autumn of 1641 he was in Edinburgh where, mistakenly believing that all men can be won by favours, he set up a Government consisting of his one-time enemies, on whom he showered offices and titles so that they would—he trusted—henceforward regard his interest as their own.

Two vital parts of his authority in England were still untouched. He had the right to choose and appoint his own councillors and chief officers of state, and he had the supreme control over the armed forces of the realm. In time of peace these consisted only of the Trained Bands, but in any national emergency it lay with him to raise and organise an army.

In October 1641 while he was still in Scotland, the emergency came. His Roman Catholic Irish subjects rose in revolt. They feared, and had every reason to fear, that the triumph of a Puritan Parliament in England would bring more repressive measures against their religion and further seizure of their land by Scottish and English settlers. Sweeping across the country and driving the settlers from their homes, they proclaimed their intention of restoring the King to his rights and asserted that they had his royal warrant for what they did.

The Irish rising precipitated the crisis. An army had to be created to suppress it, but many in the English Parliament doubted whether the King (for whom the Irish claimed to fight) could be given control of an army. The King for his part was equally determined that no one but himself should have power over any forces officially raised in his dominions. The Irish rebellion was therefore to Pym the signal for an attack on what remained of the royal power, and the message sent by the English Parliament to the King about measures to be taken against the Irish rebels contained the request that in future he would appoint no councillors save those approved by Parliament. At almost the same time in the House of Commons Oliver Cromwell, one of Pym's most reliable supporters, made a direct attempt to dictate the King's military appointments by moving that the Trained Bands in the south of England be placed under the Puritan Earl of Essex.

The King left Edinburgh on November 18th, 1641. During the week of his journey to London John Pym and his following secured in the House of Commons, by a narrow majority, the passing of the Grand Remonstrance, which condemned, in detail and at length, the King's policy in Church and State, at home and abroad, throughout his reign. Its purpose was to demonstrate beyond question that the King was unfit to choose his own councillors or to control his own army. The Remonstrance was carried by eleven votes at one o'clock in the morning of November 23rd, 1641. The King's supporters who tried to enter a protest were shouted down in a tired, ill-tempered tumult. Oliver Cromwell on leaving the House was heard to say that, had the Remonstrance been rejected, he would have sold all he had and gone overseas to America; so clearly did the supporters of John Pym recognise the significance of the political battle of which the Remonstrance was the opening cannonade.

II

When the King re-entered his capital two days later the full-throated welcome accorded him by the Londoners seemed to drown the midnight snarling of the Commons at Westminster. The King himself, with cheerful confidence, adopted his own tactics in the political battle by ignoring the Remonstrance which had been intended to draw his fire. He made no official visit to parliament, and, on the slight pretext of a sore throat, withdrew to the greater tranquillity of Hampton Court. The outcry of the Londoners, bereft of Court custom in the merry-making winter season, did not at first reach his ears. He had other things to occupy him and spent much of his time in private with the Earl of Bristol and his son Lord Digby.

Since the opening of the session, these two had adroitly guided the King's supporters in the Upper House, against the heavy-moving Lord Mandeville who was Pym's closest ally among the peers. They had aroused the resentment of a number of peers against Pym and his following and had influenced the Upper House to object to the recent demand from the Commons that in future, to prevent the choice of " evil councillors," the King should be compelled to submit his choice of ministers to Parliament.[5]

During the next weeks the King continued to rely on Bristol and Digby to further his interests in the House of Lords. Bristol was no more than a willing servant whom he did not greatly like, but George Digby rapidly became a friend and favourite. He was just under thirty years old at this time, fair-skinned, fair-haired, blue-eyed, " a graceful and beautiful person." His darting wit and fluent tongue, his elegant manners, cultivated mind and gay self-confidence endeared him to the King. He was by nature sanguine and subtle, not a downright liar but apt to withold or embellish the truth to suit himself. The King was dazzled by the ingenuity of his schemes and uplifted by the buoyant optimism with which he overleaped obstructions.[6]

Digby had friends and admirers in the House of Commons, chief among them Edward Hyde and John Culpeper, men who had supported Pym when Parliament first met but had since come to doubt his wisdom and, still more, his honesty. Both had opposed the Remonstrance. With these two was associated the gentle Lord Falkland, Hyde's especial friend. This intelligent and upright man—" of a wit so sharp and a nature so sincere that nothing could be more lovely "—was too great a lover of truth to look kindly on Digby's failings, but his disapproval did not prevent Digby from urging on the King the good use that could be made of all three to forward his interests in the House of Commons. The suggestion was not new. It had been the policy of the Court for over a century to use the councillors and servants of the sovereign to initiate and expedite in Parliament measures desired by the Crown, and to check any opposition which might arise. Under Elizabeth this system had been very highly and efficiently developed, but it had fallen into neglect, or at least had been very inadequately managed under the Stuart Kings. In none of King Charles's Parliaments had he been competently represented and supported by his own servants, and in the first session of this present Parliament he had been abandoned or betrayed by some of them. Secretary of State Vane had been frankly an instrument of Pym and not of his master the King; in the Lords his chief councillors, the Earls of Northumberland, Holland, and Pembroke had, actively or passively, abandoned him. Pym had secured the expulsion from the Commons, on one ground or another, of several courtiers and dependents of the King who might otherwise have served him. Throughout almost the whole of the first session of the Long Parliament Charles had been without organised support in Parliament, a situation which would have been dangerous even for a stronger and less vulnerable monarch, and which was disastrous to him.

He was now considering the means by which it could be remedied. Edward Nicholas, the most loyal and the most experienced of his secretaries, was in touch with Hyde and his friends. In due course, by elevating moderate-minded and respected men like these to offices of State, the King might recreate the instrument which had been allowed to decay, and have once again an organised group in Parliament to forward the policies of the Crown.[7]

The outlook was not hopeless. The stormy passage of the Grand Remonstrance had revealed a deep division in the House between those who were prepared to challenge the King to the uttermost, and those who feared further encroachments on sovereignty and distrusted the motives of John Pym. If Charles could deepen the rift in the Commons, if he could deepen also the growing rift between Lords and Commons, if he could then through his friends and spokesmen regain the initiative which Pym had seized and retained, he might at last be able to strike at his enemies in Parliament from a position of strength.

John Pym clearly saw the danger. He had succeeded so far in his attack on the King's policy and position by foreseeing every move that Charles would make and taking action to forestall it. He had not merely taken the initiative out of the King's hands, he had planned his Parliamentary tactics with a forethought and skill more ingenious, more unscrupulous, and in the event more successful than anything that had been practised before. The King's friends, and those who had in the last months been wooed to his side, were not the equal of Pym and his adherents in this dexterity and were more inclined to condemn than to imitate it. Hyde later wrote of Pym's tactics with distaste; this " thorough considering and forming their counsels " before they began to execute them seemed to him only a degree less vicious than their deliberate policy of defaming the King's friends, and of alternately bribing or intimidating their feebler colleagues in the House. Honest men, thought Edward Hyde, " would hardly give themselves leave to use those weapons for the preservation of the three Kingdoms."[8]

In his own estimation John Pym's task was indeed no less than the preservation of the three Kingdoms. In his view, and in that of his principal associates, the managing of Parliament, the propagation of every rumour of Irish or Popish plots, and the insinuation that the King was involved with the plotters were justified by the extreme danger of the situation. It might be disloyal to hint that the King had a secret understanding with the Irish rebels, but it was by no means unreasonable to fear that he had. When the Protestant Scots had revolted in 1638 he had proclaimed them traitors within a week, but more than a month after the Irish rose he had still made no pronounce-ment against them. Their leaders—Phelim O'Neill and Rory M'Guire in the North, Lord Muskerry in the South—persistently claimed that they had the royal warrant for what they did.[9] The Earl of Antrim and Lord Dillon, Roman Catholic Irish lords of influence, had at different times in the last months before the rebellion been in close attendance on the King. Two years earlier Charles had wished to use Antrim's Irish clansmen against the rebel Scots. Ever since the previous April he had tried by every available means to create or secure an army for his own purposes. It was possible that he contemplated using the Irish rebels themselves as such an army; it was more than possible that he would in the end turn any army raised to subdue the Irish against his recalcitrant subjects nearer home.

This was the danger as Pym saw it, and it was not imaginary. The King might make conciliatory statements to win the services of the honest men in Parliament whose support he needed, but this was a tactical trick to strengthen his position. At Court he encouraged the braggart young soldiers who surrounded his wife, and neither he nor his Queen left foreign ambassadors in any doubt that they intended to re-establish their authority by force at the first possible moment.[10]

Edward Hyde and his friends in the Commons were deceived

by the manœuvre. They interpreted the King's overtures to them as the welcome sign that he was ready for settlement, and deplored the intransigence of Pym because they thought he was jeopardising a sane and moderate agreement between King and Parliament on the basis of the legal reforms already achieved. They did not at this time realise that the King wanted no agreement on that basis, and it did not occur to them that he had gained them to his side only to make use of them in his coming struggle to overthrow not only Pym but all the restraining legislation to which he had been forced to consent during the last session of Parliament. Intelligent as Hyde and his friends were in their political theories, they failed to grasp the nature of the situation within which they were actors. Moderation and compromise is always, ideally, better than violence, but it postulates conditions which, in the autumn of 1641, did not exist. Those who advocated and pursued a policy of agreement between King and Parliament were in the event cheated by the King and repudiated by Pym. Hyde and Falkland may justly be respected for their ideals and pitied for their misfortunes, but they cannot justly be praised for their political judgment. King Charles and John Pym more accurately saw that no solution was now possible except by force or fraud: no equilibrium could ever be established between this King and this Parliament.

The King was over-confident. John Pym made no such mistake. He guessed the King's projects and knew his weaknesses. He had his informers at Court, though they were hardly necessary, so careless was the behaviour of the King's friends. Moreover the Parliamentary Commissioners, who had been sent to report on the King's actions in Scotland, had reassured Pym on their return that any hopes the King had of help against his Parliament from that quarter were a delusion.

Pym knew the King's weakness, but he also knew his own. He could no longer rely on a majority in the House of Commons. He was well aware that many who, a year before, had supported his attack on the royal government, on Strafford, on the prerogative Courts, on Ship-money and on monopolies had now grown doubtful and suspicious. It was undeniable that Pym and his chief supporters had by now made themselves " so obnoxious and guilty " to the King that they could never feel safe from his vengeance if he were allowed to regain his ancient power. This circumstance weakened their moral position by making it possible to interpret all their actions henceforward as the outcome of culpable fear and political expediency.[11]

Furthermore, in the summer of 1641, when so much urgent Parliamentary business was agitated at home, the Spaniards had landed in force on Providence Island in the Caribbean and utterly wiped out the English settlement there. John Pym was Secretary of the Providence Company; the principal shareholders were all leaders of the opposition to the King—the Earls of Warwick and Holland, Lord Saye, Lord Brooke and John Hampden. It was not four years since they had sunk another hundred thousand pounds in the enterprise. The association between these men in politics and in commerce was not fortuitous: the same Protestant-Puritan sea-roving tradition that made them attack the King for oppressing the Puritans at home and favouring Spain abroad, had impelled them to this private venture against the Spaniard in the Caribbean. During the long years of King Charles's personal rule they had used the business meetings of their company to discuss the means of checking royal policies which they saw as fatal alike to the spiritual and material welfare of their country. But the past significance of the foundered Providence Company was at present of less moment than the position and prospects of its shareholders. There had not yet been time fully to estimate the disaster but the liabilities of the Company were heavy and its assets few. While Parliament continued to sit, its members were privileged against arrest for debt. The malicious would certainly be willing to believe that Pym and Hampden had very strong personal reasons for wanting Parliament to continue indefinitely.[12] Insinuations of this kind had power to injure the reputation of John Pym and his chief supporters and weaken their hold on the doubtful in the House of Commons.

The Grand Remonstrance had been carried by one hundred and fifty-nine votes to one hundred and forty-eight. A motion put forward by Geoffrey Palmer that the minority should enter a protest had been so furiously shouted down by the majority that a riot had almost broken out. On the day of the King's entry to London, Palmer was voted to the Tower for his incautious conduct by one hundred and sixty-nine votes to one hundred and twenty-eight. But a further motion that he be expelled altogether from the House of Commons was defeated by a hundred and sixty-three votes to a hundred and thirty-one.[13]

The hundred and twenty-eight who voted throughout in Palmer's favour were the solid body of the King's supporters; the hundred and thirty-one who voted throughout against Palmer were the equally solid body of Pym's men. But in a House which at that time mustered only about three hundred, the shifting fears and sympathies of the odd forty could sway the issue. Of the numerous absent members, who had orders from the King to return to the House within the next few weeks, the majority were no friends to Pym. They were, as their continued absence showed, the puzzled, the indolent and the conservative. Pym was very well aware of his need to force the issue with the King before the absentees came up to Westminster.

III

The division of Parliament between the supporters and the opponents of the Court had long been a fact but the political ideas of the epoch gave no official countenance to the idea of party divisions. Parliament, the great Council of the Realm, was in theory a single, united body, comparable, according to one contemporary writer, to the seamless robe of Christ.[14]

Geoffrey Palmer was sent to the Tower for provoking division in the House—as though such division did not already exist without any provocation from him. A few days later Dr. Chillingworth, whose book on *The Religion of Protestants* had earned him the royal favour some years before,[15] observed to a lawyer friend in Clements Inn that, although Palmer was in trouble now, it would not be long before " some of the other side " were accused of treason. On a report of these words, Chillingworth was sent for to the House of Commons. He denied that he had spoken of treason, but that did not remove the offence; he had, in referring to " the other side " implied that Parliament was divided into two parties. For this innocent reference to the true state of affairs Chillingworth followed Palmer to the Tower.[16]

So long as no one admitted that two sides could properly exist within one political body, it was natural for Pym to assume that his group was the " true party of the Commonwealth " and his opponents a mere faction, bent on destroying the unity of the nation's councils. The Royalists in Parliament, for their part, thought the same of him. Much later in the century it was still possible for a statesman to say that a political party was " only a kind of conspiracy against the rest of the nation." In 1641 the more thoughtful leaders on each side naturally assumed that their policy was in the interests of all, while that of their opponents was a conspiracy of self-interested men.

Pym faced a difficult problem in the House of Commons, with his reduced and threatened majority. The problem of the House of Lords was no less troublesome, for Bristol was now marshalling the Royalist peers, in opposition to the Puritan group of whom Lord Mandeville had in the last months become the principal organiser. The able and influential Northumberland, it was true, seemed now wholly to have abandoned his allegiance to the Court. As Lord High Admiral of England, he could bring valuable help to Pym and his party but he remained an incalculable ally, one who might or might not help, as his lofty spirit moved him. The King for his part could always count on the support of the Bishops, whose ranks, recently thinned by death, it was believed he would soon strengthen with some well-chosen younger men. To deal with this menace, Pym had introduced at the opening of the session a bill to abolish the votes of the Bishops in Parliament, but this bill and any further measures to curtail the powers of the Crown might well be extinguished in the Upper House.

The maintenance of Parliament's power against the Crown might—must—depend ultimately on force. Twice before the end of November Pym's spokesmen had made a move to take military appointments into their own hands. Only a few days after Oliver Cromwell's motion that the Earl of Essex be made general of all forces South of the Trent, William Strode moved that a bill be framed for the defence of the Kingdom. Such a bill, if drafted by Pym's party, would remove altogether from the King the control of the armed forces. Over such a bill, if no sooner, the expected clash must come.

In the rapidly approaching crisis between the King's party and Pym's the removal of the Bishops from political power would play a central part because their vote, while they retained it, could block Pym's measures in the House of Lords. Pym, helped by the Puritan members for the City of London, would inevitably rouse up against the Bishops those same shouting apprentices and mariners who had, in the previous summer, hastened Strafford to the block. But the King, who firmly believed that respectable Londoners were now on his side, took measures to outwit the rabble-rousers. The approaches to the Houses of Parliament had been guarded for the last months by companies from the London Trained Bands commanded by the Earl of Essex—soldiers friendly to the London boys and a commander friendly to John Pym. Charles now replaced this guard with a company picked from the Westminster Trained Bands under the command of the Earl of Dorset.[17] On paper this was represented as a gracious gesture for the safety and honour of Parliament. In fact, it placed in the approaches to the House soldiers who disliked or despised the Londoners and officers who, being Westminster men, were friends and dependents of the Court. The King had smoothly won a key position.

Rumours that violence was intended to the House of Commons had begun even before this change of guard. On the day of the King's joyous entry, those in the City, of the opposite faction, believed that the Royalists might attack Parliament, and bestirred themselves to prevent them. Mrs. Venn, whose husband, a Trained Band captain and one of the City's representatives in Parliament who had strongly opposed the demonstrations of welcome to the King, sat weeping and wringing her hands in a neighbour's shop. She had it for sure that the House of Commons was surrounded and her husband in danger to be slain, but a valiant grocer, alternately brandishing a pistol and tapping his sword-hilt, consoled her with promises of vengeance.[18]

In the following days apprentices encouraged by Puritan masters, and glad enough of an excuse to ramble down to Westminster, congregated outside the Parliament House shouting " No Bishops " as loudly as, a day or two before, they had shouted "God Save the King." On November 29th they found to meet them not the Puritan pipe-smoking Earl of Essex and their good neighbours of the London Trained Bands, but the haughty Earl of Dorset and the smart lads of Westminster spoiling for a fight. In the ensuing rough and tumble the London boys were thrown out of the precincts with more injury to their pride than their persons.[19]

On the news of the tumult the Royalists in the House of Commons, led by Edward Hyde, demanded an inquiry into the cause of the trouble. The apprentices, they accurately averred, had infringed Parliamentary privilege by their threatening behaviour. The Royalist attack was well-conceived but Pym's friends turned their flank. By all means let there be an inquiry, argued Sir Symonds d'Ewes: let the Committee already in existence to investigate the various rumoured Popish plots also investigate the conduct of the apprentices. He knew that this Committee, dominated by Pym and his associates, could be trusted to shelve any awkward evidence put forward by the King's friends to show that Pym, Venn or any other city member had inspired the trouble.[20] Meanwhile, in ever increasing numbers, the apprentices continued their visits to Westminster " yawling and crying ' No bishops! No bishops! ' "[21] For the time being they were allowed to shout. The moment had not yet come for a trial of strength.

Methodically the King consolidated his position. He dismissed Sir Harry Vane from his place as Secretary of State and relieved the Earl of Holland of his seat on the Privy Council, thus removing from his immediate surroundings two instruments of his Parliamentary opponents. But neither he nor the Queen did anything to keep their secrets from the beautiful unscrupulous Countess of Carlisle, who was in close touch with Pym, and whose brother the Earl of Northumberland stiffly opposed the King in the House of Lords. In Vane's place, the King made the trustworthy Edward Nicholas Secretary of State, although the fact that he had no seat in Parliament lessened his usefulness. It was rumoured that he intended shortly to raise the Earl of Bristol and Lord Digby to important places at Court and in Council. Meanwhile he re-created Strafford's forfeited title and bestowed it on his young son, thus making it as clear as daylight that he revered the memory and valued the services of the great minister whom Pym had forced him to send to the block in the spring. " The good party is tottering," wrote an anxious friend of Parliament.[22]

The King's dispositions were observed with anxiety by two foreign diplomats—the Marquis de La Ferté Imbault whom Richelieu had sent to keep watch on the unfolding situation, and the Baron van Heenvliet who came from the Prince of Orange. Heenvliet was sincerely concerned for the welfare of the King and Queen to whose eldest daughter the Prince of

Orange had rashly married his only son; for their own sake, and for that of the House of Orange, Heenvliet wished to see them surmount their present difficulties and establish once again a stable and popular government. But he doubted the wisdom of the counter-attack which they were now so busily mounting, and even more their capacity to carry it out with success. The cautious reception which he gave to their frequent confidences was however entirely lost on them.

La Ferté Imbault was in a different position. His first duty was to look after the interests of France, which were not necessarily the same as those of the Queen. France was at war with Spain by land and sea; this was the policy of Cardinal Richelieu and King Louis XIII. But King Charles in the days of his power had consistently supported Spain in the European conflict and his Queen had given what sympathy and help she could to the Court factions in France which opposed the Cardinal and plotted his overthrow, often with help from Spain. In these circumstances it was very questionable whether the French Government desired to see King Charles and his wife fully restored to power. Naturally neither Richelieu, Louis XIII nor La Ferté Imbault wished to see a French princess humiliated and insulted by the English people, but the enthusiasm they felt for avenging her wrongs was moderated by their distrust of the foreign policy which she and her husband had pursued during their years of power. The intention of La Ferté Imbault was therefore to dissuade the King and Queen from any rash attempts to regain power, to work for conciliation with Parliament, and in the meantime to cultivate the friendship of Pym so that his party might be favourable to France.

Many of John Pym's Puritan supporters could see no difference between French Papists and Spanish Papists. Their suspicion and animosity was shared by the London rabble and the people of the coastal towns. After all, the French had been national enemies and rivals for much longer than the Spaniards. False rumours of French invasion were as frequent as those of

Spanish invasion, and Pym was willing enough to countenance them along with other sinister tales which discredited the King and Queen. But he himself and the better informed men of his party had a firm enough grasp of European politics to know that France was the major power in opposition to Spain, that French diplomacy was more concerned to outwit the Spaniard than to serve the interests of Queen Henrietta Maria, and that the overtures of La Ferté Imbault were therefore to be encouraged. He made himself useful, too, for he was much about the Court and very willing to maintain relations with the King's opponents by passing on anything of interest that came to his knowledge.

IV

Pym's insulting Grand Remonstrance had failed of its intended effect. He had expected that Charles would answer it immediately on his return from Scotland, and by so doing provide new occasion for an attack on his councillors and his policy. But Charles deceived expectation. The days went by and he took no notice of the Remonstrance. After a week, the Commons had to force the issue by asking permission to present it to him, together with a petition against his " evil councillors." At dusk on December 1st after a day's hunting the King received the deputation at Hampton Court, listened to their petition with an occasional half jocular interjection, said that he would answer the Remonstrance in his own time and meanwhile requested them not to publish it.[23] Next day he visited Parliament to give his consent to the Tonnage and Poundage Bill; he made no direct allusion to the Remonstrance, referred reproachfully to the disturbed state of London, and concluded: " I seek my people's happiness, for their flourishing is my greatest glory and their affections my greatest strength."[24]

Graciously as he spoke, the King did not fully appreciate the closeness of the connection between the flourishing of his people and their affections towards him. Economic distress, whatever its cause, makes a Government unpopular and a people apt to riot. London in the winter of 1641 was in distress. The King's critics had been able, for the last year, to attribute this to the royal policy: the monopolies, projects and patents of the courtiers had hampered trade; the seas had been insufficiently patrolled against pirates and interlopers; during the wars against Scotland the King had tried to seize the bullion in the Mint and had appropriated an enormous cargo of pepper from the East India Company—manœuvres which did not create confidence. Paying off the victorious Scots had been expensive and now the revolt of the Irish was swallowing up English investments in Ireland. The Londoners could easily enough be persuaded to debit their troubles, however unjustly, to the King's account. The enthusiasm with which they had welcomed him home—processions are always popular—had been damped by his tactless withdrawal to Hampton Court. Though royal spending at Christmas was not likely to bring prosperity back to the City, its absence would cause annoyance out of proportion to the real damage. Soon Sir Richard Gurney, the loyal Lord Mayor, appeared at Hampton Court with a deputation of aldermen imploring the King to return. Charles agreed to do so and graciously knighted the whole party.[25]

It was not within his power to apply any better remedy to the distress of the capital. The causes lay deeper. Dutch interloping in the fisheries, Dutch competition in the Indies and the expansion of the Dutch carrying trade pressed hard on English maritime commerce; the continual war in Europe interrupted the foreign markets for English wool; and the obviously unstable condition of English politics was said to have caused the withdrawal of foreign capital from London.[26] The substantial merchants of London were not at one in their political feelings. Only a minority were convinced supporters of John Pym; others were indifferent to, or puzzled by, the political quarrel though willing enough to support the King if by so doing peace and calm could be restored once more; others again were genuinely devoted to the King. The election of the Royalist, Richard Gurney, as Lord Mayor had reflected the waning popularity of Parliament in the summer and early autumn. But it was beyond the power of the Royalist merchants to curb the demonstrations of excitable apprentices or of the cold and hungry poor in a time of general depression. Coal was dear and scarce owing to the damage done by the Scots to the Newcastle mines; in the great river ships lay idle, and on the quaysides and in the estuary hamlets, stevedores and mariners faced a hungry winter. Apprentices were better off, for they lived in their masters' houses, but slack trade meant idle hands. In the fields south of the river the people congregated, murmuring about religion, politics and the badness of the times; an officious constable who tried to disperse one such crowd was badly manhandled;[27] they were in an angry mood and it would be easier, during the next few weeks, for Pym and his friends to raise the Londoners than for the Lord Mayor to maintain order.

A new element came into this troubled situation before the end of November. A printer issued a small quarto pamphlet, cumbrously titled *The Heads of Several Proceedings in this present Parliament*. It was a brief summary of the past week in Parliament and was followed punctually at intervals of seven days by further bulletins. To the informed few, this was no new thing in itself. Manuscript summaries of debates had been compiled in earlier Parliaments by practised scriveners for those who paid for them. But, when the abolition of the Star Chamber court relieved printers of the fear of prosecution for rash political statements, several of them gratified the news hunger of the public and the vanity of members of Parliament by issuing, in authentic or pirated forms, any speeches they could lay hands on. From this it was an easy step to issuing weekly bulletins of happenings at Westminster. Officially Parliament disapproved, and the breach of privilege was denounced in debate and in committee, but in practice it served the interests of Parliament well enough that the public should be informed, and no action was taken except when it suited the policy of the dominant party to do so. The occasional confiscation and burning of a news-sheet by the public hangman was a risk that printers were willing to take for the brisk sales and brisk profits that the times offered them.[28]

One weekly journal did not satisfy the demand. Within a few weeks rivals appeared. They warned their readers against each other, claiming that one only was authentic, the rest vile counterfeits. But soon they gave up warning the public and wooed it instead—offering as time went on more news, prettier headings, woodcut decorations, shorter and more attractive titles: *Diurnal Occurrences*, *True Diurnal Occurrences*, and in time a whole flight of *Mercuries*. Within two months of the sudden prolific birth of the English Press, one enterprising printer was publishing an Edinburgh edition only a few days behind his London issue.[29]

The close-printed octavo sheets were passed from hand to hand, were read aloud in ale-houses and brought out to illustrate points of argument, were packed into carriers' carts to keep country readers informed of what went forward in the capital. Soon they would give ammunition to both parties; at first they helped only the Puritan-Parliament side whose news alone they printed. Not for many months did the King recognise the value of this new weapon and his move to re-establish his authority during the ensuing weeks was conducted without the assistance of the Press.

After removing the Earl of Essex and his troops from the approaches to Westminster and purging his Council of Holland and Vane, the King felt strong enough to challenge Pym in the Commons, and the apprentices in the streets, by announcing the appointment of new bishops. Several bishoprics had long stood vacant, among them the Archbishopric of York. In filling these, Charles tried to please his moderate friends. The elevation of new bishops made it clear that he would not countenance any reformation of the Church which abolished them; but the character of the men he put forward suggested that he was ready to abandon the hated innovations of Archbishop Laud. Joseph Hall, who as Bishop of Exeter had consistently shielded his more Puritan clergy,[30] was translated to the difficult see of Norwich in East Anglia. The other elevations and translations all suggested a conciliatory policy. Most remarkable of all was the raising of the long disgraced John Williams, Bishop of Lincoln, to the Archbishopric of York.

The subtle, loquacious Welshman had now experienced every vicissitude of fortune. He, who had been extruded from the Royal Council for an abuse of trust, condemned for perjury, suspended from his episcopal functions by Archbishop Laud, and imprisoned in the Tower, found himself now primate of England, and for a brief, stormy moment the principal architect and guardian of the tottering Anglican Church. He had enormous misplaced confidence in his own judgment and he probably had a confidence as great and as ill-founded in the help of his friends. He was related to John Hampden and on good terms with Warwick, Mandeville and Saye. During the previous summer he had been on the Committee appointed for the reform of the Church and had been active in drawing up an abortive bill for curtailing the powers of the ecclesiastical courts. Now he trusted that his feud with Archbishop Laud and his temperate attitude towards the Laudian innovations would be a passport to favour with the multitude, who had certainly cheered him loudly when, on the collapse of Laud's policy, he had been released from the Tower.

The multitude had short memories, and for those with longer memories the critics of the Anglican Church had polemists to destroy the reputation of John Williams. A venomous pamphlet called *Two Looks Over Lincoln* suddenly appeared to remind thoughtful Protestants of the book which Williams had written some years before on the eastern position of the

Communion Table. *Holy Table: Name and Thing* had seemed
moderate indeed at the time of its publication and had greatly
annoyed Archbishop Laud. But the cautious text, combed
through by a malicious Puritan, yielded much that could be made
to look Popish, and seemed all the worse for its insinuatingly
moderate manner. [31]

The unfortunate Joseph Hall, in spite of his mildness to the
oppressed Puritan clergy, was also the object of pamphlet
controversy. He had, at the King's command, published a
defence of Episcopacy, a well-mannered and temperate book
which had been savaged a few months previously by a pack of
Puritan clergy under the collective pseudonym of Smectymnuus.
The paper warfare round and about the views of Smectymnuus
is remembered to-day because John Milton was drawn into it.
What chiefly mattered, in this December of 1641, was that it
had caused the moderation of Bishop Hall and his good offices
towards the Puritan clergy to be quite forgotten.

The pamphleteering only hastened the progress of a disease
already past cure. The new appointments in the Church might
have been better (though it is hard to see how) or they might
have been much worse; but Pym's following in Parliament
objected to any further appointments until the controversy over
Church government was settled, and the apprentices were
ready to shout " No Bishops " at the twelve apostles.

In the days following John Williams's elevation to the see of
York the crowds thickened about Westminster. The apprentices
were joined by others, mariners and dock-hands from the idle
quay-sides, hawkers and journeymen among whom trade and
work was slack:

> The oyster-women locked their fish up
> And trudg'd away to cry " No Bishop."

Vainly the Lord Mayor tried to quell the demonstrators;
vainly he published a Royal declaration calling on masters to
keep their apprentices at home. He succeeded only in rousing

the King's opponents. Substantial citizens joined the daily procession to Westminster, giving countenance in their coaches to the pedestrian rabble. A monster petition for the exclusion from the House of Lords of all Bishops and Popish peers was being prepared. It was said to be twenty-four yards long and to have fifteen thousand—or by some accounts—twenty thousand signatures. Apprentices cheerfully threatened to cut the throats of any who refused to subscribe to it.[32]

In his house at Blackfriars, where visitors from the Court were few and troubled, the King's painter Sir Anthony van Dyck lay dying. He had recorded the luminous, tranquil years that Whitehall would not see again. His sun clouding over, he yielded to the fever which extinguished him at the height of his powers and the meridian of his life. Men of dimmer vision and clumsier hands would record the worried faces of the coming decade.[33]

In the midst of the din, King Charles came back to Whitehall. He was not afraid, but he knew that the next week would be critical. Very soon now violence must meet violence in the streets of Westminster, but he did not believe that the misled rabble and a handful of rebellious members in the House of Commons could get the better of organised military force with the Royal authority behind it. The essential thing for the King was to choose the right moment to strike, when his enemies should have put themselves in the wrong; then, a swift movement from his guards could be made to coincide with a veering of public opinion in his favour.

Pym and his friends foresaw and dreaded just such a movement; so much was evident from the propositions for controlling the armed forces that they continued to put forward in the House of Commons. Following up the motions already made by Cromwell and Strode, Sir Arthur Haslerig on December 7th presented a bill for placing all military and naval appointments under the direct control of Parliament. After a debate in which the King's friends, headed by Sir John Culpeper, vehemently

called for the rejection of the measure, the Militia Bill passed its
first reading, by a hundred and fifty-eight votes to a hundred and
twenty-five. [34]

Pym's majority showed a slight increase over earlier critical
divisions. But the House was still very empty and when Charles,
a few days later, sent out a new proclamation commanding the
return of all absent members by the second week in January,[35]
it was clear that he counted on having a majority as soon as the
summons should have been obeyed. It was also clear that he
would postpone the critical decision between himself and his
opponents, if possible, until that majority was assured. For Pym,
therefore, it was of paramount importance to precipitate the
critical clash before the middle of January.

On December 9th three Royalist members, Wilmot, Ashburnham and Pollard were expelled for their part in the Army
plots of the previous summer. Next day one of Pym's party
reported a rigmarole of rumours from Whitehall: " one familiar
at Court had on Saturday last said that there should shortly be
a great change in this Kingdom; it should be seen whether a
King or no King; that the King had now the stronger party in
the City of London; that there should be shortly a change of
great officers . . ."[36] Such was the volubility of the King's
wilder followers that the report was very possibly true. The
Commons had barely digested it when Sir Philip Stapleton,
another active supporter of Pym, announced that two hundred
halberdiers had appeared in Westminster Hall, not by any order
of the House. It turned out, on inquiry, that they had been sent
along by a Middlesex Justice of the Peace who believed he was
carrying out the King's instructions in taking precautions against
possible riots. He had heard that a crowd of ten thousand people
were bringing the London petition against bishops to Westminster.
The Commons reprimanded him for an interfering busybody
and sent him to the Tower. The London Petition was subsequently presented by a small and orderly deputation, a move
on the part of its organisers well calculated to make the two

hundred halberdiers and those who sent them look like fools, or worse.[37]

The King continued to march boldly towards the crisis, confident that it would reveal the weakness of his enemies. For him the London petition with its forced signatures was no just indication of his people's views. Loyal Anglicans, imitating the tactics of their opponents, could do as well or better at procuring signatures. Petitions in favour of the bishops reached Parliament from Huntingdon and from Somerset; the latter claimed fifteen thousand signatories. Others were being organised in Nottinghamshire, Cheshire, Gloucestershire and Dorset.[38]

Testing the situation, the King gave order that the Common Prayer, already neglected and abandoned in many parishes, be read throughout England once more, without omission or change. He believed that the ignorant self-appointed prophets who swarmed everywhere had by this time proved to his subjects the dangers of religious licence. He was not wholly wrong. Respectable citizens resented the pretensions of cobblers and basket-makers to show them the way to Heaven, and were annoyed when one of the former scrambled into the pulpit of St. George's, Southwark, and would not be dislodged. Men of grammar school education heard with derision that Latin was " the language of the Beast," and grew tired of hearing the illiterate insult respectable clergymen as " Priests of Baal." Exalted spirits who declared that " the dividing of time " had come according to the prophecy of Daniel, and that the rule of the saints was at hand—meaning their own rule—met with decreasing attention. Irreverent disorder during services and wanton destruction of Church furniture caused offence to orderly people who began to question the supposed reformations; some who a few months ago had despised the Common Prayer as a mere cooked-up porridge or pottage might now be brought to agree with the Anglican divine who preached a sermon to show that this same despised pottage was " very well seasoned and crumbed with the Bread of Life." [39]

Outside London the King's order was received with calm, even with relief. "God bless His Majesty, we shall have our old religion settled again," said the good people of Dover—some of whom not so long before had been trooping to hear a prophetic stone-mason expound the scriptures.[40] Even in London the apprentices, after shouting "No Bishop" all the week, spent their Sundays hounding the sectaries. They broke into the house of the most prominent of them, the leather-seller Praise God Barbon, silenced his eloquence and beat up his congregation. Next they fell upon a wild-eyed fanatic who had interrupted the service at St. Sepulchre's Church and dragged him—still loudly preaching—before the Lord Mayor.[41]

These attacks in no way indicated a slackening of anti-Popish feeling, which burst forth in the most unlikely quarters. The French ambassador, whose services to Pym and his party depended on his maintaining some kind of credit with the Court, had persuaded the Commons to desist from protest when the King reprieved seven priests lying under sentence of death. But the other condemned men in Newgate rioted, locked themselves in and refused to be hanged unless the Fathers were hanged along with them—a sentiment of which the rabble, who soon came to hear of it, warmly approved.[42]

This situation had not been resolved when the King, on December 14th, came in state to the House of Lords, not—as had been long expected—to answer the Remonstrance, but to ask with some asperity for an end to unnecessary disputing and a hastening of supplies to Ireland. He had heard, he said, of a Bill for the regulation of the militia which involved the diminution of his prerogative. Let it be understood that the needs of Ireland could no longer wait. He would pass the Bill only if a *salvo jure* were added to safeguard his own rights and those of his people, and so postpone this quarrel until his subjects in Ireland could be relieved.[43]

V

The King spoke the bare truth. By every favourable wind appeals from the Council in Dublin reached Westminster, each one increasing the number of troops and the sum of money which must instantly be sent. The last despatch announced that the Roman Catholic population of the English Pale had joined the revolt, and set the minimum demand for help at two thousand cavalry, twenty thousand infantry and two hundred thousand pounds in money, as well as arms.[44]

The wretched Government in Dublin had hitherto suffered only defeat. A force of six hundred men—mostly refugees from Ulster—had been hurriedly armed and marched out to the relief of Drogheda, but as they were scrambling up the steep and muddy bank of the little river Nenny at Julianstown, the Irish, with blood-curdling shrieks, swooped upon them out of the mist. They fled to a man, leaving their arms for the enemy to gather up. Within ten miles of Dublin a chieftain of the Byrnes, a veteran soldier from the Spanish army, had made a strong encampment whence he raided all the country round, drove off the cattle and burnt the houses of the English. Kilkenny lay open to plundering hordes; all the Earl of Ormonde's cattle had been driven off by the Irish; refugees camped out in every room, stable and stairway of his great Castle, where his Countess, with praiseworthy calm, organised sewing for the women, lessons for the children and rations for all.[45]

In Galway, Lord Clanricarde, the greatest man in the district, remained scrupulously loyal to the administration in Dublin, but they refused to send him arms because he was a Roman Catholic. He had to watch helplessly while active young men, whom he was sure he could have enlisted for the Government, went off to find adventure in the rebel bands. " Loose people start up and none hath power to resist them "; he wrote, " many are enforced to go with them to save themselves, that would be otherwise faithful; and all discontented for want of trust and employment."[46]

In Munster Sir William St. Leger, at the head of the Government forces, had given up his one-time hope of quelling the rebels in time for the hunting season. " A company of naked rogues," he fumed, contemptuous still in words; but he had not slept in a bed for fourteen nights, nor " had leisure to shift his shirt." Irish raiders roamed the countryside and could not be put down; Cork, Waterford, Wexford and Limerick would soon be as desolate as Kilkenny if help did not come. In spite of all the chasing and patrolling, in spite of the hangings and burnings inflicted by St. Leger and his lieutenants, the three terrible Boyle brothers—ruthless sons of ruthless old Lord Cork— the rebels gained ground. At Kinsale a thousand Irish recruited for service in Spain had refused to embark, but faced about and swelled the ranks of the insurgents. Other Spanish help was hourly feared. Owen Roe O'Neill, heir to the name and fame of the great Earl of Tyrone, was in the Spanish Netherlands; if he should come to Ireland to lead the rebels, with the blessing of Spain and the prestige of a great name, it would be a dark day indeed for the English.[47]

When news of disaster came daily from Ireland, the King might justly object to the Militia Bill and ask Parliament to cut short argument and hasten supplies. Pym felt an equal justification for withholding them until the command of the armed forces was settled. The last despatch of the Council in Dublin to Parliament had contained a piece of significant information: Lord Dillon, a Norman-Irish Lord, was on his way to the King with, it was believed, an offer to quell the revolt at the head of a Roman Catholic loyalist army. Such a suggestion was calculated only to increase the distrust of the King's Protestant subjects. Dillon's relations with the rebels were highly suspect and had been already debated in the House of Commons; he had been with the King in the previous autumn on the eve of the revolt, a circumstance which could be diversely interpreted.[48] His journey now, hurrying to join the King as the crisis in London mounted, did not look innocent.

VI

For the King and for Pym, the war in Ireland was principally a weapon to be wielded in the struggle at home. The centre of conflict was not, for them, in the burning villages of Munster, in threatened Dublin or oppressed Kilkenny. It was at Westminster. Pym had already used the Irish Rebellion to discredit the Court and Royal Family; though he had been cautious of involving the King, he had repeatedly insinuated that the Queen, her priests and her friends knew more than they should. So now Charles, in his speech to Parliament, used the disasters in Ireland to make his opponents in the Commons appear remiss in assisting the English settlers. The phrasing of this speech and especially the suggestion that the Militia Bill should have a *salvo jure* clause added to it—to safeguard the rights of the King, and thus destroy its whole purpose—seems to have been suggested by Oliver St. John, the Solicitor General. St John belonged to Pym's party and his appointment earlier in the year had been designed partly to pacify the King's opponents, partly to bribe St. John himself into friendship. He may have made the suggestion in all good faith, but Edward Hyde later thought it had been a trap to enable John Pym to accuse the King of breach of privilege. A reference from the Throne to a bill still under discussion in Parliament was, Pym averred, a grave interference with freedom of debate.[49]

But he was evidently worried by the favourable impression that the King's well-judged words on Ireland might make. The Grand Remonstrance, now three weeks old, had failed of its effect in discrediting Charles because Charles had taken so little notice of it. At dusk on December 15th, when many Royalists had withdrawn (they were still unable to accept the necessity of coming to the House early and staying late), one of Pym's staunchest men, old Sir William Purefoy, the member for Warwick borough, suddenly moved that the Remonstrance be printed. The startled Royalists tried to postpone the motion but were defeated by nearly a hundred votes. They strove next to delay the printing, but although they managed to whip in a few more of their errant supporters in the interim they were again heavily defeated. More welcome to Pym, perhaps, than the vote itself was this evidence that the King's friends were still outmatched by him in the management of Parliamentary business.[50]

His next move was to persuade the Lords that the King's reference to the Militia Bill had been a breach of privilege. This did not prove difficult and the Lords joined with the Commons in a protest to which was added a demand: they desired to know the names of the " evil councillors " who had inspired the speech. In this action the moderates, hoodwinked as they were by their misplaced confidence in the goodwill of both parties, played a considerable part. Archbishop Williams took it upon himself to lead the deputation of thirty-six Commons and eighteen Lords who presented the protest to the King.[51] Although the " fell opposed opposites " were now visibly about to close with each other, those who had placed their hopes and staked their faith on compromise still sought to " beat down their fatal points " and did not realise that in so doing they served the turn of the more astute aggressors.

On the day on which Charles received the protest from Parliament, Lord Dillon arrived at Court with his message from the Lords of the Pale. Very soon it was generally reported that Dillon had strongly advised the pacification of Ireland by giving full liberty of conscience to the Roman Catholics.[52] The report did much to increase suspicion of the King's sympathy with the rebels, and to wipe out the effect of his appeal to Parliament for instant help for the English settlers.

Charles was none the less confident of his growing strength and showed it by the answer which, after three days' delay, he gave to the Parliamentary protest. Summoning the delegation into his royal presence he told them with dignity that he would not reveal the names of his councillors, for this was not a demand to be made to a man of honour. As to breach of privilege, the bill was already in print and he did not see how his reference to it could be accounted a breach; he would always maintain Parliament's lawful privileges, and he hoped they would be as careful to maintain his just prerogative. This said, he rose and with an air " confident and serene " left them to digest his answer.[53]

The London M.P.s had been working hard to undermine the authority of the Royalist Lord Mayor, Sir Richard Gurney. Complaints now reached Parliament that he had obstructed the London petition against the Bishops, but there was not matter enough in these to procure his removal, and other means had to be tried to regain control of the much divided City. The Common Council of London was in theory elective; but in practice the same substantial citizens composed it year after year. By a dexterous campaign in favour of new members, Venn and his friends organised a real election and on December 21st succeeded in ousting many of the King's friends from the Common Council and placing on it a number of Puritan-minded citizens, some of humble status—a tailor, a cutter, a dyer, said their contemptuous but defeated opponents, and even one " Riley the squeaking Bodice-maker." [54]

While Pym and his friends made sure of the City, Charles was making sure of the Tower. In the week before Christmas the House of Commons learnt that Sir William Balfour, the Scottish soldier of fortune and rabid Protestant who had long been lieutenant of the Tower, had been compelled by the King to give place to Colonel Thomas Lunsford. Lunsford, whom Pym's party clamorously described as a " very desperate " man, was such another bold and violent swaggerer as had figured among the King's friends in every real or supposed plot of the previous summer. His appointment was by no means pleasing to the King's moderate supporters and one of these, Sir Ralph Hopton, went up to the House of Lords to ask for a joint petition to the King for Lunsford's instant removal.[55]

On the day of the uproar over Lunsford's appointment Charles had sent his reasoned answer to the Grand Remonstrance. It had been drafted apparently with no official intention by Edward Hyde, seen by Digby and at once taken over by him to be issued in due course as the official reply to the accusations made against the King. The document was well-designed to disarm suspicion and strengthen the waverers in the Commons in loyalty to the King. It set forth the concessions which had been made during the last year and went on to outline a policy for the future. The King declared that he would be willing to make certain allowances in matter of religion to those of tender consciences, but the Church of England was none the less " the most pure and agreeable to the Sacred Word of God of any religion now practised in the Christian World," and he would, if called upon, seal that belief with his blood. For the rest he desired nothing more than an understanding with Parliament so that he might be a " great and glorious King over a free and happy people." [56] The paper reflected the baseless hopes of the King's group of friends in the House of Commons. They alone would be taken by surprise at each twist in the next fortnight's steep descent to catastrophe.

Christmas Eve was an anxious time for Pym. His first task was to persuade the Lords to stand with him against Lunsford. Although nothing could in fact be proved about Lunsford's religion except that he rarely went to Church more than once on a Sunday, Pym declared that his appointment showed that " the plots of the cruel and Bloody Papists " had now reached maturity, and called on " such of their Lordships as did with us apprehend the public danger " to do " what became men of honour for the public safety." The Royalist peers tried to have the question shelved until after Christmas but Northumberland revealed the extent of the opposition in the House of Lords by registering a protest against postponement in which twenty-four other Lords joined him.[57] Meanwhile Henry Marten, on behalf of Pym's party in the Commons, had sought out Lord Newport, a resolute opponent of the King, who as Constable of the Tower would have immediate authority over Lunsford. Newport gloomily told him that the King had removed him from his office, for rash and threatening words he had spoken of the Queen during the summer.[58]

With the Tower in the King's hands and the Lords divided, the Commons adjourned uneasily for two days over Christmas. They took a shorter holiday than custom permitted to the generality. The twelve days of Christmas from December 25th to January 6th were the habitual span of merry-making, the Christianised Saturnalia against which the Puritans had hitherto protested in vain. This year's Saturnalia was to be a blessed one for them. The apprentices, legitimately on holiday, surged around Whitehall in righteous high spirits shouting "No Bishops," "No Popish Lords" and "Down with butcher Lunsford," until Gurney, still trying to hold the City for the King, implored him to withdraw Lunsford from the Tower. On December 26th Charles substituted Sir John Byron, a man of better reputation no less loyal to himself. Lunsford continued in high favour at Court.[59]

On Monday December 27th Parliament reassembled and Sir William Jephson, a Munster landowner and a kinsman of Pym, reported from Ireland further evidence that the rebels had the Queen's authority to rise for the defence of the Roman Church. Pym followed this statement by reading aloud the official letter from the Lords of the Irish Pale asking for the toleration of Catholicism.[60] He was deliberately fomenting the suspicion raised by Jephson because he wished to force the issue with the King. He intended to threaten, or appear to threaten, the impeachment of the Queen. In the face of such an affront

Charles would have to attack, whether or not he was ready.
He was not quite ready.

Pym had barely finished speaking when an anxious member
—a Royalist this time—warned his colleagues that there was
fighting outside in Westminster Hall. Lunsford and some
friends, jostled by the apprentices, had lost their tempers and
drawn their swords.[61] This time no harm was done, but in
the next three days the rioting grew more serious. Down
by the river crowds blocked the stairs at Westminster and would
not let the Bishops land to take their seats in Parliament. Yelling
" No Bishops," " No Popish Lords," they held up coaches in
the adjoining streets and, in the grey winter light, thrust torches
through the windows to see who was within. Archbishop
Williams hit out in unclerical fashion at the impudent rogues,
boxed the ears of one and tumbled another underfoot, but the
apprentices were too many for him and he had to be rescued
by a brace of Protestant peers and helped into the House of Lords
with his tippet torn off. By evening the crowds had grown so
thick that the Marquis of Hertford advised no Bishop who had
managed to reach the House to venture out again, and Lord
Mandeville, for the sake of his old friendship with Williams,
smuggled several of them to his nearby lodgings for the night.
The rabble next day, finding a leader in the crazy broken-down
Sir Richard Wiseman, who had been a Star Chamber victim
three years earlier, stormed Westminster Abbey, and were
thrown back by some of the King's guards. A falling tile
killed Wiseman and sobered them for the time being.
The King denounced the rioters, sent to the Lord Mayor to
call out the City Trained Bands against them if necessary,
and ordered all his courtiers to wear swords for his and their
defence.[62]

Sustained by Digby, who was confident that all would be
well, the King serenely pursued his plans. On December 29th
he entertained Lunsford and his principal officers to a Christmas
dinner at Whitehall. As they came out, exhilarated with wine

and good company, the apprentices hanging about the palace gates greeted them with the usual parrot chorus of " No Bishops." For the second time Lunsford flashed out his sword and went for them, and this time there was a serious fight before the boys were driven off leaving some prisoners and wounded behind them. The fame of the battle went round the City and the apprentices gathered angrily in the torch-lit darkness. Even John Venn seems to have been afraid of what they might do and appealed to them not to storm the Lord Mayor's house. Instead, they broke into one of the City prisons before dispersing, exhausted, homewards.[63] During that day the offensive epithets of " Roundhead " and " Cavalier " were for the first time freely bandied about. Roundhead was an easy word of contempt for the shorn, bullet-headed apprentices, but Cavalier, which so soon acquired its gay and gallant associations, had when it was first angrily hurled at the King's men an ugly sound—" cavaliero," " caballero," Spanish trooper—brutal oppressor of Protestants and national enemy.

Next day, December 30th, Archbishop Williams took an unwise step. Digby had already attempted to move, in the House of Lords, that the threats of the rabble invalidated the present sessions of Parliament by infringing the freedom of members. The Lords had quelled this motion because, if the principle were once accepted, it could be extended to invalidate much of the legislation of the previous spring. Archbishop Williams now took up Digby's idea, possibly with his advice and connivance. In hurried consultation with his fellow Bishops he drew up a protest against their forcible exclusion from the House of Lords, implying that in their absence the House was incomplete and its acts of doubtful authority.

The King handed over the document, when it was shown to him, to the Lord Keeper, without troubling to read it—an omission which may have been mere carelessness, though it is equally possible that he knew already from Digby what the document contained.[64] When the Lord Keeper in his turn presented it to the House of Lords, it was very badly received not only by Pym's party but by the House in general, who had already expressed their views on this question when Digby had raised it, and were irritated at having it raised once again. Pym's friends saw to it that he was instantly informed in the Commons of what was happening in the Lords. With the speedy help of the lawyer John Glynne, he got the Commons within half an hour to vote the impeachment of all the bishops who had signed the protest. The Lords, offended and perturbed by this second clumsy attempt to invalidate their sessions, agreed to the impeachment, and a dozen venerable clerics were immediately hustled off to prison " in all the extremity of frost, at eight o'clock in the dark evening." That night the apprentices rang all the bells of the City and lit bonfires in the streets, but the Queen was telling Heenvliet, the Prince of Orange's envoy, that her husband would stand firm. The moment had come.[65]

Each side asserted that the other intended violence. Pym, before he turned on the bishops, had informed a rather mystified House of Commons that some villainous design was plotting against them. The King next day asked the City Trained Bands to stand ready against " the mean and unruly people " who disturbed the peace. But the House of Commons sent Denzil Holles to appeal to the King that these same Trained Bands might guard Parliament against the violence of the " malignant party."[66]

On January 1st, to show that their fears were genuine, the House went into Committee at Guildhall, as they alleged, for safety.[67] Whispers had by this time reached the King—as Pym intended that they should—that the Queen's impeachment was imminent.[68] Charles believed that he had no time to lose. A dank and rainy winter had made the roads difficult, and the additional members of Parliament, on whom he relied to destroy Pym's dominance in the Commons, had not yet reached Westminster.[69] But he thought himself strong enough to act without them, and believed that a greater danger was in delay. First he issued a proclamation denouncing the Irish as traitors, a move designed to stifle the slander which associated him and his Queen with the rebellion.[70] Then he sent Falkland to Pym with an olive branch which he knew very well would be rejected: he offered him the post of Chancellor of the Exchequer. This empty gesture was designed to please the moderates and disarm suspicion. On Pym's refusal he made Culpeper Chancellor of the Exchequer and Falkland Secretary of State.[71]

VII

They were sworn on Sunday, January 2nd. On Monday, January 3rd, 1642, the King unmasked his guns and opened the cannonade against Pym and his junto. In the House of Lords, the attorney general, Sir Edward Herbert, accused of High Treason the six principal men of the party—Lord Mandeville, John Pym, John Hampden, Arthur Haslerig, Denzil Holles and William Strode. Digby, who had inspired the project and advised the moment of attack, overplayed his part. While Herbert was speaking, he was so busy whispering his astonishment to Lord Mandeville and wondering who could possibly have advised the King, that he missed his cue. He should have risen, when Herbert concluded, to move the instant imprisonment of the accused men—as the Bishops had been imprisoned immediately after their impeachment a week earlier. He let the moment slip, then either lost his nerve or changed his mind, and hurried from the House, leaving the Lords stunned and baffled by the King's new move and with no one to indicate even to the King's friends what they should do next.

The House of Commons, apprised of what went forward almost before Herbert had concluded, sent in an immediate request for a conference with the Lords, claiming that the accusation was a breach of privilege. So also, they asserted, was the behaviour of the King's officers who had that morning invaded and searched the lodgings of Pym and Holles. In the meantime, neither House would yield up the accused men.[72]

The King, following the example set by the House of Commons when Strafford was impeached, made public the articles of treason against the accused men. They were said to have subverted the fundamental laws, alienated the affections of the King's subjects, terrorised Parliament by raising tumults, and incited a foreign power to invade the country—this presumably meant the Scots.[73] The articles, like those against Strafford a year before, had been drawn up in part at least as propaganda. They were the King's counter-charge to the Grand Remonstrance.

While Charles was organising the attack on his enemies in Parliament, the Queen sent for Heenvliet to tell him that the King and she had now decided to send their daughter, Princess Mary, to join her husband in the spring. The King, who came in while they were talking, added a hint that the Prince of Orange should make a formal request for the princess, his young son's wife, so that her journey might not look as if the troubles in England had anything to do with it. Heenvliet saw at once that this new offer would but be the forerunner to a demand for support if the King ran into further trouble.[74]

All this happened between dawn and dark on January 3rd. After nightfall two of the City members, John Venn and Isaac Pennington, urgently asked the Lord Mayor for a guard of the London Trained Bands for Parliament lest the King's soldiers should attack. Gurney was unresponsive, and about midnight he was called out of bed by a messenger from the King forbidding him to send the Trained Bands to help the House of Commons. Charles added another and more ominous word to the Lord Mayor: should any more tumults occur, he authorised the City Trained Bands to fire on the crowd.[75]

The King sent messengers also to the Inns of Court, bearing the articles of impeachment against his enemies and a request to the gentlemen volunteers among lawyers and law students to stand ready for the defence of King and Kingdom at an hour's warning.[76] Charles felt very confident. Sir John Byron was in charge of the Tower; the guards and gentlemen pensioners about Whitehall were led by the formidable Lunsford and young Lord Roxburgh who had been so hotly involved in the Edinburgh "incident" a few months before; Digby was on his way into Surrey to collect volunteers with whom he confidently believed he could march on London. The King did not doubt that Pym's apprentices would collapse before a concerted attack, and he trusted in the Lord Mayor's loyalty to prevent the City Trained Bands from giving help to the wrong side.

It must have been evident to Pym, without more specific warning, that the King intended to lay hands on him and the other accused men by force. For the details of the plan he depended on information from Court which reached him sometimes from Lady Carlisle and sometimes from Will Murray; but they do not appear to have known more than what was generally apparent—that the King would strike, but precisely when, and in what manner, they could hardly know for he was not yet certain himself. Pym therefore planned his answering strategy in the half-dark. He and his accused friends could have left the House of Commons and evaded the danger of a forcible arrest; but it was essential that the King's violent intention towards Parliament be put beyond doubt. The King would only attempt an act of violence if Pym and his colleagues were there to be seized. The trap must be baited: the Five Members were the bait.

So the House sat at Westminster, not at Guildhall, on the morning of January 4 and all the accused were present. They must be there until the King's guards were well on their way to Parliament; but they must not be there when the guards arrived. Should they be seized, the King would have secured his principal objective, whatever tumults might ensue; their party in Parliament would collapse once they were gone, and with them the directing power which made the tumults dangerous. But if they escaped, the King's attempt at violence would be nakedly revealed, and he would have gained nothing by it.

Everything depended on timing. The Commons passed an uneasy morning sending messages to the Lord Mayor and the Inns of Court to counteract those which the King had sent overnight. They adjourned nervously for dinner at noon, and Pym heard over his meal, from his good friend the Earl of Essex, that the King would certainly make his attempt that afternoon. The Commons reassembled at half-past one. Pym counted on the French Ambassador to let him know the movements at Whitehall, and at about three a breathless young Frenchman, Hercule de Langres, came hurrying through the outer Courts of Westminster with the news. The King was coming himself, with his guards about him.[77]

Had Charles succeeded, his act of inspired audacity would have been an object lesson on the might and authority of the Sovereign against the factious subject. But if there was the least risk of failure, the project was folly; the attempt, and not the deed, would confound him utterly. He should not, unless he was acting on an absolute certainty, have taken part in the arrest himself, for by so doing he cut off his own retreat; he would never be able to shift the blame.

As Charles approached from Whitehall, Pym in the Parliament House, asked leave of the Speaker for himself and his friends to go. The truculent William Strode, who had already spent ten years of his life in prison for his defiance of the King in an earlier Parliament, held them up with an untimely display of courage; he wished to confront the King and did not understand the more subtle intentions of Pym. There was no time for explanation or argument and his friends dragged him out by his cloak. At the watergate a barge waited, and the Five Members were on their way to the City by the river when Charles came in through Westminster Hall.

The King left his following in the lobby of the House and,

accompanied only by his nephew the Elector Palatine, entered the chamber. Roxburgh, negligently propping himself on the door jamb, kept the doors open so that the members could see the troops, some of whom were already cocking their pistols and playfully pretending to mark down their men. Charles, as always meticulous in little things, took off his hat as he entered the House and walked bareheaded towards the Speaker's chair, saluting some of the members as he went. The members, also bareheaded, stood in silence. They saw him look quickly to the right near the bar of the House, where Pym usually sat. " Mr. Speaker," said the King, " I must for a time make bold with your chair." Lenthall made way for him. Charles tersely explained why he had come and then asked for the members by name. " Is Mr. Pym here?" His words fell into a dead silence. Impatiently he asked the Speaker if the five members were present. Lenthall, with unwonted inspiration, fell on his knees and said that it was not his part either to see or to speak but as the house desired. " 'Tis no matter," said the King, " I think my eyes are as good as another's," and in the awful silence he continued to look along the benches " a pretty while " before at last he accepted defeat. " All my birds have flown," he said forlornly, and stepping down from the Speaker's chair, went out, " in a more discontented and angry passion than he came in "—as well he might.[78]

The intended act of strength had failed. Digby that night offered to go into the City with Lunsford and seize the accused men; this Charles refused, but with a desperate tenacity he tried once again. He made Edward Nicholas draw up a proclamation calling on his loyal subjects in London to deliver up the accused men; Littleton, the Lord Keeper, refused to seal it.[79] Charles would not be deflected. He drove into the City. The shops were closed and the streets full of people. A fanatic tossed a paper into the Royal coach headed " To your tents, O Israel "; it was an open cry for rebellion. The Lord Mayor had called the Common Council but the newly-elected Puritan members, regardless of the custom which fixed their assumption of office as the first Monday after Twelfth Night, crowded in prematurely to the meeting, and the Mayor dared not expel them for fear of worse trouble. The King promised them security of religion, a free Parliament and speedy action against the Irish rebels, but he demanded the persons of the five traitors whom he believed to be hiding in the City. Some cried " Privilege," others, but not many, set up a shout of " God Save the King."

" No privilege can protect a traitor from legal trial," said Charles, and went to dine with the Lord Mayor and Sheriffs. But he knew now that Gurney, loyal though he was, could not answer for the City. He could barely answer for himself and that very evening was set upon by an angry crowd. When Charles drove home in the winter dusk, the people who not six weeks before had cheered him home by torchlight surged round his coach, menacing and insolent, with shouts of " Privilege! Privilege! " Those with the King noticed for the first—and perhaps the only—time in his career that he was unnerved.[80]

He had cause to be. He had lost London.

On the next day the House of Commons met in Committee at Guildhall and issued a proclamation denouncing as public enemies any who assisted the King in his attempt to seize its members. (The accused men themselves were snugly in hiding in a house in Coleman Street.) The Common Council, defying the Lord Mayor, drafted a petition against Roman Catholics at Court and Sir John Byron's command of the Tower. It was hourly expected that the King's furious Cavaliers—multiplied by rumour into thousands—would attack the City; apprentices built blockades of benches across the streets; women boiled cauldrons of water to pour from the windows, and the Trained Bands mustered in readiness.[81]

At Whitehall the twelfth day of Christmas passed in gloom and disarray. The players presented *The Scornful Lady* to the little Prince of Wales and a sparse, unhappy audience.[82] No soldiers marched on the City. No one knew what to do.

The Common Council of London stretched out the right hand of friendship to the fragmentary fugitive Parliament within their gates. They formed themselves into a joint Committee for Public Safety and on Saturday, January 8th, bestowed the freedom of the City on Philip Skippon, a pious professional soldier, veteran of the Dutch wars, to whom on the following Monday Parliament gave the command of the Trained Bands, overruling the protests of the Lord Mayor and disregarding the rights of the King.[83]

The King had never contemplated the failure of the master stroke on which he had counted and planned since he left Scotland. He had felt himself secure in the support of the Lord Mayor, in the gallantry of his soldiers, in the skill of his advisers. The failure left him without policy or goal, at one moment stubborn and indignant, at the next leaning on his moderate friends for support. They, poor men, knew not what to do. Their hopes had collapsed more finally than the King's. It was not for actions of this kind that they had defended his policy and fervidly upheld his authority in Parliament. They hardly dared to attend the sessions of the Commons in the City, and they had lost heart and hope for organising their fellow members for the King. Stunned rather than gratified, Culpeper and Falkland entered on the responsibilities of the offices he had recently thrust upon them.[84]

Hitherto the apprentices and the Trained Bands had shouted loudest for Parliamentary privilege. On Monday, January 10th the port and the riverside rose. Mariners and lightermen flocked into the City, offering to live and die for Parliament. At any moment now it looked as though all London would spill out towards Westminster to demand justice or blood. This would be no mere uncontrolled thronging rabble—fearful as that could be. The Trained Bands had been mobilised and stood to their arms under the able leadership of Philip Skippon; there was marching and drilling in the City, cannon and chains across the streets. The sea-faring Earl of Warwick and young Vane, Treasurer of the Navy, had been at work among the seamen and the river was full of boats, manned and waiting.[85]

Charles hesitated, seeing that to show fear would be to weaken his remaining supporters in London. The Earls of Essex and Holland both argued with him that he should remain at Whitehall at all costs, but he did not trust either of them, knowing their sympathy with his enemies. The Queen told Heenvliet that rebellion had begun. She may have been responsible for making the King take part himself in that rash descent on the House of Commons, and she worked herself into a hysterical belief that her indiscretion alone had betrayed it to Pym. On the night of January 10th, suddenly and improvidently, the Royal pair fled from the capital, taking their three eldest children. They reached a dark and unprepared Hampton Court, late and tired, and slept—King, Queen and three children—all in one bed.[86]

Next day in London, at Three Cranes Wharf, John Pym, John Hampden, Denzil Holles, Arthur Haslerig and William Strode, stepped into a barge to the acclamations of the people. The rest of the members embarked behind them, and the Parliament men were accompanied up the Thames to Westminster by a regatta of decorated craft, of cheering citizens and mariners. With Lord Mandeville in their midst, Skippon and the Trained Bands, drums beating and colours flying, marched down the Strand to rejoin them at Westminster; as they passed the emptied palace of Whitehall they called out " Where is the King and his Cavaliers? " [87] Returning conquerors could have had no more impressive welcome. They were conquerors: they had taken the City of London and driven the King into exile from his own capital. The next time he came to Westminster, he would be a prisoner on trial for his life.

CHAPTER TWO

PREPARATIONS FOR WAR

January—July 1642

A MOOD of heroic excitement prevailed round London. A thousand horsemen rode in from Buckinghamshire, John Hampden's country, declaring that they would live and die for Parliament. The mariners offered to seize the Tower and drive out Lord Byron and his Cavaliers. Denzil Holles reported a rumour from Kingston that Colonel Lunsford and Lord Digby were mustering troops, and a boat load of saddles and arms on its way to them was stopped in the Thames.[1] It looked as though the fight for London would begin at any moment.

The ferment spread rapidly. "Every countryman's mouth almost is full of breach of privilege of Parliament," a spectator wrote. In Herefordshire it was alleged that the Papists were raising arms; Irish invasion was feared in South Wales; one of the King's soldiers, Captain Legge, had hurried to Hull on some secret mission; a French army was rumoured to be massing in Picardy for a descent on the South coast and a fleet of twenty-three great ships was reported to be making for Ireland.[2] The House of Commons sent messages to Sir John Hotham, the Governor of Hull, and to Colonel Goring, the Governor of Portsmouth, to reject any overtures from the King. They chose for their messenger to Hull, Hotham's eldest son, and gave him £2,000 to carry to his father for the necessities of the garrison. "Mr. Speaker," cried the young man, leaping to his feet, "fall back, fall edge, I will go down and perform your commands."[3] In his excited fancy, ferocious Cavaliers lay in wait with swords uplifted—" fall back, fall edge "—to smite the House of Commons and the " party of the common weal."

For nine days the King hesitated on the edge of war. He moved from Hampton Court to the more strategically placed Windsor Castle. He, too, sent—but ineffectively—to make sure of Hull and Portsmouth. He thought of despatching the Queen and her eldest daughter to the Low Countries from Portsmouth, taking with them some of the Crown Jewels to raise money for arms abroad. He himself would go northwards, where he believed the people would joyfully rise for him; thence, with foreign arms and money landed at Hull, he would sweep down on London. The Queen told the Dutch envoy Heenvliet, whom she saw at Windsor on January 17th, 1642 that her husband was beloved everywhere in his dominions except in London.[4] Heenvliet discouraged the royal plan, and rightly, for it was evident that the King was not beloved in the South. Sir Richard Onslow, Deputy Lieutenant for Surrey, raised the Trained Bands of the county, dispersed Digby's men at Kingston and took charge of the local magazine for Parliament. He also put men into Farnham to watch the Portsmouth road.[5]

This swift action in Surrey and the rising of John Hampden's tenants in Buckinghamshire, showed the King that his opponents would be quicker to raise the country than he, should it come to an immediate trial of strength. He temporised. He sent the Marquis of Hamilton to lull the suspicions of London by freely offering to the City the eight cannon and the ammunition kept at Vauxhall.[6] He wrote to Parliament from Windsor, declaring that he would " exceed the greatest examples of the most indulgent princes " in coming to an agreement with them and calling heaven to witness that he had never designed anything against them.[7] He was later to cite this message of January 20th, 1642, as proof that he had tried in vain to conciliate the

GEORGE, LORD DIGBY
on the right the Earl of Bedford
by Anthony Van Dyck

GEORGE GORING
by Anthony Van Dyck

Commons. But Digby had slipped away privately and crossed the sea to Holland where he turned up a week later, cool, cheerful and full of new projects.[8]

The failure of the attack on Pym had caused the King to hesitate, but not radically to alter his plans for the overthrow of this Parliament. He still intended that the Queen should go with her daughter to the Low Countries, there to raise money and arms, and woo the alliance of European sovereigns. He himself would in due course proceed to York, and from his northern capital march, when he was ready, on rebellious London and the rogues at Westminster. The Scots to whom he had made so many gracious concessions would, he believed, surely support him in this enterprise. Before the end of January he wrote to the Council at Edinburgh and more especially to Argyll and the Chancellor Loudoun for help; the precise nature of the help he required he conveyed more discreetly by word of mouth. Though he trusted chiefly to the Covenanters whom he had deliberately put in power, he took the additional precaution of writing at the same time to the discomfited Royalist Montrose assuring him of his continued regard. He also sent to the Earl of Ormonde, his most reliable servant on the Council in Ireland, a verbal message too secret to commit to paper.[9]

Meanwhile, the excitement in London had not abated. It was not safe for any man in a public place to utter a word against Parliament. Pym's most active supporters organised demonstrations and petitions against Papists and Bishops and in favour of the House of Commons until Heenvliet, who shared with other foreign envoys a genuine desire to prevent serious trouble, remonstrated with young Vane about the crowds of hungry, angry, idle people thronging about Westminster, and even some of the Parliamentary leaders felt a chill of anxiety for the future.[10] From time to time the Londoners expressed their Christian principles by attacking the houses of foreign Roman Catholic merchants, and on January 21st they collected in large numbers to witness the execution of two more priests. " Here's a jolly company!" said Father Alban Roe, smiling from the hangman's cart with saintly benevolence on their vindictive faces; his parting sermon and the constancy with which he and his fellow sufferer, Thomas Greene, met their end moved those who were capable of being moved.[11]

Violence seemed likely to break out round the Tower of London. The House of Commons had voted Sir John Byron out of his command. The choleric Byron snapped his fingers in the Commons' faces: he was taking no orders from them. In answer he found himself lectured to by the Sheriffs of London, refused victuals by the tradesmen, besieged by Skippon and the Trained Bands on land, and blockaded by the watermen from the river, while the Londoners petitioned for his removal, because—they said—they dared not send bullion to the mint while he was there, lest he should seize it. The King's friends sourly averred that none of the petitioners were of substance enough to have any bullion. But when Parliament sent for Byron he judged it wise to obey; on his return he found that Skippon had, in his absence, made an unsuccessful attempt to seize the Tower.[12]

The King's friends at Westminster complained that dispassionate debate was no longer possible. Yet minute quibbles of law and privilege were still from time to time respected. When the Commons voted to deprive the King's servant Endymion Porter of his command in the Westminster Trained Bands the meticulous Sir Symonds d'Ewes for once voted with the Royalist minority because he held it to be a breach of privilege of Parliament to vote Porter out of his captaincy while he was still a member of the House.[13] Such niceties apart, Pym's position grew daily stronger as the organised petitions flowed in from all over the country denouncing the King's favours to Papists, his slowness in relieving Ireland, his dependence on the counsels of evil men, his unwillingness to reform the Church. On January 26th, Pym, in a conference with the Lords, summed up these petitions as " the voice, or rather the cry, of all England." His speech, printed and widely circulated, commanded the admiration of Protestant gentry far and wide.[14]

Making allowances for political rhetoric, Pym was not unjustified in thinking that the petitions, though stimulated and organised by the active few, represented very fairly the opinion of many. The Irish rebellion had sharply increased fear and hatred of the Roman Catholic minority in England. The events of the last weeks had placed the Bishops, and therefore the Church, in the front line of the King's aggressive policy. The King's return from Scotland had been the signal for a series of disorders and disturbances which interfered with trade and made every man doubtful of the future. During the quiet summer and early autumn of 1641 the King had grown more popular and Pym less so; but the events of the last eight weeks had violently reversed the process. The King and his policies were now as unpopular as they had been a year ago, before Strafford was executed.

Public opinion is notoriously fickle. Time would work for the King, if time could be gained, and the Duke of Richmond expressed a wish that Parliament should adjourn for six months, until the situation was more normal. The House of Commons voted him a dangerous malignant for the suggestion,[15] by a majority the size of which clearly showed that the King had lost the support of the waverers. A hundred and twenty-three of the Commons voted in favour of the Duke, two hundred and twenty-three against. The numbers at this division, the largest yet recorded, disprove the Royalist contention that members were afraid to attend the House because of the menacing crowds. Without question, Royalist members were sometimes insulted and jostled. Gervase Holles, the Royalist cousin of Denzil, complained to the House of the language used to him as he passed through Westminster Hall.[16] But hard words break no bones. Most of the resolute Royalists were present during these terrible days to fight a losing battle for their King. It was not the violence of the populace which had restored Pym's diminishing majority by preventing the King's supporters from attending debates; it was the violence of the King which had alienated every wavering member of the Commons.

The hostile majority received with suspicion the seemingly gracious messages with which the King now wooed them, and responded only by demands for the abolition of episcopacy, and for the control by Parliament of the armed forces and the Tower of London. The tone of their requests very clearly indicated that they thought the King had an understanding with the rebels in Ireland; Pym had boldly implied as much. Charles played for time and put off their demands with an evasion; he could not yield to them, he said, but he would be willing to discuss them further. The Commons raged against the delay and declared that those about the King who had counselled him to make these replies were enemies to the public peace. Alone of the Royalists in the House, Sir Ralph Hopton spoke vainly against the voting of an ordinance to put the Kingdom in a state of defence.[17]

The King's attitude hardened. On February 7th he announced to Parliament his intention of sending his wife and daughter to the Low Countries, reiterated his refusal to hand over the strong places of the Kingdom, and graciously agreed to pardon John Pym and the members he had accused of treason, though without offering any explanation of his previous charges against them.[18] He rejected the moderating counsels offered him both by his nephew the Elector Palatine and by Heenvliet. He ran over Parliament's misdeeds to Heenvliet; first they wanted Strafford's death, then triennial Parliaments, then the perpetuation of this present Parliament, and now the control of the militia and the forts: "Vous voyez où leurs intentions vont." The Queen strengthened him in his resolution to beat down the opposition at any cost; she frankly told the Venetian envoy that things must be worse before they could be better.[19]

By mid-February the Royal party reached Dover, by way of Canterbury. The officer who was to convey the Queen and

Princess to Holland was John Mennes, a tough sea-captain devoted to the King and contemptuous of Parliament-men. Five of the King's warships rode at anchor ready to receive the royal ladies and their suite; the Queen herself was to embark in the *Lion*.[20] Charles, judging the loyalty of his seamen from what he saw of Mennes and his crew, felt confident of his naval strength. He was confident, too, in his wife's ability to secure by her persuasion financial help from the Prince of Orange and military help on a larger scale from the warlike King of Denmark.

The King's nephew, the Elector Palatine, who had resentfully accompanied the Court so far, was temporarily absent. Short of money for the expenses of so many journeys, he had had to pawn his Garter. His genuine anxiety that peace and a stable Protestant Government be maintained in England was strengthened by a natural concern for the future of his own income. He had lived most of his life on grants made to his family by Parliament and he took care to let his friends at Westminster know that he was not a party to the acts of violence attempted or contemplated by those about the King.[21]

During his absence his younger brother Prince Rupert appeared suddenly at Court. After three and a half years as a prisoner of war in an Austrian fortress, he had been released in the previous autumn through the intervention of the English ambassador, and had seized the first occasion of coming to England to thank his uncle. His mother, who did not want him involved in the dangerous plots of her brother's Court, had tried in vain to prevent him.[22] The eager boy whom the King and Queen had always preferred to his circumspect elder brother had grown into a man of formidable energy, hungry for action, who readily volunteered to help the Queen in buying arms and raising soldiers in Holland.

Others from whom the King had expected gratitude had failed him. His council in Scotland returned a cold, evasive answer to his appeal for help, suggesting only that the Marquis of Argyll should wait on him with advice.[23] Playing for time and acting on the suggestion of Culpeper, who believed he could weaken Pym's hold on the Commons by making a show of concessions, the King now gave in to several demands. He removed Byron from the Tower of London, which could not much longer be held without supply; more surprisingly, he passed the bill abolishing the temporal power of the Bishops, mildly adding that "he desired nothing more than the satisfaction of his kingdom." The message reached the Commons on February 14th but they were not mollified by the royal valentine. Pym and his associates realised very well that so long as the King retained his control over the armed forces, he would also hold it in his power to reverse, when he was strong, any acts that had been wrung from him when he was weak. The Commons pressed him once again to give them control of the armed forces. They impeached the Attorney General for having drawn the charges against the Five Members and they opened some intercepted letters sent from Lord Digby in Holland. Digby frankly advised the King to take forceful action against his opponents. On this evidence he was impeached for levying war on the nation.[24]

On February 23rd the Queen set sail from Dover. The King took the parting very hard. Public and formal though their farewell had to be, both were in tears, and when, with a following wind, the *Lion* stood out to sea, the King galloped along the cliffs to keep her in sight until the last sail had vanished over the wintry horizon.[25]

A fast day had been announced in London for the sins of the nation, and as the Queen crossed the sea on her warlike mission, Stephen Marshall was preaching from the pulpit of St. Margaret's, Westminster, on a text from Judges: "Curse ye Meroz, said the angel of the Lord, curse ye bitterly the inhabitants thereof, because they came not to the help of the Lord, to the help of the Lord against the mighty." In resounding words he condemned all "neuters" in the struggle which was about to begin; to seek accommodation with the malignant party was to betray the cause not of Parliament but of God. No harsh fanatic, but a warm and lively preacher, Marshall harangued the waverers into line.[26]

The Commons had consulted with the City to raise money for the suppression of the Irish revolt. Their projects were common talk some days before they were published and the King legitimately complained that he should have been kept informed. He gave his consent, none the less, to the atrocious scheme for the future of Ireland which, after his death, was to be implemented by Cromwell. It was almost the last joint act of King and Parliament. One million pounds, it was estimated, would have to be raised to suppress the revolt of the Irish and restore the property of the settlers. Ten million acres of Irish land was to be confiscated from the rebels, and one quarter of this, all profitable land—no bogs, forests or barren moors—was to be granted to those who advanced money for the war. The suppression of the revolt thus became, on the English side, a gigantic speculation in Irish land, with nearly the whole of Ireland for the prize. The scheme brought in the necessary money but it hideously justified the Irish in their revolt and gave them every cause to fight on with redoubled force. No settlement could now be acceptable to the English short of the annihilating defeat of the rebels, for no other end would ensure the necessary return on the money of the investors. The remaining loyal Irish, when they knew of " the putting this Kingdom to sale in England," might well turn away from a perfidious Government and join their fellow countrymen in arms.[27]

Consenting to this method of financing the war in Ireland, the King still postponed his answer to Parliament's Militia Bill, which would put the control of the armed forces into their hands. On Sunday, February 27th, at Greenwich Palace, where in happier times he had passed so many peaceful days with his Queen, he worked out his answer with the help of Edward Hyde. For the ensuing months he was to rely largely on Hyde's diplomatic and persuasive pen to compose replies which would consolidate for him again a following among his more temperate and conventional subjects. In a firm but persuasive statement he declared his intention of abiding by the laws and protecting the rights of his people, he denied any violent intention towards Parliament in his attempt to arrest the Five Members, but he would not " consent to divest himself of the just power which God and the laws of this Kingdom have placed in him for the defence of his people." Whatever the effect of the King's reply on men of moderation might be, the House of Commons greeted it with a shower of angry resolutions, denouncing the reply and those who advised it, and demanding the King's return to London since his absence endangered the peace of the Kingdom.[28]

The indomitable Lord Mayor, with the assistance of an equally tenacious King's man, the rich silk merchant, George Binnion, had paved the way for the King's answer by organising a petition to the House of Commons against the Parliamentary appointment of a commander to the City Militia—they meant Philip Skippon—without consent of the Lord Mayor.[29] Petitions from the King's friends were by now regularly condemned as breaches of privilege, and Pym used this one skilfully to stimulate the resentment with which Parliament received the King's rejection of their Militia Bill. The Lords, from whose sessions many of the Royalists had now withdrawn, joined with the Commons in declaring that those who had advised the King to such an action were enemies of the State.[30]

For appearance sake, the Houses once again importuned the King to pass the Militia Bill. Their messengers saw him at Theobalds on March 1st, whither he had moved, taking the Prince of Wales along with him. He spoke this time with an impatient bitterness; *they* complained to him of fears and jealousies occasioned by his actions, but let them—he said—" lay their hands to their hearts and ask themselves whether he might not likewise be disturbed with fears and jealousies? " [31]

The King's frank hostility had its effect. In the House of Commons, in a debate " full of sadness and evil augury," they resolved not to wait any more for his consent to the Militia Bill, but to issue it themselves as an Ordinance, and to take over the defence of the Kingdom without more ado. They perceived the significance of what they were doing, for this was to proclaim the power of Parliament to act for the good of the country independently of the King. " The High Court of Parliament is not only a Court of Judicature, enabled by the laws to adjudge and determine the rights and liberties of the Kingdom . . . but it is likewise a Council to provide for the necessity, to prevent the imminent dangers, and preserve the public peace and safety of the Kingdom——" so ran the preamble to the Militia Ordinance. By this action Parliament assumed to itself sovereign authority, thus indicating that the King's power, as King, was not the same as his personal and natural power. Charles Stuart, the man, might fall into the hands of evil councillors and remove himself from Westminster; but the power of the King remained with Parliament. For the rest the Ordinance provided for the protection of the country from those " Papists and other ill-affected persons who have already raised a rebellion in the Kingdom of Ireland "; the Lords Lieutenants of counties, to whom the control of all recruiting belonged, were to be appointed by Parliament and all appointments made by the King to be at once revoked.[32] The Commons resolved also to draw up a declaration in answer to the King in which their reasons for going against the Royal authority would be clearly set forth. Sir Ralph Hopton, defending his King to the last, hotly told them that they were condemning their sovereign " upon less evidence than would serve to hang a fellow for stealing a horse." For this strangely expressed objection he was voted to the Tower.[33]

From this moment onwards the last pretence of conciliation had gone. The faint rumble of threats and the occasional punitive action by which Pym had hitherto intimidated the Royalists gave place to a systematic policy of expulsion and persecution. Binnion, who had organised the petition against Skippon, was arrested for breach of privilege, and Thomas Gardiner, the Royalist Recorder of London, was sent to the Tower for having supported the levy of Ship-money. Parliament's friends in the City were meditating a further purge of the Common Council by appointing a Committee to inquire into the validity of the elections of those with whom they disagreed. A clergyman, Dr. Howell, was in trouble for calling the honourable House of Commons "a company of giddy heads" and a pot-valiant cavalier who had been heard, at the Spread Eagle Tavern, threatening to cut King Pym in pieces found himself sternly called in question by the House. Robert Trelawny, member for Plymouth, was expelled from the Commons for criticising Parliament's behaviour to the King in a private conversation, and poor deluded Sir Edward Dering was marched off to the Tower, with the rabble hooting at his heels, for publishing his own speeches, some of which were critical of Pym's conduct. Farther afield, in Oxfordshire, Lord Saye laid by the heels some gentry whom he found organising a Royalist petition. Over all the country, neighbours and families quarrelled over politics, brawled in the streets, argued in their homes, and peaceable men began to go armed.[34]

Charles continued his journey northward. He was at Royston when Parliament defiantly issued the Militia Ordinance. He was at Newmarket when the shifty Pembroke and the shiftless Holland reached him with the text of Parliament's declaration in answer to his rejection of their bill. He stared angrily at the two Lords who had once been his courtiers, interrupted the reading of the Declaration, and quelled them when they had done. "What would you have?" he snapped, with none of his usual hesitation, "have I violated your laws? Have I denied to pass any one bill for the ease and security of my subjects? I do not ask you what you have done for me." Later, the Earl of Pembroke tried once again to persuade him to agree to Parliament's control of the militia, if only for a time. "By God, not for an hour!" said the King.[35]

Pembroke and Holland took coach for London, and Charles, with his eldest son, turned northwards. The extremists of both parties had got their way. The rift was absolute.

II

All through these troubled weeks, dismal news from Ireland had not ceased to come in. The crisis between King and Parliament had begun in a dispute over means to put down the Irish revolt. It now seemed that a Civil War would have to be fought in England before either Parliament or King could send help to the settlers in Ireland.

Region by region, the island foundered into anarchy. "Ireland is in good estate and universally revolted," wrote a jubilant priest.[36] In the North, the O'Neills, M'Guires and M'Ginnes were up in arms. The Earl of Antrim, who had so long and loudly boasted the prowess of his Macdonnells, had chosen this moment to visit friends in the South, but five hundred men of his clan found a leader in Alaster M'Coll Keitach, a bold and brawny giant of eighteen.[37] Over the whole of Derry and Antrim, barns, farmsteads, and stacks went up in flames; the roving Irish drove off the cattle and carried away what goods they did not destroy, while the settlers abandoned their homes and crouched inside the walled towns, short of food and fuel and arms.[38]

In Munster, the MacCarthies under Lord Muskerry overran the country, driving the settlers to take refuge in Cork and Kinsale, Youghal and Bandon Bridge.[39] What would now become of the market towns and Protestant churches, the settlements of industrious English that the Earl of Cork in his active lifetime had imposed on the green land, not to speak of the income of twenty thousand pounds a year that he drew to himself from the spoils of the Irish? From his stronghold at Lismore on a winter night a watcher counted five hundred several fires between the Blackwater and Dungarvon. "We are now at our last gasp," the old scoundrel lamented; "if the state of England do not speedily help us, we are buried alive."[40] But so far all the help that had come from England was three small contingents of foot soldiers, one of them under Colonel George Monk, and four hundred horse under Sir Richard Grenvile. Grenvile bore a famous name that he was to make infamous; Monk bore a name which had yet to become famous.

One important clan, in the South, had not joined the insurgents. The chief of the O'Brien, Lord Inchiquin, was married to the daughter of Sir William St. Leger, Lord President of Munster, and in the hope of succeeding to this office, Inchiquin put his ferocious energy at the service of the English.

The settlers were slow to organise their defence. In the North the Scots suspected the English and the English mistrusted the Scots. Anglicans mistrusted Presbyterians, and both looked with doubt on the loyalist Roman Catholics. At Galway the great man was Lord Clanricarde, a Norman-Irish Catholic, half-brother, through his English mother, to the Puritan Earl of Essex. He refused all overtures from the Irish and kept the citizens of this valuable western seaport true to the Dublin Government which, for all reward, refused to send him any arms. But the local garrison was under the command of a Puritan professional soldier, Captain Willoughby, who provoked the Irish to revolt by plundering them to feed his garrison, openly hated Clanricarde as a professing Papist, thwarted him in his plans for pacifying the town, fired on its citizens and slandered Clanricarde to the Council in Dublin.[41]

In County Clare, Lord Thomond, less competent, and less loyal than Clanricarde, undertook to defend the property of the English with the help of Irish troops, but they first disarmed and then plundered those whom they were set to protect. Many settlers fled; a few, like the stubborn Maurice Cuffe at Ballyally Castle, took their own measures of self-defence.[42]

With distrust everywhere, and anarchy almost everywhere,

fugitives from the Irish raiders found little help on their wintry marches to the hoped-for safety of the towns. The Irish, who naturally took what they needed for their own ill-equipped, half-naked forces, seized the clothes and money, carts, horses, and stores of their prisoners before turning them loose to trudge to the nearest stronghold through a hostile country, in winter, without shoes to their feet or coats to their backs. Some of the Norman-Irish gentry tried to help. Ulick Burke of Castle Hacket sent out his coach and coachmen to scour the countryside for wanderers; he came back with two men, three women and three children whom he had found almost naked, huddled together, exhausted, in the snow. Thawed and clothed again, they were revealed as the Bishop of Killala, his wife and family.[43] Four hundred women and children who had made their way to Waterford had been shipped thence to Youghal; but the Earl of Cork had enough to do without destitute refugees to care for, and all who came thither were sent on to England.[44] Bristol, Chester, and the little ports of Scotland's south-west coast, which had at first taken in the richer fugitives, received, as the winter deepened, boatloads of sick, hungry, ragged people, wives who had lost their husbands, children who had lost their parents during the desperate flight.[45] The lamentations of these people swelled the tale of Irish atrocities—the hangings, the murders, the mutilations they had seen, or had come to believe that they had seen.

Cold and hunger in that long hard winter destroyed more of the fleeing settlers than the Irish killed, either in fight or in cold blood. But it was, from the start, a vindictive and bloody war. What else could it have been where difference of religion, race and culture was added to the bitter hatred of the dispossessed native against the intruding colonist? In England almost at once Parliament authorised the publication of atrocity stories against the Irish; the Dublin government followed the bad example a few weeks later.[46] The Protestant public read with fascinated horror of settlers hanged before their plundered farmsteads, of families burnt alive in their homes, of women raped and murdered, of children drowned in bogs or spitted on long knives before the eyes of their parents. The refugees added to the tales; a woman in Scotland claimed to have seen her husband crucified.[47] The appetite grew with what it fed on. No crime was too atrocious for the " bloody Irish butchers," and the reputed numbers of their victims had, within weeks, passed a hundred thousand, until Ireland, drenched in blood, seemed scarce " tomb and continent enough to hide the slain."

These fearful tales proliferated from seeds of truth. There had been deliberate drowning of women and children at Portadown in Ulster and at Shrule Bridge in Galway. The Irish burnt and plundered with careless ferocity and, on occasion, as in the premeditated massacre of the settlers at Island Magee, killed in cold blood. Their leaders genuinely strove to have civilian prisoners escorted to places of safety but could not always provide a guard strong enough to protect them against the bands of raiders who ferociously roamed the country. Not every beggar woman in the streets of Dublin, Bristol or Chester who claimed to have seen her husband's throat cut by the Irish was telling the truth: but some of them were.[48]

The English and the Scots retaliated. " No quarter " became the common rule: prisoners were hanged, women drowned: " a thing inhuman and disavowable," wrote a Scots soldier of fortune in disgust, " for the cruelty of one enemy cannot excuse the inhumanity of another." [49] In Leinster the Government troops set fire to the heath and furze in which the Irish took shelter and burnt not the active raiders but their women and children who could not escape. In Munster Sir William St. Leger, with his terrible Irish son-in-law Lord Inchiquin—Murrough of the Burnings, as the Irish half-admiringly called the renegade chief—hunted the insurgents without mercy for man, woman or child. Lord Cork's three younger sons joined with enthusiasm in the chase, and St. Leger approvingly reported to the gratified father when the youngest of them burnt down an Irish stronghold with every living creature in it.[50]

In this fury of destruction and hatred, some of both parties still behaved like Christians and men of honour. The Protestant Bishop of Kilmore, William Bedell, with his house full of quaking refugees, calmly confronted the insurgents, his pastoral staff in his hand. He secured quarter for himself and his little flock, and when a few weeks later he died, the Irish soldiers gave him a guard of honour to his grave and fired a salute over the coffin of the austere, undaunted old man.[51]

The Earl of Ormonde, general of the forces of the Dublin Government, refused to lay waste Irish villages or kill civilians. The greater number of his Norman-Irish family were in sympathy with the rebels; his mother was a Roman Catholic, his brother was in arms with the insurgents. He had other anxieties, for the King had certainly communicated secrets to him that he would have been happier not to have known and he, if anyone, knew the extent of Charles's inept tampering with the Irish. His competence and popularity with the Government forces made him indispensable, yet there were those on the Council who suspected him of complicity with the rebels. But Ormonde stood with great steadfastness, for law, order and loyalty to the Crown, and rebutted the whispered slanders: "I will go on constantly," he wrote, "neither sparing the rebel because he is my kinsman, or was my friend, nor yet will I one jot the more sharpen my sword to satisfy anybody but myself in the faithful performance of my charge."[52]

His wife was cut off in Kilkenny Castle with her children and the hundreds of fugitives whom she had received and relieved there. The Irish leaders threatened to destroy them unless Ormonde abandoned his command of the Government forces. The English responded that if the Countess and her children came to harm, no Irish woman or child would be spared. But Ormonde, not slackening his preparations for the spring campaign, proclaimed a different answer. If his wife and children, he wrote, " shall receive injury by men, I shall never revenge it on women and children; which, as it would be base and un-Christian, would be extremely below the price I value my wife and children at." [53]

Ormonde was a competent rather than a gifted soldier, but he understood the strength and weakness of the Irish. He had opposed the Government's attempt to relieve Drogheda which had ended in disaster at Julianstown. The troops, a pack of demoralised Ulster refugees, without, in Ormonde's phrase, " soldiers' faces," had hardly known how to use the muskets hurriedly put into their unpractised hands.[54] Against such forces the shock tactics of Phelim O'Neill's Irish, surging down on them out of the mist, had been bound to succeed. But at Drogheda itself Sir Henry Tichborne, an experienced professional soldier with a disciplined garrison, had held out in spite of hunger, treachery, repeated attacks and even infiltrations by the enemy. The long defence revealed the superiority of a small well-ordered force over the undisciplined numbers of the Irish. By the beginning of March Ormonde had assembled, trained and armed about three thousand foot soldiers and five hundred horse. Phelim O'Neill's numbers outside Drogheda were larger but he was too wary to risk fighting with an organised army. As the Government troops approached from Dublin, he drew off to the safety of Ulster and on March 11th, 1642, Ormonde entered Drogheda.[55] It was, for the English, the first good news out of Ireland in five appalling months.

III

The varying fortunes of their compatriots in Ireland were now only the background to the shocking situation in England. " Beacons are new made, sea-marks set up, and great posting up and down with packets; all symptoms of the ensuing war," wrote a Parliament man.[56] Charles, from Huntingdon, warned his subjects not to obey any ordinance to which he had not given his consent. Both Houses of Parliament, highly offended, declared that any who questioned their authority would be guilty of breach of privilege.[57]

The King continued his journey northwards, not without the pleasures and diversions of more tranquil times. At Cambridge he visited Trinity College and St. Johns, and the Prince of Wales was entertained with a play.[58] On a day of mild sunshine the royal party called on the Ferrar household at Little Gidding; the King shot a hare in the neighbouring fields; the Prince of Wales munched cheese-cake and apple pie in the pantry. At parting, the King gave the Ferrars for their charities five pounds which he had won at cards the previous evening from his nephew the Elector Palatine. His last words betrayed for a moment the anxiety on his mind. " Pray, pray for my speedy and safe return," he said.[59]

Edward Hyde, who with Lord Falkland did what he could at Westminster to sustain the King's few remaining friends in the Commons, kept the King informed by letter, offered him advice and drafted statements for him to make in the war of printed papers he now waged with Parliament. Hyde still deceived himself that moderate councils could prevail to hinder the clash which the King and Pym, in their different ways, were both seeking.[60] " Your Majesty well knows," he wrote, " that your greatest strength is in the hearts and affections of those persons who have been the severest asserters of the public liberties, and so, besides their duty and loyalty to your person, are in love with your inclination to peace and justice." He urged the King to give not " the least hint to your people that you rely upon anything but the strength of your laws, and their obedience."[61] The King saw the wisdom of maintaining this pose both to gain more support for himself, and to make more apparent to the world the fact that Pym and his following had by their rebellious intransigence caused the troubles which had come upon the nation. At Stamford he proclaimed the strict enforcement of the laws against Roman Catholics,[62] a move to please his Protestant subjects, which would not cost him the loyalty of the Catholics who well knew that, however hard their lot, he was more their friend than his opponents would ever be.

Hyde meanwhile had drafted a more conciliatory answer to the propositions that Charles had rejected with such asperity at Newmarket. It was issued in the King's name soon after he entered his northern capital of York. In the measured phrases of this document, the King reproached Parliament for lack of trust in him. Once more he proclaimed his " faithful and zealous affection to the true Protestant profession and his resolution to concur with Parliament in any possible course for the propagation of it and the suppression of Popery." Once more he condemned the Irish rebellion and all who had abetted it. He denied all the rumoured plots that foreign powers were being called to his help, reminded them of his many concessions, declared his willingness to return to London if he could feel secure in so doing, and announced that he wished for nothing more heartily than the " peace, honour and prosperity of the nation." [63]

This was the last conciliatory message he was to send and it did not fail of the effect that Edward Hyde intended. Many uncertain and troubled men, in Lords and Commons, and in the country at large, were moved by these royal expressions of moderation to judge that, in this last resort, Pym and his faction were the aggressors and to take part henceforward, actively or passively, with the King. The persuasive power of this document arose from the sincerity with which Edward Hyde had composed it. He truly believed that the King might still agree to a compromise settlement and he put all his moral convictions as well as his intellectual gifts into what he did. The King for his part knew the value of these moderating gestures but had not wavered at all from his conviction that the faction in power at Westminster would yield only to force. They had already claimed that the authority of the King and the authority of Charles Stuart were two different things, and that the kingly authority belonged properly to them. It was the natural response for the King to see " a necessity to defend Charles Stuart if he desired to save the King." [64] On that necessity Charles acted, and the message sincerely drafted by Edward Hyde was, for the King, a weapon of war, intended to undermine the position of the enemy.

Aware of the danger, Pym's party were menacingly watchful, and were already muttering against Edward Hyde.[65] Recently they had extended the methods by which they stifled the influence of the remaining Royalist sympathisers at Westminster. Committees multiplied—for Defence, for Information, for the Navy, for this, that and the other inquiry and accusation. In all of these Pym's men dominated, and through their hands passed the chief business of the House.

Outside Parliament the Royalists were learning how to organise. From Lancashire a petition was reported against the Lord Lieutenant appointed by Parliament, the Puritan Lord Wharton, and in favour of Lord Strange, a devoted King's man. The House of Commons received the news with censorious comment on the pressure which had been put on the honest folk of Lancashire to subscribe to it.[66] Oliver Cromwell drew attention to a report from Monmouthshire that the Puritan clergy of the region feared that a rising was plotted by the local Papists.[67] They were certainly very strong in the neighbourhood, which was dominated by the richest Catholic peer in the realm, the Marquis of Worcester. In Kent, a Royalist judge, Thomas Malet, had persuaded the Grand Jury at Maidstone to adopt a petition that all military power be restored to the King, and that Parliament remove from the vicinity of London to some place where members need fear no interference from the populace.[68]

Pym's party had other fears. Their attention was anxiously divided between Hull, the Low Countries and Denmark, for if Charles intended to declare war from York and draw help from abroad, Hull was the port that he must secure. King Christian IV of Denmark, though advanced in years, was still an active, and had once been a famous. war-lord by land and sea. He was

King Charles's uncle, his mother's brother, and it was known that the Queen had urgently appealed to him for help. Rumours of invasion—especially from Denmark—were rife during all those months. The busy little Queen spent her time at The Hague raising money on the security of the royal jewels that she had carried away with her, collecting arms and volunteers with the able assistance of Prince Rupert, and seeking by every means in her power to interest the Prince of Orange as well as the King of Denmark in her husband's cause. She was not well. Her toothaches, headaches, coughs and colds made a plaintive accompaniment to the tender protestations of love with which she filled her letters to the King. But her advice was not plaintive. She warned him against the half-hearted who advised moderation and she repeatedly urged upon him the importance of securing Hull as a key point in the strategy of their joint design.[69]

The King held Court at York with something of the old elegance and ceremony. He had sent for his musicians from Whitehall but their salaries had been two years unpaid and they could not afford the journey.[70] The Earls of Holland and Essex formally refused to join him, and were dismissed from their posts at Court,[71] but a great number of the nobility were now rallying to his side. They left the House of Lords a diminished handful, almost all of Pym's party, and went some to York, some more cautiously to their own estates to await events.

A temperate gaiety prevailed in the halls and gardens of the great houses at York where the King and his friends dwelt. Innkeepers and farmers did well and markets were brisk. But the King deceived himself if he counted on general support in the North. The country was fiercely divided, by religion, by the feuds and rivalries of great families, by the hard feelings that Strafford, that formidable Yorkshireman, had left between those whom he had favoured and those whom he had offended.

Occasionally, too, local grievances were aired in defiance of all parties. A gang of women, to the music of pipe and tabour, levelled the fences round a recent enclosure and feasted on cakes and ale to celebrate the act before they were caught and sent to jail by an angry magistrate.[72] By timely favours Charles had won over Lord Savile, whose family were strong in the West Riding, but he could not win the influential Lord Fairfax and his soldier son Sir Thomas. Some of the gentry offered him declarations of loyalty; others petitioned him to return to Westminster and be reconciled with Parliament. Rival groups ran foul of each other in the streets of York with rough words and rough handling. Refugee settlers from northern Ireland, put ashore at Liverpool, drifted begging across the country and spread tales of horror and dread. Humble Puritan households prepared with fasting and prayer for an invasion of the Popish-Irish and for death at their hands. " O what fears and tears, cries and prayers, night and day, was there in many places, and in my dear mother's house in particular," wrote a Bradford man long after. " I was then about 12 or 13 years of age, and though I was afraid to be killed, yet was I weary of so much fasting and praying." [73] The ignorant were not alone in fearing Irish-Popish massacres: a Protestant gentleman wrote to Lord Fairfax: " it concerns us all to endeavour the prevention of the like in this Kingdom." The Puritan gentry looked with dismay at the volunteers the King was gathering in York from among their recusant neighbours; they called them " the Popish army." [74]

Charles, still trying to convince his subjects that he was a sound Protestant, sacrificed two priests. They were a tranquil and harmless pair who had been quietly ministering to their co-religionists in Yorkshire for years past while the law slept. Both were hanged in York, though one of them, Father Lockwood was nearly ninety years of age.[75]

Charles, to give more popular colour to his recruiting, now declared his intention of proceeding to Ireland in person to put down the rebels. In London, Parliament instantly objected, and the Council in Scotland, though in more guarded terms, also opposed the plan.[76] The King's attempt to assume the part of Protestant champion and protector of the settlers in Ireland convinced few of his friends and none of his enemies. The Council in Dublin had recently questioned two eminent prisoners under torture, and one of them, Hugh MacMahon, the young chieftain whom they had seized on the eve of the rising, stated on the rack that as long ago as the previous May he had heard that the King would support an Irish rising.[77] The second victim, Colonel John Read, an English professional soldier, was more guarded than MacMahon, and admitted little, but his reticence was interpreted to imply the King's guilt. The Dublin Council showed its own opinion by reporting the examination of these prisoners to Parliament alone, thus making it clear that they no longer looked to Charles for guidance or help.[78]

Neither the Council in Dublin, nor Parliament in London, nor the Puritan gentry of Yorkshire were altogether wrong in suspecting that if Charles went to Ireland he would not quell the insurgents, but join them. The Queen, who must have understood her husband's plans, wrote urgently from The Hague: she had heard that he intended to go to Ireland by way of Scotland; this, she pointed out, would be a grave mistake as the Scots were unlikely to help him; he would be wiser to go through Wales. She assumed without question that his final intent was to put himself at the head of the Irish. But she had the wisdom to give no official countenance to the idea that her husband would join the rebels, and when an Irish Franciscan Father in Brussels tried to secure an answer to this question she was commendably discreet.[79]

Observers in Europe none the less assumed that the King of Great Britain, threatened by the revolt of Parliament in England, would enlist the willing help of the Irish Catholics and so carry out to its logical conclusion the policy of favour to the Roman Church which had marked his days of power. His unhappy sister, the Protestant Queen of Bohemia, as she watched the activities of Queen Henrietta Maria in The Hague, and read the depressing news which her eldest son the Elector Palatine sent her from York, could see things in no other light. She strove at least to extricate her younger son, Prince Rupert, from a quarrel that she could not approve by appealing to the Venetian envoy in the Netherlands to recommend him for a place in the armies of the serene Republic.[80]

She acted too late. Prince Rupert had already pledged his services to the King; while he assisted Henrietta Maria with her recruiting in the Low Countries, King Charles at York had called a Chapter of Knights of the Garter to elect him one of their order. For some days the King was so deeply absorbed in these ceremonial proceedings that he scarcely had time to read reports from the rest of his dominions. His plans were, however, rapidly maturing. Early in April the Marquis of Hertford, rousing himself from his natural lethargy and disregarding the impertinent commands which Parliament sent after him, brought to York the King's younger son who had been left in his care. The little Duke was welcomed with blazing bonfires and met by a guard of nine hundred well-mounted troops. In the next few days he was formally elected a Knight of the Garter together with his absent cousin Rupert,[81] and on April 22nd he was sent, with a party of Lords and gentlemen, to visit the Governor of Hull.

IV

It was the King's first move in the war. Sir John Hotham, the Governor of Hull, suspected from the first that there was something behind this friendly visit, but he could hardly refuse to receive the royal child and his companions. Next morning Sir Lewis Dyve, George Digby's half-brother, rode into the town announcing that the King was on his way to rejoin his son in Hull with a troop of horse. Hotham saw the trap. If he let in the King and his men they would certainly take charge of the castle and magazine which he had agreed to hold for Parliament. The townsfolk were of divided sympathies, and the mayor was a royalist; with the Duke of York already in the town it would be doubly difficult for Hotham to exclude the King if he appeared at the gates. Tremulously he begged Dyve to make his excuses; he could not receive so many . . . he was quite unprepared. . . .

Hotham was experienced in local politics, ambitious and choleric; he had quarrelled with Strafford. He had no settled convictions except the not unusual belief in the importance of his family and the resolution to see that, whichever party won, the Hothams would have to be reckoned with in the East Riding of Yorkshire. The Commons flattered and spied on him— Hampden wrote him friendly letters, but his son, Captain Hotham, was encouraged to report on his conduct, and Peregrine Pelham, the member for Hull, travelled up and down from Westminster to keep in touch. Pelham was in the town when the King announced his visit, and stiffened the fretful Hotham in his loyalty to Parliament. When the royal party appeared, Hotham closed the gates of the city, came out on the wall and told the King that he could not enter. For a few minutes the decision hung in the balance; some of the King's men, seeing their friend the mayor also on the wall, called on the people of Hull to throw Hotham down to them and open the gates themselves. No one acted on this encouragement, and the Duke of York's companions, who might have been expected to give a lead to the Royalists in the town, were quietly at dinner and do not seem to have known what was happening. The King, astonished and angry, could only accept the rebuff and withdraw, followed at a little distance by the Duke of York and his crestfallen party of decoy ducks.[82]

One of this party was the King's eldest nephew, the Elector Palatine. The King had as usual included him in the group because of his unimpeachable association with the Protestant cause in Europe. He probably believed that his nephew would use his best endeavours to persuade Hotham of his duty to receive his sovereign. The Elector, who doubted his uncle's wisdom and resented the use that was made of him, did nothing or worse than nothing. It is certainly odd that the Duke's little party at dinner never noticed, or guessed the reasons for, the Governor's absence when he went on to the wall to speak to the King. Someone, surely, must have set an example in preserving such total indifference to the parley outside. Whatever part he had played, the incident decided the Elector to dissociate himself finally from the King; he calculated that, if it came to war, his wisest course was to remain on terms with the wealthier and more Protestant party—Parliament. Soon after the adventure at Hull where, in his resentful phrase, he had been " sorely catched in," he slipped away from York without leave-taking, asked Sir Symonds d'Ewes at Westminster to explain and excuse to the House of Commons his conduct in apparently abetting the King and crossed unobtrusively to the Netherlands.[83]

The King had withdrawn to York, sending Sir Lewis Dyve hurriedly away to the Queen in Holland with news of the check at Hull.[84] Maintaining the thin pretence that he was still on terms with Parliament, he asked them to punish Sir John Hotham for an act of treason, a request which was instantly ruled to be a breach of privilege.

The tension in London and Westminster had hardly abated since he left. Early in April the scare of an Irish invasion mounted again with news that the insurgents had taken Waterford. The execution of yet another priest, Edward Morgan, only temporarily assuaged the vindictive anti-Popery of the populace.[85] News of the King's attempt on Hull came into an atmosphere charged with anger and fear. At about the same time a party of Kentish Royalists entered the town: they came up Fish Street Hill " many hundred of them on horseback, with their protestation sticking in their hats and girdles," led by the courtier Richard Lovelace, reputed the handsomest man in England. The " protestation " that they carried was the petition for restoring the army to the King which Sir Thomas Malet had initiated at Maidstone Assizes in the winter. When they appeared at the doors of the House, Pym's party could think of no better way of refusing to receive their petition than by hurriedly rising before it could be presented. Next day the Commons voted it subversive and committed some of its sponsors to prison as dangerous malignants, an outrage which inspired Lovelace soon after to distil from the stone walls and iron bars of his confinement one of the loveliest lyrics in the English language.[86]

It was now only a question of time before the animosities which had spread throughout the country found a violent outlet. Already at Norwich bloodshed had been narrowly avoided on Shrove Tuesday when a rumour that the apprentices intended to break up the organ had caused the clergy to set a guard on the cathedral. An angry incident had occurred at Wells when a visiting Puritan threw a stone at an ancient Saxon crucifix. A group of godly image breakers had been ignominiously routed at Kidderminster and had fled with their minister, Richard Baxter, to join the " civil, courteous and religious people " of Gloucester. At Blockley the Puritan Vicar celebrated Easter Monday by knocking down the constable, tearing out his hair and kicking him into the ditch because he presumed to ask for money for a loan to the King. The lads of Ludlow on May-day set up " a thing like a head " on a May-pole and pelted it in derision of Roundheads; not far off other young rowdies were pelting in earnest a Puritan clergyman who had omitted the prayer for the King. Even in London the Royalists sometimes had their say, and no one intervened to help a godly brush-maker when a drunk Cavalier, at the dagger's point, made him kneel to Cheapside Cross and say a prayer for the Pope.[87]

Quiet-loving men stood by deploring the feverish state of the country, for which, as they medically put it, the only cure was by blood-letting. " The demands on both sides so ungrantable as there's little hope of any loving accordance. Yet both strive for the maintenance of the laws, and the question is not so much how to be governed (by the laws) as who shall be master and judge of them. A lamentable condition to consume the wealth and treasure of such a Kingdom, perhaps the blood too, upon a few nice wilful quibbles ": [88] the words of poor Sir Thomas Knyvett hit the mark near enough, but when the " nice, wilful quibbles " in dispute between two authorities are nothing less than the control of the armed forces, war has as good as started.

V

In this interval of confusion, few men were more to be pitied than the Earl of Ormonde to whom, as the general of the Dublin Government, fell the task of defending the English settlers in Ireland. By birth a Norman-Irish aristocrat whose mother and brothers had remained true to the old religion, Ormonde had been expected by many of the insurgents to join them as most of the Norman-Irish did. But he had been educated under the care of the English Crown as a Protestant, a religion to which he remained faithful; he had been trained in the responsibilities of civil government by the Earl of Strafford whose administrative gifts and material work for Ireland he never ceased to respect. His experience and still more his religion aligned him against the Irish rebels. But he was, on the other hand, deeply loyal to the King and distrustful of the speculators in Irish land who had ruined Strafford, who dominated the Council since his fall, and whose predatory policy had provoked the rebellion.

He was at this time about thirty years old, strong, tall and fair (James the White, the Irish called him) with a grace and charm that few could resist. He concealed his troubles under a manner calm, civilised and cheerful, but his troubles were many. An intelligent man with a high sense of duty he lived in an epoch when conflicting loyalties hampered the exercise of his judgment, and he was compelled to waste his administrative talents in a war which laid waste the country he loved, and ruined the master whom he asked only to serve.

On his return to Dublin after the relief of Drogheda he

found a ship newly come in with his wife and children aboard. The Countess had been allowed to leave Kilkenny, taking with her the fugitives in her care, to embark at Waterford. Arrived in Dublin she immediately applied her organising talent to the relief of the refugees. The women were formed into sewing parties to make shirts for her husband's soldiers and the children were sent to school. A little band of selected orphans she took into her personal care.[89]

Ormonde had time only to greet his wife and children before marching against the rebels in Kildare, where they abounded " like swarms of bees in the woods, bogs and other places of advantage." They scattered to their hiding places at his approach and would not be drawn to fight, but he drove off their cattle, hoping to destroy the nomadic economy by which they lived. The captured herds were shared out among the Ulster refugees, to each of whom was allotted a small plot of land and a sack of seed corn with orders to provide cheese, milk and (in time) grain for the supply of the army.

Roused by Ormonde's advance, the Irish from Kilkenny, a huge, ungoverned rabble surged out to meet him, led by Lord Mountgarret, the veteran leader of the Elizabethan rising. Ormonde intercepted them at the low-lying hamlet of Kilrush. On the uplands a little way off stood Maddingstown, the house of young Lord Castlehaven. Castlehaven owed his Irish land and title to a Jacobean grant but he was a Roman Catholic by conversion. He had seen service in the armies of the Duke of Savoy, had come home when King Charles called for volunteers in the Scots War, and had done nothing since. In this springtime of 1642 he was entertaining the frivolous Antrim and his equally frivolous wife, the Duchess of Buckingham. When the forces of Ormonde and Mountgarret closed in battle less than three miles away, the house-party at Maddingstown was rudely startled.

The Irish were more numerous than the Government troops, and they relied, as they had done all the winter, on the speed and force of their attack, their bright banners, their long dirks, and the terror they struck into the hearts of the settlers. Ormonde checked their onslaught with a cannonade; they had not faced artillery before. Ormonde's cavalry under the ferocious Charles Coote followed up the advantage, and Mountgarret's forces fled in confusion to the spongy safety of a neighbouring bog.[90]

The fighting was over by late afternoon and Ormonde announced himself and his staff as guests for dinner at Maddingstown. Castlehaven and Antrim received the victors with civility, but the Duchess of Buckingham caused embarrassment by calling Sir Charles Coote a bloodthirsty bully and low-born at that. Immediately afterwards Antrim vanished, having fled presumably to join his revolted clan in Ulster. His disappearance may have had something to do with this confrontation with Ormonde. Years later Antrim was to produce a strange story —namely that the King had instructed him and Ormonde in the summer of 1641 to keep together Strafford's disbanded army, to seize Dublin Castle, declare for the King and denounce the English Parliament, confident that the Irish nation would support them. But the Irish chiefs, forewarned by Antrim, and impatient of delay, began the war too soon and Ormonde had no choice but to dissociate himself from their violent and ill-timed rising. If this had indeed been so, then Ormonde knew things about Antrim which made his flight advisable in the event of a Government victory.[91]

Castlehaven too was sent for and questioned in Dublin, on a suspicion that the roast chickens he had served to Ormonde had been sizzling on the kitchen spits for Lord Mountgarret's dinner before the battle started. Castlehaven denied this, but was arrested none the less. Soon after he contrived to escape and return to his lands, but a mile from Maddingstown he saw the flames rising. Sir Charles Coote had fired the house. Castlehaven rode to Kilkenny and joined the Irish.[92] His defection and Antrim's return to Ulster were the unhappy after-effects of a battle which at the time caused great rejoicing to the English.

The engagement at Kilrush was held to prove that the Irish rebels would not be able to stand against a sufficient force of well-disciplined troops, although Ormonde, with sober realism, foretold that if the Irish could get arms, ammunition and a few more professional leaders, they would be able to defy the English indefinitely. As he saw it, the only hope of ending the war was to end it before too many good officers and supplies reached them from their friends abroad.[93]

In England they had other worries and did not look so far ahead. The King expressed his warm appreciation of Ormonde's services, the House of Commons voted him a jewel worth five hundred pounds and recommended that he be made a Knight of the Garter.[94] King and Parliament, as they approached the final breach, were equally anxious to retain the services of so valuable a man. Congratulations from York and presents from Westminster did nothing to ease the difficulties of Ormonde, an honourable man entangled in a web of plot and counter-plot. The King had acted with culpable indiscretion towards the Irish, but the Council in Dublin was now openly in favour of the English Parliament which had revolted against the King. Ormonde conscientiously performed his military duties, watched and waited.

VI

The King at York continued to exchange public recriminations with his Parliament at Westminster. Neither he nor they did anything to resolve the Irish problem. Charles was more concerned with Scotland. In the six months since he had left that country, the " rigid lords," dominated by Argyll, had consolidated their power, working in close alliance with the Church. Regular local synods maintained a firm hold on the morals—and through them on the politics—of the people. The Church of Scotland was controlled, in the last resort, by the elders who since the elections to the Glasgow Assembly three years earlier had been chosen overwhelmingly from the friends, clients and supporters of the party in power. Nearly all ministers and schoolmasters who had wavered towards episcopacy had by this time been removed or brought rigidly into line.[95] The unanimity between State and Church in Scotland had rarely been more complete, and the actual dominance of the secular over the spiritual arm was masked by the genuine religious fervour of Argyll, which set the tone for other less pious lords. The days when the Covenant party had been led by the openly ambitious, loud, cheerful, jesting Rothes seemed far away. The austere and searching spirit of the present rulers allowed for little deviation, and those who sought to gain or hold power adapted themselves to the example of Argyll and the precepts of the ministers.

The endemic troubles of the Highlands gave further opportunities for the extension of Argyll's authority and the power of the Church. A new Justiciary Commission on which Argyll was naturally prominent had recently been set up to control these regions, by holding Courts twice yearly to inquire into and punish disorders.[96] The political use that might be made of such Courts was obvious, and there were other opportunities for extending the authority of Church and State. When, for instance, the unruly MacGregors fell to raiding the Gordon country, the outbreak provided an excuse for patrolling a region notoriously unfavourable to the Covenant. It was perhaps with the intention of preventing Royalist plots and gatherings that the Presbytery in Aberdeen forbade all merry-making at Easter and arbitrarily prolonged Lent for three weeks.[97]

Argyll was not only concerned to maintain order; he lent his authority to the efforts of the ministers to elevate the moral character of the Highlanders. The synod of Argyll, " by the happy reformation of these days," abolished the giving of presents at Christmas and Easter; it fulminated against the idolatry and loose living of the people of Lochaber and the

Island of Skye, and threatened with the jougs any ignorant women who still presumed " to howl their dead into the graves, which commonly is called the coronach." [98]

The Edinburgh Government during the last months had been principally concerned to set an army on foot against the Irish in Ulster. The King had given Argyll authority to act against the rebels, a military commission which he would in time most bitterly regret. So far, however, Argyll had proceeded with his usual efficiency; controlling, as he did, the coast and islands facing towards northern Ireland he managed to keep the sea passage open and to furnish the Ulster ports, still held by the settlers, with supplies of meal and salt fish. A well-equipped force of more than two thousand men under Robert Monro, a professional trained in the Swedish service, landed at Carrick-fergus in mid-April, just about the time of Ormonde's victory over Mountgarret at Kilrush.

Jealous for the stores and supplies, the English at Londonderry refused to co-operate. Monro turned south towards Newry, driving off the Irish cattle as he marched, and using their oxen for his gun teams. Brushing off a band of Irish under Rory M'Ginnes he reached and took Newry where he shot and hanged sixty of the citizens and two priests for helping the rebels. A general massacre of the women prisoners was prevented by the more humane Colonel James Turner. A day later Phelim O'Neill burnt the town of Armagh, some said to save it from Monro, others out of revenge for the shootings at Newry. The hatred felt by the Covenanting soldiers for the Popish Irish was deepened by superstitious fear. Violent storms and bitter cold came down on them; in the high wind they could not pitch their tents and some died of exposure in the open fields. Such weather in early May they thought must be procured by Irish witchcraft.[99]

The character of the Scottish army to be raised for Ireland had been agreed on in consultation with the English Parliament; Monro had not transported the whole of it and the oppressed

PRINCE RUPERT
by Gerard Honthorst

ROBERT DEVEREUX, EARL OF ESSEX
from an engraving by George Glover

Royalists in Scotland viewed with anxiety the still very considerable army that the Covenanters maintained at home under Lord Leven's command.[100] The King was less perturbed by this because he thought he had secured Leven's friendship when he gave him his title, and he hoped that the Covenanting army, if it was used at all, would be used in his interests. He was anxious to conciliate rather than to challenge a party which had so much power at its command. When some of the Scottish Royalists, Montrose and his cousin Airlie, tried to come to him at York he forbade their approach.[101]

He received instead Argyll's spokesman, the Chancellor Loudoun, and heard from him the unwelcome news that his Scots Council considered the English Parliament to be in the right in the present unfortunate quarrel. " We do not require of you that ye sit as judges upon the affairs of another Kingdom," Charles replied with some asperity, and sent Loudoun back with a new exposition of the royal case.[102]

On his return Loudoun found Edinburgh crammed with intruders. The Royalists had worked up a petition in favour of the King against Parliament, and their lords and gentry came into the capital with a considerable following. A rumour, possibly spontaneous, probably inspired, accused them of " a wicked design against Argyll's person." At this " the gentry and ministry of Fife " took alarm and came into the town " running over in thousands," while a regiment of men at arms was brought in to guard the Council. In this atmosphere, the old Earl of Morton pleaded in vain the rights of the King— *their* King and fellow countryman—against the pretensions of the arrogant English Parliament. The Council welcomed a petition from the Covenanters, rejected that of the Royalists, and informed the King that they would use all their endeavours to make a happy concord between him and his Parliament. Even this failed to discourage Charles; still convinced that the Covenanters were at heart his friends, he despatched Hamilton to reason with them.[103]

VII

The King's foreign diplomacy had meanwhile foundered. The Queen could get little help from the Prince of Orange because the Dutch Estates were now openly on the side of Parliament.[104] The King of Denmark was too deeply involved in the German wars, where he was trying to set himself up as an arbiter and mediator, to have time—still less, money—to spare for his nephew of England. The Queen's appeal to the Spanish Netherlands was equally ineffective. From Westminster, the French Ambassador, La Ferté Imbault, pursuing the interests of France, crossed the King's efforts to maintain relations with the Habsburg dynasty in Austria; he informed Pym that Charles's ambassador in Vienna was about to make an alliance with the Roman Catholic imperial party in Germany. Charles's ambassador, the veteran Protestant diplomatist Sir Thomas Rowe, had no such thought in mind. He was only doing what he had been doing for the last fifteen years—trying to use his master's dwindling prestige in favour of a just settlement of the German religious wars and the restoration of the King's sister and her children to their rights. The storm of anger aroused by the French envoy's imaginative statement caused Charles to recall Rowe since the advantage to be gained by his continuance at Vienna was more than cancelled by the harm it was doing him at home.[105]

Foreign diplomatists already reckoned with Parliament as a more effective factor in the politics of Europe than the King. London was the commercial capital where the trading nations —the Dutch, the Venetians, the French, the newly liberated Portuguese, and even the Spaniards—must evidently keep their representatives. The Venetian Resident all this spring and summer had been troubled over the importation of currants; many Aegean islands, under Venetian rule, lived on the sale of currants, but the City of London, early in 1642, had prohibited their further importation because the Venetians were obstructing the sale of English cloth in the Adriatic ports. The Resident accused Samuel Vassell and Thomas Soame, both members of Parliament for London, of having engineered the prohibition in order to sell their own stocks of currants at exorbitant rates. He appealed to the King at York, but even if Charles had had time to consider the problem—in which he showed little interest —he could have done nothing about it.[106] The competent authorities were at London or at Westminster. The King, as all foreign states were quick to realise, would be of little account in the affairs of Europe until he had regained his capital and greatest seaport.

VIII

King and Parliament now moved fast towards war. On May 8th Commissioners reached York from Westminster ostensibly to discuss with the King the incident at Hull. Charles rightly suspected them of intending to interfere with his recruiting plans in Yorkshire and ordered them to leave. They refused to do so. On the 12th the King summoned the Yorkshire gentry to attend him in arms; immediately a group of them, headed by the Parliament men, Stapleton and Cholmley, lodged a protest.[107]

In London, on May 10th, the City regiments were reviewed by Philip Skippon in Finsbury Fields and all the leading members of Parliament rode or drove out to view them.[108] Charles, from York, struck now at what he believed to be a vulnerable point in his opponents' schemes: he ordered the removal of the law courts to the North. At this news, on May 17th, Parliament with Lord Keeper Littleton's approval declared the King's interference with the law courts illegal. But a messenger from the King managed to persuade the Lord Keeper to second thoughts. He despatched the Great Seal to York, following after it as unobtrusively as he could. Bluffing his way past an officious constable who tried to stop him at Woburn, he rejoined the King.[109]

Charles now had the greatest law officer in the Kingdom on his side, but had he the law on his side? So long as the Great Seal remained with them, Parliament could sneer at the King's proclamations as mere printed papers. Once he had the Great Seal, the legal position was dangerously altered, and they had to act at once to redress the balance in their own favour.

On May 27th they declared that the King, seduced by wicked counsellors, was making war on his Parliament. In this chaos of the constitution, therefore, lawful authority for preserving the peace and governing the Kingdom devolved upon them, and the King's subjects were instructed henceforward to accept no order as valid that did not come from the two Houses of Parliament. From this stupendous claim there was no going back; in order to preserve the King's peace Parliament had declared war on the King.[110]

The last barrier was down and the two claimants to sovereignty, King and Parliament, faced each other in open defiance. Nineteen propositions on the future government of the country were agreed to by both Houses on June 1st. They demanded for Parliament the control of all the high offices military and civil, in the Kingdom, the prosecution of the laws against the Roman Catholics and the reform of the Church, the control of all fortresses, effective support for the Protestant Cause in Europe, and the clearing of the Five Members of the monstrous charges against them. The nineteen propositions were the ultimatum on the eve of war. No one regarded them as anything else.[111]

On June 3rd the King rode out to Heyworth Moor with his two sons to receive a demonstration of loyalty from the gentry of Yorkshire organised by Lord Savile. But the Fairfaxes had also been busy and contrary to expectation several hundred of the opposite party appeared with a petition asking Charles to return to Westminster. Savile tried to prevent their approach, but Sir Thomas Fairfax out-manœuvred him and pushed the petition on to the King's saddle. Charles, pretending not to see him, almost rode over him, an act of discourtesy which was long and angrily remembered in Yorkshire.[112]

In London, the same week, Parliament's appeal for loans of plate and money at eight per cent interest met with an enthusiastic response. Their friends were raising troops over all the country-side. Puritan clergy urged young men to take arms for the Lord, Puritan gentry laid in powder and stores, and armed their tenantry.[113] Sir Thomas Knyvett, a harmless loyalist from East Anglia, meeting the Earl of Warwick at Westminster, was commanded to raise a foot company for Parliament; he accepted the charge because " 'twas no place to dispute"; privately he was wondering if he could slip away to the King, foot company and all.[114]

Charles now denounced and rejected the nineteen propositions which were framed, he said, by " raisers of sedition and enemies to my sovereign power."[115] He persuaded the peers who had joined him at York to sign a protestation declaring themselves fully satisfied of his peaceful intentions; and that they had seen no " preparations or counsels that might reasonably beget the belief" that he had any design of making war on his Parliament. Strong in this confirmation of his peaceable intentions, the King next day issued Commissions of Array to all the Lords Lieutenant throughout the Kingdom: it was the general call to arms.

Parliament, equally determined to be in the right, called in the authority of John Selden, who gave it as his opinion that the King's Commissions of Array were unlawful. This dictum was respectfully received, but when he expressed the view that Parliament's Militia Ordinance was not lawful either, his opinion was disregarded. Not caring for this disparaging treatment, he said no more about it.

For all the thousands of small men from Justices of the Peace downwards on whom the peaceful order of the country rested some kind of choice could not long be postponed; they would have ultimately to implement the orders of either King or Parliament. "Now there is so much declared as makes all officers in the Kingdom traitors of one side or the other," wrote Sir Thomas Knyvett, "neither are standers by in any better condition."[116]

At York offers of help flowed in; forty peers each agreed to pay a troop of horse for three months. (Some of them, including the Marquis of Hamilton, later defaulted.) The violent young men rejoiced, and Harry Wilmot wrote blithely to a friend that there would be pickings to be had from the fat estates of the Parliament men when the war was won.[117]

But they were still a long way from conquering London and the fat estates. The Lord Mayor, loyal to the end, had the King's Commission of Array read in the City, and was soon after deprived of his office and clapped into the Tower by Parliament.[118]

Now, all over the country, the great lords and gentry of each party manœuvred for position, wooed or commanded the support of tenants and neighbours, and tried to secure whatever magazine of arms was kept for the use of the local levies in time of war. Clashes occurred over the Commissions of Array, with defiance, resistance, high words and blows. In Yorkshire the Fairfaxes and their adherents were insulted by the King's officers. In Gloucestershire, Lord Chandos, who tried to read the Commission of Array, was driven out of Cirencester and his fine coach broken in pieces. Henry Hastings, the spirited younger son of the Earl of Huntingdon, was more successful in proclaiming the Commission in Leicestershire, though he failed to seize the city of Leicester with a party of newly-recruited miners from the family estates in Derbyshire.[119] Members of both Houses left Westminster to work up the cause of Parliament in the countryside. The Earl of Warwick approvingly watched the Essex levies drilling, and in London five hundred cavalry were trying to master the art of war in Tothill Fields.[120] In Hereford the Royalist gentry assembled the local levies, but could not think what to do with them next; one of the greatest men in the region, the Puritan Sir Robert Harley, was at Westminster, but Lady Harley fortified his castle at Brampton Bryan against her malignant neighbours and sent the family plate to London for Parliament's use, not forgetting to add a wholesome home-baked cake for her husband.[121]

Intimidated by the Puritan Lord Willoughby, the Mayor of Leicester rejected the King's Commission of Array and arrested his messenger, but when Willoughby's back was turned he slipped away with his prisoner and joined the royal following at York. At Warwick, Tibbott, the armourer, boldly defied the local Puritan magnate, grim Lord Brooke, and would not give up to him the arms which Royalist gentlemen had left in his shop for repair.[122]

At York the King received offers from North and South Wales—Sir Richard Lloyd for the North promised ten thousand men, and Lord Herbert of Raglan, son of the enormously rich Marquis of Worcester, put his own and his father's fortune unreservedly at the King's disposal. He had advanced more than a hundred thousand pounds to the King in the course of the summer.[123]

Before the end of June the Earl of Newcastle, acting for the King, had made himself master of the town whose name he carried. By securing Newcastle-on-Tyne the King hoped to gain valuable revenues from the export of coal. But unless he had the Navy at his command he would be cut off from the advantages of foreign commerce and foreign help.

The King had failed to secure his Navy. The care he had lavished on it in the days of his power had counted for little with the majority of his seafaring subjects because his policies abroad had offended against the traditions in which they had been bred. When the mariners had joined the demonstrations against him in January they had offered a petition which contained significant phrases: " That great vessel the Parliament House which is so richly fraught with no less than the price of a kingdom is fearfully shaken and in great danger. Rome has rocks and Spain quicksands to swallow her up."[124] The majority of the captains and the crews of the King's own fleet thought that he had piloted the ship of state towards the Roman rocks and the Spanish quicksands.

The king was also at a practical disadvantage because the principal naval dockyard and magazines at Chatham were in the hands of Parliament. But he could at least have hampered his opponents by removing the Earl of Northumberland from his post as Lord High Admiral. This proud and able man who had been one of the King's principal councillors throughout his personal rule had quietly and consistently opposed him ever since Parliament met. The reasons for his conduct are not easy to define; he had felt himself to be undervalued by the King, and his unbending nature led him to despise the tricks and subterfuges of the royal policy. Writing to Sir John Bankes, he expressed views on the character of Parliament which he seems to have kept to himself during the King's personal rule: " We believe that those persons who are most powerful with the King do endeavour to bring Parliament to such a condition that they shall only be made instruments to execute the commands of the King, who were established for his most supreme council."[125]

When the King went to York and the danger of Civil War was apparent, Northumberland conveniently evaded his responsibilities by falling ill. Charles wished him to appoint the Royalist Sir John Pennington as his Deputy, but Northumberland preferred to appoint the Earl of Warwick. So matters stood until the end of June when Charles, recognising very late that Northumberland was his enemy, dismissed him, and ordered Pennington to take command of the fleet, then riding in the Downs, and bring it to Bridlington Bay. Parliament instructed Warwick to continue in charge of the fleet and to forestall anything that Pennington might try to do. The King's candidate was out-matched from the start. He had never been a man of great initiative, and while he waited for more explicit orders, Warwick, on July 2nd, was already with the fleet.

Warwick was an active and adventurous seaman, with all the Elizabethan hatred of the Spaniard. When the King had made peace with Spain, Warwick had organised his own pirate fleet, under the flag of the Duke of Savoy, to prey on Spanish ships. He had been a principal shareholder in the Providence Company and had freely spent his money and his energy to secure for his countrymen a share in the riches of Spanish America. In that very summer he had authorised Captain William Jackson, with three ships, to set forth on a voyage of piracy to the Caribbean.[126] Tough and quick-witted with a vigorous, open manner which made him popular with the seamen, Warwick had little difficulty in securing the navy for Parliament. Five captains only refused obedience. Warwick had their ships encircled whereupon three of the five weakened. He fired warning shots over the remaining two, then easily boarded and overpowered the captains. The King had lost the fleet, and with it his remaining reputation in Europe; a King of Great Britain without a navy was, in all the interchanges of diplomacy, no King at all.[127]

Of all his great fleet, there remained to the King only a few lesser ships which had not been in the Downs at the time. The *Providence*, a fourth rate of three hundred tons which had attended the Queen on her journey, was bringing a supply of gunpowder to him from Holland. She was chased and captured off Hull by the more powerful *Mayflower*, an armed merchantman in the service of Parliament, but her captain, with great skill slipped from his guard in the Humber estuary and sailed the *Providence* into a narrow creek where the *Mayflower* could not follow. Here on the muddy shore some of the King's men successfully unloaded her cargo.[128]

The *Mayflower* was left with no larger prize than a small ketch which was seized in the estuary with a seasick Frenchman on board, who was sent a prisoner to Sir John Hotham at Hull.

There he joyously revealed himself to be neither French nor seasick, but Lord Digby in the best of health and spirits. He had been secretly with the King at York, and by his account of the royal plans and prospects he now beguiled Hotham into agreeing to yield Hull. All that the fickle Governor asked was that the King should come against the town in sufficient force to give to the agreed betrayal the appearance of honourable surrender.

The King therefore in the first week of July came with his army to Beverley, dug trenches, made a show of encircling Hull by flooding the adjacent fields, and raised batteries against its walls. But Hotham failed him. Parliament, suspicious of his intentions, had sent Sir John Meldrum, a Scottish professional, to his assistance. Meldrum took charge of the defences, made a sally against the King's men and drove them from their trenches.[129]

Amid the sights and sounds of war, Charles received Commissioners from Parliament led by the Earl of Holland who, for the last time, asked him to return in peace to his capital. Let them order the delivery of Hull into his hands, said the King, in earnest of their intentions. They refused. " Let all the world now judge who began this war," said the King.[130]

In the same week Royalists and Parliament men had clashed in Lancashire. Lord Strange had proclaimed the King's call to arms at Preston and had seized the magazine at Liverpool. He was powerful in the county, where he had great possessions, spread wide about his palatial mansion of Lathom House; but he was not loved. Lord Wharton, acting for Parliament, was also raising levies. Both converged on the town of Manchester where was another local magazine of arms. It was a place of hard work and no pretensions, " the very London of these parts, the liver that sends blood into all the countries thereabouts "[131]—in simpler words, the centre of the fustian industry. Its people were strong in the militant Puritanism which so often characterised the clothiers and weavers of England. Here was daily preaching and singing of psalms, and the little town had already received a number of Puritan refugees from Yorkshire who told horrid tales of the excesses of the King's cavaliers.[132]

Lord Strange with a small party of horse reached Manchester before Lord Wharton, on July 15th, 1642. The town had few and weak defences, and some of the citizens asked him in to dine, hoping that all would go off pleasantly. Other citizens, alarmed, began to get out their muskets and muster their neighbours in the streets. The fighting started no one quite knew how, with men on horse and men on foot slashing and firing wildly in the mean muddy streets under the pelting rain. Strange and his men were driven out, leaving some of their own men wounded and one of their assailants dead.[133] Later Lord Strange was impeached and charged with killing the first man in the Civil War.[134] But the charge is disputable, for in the summer of 1642, casually and dispersedly, over all England, Civil War had begun.

CHAPTER THREE

AUTUMN CAMPAIGN

August—November 1642

IN accident and miscalculation the King had begun his war. The divided North gave him no assured base for his march on London; he had not secured Hull; no help came from Scotland. He sent in turn Hamilton and Will Murray to win the support of Argyll, but whatever these two did in Edinburgh —and the King's friends thought they did only harm[1]—the Covenanters were too wary to move.

The Marquis of Argyll was now in effect the ruler of Scotland. Clear-sighted and laborious, persuasive in argument and sure in his judgments, he dominated the Council with the discreet assistance of his kinsman, the Chancellor Loudoun. Argyll had never been deceived by the King's concessions to the Covenanters; he understood very well that Charles would favour them only so long as he needed their help against his English Parliament. When Pym was overthrown, their turn would come. Argyll would rather have seen the King come to terms with his opponents than make war upon them, but if war there had to be, then, in the interests of the Covenanters, and in what he sincerely thought to be the true interests of his country and his King, Argyll was on the side of Parliament.

News from Ireland deepened his distrust of the King. His lands lay on the Western seaboard, facing towards Ulster. Over the years his own ships and those of his people, fishing in home waters, or trading abroad, had been troubled by the lawless interventions of the Irish Macdonnells and the Macdonalds of the Isles and the Western Highlands. The Irish language, the Catholic religion and the deep loyalties of the clan bound these people together; it was possible that, through them, the Irish revolt might spread to Scotland. The Earl of Antrim, chief of the Ulster Macdonnells had, only a few years before, secured the royal permission to invade and seize Argyll's land of Kintyre.[2] This outrageous grant was brought to memory during the summer of 1642 when Robert Monro, general of the Scots forces in Ulster, captured Antrim's own Castle of Dunluce with the Earl inside it. The candid and loquacious Antrim informed his captors, who passed on the news to Edinburgh, that the King had instructed him to hold Dunluce at all costs and had promised to make him " general of all the Roman Catholic forces in Ulster." [3]

In the face of this further evidence of the King's interest in the Irish rising, the Council at Edinburgh returned circumspect answers to his requests for help, redoubled its watchfulness on the Highlands, tightened the precautions against Roman Catholics and ordered the seizure of all suspect priests and Jesuits " being crafty and politic heads and traffickers in matters of state." [4]

The Assembly of the Church met at St. Andrews in July and was attended by several representatives from Ulster,[5] bitter alike against the King and the Irish. Throughout the meetings Argyll set an example of punctuality and helpfulness much and rightly commended by the ministers. " All the diets of our Synod he kept and did give most and best advice in every purpose . . . Our Privy Committee before or after the Assembly, he never missed . . . and yet never complained of weariness." In response to a message from the English Parliament, the Assembly appointed a commission to consider the reformation of the Church throughout Great Britain.[6] The principal commissioner chosen to forge this new link between the Covenanters and the King's enemies in England was John, Lord Maitland, a bulky red-headed young man of great learning and prodigious memory, a cold heart, a shrewd head, and a wrathful, spluttering eloquence. The decisions of the Assembly were ratified by the Council on a day when Hamilton, who ought to have defended the King's interests, was tactfully absent,[7] and the sending of Lord Maitland to Westminster marked the end of the King's misplaced hopes of help from the men he had raised to power in Scotland.

The process by which his Council in Scotland abandoned him was a model of candour compared with the conduct of his Council in Ireland. The harassed Government in Dublin, without money to pay the troops, or to keep them armed and clothed and shod, looked to Parliament for military help—since the King could send them none. The Irish could count on surreptitious help from both the two great rival powers in Europe, since neither France nor Spain would allow the other to make an exclusive claim on the gratitude, and future alliance, of a free Roman Catholic Ireland. Both Governments permitted Irish commanders and troops in their service to withdraw and gave them transport to their native land, while the Spaniards sent arms and supplies.[8] In the course of the summer two distinguished generals came home to organise their warlike countrymen. Thomas Preston, son of a Norman Irish nobleman, who had risen to a position of high trust in the Spanish Netherlands, and won recent laurels at the siege of Genappe, landed at Wexford. More secretly, in the North on the shores of Lough Swilly, landed Owen Roe O'Neill, the Red O'Neill, chief of the clan, nephew to the great Tyrone of Elizabethan fame. Trained from boyhood in the discipline of the Spanish Army, he soon turned the fierce raiders of Ulster into a formidable army.[9]

All this while the King had sent no help to the settlers, and Parliament, very little. The hungry troops were mutinous, the city of Dublin crammed with sick and homeless fugitives.[10] A small naval expedition, financed by the company of Merchant Adventurers, after battling through dirty weather, escaping shipwreck off the Scilly Isles and lying long becalmed by sea-fog off the Irish coast, reached Munster in mid-July. It was led by a Scottish professional, Lord Forbes, an angry Calvinist trained in the German wars and convinced that the Irish were less than human, the settlers incompetent or treacherous. His chaplain, an eloquent, resolute, bustling little man, Hugh Peter, had newly returned from America and felt about the Irish much as he did about the Redskins.

Forbes and his men fell on the South and West coasts like a cloud-burst. They landed at Kinsale and scoured the country round without regard to friend or foe. At Timoleague, a little village with a great abbey which had done no harm to anyone, Forbes, with grim enjoyment, " burnt all the town and their great abbey," and allowed his men to torture and kill two prisoners on suspicion of being spies: " the rogues slight death, for we could get nothing out of them," he recorded. Invited to Galway, by a Puritan officer who governed the castle, in flat defiance of Lord Clanricarde, who was with difficulty keeping the town neutral, Forbes sacked the town, plundered the outlying villages, and desecrated St. Mary's Church. The settlers at Tralee, beseiged by the Irish, hoped for his help, but he stopped on the way to plunder the Aran Islands and arrived too late. Sailing south again he made landings on the coast of Clare to burn houses and destroy crops before unloosing his men in a last destructive raid up the Shannon Valley. " These kind of proceedings," reported the gentle Clanricarde from Galway, " make such assistance more destructive than beneficial to us," and Lord Inchiquin, who commanded in Munster, wrote in a fury to the Council in Dublin to ask by whose authority this bloody, rash, uncivil and incompetent fellow had been inflicted upon him in lieu of help.[11]

" By whose authority " was a question which gravely troubled some members of the Council in Dublin. It had been an uneasy, divided body since the fall of Strafford. His supporters and disciples, of whom Ormonde was the chief, had little love for their colleagues who had engineered his fall or risen by it. Of the two Lords Justices who headed the administration, one, Sir John Borlase, was a cypher; the other, Sir William Parsons, a rapacious speculator in Irish land who had at first greeted the rebellion with unconcealed pleasure as a new excuse to despoil the Irish of their possessions. Things were certainly not going according to Sir William Parsons's hopes, and he was not the only one at the Council table in Dublin who suspected the intentions of the King. Official reports from the Dublin Government still went to Parliament at Westminster and not to the King in the North. On August 13th, 1642, Ormonde wrote to Secretary Nicholas at York telling him of his doubts of his colleagues' loyalty. He advised no action, for the position was too delicate and the Council too much divided; but he implored the King to be watchful.[12]

II

By the time Ormonde's letter reached York the King had formally declared war. All July and August King's men and Parliament men over the whole country had been active to secure the adherence of their neighbours, the custody of the strong places, the possession of the stores and arms belonging to the Trained Bands of each county, and wherever possible the precious metals which are the sinews of war. In the University of Cambridge the Royalists packed up their plate for the King; one cartload reached him, but Oliver Cromwell, active to prevent any more such escapes, occupied the town, held back all the rest and shortly after arrested and marched off to prison several heads of colleges.[13] In Oxford the students, marshalled by some of the King's soldiers, exercised themselves in arms to the annoyance of peaceable citizens, and when the Members of Parliament for the town came down to interfere, drove them out with ignominy.[14]

At the town of Watlington below the Chiltern hills, John Hampden prevented the Earl of Berkshire from reading the King's Commission of Array. The Royalist call to arms was silenced at Cirencester by the Puritan populace and at Worcester, where the people were more sympathetic, by the timely arrival of the two active Members of Parliament for the county. The Marquis of Hertford and Sir Ralph Hopton failed to raise Somerset for the King and withdrew to Dorset where, for a little, it seemed they might do better.[15] But the county was bitterly divided, and at Dorchester violence of another kind broke out when Hugh Green, a Roman Catholic priest, was hanged in the Roman amphitheatre and the faithful who tried to secure relics fought across the martyr's body with their Puritan neighbours.[16]

In other regions the Cavaliers fared better. At Nantwich they rode into the town in " a bravado, with great shouting and rejoicing," and kept out Sir William Brereton who was raising men for Parliament. He had been equally unfortunate in Chester when he tried to recruit there.[17] Near Banbury, far-famed for its Puritan austerity, the Royalist Lord Northampton intercepted and seized five cannon from one of Lord Saye's sober-sided sons.[18] At Portsmouth, to the momentary dismay of Parliament, Colonel Goring, who had successfully convinced them of his devotion, threw off the mask and declared for the King.[19] But without a Navy Portsmouth was of little value, and Goring, once Parliament blockaded him from the sea, could do nothing to solve the King's now vital problem of communication with the friends abroad from whom he expected arms, money and men. While the Queen did her utmost to raise all three, the seas between her and her husband were assiduously patrolled for Parliament by the fleet which he had so lovingly built on the proceeds of Ship-money.

He had at least not authorised the taxes which his subjects were to pay for the war against him; he had refused to pass the Annual Tonnage and Poundage Bill offered to him at York just before the breach with Parliament became absolute. Parliament was therefore without any legal instrument for the enforcement of customs duties, and on August 1st issued an ordinance, couched in persuasive phrases, declaring that although no subject was "compellable," it would be counted " an acceptable service to the Commonwealth " if they would pay the duties prescribed in the Bill as if the King had passed it. The money they needed for the Navy alone amounted already to nearly £200,000, but as every merchant in London, whatever his politics, knew that trade depended on the security of the seas, it was probable that the imposts would be paid.[20]

Early in August Prince Rupert, with his brother Maurice and a staff of professional soldiers, mostly English or Scots, sailed from Holland; challenged and fired on by a Parliamentary ship, they out-sailed the pursuer and put in to Tynemouth which, with Newcastle, held out for the King.[21]

The active on both sides were still the minority. Small bodies raised by men of influence and ardour seized on the stores of the local militia and fought each other for possession of arms and strong places. But many of the gentry still hoped that they could divert the war from their borders. In Lincolnshire, after at first obediently putting the Commission of Array into force for the King, they resolved " not to embark further by sending any forces out of the county " but to work for an accommodation. In Yorkshire, Cheshire, Staffordshire, Cornwall and Devon for the next six months there were to be local pacts of non-aggression, vain attempts to secure a limited neutrality for themselves whatever their neighbours might do.[22] The militia was generally unwilling to bestir itself for either side and the enthusiasts of both parties appealed instead for volunteers. John Hampden armed his tenantry, a full regiment all in dark green. A retired sea captain at Gravesend raised a troop of " well affected and stout youngsters." Oliver Cromwell called on the fen men to take arms for " the freedom of the gospel and the laws of the land," but it was commonly thought that they enlisted " the rather

because they hope Parliament will give them their fens again "
and curb the speculators who were draining and enclosing them.
In regions where trade had long been depressed, in Essex among
the hungry weavers and in London and the suburbs, recruiting
went well, but new coats, boots, food and the prospect of plunder
drew in the men, rather than the desire to defend the gospel and
the law. In that unruly autumn there was plundering of larders
and poaching of deer wherever Parliament's army went;
smashing of church glass, burning of altar rails and destruction
of images were added to demonstrate the religious fervour of the
troops. Soon the Commons had to issue an order forbidding the
plunder of the " disaffected " because their houses and property
were the patrimony of the Commonwealth and would be
more serviceable if not destroyed, and Hampden, after seeing
some of the troops' handiwork in Northamptonshire, wrote
urgently suggesting that martial law be applied to check their
excesses. [23]

Some companies and troops were more respectable. Volunteers from the Inns of Court, young men of good family like
Edmund Ludlow and Charles Fleetwood, or humbler enthusiasts,
clerks and messengers like Thomas Harrison and Matthew
Tomlinson, formed themselves into a lifeguard for the Earl of
Essex.[24] This veteran of the Dutch wars, this sober, god-fearing,
pipe-smoking nobleman who had steadfastly supported Pym's
party in the House of Lords had been appointed—it was the
inevitable choice—general of Parliament's forces early in July.
He was a strange heir to his father, that turbulent and passionate
Earl of Essex whom Elizabeth had sent to the block forty years
before, but the King, to whom all rebellions seemed much alike,
was constantly thereafter inclined to draw comparisons between
father and son and to cite Queen Elizabeth's handling of the
Essex affair as though it provided a useful precedent for his own
conduct.[25]

There was deceptively something of a feudal family atmosphere
about a war, in which the chief commanders by land and sea

both sprang from the one ambitious stock, for Warwick was the son of Penelope Devereux, sister to Elizabeth's Essex and the Stella of Sir Philip Sidney's poems. But the King grasped only what was least important in the situation; it was not very remarkable that Essex and Warwick were cousins, but it was significant that both had been reared in the Elizabethan tradition of Protestantism and expansion.

While Parliament's chosen leaders made ready by land and sea, Pym tautened the procedure at the centre. Every message to the front could not be discussed in both Houses; the immediate conduct of the war must be confined to a few. On July 4th, 1642, the Committee of Safety came into being for this purpose. It was a body consisting of members of both Houses chosen by vote,[26] a body into whose hands gradually the effective power of Parliament would be delegated.

With the near approach of war almost all eminent Royalists had left London and the neighbourhood to offer their services to the King. By order of Parliament their houses were searched for arms, and plundered of anything else the searchers fancied. In the City the occasion was almost openly used for paying off old scores against rivals. All the Duke of Richmond's fine Barbary horses were taken from his stables at Cobham, Lord Dorset's stores at Knole were rifled, and in Hertfordshire the young Earl of Bedford descended on the houses of his Royalist neighbours, Sir Thomas Fanshawe and Sir Arthur Capel, and sent their valuables to Parliament.[27]

The King's advance on London was daily feared, but in the North Charles hesitated. He briefly reconnoitred the midlands in late July, then returned to Yorkshire, where he contemplated seizing Lord Fairfax and his son, the two most active organisers of the opposing party, before he again marched South. He abandoned this design for fear of antagonising the quiescent or neutral northern gentry,[28] and at last, after appointing for his lieutenant of the North parts the Earl of Cumberland, the mild scion of the once formidable family of Clifford, he turned southwards. Proclaiming the Earl of Essex a traitor, he advanced into the midlands. His forces numbered a few hundred only, but he counted on the ready support of the local magnates, the Earl of Northampton, Sir John Byron, the energetic Henry Hastings, and most of all on the Earl of Lindsey who had promised strong support from his tenantry in Nottingham and Lincolnshire. But rival influences had worked for Parliament and the King was coolly received. He had hoped to catch Sir Arthur Haslerig, one of the Five Members, who had been raising men on his Leicestershire estates and was said to be still "lurking thereabouts," but Haslerig, forewarned and well-friended, eluded him. At Leicester he captured instead an old enemy, crop-eared John Bastwick who had stood in the pillory five years before for attacking the bishops. Charles would have arraigned him at once for high treason but was dissuaded, for fear that a local jury would acquit him.[29]

His intention now was formally to raise the Royal Standard and call on all loyal subjects to restore him to his own. Lord Strange had urged him to choose Warrington for this gesture, a town in the protecting shadow of the feudal-royalist Stanley domains. But Warrington was too remote from the help which the King still expected from his wife in the Netherlands. He chose instead Nottingham, reachable from the Humber estuary by the navigable Trent, commanding a critical bridge in the road complex of the midlands, and near—as he thought—to the country where his supporters could raise men.[30] It was a place of about five thousand inhabitants, prosperous enough as the centre for the cattle trade of the Trent valley, a busy town scrambled untidily on two lumpish hills, dominated by a ruinous medieval castle, and noisome with the stench of tanneries.[31] But first, ill-advisedly, the King marched on Coventry meaning to dislodge a Parliamentary force which had besieged it. They were an undisciplined rabble who poached the deer, stole the church vestments, playfully ducked a troublesome whore, and shouted that they would eat a "mess of Cavaliers" for supper;

" very cannibals," as one of their officers commented with approval.[32] The King's forces were better disciplined, but much smaller, and he did not allow them to engage.

On August 22nd he withdrew to Nottingham and here, in an atmosphere of indifference rather than hostility, went through the formality of raising the Royal Standard and proclaiming the Commons and their soldiers traitors. It was a confused, inglorious business. The weather was dismally wet; the King, sunk in gloom, changed his mind about the form of the proclamation and altered it so obscurely that his herald could barely read it. Later in the week the standard blew down. Very few recruits joined his forces.[33]

The lack of enthusiasm to enlist for the King was partly to be explained by the season of the year; it was harvest time and everyone was fully occupied in the fields. But it was also partly the fault of his advisers, who persuaded him to make one last offer of peace—a gesture intended to strengthen his moral position, since it was certain it would be rejected. Charles, who at first resisted the suggestion and only yielded with tears, was for once right. These last minute messages to Parliament, coldly rejected by them, were interpreted in the midlands as a sign of weakness, which made the loyal gentry unwilling to join him. They were not anxious to be welcomed as his true champions in one week, only to be delivered over in the next, to the vengeance of their numerous and active Puritan neighbours because he had decided to make a compromise peace.[34] In these early months of the war his betrayal of Strafford told heavily against the King.

Charles had other cares. Prince Rupert, acting in the manner long authorised by European military practice, demanded two thousand pounds of the citizens of Leicester as the price of immunity from plunder. In a fright they sent him five hundred pounds. The King repudiated the action, though he kept the money, and Rupert, who was quick to learn, never repeated the mistake. But the story lost nothing in the telling and served

to stimulate the ire of all propertied citizens against the King
and his " malignant " followers.[35]

Money was the King's chief problem. The Oxford colleges,
forward in devotion, sent him the best part of their plate, and
the King's rich sympathisers everywhere were asked for help.[36]
The Queen bought ammunition abroad but the Dutch Estates,
more friendly to Parliament, obstructed the sailing of the ships
which carried them, and Parliament patrols off the East Coast
made it hard for them to land at Newcastle or on the south bank
of the Humber estuary. On the coasts, disaster abounded.
Bristol and Plymouth declared for Parliament, and Dover Castle
was seized despite the efforts of the Royalist townsfolk to
recapture it.[37] A squadron under Captain Swanley sailed threateningly round the Isle of Wight and landed men and guns at Cowes.
The stout-hearted Governor of Yarmouth, Barnabas Burley,
came out on the sea wall, match in hand, and threatened to blow
up the castle rather than yield.[38]

In Guernsey, Sir Peter Osborne fortified his castle and held
out for the King much against the inclinations of the people.
The French-speaking Calvinist Channel Islanders generally
disliked the King's policy and leaned towards Parliament. The
people of Jersey petitioned the Commons against their Royalist
Governor, Sir Philip Carteret, but he had filled the key posts
in the island with his friends and defied alike the petitioners and
Parliament.[39]

The gravest blow to the King was the loss of Portsmouth.
It had been a part of his strategy that Goring should hold this
valuable haven in readiness for the landing of help from France.
But the plan had miscarried; Cardinal Richelieu had refused to
countenance any pleas of the Queen for French help, and Goring
had never contemplated holding Portsmouth with the Navy
against him and the Isle of Wight in the hands of the enemy.
Attacked by land from Gosport and Southsea, blockaded on the
seaward side, and faced by general mutiny within, he surrendered,
and in so doing made further resistance by Captain Burley,

isolated in the Isle of Wight, impossible. Goring himself sailed to Holland, undiscouraged, to assist the Queen.[40]

Over all the country now there was sporadic fighting. On Sunday, 28th August, Sir John Byron and his Cavaliers were chased out of Brackley by the Parliament forces. Turning retreat to advantage, they presented themselves at Oxford. The townsmen tried to close the gates, but the vice-chancellor came to Magdalen Bridge with all the dignitaries of the University and the students in arms, crying: " Welcome, Gentlemen! " and Byron occupied Oxford in the biggest " town and gown " row the ancient city had seen for many a long year.[41]

The Earl of Bedford, accompanied by Denzil Holles, marched down into Dorset to dislodge the Royalists, Hertford and Hopton, from Sherborne Castle. When the Castle guns opened fire, the Parliamentary troops—country lads unused to such doings— " fell flat on their bellies " and were loath to move again. At nightfall they began to desert and Bedford was compelled to retreat.[42]

III

On September 9th, 1642, the Earl of Essex left London amid the plaudits of the people, and twenty-four hours later joined the midland forces at Northampton, whence he appealed to the City for a loan large enough to " finish this great work." Parliamentarians claimed that he had fifteen thousand men, which was an exaggeration. His troops were undisciplined, untrained and greedy for plunder. Little attempt had been made to organise them into regiments. Captains and companies acted independently and the confusion was great. But the supreme command, at least, was undisputed and the authority of Essex paramount.

On the King's side confusion was greatest at the top. No commander-in-chief had been appointed. The Earl of Lindsey, in recognition of his not very successful efforts to raise the northern midlands, held the rank of General-in-Chief but his authority was recognised only by the infantry, which consisted for the most part of the men he had himself brought in. He was sixty years old, had won his reputation and a Knighthood as a mere boy at the capture of Cadiz in 1597 but had seen no active service by land for nearly twenty years. Prince Rupert as Lieutenant General of the horse was understood to be independent of his interference, and Harry Wilmot as Commissary General assumed a like independence.

At the approach of the far superior forces of Essex, the King retreated to the Welsh marches where he hoped to recruit his strength.[43] All hope of peace was now finally abandoned but, as he fell back, he sent one last mournful message to the rebel Parliament: "the God of Heaven direct you," he wrote, "and in mercy divert those judgments which hang over this nation, and so deal with us and our posterity as we desire the preservation and advancement of the true Protestant religion, the law, and the liberty of the subject, the just rights of Parliament, and the peace of the Kingdom." At Wellington, on his march, he reviewed his small army and once again in much the same terms solemnly averred the moderation of his objectives and the justice of his war.[44]

In the iron regions of Staffordshire the King found some friends to organise the manufacture of arms and bullets. Occasionally there were lighter moments: at Stafford Prince Rupert showed off his marksmanship with a pistol by picking off the weathercock on St. Mary's steeple.[45] As Charles retreated, Essex came on, but cautiously. His orders were "to rescue His Majesty's person, and the persons of the Prince and the Duke of York out of the hands of those desperate persons who were then about them" and to bring the sovereign home again to his loving Parliament.[46]

The Royalists wasted neither time nor men in attempting to hold the places they had at first occupied. Oxford was speedily sacrificed. Byron and his cavalry scampered out on the Worcester road, taking with them some of the University plate and as many students as could find horses to carry them. The rest were left to the mercy of the indignant townsfolk and the Parliamentarian troops.[47]

At Worcester, Prince Rupert joined Byron to cover his retreat, while the King hastened on to the Welsh border where about five thousand infantry were said to be mustering for him at Shrewsbury.[48] Worcester enjoyed the brief glory of the Cavaliers' first triumph. On September 23rd Rupert and some of his chief officers were reconnoitring between the Severn and the Teme, near the village of Powicke, when they became aware that a party of enemy horse had crossed the Teme at Powicke Bridge in their rear with the evident intention of cutting them off. The manœuvre was not ill-conceived but it was lamentably executed. The Royalists were in an open field, to reach which the Parliamentary troops had to advance through a narrow lane between hedges, in which Rupert had hurriedly placed a few dragoons to harass them with their fire. With the brief delay he had thus procured the Prince drew up his men ready to charge on his attackers, as soon as they emerged from the lane and before they had time to deploy. The untried Parliamentarians were thus exposed to the full force of a cavalry charge as they came blinking out into the open, and were driven back on to their comrades still struggling up the lane. Someone gave the order to " wheel about," as if such a movement had been possible in so narrow a place, and the Parliament men " not yet well understanding the difference between wheeling about and shifting for themselves " fled in disorder, leaving the Royalists masters of the field.

The effect of the skirmish at Powicke Bridge was out of all proportion to its military importance. The superior and advancing forces of Essex had been ignominiously defeated by far inferior numbers at their first contact with the Cavaliers. In a moment the untried, unknown Prince Rupert was the hero of all the bold young men who served the King, and the terror of Parliament.[49] It was a position that this austere, energetic, single-minded young warrior was long and justly to maintain.

Next day the Earl of Essex issued instructions to his officers that they were to waste no time " practising the ceremonious forms of military discipline " but to instruct their men without delay " in the necessary rudiments of war, that they may know to fall on with discretion and retreat with care." [50]

Victorious though they had been, the Royalists did not intend to hold Worcester. In the peaceful generations since the last wars in England, its walls and gates had decayed and it was indefensible against superior numbers. The Cavaliers fell back to join the King in the Welsh marches and, in a dismal downpour of rain, the Parliamentarians entered the " papistical, atheistical, abominable " town, arrested the Mayor, sacked the Cathedral, and tore down the sweet-toned organ that had been the joy and pride of the region.[51]

IV

While the Parliamentary troops desecrated Worcester, a fury of iconoclasm and anti-popery was sweeping the south-eastern parts of the country. At Colchester, a Puritan town embittered by years of distress, an angry crowd plundered the house of the Lucas family, rich and Royalist, tore down the hangings, smashed the glass and ornaments in the private chapel, broke open the family tombs and scattered the bones of the dead. They set upon and nearly killed the aged vicar of Holy Trinity Church, and then poured out of the town towards the country house of the Roman Catholic Lady Rivers. She sent for neighbourly help to the Earl of Warwick's steward, but he failed her and she fled for her life to London, leaving her house to its fate.[52]

The frenzy crossed the Thames estuary and raged next in Kent. The houses of Catholics and suspect Cavaliers were forcibly entered and searched; arms, horses and plate were taken. Barham Place, the house of Sir William Boteler, was sacked and while some of the invaders tortured his steward others consumed all the stores in his larder. A gang of seamen battered down the images and glass of Rochester Cathedral, and destroyed the cherished library accumulated by the poet Dean, Henry King. At Canterbury soldiers of Parliament tore up the illuminated service books, slashed the tapestries and discharged their muskets at the Crucifixion over the South Gate. In London another living victim was sacrificed to the frenzy of anti-Popery when Thomas Bullaker, a priest who had been captured while saying Mass, was hanged at Tyburn.[53]

Puritanism, which showed so ugly a face in its fanatical triumphs, showed to better advantage in moments of danger. The stubborn people of Manchester, since their first bloody clash with the Cavaliers in July, had resolutely held their town against all assaults. The coming of the King to Chester, on a visit from Shrewsbury, was the signal for a new surge of Royalist energy in these parts, and Manchester was to face another test.

The smiling monarch with his following of gallant officers was joyously received by one-half of the population, but the others cursed under their breath the " hell-bred Cavaliers " and the Popish lords in the royal retinue.[54] The region had for three generations sent many settlers into Ireland and many of the people had kinsmen now in difficulty and danger. Fear and anxiety about the outcome of the Irish rebellion had been acute here for the last ten months, and Chester itself was full of refugees telling bitter tales of the Irish-Popish massacres. These people were shocked when the King detained for his own use some waggons and draft horses awaiting shipment to the English troops in Ireland, and they were appalled when he gave permission to the local Roman Catholic gentry to bear arms for his defence.[55]

The King's men now gave the Puritan gentry some of their own medicine; two of the most important were arrested, their houses searched, their horses, arms and valuables seized, while the handsome young Lord Grandison flashed with a troop of horse into Nantwich, plundered the houses of Lord Crewe and other disaffected gentry and took their horses for the King.[56]

Lord Strange, who in September had succeeded his father as Earl of Derby, assembled the Cheshire levies to join in the siege of Manchester. "I believe all the Papists in the country were forward in giving assistance against the town," wrote a staunch Lancashire Puritan.[57] But the Cheshire men, when it came to the point, refused to fight outside their own county, a limitation on loyal enthusiasm which was on many other occasions to give trouble to the commanders of both parties. Even so, Manchester was close-beset, but the drenching rain which damped the gunpowder, and the spirits of the attackers, proved a faithful ally, and the besieged kept up their hearts by singing psalms whether on duty in the wet, or off duty in the ale-house. After a week's intensive attack and ten weeks' blockade the Cavaliers gave up, leaving Manchester "compassed about with songs of deliverance."[58] Its stubborn resistance had preserved a valuable Parliamentary outpost in a barren and difficult country soon to be overrun by Lord Derby's undisciplined roving bands.

In Yorkshire the Parliamentary party was making head. The King's commander, Cumberland, an amiable scholar with no desire to make enemies, did little to hinder them. The bustling Archbishop, John Williams, who had been installed in his Episcopal chair at York in June, seemed at first eager to help the King; but he was dismayed by the ease with which his castle of Cawood on the Ouse, midway between York and Selby, was seized for Parliament. A Royalist party who set out in the dusk of evening to resume possession mistook a windmill in a field of bean-stooks for the defending force and, unlike Don Quixote, turned and fled.[59] At this, John Williams decided he could serve the King better in his own country of North

Wales than in the archbishopric where he had too few friends and too little influence. He withdrew from York and fortified himself in Conway Castle.[60]

The northern Cavaliers cast about for a more effective leader than poor Cumberland to combat the family alliances, the territorial influence and the zeal of the Fairfaxes in the cause of Parliament. The Peak district and the low-lying region along the Trent to the Humber was dominated by the great family of Cavendish. The head of the house, the proud and elegant Earl of Newcastle, had shown unexpected qualities during the summer. As Governor to the Prince of Wales and as a commander in the Scottish wars he had seemed more concerned with his own dignity than with the best interests of the King.[61] But in the last weeks he had shown a new energy and competence, and had secured Newcastle-on-Tyne and the surrounding coal-fields for the King. To him, therefore, the northern Royalists now appealed to take Cumberland's place in organising their forces against the enemy.[62]

The King had hoped to secure the revenues from export duties on Newcastle coal. But the possession of the mines and the port were of little avail when he had not the command of the sea. This fatal loss hampered him at every turn. The only remaining ships of his fleet which had evaded the Earl of Warwick's control, the *Bonaventure* and the *Swallow*, were captured early in October as they tried to run the blockade into Tynemouth. Almost at the same time a merchant ship sent by the Queen carrying munitions, arms and a number of professional soldiers was captured off Yarmouth; the men were held for questioning and the cargo was diverted to the Parliamentary magazines.[63]

The King, far inland at Shrewsbury and surrounded by his soldiers, took too little account of his misfortunes by sea. His spirits rose in the congenial atmosphere of the busy little town where, on market days, the musical idiom of his Welsh subjects mingled with the accents of England. The loyal gentry of

Montgomery and Radnor began to come in with their following. Their livelihood was the fleeces of the sheep on their
mountains and the light woollens woven in their villages to be
marketed by the merchants of Shrewsbury. The King, in his
time of power, had protected their rights against the greedy
claims of the Merchant Adventurers of London to the monopoly of commerce in wool.[64] The region, which owed its
recent and considerable prosperity to him, now showed its
gratitude.

Farther south, in Monmouthshire and Glamorgan, the Earl
of Worcester's dilettante son, Lord Herbert of Raglan, had
abandoned his speculations on submarine transport, pedometers
and water-power, and was raising an army. The old Earl of
Worcester was as rich as he was loyal and the King now offered
him a Marquisate for twenty thousand pounds; more gracefully,
he sent the twelve-year-old Prince of Wales on a visit to Raglan.
Young Charles made merry with the Welsh gentry in the Earl
of Worcester's great banqueting hall, gratefully received their
family plate for his father's treasury, drank home-brewed
metheglin to the health of his " Ancient Britons " and swore to
be always their own true Prince of Wales.[65]

At Shrewsbury, the King was joined by Patrick Ruthven,
the veteran soldier who had held Edinburgh Castle for him
against the Covenanters in 1640. Created Earl of Forth in the
spring, he had been in Germany since then, and now rejoined
the King with some professional Scots officers. Forth was a
soldier of experience and distinction, who had held high commands in the Swedish army. Although nearly seventy and
hampered by deafness and gout, he was a more modern and
more active commander than Lindsey, and had, in spite of his
age, far more in common with the young and vigorous Rupert
who was daily drilling the King's cavalry into shape in the
meadows by the Severn. Forth's arrival, and the gathering of
the Welsh infantry, who soon outnumbered the English, lessened
the influence of the Earl of Lindsey, still nominally General-in-

Chief, though the work was done and the authority was exercised more zealously by the other two.

Meanwhile Thomas Bushell, engineer and speculator in the Welsh mines, joined the King; he undertook to clothe three regiments at his own charge, to provide cannon and shot from his foundries, and to coin silver—some from his mines, the rest from melted plate—at the rate of £1,000 a week towards the pay of the troops. Some of this money vaunted the legend *Exurgat Deus, dissipentur inimici;* others carried the more sober phrase: *Pro religione et Parliamento.*[66] The latter inscription bore out the theory officially stated by the King that he was defending the true religion and the just rights of Parliament against a conspiracy of rogues at Westminster. But moderate-minded men, who had abandoned Parliament to serve him, weighed the devices on his coinage and his unimpeachable public statements against the evidence of the company he kept. He was surrounded by professional soldiers, by his Roman Catholic subjects in arms, even by lords from Ireland—Dillon and Taaffe—who were suspected of complicity in the rising and on whom he now bestowed commissions in his army. Seeing such things, men of moderate views feared his victory only a little less than they feared his defeat.

Lord Spencer, writing from the King's quarters to his wife, revealed a young man's dilemma which must have afflicted others beside himself: " Unless a man were resolved to fight on the Parliament side, which for my part I had rather be hanged, it will be said without doubt that a man is afraid to fight. If there could be an expedient found to solve the punctilio of honour, I would not continue here an hour." The growing influence of the Papists deeply perturbed him. The King, he thought, would be in London before the year was out; this would bring the triumph of extreme and violent men, and there would be no alternative for those, like himself, of moderate and Protestant views, but to go into voluntary exile. His letter ended on an unexpected note. " I never saw the King look

ROBERT RICH, EARL OF WARWICK
by *Anthony Van Dyck*

EDWARD MONTAGU, EARL OF MANCHESTER
by Peter Lely

better," he wrote, " he is very cheerful, and by the bawdy discourse, I thought I had been in the drawing-room."[67]

The excitement and the open air life suited the King's restless nature. After two years of discouragement and defeat, he felt that he was about to strike a blow for the things in which he believed, and he was encouraged in his resolution by letters from his wife exhorting him to pay no heed to those half-hearted councillors who spoke for peace or compromise.[68]

At Shrewsbury he had assembled six thousand infantry and fifteen hundred dragoons, as well as the cavalry that his nephew Rupert was training.[69] His misfortunes, moreover, inspired in his servants a fervour he had not known in his days of power; their devotion quickened his inhibited affections and was balm to his injured self-esteem. The atmosphere of war had already softened something of his rigidity; to men who were ready to die for him, much could be forgiven, even talking bawdy.

V

The feared Civil War was now a fact, and as the armies of King and Parliament made ready to march, anxious men and women searched their hearts to justify the choice they had made, or must soon make. It was possible for an honest partisan of either side to argue a convincing case although the political theory in which most Englishmen had been reared gave little help. Since King and Parliament made up the body politic it was a clean impossibility for the two to be at war. Each man solved the problem by deciding to the best of his judgment which of the two had temporarily forfeited his function. Was the King, seduced by evil councillors, no longer in possession of his judgment, so that his authority was merged, for the time being, in that of Parliament? Was Parliament, controlled by a mischievous faction and intimidated by the rabble, no longer fit to represent the nation so that its powers were resumed by the King?

For some, like Sir John Oxinden, the King could have no existence as a King except in relation to the Commonwealth; those who stood for the Commonwealth, he argued, " in so doing stand for the King and consequently both for King and Commonwealth." [70] This was the argument of Pym, Hampden, Essex and all the leaders of the Parliamentary party: they reverenced the person of the King and fought to restore him to his Parliament and to reintegrate the threatened state.

This argument perplexed the more moderate Royalists and enraged the more vehement. The distinction between Charles as a man and Charles as King seemed a dangerous sophistry. " I beseech you to consider that Majesty is sacred," wrote young Edmund Verney to his elder brother who had chosen to stay with Parliament, " I believe ye will all say ye intend not to hurt the King, but can any of ye warrant any one shot to say it shall not endanger his very person?" [71] A satirical parody of the Roundhead contention was crystallised in a piece of Cavalier ballad mockery:

> Tis to preserve His Majesty
> That we against him fight.[72]

Those who could not accept the idea that there was a distinction between Charles Stuart and the King were bound, even if they had disapproved his acts and policies, to range themselves in his defence when Parliament made war on him. The progress of the moderate men into the Royalist camp was hastened by their growing dislike and suspicion of the Parliamentary leaders. The studied moderation of the statements which Hyde had drawn up for the King in the last months contrasted favourably with the more harshly phrased protests of Parliament and made Pym and his party appear more intransigent than the King. The indignation which many had felt when Charles came in force to arrest the Five Members had cooled during the summer, as it became apparent that Pym and his friends had not only escaped the threat but made use of it to strengthen their position, discredit the King and drive him from his capital. Their cleverness in seizing the Navy, the principal seaports, the royal dockyards and magazines might provoke an unwilling admiration, but it made no appeal to the heart. The King's plight gave him an instant claim to chivalrous and disinterested loyalty; Parliament could inspire no such feelings. To pious exclamations of " God save King-and-Parliament," the cynical were apt to respond: " God save the King; Parliament will look well enough to save themselves."

There were some who thought that Pym and his junto had made the war for no other purpose than to preserve themselves against a King whom they had irretrievably offended. But outside the relatively small circle of the well-informed, the questioning and the critical, humbler folk made up their minds on the issues of faith and loyalty as they saw them, on simple and simplified recollections of the politics of the last decade. Londoners still remembered the bleeding ears of Prynne, Burton, Bastwick and the stripes suffered by Lilburne, and were not allowed by the Puritan preachers to forget the oppressions and interferences of Archbishop Laud. If Parliament was now asking for money to finance its troops, the demands of the King for Ship-money and the two wars on Scotland were still vivid in memory. So were the inconveniences of his soap, salt and tobacco monopolies. A doggerel ballad summed up a score of plausible reasons for supporting Parliament—" The King's Great Counsel "—against the King:

> With taxes and monopolies oppressed
> Ship-money, soldiers, Knighthood and the rest,
> The Coat-and-Conduct money was no jest,
> Then think, good neighbours, how much we are blest
> In the Great Counsel of the King
> And the King's Great Counsel.

Who did regard our poverty, our tears?
Our wants, our miseries, our many fears?
Whipt, stript, and fairly banished as appears—
You that are masters now of your own ears
Bless the Great Counsel of the King
And the King's Great Counsel.[73]

Parliament's claim to stand for the liberties of the subject seemed more plausible than the King's protestation that he did so, for his numerous infringements of his subjects' liberty were well-remembered and well-advertised, while those of Parliament had so far affected only a minority. The same was true of the King's assertion that he stood for the true Protestant religion: whatever the purity of his personal faith, he had shown over the last twelve years that he preferred Papists to Puritans and by so doing had brought the Church of England under suspicion with large numbers of his subjects. This was the issue on which a great many earnest Protestant Christians made their choice when it came to war. "When I put my hand to the Lord's work in 1642," wrote a Puritan soldier, "I did it not rashly, but had many an hour and night to seek God, to know my way." [74] Devout sons of the Church of England, who prayed no less ardently, received a different answer and joined the Cavaliers.

But active participation was still confined to a minority. Even those who most ardently took up the cause of King or Parliament anticipated no more than a single brief campaign. The majority throughout the country still hoped that the storm would pass over before they were called upon to decide for either party.

King and Parliament both counted on a short war, a single trial by battle, from which there would be, for the defeated, no further appeal. The King's objective was to destroy the army of Essex and to re-enter his capital, if not as a conqueror, then at least as an unquestioned master. Once he had established his superiority in arms, it should be an easy matter to silence Pym and his junto (the rogues might make it easier by fleeing the country), to get this Parliament to dissolve itself, and to begin his reign anew with a Parliament made tractable by the lesson he had taught its predecessor.

Parliament's objective was even simpler: to destroy the King's army, to bring him back to Westminster with honour and safety (but no liberty) and there to secure from him the ratification of their two demands—Parliamentary control over the armed forces of the realm and over the appointment of his Councillors.

The King was sincere in averring that he wished to protect Parliament and the liberties of his people. The Parliamentary leaders were equally sincere in protesting their respect for the King. But the meaning of such words as " protection," " liberty " and " respect " was not the same for both parties. The King wished to make an end of this particular Parliament but not to destroy Parliament as an institution. The Parliamentary leaders were ready to respect his person, but not the prerogative that he claimed. Each side was resolved to make the other dependent and therefore harmless. Both were convinced that within a few weeks—or months at most—God would have blessed the righteous cause.

VI

By the middle of October the King began the march to London. At Bridgenorth the people cheered him through the streets and the bells rang welcome.[75] Recruits were still coming in. " Dear Mother," a Cheshire boy apologised for running away to the army, " it did much trouble me to depart from you as I did, but I thought it better to do so than to take a more serious leave, which might have occasioned more compunction and have prevailed nothing to alter my resolution." [76] At Wolver-

133

hampton the last of the Welsh levies joined the King, who now had something over thirteen thousand men. They were in good heart and under reasonable discipline but poorly armed. The magazines of the local trained bands had not met their needs; the infantry were short of swords, the cavalry of body armour and firearms; they had no tents and too few baggage waggons.[77] At Kenilworth the King appointed Sir Robert Heath Lord Chief Justice, since the cautious Bramston had pleaded illness and refused to join him, and had a charge drawn against the Earl of Essex for high treason.[78]

The Parliamentary army had marched, meanwhile, from Worcester to Warwick to intercept the Royal army. Hampered by lack of draft horses, Essex only reached the little market town of Kineton, a few miles south of Warwick, by the evening of Saturday, October 22nd, with much of his artillery still a day's march in the rear. The King was at Southam that night, Rupert with the advance guard at Wormleighton, where he had a brush with some of the Parliamentary cavalry on a foraging party. Essex, to whom Rupert's position must have been reported by them, did not stir, perhaps thinking that daylight would reveal more clearly the King's strength and movements. Next morning, just as he was going to Church, his scouts reported a great part of the Royalist army three miles to the south, on the dominating escarpment of Edgehill, between him and the main road to Banbury, Oxford and London. During the night the swift-thinking Rupert had sent word to the King, and by a hurried march in the dark had occupied with his cavalry the summit of the hill where he was now waiting for the infantry to come up.[79]

Edgehill commands one of the loveliest views in England, spacious landscape of green pastures and fertile fields unfolding towards the Avon valley. But on that bright and cold October morning the King's officers were more concerned with getting their infantry into position and with the movements of Essex below them than with the rich, rural distances in the autumn sunlight. The summit of the ridge affords a dominating view of the plain below, but the slope is too steep for cavalry action. Essex therefore moved into position unhindered, while Rupert, seeing that the enemy meant to fight, brought his men down from the crown of the hill to the smoother slopes below. The Cavaliers had the advantage of the ground, and Essex was perturbed to find that he had not, as he had been led to suppose, a marked superiority of numbers. The armies were fairly evenly matched, Essex having an effective force of about two thousand cavalry and eleven thousand foot, the Royalists something over three thousand cavalry and dragoons, and about nine thousand foot.[80]

But Essex had the advantage of being able to rely on the trust and obedience of his officers. His command was undivided and, although he was no genius, he was competent, calm and determined. He got his forces into position, with the right flank of his cavalry resting on the hamlet of Radway and somewhat protected by the lane and hedges that ran up that side of the hill from the village. The foot in the centre, with such of his guns as had reached him, had the advantage of slightly rising ground; only the left wing was fully exposed to the enemy.

The Royalists were in the stronger position but for the last two days they had come through hostile country where food and shelter were hard to find.[81] The troops were hungry and the tempers of the leaders were at breaking point. Lindsey, who had advised marching through the enclosed land in the valleys among the villages, in the interests of the infantry, had been overruled by Rupert, and the advance had been made through the open country on the higher ground where the cavalry could move —and see—best. In the swift seizure of Edgehill and the drawing up of the battle Rupert's advice had again prevailed. Lindsey refused to allow him to direct the ordering of the infantry on the field. Rupert, with more military judgment than social tact, protested that the battle could not be planned piecemeal and further insisted that pikemen and musketeers be interspersed with each other in the modern Swedish fashion. Lindsey's sulks flared into rage. In front of the troops, he flung his baton to the ground and declared that if he "was not fit to be a general he would die a colonel at the head of his regiment." [82] In the embarrassing circumstances, his place as commander of the foot was taken by Sir Jacob Astley, a mature and competent soldier who had once been Prince Rupert's tutor and understood how to get on with him.

The quarrels concluded, they completed the ordering of the field. Rupert with four cavalry regiments and the King's lifeguards, was on the right wing, Wilmot with five regiments of horse on the left, the infantry in the centre. The King's standard, borne by Sir Edmund Verney, floated at the head of his red-coated foot guard. His lifeguard of cavalry, under his cousin and Richmond's brother, Lord Bernard Stuart, had asked and been given permission to serve with Prince Rupert.

The King, in a black velvet cloak lined with ermine, now rode along the lines with words of encouragement. He had already briefly addressed the principal officers in his tent: "Your King is both your cause, your quarrel and your captain," he said, "come life or death, your King will bear you company, and ever keep this field, this place, and this day's service in his grateful remembrance." [83]

Rupert also addressed his troops, not on politics, but on tactics. He knew that his cavalry, short of firearms and scantily trained, must achieve the utmost by the impact of their first charge, and consequently instructed them to ride in the closest possible formation, and to hold their fire until they had closed with the enemy.[84]

It was afternoon before both armies were in position and Essex, hoping to gain the initiative and cause some preliminary disorder in the King's lines, opened fire with his cannon. At this the King with his own hand ignited the charge and the Royalist guns gave answer.[85] Sir Jacob Astley uttered a brief prayer: "O Lord, thou knowest how busy I must be this day. If I forget thee, do not thou forget me." Rupert waited no longer, and suddenly Essex saw the Royalist horse on his left sweep down the slope and hurl themselves upon his wavering lines. Rupert's men came in at an oblique angle, riding down not only the Parliamentary cavalry on that wing, but some of the infantry nearest them. The opposing forces made no stand but fled " with the enemy's horse at their heels and amongst them, pell mell." In their flight they battered their way through their own reserve drawn up in the rear, and although Denzil Holles gallantly " planted himself just in the way " and tried to rally the fugitives he brought very few of them to a stand. The rest shamefully scattered with Rupert's men hallooing after them. Some stragglers made a wide cross country circuit and carried the news of Parliament's defeat down the London road as far as Uxbridge. Most fled to Kineton and were beaten through it by the Royalists. A mile beyond the town John Hampden and his regiment, marching up with the rest of the delayed artillery, met the dismayed rout, and by expeditiously planting a battery across the road checked or at least deflected the pursuers.

All this time on the slope of Edgehill the King's forces were faring badly. Contrary to instructions the very small reserve of cavalry on the right wing, which should have stayed to give cover to the infantry, had followed Prince Rupert's charge and joined in the pursuit, leaving the centre, with the infantry, the guns, and the King's standard, bare of defence on one side. Before the Prince and his few experienced officers could extricate their men from the enjoyable chase and bring them back to the field, the infantry had been very roughly handled.

The resolution of Essex and the skill of the old Scottish veteran, Sir William Balfour, had prevented the total defeat of Parliament. Wilmot, on the Royalist left, had charged when Rupert did, and had driven the greater part of the opposing cavalry from the field, but the wily Balfour, with a party of Parliamentary horse, drew out of the range of Wilmot's onslaught, and while the Royalists pursued the fliers, he made his way up the hill under cover of the hedges until, with a sudden charge, he fell upon the King's guns and the infantry in the centre. At the silencing of the Royalist guns, the Parliamentary infantry took heart and closed with the now defenceless and disordered Royalist centre, who manfully stood their ground. Lindsey, badly wounded, was taken prisoner; the King's standard bearer Sir Edmund Verney was killed and the standard taken. The Prince of Wales, to his joy, found himself almost at grips with the rebels. "I fear them not," he shouted, and cocked his pistol, but his startled attendants hustled him to the rear.[86]

Some of Rupert's cavalry were now returning, by scattered parties. Captain John Smith rounded up a couple of hundred men and fell in on the Parliamentary flank, diverting them from their prey. Sometime in this hot action he retrieved the King's standard in a hand-to-hand struggle with several of the enemy.[87] Exhaustion, and the harassing onslaught of the returning Royalists, forced the Parliamentary infantry to give ground and fall back as the early darkness fell.

Both armies camped in the field, neither being willing to allow the other to claim sole possession. Through a night of bitter frost they strove, vainly, to keep warm, and on the next day Essex, while formally announcing his victory, drew off towards Warwick. His cavalry was in total disorder; he had lost about fifty colours and much baggage and equipment. On the retreat to Warwick, Rupert's cavalry harassed him all the way, forced him to abandon some of his cannon and blew up four of his ammunition waggons. The Royalists were now between him and London with an almost clear road, and he wrote urgently to Westminster to call out all available troops to defend the capital. But his claim of a " victory " had this much truth: he had, with Balfour's invaluable help and by his own calm and tenacity, retrieved his army from what might easily have been irremediable disaster.[88]

VII

The Royalist prisoners in the Parliamentary camp were among the few who at first truly believed in the Parliamentary claim of victory. Lord Lindsey, angry and in pain, declared that he would never fight in a field with boys again; he never did, for he died that day.[89] Those who had watched Prince Rupert's charge from the other side cursed this boy of twenty-three for a different reason. He was a soldier to be reckoned with, and his men had a spirit which needed only a little more discipline to make them irresistible. Oliver Cromwell in later years recorded a conversation that he had with his cousin Hampden about this time: " Your troopers said I, are most of them old decayed serving-men and tapsters, and such kind of fellows. Their troopers are gentlemen's sons, younger sons and persons of quality . . . You must get men of a spirit that is likely to go on as far as gentlemen will go, or else I am sure you will be beaten still." [90] Cromwell was not altogether fair to the quality of the Parliamentary cavalry or the sources whence it came, but he saw that the Cavaliers, at Powicke and again at Edgehill, had established a superiority that it would be very hard to challenge.

In London the citizens swayed from terror to resolution. Some clamoured against Parliament, others—men and women alike—volunteered to work on the defences. Posts and chains were set up across the streets; to assist recruiting an ordinance was hurriedly issued to secure apprentices and their masters against breach of contract or loss of rights when the boys enlisted; at a general meeting at Guildhall the Parliamentary leaders made an impassioned appeal for money to prosecute the war; [91] the Trained Bands stood to arms; a small garrison was despatched to Windsor, and John Milton, alarmed at the tales of plundering Cavaliers that were assiduously reported in London, meditated a sonnet to soften their hearts:

Captain or colonel or knight in arms
Whose chance on these defenceless doors may seize—

The King lost his opportunity. He was shaken by what he had seen, the violence and the losses—his young cousin Lord d'Aubigny mortally wounded; Lindsey dead; Verney dead; sixty of his footguard piled dead on the patch of ground where his standard had been.[92] When he called a Council Rupert and Lord Forth were for racing on with the Cavalry to seize London and forcibly dissolve Parliament. But the Earl of Bristol voiced the opinion of moderate men, and disadvised so violent a move. Charles yielded to the milder counsel. Convinced that his subjects would see for themselves the folly of opposing him, he preferred not to enter London by force.[93]

While Rupert and the professional soldiers fumed in frustration he refreshed himself at Aynhoe and on October 27th advanced to Banbury. The garrison, raised by Lord Saye, the greatest magnate of those parts, instantly surrendered and re-enlisted in the King's army. Charles made the rival local magnate, Lord Northampton, Governor, helped himself to cloth, stockings, shoes and victuals for his men[94] and marched at a comfortable pace to Oxford. The loyal, resilient University made haste to greet him: " Our Oxford hath now thrown off all clouds of discontent, and stands clear, gilded by the beams of Your Majesty's royal presence," ran the official welcome, though the influx of so large an army and the unfamiliar presence of an artillery park in Magdalen Grove was a little disturbing.[95]

At Westminster both Houses discussed the possibility of a treaty but they were thinking not so much of surrender as of a delaying action. They moved the King's two younger children, Princess Elizabeth and Prince Henry, from suburban, indefensible St. James's to a house within the City—an action which indicated their intention to resist to the uttermost and to use such valuable hostages if need be. The response to their appeal for cash had been disappointing, and they had had to arrest more than seventy citizens who refused money for the war.[96] They sent, with increasing urgency, to the Scots for help against the Popish malignant army of the King, and at the same time they wrote to the King offering to treat.[97]

Charles received the request at Reading, asked them to name commissioners for a treaty, and continued his advance on London. Rupert and his flying cavalry attacked Windsor, hoping to cut off the water traffic from the Thames valley to the capital; failing in this because the castle had been occupied for Parliament by the truculent London M.P., John Venn, he scoured the Vale of Aylesbury for food and forage before rejoining the King at Egham.[98]

Essex, taking the northern route and keeping outside Rupert's striking distance, had crossed the Chilterns at their eastern extremity and was approaching London. He wrote from Markyate Street in terms of studied mildness to call in the deserters who had left him since Edgehill, and were now skulking in or near London. "I doubt many are gone to visit their friends," he wrote, "but I am confident that those who fought so gallantly will not quit their colours." In every official statement he had tactfully minimised the ill-conduct of the fugitives and claimed the battle for an unquestioned victory. When, on November 7th, he entered London, he was received as a victor and voted by Parliament a special gift of £5,000 as a mark of confidence.[99]

A few days later, while Pym was at Guildhall urging the Common Council of London to vote further supplies of money, Parliamentary Commissioners were received by the King at Colnbrook. As yet they discussed no terms, but merely the preliminaries of a conference, pending which they agreed to a "cessation of arms." The meaning of the phrase was left undefined, and on Friday 11th November, Essex and his cavalry and Philip Skippon with the London Trained Bands marched out of the City towards the King, with drums beating, colours flying, and all the girls from Cheapside to Hammersmith running out with baskets of baked meats for the gallant boys.[100]

At this, the King moved his advance posts to the outskirts of Brentford. The little town was held by the regiments of Lord Brooke and Denzil Holles, "all butchers and dyers," sneered the gentlemen Cavaliers. Rupert, assuming that the advance of Parliament's forces had ended the truce, attacked in the mist early on Saturday morning, November 12th. He took the defenders by surprise. Holles's men fought, but Lord Brooke's regiment fled, all except one of their captains, who, attempting to take command in the absence of his superiors, seized the colours and exhorted the men to come back to the help of their comrades. Few obeyed and the young captain himself was soon after captured; his name, familiar already to the Cavaliers, was John Lilburne.[101]

In Brentford the Cavaliers and Holles's "butchers and dyers" fought furiously, wrecking the well-tended orchards and gardens, firing a house or two, shooting in and out of windows and up and down the muddy footpaths that slanted to the river. The Cavaliers cut the defenders down or drove them into the water; the prisoners they herded ignominiously into the pound, like strayed hogs. The fighting over, they broke into cellars and larders, carried off linen, stores and plate, ripped up the beds and set the feathers flying. They were young, drunk, victorious and out of control.[102] Outraged Puritans were to declare that the sack of Brentford was worse than that of Magdeburg—citing the most infamous disaster of the German wars.[103] It was not remotely comparable: Magdeburg, a town of 70,000 inhabitants, had been reduced to ashes; no civilian life seems to have been lost at Brentford, but the rowdy destruction, the firing of thatch and the breaking of windows, was long remembered against Prince Rupert.

The news travelled fast. On that same Saturday afternoon the attack was reported in the House of Commons, causing an outcry against the King's breach of the truce.[104]   On Sunday morning Essex sent barge-loads of ammunition up river to help the remnant still before Brentford, but Rupert's men fired on them from the gardens of Syon House, sank some and blew up one in mid-stream.   The explosion completed the demoralisation of the Parliamentary troops in the region, and the King's army continued to advance.[105]

But Essex, reinforced by the Trained Bands, had twice their numbers entrenched in the fruit gardens, bean rows and out-buildings of London's outer ring of villages, and drawn up on Turnham Green.   It would have been folly for the King to risk a general engagement against odds so heavy and in ground so much enclosed and therefore so favourable to the defence.   Besides, the King's men were by now tired, cold and hungry after long marches, while the Parliament troops were plentifully supplied from London.[106]

The Royalists fell back, Rupert's cavalry covering the with-drawal of the tired infantry, while Essex was too cautious to attempt to cut off their retreat.[107]   The King went by way of his palace at Oatlands to Reading, while at Westminster both Houses debated whether or not to go on with the treaty.   The Lords were willing, the Commons less so.[108]   Pym and his Committee of Safety did not slacken their measures for the prosecution of the war.   On all the roads into London waggons were commandeered for their army, to the great disturbance of market folk and carriers.[109]   Captain George Wither, once a frivolous poet but now regenerate and God-fearing, rode into Kent with orders to seize the horses of all who were disaffected to Parliament.   " Mr. Dixon of Hylden, a notorious malignant, hath good coach horses," he noted down.[110]   The Commons made plans to assist the work of the Navy by encouraging privateers to prey on ships carrying arms or supplies either for the King, or towards Ireland.   Repeatedly and gravely they considered how to impose a general assessment to raise money for the continuing war.[111]

The King lingered at Reading where the Prince of Wales, who had hitherto greatly enjoyed the war, sickened with measles.[112] He received an envoy from his uncle the King of Denmark, who had proved less willing to help him than he had hoped; he drew up regulations for the discipline and maintenance of his army for the coming winter, and in the last week of November rejected the terms which Parliament proposed as a basis for a treaty—namely that he should return to Westminster and abandon all delinquents to justice. Such an offer from Parliament represented a victory of the war party against the waverers, for no one can have supposed that the King would treat on any such basis. Leaving a garrison at Reading to command the approaches from London, he withdrew to establish his Court and his headquarters at Oxford.[113]

That same week a gentleman was stopped as he tried to slip through London by water with a concealed letter for one of the King's secretaries. It came from someone in the Queen's suite, possibly George Goring, and outlined with equal optimism and conviction the substantial help that was soon to come for the King from Denmark, France and the Low Countries, and the conviction of the Queen and her friends that the war would rapidly end with the conquest of London.[114] Parliament could not have had better propaganda to prove their wisdom and courage against the unscrupulous methods of the King's evil councillors. On the strength of this discovery, the public accepted with less protest than might have been anticipated an Ordinance of Parliament assessing all men of property for compulsory contribution towards the expenses of the war. The money thus forcibly to be borrowed was guaranteed by the " public faith " —a phrase soon to be uttered with bitter derision by all unwilling lenders.[115] This was the largest general forced loan yet to be imposed on subjects, and those who voted for it in Parliament had, many of them, protested with vigour and sincerity against the Forced Loan demanded by King Charles in 1626 and the extension of Ship-money ten years later. For fifteen years a recurrent theme of their grievances had been taxation by the King without consent of Parliament. In future there would be, outside the walls of Westminster, complaint louder, longer and more widespread against taxation by Parliament without consent of the King.

CHAPTER FOUR

WINTER OF DISCONTENT

November 1642—April 1643

BOTH parties now faced a prospect that neither had expected. Each had appealed to arms in the confident conviction that the other would speedily submit. Neither had anticipated a long war. The King and his Council at Oxford, Parliament in London, had now to reckon with the serious problem of raising money to maintain their armies indefinitely, with complex questions of internal administration in a country with two rival governments, and with the intricate formality of foreign relations.

King and Parliament each had to be on terms with foreign powers if only to prevent the other gaining help from them. The situation for foreign diplomats in England, and for English diplomats abroad was extremely perplexing. Spanish, Portuguese, Venetian and French representatives continued to reside in London looking after the affairs of their countrymen, suffering insolence from time to time from anti-Popish demonstrators, but keeping on good terms with Parliament so long as Parliament controlled the principal port of the kingdom and the Navy. Only the Portuguese envoy, Antonio Sousa, anxious to detach the King from his Spanish friendship and to ensure his support for the newly-liberated Portugal, made himself useful to Charles surreptitiously and continually.[1] The Spanish envoy, Alonso de Cardeñas, played against all the odds for the friendship of Parliament, nor was it in fact able to do without the discreet help of the national enemy. Scarcely another word was to be heard in public about the treaty once made by King Charles for the transport of Spanish silver to Flanders on English vessels, the treaty so profoundly disliked by Puritans; but nothing was done to end an arrangement which brought silver into the Mint for Parliament's use.

Abroad, rival envoys from King and Parliament strove to make good their claims. Thus in Paris Sir Richard Browne, who had long represented the King, was offended by the interference of one Angier, an Anglo-French merchant whom Parliament had appointed to protect their interests.[2]

In The Hague, the Queen protested in vain against the attention paid by the Dutch Estates to Parliament's envoy Walter Strickland, who made constant trouble for the Royalists and annoyed old Sir William Boswell who had represented King Charles in Holland for the last fifteen years.[3] The same quarrel was echoed at Campveere the principal Dutch port for the Scottish wool trade: the Covenanting merchant, Thomas Cunningham, tried to oust Sir Patrick Drummond, a Royalist, who had long represented the Scots merchants there, and made use of his interest with the Dutch to raise loans and buy arms for Scotland.[4] The sympathies of the Dutch were divided; the Prince of Orange favoured the King, but the majority of his subjects were for Parliament against the " spaniolated " Charles with his Popish sympathies. Parliament saw to it that plentiful propaganda for their cause was printed in Holland: were not these two great Protestant nations like Ephraim and Manasseh, close as brothers one to another?[5] So argued one pamphleteer, but in less fraternal mood the Dutch were glad enough to see the war in England prolonged since it hampered the English from competing with them in the Indies trade.

The goodwill of the United Provinces was of signal importance to both King and Parliament. Their sea-power was paramount in the Channel and the North Sea; through their help, the King might hope to nullify Parliament's possession of the Navy; without their help he could not hope for arms from Europe, and scarcely even to see his wife again. Both the Queen and Parliament wooed the Amsterdam bankers, and both alike bought arms through the Dutch and recruited experienced professional soldiers from their armies.

At home the divided governments of King Charles's three kingdoms—England, Scotland and Ireland—presented a constitutional picture of exquisite complexity. In England the King had declared Parliament to be under the control of a minority who maintained themselves by intimidation, while Parliament had declared the King to be enslaved to a " malignant faction " and incapable of exercising sovereign power.

Each therefore claimed to be the only just and authentic government. Of the insignia and instruments of civil power, the King had the Great Seal with him at Oxford, but his order that the Law Courts remove from Westminster had been disobeyed and Parliament paid no heed to the new Lord Chief Justice, Robert Heath, whom Charles had appointed in place of the timorous John Bramston. To emphasise his incontrovertible and inalienable rights the King had ordered the collection of evidence for the arraignment of Essex for High Treason, and he had the captured John Lilburne tried and condemned on that charge.[6]

His master of the Mint, had joined him with the authentic dies of his coinage, and much of the bullion from the Tower, which, with what Thomas Bushell was bringing from Shrewsbury, would serve him for some months. The King was also glad to have with him still the medallists Thomas Rawlins and Nicholas Briot, notable artists in their kind, so that what came in these years from the Oxford Mint was worthy of his fastidious taste.[7]

As for the Government of England, the King issued proclamations as he had done during his personal rule: Parliament issued ordinances. The King's practice was authorised by custom; in the intervals between Parliaments, the monarch had always conducted the Government in this way. Parliament was here the innovator. But the obedience given to either depended not on the legality of the procedure but on the occupying forces in any region, and the sympathies of the Justices of the Peace.

In Scotland the Council appointed a year earlier by the King refused him any help but continued to protest its willingness to reconcile the disputing parties and its insistence that the Presbyterian order of Church government be imposed throughout the British Isles. In November it received from the English Parliament a letter blaming the King for his favours to Papists and the "Spanish faction" and accusing him of planning to employ foreign troops against his own natural subjects. For six weeks the Council let the letter lie; then Hamilton's younger brother arrived with a message from the King protesting against the "horrible scandals" laid to his charge. The Council, yielding to pressure from the Hamiltons, published the royal denial and held back Parliament's accusation.[8]

Whatever the Hamilton brothers had intended, the result was disastrous for Charles. "The King's letter hath awakened those that have been asleep," wrote a Parliamentary agent in Edinburgh. The Covenanters petitioned to know what accusations had been made against the King, that he had to defend himself in such terms, and the Council to satisfy them revealed the contents of Parliament's letter.[9]

"The coals now want only blowing from England, and this Kingdom will be soon on fire," wrote the Parliamentary agent; in Edinburgh there was an outcry, part spontaneous, part inspired, for a closer friendship with Parliament and a joint effort to rescue the deluded King from his malignant and Popish councillors. The Scottish Royalists were leaderless and bewildered. Huntly ("that feeble, effeminate, foolish atheist," sneered the Covenanters,) stood aloof in the North. Montrose was too deeply suspect to make any public move. The Earl of Home sponsored a mild petition, for which Hamilton's defenders later claimed his authorship, calling for restraint in the present troubled state of His Majesty's affairs. But this so-called Cross

Petition—which crossed the policy of the Covenanters—was condemned by the standing Committee of the Assembly of the Church and denounced from the pulpits of Edinburgh.

Hamilton, pleading that pressure of business kept him from the Council, worked off his worries in the tennis court, while the Council, controlled by Argyll and Loudoun, wrote urging their royal master to return to his loving Parliament and despatched Commissioners to reason with him in Oxford.[10]

In Scotland a Government which the King had himself appointed betrayed his interest, but in Ireland a Government which he refused to recognise set itself up in his name and protested its loyalty. The Irish insurgents had in the autumn convened their own Parliament at Kilkenny, and had given formal existence to the new state, the Irish Catholic Confederacy. The constitution of the new Ireland had been drawn up by an able lawyer, Patrick Darcy, who had experience as a member of Parliament, in consultation with the lords, the gentry, the Catholic bishops and abbots who would in future be the national leaders. The General Assembly, as the Irish Parliament was called, consisted of lords, clergy and Commons, sitting all together in one room; the Government was concentrated in the hands of a Supreme Council of twenty-four, elected by the Assembly, much as in Scotland the Committee of Estates was elected by the Scottish Parliament. The term "Confederacy" had been chosen to emphasise not the union between the separate provinces of Ireland, but the Union between the Old Irish and the Catholic Anglo-Irish, mostly of Norman descent, who had joined with them in the struggle against the Puritan Parliament at Westminster and the aggressive English and Scottish Protestant settlers of the last two generations.

Though the clergy were prominent in the Assembly and had for the last six months warmly co-operated with the Irish and Anglo-Irish lords and gentry, the Confederacy by Patrick Darcy's constitution embodied the political and legal, rather than the religious, aspirations of the Irish. It established the legislative and political independence of Ireland, desired alike by the Old Irish and the Anglo-Irish, by the clergy and the laity. Time was soon to show that, while the Anglo-Irish were content with political independence, the desires of the Old Irish and the clergy did not stop there, but in the autumn of 1642 the divisions of the two factions were temporarily stilled, and it looked as though resurgent Ireland, with a sound constitution, an increasing army and intelligent leaders might establish itself as an autonomous nation.[11]

The revolt was against the English Parliament, not against the King, whom the Irish continued to recognise. The official standard of the Confederacy carried the Irish harp surmounted by the Crown and the letters C.R.; the official seal bore the inscription " *Hiberni unanimes pro Deo, Rege et Patria*—Irishmen united for God, King and Country." The new Government at once set in motion plans for taxation, for organising their armies, for printing and distributing their official documents. They appointed ambassadors to Paris, Madrid and the Vatican, whence they expected help in money and arms to continue the war. They wrote with all duty and humility to the King at Oxford, blaming the misgovernment of Lord Justice Parsons as a principal cause of their rebellion, and the aggressive conduct of Puritan English and Scottish settlers, and asking the King to receive their representatives and hear their grievances.[12]

The King continued officially to disregard these embarrassing allies, although their claims to be his true friends were made, not only at Kilkenny, but by the Irish friars abroad, who in Italy, France and the Spanish Netherlands formed a wide network of diplomatists for liberated Ireland. The Queen was already urging him to counteract the danger from Scotland by giving the Irish freedom of religion and making use of their vigorous troops for his war at home.[13]

Pym and his party, as convinced as the Irish that the King's sympathies lay with the Confederates, set traps to entangle him by inspiring appeals to him at Oxford from the Protestant settlers, and watching for any sign in his response that would betray his relations with the rebels.[14] Meanwhile the Government in Dublin continued its devious course; Royalists and Parliamentarians on the Council uneasily spied on each others' movements and were united only in deploring that the breach between King and Parliament had cut off all hope of help from either.

II

The repulse of the King's forces before London impressed the whole country with the strength of Parliament. They kept the news-sheets well filled with their successes and took pains to advertise through their friends, everywhere, their irresistible strength. As far north as the Scottish border, many of the country folk believed their victory was assured.[15]

The impression began to evaporate with the disasters of the ensuing weeks. In Lancashire Parliamentary garrisons and Puritan villagers resisted with difficulty the growing strength of Lord Derby's violent, undisciplined forces.[16] In Yorkshire the Earl of Newcastle, ably seconded by the dour Sir Marmaduke Langdale put new life into the King's cause. He surprised and defeated the younger Fairfax at Tadcaster, and forced him to withdraw to Selby, while the Royalists invaded the West Riding and cut off the help in food and contributions on which the Fairfaxes had counted from the industrious Puritan clothing towns. The local Royalists rose to help him and the projected truce, which was to have kept Yorkshire out of the war, was denounced by both parties. Distractedly the elder Fairfax appealed to Parliament: " the enemy is mighty and master of the field, plentifully supplied from His Majesty and the Papists and malignant parties, with money and all necessities." [17]

In the western midlands Parliament's commander, the Earl of Stamford, with troops of his own raising, was repulsed at

Hereford and retreated to the safety of Puritan Gloucester.[18] The centres of the woollen industry, Shrewsbury excepted, were predominantly Puritan in sympathy. For every reason, the King's party would do well to block the traffic of wool to the distribution centres, and of cloth to London. Partly with this in mind, partly to open a line of communication from Oxford to the south-west, Digby proposed to Wilmot an attack on Marlborough, to give the Roundheads " a warm breakfast."[19] Each was willing enough to perform a daring stroke for the King without sharing the glory with Rupert.

They attacked with a party of dragoons in the small hours of Monday, December 5th. The town was built along a broad high street, with three or four great inns whose generous stabling offered vulnerable angles and points of entry which could not all be guarded. Through one of these hostelries some of the Cavaliers forced their way in, while others attacked at each end of the long high street. The defenders fought from barricades and fired from windows but were overpowered. The conquering Cavaliers merrily plundered barns, stables and store houses, carried away bales of cloth to furnish the King's army, and " two hundred pounds worth of cheese, every pennyworth." Prisoners they roped together and sent to Oxford. The defence-less townsfolk made their peace with money, not without considerable affright. A citizen who pleaded poverty because he had eighteen children was told by a wicked Cavalier (Lord Digby in person, he thought) to go and drown them.[20] London pamphleteers made as much of the sack of Marlborough as they had of Brentford, but the serious aspect of the matter, for Parliament, was that the Royalists could now divert the wool and cloth of the Wiltshire Downs from London and strangle the trade on which so many of Parliament's supporters depended.

As the news grew more gloomy Pym's hold on the fickle sympathies of the Londoners weakened. Many of the Royalists in the City had been excluded from the Common Council, but some remained in the government of the City, and many more were merchants of substance who commanded the obedience of apprentices and the support of friends. Isaac Pennington, who had been chosen as Lord Mayor on the removal of the Royalist Sir Richard Gurney, was re-elected in November 1642 for the ensuing year. Extremely rich, with interests in cloth as well as in the East India and Levant trades, Pennington generously supported Parliament, and proved an energetic leader in the most critical months of the war, though he had to endure occasional insults from "wicked, debauched Shaga-muffins" of the King's party.[21]

With the theatres closed, the Court gone, the traffic in and out of the City strictly controlled and a monthly fast day imposed, London was chill, drab, and uneasy with suspicion. Food was dear because of disturbances on the roads and water-ways into the City; trade was sluggish and the shops had been shut for ten days during the King's advance in the autumn. Coal was scarce because of the blockade of Newcastle, although a pamphleteer, assuming the character of a London wife, wrote that "coals are not so necessary as husbands, warm in bed and comfortable at board," and predicted a revolt of the women if the men stayed any longer in the armies.[22] More than eight hundred citizens were said to have been black-listed as Royalists, and the disarming of suspects and searching of their houses was frequent.[23] Repeated demands were made on the charity of the citizens—to relieve wounded soldiers or their wives and children, to help the victims of plunder, to assist the poor people of Brentford and other distressed parishes. The ordinance for a general assessment, issued on December 8th,[24] was the signal for four days of disturbance. It began with trouble in the courtyard of Haberdashers Hall—now commonly called Plunderers Hall, because the Parliamentary Committee for Advance of Money held its sessions there. Puritan merchants were jeered and jostled as they went in. Next the Royalist merchants drew up a petition for peace, but were forbidden by the Common Council of London to present it to the House of Commons. At this the petitioners, like others before them, enlisted the help of the people. Inspired by such popular characters as the warden of the bear-garden and a clown from the recently closed Bull Theatre, they advanced on Guildhall, where the Common Council was in session, filled the approaches, besieged the doors, manhandled a servant of General Skippon who tried to push his way through them, and had to be dispersed in the end by the Trained Bands.[25]

At this moment King Charles, from Oxford, issued a Declaration persuasive enough to shake every wavering supporter of Parliament. In measured terms, which suggest the phrasing of Edward Hyde, he denounced the iniquitous taxes imposed by Parliament without consent of the subject, the confiscations of property and the arbitrary imprisonments of which the Londoners had seen so much in the last months. All this the King truly stated was done not by Parliament but by a wretched fragment which usurped the name—a fifth part only of the House of Lords, and the eighty or so members who had made themselves masters of the Commons: even the Government of the ancient and proud City of London had been, he pointed out, overpowered and seized into the hands of a few.[26]

Pym's party stood in dire need of a victory to divert public attention. Fortunately on December 13th Parliamentary dragoons in Hampshire under Sir William Waller fell upon the small force of Royalist cavalry which had occupied Winchester and penetrated the town as rapidly as the Cavaliers had done at Marlborough. The Royalists were allowed to withdraw to Oxford but the townsfolk, who had been exasperated by their demands and disorders, stoned them out of the place. The forces of Parliament proved more respectful of secular property than their defeated foes had been but celebrated the victory by destroying the tapestries, vestments and books in the Cathedral, tearing up the muniments and breaking the organ in pieces.[27] At the news, Parliament ordered bells to be rung and bonfires to be lighted, rejoicings which emphasised rather their need for a victory of any kind than the importance of this particular success.[28]

III

The King at Oxford was confident and serene in the crowd and bustle of war. Townsfolk and students laboured together in the trenches and earthworks that were to strengthen the fortifications. A mill for gunpowder was set up at Oseney and a sword factory at Wolvercot. New College was the principal magazine; the Music and Astronomy Schools were stocked with cloth and coats for the soldiers, the Law and Logic Schools with oats for their horses, and rope bridges and other tackle were piled up at the ancient School of Rhetoric. Stray and plundered cattle were penned in the great quadrangle of Christ Church to be resold or slaughtered, according to the army's need. In the circumstances the town throve—for never had the citizens been able to sell food, drink and beds so dear—and the University languished.[29] Few freshmen came up in those troubled years, and few students stayed at their books. Some had already ridden out with Byron in the late summer. In October, as the King approached, Anthony Wood records that his elder brother " left his gown at the towns-end and ran to Edgehill."[30] He was probably not the only one who did so. Of those who still remained when the King made his headquarters at Oxford a month later few can have kept aloof from the drilling and exercising, the drinking and swearing of the soldiers. Even men of learning and professors changed their gowns for buff-coats. William Beau of Merton College (later a divine and a bishop) took up arms and equipped at his own expense several of his pupils, and Peter Turner, the Savilian Professor of Geometry, though well over fifty, was one of the first to follow the drum.[31]

All that winter the Royalist gentry were coming in to the

King, some at the head of troops and companies of their own tenantry, others as single volunteers, like the loyal poor gentleman from Wales who could offer his King only " a Spanish blade at his side and a Welsh heart in his bosom." [32] Overcrowded with troops, the town was noisy with brawling; duels were frequent among the high-spirited young officers, and drunken fights disturbed and shocked peaceable citizens until some limit was put to the nuisance by prohibiting the sale of drink after nine in the evening. A Parliamentary spy reported Prince Rupert himself parting two combatants with the blunt side of a pole-axe. [33]

For the reward and encouragement of valour the King adopted Thomas Bushell's suggestion and had the beautiful " Forlorn Hope " medal designed by Thomas Rawlins for presentation to those who had volunteered for dangerous service. The silver oval showed the King on one side, the Prince of Wales on the other. It was probably the first military decoration to be given in England. Other medals presented for special services carried the head of the Queen, and one of peculiar elaboration was taken from the portrait Van Dyck had painted of Prince Rupert five years before. [34]

Already the Cavalier legend was growing. Although money was short, many of the officers spent lavishly on the equipment of their men. The King's Lifeguard under his blond young cousin Lord Bernard Stuart so dazzled the eye with shining armour and battle-axes that it was commonly called the " Show Troop," and one cornet who fought in it claimed that he shaved only in sack. [35] The atmosphere engendered by the courtier-soldiers was gay and devoted, although in London there were reports of disagreement between the professional officers and the noble amateurs.

The King appointed a Master of the Revels and brought his sergeant-painter William Dobson to Oxford. He kept the Christmas season with ceremony and splendour at Christ Church College, which was henceforth his residence. The Vice-Chancellor of the University offered him as a New Year's gift a cup filled to the brim with golden coins saying: " Our wishes desire it were an inexhaustible Indies." [36]

Prince Rupert was the informing genius of the King's army. Since the action at Powicke Bridge his reputation had rapidly grown. Parliament selected him for a villain, the Cavaliers for a hero; he was credited with movements swifter than the wind, with being in several places at once, with doing his own scouting in a number of ingenious disguises, with being impervious to bullets, in league with the Devil, and a cannibal. To his own party he became at once a second Black Prince, while the white dog which went everywhere with him was popularly elevated to military honours as Sergeant-Major-General Boy.

The Prince was twenty-three years old, tall, spare and black browed. His naturally frank and generous disposition had been overlaid with austerity and reserve during his three years' close imprisonment in an Austrian fortress, a long frustration which had also sharpened his naturally hasty temper. But at the Viennese Court after his release he had impressed the Venetian envoy by the " nobility of his ideas "; the observation was just and penetrating, for the Prince was distinguished among the many ambitious and frivolous men about the King by an elevated and candid spirit, free from deceit and selfishness. He had wanted to be a sailor and was more deeply interested in the mechanical part of his profession—artillery, fortifications and siege warfare—than in the cavalry fighting for which he had so immediately established a reputation. The speed with which he took decisions and acted in the field, and his impatience with the King's older and slower advisers at the Council table reflected the quickness of his intellect, for he could be thorough and patient when occasion required, as for instance in the training of his men. (Later he was to acquire great skill as an engraver, an art which demands unlimited patience and concentration.) With so many qualities, he lacked the easy social gifts, and was apt to show his uneasiness with courtiers and politicians by a sardonic wit and a contemptuous manner. But he inspired in those who knew him best a deep and lasting loyalty, and he easily gained and held the affection and respect of his troops, for he was enduring in hardship, fearless in danger, quick to recognise merit, and as indifferent to praise himself as he was generous in giving credit to others.

But he cared too little for the opinions of his colleagues and he had the young man's fault of yielding too easily and too openly to his likes and dislikes. From the first he did not care for the sly ambitious Wilmot, Commissary General of the Horse, and was already on bad terms with George Digby, whom he had unwittingly deposed from the first position in the King's favour. But he had made a valuable friend in the Duke of Richmond whose restraining influence did something to mitigate the ill-effects of his hasty and unsocial temper.

In military matters he was very sure of his opinions. He advised the King to fortify the loyal towns and thus compel the rebels to wear themselves out in siege warfare. If the strong places were used to immobilise a great part of the opposing forces, the King's skirmishing cavalry could harry their flanks, cut off their convoys and raid the country they left undefended. The drawback to this plan—which had been successfully adopted in the Dutch war against the Spaniards—was the expense of fortifying the strong places. Rupert thought poorly of the amateurish earthworks which had been thrown up at Reading. If the expense of so much building was beyond the King's resources, then his best hope was to increase the strength of his infantry; he might even persuade the Prince of Orange to release the four English regiments now serving under him. Well-equipped professional infantry were essential, for no war could be won by cavalry alone.[37]

Rupert took too little account of the political complications. English soldiers in the Dutch service, if they should be released, might very well prefer fighting for Parliament; the greater number of the professionals now offering to join the King were,

significantly, from the opposing side—Roman Catholics or
their sympathisers from the Spanish service in Flanders. In
Brussels Sir Henry Gage, veteran English commander with a
long and distinguished record, was using his endeavours to get
his compatriots released to join the King's forces.[38] Inevitably,
both by sea and land, the King became linked in war (as he had
been in peace) with the Spanish-Flemish-Austrian alliance in
Europe. His eldest nephew, the Elector Palatine, in his own best
interests as a Protestant Prince, thought it advisable publicly to
denounce his brothers, Rupert and Maurice, for joining the
Cavaliers and compelled his mother, the Queen of Bohemia, to do
likewise.[39]

By sea, for the last year, the Dunkirk privateers, operating
under Spanish protection, had carried arms and men to the
Irish insurgents and freely used their ports as bases whence to
prey on Dutch and English shipping. The Confederate Irish at
Kilkenny now made one of these pirates their official vice-
admiral; for the next seven years Wexford became the principal
base for an Irish-Dunkirk fleet of nearly ninety ships. They also
used the Breton ports, in despite of the French Government, and
so infested the western approaches of the Channel against all
vessels bound for London or the Dutch ports. The Irish-Dunkirk
pirates were not yet the open allies of the King, but they did not
attack his ships, and Royalist mariners and sea captains knew them
for friends because they shared a common enemy.[40]

The Royalists by this time had begun to challenge Parliament's
control of the sea. Loyalists in the West Country placed their
ships at the King's service; the governors of Guernsey and
Jersey were both for him, held the strong places of the islands
and kept the ports open for him in despite of the people; Lundy
Island, the Scilly Isles, Lord Derby's Isle of Man, all gave shelter
or mounted guns for the defence of Royalist ships. The Sussex
Cavaliers had seized and briefly held Chichester, and though
they were driven out by the end of December[41] the danger of
more such attempts was ever present. The Royalists could not

JAMES BUTLER, EARL OF ORMONDE
by Justus Van Egmont

Scotland's Glory, Britain's pride
As Brave a Subject as ere ser Monarch dy'd
KINGDOMS in Ruins often Lye
But great MONTROSS's Acts will never dye

THE MARQUIS OF MONTROSE
from an engraving by William Faithorne

challenge the command of the sea, but they could make it very unsafe for all vessels bound to Parliamentary ports. London merchants clamoured for better protection, but the Earl of Warwick and the Navy were fully employed patrolling the North Sea and the Channel against ships carrying arms for the King to Newcastle or the Cornish coast.[42]

IV

Fear and discontent grew in London, and angry complaints at the increasing taxes. The King had proclaimed that any man paying customs duties not authorised by him was guilty of treason. The prohibition discouraged the farmers of the customs who announced early in January that they could advance no more money to Parliament.[43] Citizens who, under pressure, or with ephemeral enthusiasm, had subscribed to loans in the summer were by now disheartened at the prospect of the lengthening conflict.

In the House of Commons a sullen mood prevailed. Denzil Holles, injured and depressed by the defeat of his men at Edgehill and at Brentford, inspired the demand for a negotiated peace, and was supported by the lawyers Maynard, Whitelocke and John Glynne. Against these worried men were ranged the extremists, the austere young Vane, the irrepressible republican Harry Marten, Alexander Rigby, the Puritan member for Wigan, bitter against the excesses of Lord Derby in Lancashire, and others like them. There was no unity among the two hundred members of the reduced House of Commons and Pym's leadership alone prevented its dissolution into anarchy amid the disputes of the factions. The Committee of Safety was as divided and as quarrelsome as the House, and the violent utterances of the extremists threatened to make a permanent breach with the more conventional, more pacific House of Lords.

Once again John Pym by his patient subtlety navigated the

dangerous passage. He was not, like Vane and Marten, prepared to go to all extremes against the King; he believed sincerely in the phrases of the Parliamentary Commission issued to the Earl of Essex and wanted the King restored to his faithful Parliament to rule under such safeguards as they thought fit. But he saw with a clarity denied to Holles and others that this could not be achieved by a negotiated peace that winter. The King would have to be defeated in the field before he would agree to that lopping of his power that Pym desired. (Pym was not to know that even defeat in the field would make no difference to the King's attitude, that he had, on December 2nd of this year, 1642, put it upon record in a private letter—half jesting, yet wholly serious—that he would be " a Glorious King or a Patient Martyr ";[44] no other part would satisfy him.) But for Pym, who assumed naturally enough that the King would accept the logical consequences of military defeat, the problem remained that of fighting and winning the war against him.

But the war could not be waged if Parliament was divided, and the surest way to divide Parliament was to let the war party have their will and block all overtures to the King. This intransigence would alienate the Lords, frighten the perplexed and uncertain into joining the peace party or withdrawing from Parliament altogether, and cause misgivings among the doubtfully loyal or neutral in the City whose money and support were needed. The war party, left to themselves, would defeat their own end. As he had done a year ago, so now again, Pym saw that he could command a majority for the measures that were really needed only by reassuring and retaining control of the uncertain voters in the House, the men who were frightened by extremes. With cool dexterity throughout that winter he supported the demands of the peace party for a negotiated peace, but mobilised support for the war party on every motion concerned with the actual prosecution of the conflict—the voting of money, the organisation of forces, the maintenance of good relations with Scotland.[45]

He was strong in the conviction that the King, as things now stood with him, would neither offer nor accept satisfactory terms; and the City of London was already too committed to the Parliamentary cause to withdraw support when it came to war again. Thus he inspired his friends in the City to request a treaty with the King, by a gesture which had the outward appearance, but not the inward substance, of an offer of peace.

The old contempt of Court for City had not lessened under the impact of war. When a deputation of London aldermen, in Christ Church Hall, assured the King that they desired only that he would guarantee the liberties of his subjects and return to London, the surrounding courtiers broke into mocking laughter. The King himself answered courteously: " I know not how to make you confide in me," he said, " but you shall do well to believe those that lie least." With this reflection on the veracity of the Parliament men, he dismissed them, promising a written answer in due course. As they left the town, they attempted to bestow a gratuity on the sentry at Magdalen Bridge, who rejected it, saying he would take nothing from a Roundhead. For this loyal gesture the King later rewarded him.[46]

V

The visit of the City delegation coincided with a new departure in the King's policy. George Digby, who still dominated his political, though not his military, strategy, suggested the publication of a Royalist news-sheet to answer the official and unofficial bulletins which poured from London, damaging the King's cause with tales of atrocities and reports of defeat. In January 1643 appeared the first number of the Cavalier news-sheet, *Mercurius Aulicus*. It was published thereafter weekly in Oxford at a penny and regularly smuggled to London—mostly it would seem by women, who wandered the roads in the guise of strolling beggars and picked up and passed on packages of forbidden Oxford pamphlets left in agreed places. To meet the London demand more copies, not always wholly identical with the Oxford prototype, were printed secretly by Royalists in London, and sold to sympathisers for as much as eighteen pence.[47] *Aulicus* was usually worth the money. The editor was John Birkenhead, a young Fellow of All Souls, whose lively, unflattering portrait was sketched by John Aubrey: " he was exceedingly confident, witty, not very grateful to his benefactors, would lie damnably. He was of middling stature, great goggly eyes, not of a sweet aspect."[48] George Digby saw to it that he was supplied with information, but Birkenhead rapidly made his news-sheet into something more than a calendar of events. He was fluent in derision and quickly turned the Parliamentary newsmongers to ridicule: " Sir Jacob Astley lately slain at Gloucester desires to know was he slain with a musket or a cannon bullet." But it was a London imitator of his manner who averred that a preacher had recently called upon the Almighty: " O God when wilt thou take a chair and sit among the House of Peers, and when, O Lord, when I say, wilt thou vote among the Honourable Commons?"[49]

The flood of Cavalier mockery had begun. In a hundred ribald ballads, as the war went on, they preposterously parodied the solemnity of their opponents. Thus the Roundhead Colonel exhorts his men:

> Fight on, brave soldiers, for the Cause,
> Fear not the Cavaliers;
> Their threatenings are as senseless as
> Our jealousies and fears.
> 'Tis you must perfect this great Work,
> And all Malignants slay,
> You must bring back the King again
> The clean contrary way.

At Kineton, Brentford, Plymouth, York
And divers places more,
What victories we saints obtain,
The like ne'er seen before,
How often we Prince Rupert killed,
And bravely won the day,
The wicked Cavaliers did run
The clean contrary way.[50]

The Royalists cheerfully took to themselves the once opprobrious name of " Cavaliers." The King himself authorised its use: " the valour of Cavaliers hath honoured that name . . ." he said, " it signifying no more than a gentleman serving his King on horseback." [51]

In answer Parliamentary writers tried to change " Roundhead " into " Soundhead," or if heads must be brought in, to call the Royalists " Rattlepates " or " Shagpolls " or some belittling name with no honour to it. " Though we be roundheaded we are not hollow-hearted " a pamphleteer averred, but their propaganda and even their atrocity stories were singularly flat: hoary tales of maidens raped and babies roasted, of pacts with the Devil and judgments from Heaven, and once in a way a Cavalier burned to death because the flame of his pistol set fire to his lovelocks, thus proving what God thought of these unseemly tresses.[52]

It was natural that the best ballad-makers should be Royalists. Taylor, the popular doggerel poet, and Martin Parker, the best known writer of topical songs, were staunch King's men, and Parker soon gave to his expectant public the ballad which to a familiar tune was to be the unofficial anthem of the Cavaliers: " When the King enjoys his own again." [53]

The Parliamentarians encouraged, not at first very successfully, a solemn godliness among their men. " Is any merry? Let him sing psalms," advised one writer, and many little books were issued to comfort the troops: "A Spiritual Knapsack" was packed up by a helpful minister, and London's General, Philip Skippon, published his private devotions under the title of "The Christian Centurion." While Martin Parker and John Taylor put their facile talents at the King's service, Parliament used George Wither to celebrate their victories and advertise their cause. But they had no effective answer to *Aulicus* until the inception in London—not officially authorised, but encouraged and inspired—of *Mercurius Britanicus* "a fine new thing born this week," sneered *Aulicus*. This, with its misspelt name, was the most continuous of the satirical news-sheets on the Parliament side. Its successive editors, Thomas Audley and Marchamont Nedham, were as quick as Birkenhead to fasten upon the weaknesses of their opponents and turn their statements to ridicule. As the war progressed the duel of wits between *Aulicus* and *Britanicus*, challenging, deriding, and scoring off each other week by week became an accepted and enlivening accompaniment to the conflict.[54]

These developments were to come, but in this first winter of the war the Royalists acquired a facility for timely and intelligent propaganda. The King's denunciation of Parliament in December on the occasion of their first major attempt to levy taxes had made a considerable effect; in January an anonymous pamphlet which elaborated the same themes was widely circulated in London to coincide with the Royal answer to the City propositions of peace.

A Complaint to the House of Commons purported to be the work of those in London and Westminster who desired peace. It accused Parliament of prolonging an unnecessary war, because the King had passed more than a year ago a number of "good and profitable laws" and put an end to the tyranny of the Bishops and the Star Chamber. Tyranny there still was, and infringement of the liberties of the subject, but the King had no part in it. Parliament now imprisoned men without trial, sequestrated their land and seized their property. Parliament levied and forcibly collected taxes and customs. Parliament, after denouncing monopolies and expelling from the House of Commons monopolists who were the King's friends, favoured and encouraged monopolists who offered them money. Since all who opposed Pym and Hampden in Parliament had been silenced or expelled, there was now neither law, justice, nor a free Parliament, but a faction which bought and sold power by " siding and engaging one another," which plundered the citizens to maintain an unjust war, which advanced "schismatical beggarly sectaries" to be officers in its army, which, by a subtle combination of force and fraud, "under pretence of defending our laws and religion" . . . had found " a new way to deprive us of laws, liberty and property." [55]

While arguments such as these stimulated political discontent, the messenger who brought King Charles's answer to the peace petition of the City spread tales of the dangers now gathering against London. He told the Venetian envoy, no doubt with the intention that it should be repeated, that the King's forces in the spring would advance simultaneously into Essex and Kent, and hold London in a pincer grip by commanding both shores of the Thames estuary below the City and cutting off supplies.[56]

The King's answer to the peace petition was formally read out at Guildhall on January 13th, 1643. It was, in the circumstances, too aggressive; the King should have undermined the already disquieted citizens by persuasive words. Instead, he accused the Lord Mayor and three aldermen of treason. Pym, who was present with other representatives from Parliament, used this to prove the danger of treating with the King. The answer weakened the position in the City which the Royalists had assiduously built up, though they made one spirited effort to redeem the situation at a Common Council called for the raising of money three days later. Alderman Garraway (who had striven so resolutely as Lord Mayor to help the King in 1640) led the attack. He accused Parliament of robbing the citizens, declared that the King was the true protector alike of liberty and property, and demanded the arrest of those whom the King had accused as the creatures who were selling the City to a corrupt Parliamentary faction. A colossal din followed this attack with shouts of "No money! Peace! Peace!" and the Council broke up in disorder.[57]

But Garraway overlooked the real strength of Parliament in the City—Philip Skippon was staunch to them, and while he commanded the Trained Bands, Pym's friends in the City were secure. Isaac Pennington remained Lord Mayor and the principal outcome of the tumult was that Pym strengthened his position by replacing the recalcitrant farmers of the customs by men more willing to serve the Parliamentary cause.[58] This was to be the repeated pattern of Royalist efforts to regain the City; they were strong enough to create a tumult but not to overpower the others, while the half-hearted whose help they needed proved always in the last resort unreliable. Opinion veered away from the Royalists at the critical moment, and each new attempt they made to gain control served only as an excuse for more arrests and persecutions.

The King's answer was rejected in the City, but Pym cautiously played out rope to the peace party in Parliament; he saw that nothing was to be lost, and much to be gained, from a period of slackened hostilities. He wanted time to put the finances of the war on a more regular footing, and saw how he could use an interim of negotiation to push through Parliament the ordinances that would be necessary to maintain and enlarge the army. He was therefore willing enough that commissioners from both Houses, headed by the Earl of Northumberland, should once more approach the King for a treaty.

In Oxford the Parliamentary deputation hinted in private to the King's Councillors that, if permission were given to treat, they would undertake to control, or suppress, Pym's outrageous war-party and offer His Majesty reasonable terms.[59] They spoke unwisely, for the temper of the House altered almost daily, and Pym played very skilfully on the fears and prejudices of the waverers. While they were on their mission to Oxford, reports from Fairfax in Yorkshire that the Earl of Newcastle was arming recusants and freely employing them as officers in his forces caused alarm and indignation at Westminster and sensibly weakened the case of the moderates for peace.[60]

The King, for his part, was as ready as John Pym to exploit a delay in the war for his own ends. He had no illusions as to the ultimate intentions of the Parliamentary leaders, because he had no illusions about his own. "No less power than his who made the world of nothing can draw peace out of these articles," he wrote frankly to Ormonde. Like Pym, he planned for war. Surreptitiously a scheme was whispered about the Court that the Irish insurgents might fight for the King of England. This extremely dangerous idea had been suggested in a letter of the Queen's to her husband and was being pressed by Lord Taaffe, one of the Lords of the Pale, who was serving in Rupert's cavalry. But whether or not Charles would consent to this plan, he saw himself that he could release, and bring into his English armies, many of the Government troops from Ireland if only the fighting there would cease. With this in view, he now wrote to his Council in Dublin commanding them to make some kind of peace with the insurgents.[61]

In Oxford, playing for time, he encouraged his moderate Councillors and allowed the preliminary moves towards a treaty with Parliament to be made in apparent good faith. His initial demand—which he knew would cause useful delays—was for a cessation of arms during the treaty period.[62] He made his request from a strong position, because the arrival of the Parliamentary Commissioners in Oxford coincided with a Royalist victory.

VI

Good news had come unexpectedly from the south-west. Driven out of Dorset and Somerset, the Marquis of Hertford, a baffled amateur warrior, had taken ship at Minehead and transferred his activities to South Wales, to recruit men and dispute about precedence with another noble amateur, Lord Herbert of Raglan. He had left the King's affairs in the south-west in the hands of two more tenacious professional soldiers, Sir Ralph Hopton and Sir John Berkeley.[63] They retreated to Cornwall with a handful of cavalry, and were there joined by four of the Cornish gentry, Sir Bevil Grenvile, Sir Nicholas Slanning, John Trevanion, and John Arundel, all valiant, resourceful and of influence in the county. Between them they raised fifteen hundred men, and with these made ready to resist a Parliamentary force sent against them from Devon. The outlook for the Cornish Royalists was not cheerful; the county was divided in its loyalties; they were outnumbered and poorly equipped, though Slanning was busy with a plan to buy arms in France in exchange for Cornish tin, and had shipping ready for the purpose. Just at this moment four vessels with cargoes of arms and money bound for London were driven inshore by wind and weather not far from Falmouth. Slanning's small craft took advantage of their difficulties to harry them within range of the guns of Pendennis Castle, which John Arundel held for the King. Seeing no safety elsewhere, they took refuge in Falmouth harbour, where Hopton's men boarded them and took over their precious cargo. Thus strengthened, the Cornish Royalists marched against the Parliament forces, which after occupying Lostwithiel had turned northwards over the high ground towards Bodmin to cut them off.

The Parliamentarians felt strong in superior numbers and, as they thought, superior equipment; they had near at hand the extensive estates of the friendly Lord Robartes, a great Parliament man, whose splendid mansion of Lanhydrock bore notable witness to the magnitude of his fortune. On the deceptively uneven brow of Braddock Down, among the gorse clumps, they saw what they took to be the miserable remnant of Hopton's Cornishmen, and immediately advanced at a smart trot, confident that a single charge would settle the business. But Hopton had concealed the greater part of his forces in the broken ground and had masked the six good cannon he now possessed. An unexpected cannonade halted the oncoming force and hesitation turned to rout when the Cavaliers sprang in force from the gorse bushes. The Parliament troops fled helter skelter down the steep rutted tracks back to Lostwithiel, their cavalry overrunning and trampling their infantry in the narrow lanes; in the town they failed to rally, but fled leaving their wagons, their money, nearly a thousand muskets and " four choice pieces of ordnance " to be taken up by the victorious Cornishmen.[64]

The news which reached the King from other quarters was less favourable. The town of Chester remained loyal to him thanks to the influence of Bishop Bridgman and his son Orlando, once a successful barrister, who now spent his fortune on paying the garrison and fortifying the town [65]; but the rest of the county, after a vain attempt to proclaim its neutrality, had been mobilised against the King by Sir William Brereton, who thrust the Royalists out of Nantwich and established the predominance of Parliament.[66] In Lancashire, Lord Derby's brutal pressing of unwilling recruits started a flow of young men to the garrisons of the Puritan towns, where they were better armed, better lodged and more humanely treated. Making head, the Lancashire Puritans seized and fortified Lancaster Castle, occupied Preston, and dourly held Bolton against the attacking Cavaliers.[67]

In Yorkshire the stubborn fight went on for control of the West Riding, with its valuable commerce in woollen cloth. The Royalists lost Bradford on January 18th, 1643 when the country folk, armed with scythes, rose to assist a small Parliamentary force which had taken possession of the church. In eight hours of obstinate skirmishing in the streets of the little town and over the neighbouring moor, they drove off the Royalists with some loss of men and more of arms and money.[68]

A week later the young Fairfax took Leeds. The town had been well fortified but the Parliamentary troops were strengthened, as they had been at Bradford, by local volunteers—called clubmen from the character of their weapons. These fought with a stubborn zeal born in part of religion, in part of local rivalry; the greater number were Halifax men, and Halifax, the older town, resented the rising importance of Leeds in the woollen industry. Fairfax, " the man best beloved and relied upon by the rebels in the north," understood and shared the religious fervour of his men. He chose " Emmanuel " as the word for the day and the attack began to the sonorous singing of the sixty-eighth psalm: " Let God arise and his enemies shall be scattered." By the late afternoon the town had been so far infiltrated that further resistance was impossible, and the Royalists escaped as best they could towards Pontefract, meeting on the way their comrades from Wakefield, who had not stayed to fight. About four hundred and sixty were taken by Fairfax, but released on swearing never again to fight against Parliament.[69] This procedure, which had also been adopted with the prisoners taken at Chichester,[70] was to become in time a serious drag on Royalist recruiting.

The contribution in cloth, cash or kind which the West Riding could make to either party depended on the maintenance of manufacture and commerce and that in turn depended on the complicated co-operation of sheep farmers and clothmakers. Between them moved the middle-men who bought the raw wool, distributed it in the villages where it was washed, spun and woven, and later collected and marketed the cloth; they went their rounds over winding roads, from upland farms to scrambling villages in steep hollows where the streams drove the fulling mills, and on to the market towns, their packhorses burdened with sacks of wool and bales of cloth. The economy of the whole region depended on their visits. But in the last months the roads were unsafe with rival soldiery, the cloth might be seized, the flocks scattered; until one party or the other could wholly secure the West Riding, it was of little use to either. Meanwhile the winter was one of pinching anxiety for farmers and merchants, of idleness and hunger for the poor. In the West Riding cottages, looms were empty and spinning wheels at rest, while in the chattering becks the mill wheels turned in vain.[71]

For able-bodied, hungry men, the armies of both sides offered food, a chance for licensed robbery and—for the scorned and angry—a revenge on fat farmers and tight-fisted tradesmen. The dangerous mood was noticed by Sir John Hotham's son. "The necessitous people of the whole kingdom will presently rise in mighty numbers," he gloomily prophesied. "If this unruly sort have once cast the rider it will run like wildfire in the example through all the counties of England."[72] Something of the same kind had indeed been noticed by gentry in other regions, when arms were put into the hands of the common people and they were instructed to fight their betters; small wonder if it gave them ideas of revolt against the traditional order of society. "The gentry (say they) have been our masters a long time, and now we chance to master them," a Royalist summed up their opinions, and added, "now they know their strength, it shall go hard but they will use it."[73]

Captain Hotham expressed his doubts, indiscreetly, in a letter to the Earl of Newcastle; his action in corresponding with the Royalist commander was typical of the renewed desire for some kind of accommodation, if not throughout the country, then at least in Yorkshire. So Sir Hugh Cholmley, Parliament's Governor of Scarborough, reporting to the House of Commons his defeat of the Royalists at Gisborough, wrote: "I am forced to draw my sword not only against my countrymen but many near friends and allies some of which I know both to be well-affected in religion and lovers of their liberties."[74]

Honourable doubts, less honourable fears and forebodings were taking hold on both sides. The uncertain Royalist Lord Savile was arrested by Newcastle in the North on suspicion of entering into a conspiracy to seize the Queen when she landed in England and hand her to Parliament as a hostage until the King made peace.[75]

The Queen was on her way home. She had raised on the Crown jewels, partly in the Spanish Netherlands and partly in the United Provinces, loans of about a hundred and eighty thousand pounds. The Flemish moneylenders demanded interest at twelve per cent; the city of Amsterdam, on the other hand, offered her a small free gift.[76] One way and another, she had by January, 1643, several shiploads of arms for her husband and a number of distinguished professional soldiers waiting to sail for England under the escort of Admiral Tromp. Her first attempt was defeated not by the vigilance of Parliament but by the forces of nature. For six days her convoy battled with the storm. The Queen's ladies strapped to their beds, filled the narrow, shuddering cabin with cries of terror. She herself was in heroic mood; sea-sick but undaunted, she assured them that Queens of England were never drowned, and laughed to hear them prepare for death by confessing their most intimate sins in voices raised to carry above battering waves and creaking timbers. Beaten back at last, they landed again in Holland, the " rose and lily Queen " exhausted, sick and dirty, but resolved— to the admiration of Tromp—to sail again as soon as he could repair his damaged ships.[77]

The Queen longed to be with her husband to strengthen him against the moderate men who urged him to treat, and whom she distrusted. She need not at this juncture have feared that he would weaken. He had just had published in Oxford the Readings on Treason of Sir Robert Holborne which were largely devoted to the Essex rising of 1601 and the fate of those involved in it, and his coolness to the Parliamentary Commissioners newly arrived in Oxford showed how little hope there was of any treaty. Good news from Hopton in the West and from Rupert nearer at hand encouraged the King to demand much and offer little. On a desolate February day, the Commissioners saw a great crowd of prisoners, half-naked, starved and frozen, driven through the streets of Oxford and herded into St. Michael's Church—all that were left of the Parliamentary defenders of Cirencester.[78]

Rupert had taken the town two days before. Its capture was essential to the Royalists, to open up their line of communication to the south-west. They also hoped to hold up the transport of wool to London and to Gloucester, and if possible to divert the profits of the trade and the contributions of the wool-men and clothiers into the King's coffers. Furthermore, the King's growing armies needed food, fodder and clothing, and these could best be drawn from the farms, barns and store houses of the Cotswold country. Rupert had planned an attack early in January in conjunction with the forces the Marquis of Hertford had raised in South Wales, but Hertford did not arrive in time and the attempt failed.[79]

A heavy snowfall late in January prevented the Parliamentarians from reinforcing the garrison at Cirencester. Like most of England's peaceful towns, its ancient walls were not designed for modern warfare, and it was surrounded by gardens, houses and outbuildings which gave cover to an attacker. Rupert brought up cavalry and guns from Oxford, and was, this time, successfully met by Hertford, the snowfall notwithstanding. On the morning of February 2nd, 1643 they launched a joint attack. Rupert himself, with the main body, on the south-west of the town forced a way through the straggling suburban street to the main gate. He had directed a smaller body of horse to attack on the north side, so that the overburdened garrison would be dragged in two directions. Meanwhile his great cannon " made a terrible ruffling among the houses." The defenders put up a stubborn fight, musketeers fired from the small windows under the thatched eaves, and every street was barricaded with wagons, harrows and other country gear. But all was useless against the energy and numbers of the terrible Cavaliers and in less than two hours the town was stormed, penetrated and taken.

Charles used the victory to maintain his advantage over the Parliamentary Commissioners. He also sent to Rupert for supplies of wool and linen, of brimstone, flax, hemp, iron, harness and cheese for his growing army. Rupert, who on his march to Cirencester had acquired about two thousand horses for his cavalry by the simple process known as "sweeping the commons," now summoned the gentry and farmers of the region and got from them an agreement to pay four thousand pounds a month, in cash or kind, to sustain the King's forces.[80]

The news increased the desire for peace among the half-hearted in Parliament, especially the Lords, and stimulated in the more fanatic opponents of the King, whose chief spokesman was young Vane, the demand for a more vehement prosecution of the war. On February 11th this party in the Commons succeeded in voting down the request of the Lords to go on with the Treaty in spite of the little encouragement they had from the King. The Lords, ruffled by this insult from the Commons, refused to pass a bill fixing the amount of the assessment on each county to pay for the war. Vane was for precipitating a breach with the Lords, but Pym and his Yorkshire henchman Philip Stapleton prevented this. A second vote in the Commons secured the continuation of the talks with the King, in return for which the Lords, persuaded by Pym's friends, confirmed the assessment bill. In this complex transaction the Lords and the moderate party had gained an imaginary advantage only, but Pym had gained a real one. *They* went on with negotiations that would never lead to peace, but Pym had made a necessary advance towards the financing of the war.[81] He needed it; demands for pay and arms grew ever more urgent and he thought it wise to write himself to Sir John Hotham at Hull to beg him to be patient until money should be forthcoming.[82] It was a

constant anxiety that men of doubtful devotion would change
to the side best able to pay them.

Besides the immense advantage gained by passing the assessment ordinance, the advocates of a stronger war policy, in and
out of Parliament, now made another move to redeem the
disaster at Cirencester. They appointed Sir William Waller,
a member of the House and an influential landowner, who had
been a professional soldier in his youth, to be Major-General in
Gloucestershire,[83] to consolidate the rich Puritan Severn valley
before it was too late and thrust a barrier between the victorious
Cavaliers at Oxford, the oncoming Cornish forces, and the troops
which Lord Herbert was raising in South Wales.

VII

In the last week of February the Queen, defying her
astrologers who warned her of a dangerous conjunction of
planets, again put to sea. She had used her enforced stay in
Holland to insist that the Dutch release a ship carrying arms to
the King which had been held up at the request of Parliament's
ambassador. Now she vowed to Our Lady of Liesse—a favourite
shrine of her family's—a ship of pure silver should she come safe
to shore; Our Lady, through the agency of Admiral Tromp,
brought her safely to Bridlington Bay. Parliamentary ships,
armed colliers from the patrol off Newcastle, arrived too late
to stop her landing, but bombarded the houses near the quay
until Tromp threatened to return their fire, whereupon—either
out of fear, or because the tide carried them out of range—
they ceased. The Queen was unmoved by the danger; persuaded
to leave her bed and take refuge in a ditch, she went back to
fetch her lap-dog, which her ladies had forgotten.[84]

Her hopes rose high next day when Captain Hotham arrived
on the excuse of exchanging prisoners; his wavering loyalty
to Parliament's cause and his jealousy of the Fairfax family were

evident to the Queen and her advisers who believed they could win him over.[85] When in the course of the next few days she was escorted to York, it was noticeable that the Hothams made no attempt to intercept her. At York the Queen lodged in splendour at the palatial house of Sir Arthur Ingram, hard by the Minster; here she received a number of Scottish Royalists, Huntly's younger son, Lord Aboyne, and Airlie's son, Lord Ogilvie, who had come with Montrose to assure her that the oppressive rule of Argyll was unpopular in Scotland. The Royalists awaited only a sign from the King to rise against a government which usurped his authority. The Queen who had, only a few weeks before, urged upon the King the necessity of making a military party for himself in Scotland, was delighted to find her hopes and projects thus confirmed.[86]

She thought of nothing less than peace, and at York she saw war conducted with an elegance that appealed to her. The civilised conversation and good manners of the Court maintained at York by the Earl of Newcastle did not make so good an impression on every observer. A spiteful critic wrote of him that this " sweet general lay in bed until eleven, combed till twelve, then came to the Queen, and so the work was done." [87] Even the kindly Philip Warwick, writing at a later time his memories of the war, was doubtful of Newcastle's fitness: " He was a gentleman of grandeur, generosity, and of steady and forward courage, but . . . he had a tincture of romantic spirit and had the misfortune to be somewhat of a poet. So he chose Sir William Davenant, an eminent good poet and loyal gentleman to be his lieutenant general . . ." [88] These comments are unfair to Newcastle who had, so far, done well in putting heart into the Yorkshire Royalists. He employed professionals to supply the gaps in his own knowledge, gave unqualified support to Sir Marmaduke Langdale [89] and George Goring, both able cavalry commanders, and welcomed a distinguished veteran from the Swedish armies, General James King, whom the Queen brought with her, and who soon became his right-hand man.

In these congenial surroundings the Queen could take stock of the situation in the North. In Lancashire the Earl of Derby had taken and savagely burnt the town of Lancaster, though he had failed either to drive the rebels out of the castle or to hold the town for long. He retook Preston, which the Parliamentarians had briefly held, he sacked Blackburn, drove off the cattle and horses of Puritan farmers and forced their sons into his ruffianly forces. A Spanish ship carrying troops and guns to the Netherlands was storm-driven into the estuary of the river Wyre. Before Derby could reach it, the Parliamentarians fell upon it as it lay helpless and seized eight brass cannon. Then Derby swept down; having no means to carry off the cargo, he burnt the ship to the waterline, and—as he rather oddly put it—" freed the Spaniards "; he landed them, four hundred in all, on the unfriendly shore and left them to fend for themselves. The rest of the cargo, cannon and arms, were recovered from the floating hulk by the Parliamentary soldiers.[90]

The Earl of Derby was narrow-minded, vain and silly; his warfare was brutal because he felt, and encouraged his men to feel, that rebellion in Lancashire was a personal affront to the House of Stanley, a revolt of ungrateful and treacherous bondmen against their rightful lord. His manner of campaigning was resented and criticised by the wiser Royalists of Lancashire who saw what damage he was doing to the King's cause, but it was reported at York as a stream of glorious victories.

In Yorkshire, George Goring had taken the field at the head of cavalry raised by the local gentry. This ambitious, erratic soldier was, at his best, a skilful commander popular with his subordinates alike for his ingenuity, gaiety and courage. He had joined the Queen in the Low Countries after his surrender of Portsmouth in the previous autumn and had had no great difficulty in explaining his conduct. His father, long a favourite with her, had no doubt helped him back into her good graces, and both father and son had worked hard to negotiate loans and buy arms on her behalf. His first exploit in the spring of 1643 was to surprise the younger Fairfax on Seacroft Moor as he was effecting the withdrawal of his father's troops from Selby to secure the West Riding. Goring drove him back to Leeds with considerable loss. He would have followed this up by an assault on the town, but his older professional colleagues, especially General King, did not believe the place could be carried by storm and, as they had neither resources nor machinery for a siege, the project was abandoned.[91]

The Queen scored a bloodless success when Sir Hugh Cholmley, Parliament's Governor of Scarborough, after some months of heart-searching and doubt, declared for the King. A fortress and harbour of considerable value was thus gained for the Cavaliers. Cholmley's example might, they reasonably hoped, be followed by the Hothams at Hull. The outlook for war seemed to the Queen far more radiant than the arid prospect of a negotiated peace with Pym and his junto. When she announced the winning over of Cholmley to her husband, she added a warning: let him never make peace without dissolving " this perpetual Parliament," for should he do so, " I am absolutely resolved to go into France, not being willing to fall again into the hands of those people."[92]

The outlook for the Royalists in the Midlands was considerably less favourable. Parliamentary forces under Lord Brooke seized on Lichfield, carrying the last stronghold of the Cavaliers in the Cathedral itself only after a desperate assault. Lord Brooke was killed by a stray shot, in an interval of the fighting, as he sat at an open window: a judgment, the more pious Royalists thought, because it was Saint Chad's Day—the patron saint of Lichfield. The loss to Parliament was a serious one, for the energy and influence of Brooke was paramount in the Midlands.[93] An equally grave loss to the Royalists occurred a fortnight later. Secure at Lichfield, the Parliamentary commanders saw the possibility of linking with Sir William Brereton's forces from Cheshire, and consolidating the northern Midlands. As Sir John Gell advanced across Staffordshire to join with Brereton, the

Staffordshire Royalists called for help on the Earl of Northampton who, hurrying to their rescue, came up with Brereton and Gell on Hopton Heath near Stafford. In spite of bad ground, treacherous with rabbit holes, Northampton's cavalry checked the Parliamentarians and forced them to withdraw with the loss of nearly all their artillery. But Northampton himself, a man no less influential for the King than Brooke had been for Parliament, was killed early in the battle. Brereton and Gell refused to return his body for burial unless the Royalists would, in exchange, give them back their guns. Lord Northampton's fiery son, who had taken over his father's command, refused and the Cavaliers long remembered the uncivilised bargain that Brereton had tried to make.[94]

In the south-west Rupert moved against Bristol. If the King could take this, the second seaport of the realm, he would greatly improve his position both by sea and land. But Bristol was strongly garrisoned and a plot by the Royalists of the town to open one of the gates to him was discovered in time by the defenders. Over eighty suspects were arrested in the town, thus putting an end to any further hopes of the Cavaliers for help from within.[95] Rupert fell back to mature other plans.

By this time Parliament's Major-General for Gloucestershire, Sir William Waller, had raised a substantial force among the Puritan yeomen of the district, and marched to Bristol to strengthen the Governor, Lord Saye's son Nathaniel Fiennes, with advice and men. Next he thrust the Royalists out of Malmesbury and turned towards the Severn to deal with the army that Lord Herbert was bringing to the King from South Wales. This considerable force had remained inactive for five weeks at Highnam, just across the river from Gloucester, unable to cross because Gloucester was garrisoned for Parliament, and apparently unwilling to move until Rupert or some experienced soldier came to their help. Waller, with professional skill and speed, crossed the Severn estuary a little below Gloucester on an improvised bridge of boats, marched through the Forest of Dean,

and came on Lord Herbert's forces in the small hours of March
24th. Lord Herbert was not with his troops in person, and no
officer of experience had been left in charge. Their scouting was
so bad that they did not know Waller had crossed the Severn, and
were astounded when his army suddenly appeared on the Welsh
bank of the river, cutting them off from retreat into their own
country. As Waller closed in, the garrison from Gloucester
made a sharp sally. The Royalist cavalry, few in number, fled
from the closing trap, and the whole force of Welsh infantry
surrendered without fighting. The King lost fourteen hundred
men and Waller gained a valuable supply of arms, powder and
artillery.[96]

While Waller redeemed the situation for Parliament in
Gloucestershire, Oliver Cromwell stamped on the glowing
embers of Royalism in East Anglia, by marching within a week
on the disaffected towns of Lowestoft and King's Lynn. At
Lowestoft he surprised a group of Cavalier gentry who had
hoped to secure the little port for the King, and carried them off
prisoners to Cambridge. Here he found the Consistory in
session, surrounded them, and kept them prisoners through a
long cold night until they voted help to the Parliament forces.[97]
The purging of the University was shortly to follow.

VIII

These checks, notwithstanding, the King felt himself to be
strong. Rupert's cavalry controlled the country round Oxford
and his raiding parties scoured the Chilterns for fodder, horses
and cattle as far as Aylesbury.[98] In Oxford itself, early in March,
the King received the Parliamentary Commissioners led by the
Earl of Northumberland, who caused some merriment among the
Cavaliers by bringing large supplies of food, in the mistaken
belief that the King and his party were on very short commons.[99]
The terms put forward by Parliament were: the abolition of

episcopacy, the enforcement of penal laws against the Catholics, and the punishment of the principal delinquents, by which they meant the King's present advisers, especially Lord Digby and Prince Rupert. The King for his part asked that all strong places in the Kingdom be yielded to him, all the Parliamentary forces be disbanded, and Parliament be transferred from Westminster to some neutral region where it could meet without fear of violence.

The terms were wholly incompatible with each other and it was clear to men of perception on both sides that they were neither sincerely offered by Parliament nor sincerely entertained by the King. Secretary Nicholas summed up Pym's policy in a letter to Rupert: " The truth is Parliament is not willing to treat but would gladly have the people believe they could not obtain a peace." [100] The King, in his letters to the Queen, made it clear that he considered Parliament's terms not worth discussing, but was anxious to throw on to them the onus of a final breach. She, in return, fiercely reiterated her earlier advice: " Do not suffer your army to be disbanded, or any peace to be made, till this Parliament be ended . . . Remember that you are lost if you consent to a peace before this Parliament be dissolved." [101] Both the King and Queen hoped—and to a great extent believed —that the war could be won within a few months by so resounding a victory over their enemies as would put them in a stronger position than ever before to elevate the monarchy to that splendour of unquestioned and God-given authority in which they believed.

During the negotiations a grudging succession of four-day truces maintained an uneasy quiet between the armies of Essex and Rupert. The unwillingness of either side to impose any more durable cessation of arms was the index to the true feelings of their leaders. To the Parliament men also the frequent presence of Rupert at the negotiations seemed very significant. He sat silently with the older and more learned civilian representatives of the King, but he was known to have risen, in the last weeks, very high in the King's favour, and to be for the time being "absolutely the favourite of the Court."[102]

Rupert's martial presence, rather than anything he said, added to the impression that Charles had no serious intention of making peace. Far more damaging was the interception by Parliament of a letter from the King to the Queen, frankly admitting that he cared nothing for the treaty, but was full of "fine designs" for continuing the war.[103] Parliament must also have known from the reports which came to Westminster from their various friends in, or near, Dublin that Charles was planning help from Ireland. Charles's private letters to Ormonde might be safe from prying eyes, but his commission to his Council in Dublin to treat with the Irish rebels was a matter of public knowledge; so was his peremptory order issued from Oxford in March, that Parliament's two commissioners in Dublin be expelled without delay.[104]

In all this, the King played into Pym's hands. With no more intention than the King of making a permanent peace, Pym could safely allow the moderate and wavering men at Westminster to play at treaty-making until they were finally disillusioned. Meanwhile, he used every fresh discovery of the King's double-dealing to stimulate the voting of the necessary ordinances for waging the war.[105] Before the end of March he achieved his most important measure for the raising of ready money, a general order for the sequestration of all Royalists' estates. Committees were appointed to see to this in each county, their costs to be defrayed out of the property seized. In effect this measure authorised and made general a practice which had already casually grown up, since in any region controlled by Parliament their leaders naturally seized on the stores and money of the opposite party before they troubled their friends.[106] This ordinance for licensed robbery was not very different from the measures authorised by the King for diverting the rents of "disaffected" landlords to his own coffers and the seizures of their goods and live-stock to supply his own needs.[107] Between them, both parties were shaking the structure of English rural society by loosening the deep-rooted property rights on which it rested. But neither of them at the moment had leisure to think of the after-effects of their work.

In one thing alone Pym seems to have been temporarily outwitted by one of his own moderate men. Neither he nor the other Parliamentary Commissioners in Oxford guessed that one of their number was conducting private negotiations with the King of a different kind. Edmund Waller, Member of Parliament for the Cornish borough of St. Ives, poet, one-time courtier, friend of Falkland and of Hyde, was not altogether at home in the Parliamentary party. He genuinely desired peace and he saw that peace was not Pym's intention. He was in touch with the London Royalists who were still hopeful and still active, and under cover of the negotiations at Oxford he discussed with Falkland a plan for regaining London for the King and so automatically ending the war. The details were confused. The King's friends in London were apparently to stand in readiness for a sudden and city-wide demonstration. Rupert and his cavalry would approach as close as possible to London; since the King held Reading he would have no trouble in coming almost to the outer defences. At a given moment, the King's Commission of Array would be read in the City, the Royalists would acclaim it, and Parliament, caught between invasion without and revolt within, would be helpless. The war would be over in an instant. The architects of this too sanguine "peace plot" took insufficient notice of Philip Skippon and the London Trained Bands devotedly loyal to Parliament, and seem to have left out of their reckoning the powerful line of fortifications which all that winter had been built round the outer circuit of London, and the internal defences of the city, the breastworks or musket-proof turnpikes at every strategic place planned for a street to street defence.[108]

The King had not lost his fondness for a variety of plans, and his projects during March and April included Scotland and Ireland as well as the London plot. The Scots Commissioners had by this time reached Oxford—Chancellor Loudoun as the messenger from the Council in Edinburgh and Henderson from the Assembly of the Church of Scotland—bearing their petition for the thorough and immediate reform of the Church of England. Loudoun conveyed to the King that if he would accede to this request he could count on the support of his Council in Scotland in the present war; if he refused, then Loudoun would offer no more than his good offices to mediate between King and Parliament.[109] The King had been advised by Hamilton to treat the Commissioners courteously but to prevent them from going to London. He took the second advice but not the first. He received them only in public and with marked coldness; he even considered arresting Henderson who, unlike Loudoun, had no safe-conduct. Following the King's example, the Cavaliers insulted them in the streets; all their letters were opened and their offers and petition were alike rejected.[110]

The King's treatment of them suggested that he intended to break with the Covenanters and adopt the plan for a Royalist rising in Scotland put forward by Montrose, Aboyne and Ogilvie to the Queen at York. On the contrary, he believed himself to be following Hamilton's advice and, with typical inconsistency discouraged the Queen from accepting Montrose's offers until she could have the benefit of Hamilton's opinions on them. He, when he reached York from Edinburgh, assured her that he could vouch for the neutrality of Scotland at least until the end of the summer, unless some Royalist rising were to precipitate a crisis. As the war in England would in all likelihood be over by the autumn, it would be folly to accept Montrose's plan, involving as it did an unnecessary additional war in Scotland.[111]

The King therefore discouraged the Covenanters at Oxford, while pressing his wife to placate them from York. Accepting Hamilton's view that the Scots could be kept neutral, he did not realise that they would not remain neutral indefinitely, if the war were to continue for more than another year for instance, and still less so if he persisted in his present policy of making peace with the Irish.

The Covenanters, and more especially Argyll with his westward-facing coastal lands, vulnerable to Irish raiders, would never accept any conclusion of the revolt in Ireland except the utter defeat of the " Popish-Irish butchers; " any compromise the King might make with them must force Argyll and the Covenanters into closer friendship with Parliament.

Spring came early in 1643, with mild and open weather, " fair, calm and growing " wrote a Royalist squire in his diary and added " God help and deliver us from these troubles and tribulations."[112] But the armies, except in the truce area between London and Oxford, continued their activities. In Lancashire the Parliamentarians took and immediately lost Wigan, and the Manchester men, after a repulse at Warrington, retired within their fortifications and fell a-praying, while Lord Derby's undisciplined bands terrorised the county. But sudden retribution was at hand. Ralph Assheton, the member of Parliament for the county, had gathered his neighbours in Rochdale, put heart into them, and set on foot a force stiffened by several companies of musketeers, properly armed and with some understanding of their weapons. Lord Derby thrust through the hilly country to challenge and destroy them. At Whalley Abbey he crossed the Calder and leaving the main of his forces in the low ground by the water with the cannon, despatched a party of horse and foot uphill towards the village of Padiham to find out the enemy. The country thereabouts is steep and hilly, with narrow roads flanked by drystone walls. Assheton's musketeers lined the walls, unseen, and met the carelessly advancing Cavaliers with a stinging fire which put their horse to flight. The musketeers now advanced, followed by the rest of Assheton's forces; at the sound of the firing the cautious country folk peeped from their cottages, and when they saw Lord Derby's men fall back, seized what weapons they could and joined Assheton's army. The main body of the Cavaliers, in the low ground, saw and heard with terror the shouting, angry crowd of soldiers and countrymen surging down the hills towards them. The rabble foot fled pell mell, dropping their arms and wading the river; at this the cavalry made no attempt to stand. Derby with difficulty escaped, saving a few of his guns and a handful of troops. He never raised another army for the King.[113]

Better fortune attended the Royalists in the Midlands. Rupert's first concern, as the negotiations for peace faltered hopelessly on, was to clear a passage between Oxford and the North so that they could communicate more freely with Newcastle's forces and the Queen. Taking a train of artillery and some of his best cavalry, he set off to recapture Lichfield. On April 3rd, Easter Monday, he was before the hostile little town of Birmingham, given over to the manufacture of ironware and cutlery, and, since the war began, busily making swords for Parliament. With foolhardy faith in the Lord, the citizens refused him entry. Rupert battered his way in, setting fire to a suburb and shooting up civilians who resisted.[114] Subjugated, the place might well be useful for the manufacture of arms for the Royalist troops. Three days later Rupert summoned Lichfield; the Parliamentary garrison, lacking the vigorous leadership of Lord Brooke, withdrew from the lower town and made themselves strong in the Cathedral Close, while Rupert began to drain the muddy stretch of water below the Cathedral hill on the southern side, and set up his batteries to dislodge them.[115]

The Earl of Essex, somewhat slower to move, had by the second week in April closed in to besiege Reading. Ephemeral hopes of peace now vanished. On April 7th the King in Oxford finally told Loudoun that he would not tolerate the meddling of the Scots between him and his English subjects; there should be no mediation.[116] On April 8th Parliament declared that the King's offers were not acceptable; Charles, shifting the onus of the breach on to them, made slightly modified offers which were in turn rejected. On Saturday, April 15th,

Parliament recalled the Commissioners.[117] Next day the guns of Essex thundered against Reading and Rupert loosed his assault parties on Lichfield with scaling ladders and hand grenades.

Charles from Oxford wrote a restraining letter to Rupert, for the burning of Birmingham had given fresh material to Parliament pamphleteers; he urged him to eschew bloodshed and seek to reclaim rather than to punish his misled subjects, to "take their affections rather than their towns."[118] But graciously as the King expressed himself on paper, his prosecution of some of the leading prisoners and his indifference to the fate of the others more truly reflected his feelings towards his rebel subjects. John Lilburne, sentenced to death for treason, had been saved from the gallows only because Parliament threatened reprisals; it was evident, if not to the King, at least to the commanders of his army, that the trying of prisoners of war would set a most dangerous example. Ordinary prisoners who would not re-enlist in the King's army, were herded together in the Oxford churches and in Oxford Castle without fire or bedding, sometimes with so little water that they drank the puddles in the wretched enclosures allotted them for exercise. Surgeons were refused them, and townsfolk who tried to help were driven away, while the Governor of the Castle beat and ill-used them to compel them to join the King. A more effective form of persuasion was the offer of pay and food if they would work on the fortifications of the city.[119]

The King made ready to wage the war to an end by every means in his power. On the failure of the treaty he wrote to his Scots Council denouncing his English Parliament and warning them against the overtures and pretences which it had made to them. "We never denied any one thing that by law we were required to grant, or asked one thing but what by known law was unquestionably our own." The terms of peace had been "absolutely and scornfully rejected" by the wretched minority that usurped the name of Parliament. Let not the Scots be deceived into believing that Pym and his friends had the interests of the Presbyterians at heart. Their ranks, he said, were stuffed with Anabaptists who would bring only disorder, destruction and anarchy to the Church of Scotland.[120] He wrote in the same vein also to the town of Edinburgh, reminding them of all his past favours shown to them and warning them against the lies and flatteries now flowing from London.[121]

Immediately after, on Sunday, April 23rd, 1643, Saint George's Day, he wrote twice to the Earl of Ormonde in Dublin: an official letter urging once again the necessity of a truce with the rebel Irish, and a private message commanding him to enlist for the royal service in England, as soon as the truce was made, as many troops as he could, English or Irish.[122]

The fatal confusion deepened. In the Narrow Seas the Dutch Admiral, Maarten Tromp, was stopping Dunkirk pirates who now defiantly claimed that they were legitimately operating under the authority of the Irish Confederation or the King of England, and sometimes of both.[123] The King's Cause was just, Protestant and constitutional when he defended it on paper, but for its defence by sea and land he was willing to call in lawless sea-rovers and Irish rebels. For these things there were some among his subjects who would never forgive him.

BOOK TWO

THE FIRST CIVIL WAR

April 1643—October 1645

CHAPTER ONE

THE EQUIPOISE OF FORTUNE

April—September 1643

THE first important news to reach Westminster after the collapse of the treaty was disheartening. The invincible Rupert had taken Lichfield Close. He had made a causeway over the muddy strip of water below the hill on which the Cathedral stands, and had mined the wall of the Close. Before firing the mine he offered the garrison one more chance to surrender. They refused, and on April 20th, 1643, Rupert sprang the first mine in England and launched the assault in the smoke of an explosion which blasted skyward several tons of masonry and Staffordshire clay. The Parliamentarians defended the breach all day but when night came they knew they could fight no longer and sued for terms. Rupert allowed them to march out with the honours of war and gave them safe passage to Coventry.[1]

From Lichfield, the Prince hastened back to Oxford in answer to an urgent summons, for the Parliamentary forces had closed in on Reading. Commanding the main road from London to Oxford, the Thames valley and the widest gap in the Chiltern Hills, it was a key position in the King's strategy, and since the previous December, Rupert had urged in vain that it be more effectively fortified. Sir Arthur Aston, the Governor, a professional soldier with a good conceit of himself, did not care to risk his reputation on the defence of a town under-manned and poorly fortified; injured by a falling tile early in the siege, he was conveniently struck dumb. Responsibility devolved upon his second-in-command, Richard Feilding.

The King failed to reinforce the garrison by barge from Oxford because the batteries of Essex covered the river. He failed again with heavy loss in an attempt to introduce a relieving force over Caversham bridge, and finally, with the help of Rupert newly come from Lichfield, he tried once more to combine an attack on Essex with a sally from the town. A scout swam the river with a message for Feilding, but he failed to respond, and the Royalists after some wasteful skirmishing withdrew.[2]

Feilding surrendered next day. The garrison was granted the honours of war and safe passage to Oxford but Essex, unlike Rupert at Lichfield, could not control his men who insulted and robbed the defeated Cavaliers. When they reached Oxford, with Sir Arthur Aston still speechless in a litter, their resentment had hardened against Feilding. Tried by Court Martial, he was sentenced to death for failing to obey the orders to co-operate with the relieving force. In his defence he pleaded that he had at the time agreed to a truce with Essex pending negotiations and had thought it dishonourable to resume hostilities without warning. The generous Rupert alone recognised that the dilemma was a genuine one and, by the intervention of the Prince of Wales, obtained his pardon from the King. Sir Arthur Aston, who had recovered his powers of speech, was soon after rewarded with the Governorship of Oxford.[3]

The fall of Reading was a major disaster. Though the King had garrisoned Abingdon and Wallingford, Essex was now perilously near to Oxford. Parliament had other lesser but satisfactory gains. Waller, after capturing Lord Herbert's Welsh army at Highnam, had put small garrisons into Monmouth and Chepstow to hamper Royalist recruiting in those parts, briefly occupied Hereford, seized Wardour Castle from its Catholic owner and placed the stalwart young Puritan Edmund Ludlow in command.[4]

The Parliamentarian propagandists made even more of a small engagement in the West, where Sir Ralph Hopton had been surprised on a dark and stormy night on the hills above Okehampton. James Chudleigh, a young Devon gentleman who had served already in the Irish war, ambushed the advancing army with a small party of horse. Hopton's army—three thousand foot and six hundred cavalry and dragoons—walked straight into the trap, and in the confusion of darkness, storm and surprise fled leaving in Chudleigh's hands a thousand muskets, five barrels of powder and, most serious of all, Hopton's portmanteau with papers naming the loyal gentry who had contributed to his army.[5] In London the pamphleteers made much of the Western Wonder, until the Cavaliers turned it to ridicule.

> Do you not know, not a fortnight ago,
> How they brag'd of a Western Wonder?
> When a hundred and ten, slew five thousand men,
> With the help of lightning and thunder?
> There Hopton was slain, again and again,
> Or else my author did lie;
> With a new thanksgiving, for those who are living,
> To God, and His servant, Chudleigh.[6]

The Cavaliers, in spite of these lesser setbacks and the loss of Reading, had cause for gaiety. Essex accepted his victory with unexampled gloom. All through the winter deserters had been slinking away and now disease broke out in the diminishing army. Lord Brooke's regiment had evaporated after the death of its colonel and paymaster; the regiment of Denzil Holles, badly damaged at Brentford, had disintegrated when Holles (it was said at the nagging of his " bitch wife ") had forsaken the field and gone back to Westminster.[7] In the circumstances Essex could undertake no further action until Parliament sent him money to pay his troops and recruit his forces.[8]

London, in that latter half of April 1643, was a dismal town. Wounded men with women and children claiming to be victims of the war swelled the number of beggars. Householders were now paying towards the relief of war distress, the cost of fortifying London, and for men, horses and arms for Essex. Richer citizens were compelled to lend money on the feeble security of "the public faith" a phrase already spoken with contempt. On Sundays from the pulpits they were exhorted to give alms for stricken Brentford, for refugees from Ireland, for the sick, wounded and orphans. Food was not yet scarce, but housekeeping had become difficult as the smooth transport of supplies from the neighbouring counties was lessened or interrupted by Royalist foraging in the Chilterns and the Vale of Aylesbury, by the aftereffects of destruction, most of all by the confiscation of horses and waggons which hampered the carriers' trade. Fuel was the worst problem; no coal came from blockaded Newcastle, and neither the coal from the Scottish mines nor the available wood on which London was now forced to rely could meet the demand. The price of coal soared beyond the reach of the ordinary household and far beyond the price fixed by Parliament. The patience of the Londoners was near to breaking.[9]

Some of the London discontent was vented on the remaining monks and priests now deprived of the protection and alms of the rich Catholics who had left with the Court. The rabble invaded the quarters of the Queen's little community of Capucins at Somerset House, broke up their chapel, destroyed the altarpiece by Rubens and burnt an image of that "deceiving warlock" St. Francis of Assisi. Some of the friars found asylum with the Portuguese envoy; others were deported to France. On April 17th a young missionary priest, Father Henry Heath, was hanged and disembowelled at Tyburn. Other priests remained in prison, in great want for lack of alms, patiently awaiting the day when Parliament would think it politic to immolate another victim.[10]

The people kept themselves warm by breaking into St. Margaret's, Westminster—or "Margarets" as it was now called to avoid the taint of Popery—where they "battered the windows to pieces." Parliament thought to cheer them further by having that "monument of idolatry" Cheapside Cross pulled down; the lead and metal about it could be used for arms. But this act of Protestant piety misfired: some of the Londoners were fond of their Cross and a troop of horse had to be sent to prevent a fight over its demolition.[11]

Suspicion and slander grew. It was freely said that the Parliament men feathered their own nests, helping themselves to pickings from the money and plate that passed through their hands and keeping back the best horses seized from Royalist stables. No doubt some of them did. Standards of honesty in public affairs were elastic, and it had always been understood that tax farmers, commissioners for the Navy, and other officers of the central administration defrayed their expenses out of perquisites.

On the return of the Parliamentary Peace Commissioners from Oxford a quarrel between Lords and Commons was narrowly averted. The Earl of Northumberland, incensed because a private letter of his had been opened by Henry Marten, one of the most extreme of the Commons, hit the little man in the face with his cane. But Pym did not want a quarrel over "privilege" and the untoward incident was smoothed away.[12]

II

Both sides were now facing the realities of a long war. Their armies would have to be kept on foot indefinitely, or certainly for not less than another year, and money must be found somewhere, by force, by persuasion, or by borrowing.

The organisation of the armies, when the war began, was haphazard. Gentlemen who paid and equipped foot companies or troops of horse liked to exercise the command themselves. Though the ardent and wealthy—Brooke, Hampden, Holles— had raised whole regiments, the army of Essex in the first months of the war consisted very largely of troops and companies privately raised and not formed into regiments. Gradually, as they realised the demands of the service, many of the independent captains withdrew leaving their places to professionals or to those with an aptitude for soldiering. Often the men went home with the masters, leaving to Essex only the worst recruits, the masterless and unemployed who were better off, even unpaid, in his forces than they had been in peace-time.

In the counties the action of enthusiasts had created garrisons and small independent forces in great numbers. Fortunately, the more astute local commanders soon saw that valuable energy would be wasted if every county conducted the war in isolation from the next. Members of Parliament, Lords and Commons, locally active in the field, came up to Westminster with plans for co-operation, and in the course of the winter authorised the association of certain groups of counties for the purposes of the war; of these groups the Eastern Association was to become the most famous. Lord Mandeville, now by the death of his father Earl of Manchester, was made general of the Eastern Association. Lord Grey of Groby, the youthful son of the Earl of Stamford, was appointed general for the Midlands where the death of Lord Brooke had left a grave gap in leadership. In the North Lord Fairfax and his son Sir Thomas organised the war for Parliament; in Cheshire and on the Welsh border Sir William Brereton; in the South Sir William Waller.

The main army was still that of Essex, though the extent of his power over these other generals was necessarily vague. He and Manchester both had seats on the Committee of Safety in Westminster, when they could spare the time. But the situation had entirely altered since that day in August when Essex had taken command of the cheering thousands at Northampton and had marched at their head to release His Majesty from the " malignants " and bring him home to his faithful Parliament. The expanded organisation was more effective and more comprehensive, but it had lessened the importance of Essex and had gravely weakened his army. Many of his best officers had been absorbed, with their men, into the new formations; Oliver Cromwell, for instance, who was now a Colonel under Manchester, and rapidly becoming his right hand. It was rumoured, not untruly, that Essex was resentful of Manchester and the Eastern Association and, increasingly, of Sir William Waller in the south-west.[13]

John Hampden, in these difficult months, acted as the liaison between Essex and the House of Commons. He had great faith in him—understandably, for at that time it would have been hard to find a man of equal experience, influence and resources. With his habitual tact and goodwill he smoothed down the asperities of the general's complaints and kept before the House the necessity of properly supplying his army, which covered London and kept open the vital communications of the capital.[14]

Money was the eternal problem. Secretary Nicholas had sagely predicted that the City men who had lent money to Parliament would press for continuance of the war to get their money back. But even the most sanguine must ultimately begin to weigh the wisdom of lending more against the chances of seeing any return, ever, on their investment. Heavy rates of interest—eight and twelve per cent were now usual—might defeat their purpose, as more money had to be borrowed to pay the interest. Representatives of the great banking houses of Amsterdam had been in consultation with City and Parliament men in the spring. Some of these houses had links with Scotland. Behind the finances of the war could be detected Pym's constant pressure on his colleagues at Westminster and on his friends in Scotland to make an armed alliance against the King.[15]

As fresh sums were groaningly raised ordinary men learned, as they have in other times, a puzzling truth. John Greene, a barrister, wrote in his diary: " We begin now to see that a kingdom according to human discourse, is not so easily ruinated, and will commonly hold by stronger roots than we imagined; we may hold out, if God have not determined otherwise, two or three years longer at this rate—only grow poorer and poorer."[16]

Some way more continuous and reliable than loans had to be found to finance the war. While the peace negotiations caused a welcome delay, Pym had gained consent to ordinances for the general assessment of the country, and the sequestration of Cavaliers' estates, which ensured a steady flow of money to the Parliamentary troops. Local committees were responsible for raising the weekly sum for which each county had been assessed at Westminster; it lay with these committees to distribute the burden fairly, and to see that the rents and profits of Royalist landowners in regions held by Parliament flowed into the committee's hands, leaving only an allotted minimum for the family to live on.[17]

The management of the assessments and sequestrations varied with the efficiency and zeal of the local gentry. Deceptions and evasions were sometimes successfully practised. " I am loth to eat in pewter yet," confessed the Countess of Sussex, " but truly I have put up (i.e., hidden) most of my plate, and say it is sold."[18] The notoriously Royalist Marquis of Worcester was said to have let the local Committeemen enter Raglan Castle, then to have had a servant turn on one of his son's noisy hydraulic engines and announce with well-simulated agitation " the lions are all got loose "—whereat the gentlemen of the Committee hurriedly withdrew.[19]

It was remarkable on the whole with what ease the nation-wide system of taxation began to work, and how quickly it became an accepted, though unloved, part of local life. The county Committees were new in name—or names, for there were sometimes two or three: a Committee for Assessment, a Committee for Sequestration, a Committee for Accounts, and later possibly a Committee for Compounding—but they were not new in nature. Parliament depended during the war, as the King had depended during the peace, on the goodwill and intelligence of the local gentry, the deputy-lieutenants, the justices of the peace. In the old days when subsidies had been voted, these were the men responsible for raising the money, region by region, hundred by hundred. In the 'thirties they had been responsible for raising Ship-money; now they were responsible for raising the assessments to pay for the war. But this new demand was both urgent and continuous, nothing less than a weekly levy, constantly paid in, constantly going out again, to Westminster for the expenses of the nation, or more directly to the head-quarters of the local troops: it was therefore necessary for the gentry responsible to meet regularly and to have some kind of administrative centre and staff. The Kent Committee took over Knole, paying no rent to the Royalist Sackvilles, but making free of their great house as a " glorious seraglio," said the Cavaliers, but in sober truth as a combined office and hostel, where a great deal of work was more or less efficiently done.[20] Administrative efficiency and administrative costs (subtracted from the assessment money) varied from county to county. Sir William Boteler applied logarithms to the finances of Bedfordshire[21] but simpler methods were more usual.

The amount of the Weekly Pay expected from each county had been fixed at Westminster according to the supposed re-sources of the county. Devonshire, with its rich husbandry, led all the rest with an assessment of £1,800 a week; remote and barren Westmorland brought up the rear with a proposed contribution of twenty-seven pounds and five shillings; the whole of Wales was assessed at only a little over four hundred pounds.[22] It remained for the Committees to work out the proportion due from each property owner. Over and above this allotting and collecting of the Weekly Pay, they were responsible for administering the sequestrated estates of Royalists, a source of revenue which in the long run proved less profitable than the direct levy.

The network of Committees extended over all the country where Parliament held undisputed, or disputed, sway. In some counties Royalist Committees also existed though these were commonly less effective, and more dependent on the assistance of their soldiers to bring in any money. The frontiers between the two parties were in many districts uncertain, constantly changing, with enclaves in each other's territory, deep infiltrations, regions which seemed almost to be under dual control, and paid alternately the Weekly Pay to the County Committee or the levy for the King's troops; but the parish authorities were usually stubborn enough to stand up for themselves and it was rare, if not absolutely unknown, for them to submit to being mulcted by both sides in the same week.[23]

The severity with which opponents were treated, and the general justice or injustice of the assessments varied from county to county with the character of the men who dominated the Committees. "Affinity and consanguinity mars all," wrote a Parliament man, angry at the forbearance of some of his colleagues.[24] But affinity and consanguinity were a saving grace which often prevented the embitterment of the conflict. At other times local feuds and private quarrels aggravated the ill-effects of the war. " If this be the privilege of Parliament and liberty of the subject, I pray God amend it," cried a mulcted Royalist in Staffordshire.[25] "One extravagant word spoken but by one man is enough to confiscate the goods of a whole family," lamented a Royalist who suffered from malicious neighbours; [26] it was painfully true, as at all times of political strife, that one envious informer could do damage that the good nature of hundreds would not wipe out. A vindictive man on a Committee could always find reasons for persecuting his enemies, no matter how neutral and harmless they tried to be. On the Kent Committee, old angry, venomous Sir Anthony Weldon unmercifully harried Sir Roger Twysden whose mild Royalism would not, in his phrase, allow him to " approve and run mad in complying with their horrid ways." [27] In Norfolk, poor feckless Edward Benlowes, the poet, protested against the demands of the Committee inspired, he believed, by a private enemy: " I fear that these things arise from some personal differences . . . wherein passion may overact." [28] In some counties the ablest and the best men were away fighting, leaving the more grasping and less gallant to do the work of the Committees. The Earl of Manchester, appealed to by Lady Paston, whose husband had fled abroad, tried to assuage the hard feelings provoked by the grasping Committeeman Miles Corbet: it was his desire, he wrote, to win by civility rather than by harshness. [29]

The military commanders sometimes set the tone, especially when as often happened they were also members of the Committee; in the Western Midlands Brereton for Parliament and Byron for the King were both harsh and unyielding. In the North, Newcastle and the Fairfaxes competed in courtesy, although their subordinates did not always imitate them. The appeals of Cavalier gentry to the Fairfaxes, sometimes claiming kinship, were always kindly received, and they treated with special consideration the widow and daughters of Strafford, "that poor broken family at Woodhouse." [30] In Lancashire Sir Ralph Assheton did what he could to protect from plunder the households of his Royalist neighbours, when his own party was in the ascendant. [31] Even quite late in the war Colonel Herbert Morley, an active soldier for Parliament, could write to a Sussex neighbour, in the King's army, with suggestions for a safe place for his wife's lying in. [32]

The King's military and economic problems were much the same as those of Parliament, only less easy to solve. Many of his troops, and nearly all the cavalry, had been raised on the estates and by the munificence of loyal lords and gentry. Sir William Pennyman, an old friend of Strafford's, brought in, equipped and kept in pay a regiment of horse and another of foot, [33] and the fabulously lavish Bushell clothed the Life Guard and three other regiments and gave twenty-six cannon to the King besides unlimited lead for bullets. [34] But the ardour of some amateur captains who had joined the Royal army with three score horse in the mild autumn weather grew cold when the war did not end at Christmas. Many went home after the first campaign; others, with estates in threatened parts of the country, withdrew when the sequestration order came in, on the reasonable plea that, by staying in arms, they merely delivered their lands and rents to the management of the rebels for use against the King. But many others stayed in arms, expecting to be treated by their professional colleagues and military superiors with a respect becoming to their social rank and to the material help they had brought to the King's cause.

Some local gentlemen fortified their houses, armed their servants and saw to it that no help in cash or kind went to Parliament from anywhere near their little stronghold. The same thing was done for Parliament by others so that small local wars between such rival garrisons were a lesser feature of the war. Sir Robert Harley's Brampton Bryan was a Parliamentary fortress in Royalist Herefordshire. The Midlands were infested with such strong points, of which Rushall Hall near Birmingham was one of the most famous, long held by the Royalists, whose brigand cavalry did constant damage.[35] Other Royalist strongholds were Sir John Winter's house in the Forest of Dean, " the plague of the Forest " and a goad in the flank of the Parliamentary garrison at Gloucester, and the lovely mansion of Abbey Cwm Hir in Radnorshire which threatened any movements of Parliament sympathisers thereabouts. Such independent garrisons were, as the war progressed, to become something of a plague even to the side they supported, for their commanders took toll of the neighbourhood and would not allow even friendly troops to share in their profits; in North Wales it was complained of some Royalist colonels that " they drink their ale in these heaps of stones not permitting any army to quarter near unto them for fear of hindering their contributions."[36]

The King's volunteer champions were difficult to bring under discipline, for they seldom abandoned the hierarchy of rank which had governed their conduct in peacetime. A Cavalier with old friends among the Roundheads who had been taken prisoners, cheered their confinement by carousing with them half the night, and when he was requested to leave by the Royalist officer in charge of the prisoners, drove him from the room with insults.[37] Rupert's cavalry captains, though indifferently obedient to their own commanders, defied and insulted the infantry officers. "The officers of your own troop will obey in no kind of thing, and by their example never a soldier in that company," wrote the distracted Governor of Abingdon to the Prince. Rupert himself strove to maintain discipline but was frequently crossed by the ill-example of his arrogant, nobly-born colleagues. "Give me leave to tell your Highness I think myself very unhappy to be employed upon this occasion," Wilmot insolently complained of his orders.[38]

Difficulties of rank were no less troublesome on the Parliament side. "He scorned to march below me and did upbraid me . . . concerning my profession, being a Tradesman," a Roundhead officer complained of an insolent subaltern, but "I told him though I were a Tradesman, I were a gentleman, and I can show my coat of arms."[39]

The rank and file on both sides were strangers to discipline. The Parliamentary troops in the first months of the war had been entirely beyond the control of their inexperienced and often frightened officers who "durst use no instrument of correction in their hands except their hats." Essex at the fall of Reading had not been able to stop his men plundering the vanquished. The King's men were little better. The Cornish infantry—soon to be the most famous for valour in the whole war—followed their leaders readily in action, but at other times did much as they pleased; nor were other units of the King's forces very different. A cavalry officer thus describes his efforts to marshal his men: "I desired them with all importunity for command was now laid asleep"; and another declared that "our men are not very governable, nor do I think they will be unless some of them be hanged."[40]

The Earl of Forth, Prince Rupert and Sir Jacob Astley all

worked hard to establish higher standards of discipline but there remained in the King's forces throughout the war too many commanders who interpreted their duties to suit themselves, and the ill-feeling between professionals and amateurs, whose money and titles had bought them advancement, continued and grew in bitterness.

In the North the Earls of Derby and Newcastle exercised independent commands. In South Wales, Lord Herbert, by virtue of his father's great fortune, raised his own army—and having lost it fell to raising another.[41] His father, the Marquis of Worcester, was not always so willing to throw his fortune away and there were fervent arguments, family scenes, and some wonderfully unscrupulous manœuvres by Lord Herbert. " You have made it your profession all along," cried the old lord, " to deceive your father to help the King."[42] Lord Herbert bitterly resented interference of any kind in the management of his military affairs but his performance continually fell short of his promises. He offered twenty thousand pounds for ammunition but only four hundred arrived. " I verily believe if he had a million he would disburse it to serve His Majesty, but moneys fail him," wrote Sir William Vavasour, his principal recruiting officer, but Vavasour, a capable soldier who had served in Ireland, soon awoke Herbert's irritable jealousy.[43]

The Marquis of Winchester, the other rich Catholic nobleman whose fortune was at the King's service, turned his great mansion at Basing House into a fortress astride the main road from London to the Wiltshire Downs. The geographical position of Basing made his generous, but independent, expenditure less wasteful than that of Lord Herbert on the army which had been lost at Highnam. Basing played a significant part in hampering the London wool trade, though it is questionable whether, in money and effort it did not cost more than it was worth. It was Charles's misfortune that his most generous supporters were resolved to help him only in their own way.

The King's money problems were graver than those of

Parliament. Of the revenue from the customs on which the Crown so largely depended, he could collect only what was paid at the few ports in Royalist hands. He had lost the duties on Newcastle coal when Parliament blockaded Newcastle. But he had retained, in part at least, one of the least popular sources of the revenue of the Crown—the Court of Wards. Parliament had not abolished this source of income during the previous two years, for the very simple reason that Lord Saye, who had been made Master of the Court, did not wish to lose his revenues. The King ordered the removal of the Court to Oxford, and Parliament forbade its removal. In the upshot, the Court officials divided and both Oxford and Westminster had a Court of Wards through which to extract what they could from the estates of minors during the war. The King hardly did as well out of this as he had done in peace-time, but his remnant Court of Wards brought him in about £26,000 in two years.[44]

For the rest he sequestrated the estates of his enemies when they fell into his power; he sold their timber, used up their stores and ate their game. He followed the Parliamentary system of assessing districts, towns and villages in his control and quartering his troops free; the town, county and university of Oxford contributed under this system £2,700 a month. Military operations round Oxford and Marlborough, and continually in the Aylesbury vale, were often no more than horse stealing or sheep and cattle raiding, designed to hold up supplies to London and bring food and money into the King's quarters. The stolen livestock was penned in Christ Church quadrangle to be sold next market day and farmers could buy back their own. In theory the King was anxious to keep the law and spare the civilian; in practice he could rarely afford to do so.

In the paying and quartering of troops endless confusion arose. Already by the winter of 1642-3 shoes and coats were wearing out, and the cavalry, short of pay, could not afford to have their horses shod.[45] Troops would arrive to take up quarters in a village already fully occupied and fight each other for the right to stay. Regions were assigned to regiments and garrisons from which they could draw supplies in cash and kind, but double assignments were frequent, leading to high words between colonels and fights between foraging parties.[46] There was a further complication. Royalist officers, who were paying their own troops, sometimes found that their tenants had already been so mulcted that they could not pay their rents. Lord Northampton pointed out to Rupert that his ability to maintain the troops he had raised for the King depended on the continued prosperity of his estates. If other colonels bled his tenants white, he would have no income left.[47]

Northampton spoke plain English that was well understood by both parties. In spite of casual plundering and destruction, deliberate horse and cattle raiding, sheep stealing and the exactions of free quarter, both sides knew that they could not ruin the country without ruining themselves. They could take the surplus but not the very livelihood of the people. If taxes were to be paid and assessment met, harvests must be sown and reaped, pigs fattened, lambs reared, markets kept open. Both parties continually issued orders for the better discipline of the troops, for the sparing of green corn, cultivated land, fruit-bearing trees.[48] Both did what they could to keep the life of the country going. In this they were greatly helped by the toughness, experience and common sense of the Justices of the Peace and the parish authorities.

The ordinary Justice of the Peace had nothing remarkable about him; much could be said against Robert Shallow Esquire in the country or Justice Overdo in the town, but these commonplace men had behind them a long tradition of meeting emergencies. They knew what to do when the harvest failed, or murrain destroyed the cattle, or fire consumed the barns, or floods drove cottagers from their homes. It was their natural task to relieve want and prevent disorder, to keep the pulse of the country beating. In conjunction with one party or the other, or with both, or with neither, they saw to it that the burden of war did not become intolerable and the framework of order and justice was preserved.

Parliament, with the principal ports of the kingdom and the resources of London, was much better off than the King. He strove to counteract this by choking the traffic between London and the kingdom, by straddling the roads to the wool districts, diverting Cotswold wool, and forbidding the regions he controlled to trade with the Londoners. He was not altogether successful. Between London and Oxford the ordinary carriers went through High Wycombe, and most contrived to have double permits, from Oxford to Wycombe in the King's name, from London to Wycombe in Parliament's. As the clearing station for this illicit traffic Wycombe enjoyed unusual prosperity.[49]

Better off for money, Parliament was also better supplied with arms than was the King who had begun the war by losing all his principal stores and arsenals. Sussex, the greatest iron region of the country, was in Parliament's hands, and the swordsmiths of Hounslow worked for them. The King had the Forest of Dean where Sir John Winter cast cannon for him; he had the lead mines of Wales and foundries working for him in Staffordshire and Shropshire; but he had been unable to hold Birmingham, whose principal swordsmith supplied the Parliamentary army.[50] The tin of Cornwall was in his hands and, thanks to the ingenuity of Sir Nicholas Slanning and George Carteret, the Governor of Jersey, was regularly sold in Normandy and Brittany and the proceeds laid out on arms.[51] Newcastle coal, on which Charles had also counted for revenue, was locked up by the naval blockade.

The decision to support one side or the other could no longer be confined to a minority. The whole country was now involved in the conflict. For most of them it was an unwelcome disturbance in which they would gladly have avoided taking sides; there was hardly anywhere a spontaneous political rising. The men who had ridden in from Buckinghamshire to support John Hampden after the attempted arrest of the Five Members for the most part agreed with the policy for which he stood, but they had risen essentially because he was John Hampden, the great man of their neighbourhood, influential and beloved. The Kentish petitioners in favour of the Common Prayer were certainly for the King and against Parliament; but what had brought them together in such vehemence and numbers was the natural unwillingness of Kentish men to be dictated to by a Parliament consisting of strangers from all the other counties of England. So again when the Cornish army came into being for the King, the gentry who led it were convinced Royalists, but their men were first and foremost Cornishmen resolved to demonstrate the valour and vindicate the honour of their county. They disliked and despised their fellow Royalists only a little less than the enemy they came to fight.[52] The best soldiers in the early days of the war were those inspired by local pride and loyalty, yeomen's sons resolved to do honour to the place that bred them, or tenants who felt an obligation, even a devotion, to an ancient family or a good landlord. This feudal influence was strong on both sides; Royalists like Henry Hastings in Leicestershire and Bevil Grenvile in Cornwall could be paralleled by the Parliamentary Fairfaxes in Yorkshire, Ralph Assheton in Lancashire, Brereton in Cheshire.

There were, however, some regions where Puritanism had a deep hold on the people and directed their choice: round the coasts, especially the south-east: in the wool districts; and in the North, where Catholicism was still deeply rooted and therefore feared. The popular resistance of Manchester and of Bolton to the Cavaliers was inspired by religious conviction, and many of the prisoners taken at Cirencester refused to fight or work for the King in spite of the cruelties to which they were subjected. Prisoners taken from the army of Essex, on the other hand, had as a general rule agreed to join the King's forces, and the garrison of Banbury changed sides after Edgehill, an incident which suggests that Lord Saye, who had created it, was not a landlord able to inspire his dependents with his own strong political feelings.

In the earlier years of the war religious and political conviction was chiefly to be found among the officers. The Royalists could often imbue their men with loyalty to their leaders or to the more remote, but impressive, figure of the King. The Parliamentarians might seem at first to have a harder task, for the idea of King-and-Parliament could not be explained simply and was too cumbrous a concept to inspire much enthusiasm among the uneducated. But their strength lay in the religious fervour of the few, the Protestant prejudices of the many, and the accumulating influence of Puritan preachers on the soldiers. Those who could read would have knowledge of the Bible and of Foxe's *Book of Martyrs* and of little else.[53] The Bible was full of statements about righteous wars that they could apply to themselves; Foxe's *Book of Martyrs* told them not only of the heroic sufferings of their Protestant forefathers, but clearly preached the mission of England to fight Antichrist.[54] The material in these men's minds might be meagre, but it was consistent and could be developed into a righteous and crusading faith.

There was nothing so firm and simple to unite the Royalist forces. The personal loyalties which were helpful in the early years of the war were ultimately to become a dividing element, and the Church of England made an appeal to men of intellect rather than to the rank and file. The chaplains, moreover, were often hangers-on of great men, sometimes the secretaries of the officers, almost always their dependents; whereas the Parliamentary chaplains were more often (like all Puritans) great preachers, wanting to communicate with and influence as many of the men as possible.[55] All this was, gradually, to tell against the King.

Men of education and position were very evenly divided between the two parties. The Court and its hangers-on, with a very few exceptions, followed the King, and this gave his party an aristocratic veneer, a surface elegance which might give a false impression that he had the aristocracy of the kingdom largely on his side. It was not so: though he had most of the "place-men," those who had held positions of profit under the Crown whom gratitude or self-interest prompted to stay with him. There were dissidents even here: most notably the elder and the younger Vane, whose professional connections with the Court prevailed nothing against the self-interest of the father and the fanaticism of the son. Sir Humphrey Mildmay, too, the Keeper of the King's Jewel House, gave his support (and some of the King's jewels) to Parliament.

Only a minority of the lords remained at Westminster, but of those who withdrew few actively joined the King, nor is it possible to generalise on the quality and interests of the peers of either party. Of the two most powerful feudal noblemen left in England, the Earl of Derby was for the King, the Earl of Northumberland for Parliament. The great lords who had built their position during the economic revolution of the last generations, on crumbling monasteries and expanding trade, were by no means all to be found on the same side: Northampton and Craven for the King, Clare in a state of dubious neutrality, Pembroke, Salisbury, Manchester for Parliament. The leading citizens of the great cities were equally divided, not least in London, where Parliament had indeed placed its supporters in key positions, but where Royalist citizens of considerable eminence were a continuous drag and an intermittent danger. Other causes besides religious and political conviction were at work. The merchants of the East India Company had cause to hate the King because he had tried in his time of power to create a rival company in his own interests, but he also owed them a hundred thousand pounds borrowed in 1641; Parliament refused to accept liability, thus giving the Company a strong interest in the King's victory.[56]

Each army represented a fair cross section of the population, and the lines of division—if distinctions so various and confused could be called lines—were those of group and sectional loyalties.

The face of the country at war reflected, in the complexity of interlocking or conflicting interests and loyalties, the face of the country at peace.

Problems of organisation, of finance, of supply stretched drearily ahead of both combatants, but the King's prospects, unless he could get substantial help from overseas, were darker than those of Parliament. If he did not win the war within a year, he was unlikely to win it at all. Parliament had the staying power.

III

The King hoped for help by sea from Denmark and was offering to cede the Orkney Islands in return for the services of the Danish fleet.[57] He was in touch with the Portuguese envoy, who was buying arms in Holland ostensibly for the King of Portugal but actually for the King of England.[58] But his more immediate hope was fixed on Ireland whence he eagerly awaited news of the truce which would release troops for him to use. The Queen, still at York, pursued her own sanguine designs, greatly encouraged by the Earl of Antrim. Taken prisoner in his native Ulster, he had escaped again and now appeared in York offering to make peace between all parties in Ireland and raise twenty thousand men to march against the Covenanting Scots.[59] The Queen, much taken with the plan, authorised him to proceed with it at once, while she in York urged Montrose, Aboyne and the other Royalist Scots to pursue their project for a rising in Scotland. Their plan had, it was true, been officially rejected on Hamilton's advice. But she saw no objection to its surreptitious continuance. Some of them were willing, but Montrose, who disliked such underhand proceedings, refused to go on with any design not formally authorised by the King, and left York under the Queen's disfavour and at odds with his fellow Royalists.[60] In spite of this disappointment, the Queen was aglow with hope. "*Il y a fort longtemps que je n'ai été si gaie et si satisfaite que je suis,*" she wrote to the King on May 17th, 1643.[61]

Three days later, on Whitsunday, the Royal fortunes of war in the North took a sudden turn for the worse. Sir Thomas Fairfax, his forces swelled by young volunteers from the Puritan cloth-making villages of the West Riding, launched a sudden attack on Wakefield. He had been compelled to action by the discontent of the poor people. After his defeat a month before, the Cavaliers had held the prisoners to ransom; those who could had bought their freedom, but many were still captive, starved and ill-used by their captors in the hope that their kinsfolk would scrape together a ransom for pity's sake. Their wretched wives now flocked round Fairfax appealing for help and the attack on Wakefield was undertaken chiefly to make prisoners who could be exchanged.[62] The town was strongly held, with George Goring in command, but Fairfax forced an entry at a weak point in the defences, held to his advantage with ferocious tenacity, and by dispersing his men in parties about the winding streets, convinced the Royalists that the town was taken before it could truly be said to be so. They lost confidence, and after an hour or two's desultory fighting, surrendered. "It was," said Thomas Fairfax, "more a miracle than a victory." [63]

Guns, arms and stores in abundance fell into his hands, and as many prisoners as he wanted, including George Goring, the ablest of the King's cavalry officers in the North. It was not, however, the intention of the Fairfaxes to hold Wakefield itself, and they fell back, heavy with spoil, the elder to Leeds, the younger to Bradford.

The Queen was dismayed neither by the defeat at Wakefield nor the news which soon after came from London: the House of Commons had formally impeached her of treason. Only a few weeks before she had been the astonished recipient of a letter signed by Pym, Hampden and others, asking her to use her influence with the King for peace. At the time it might have been taken for an indication of weakness on their part; it was more probably a preliminary move—a last chance given her—before her impeachment. Safe among her valiant and flattering retinue of soldiers, she could afford to laugh alike at pleading or threats, while she urged the King to lose no time in proclaiming the present junto at Westminster to be no true or free Parliament.[64]

In the West, Hopton had recovered from the check inflicted on him by Chudleigh and was about to lead his Cornishmen over the Devon border. On May 16th, 1643, he caught the Earl of Stamford, the Parliamentary commander in the West, between the hills and the coast at Stratton. In a hard fought engagement the Cornishmen swept Stamford out of their way and scattered his forces with heavy loss, taking prisoner young Chudleigh himself. Stamford hastened to Westminster to accuse Chudleigh of failing to support him in the battle, an accusation which received an implicit confirmation when Chudleigh accepted a commission in the King's army.[65] At this his father, a leading Devon landowner, also withdrew from the Parliamentary forces, Hopton's Cornishmen advanced unopposed through a divided Devon—raiding Totnes on a market day and taking all the horses they needed—while from Oxford the King despatched the Marquis of Hertford and Prince Maurice to join them. It looked as though the whole south-west would soon be held solidly for the King.[66]

The news of Hopton's advance reached Sir William Waller, successfully campaigning for Parliament in the Western Midlands. Not wishing to lock up troops in garrisons, he had evacuated Hereford and was now before the much-tried Worcester, which the Royalists had once again occupied. The town put up a resolute defence, but was saved rather by the news of Hopton's advance in the West than by its inherent strength. Waller abandoned the siege to go to the rescue and prevent, if he could, the junction of Hopton and Hertford.[67]

The Parliamentary disaster at Stratton drew attention away

from a minor engagement in the same week in another part of England. In the county of Lincolnshire, where both parties disputed the mastery, Colonel Oliver Cromwell, patrolling the region of the Great North Road, was surprised by a superior force of the King's men in the hilly country north of Grantham and near the small village of Belton. They had, he estimated, twenty-one troops of horse and three or four of dragoons. He had twelve troops of horse, mostly his own East Anglian men. They faced each other doubtfully in the waning light of the spring evening. The musketeers of both parties exchanged a few shots but the Cavaliers thought it too late in the day for fighting to be advisable. Just before the light went, Cromwell charged; he brought his men down on the slack Royalist forces "at a pretty round trot," startled them into sudden flight, and took four or five standards.[68] The episode, more disgraceful than damaging to the Cavaliers, proved that Cromwell could make his recruits into soldiers to be reckoned with.

Cromwell, a reliable rather than a prominent member of Pym's party in the House of Commons, stood out among the gentry of East Anglia for his energy and initiative. He was in his forty-fourth year, a largely built, angular, raw-boned man, whose formidable powers of intellect and spirit had found no outlet in the life of a country gentleman, packed into a small house with a dominating mother, a thrifty wife, and a growing family of children. In his early years his practical and organising ability had been confined to local politics and the management of a small estate, and his brooding intelligence had had little to feed on except his own condition and the word of God. Meditative and obscurely unhappy in a life which repressed his natural powers, he was melancholic, hypochondriac, at times even given to delusions. In his thirties he had experienced the agony and release of a religious conversion; he had in his own words "lived in and loved darkness" and had with difficulty battled his way out into the daylight of faith.[69] He had found God by hard unaided wrestlings of the spirit and he believed with all the passion of his intense being that every man had a right and a duty to find his own way to God.

The war gave him at last an outlet worthy of his abilities. Within a few months he was generally recognised as the most active man in the Eastern counties. With no previous experience of fighting he rapidly mastered the technical knowledge necessary to his task, and his first small victory at Belton proved what he had always believed—that men who feared God and knew what they were fighting for " would go as far as gentlemen would go " and beat the Cavaliers.

Cromwell was neither modest nor vain but he felt God's hand upon him marking him out, and he gave the glory to God by mightily advertising his victories. His enemies, who took this for personal vanity, did him an injustice; but he was nothing so simple as a hypocrite or a self-deceiver. He strove after a rigid honesty, a pure and direct relationship with his Maker, and every letter he wrote, every troop he organised, every garrison he strengthened, every village he occupied or skirmish he won was for him part of a psalm in action, a ceaseless glorifying of God.

The godly character and good discipline of Cromwell's troopers soon attracted attention. " The countries where they come leap for joy of them," wrote one of the London journalists,[70] but there were exceptions. Cromwell from the first had insisted on worth rather than rank in his subordinate commanders. His men were for the most part " freeholders and freeholders' sons, who upon a matter of conscience engaged upon this quarrel,"[71] and his captains, when they were not of his own kindred, were not always gentry. This flouting of the social order enraged young Hotham, whose troops occasionally came into contact with Cromwell's on foraging parties on the borders of Lincolnshire. So far from leaping for joy at their approach, Hotham threatened to fire on them if they trespassed into his territory.[72]

In mid-May the Earl of Essex came up to Westminster from

his wasted and disease-ridden forces, and confronted Parliament and the City with an immediate demand for more than a hundred thousand pounds. A third of what he needed was, with difficulty, found for him. Extraordinary measures were contemplated: the Dutch word *accijs*, anglicised as " excise," was spoken now and again in the Commons debates. It meant a purchase tax and had been at first rejected in Parliament, but was now under consideration by a Committee.[73]

With the spring weather London was superficially more cheerful than it had been for some months. Parties of volunteers, in the lengthening evenings after the shops closed, marched out spade on shoulder to the sound of martial music to work on the fortifications. Girls were encouraged to join them, perhaps not so much for the work they could do as because their presence was an attraction to the men.[74] Meanwhile Edmund Waller had been busy ripening the plot which had been planned under cover of the treaty negotiations in Oxford. On May 19th Lady d'Aubigny, the sprightly widow of the King's cousin who had been killed at Edgehill, arrived in London ostensibly on private business. She had concealed about her person the King's Commission of Array. This, by arrangement with various influential loyalists in the City, was to be proclaimed as soon as the King sent word of an advance on London. The Tower was to be seized and several of the Parliamentary leaders to be secured as hostages. Waller had tried to involve the Earl of Northumberland, who remained indifferent, and the Earl of Portland and Lord Conway who seem to have entered rather more rashly into his projects. He may have known something of parallel designs sponsored by the immensely wealthy Sir Nicholas Crisp, Royalist merchant and customs-farmer who had escaped to Oxford in the winter, but kept in contact with the King's friends in London. Whatever was intended by the conspirators, nothing came of it, for like every other plot in this indiscreet society, it leaked out. On May 31st, 1643, Waller and other suspects were arrested.

Lady d'Aubigny scurried to the house of the French ambassador and claimed protection. (Her husband, as the sieur of Aubigny in France, had had some claims to rank as a French subject.) Parliament would have none of it and fetched her away in high-spirited indignation to the Tower. Her sex and rank protected her from further danger, and Edmund Waller bought his dishonoured life by naming all who had been his accomplices, and even abjectly imploring them to substantiate his charges. So detailed was his statement that the Venetian agent believed the plot to be a fabrication, arranged between him and the House of Commons, as an excuse for the arrest of suspect Royalists. Three London citizens were hanged for the conspiracy, but Waller, after fifteen months in prison paid a fine of ten thousand pounds and went into exile.[75]

The substance of this abortive plot was less important than the use made of it. Waverers and moderate men and those who had hoped for a negotiated peace were frightened by the threat of betrayal from within. An agreed settlement with the King was one thing, but his triumph through the treachery of their colleagues was quite another. A new oath of loyalty to the Parliamentary cause was drawn up and imposed on all members of Parliament and men in places of trust. Pym urged yet again on his colleagues the need for a closer understanding with the Scots, and the Lords, embarrassed by the suspicions that had fallen on some of their number, were pressed to join with the Commons in choosing commissioners to go to Edinburgh on Parliament's behalf.

More important was the decision now taken by Parliament to indicate their desire to bring the Church into closer harmony with the word of God. In accordance with this they set out an ordinance for an Assembly of Divines to consider the reform of the Church in accordance with the example of Scotland and other Protestant countries.[76]

The advent of the Assembly was celebrated in the London press by a burst of derision against Archbishop Laud, still a helpless prisoner in the Tower. William Prynne, to whom fell the congenial task of preparing the charges to be brought against him, had recently searched his room at the Tower and carried off his private papers including the diary in which he had, from time to time, noted down his dreams. These intimate scribblings were later revealed to the public with appropriate comment.[77] Pilloried Prynne was the master of Laud's fate; Dr. Burton preached to full congregations; the Star Chamber and High Commission Court, the organs by which the King and the prelates had disciplined their opponents, were both gone. It was Parliament's turn to feel the need for some way of restraining the dangerous freedom they had created; undaunted by fear of prosecution, pamphleteers now printed views which, in the opinion of the Calvinist-minded, God-fearing majority, threatened alike the stability and morals of society. On the day after the Assembly was called, Parliament set up by ordinance a body of censors without whose licence nothing was, in future, to be published. Printers and pamphleteers, intoxicated with the freedom they had enjoyed for the past two years, took very little notice.[78]

The dangers of betrayal from within were not yet over. A fortnight after the discovery of the London plot, the underhand negotiations between the Earl of Newcastle at York and the Hothams at Hull reached their climax. The elder Hotham, jealous of the Fairfaxes and incensed by the behaviour of Cromwell, was ripe to hand over Hull and join the King's party. His son, though no less willing than his father to betray his trust, was troubled by doubts; he protested to Newcastle that too many of the King's officers were violent, ill-conditioned men with whom he did not wish to serve.[79] While the Hothams hesitated, their colleagues grew suspicious. At Nottingham on June 18th the Governor, Colonel Hutchinson, had Captain Hotham arrested. He escaped to Lincoln but was recaptured. His father, alerted, tried also to make off, but a fall from his horse prevented his escape and he was sent to London, an angry prisoner with a bad conscience and a black eye.[80]

Disaster had been narrowly averted at Hull, but from the Thames valley, the Chiltern hills and the West the news was bad for Parliament. Sir William Waller, too late to prevent Hertford, Prince Maurice and the Oxford cavalry from joining Hopton and the Cornish army, threw himself into Wells and called on the Somerset men to join him. But the Cornish forces came steadily on; the local troops gave way to them at Taunton and they marched unhindered through the Vale of Avalon to Wells. Waller, in undignified haste, pulled out of Wells before them, but Prince Maurice and Lord Carnarvon, with the cavalry, came over the Mendip Hills hard on his heels, and in a running fight, in which Maurice himself was captured and rescued, startled, galled and mortified him.[81]

The West country news was far enough away to cause only a vague uneasiness in London. It was different with the news from the Thames valley and the Chiltern hills. Essex continued to appeal for more money and more men, and was energetically seconded by the letters from Hampden to his private friends. Cromwell in mid-June reported that the Queen would soon be on her way from York with twelve hundred horse and three thousand foot, and every effort must be made to intercept her.[82] Essex, stung to activity, tried to close in on Oxford, and reached Wheatley five miles away but was repulsed when he tried to cross the Thames at Islip. His further action was paralysed by the counter attack of Prince Rupert, who slashed in a sudden night raid through the very heart of his quarters.

Acting on information brought by a distinguished deserter from the Parliamentary forces, Colonel Hurry,[83] Rupert left Oxford on the afternoon of June 17th with about a thousand picked cavalry, and eight hundred dragoons and foot, crossed the Thames at Chiselhampton and under cover of night marched silently through the country occupied by Essex, fell upon the quarters of Sir Samuel Luke at Stokenchurch on the height of the Chiltern ridge, and about dawn surprised the sleeping village of Chinnor where Essex had quartered some troops newly come from Bedfordshire. The Cavaliers scared and scattered these, only narrowly missed a convoy carrying money for the troops and bound for the headquarters of Essex, and spread alarm and dismay through all his quarters. This done, Rupert fell back in good order towards Oxford, sending a party in advance to secure the bridge at Chiselhampton and keep open his line of retreat. Sir Philip Stapleton who, in the absence of Essex, was in charge at Thame, put heart into his forces, sent out for all who could be spared from neighbouring outposts and, with the help of John Hampden, came after the Cavaliers. Rupert drew them on by falling back, until he had them at a disadvantage in Chalgrove cornfield, then attacked with all his cavalry and routed them. He was back in Oxford early in the afternoon of June 18th having brilliantly achieved his purpose of disordering the forces of Essex and frightening him into abandoning the attempt to blockade Oxford.[84]

Early in that confused and violent fight John Hampden was wounded in the shoulder. He made his painful way back to Thame, where six days later he died. " Poor Hampden is dead," wrote Pym's nephew and right-hand man, " I have scarce strength to write the word. Never kingdom received a greater loss in one subject. Never man a truer and faithfuller friend." [85] He had never faltered in his loyalty to Pym or his conviction that the King must be defeated in war. He, more than any other, had with consummate tact and unflagging energy smoothed the difficult relations between Essex and Parliament, maintained trust in the general, supported his demands for money, excused and explained the querulous tone of his letters. With him died the most persuasive and most generally popular member of the Parliamentarian party, but also one who was widely felt to be its noblest representative. A man of great political acumen, skilful in the management of his own affairs and those of Parliament, he was unreasonably hated by those, among them Edward

Hyde, who had been as they thought deceived by his honey-tongue into supporting policies that they later regretted. But he was also much and widely beloved, and the character for un-blemished patriotism which he had acquired during his resistance to the King over Ship-money stayed with him to the end. Sincere beliefs may be combined with intelligent calculation and noble vision is not always incompatible with astuteness in the daily struggle of politics. John Hampden was a good Parliament man in the political sense, but he was also in the widest sense a *good* Parliament man.

> His purer thoughts were free
> From all corruptions: he not valued friends
> A fair estate or self-propounded ends,
> Airy preferment, or ought else above
> A quiet conscience, and his nation's love . . .[86]

The anonymous poet who published this elegy in London wrote truly and the fellow soldiers and fellow Parliament men, who a few days later, followed his body to its quiet resting-place among the beech woods of his home, knew the value of the leader they had lost.

Using the knowledge he had gained from Hurry, Rupert intensified his raiding in the Chilterns and on the roads to London. His troops foraged merrily in Buckinghamshire and Berkshire, drove off cattle and the plump sheep from the Vale of Aylesbury, flashed through the Parliamentary outposts and plundered the villages that supplied London. A week after Chalgrove a party under Colonel Hurry struck right across the Chilterns and raided West Wycombe, while the Londoners in panic stood to arms all night. Without John Hampden to restrain them, the Commons responded to London's clamour, and sharply called on Essex to deal with Rupert. Essex, tormented by the Cavaliers and by sickness among his men, hardly able to keep order, weakened by desertion and always short of money, snapped back at them with a threat of resignation. Pym, adding

Hampden's burden to his own, restrained the Commons, flattered the general and temporarily restored a calm.[87]

He had hardly done so before the worst disaster yet was reported from Yorkshire. Lord Fairfax and his son, hoping to secure the West Riding once and for all against the Cavaliers, drew together all their forces from Leeds and Halifax towards Bradford, towards which Newcastle's ill-armed but considerably larger army was fast approaching. Sir Thomas Fairfax, giving precedence to his father in the ordering of the battle, himself commanded the cavalry only. On June 30th they faced the main body of the Royalists, about fifteen thousand foot and four thousand horse, just beyond Bradford on Adwalton Moor. The Cavaliers had occupied the lanes and cottages fringing the moor but were driven from them by the resolute attack of the Parliament men. The advance was sadly misconceived, for the Royalists, with twice their numbers, still commanded the height of the moor, and Newcastle detached a party of horse which, making a circuit under cover of the lanes, hedges and little hills, suddenly fell upon the Parliamentary rear. Thinking themselves surrounded, the tired Parliament men gave way to panic. The younger Fairfax got some of the cavalry away to Halifax, but the infantry scattered to the four points of the compass, much of the artillery was lost, and the elder Fairfax, with great difficulty and some good luck made the best of his way back to Leeds.[88]

Giving up the West Riding for lost, the Fairfaxes resolved to fall back on Hull until they could recruit their strength. Sir Thomas with great dexterity evaded the Royalist forces and got back into Bradford in the hope of bringing off the troops who had been left there together with his wife and child. The town, bereft of almost all ammunition, was already encircled and "the Queen's pocket pistols," as the Royalists called their cannon, pounded its defences. The break out was carefully planned and boldly executed but the odds were too heavy, and few of the troops got through. Lady Fairfax was captured before her husband's eyes, though the little girl and her nurse escaped. Joining the troops from Halifax and Leeds, Fairfax made to cross the Ouse at Selby, but was intercepted by the Royalists and driven towards the Lincolnshire shore of the Humber estuary. Leaving the infantry to quarter there, he got shipping for the poor remnant of his cavalry to Hull, where he arrived spent and bloody; he had been forty hours in the saddle, had been wounded in the arm at Selby, and had seen his daughter, as he thought, dying of exhaustion before his eyes. At Hull he found a temporary respite, and Hotham's treasure chests from which to pay his troops. Lady Fairfax came back to her husband by the courteous Newcastle's express wish, conveyed in his own coach, and the child after a night's sleep was none the worse for her adventure.[89]

The time for rest was short. Newcastle, now in almost undisputed command of Yorkshire, opened the sluices which kept out the sea from the low-lying shores of the Humber estuary and flooded the country round Hull. There was neither fodder nor drink for the cavalry of Fairfax and he had no choice but to leave the town to its own resources and take his troops across to Lincolnshire to consult with Cromwell.[90]

The Queen, "Her She Majesty Generalissima," as she gaily styled herself, was on her way from York to join the King with three thousand infantry, thirty companies of horse, and six good cannon.[91] As her army moved southwards, the Parliamentarians, stunned by the defeat of Fairfax, argued, hesitated and failed to intercept her.

IV

In the south-west, Sir William Waller had fallen back to Bath; here he received a request from Hopton to meet him for a personal interview. Twenty years before in the German wars they had been comrades in arms; it was natural for Hopton to believe that Waller, like so many others, might be sensible to arguments sincerely urged by a friend whom he respected. But Waller refused the interview in terms which nobly convey the distress of many honest men on either side:

" Certainly my affections to you are so unchangeable, that hostility itself cannot violate my friendship to your person, but I must be true to the cause wherein I serve; the old limitation *usque ad aras* holds still, and where my conscience is interested, all other obligations are swallowed up. I should most gladly wait on you according to your desire, but that I look upon you as you are engaged in that party, beyond a possibility of retreat . . . That great God, which is the searcher of my heart, knows with what a sad sense I go upon this service, and with what a perfect hatred I detest this war without an enemy . . . We are both upon the stage and must act those parts that are assigned us in this tragedy; let us do it in a way of honour, and without personal animosities, whatsoever the issue be . . ."[92]

A few days later he wrote urgently to Parliament for money. Help of another kind—a regiment of five hundred " prodigiously armed " horse, Sir Arthur Haslerig's " Lobsters "—had reached him, but without money he doubted if he could maintain the discipline or the numbers of his army.[93] Meanwhile the Royalists were fast approaching and Waller made ready to hold them, if he could, in the steep country near Bath. They for their part crossed the Avon at Bradford-on-Avon and turned northwest towards Bath to cut his communications with London. Waller put a party across the river and ambushed their advancing force at Monkton Farleigh on July 3rd, but the Royalists beat them back. Aware of Waller's main army, just across the river and south of Bath, they resolved to swing round to the north of the town and occupy the dominating ridge of Lansdown, but exhausted with the efforts of that day they camped for the night at Batheaston. In the night Waller moved and by daybreak of

July 4th had occupied Lansdown ridge himself. The Royalists tried to draw him by moving their headquarters farther north to Marshfield which commands the Bristol road.

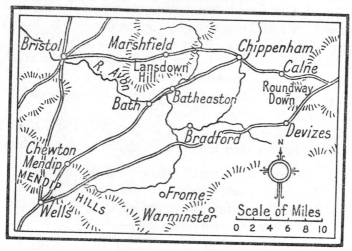

BATH AND DEVIZES

Between Lansdown and Marshfield the ground falls steeply with fringes of woodland and winding lanes to a muddy bottom, and rises again as steeply. Waller lined the copses and lanes with musketeers and when, on July 5th, the Royalist cavalry advanced on his position, they were at first checked by the firing and, as they retreated, thrown into disorder by a cavalry charge. The Cornish foot, however, stood their ground until the cavalry rallied, and the Royalist forces again moved forward. This time the Cornish, in a stubborn hedge to hedge advance, forced Waller's musketeers to withdraw while the Royalist cavalry gradually exhausted and dispersed or forced back the opposing horse. But, though he had lost the lower slopes, Waller's army with its formidable artillery and a considerable body of cavalry still held Lansdown Ridge. A professional soldier would have deemed the position impregnable, but the Cornish infantry, who were not professionals, shouted that they would " fetch those cannon." Sir Bevil Grenvile led them on at the head of his pikemen with a body of musketeers on his left. Three times, through smoke clouds so dense that no man could see daylight, the Cornish foot forced their way to the top of the ridge, and twice were beaten down again by cannon fire and the hurtling charges of Waller's horse. They fell on a third time, undaunted, Grenvile still leading. This time the Cornish pikemen reached the ridge, formed a square and held their ground, standing " as upon the eaves of a house for steepness, but as unmovable as a rock " before the deadly onslaught.

Here, in the rattle of shot and blackness of smoke, Grenvile was killed, but his men fought on with the greater resolution.

> This was not Nature's courage, nor that thing
> We valour call, which time and reason bring,
> But a diviner fury, fierce and high,
> Valour transported into ecstasy—

Afterwards, in Oxford, poets would celebrate the heroic ascent; later still romantic and reverent posterity would crown with a monument the steep height where Grenvile died. The attack and endurance of the Cornish pikemen achieved the impossible, while the Royalist cavalry, scattered and disorganised, failed to give them support. But the musketeers now came on again, drove off Waller's tired cavalry with their unceasing fire and formed on the ridge beside their comrades. Waller gave ground sullenly to take up a defensive position behind a stone wall, and darkness fell with both armies facing each other on the flat top of Lansdown.

Through the night sporadic firing kept the Royalists alert. From Waller's position camp fires seemed to flicker. But Royalist scouts, in the small hours, reported that he had retreated, leaving only here and there burning matchcord hung on walls and hedges to deceive them. On the field and in the camp the victors found five hundred muskets, fourteen barrels of powder and a stand of pikes to replenish their stores. The London papers, with some ingenuity, reported that the Cavaliers had "now learned by experience that our giving ground hath been much to their disadvantage," but in Oxford *Mercurius Aulicus* more justly claimed a victory.[94]

Their triumph, clouded by the death of Grenvile, was short-lived. Waller had been checked but not defeated; he made good his losses with men and arms taken from Bristol and on July 7th marched out against the Cavaliers. They were in no condition to fight again. Much of the cavalry had scattered; they were very short of ammunition for muskets and cannon; Hopton had been seriously wounded the day after the battle by the explosion of a powder waggon; disheartened by this mischance, and weakened by their losses at Lansdown, they found the country hostile and could get little food and less information from the people. Three miles from Devizes, on Sunday, July 9th late in the afternoon, Waller's advance guard of cavalry fell on their rear. Prince Maurice, with some difficulty, rallied the Royalist horse and by a delaying action gave the infantry time to retreat into Devizes.[95] Waller immediately occupied the commanding chalky eminence of Roundway Down, whence his batteries commanded the low-lying, unwalled town where the Royalist army lay.

Their position seemed desperate but Hopton, half blind and muffled in bandages, kept a clear head. At a council of war that night he agreed to hold the town with the infantry, while Maurice, with the Marquis of Hertford and the Earl of Carnarvon, rode to Oxford for help. They set out with the cavalry as though retreating in the direction of Salisbury; but once clear of Waller's outposts the chosen party broke away and galloped for Oxford. Here they arrived early in the afternoon of Tuesday, July 11th, to find the town half-stripped of cavalry because Rupert had gone to meet the Queen as she traversed the dangerous Midlands. All the horse that could be spared made only about eighteen hundred. Wilmot and Sir John Byron were to command; Hertford was unequal to another night in the saddle, but Prince

Maurice went back as a volunteer. They left late on the Tuesday night and sighted Waller on the downs above Devizes at three o'clock on the Thursday afternoon.[96]

They were just in time. The Royalists in the town had held out two days and two nights of fighting, with one short truce while Hopton negotiated and his exhausted men slept. Waller, with his far larger numbers, could maintain the attack almost continuously. In the town they were melting the gutters for bullets and using bed-cords for match, and their powder was nearing exhaustion. Waller's men had penetrated the outer defences, but the heavy rain prevented him from effectively using his artillery. Over-confident, he took his time, ordered up a cheering supply of beer, sack and brandy from a neighbouring inn, and trusted that Essex would prevent any relieving force from leaving Oxford.[97]

Apprised by a scout of the approaching Royalists, Waller had just time to draw up his forces on Roundway Down. But Wilmot seems to have turned his flank, and with his smaller, but much more nimble forces, threw the Parliamentarians into confusion almost at the outset. Even Haslerig's stout-hearted Lobsters, after rallying once, collapsed when Byron seconded Wilmot's charge and fled pell mell down the precipitous chalky slope. Sir Arthur Haslerig himself was all but captured by a Royalist captain who pursued him a great way trying in vain with pistol and sword to pierce his carapace—an exploit which later caused the King to say, with one of his rare jests, that had Sir Arthur " been victualled as well as fortified he might have endured a siege." Left naked of cavalry cover, Waller's infantry, exposed to the onslaught of the Royalist horse, threw down their arms and scattered when the Cornish infantry, sallying from Devizes, attacked in the rear. The overthrow of Waller was sudden and complete. He lost thirty-six standards, fourteen hundred men taken or killed, all his cannon, all his ammunition and all his baggage—and this to a force less than half his number, consisting entirely of cavalry, many of whom had ridden forty miles from Oxford before the battle. " No men ever charged better than ours did that day," a captain under Prince Maurice reported with justifiable relief and pride.[98] " We must needs look upon this as the hand of our God mightily against us," wrote a puzzled Parliamentary officer, " for it was he only that made us fly." [99] Others, less philosophic, broke into recrimination, and Waller indignantly blamed Essex for letting through the Royalist cavalry. Whoever was to blame the disaster to Parliament's western army was complete.

On the afternoon when his cavalry broke Waller on the Wiltshire Downs, King Charles rejoined his Queen on the site of that earlier great cavalry charge, on Edgehill. She had been met by Prince Rupert at Stratford-on-Avon, where she had spent the night at New Place as the guest of Shakespeare's granddaughter. She had greatly enjoyed her summer journey, the informal way of travelling and the *al fresco* meals among her gallant soldiers. It was not, however, for a soldier but for her platonic admirer, her secretary, chamberlain, master-of-the-horse, and right-hand man, Harry Jermyn, that she immediately asked the reward of a peerage.[100] The King merrily agreed, and their joyful cavalcade entered Oxford on July 14th to be met by the news of Roundway Down and the poetic compliments of the University wits. In deft and delicate imagery, from many a young poet, the triumph of royalty and beauty was celebrated:

> Shine forth with doubled light, that rebels may
> Or sleep in darkness, or else see 'tis day:
> And treason stoop, forc'd by commanding charms,
> Either to kiss your hands, or fear your arms.[101]

The welcome supplies brought by the Queen strengthened the King's position and an early victory seemed almost sure. Charles none the less continued to pursue his plan for bringing over the Government troops from Ireland to fight for him. He had realised in the last weeks that this project would never thrive while the Council in Dublin was stuffed with men friendly to Parliament. Against their opposition, Ormonde could achieve neither a truce with the Irish Confederates, nor the sending of forces to join the Royal army in England. Some days before he met his Queen the King had, therefore, written to Ormonde commanding him to arrest four of his fellow councillors, thereby to assure the loyalty of the Dublin Government and its co-operation in his future plans.[102]

While everything now seemed to move in the King's favour, the defeated Waller had fallen back to Bristol, then moved hesitantly to Gloucester. Rupert, leaving Wilmot to guard Oxford, went in pursuit, taking the best of his cavalry, fourteen regiments of foot and a formidable train of artillery. As he approached, Waller fled with " fifteen pitiful weak troops of horse," the remnant of his army, to Evesham. Thence, temporarily delegating his command, he hastened to London to denounce Essex and demand help.[103]

On Sunday, July 23rd, Rupert made a junction with the Western army two miles from Bristol and before the end of the day he had taken up his position north of the town and fixed a battery on Clifton Church, while the Western army lay to the south, on the farther side of the Avon. The defences of Bristol were well-planned and very strong, especially on the southern side; a wall and ditch " full five miles " in length protected the town, starred with forts mounting cannon. But the garrison had been perilously reduced by Waller when he replenished his forces after Lansdown, and only about eighteen hundred men were left to man this extensive circuit. The Governor, Nathaniel Fiennes, Lord Saye's favourite son, was unpopular and was gloomily convinced that he could not hold the town. He rejected Rupert's summons none the less and on July 24th the Royalist guns opened fire in a preliminary day-long cannonade designed to exhaust the defenders. The captains of eight ships lying in the river just beyond the city, and loaded with plate and valuables of Bristol merchants, yielded to the persuasions of some of the Cornish officers and declared for the King.

Meanwhile at Knowle, at the headquarters of the Western army, Rupert held a Council of War. Prince Maurice and the Cornish leaders were in favour of mining the approaches, investing the town more closely and starving it into surrender; on the south side, which was almost impregnable by assault, this would undoubtedly have been the wisest and most economical method of attack. But on the north, the soil was unsuitable for mining and Rupert and the Oxford commanders were convinced that the defences, badly undermanned, would be easily carried by assault. This opinion prevailed, and before daybreak on July 26th, in the twilight of the short summer night, the storming of Bristol began.

The defenders, even on the weak northern side, met the attack with a deadly fire and at one time Rupert's presence alone seems to have prevented a general retreat. But at last Colonel Washington shot his way in through a breach and managed to clear a passage for the cavalry. The Royalists were now within the outer defences on the northern side. An inner line still had to be carried, formed by the river Frome, and part of the circuit of the old city wall ; beyond this again was the fortress-castle, where Fiennes had his headquarters. On this shortened line, the defenders fought with redoubled vigour, and Rupert sent word to Maurice that he had breached the outer defences and now wanted a thousand Cornish infantry to help him press home the victory. But on the southern side the heroic Western army had stormed in vain and with appalling loss. Maurice had not a thousand men to spare; he came with five hundred. By that time Rupert's men had forced the defenders back over the Frome. Fiennes sent out for a truce and a parley. He lacked the ammunition to hold out in the castle, and the citizens were unwilling to agree to a resistance which would have destroyed their town. The terms of the surrender were signed that night. Leaving his ammunition, arms and sixty cannon to the conquerors, Fiennes marched out next morning with his dispirited men. "Where is your King Jesus?" the Cavaliers blasphemously shouted, and imitating Puritan preachers nasally chanted "Where wert thou at Runaway Hill, O Lord, and where art thou now?" The men of the Oxford forces, remembering the ill-usage they had had from the Parliament men at the surrender of Reading, broke ranks and fell to plundering the defeated until Rupert, in a towering passion at this indiscipline, beat them off.[104]

Bristol had been dearly bought. The losses had been heavy on the northern side where Rupert led the assault, heavier still on the southern side where the Cornish, exposed for hours to the fire of the defenders, had vainly tried to escalade the wall. Not only was the Cornish force now very gravely reduced, but several of their most distinguished officers had been killed or wounded beyond hope of recovery. In a war where so much depended on the influence and character of the local leaders, the extinction of such men could be disastrous. As early as February the Cornish had lost Sidney Godolphin, killed by a chance shot in Chagford; at Lansdown the incomparable Grenvile died. At the storming of Bristol Sir Nicholas Slanning and his friend John Trevanion were both mortally wounded. Slanning's place as organiser of the West Country shipping for the King would be taken by Sir Francis Basset, and other loyal gentlemen would fight bravely on, but the Cornish would never know again such a team of leaders as commanded them in those first heroic months.

> Gone the four wheels of Charles's wain
> Grenvile, Godolphin, Slanning, Trevanion slain . . .[105]

The taking of Bristol brought to a crisis the discontent between the King's principal commanders. The slow, elderly and dignified Hertford felt himself slighted by the two Princes. The brothers, both professional soldiers, had neither the time nor the temperament to consider his feelings, and had conducted operations in their own manner without, he complained, any reference to him. On the capture of Bristol he re-asserted his jeopardised authority by immediately and without consultation appointing Sir Ralph Hopton as Governor. But Prince Rupert had already written to the King requesting that honour for himself. Charles, aware of the tension between his commanders, for once achieved a tactful solution. Assuring Hertford that he could no longer spare so wise a councillor from his side he recalled him to Oxford. Hopton remained the effective Governor of Bristol as Rupert's deputy, and Maurice succeeded to the command of the Western forces.[106]

The King, aglow with family pride in his nephew's prowess, now came to Bristol where the citizens, who had cheered Waller not a month before, welcomed him with bonfires and acclamation.[107] Theirs was a divided city but, on the whole, more favourable to the King than Parliament. Both their representatives in Parliament, merchant princes of great wealth and influence, had been expelled, a measure which Pym would hardly have allowed if he had not suspected their loyalty to his party.[108]

In the days before the war Bristol merchants had resented the King's interference, and his ruthless attempt to destroy their manufacture of soap; but they were also jealous of London and glad, in the difficult time of war, to take advantage of the King's desire to destroy the trade of London and cherish theirs. To achieve this he shortly after issued a charter to Bristol to become in place of London the staple port for the Levant Company, the Eastland Company, the Russia Company and the London Merchant Adventurers; naturally this had no effect on members of these companies dwelling in London who were strong Parliament men, but it opened up new possibilities for Royalist merchants, of which some availed themselves. The advantages of being turned suddenly and deliberately into London's rival might seem at first considerable, but Bristol was to find the King and his army costly to support when the large gifts with which the corporation first tried to propitiate him were seen to be only the beginning of expenditure, and the city was assessed at four hundred pounds a week for the payment of the garrison alone.[109]

V

The loss of Bristol was a heavy blow to Parliament's staggering cause. It was followed within a few weeks by the surrender of Poole, Dorchester, Portland, Weymouth and Melcombe; when the greatest city had fallen " the lesser garrisons came tumbling to the obedience of the King." [110] Already the Navy under the Earl of Warwick was unequal to guarding the western approaches; the Irish-Dunkirk pirates and the Cornish sea captains darted from the ports and islands across the mouth of the Channel. The Governors of Jersey and Guernsey were for the King; the Scilly Islands gave shelter to his vessels; there were plans for rebuilding the ruinous castle of Lundy (which belonged to the ubiquitous financier Thomas Bushell) and making the island into another useful base. The French Government allowed the King's ships to use the havens of the Norman and Breton coast. Fishing boats and small merchant ships from Parliamentary ports were repeatedly plundered or towed away by the King's pirates. To add to all this, the King now controlled the second greatest seaport in the Kingdom, with all its wealth, supplies and far-spread trading interests, and had taken, in Bristol roads, four ships of the Navy. When he lost the fleet at the beginning of the war, Charles had lost the respect of foreign sovereigns. With the capture of Bristol and the revival of his sea power he began to count again. He chose the moment to issue a general declaration of his devotion to the Protestant religion and the liberties of his subjects and an offer of pardon to all who had been misled by his enemies. This, with the proclamation he had made a month earlier from Oxford condemning the remnant at Westminster as no free Parliament, was intended to undermine its authority, and did indeed threaten to do so.[111]

Angry gloom pervaded London and Westminster. The King's outposts on the main roads checked the flow of food and goods to the capital. Smithfield market lacked for cattle, Blackwell Hall for cloth; grain, cheese and vegetables were short. For a week, from July 18th, a Royalist rising in Kent threatened the Thames estuary and the port of London itself. Angry, armed crowds took possession of Tonbridge and Sevenoaks, plundered the houses of rich Parliament men, took prisoner Sir Harry Vane, who had gone down to reason with them, surged towards the river and seized some of the artillery from the Parliament ships. So in past centuries the lawless bands from Kent—under Wat Tyler, under Jack Cade—had marched on London. Their legend lived and the distracted city trembled, for although the rising was said to be for the King, plunder soon became its object. "We must plunder none but Roundheads," a scrupulous rioter was heard to say, but another answered: "We will make every man a Roundhead that hath anything to lose."[112]

At the height of these anxieties, Parliament had issued a measure that had been long and anxiously discussed, the Excise Ordinance. The continued cost of maintaining the army and the navy was estimated to be nearly three and a half million pounds a year; to meet this intolerable burden the Excise Ordinance imposed a purchase tax on wine, sugar, beer, linen, leather and other goods, selected because they were in common demand but not prime necessities of life.[113] As the war went on the Excise was to be extended to these as well; but at first it was hoped that extreme measures could be avoided.

Immediately after the imposition of the Excise, under strong pressure from the Earl of Manchester and Oliver Cromwell in the Eastern Midlands, Parliament put out a further ordinance for the immediate raising of seven thousand horse.[114] It was high time; the cavalry of Fairfax and Waller had been destroyed, and that of Essex was demoralised with sickness and want. On the disastrous news of Bristol's fall, Pym further tightened the management of the war. The Committee of Safety was proving too slow and disputatious in taking decisions; on August 2nd Pym brought into being a Council of War composed of a smaller group of members of Parliament, all resolute for the continuation of the war, and some merchants and soldiers for additional practical advice.[115]

Quarrels and jealousies divided Parliament and paralysed the armies. Pym, in the fear and exasperation of the last weeks, had joined in the general criticism of Essex only to realise the dangers of this course. Essex, after threatening to resign, had early in July indicated in a complaining letter to the Speaker that he thought it advisable to re-open negotiations with the King.[116] This had greatly encouraged the peace party in the Lords, led by the Earl of Holland, cousin of Essex and half-brother to Warwick. It had also, in another direction, stimulated the extreme war party in the Commons, which, following the irresponsible leadership of Harry Marten, broke away from Pym and acclaimed Waller as the only possible saviour and hero. When he rode into London as dapper and cheerful as if he had never lost an army on " Runaway Hill," he was loudly applauded. Essex alone, he claimed, was the author of his defeat because he had not prevented the King's cavalry from leaving Oxford. On the surge of mistaken enthusiasm he was voted an army independent of Essex, to be raised in London by a Committee headed by Harry Marten.[117]

At this Essex, tried beyond endurance, demanded an investigation of the disasters in the West before a new army was voted to a general who had already lost one. He asked that pay be sent for his own hungry plague-stricken troops. Demoralised by the attack on him, his men deserted, his officers defied him. Why, he and his friends began to ask, was Essex to be blamed for other men's mistakes? Where was Fairfax and where was Cromwell when the Queen and her supplies passed without hindrance from York to Oxford? How came it that Waller, with all his cavalry, infantry and guns, had been annihilated by a handful of the King's horse?[118]

John Pym had almost lost control of the situation. Marten and the extremists in the Commons scared their more moderate colleagues into the peace party which was now dominant in the House of Lords. The Earl of Holland, that confused courtier-politician, who had somehow got himself stranded on the Parliamentary side of the fence when the war began, now led this group and had promised them that Essex himself would support them. The terms they proposed to suggest amounted to surrender: they were prepared to give back to Charles the control of the armed forces, the very crux of the whole dispute between King and Parliament. Their fears were understandable, if not admirable. The King was everywhere victorious; the quarrel between Essex and Waller and the hot-headed elevation of Waller had hopelessly confused Parliament's efforts to stabilise and consolidate their forces against the Royalists. Into the midst of quarrels, confusion and recrimination, came the stunning news that Bristol had fallen. It looked as though the war was over, and a humble plea for peace the best way out of the disaster for the half-hearted, while the hot-heads wasted their energy on rhetorical speeches and furious quarrels, and recruits failed to come in.

In this most desperate hour, Pym kept his head and guided the Commons into wiser and stronger courses. He saw that the disputes must cease, that confidence must be restored in Essex, and Essex himself be prevented, by renewed and generous support, from yielding to the nervous persuasions of his cousin Holland and the peace Lords. He saw also that the alliance with Scotland which he had often urged on his colleagues was, since the defeat of Fairfax in the North, an urgent necessity.[119]

The Covenanters had come, at the same time, to the same conclusion, and in these last stormy days of July a proposal for a formal alliance reached Westminster from Edinburgh.[120] Ever since the return of Loudoun and Henderson from the hostile King in Oxford the Marquis of Argyll had seen unmistakable signals of approaching danger. The Earl of Antrim, unlucky again, had been captured by a Scots patrol as he recrossed the Irish Sea after leaving the Queen at York. From letters on his person and the admissions of a servant his captors learnt of the scheme to raise his clan, the Macdonnells of Ulster, for the invasion of Scotland. This proof of the King's tampering with the Irish they passed on at once to London where it did not fail of its effect in the critical summer days. They learnt also the names of the Royalist Scots concerned in this plan and that Montrose had refused to be a party to it.[121]

Rumours of secret Royalist meetings were frequent that summer in Scotland. Montrose spent three days with Huntly but could reach no agreement with him for joint Royalist action. Foiled twice in his effort to lead the Royalists in his own manner, Montrose was reported to have withdrawn in anger. Argyll, for once incautious, believed the tale and sent privately to sound his feelings. Alexander Henderson, who had returned from Oxford with no illusions about the King's policy, reasoned with him for two hours walking by the water side near Stirling. He made it clear that, in the army which was to be raised to quell the Irish and malignant forces, and invade England if necessary, Montrose should have a very high command. Montrose withheld his answer, and a few days later it was known at Edinburgh that he had fled the country. The news spread consternation; in the hope of winning him, they had let him know too much. He was surely on his way to carry his dangerous knowledge to the King.[122]

In the shade of these anxieties, Chancellor Loudoun had convened the Estates. Forbidden to call a Parliament by the King, he had consulted with the venerable and wily Lord Advocate, Sir Thomas Hope, who had declared that in an emergency a Convention of Estates for voting money (but not for legislating) might be called without waiting for the sovereign's consent. The Hamilton brothers, at a loss as usual, merely withdrew their presence. But the Convention, when it met, found to their chagrin that their English brethren, overwhelmed with their own troubles, had sent no commissioners to consult with them.[123] It was the Scots' turn now to recognise that they must make common cause with the English before it was too late. In all the North of England, the King's forces triumphed; an invasion of Scotland with Irish forces had evidently been planned; Montrose's arrival in the King's quarters with his dangerous knowledge might easily be the signal for Charles to turn upon them. Such were the fears underlying the formal proposal of alliance which they made to Parliament and which, at the end of July, was grasped like a life-line by John Pym in the turmoil at Westminster. He sent a deputation to Edinburgh, with young Vane at its head. It was a judicious choice, for Vane's earnest and zealous character would do well with the Scots; but he had also vehemently criticised Essex, and his presence in the House while Pym tried to restore confidence in the Lord General would have been an embarrassment.

While Vane and his colleagues boarded the *Antelope* and sailed for Leith—the land journey was barred by the King's armies—the northern Royalists advanced into Lincolnshire. Cromwell's troops from the Eastern Association were unable to relieve the Parliamentary garrison in Gainsborough. The Earl of New-castle's artillery bombarded the town, the Royalists of the region flocked to him with men and money, Gainsborough surrendered and what was left of the Parliamentary force retreated fast from Lincolnshire. Panic spread in the threatened counties; troops deserted. Cromwell pelted the wavering authorities with exhortation and command: "It is no longer disputing, but out instantly, all you can. Raise all your bands; send them to Huntingdon; get up what volunteers you can; hasten your horses. Almost all our foot have quitted Stamford; there is nothing to interrupt an enemy but our horse." And again: "You sent indeed your part of the two thousand foot, but when they

came, they as soon returned. Is this the way to save a kingdom?
. . . Haste what you can . . . The enemy in all probability
will be in our bowels else in ten days."[124]

While Cromwell strove to consolidate a crumbling front,
Pym had regained control at Westminster. Harry Marten's
mismanagement of the levies to be raised for Waller brought
the extreme party into disrepute. The hubbub of criticism
against Essex died down. A new appeal for supplies for his
army was sympathetically received in the Commons and a
vindication of his conduct was officially published by the Lords.[125]
Fickle opinion veered away from Waller. Reassured, Essex
withdrew the encouragement he had given to the peace party
in the Lords, and their pusillanimous proposals for a treaty were
voted down by a narrow majority in the House of Commons
on August 7th, 1643. The city ministers preached the necessity
of the war; Royalist suspects, amid demonstrations of hostility,
were temporarily removed from the prisons and put, for greater
isolation, under hatches in ships on the river; a shocking
proposal that they should be sold for slaves in Barbadoes was
flung up in the ferment of fear and anger; the Lord Mayor
organised a petition against a treaty and crowds flocked to
Westminster crying " No peace! No peace!" Their support
was merely vocal, for recruiting still went badly. " No fewer
than fifteen stout fellows " had actually enlisted, sneered *Mer-
curious Aulicus*. [126]

The strengthening of the army would follow, as Pym well
knew, once he had restored confidence in the existing command
and silenced the extremists whose attempts to elevate Waller
would have destroyed the army of Essex before another could
be raised, and left the Parliamentary Cause with none.

A tragic epilogue followed. When the peace terms had
been voted down and the multitude had dispersed, a crowd of
poor women came clamouring to Westminster asking too late
for peace. When they would not go away the guards dispersed
them with blows and some reckless firing. There were casualties,

among them a young girl, who had no part in the demonstration but had slipped out to draw water.[127]

In the King's quarters the march direct on London had been canvassed before, and after, the taking of Bristol. It was argued, chiefly by the civilian councillors, that London was ripe to fall and that the Kent rising should be powerfully seconded. But the soldiers doubted that the King's army had the strength for such an undertaking and advised him to consolidate his position by taking Gloucester, and drawing into his army the new forces raised for him in South Wales by Lord Herbert before he began the long march to London. The defiant Puritan city, the centre of the Cotswold wool trade, was in a commanding position on the river Severn, blocking this valuable waterway from Royalist Shrewsbury and Worcester down to the Bristol estuary and barring also the nearest way from the King's main armies to the iron foundries of the Forest of Dean and the region of South Wales where the Marquis of Worcester and his son were still recruiting. But the decision to move against it was not unanimous and the King's army lost several days before they began to march. This delay, a Puritan writer was later to aver, gave the quarrelling factions in London time " to piece up their discontents " and make good their cause once more. But the siege of Gloucester gave them something more than time; it gave them inspiration.[128]

Colonel Edward Massey, Governor of Gloucester, was, like Prince Rupert, only twenty-three years old. The younger son of a Cheshire gentleman, he may have served for a short while in Holland before joining the King's army as a captain of pioneers in the Scots war of 1640. Disturbed by the favours shown to Roman Catholics, or those whom he thought no better, he had withdrawn from the Royal service in the summer of 1642 and taken a commission from Parliament. Nothing in his record made his masters at Westminster suppose that he would do any better for their cause than Nat Fiennes had done at Bristol, and when, shortly after the fall of Bristol, Massey tentatively offered to negotiate for a surrender, it was widely believed that he, like Cholmley and the Hothams, was about to betray his command. The King, indeed, was sure of it and decided to march on Gloucester in the belief that it would at once capitulate, but Massey, cut off from relief and news, was only playing for time. When the King appeared before the town on August 10th, he found the young commander resolute to resist him, supported by the townsfolk, who had for the last days worked shoulder to shoulder with the garrison to strengthen the city's defences.

It sometimes happens, when a series of defeats has all but destroyed a nation or a party at war, that a new threat will inspire a heroic effort and revive an all but broken cause. An effort of this kind had restored the desperate fortunes of the Dutch in their war against Spain at the famous siege of Leyden in 1574. The siege of Gloucester was to play the same part in the English Civil War.

Gloucester stood firm against the King; and, suddenly, out of the pit of anger and gloom, London rallied to the help of her sister city. The Trained Bands must be marshalled, new regiments be raised and the Earl of Essex must lead them to the relief of Gloucester. Waller's friends watched, silent and mortified, as apprentices flocked to the colours; a month before Henry Marten's Committee, claiming to raise London " as one man," had raised little more than one man. Now, " this gallant city, considering the distress that Gloucester is in, hath enabled His Excellency to march with five new regiments of foot, at least a thousand horse, clothes for all his old army, and thirty thousand pounds in money to pay them." The existing city regiments of infantry were brought up to strength, three new ones sprang into being, a regiment of horse was formed.[129] Henry Marten, deserted by his following in the House, found himself taken up suddenly on one of his more indiscreet republican utterances and packed off to the Tower for offending against the avowed intentions of Parliament to respect the person of the King. It was a good riddance for Pym.[130]

In the midst of the bustle and recruiting, news reached Westminster from Ireland. Ormonde, choosing his time with care, had acted on the King's command and by a sudden stroke removed Sir William Parsons and the sympathisers of Parliament from the Council board in Dublin. His personal influence in the army, without which the Dublin Government could not have existed, enabled him to carry out the coup and his power was now paramount. This he had done at the King's request principally to expedite a truce with the Irish so that he could release the troops to go to England. News which, a few weeks earlier, would have dismayed the Commons now served to stimulate and strengthen their endeavours against the King and his malignant, Popish policies.[131]

On August 22nd Essex met the London regiments on Hounslow Heath, " riding with his hat off and bowing to them." In their knapsacks were bread and cheese for a week, and the country through which they passed supplied them with beer in " great plenty." In good heart, they took the road for Gloucester.[132] But the siege had lasted twelve days already and Nat Fiennes, justifying his capitulation at Bristol, predicted that Gloucester would never hold out till relief came.[133]

The King's great batteries, north and south of Gloucester, gave the defenders little rest. Rupert had wanted to take the town by assault, as Bristol had been taken, but was overruled for fear of a repetition of the same heavy loss of life. Instead, it was decided to breach the walls of Gloucester by mining, although Rupert refused to take responsibility for the outcome, because he thought the ground too wet for success.[134] Miners from the Forest of Dean were hastened up to assist and in the meantime the King's pioneers first cut the pipeline that carried drinking water to the citizens, then diverted the stream which drove their flour mills.

Massey had drinking water pumped in from the Severn and set up treadmills for the grain. He went about the city with calm good-humour, and the citizens, heartened by his confidence, cheerfully defended their town. Milkmaids drove their cattle to pasture in spite of enemy gunfire, and housewives with pails of water ran out to extinguish Royalist hand grenades. The walls were strengthened with earth and turf against the King's artillery, and the impact of the bombardment at the more exposed points was deadened by sacks of wool.

Outside the city the King held formal Court in the evenings at Matson House and by day rode round the works, leaving his two sons locked up with nothing to do but carve their names on the panelling. Prince Rupert slept at Prinknash Park, when he slept, but night and day he worked with the miners in the trenches, where sometimes also the mathematical skill of Dr. Chillingworth was in request. Sometimes a deceptive quiet prevailed, and Chillingworth one evening accompanied Falkland to dine at his cottage-billet with Lord Spencer. The three friends could forget the troubles in their hearts when the guns were silent, and they sat far into the night discoursing of theology as they had done in happier times at Great Tew.[135]

On August 24th the King gave Massey one last chance to surrender before the mines were fired, his walls were shattered and the city was exposed to the conquering Cavaliers. Massey trusted in God, in Parliament and in the works he had set up for the inner defence of the city. That night a beacon to the north on Wainload Hill signalled to him that a relieving force was on its way. Before morning, a fortnight's spell of clear weather, the longest that summer, ended in a deluge of rain. The King's mines were flooded and could not be fired. Fourteen days had been lost and all was to do again.

But the relieving force moved slowly and the city was hard beset. The King's troops harassed them with continual firing, and shot in papers of bad news fixed to arrows. " Your God, Waller hath forsaken you; Essex is beaten like a dog; yield to the King's mercy." What were they to think, cut off from all other news, waiting for a relieving force that had been signalled, but never came? Massey continued impassive, firm, confident, watching the empty hills to the east, day by day, for the first sign of the approaching army.

In the camp before Gloucester, Montrose and his cousin Ogilvie had arrived from Scotland, with their story of the Covenanters arming to join with the English rebels. They found the King preoccupied, about to leave with Rupert on a visit to Oxford, scarcely willing to listen, though Montrose persisted and rode with Rupert all the way. Charles would not hear of a Royalist rising in Scotland; Hamilton had promised he could hold the Scots neutral until the winter and by the winter the war would be over.[136]

In the two days he spent in Oxford the King saw the Earls of Bedford, Holland and Clare, newly come from Westminster. He was uncertain whether he should pardon these penitent renegades, and the Queen expressed vehement displeasure when Rupert, who saw nothing to be lost by encouraging them, introduced them into the royal presence. But if nothing was to be lost by receiving them, neither was anything to be gained. A month before, their party in the Lords with the support of Essex might have compelled the Commons to a peace, but now all was changed; the three lords had neither influence nor information that could help the King, and the King was convinced that he would win the war in the next few weeks without their help.[137] On the 28th the King and Prince returned to Gloucester. Meanwhile the relieving force was on its way. On September 1st the London regiments joined Essex and the main body at Brackley. From thence they had about sixty miles to go across the Cotswold Hills, where every shoulder might conceal the King's demon cavalry. The weather was cold for the time of year; their rations were running out and they dared not light fires at night for fear of betraying their position to enemy patrols. But their spirits were firm. Wilmot, with cavalry from Oxford, tried and failed to check their advance. Rupert, collecting the horse he had at Gloucester, fell on them just below Stow on the Wold, but they outnumbered him;

the pikemen stood their ground and the firing of the musketeers broke the force of his attack. He drew off towards Cheltenham and they continued their march.

On the dank evening of September 5th from the brow of Prestbury Hill they saw at last the wide valley of the Severn, the glimmering line of the river and the great cathedral tower of Gloucester. Essex fired a salute and heard the distant answering shot from the city. In gathering dusk and falling rain he tried to march on, but his waggons stuck and some overturned on the steep descent. He halted the advance until morning, when he saw smoke rising before Gloucester and concluded that the garrison had made a sally and was engaged with the King's army. But as the relieving force approached through the unceasing drizzle, they saw that the King's army had withdrawn in the night, leaving only waterlogged trenches and heaps of refuse sullenly burning.[138]

VI

Gloucester was saved: but at what price? Essex paused warily. Somewhere in the sheltering, concealing hills over which he had come was the King's army, horse, foot and guns, lying in wait to destroy him on his return journey. To relieve Gloucester was the first part of his task; to get back to London was the second and more difficult part. "Essex is here in a strait and wishes himself at London again," reported a watchful Royalist.[139] If his army should be annihilated as that of Waller had been annihilated, London would lie bereft of almost all defence, an easy prey to the Cavaliers.

This was indeed the plan agreed upon by the King and Lord Forth when they left Gloucester, and they had sent to Rupert for his co-operation in fighting with Essex " as soon as may be." [140] But though Rupert was eager to respond, the plan was held up, for the King lapsed into a despondent mood. On the march from Gloucester tradition has it that he rested on a mile-stone and when one of his sons asked if they might not now go home, said " We have no home." [141] The disappointment at Gloucester darkened his eyes to the very real hope that the war could still be won if he moved resolutely to intercept Essex. While Rupert sent his cavalry on scouting parties and fretted at the delay, the King pondered gloomily over his prospects.

After the fall of Bristol the valiant Cornish army, deprived of its best leaders and weakened by heavy losses, had withdrawn from the operations and Charles now belatedly tried to re-animate it by drawing up an elegant letter of thanks—the work of Falkland—to be published throughout Cornwall.[142] The consolidation of the West continued. While the main forces of the King's army were before Gloucester, Prince Maurice had laid siege to Exeter. Parliament had sent the Earl of Warwick to strengthen the town from the sea, but Exeter is situated on a narrow estuary and the relieving ships could be enfiladed and fired at from both sides by the besieging force. The Earl of Warwick was helpless and the city surrendered to the Cavaliers on September 4th.[143] The Royalist capture of Exeter hardly balanced the check at Gloucester but it gave them a western capital, a city of influence and distinction where, in due course, the King set up a mint, and whence he could effectively direct the administration of the war. Meanwhile on the north coast of Devon, Barnstaple and Bideford also surrendered.

The consolidation of the West was doubly important if the King's Irish plans were to mature, and in the days after his withdrawal from Gloucester he wrote again urgently to Ormonde to hasten the truce with the Irish and release troops to help him in England.[144]

The King's project for raising help in Ireland moved more slowly than Pym's plan for the Scottish alliance. The English Commissioners, led by Vane, had reached Edinburgh on August 7th. A doubting party in the Assembly of the Church still argued that any intervention in England should be undertaken only in a spirit of strict neutrality between the combatants, but Warristoun, with arguments at once vehement and practical, " did show the vanity of that notion and the impossibility of it." [145] The next obstacle was created by a difference in outlook between the Scots and the English. The English wanted a conventional political alliance, but nothing would satisfy the Scots but a religious oath; both nations must unite in a Covenant sworn not to each other but to God.

Argyll and Vane were well-matched. Both men were fanatical in their beliefs, but cool, clear-headed and ingenious in political action. From the first they understood and respected each other. Both also understood the urgent danger of their situation. Within ten days the formula of the Solemn League and Covenant to be sworn by both nations had been laid down, and within a fortnight, while Charles was still before Gloucester, the Scots Estates ordered all able-bodied men to stand ready for service at twenty-four hours' warning, and despatched the text of the Covenant to Westminster. Parliament debated it while their army marched for Gloucester over the Cotswolds, and Charles, a few days after his withdrawal from Gloucester, roundly denounced it and forbade his subjects to sign it. [146]

Meanwhile Essex had withdrawn from Gloucester to Tewkesbury and was waiting the moment to begin his return journey. On September 15th he made a feint towards Worcester, then at dusk struck unexpectedly southwards, marched through the night and at three in the morning on September 16th surprised and scattered the Royalists occupying Cirencester and cut off a convoy of provisions bound for Oxford. Exhilarated by this achievement, his men raced for the London road by way of Cricklade. Rupert was meanwhile searching the Cotswold countryside for the King and Lord Forth who at this critical moment had lost touch with him. By the time he found them, sitting together over a game of piquet, Essex was well away and their task was no longer interception but pursuit. Rupert went ahead with the cavalry to harry and hold up the retreating enemy. Charles and Lord Forth with the infantry and guns were to follow after with all speed in the hope that they might yet bring Essex to fight. Through blustering weather, with lashing rain, the King's army pushed rapidly forward. On the night of September 17th Rupert's cavalry were beyond Faringdon at Stamford in the Vale, the King and the infantry some miles behind at Alscot, striving to keep up though hungry, footsore and " pickled " with the wet.[147]

Essex was at Swindon. His troops had now used most of the provisions taken at Cirencester, were adding to their rations by pulling nuts, blackberries and hedgerow apples as they went along, but were much dispirited, especially the infantry. In the mud and the wet their progress was slowed down by the plundered sheep and cattle they were herding with them. Rupert conceived that he might, by a swift move south, cut off their cavalry from the rest of the army and delay the retreat. On Monday, September 18th, early in the morning he fell on the Parliamentary horse as they crossed the green uplands of Aldbourne Chase, King John's old hunting forest, but though startled, they retired in good order to their infantry and Rupert was unable to do much damage against the steady firing of their musketeers. He had, however, slowed down their march and concentrated now on racing Essex to Newbury and blocking the London road. His friend, the Duke of Richmond, took his part with the King and stimulated his flagging spirits, so that the Royalist infantry put forth a last effort. When on the evening of September 19th Essex and his men, wet through, worn out, and very short of food, approached Newbury, where they had hoped for dry quarters and plentiful supplies, they found the Cavaliers were there two hours before them.[148]

The King had been joined by fresh cavalry from Oxford and by some from the West under Prince Maurice. In horse and guns he had the advantage of Essex and his infantry was not much inferior, but ammunition was perilously low and fresh supplies had not come from Oxford. At the Council of War in Newbury that night Rupert was against fighting on the following day. Essex was immobilised, and they could afford to wait until the ammunition came.[149]

Rupert was overruled. Next morning the Cavaliers occupied the rising ground at Wash Common, just to the south-west of the town. Essex, whose headquarters were at Enborn, sent forward Hampden's veteran regiment to seize and hold Bigg's Hill, a vantage point on their flank, whence he believed he could engage and hold some of their cavalry. His infantry meanwhile advanced on the flat ground between the town and the Common, using with great skill the opportunities afforded by hedged lanes and enclosed vegetable gardens to infiltrate the enemy position. Very soon the Royalist musketeers, as tired and wet as their opponents, began to run short of ammunition and could no longer make any effective resistance, although the ground was admirably adapted for the musketry but too enclosed to be favourable to cavalry and impossible for the manœuvres of pikemen. Rupert brought his cavalry to the rescue, outflanked the enemy, and stormed their infantry in the rear with a hail of sharp onslaughts. The London Trained Bands, who were the first to be exposed to this new danger, began to waver, but Essex reached them in time, rallied their pikemen and encouraged their musketeers. In that enclosed ground, the Cavaliers could not charge on a wide front and the Parliamentary musketeers wrought terrible havoc among Rupert's small attacking parties.

As the day wore on the King's men, crippled for lack of ammunition, gave ground. They fell back from Wash Common before the resolute firing that they could not return, and under cover of the falling night retired within the town. Their losses were terrible. All that night carts brought in the dead and dying from the lanes about Newbury. Prince Rupert, in the saddle from dark to dawn, reassembled his cavalry to attack the enemy if they moved for London in the morning. Some time in the restless night he wrote briefly to Essex desiring to know if the Lord Viscount Falkland was a prisoner in his hands, or if he had his dead body.[150]

A musket ball had ended Falkland's life, made desolate by divided loyalty and extinguished hope. What he had thought or felt in those last days rests alone on the conjectures of poor stricken Edward Hyde, who was never again to know such a friend. All chance of a negotiated peace had gone in April, and the last illusory hope had to be relinquished in the summer, when the peace party in Parliament finally collapsed. In the weeks since then Falkland had watched the King's plan for Irish help steadily maturing; he had heard the news out of Scotland. He had taken part in the frantic pursuit of Essex during which Rupert and the hot-blooded soldiers had governed the King's councils and even the gentle Richmond had joined in the excitement of the chase. All this was utterly repellent to Falkland. He saw the war extending over all the King's dominions, the parties becoming irreconcilable, the disorder and destruction continuing without end. Or if, by the fortunes of war, the King were to triumph at Newbury and sweep on to London, he feared an intemperate victory that would destroy the legal and moderate government in which he believed. In this mood he had fought at Newbury as a volunteer in the King's cavalry and had ridden to his death.[151]

Two other noblemen were among the dead—the Earls of Sunderland and Carnarvon, both well-known to the King. Later it was said that the King came into the inn where Carnarvon lay dying and " would not stir from the bedside 'till he saw all hope of life was gone." Carnarvon, a high-tempered young man with a mop of yellow curls was no particular favourite of the King. He may have mourned in him the many brave and young, known and unknown, who had so fruitlessly died that day in the damp lanes, or under Bristol walls, or on the slope of Edgehill.[152]

Next day, the Earl of Essex listened in vain for a sound from the King's quarters. Shortly before midday he resumed the march for London, rightly believing that the King's musketeers and batteries were out of action. The only danger was from the cavalry. Essex placed his tired infantry in the middle of the column, guarded by detachments of horse before and behind. Three miles beyond the town, "at the heath's end" in a narrow hedged road, Rupert's cavalry fell on his rear and momentarily disordered the retreat.[153] The Parliamentary horse took panic and almost rode down their own infantry, but the musketeers manned the hedges and their firing checked the Royalist attack. There were small disordered skirmishes and much hand to hand fighting. Sir Philip Stapleton, a weedy little man with a stout heart, rode up to Rupert and fired in his face point-blank. The pistol failed to go off and Stapleton wheeled off in dismay from the indestructible Prince.[154] Battered, but not seriously damaged, Essex got his army away to Reading, decided that the town could not profitably be held, evacuated the garrison and completed the march to London. He was received with enthusiasm and congratulated, in his great house in the Strand, by the Lord Mayor and the Speaker with deputations from the City and the House of Commons. His men, with laurels in their hats, marched through streets lined with cheering crowds.[155]

The King put a garrison into Donnington Castle above Newbury to block "the great road through which the western trade was driven to London." He also, with a new and generous wisdom, made arrangements for the care of the wounded prisoners in Newbury.[156] Then he returned to Oxford, where bonfires blazed out his royal triumph. But he knew that after thirteen months of war he was no nearer to victory. Parliament still had an army in the field and still held the capital. In London, the victory parade diverted attention only for a while from continued anxieties. Gloucester saved, but Bristol lost, Exeter lost, Reading abandoned; the end of the war remote and unforseeable. "All were Englishmen," wrote Bulstrode Whitelocke of the battle at Newbury, "and pity it was that such courage should be spent in blood of each other." [157]   But in future all would not be Englishmen, for both sides had called in other allies. The King's plan for Irish help and Pym's plan for Scottish help matured at the same time.   Henceforward the politics of Ireland and of Scotland would divert the course, alter the objectives, and prolong the duration of the war.

CHAPTER TWO

THE COMING OF THE SCOTS

September 1643—March 1644

ON September 25th, 1643, while London rejoiced at the news from Newbury, the members of both Houses of Parliament, with the Commissioners from Scotland, signed the Solemn League and Covenant at the Church which was now called Margarets Westminster. This was no ordinary secular alliance but, in the words of Philip Nye who preached the sermon for the occasion, an oath of " fealty and allegiance unto Christ the King of Kings."[1]

The agreement with the Scots was a compromise between irreconcilable ideas, a treaty born of necessity and nourished by illusory hopes. The King's approaching victory menaced the Covenanters in Scotland only a little less than it did the Parliamentarians in England; they closed their ranks in face of a common danger. But they had little else in common.

The Scots were later to accuse the English of deceiving them, but at the time both parties were open-eyed. Sir Harry Vane, who had conducted the negotiations, was not and did not pretend to be a Presbyterian; fanatic though he was, he disliked the idea of giving to a political treaty all the spiritual force of a religious undertaking. He had insisted that the word " League " be set alongside the Biblical term of " Covenant," so that the true character of the treaty was not concealed. The Scots had given in to this; they had also after prolonged argument given in to a modification of their religious terms. In the first place they had demanded the abolition of Episcopacy in England (to which Vane willingly agreed) and the imposition of the Presbyterian discipline, at which Vane demurred. At this point in the negotiations the minister of Stirling, Henry Guthry, who was known to have Royalist sympathies, tried to break up the alliance by an impassioned denunciation of the English for the ambiguity of their religious intentions. The hint that the English would favour the sects rather than the Presbyterians was hardly necessary; most of Guthry's colleagues were well aware of it, but they suspected his motives, so that his opposition to the alliance went far to convince them of its necessity. At length they forced upon the English a clause binding them to bring the Churches of God in the three Kingdoms into conformity with each other: they meant into conformity with the Church of Scotland, but Vane insisted on adding the phrase that this joint reformation should be "according to the Word of God."[2]

The Word of God might be interpreted by Sir Harry Vane or other Englishmen to mean something very different from Presbyterian government. The Scots perfectly understood the purpose of the interpolation, but they believed they could render it harmless partly by offering theological proof, in which they themselves most passionately believed, that the Presbyterian discipline, *and no other*, was according to the Word of God, and partly by the overwhelming influence they would wield in English affairs when invincible Scottish soldiers had won the war. A dispensation of Providence, as wonderful as it was gratifying, had humbled the English into supplicating for their help against "a generation of brutish, hellish men . . . under whose cruelties we bleed and" so the entreaty ran, "if present mercy step not in we die."[3] Who could doubt that God, who had brought this thing to pass, would continue his blessing on their work? In this conviction, at once religious and practical, the Covenanters conceded the minor points to Vane and made ready to support the English in arms as soon as the practical details could be agreed on.

An order was sent out calling all men from sixteen to sixty to the colours with forty days' provision for their march. The younger of the Hamilton brothers, the Earl of Lanark, as Secretary of State, let it go out in the King's name. The harvest that year had been gathered early so that it was confidently believed the new levies would quickly come in. Lord Leven consented to be commander-in-chief; he had sworn to the King, two years before, that he would never more draw sword against him, but he regarded the present emergency as outside the meaning of his oath. The Assembly of the Scottish Church— as particular in this as the Parliament of England—sent a message to the King assuring him that the Scots were entering the war entirely in his own best interest. The Convention of Estates voted money towards the expenses of the army, and Argyll topped the list of private loans with a subscription of twelve thousand pounds. Edinburgh set an example by offering to raise and " rig out " at the city's expense twelve hundred men summoned to appear " by tuck of drum in their best armour," and further to prove the solidarity of the two nations made Sir Harry Vane a burgess.[4]

But both parties recognised the division underlying their present unity. The choice of Philip Nye to preach on the occasion of the formal signing of the League was itself significant. He had already given offence in Edinburgh by a sermon of strong independent colour. Now at Westminster, he emphasised that the goal they had to set before them was the purification of religious worship according to no national model, but by " whatsoever the Word shall discover." Alexander Henderson, speaking for the Scots, gently but firmly added his own words of exhortation when Nye had done, and drew the attention of all to " the near and neighbouring example of the Church and Kingdom of Scotland."[5]

For the moment, the unreconciled division could be overlooked. The dangers to their joint cause grew hourly more serious. Argyll at Edinburgh and Pym at Westminster both knew before the end of September, 1643, that the Marquis of Ormonde in the King's name had made a truce with the Irish. If Charles was willing to take these " idolatrous butchers " by the hand while he waged war on his sober, godly subjects, it was, by every Covenanter's reckoning, " high time for all true-hearted Scottish men and good patriots . . . to take up arms." [6]

Ormonde, with the help of the Roman Catholic loyalist Clanricarde, had concluded a truce with the Confederate Irish, the Cessation as it was generally called, on September 15th, 1643. Quite apart from the King's urgent need to employ Ormonde's troops in England, there was much to be said for making a truce in the Irish war. It had degenerated into an aimless, bloody deadlock in which neither side seemed likely to gain a permanent advantage. Ormonde in the spring had tried to reopen communications between Dublin and the Munster loyalists by taking the town of New Ross, but his temporary success had been followed by the retaliation of the Confederate general, Thomas Preston, a Spanish-trained professional, who had overrun the surrounding country, driving a fresh flight of homeless settlers to seek refuge in overcrowded Dublin.[7]

The Irish were rarely victorious in pitched battle, but they roamed at will over the wilder parts of the country, raided open towns and villages or reduced, isolated strong-points. Neither Ormonde's forces round Dublin, nor those of Inchiquin in Munster, nor the Scots under Monro in Ulster could drive the Irish from their fortresses or bring their raiding under control, but they were strong enough to prevent what had at first seemed likely—the conquest of all Ireland by the Confederates. Lord Muskerry was repelled from Cork by the angry, ancient patriarch the Earl of Cork himself, conducting the defence of his town.[8] Owen Roe O'Neill was defeated by Monro when he tried to trap and deal with the Scots army in Ulster.[9] In spite of the professional soldiers who were now for the most part leading the Irish bands, it proved impossible effectively to organise the

Confederate army. Raiding was the kind of fighting the troops understood; in the north O'Neill allowed a great part of his forces to remain in their natural clan formation and to march with their creaghts, the cattle which they drove nomadically with them. It was impossible even at the Confederate head-quarters to keep the effervescent Irish together as an army during the slack months of the winter; they would be forever " riding up and down to see their friends," wearing out their horses.[10]

Irish warfare was terrifyingly unconventional, sometimes comically so, for what else can be made of the experience of the small government garrison put into Ballymarter Castle who were plagued to death by poltergeists " like creatures in white shirts " who pulled the clothes off their beds and otherwise annoyed them, till one of them going into the cellar found " Gibbaloney the great divell himself sitting at the barrel's head with a candle in his hand taking tobacco," after which there was no further staying at Ballymarter.[11] But such lighter moments apart, the English and the Scots were much inclined to suspect the Irish of occult powers, a dark fear which sometimes found an outlet in the ill-usage of prisoners.

If troops and money had been poured in from England the Irish war could have been ended (as it was ultimately to be ended) in a few months. But that was now impossible; the government forces were unpaid, ill-equipped, mutinous and deserting.[12] The war might drag on for years without ultimate advantage to either side. This was evident to some at least of the commanders who were glad to welcome a truce. But the Irish priests thought differently; they believed the country to be virtually liberated already and would hear of no terms with Ormonde that did not restore Catholicism as the religion of Ireland, together with all the property of the Church. In this they were strongly supported by an emissary from the Vatican, Pier Francesco Scarampi, who reached Ireland in the summer of 1643.[13] Already in the negotiations which preceded the truce, lines of division between the Confederates began to appear. The priests, supported by the bulk of the people, were for the absolute restoration of the Catholic faith; most of the nobility, with the lawyers and professional men (a small group among the Irish, but influential) were for a compromise settlement. The line of division of interest coincided very closely with the racial line between the Old Irish and the Norman or Anglo-Irish. Just as the virulent policy of the English Parliament had, at the beginning of the Rebellion, driven the Lords of the Pale, the Norman and Anglo-Irish Catholics into alliance with the insurgents, so now the fear of prolonged disorder, of excessive Irish demands and above all of the loss of their lands to the Church, was driving the Anglo-Irish back towards the idea of a compromise settlement with the Dublin Government under Ormonde. The character of that Government had, after all, been radically changed by the removal of Sir William Parsons and the Puritan councillors.

Whatever might be said against these Anglo-Irish—the "Ormondists" as they later came to be called—as Irishmen or as Christians they had a more sane and worldly understanding of the problems which faced their country. They knew that what the priests hoped for would never be granted by Ormonde or any other Lord Lieutenant, and they thought it wiser to seize and consolidate the advantages they had won by making a compromise settlement which had some chance of being accepted in England when the war was over. Their influence secured the Cessation, but the sharp divisions of the Irish and the intransigence of the religious made it, in effect, nothing more than an agreed interval in the fighting alike by land and sea, a year's armistice with mutual release of prisoners during which both parties were to hold, and govern according to their own ideas, the country which they occupied; no peace terms were foreshadowed, no basis of discussion was suggested.[14]

The divisions of the Irish were for the moment less troublesome to Ormonde than the divisions of the settlers. If the Irish priests objected to the armistice, so did many of the settlers. In England, Parliament had denounced it.[15] The Council in

Dublin, purged of Parliamentary sympathisers, might defend it reasonably enough on the grounds that too little help had come from Westminster to enable them to continue fighting. But the settlers far and wide soon found that the Confederate leaders could not control the raiding parties of the Irish and that they were, by virtue of the Cessation, left defenceless against " these merciless bloody villains." In Ulster the government troops in agreement with the Scots described the armistice as " a master-piece of the Devil." At this Ormonde stopped their pay, but the Confederates—for their part—authorised O'Neill to go on fighting.[16] The suspicion of the settlers that the King desired not merely a truce but an alliance with the Irish rebels was justified. Though at first the King's official policy was to bring over only government troops to fight for him, the Confederate Irish immediately after the Cessation voted him thirty thousand pounds, mostly in kind and cattle. Within a month of the armistice Lord Taaffe said he had a force of four thousand Irish ready to send to the King and was asking only if he might first have " liberty to destroy " the troublesome Scots in Ulster. The King himself had no compunction in the matter; he was cynically willing that the Scots in Ulster should refuse the Cessation and thus fall a prey to the Irish, rather than accept it and come home to swell the army of the Covenanters.[17]

With so thick a confusion between loyalist and rebel, Catholic and Protestant, English and Irish, it was not surprising that a murmur of resentment, rising here and there to mutiny, spread among the King's English forces when the new auxiliaries began to arrive from Ireland. The first to come were Ormonde's government troops, nearly all Protestant and English or of English descent. They landed, inevitably, at the ports of the Bristol Channel or at Chester, the very regions which for two years had been receiving boatloads of fugitive settlers in great distress. Cheshire had, furthermore, in the past two generations sent many colonists to Ireland so that the gentry of the region resented the Cessation with unusual bitterness as a betrayal of the settlers. Trouble began at once. The new troops were constantly referred to as "Irish" and refugees in Chester claimed to recognise among them the murderers of their husbands and sons. Everywhere the people were hostile and unwilling to house or feed the newcomers. In the West Country, the Royalist troops at Bridgewater mutinied and would not serve with them. Sometimes, to confuse the issue further, the government troops from Dublin who had, after all, been fighting a hard war against the Roman Catholic Irish were indignant to find Catholic officers in the King's English army; one company strongly objected to assisting the Popish owner of Wardour Castle to recapture his own home from the Protestant garrison which was holding it for Parliament.[18]

In Ireland Ormonde had trouble with some of his officers. Colonel Michael Jones resigned his commission after first presenting a petition against the truce. Ormonde was compelled to arrest Lawrence Crawford, a Scottish professional, who furiously resented the transfer of his troops to England to fight alongside the Papists. The one time Governor of Dublin, a man well-known and well-liked in all ranks of the army as "honest George Monk," refused the special oath of loyalty to the King tendered to all officers leaving for England. Ormonde, anxious that the King should not lose a professional soldier of great value, sent Monk in honourable custody to England in the hope that a personal interview with His Majesty might clear his doubts.[19]

II

The situation for Parliament in the autumn of 1643, though greatly eased by the relief of Gloucester and the safe return of Essex, still gave cause for anxiety. Reading had been evacuated and Rupert's cavalry was free to raid in the Chilterns and endanger the approaches to London. It was indeed still possible that the king might compel his capital to surrender before the Scots could come to the rescue.

While Hopton, empowered with a commission to raise the counties of Surrey and Sussex, tried to push forward south of London, Rupert planned to cut its supply line from the Midlands. On October 6th a Royalist force under Sir Lewis Dyve seized Newport Pagnell. Essex had been counting on the snug little town in the reedy flats of Buckinghamshire to be " a warm nest " for his tired men during the winter months. But Newport was something more than a convenient centre for his winter quarters; it was a key point in the road and river communications by which the contributions and the produce of the eastern counties reached London. By holding it the Royalists would stop up one of the main channels by which the city lived.[20]

Parliament still pressed its demands for money, over and above the regular assessments. Owing to the slackness of trade the excise were bringing in far too little.[21] They could not meet the legitimate demands of the army and navy, and they needed still more to hasten the preparation of the Scots. A Forced Loan of nearly seventy thousand pounds was imposed. The Merchant Adventurers came forward with another thirty thousand, but the resources of the City were strained to the uttermost, while Royalist piracy on the high seas menaced all merchandise bound for London, and the competition of Bristol was now beginning to be felt. The fuel shortage, which greatly depressed the people, would be a serious problem when the cold weather came; an order went out for the felling of trees for sixty miles round—beginning with the Royal parks—to keep the London fires burning, and Parliament's Scottish allies drove the Fifeshire miners to work for longer hours and diverted the bulk of the coal to London, regardless of the claims of their own more hardy countrymen in the coming winter.[22]

From the Welsh marches, Brereton reported gloomily that Shropshire was " rotten " with Royalism, and from Gloucester, Massey complained that his men, for lack of pay, were deserting to the opposite party.[23] The revolt in Kent that summer left an uneasy fear of further trouble, especially if Hopton managed to advance south of London, and there were alarms of Royalist agents at work.[24] In the heart of the Eastern Association there had been grave trouble when the people of King's Lynn refused to pay their part of the assessment and then, suddenly, declared for the King and held the town with great resolution for nearly a month under the command of the Norfolk Royalist Sir Hamon Lestrange. They had counted on help from the Marquis of Newcastle who was by August undisputed master in the North. Had he immediately come to their relief, which he could have done after the taking of Gainsborough, he could have overrun the Eastern Association before Cromwell could marshal troops for its defence. Instead he listened to the pleas of the Yorkshire Royalists who wanted to see Hull reduced, and allowed his forces to be locked up in the siege of a town which was pretty well impregnable unless he had had control of the sea. The heroic rising at King's Lynn ended in capitulation on September 16th, and one of the greatest opportunities of the war was lost.[25]

Crossing the Humber, which Newcastle could not patrol, Cromwell got into Hull to consult with the two Fairfaxes. Lord Fairfax remained there as Governor but his son, Sir Thomas, returned across the estuary to Lincolnshire with Cromwell, bringing with him the remnant of his horse and dragoons.[26] In the crisis of the late summer the Earl of Manchester had replaced the young and incompetent Lord Grey as general for the Eastern Midlands as well as the Associated Counties, and during these urgent weeks he worked with the enormously active and effective Cromwell to restore the confidence and strength of the army, on which the ultimate relief of Hull and the safety of the Eastern Midlands now depended.

In the second week of October the Scots professional who governed Newark for the King, Sir John Henderson, marched with eighty companies of horse and dragoons against the now growing forces of Manchester quartered about Horn-castle. Manchester had both Fairfax and Cromwell with him, and some infantry and artillery to support his cavalry. His whole force was less than half of Henderson's strength but he thought it wisest to take the initiative. He intercepted him at Winceby on the edge of the Lincolnshire Wolds. Confident in his well-disciplined cavalry Cromwell charged first; his horse was killed under him but so effective had his training been that his men came on undaunted alike by the accident to their leader and the firing of the Cavaliers, and the King's men broke before them; at this Fairfax brought his cavalry in on the flank and completed their discomfiture. After this second charge, Manchester reported, " our men had little else to do but to pursue a flying enemy, which they did for many miles." They took more than eight hundred prisoners as well as horses and arms and twenty-six colours. The battle at Winceby was the quickest and easiest victory yet won by either party and although the Royalists alleged that culpable cowardice on the part of a few had caused their overthrow, they admitted that the Parliamentary cavalry was now, beyond their expectations, well trained and well armed. Cromwell's methods had begun to tell.[27]

At the same time the veteran Meldrum had relieved Hull. A high tide which flooded the Royalist siege works and a sally from the garrison compelled Newcastle to withdraw leaving some of his cannon in the enemy's hands and some stuck in the mud. Manchester, profiting by the general disorder among the Lincoln-shire Royalists, summoned the town of Lincoln which instantly surrendered with a considerable supply of arms.[28]

This remarkable recovery of the Eastern Association forces, the joint work of Cromwell and Manchester, would have done little service to the Parliamentary cause if the Royalists had made good their hold on Newport Pagnell and so cut them off from London. But everything depended on the speedy despatch of ammunition to Sir Lewis Dyve and his garrison, and at Oxford there were no wagons available. Rupert sent a storm of messages urging haste, but at the King's headquarters they did not put themselves about. By the time they had found the necessary carts it was too late. Someone had neglected to inform Dyve that supplies were on their way and on October 27th he evacuated Newport before the advancing Parliamentary forces, either because he had no means to resist them or because he had been sent a wrong order. Rupert was a man of few words, but some bare jottings by his secretary reflect his mood: " the mistake about Newport Pagnell, which spoiled all." [29]

The significance of the failure at Newport Pagnell was not immediately apparent to the King, who gave little support to Rupert's urgent efforts in the next month to fortify Towcester, to the north-west of Newport, and use it in the same way to hold up the flow of supply to London.[30] At Oxford they consoled themselves with good news from the south. Hopton was pushing on towards Surrey, and Waller had suffered another check at Basing House, the massive Royalist outpost which barred the road to London from the wool districts of the south-west. His men, discouraged by the ferocious resistance of the garrison, and depressed by cold and blustering weather, began to desert; whole companies of London recruits set up a cry of "Home! Home!" and marched away. With what was left of his army he dragged through pelting rain to Farnham, and having got his men under cover, wrote urgently to Parliament for ammunition, clothes and pay.[31]

But though the discomfiture of Waller was gratifying, the Royalist leaders were perturbed by a sudden and successful move of their enemies in the Welsh marches. Here, on November 9th, 1643, Brereton made himself master of Wrexham, a point from which, they feared, he would be able to intercept the expected troops from Dublin, whose shortest route lay across North Wales.[32]

As the second winter of the war closed in, the combatants faced each other in a mood in which hope and fear were evenly balanced. Neither could be certain of victory, but neither had need to despair of it, and neither had anything to gain by negotiating for peace. The French envoy, the Comte d'Harcourt, sent that autumn with some idea of mediation between the combatants, wasted his time. The government of France had changed in name but not in nature since the outbreak of the English war. Cardinal Richelieu died in December, 1642, and his master Louis XIII five months later, just at the time when his forces won their first decisive victory over the Spaniards at Rocroy. From this change King Charles and his Queen hoped much, but Richelieu's disciple and successor Cardinal Mazarin soon acquired a more secure and more intimate mastery over the new ruler than Richelieu had ever exercised over King Louis XIII. The new ruler, in the name of the child Louis XIV, was the handsome and susceptible Queen mother, Anne of Austria; the wise, worldly, gallant Mazarin played the part of her devoted and respectful admirer and was rewarded by her affectionate trust. No change of policy, therefore, occurred between the two reigns, for Mazarin had been trained in politics by Richelieu, and he miraculously persuaded this devout Roman Catholic, Habsburg princess to work as her husband had done, in alliance with Protestant Swedes and Dutch, against Catholic Spain and Austria, for the European influence and national expansion of France.

All that mattered to Mazarin, and to the envoy whom he presently sent to England, was that the outcome of the English war should not be disadvantageous to France in her European policies. The Comte d'Harcourt suffered a rude initiation into English wartime politics. Though he was well received by the London crowd, he found that Parliament had removed all the furniture from the Queen's palace of Somerset House, where he was to lodge, and he was further troubled when unpaid troops broke in and stole his plate. In his suite, disguised, he had the Queen's Catholic favourite, Wat Montagu—the Puritan Earl of Manchester's converted brother—who was hoping to rejoin the Court at Oxford. Parliament ferreted him out, scoffed at diplomatic immunity and sent him to the Tower.[33] But Harcourt, in spite of so much discourtesy, realised that the interests of France would be best served by keeping on terms with Parliament.

When he reached Oxford, the King received him civilly and the Queen, who had attached much importance to his coming, sent warm messages to Anne of Austria; but Harcourt reported that the Court swarmed with friends of Spain. Many of the King's commanders had come from the Spanish service in Flanders; Flemish arms and Dunkirk vessels were sustaining the King's cause by land and sea. No doubt the French could have given Charles enough support to make him independent of Spanish or Flemish help, had it been worth their while to do so. But Harcourt did not think that it was. The task would be too expensive and while Parliament controlled the navy it would be unwise to add to the difficulties of France by making an unnecessary enemy of them. As for mediating a peace, the King was indignant at the mere hint of such a thing. In a letter to Prince Rupert, he had declared he would consider no way of treating in future except with Essex personally, " being the chief rebel," an attitude which was the logical outcome of his declaration in the summer that he no longer recognised the remnant at Westminster as in any sense a Parliament. In the circumstances Charles parted from the French envoy with mutual compliments and mutual dissatisfaction.[34]

The King's relations with Antonio de Sousa, the Portuguese representative, were more cordial. Parliament was suspicious of this secretive, industrious man who more successfully than any of his colleagues contrived to be useful to both parties. He was one of the principal channels through which the King communicated with his friends in London, but Portugal had been for the last three years in revolt against Spain, and Parliament could hardly take action against the representative of a nation which was fighting their own traditional enemy, the more so as their trading relations with Portugal were of considerable importance. Sousa therefore made good use of a pass to Oxford where, after a friendly talk, he arranged to keep King Charles's favour by sending him arms, bought with Portuguese money in Holland, to the port of Falmouth. One thing in these elaborate plans proved to be outside his reckoning; when the arms were ultimately shipped in a Dutch vessel the captain, mindful no doubt of King Charles's favours to Spain and to the hated Dunkirkers, refused to put in to Falmouth and carried the cargo instead to Lisbon.[35]

The King's plans for foreign help were generally ill-fated that winter. Neither the Dutch Estates nor the Prince of Orange were anxious to do more than mediate a peace, although the King hinted at a marriage between the Prince of Wales and the Prince of Orange's daughter. These hints did not prevent other tentative moves being made in the direction of the only available French princess, the Duke of Orleans' daughter; nor was either of these plans wholly abandoned when a third bride, the five year old Infanta of Portugal, was later added to the possibilities. But the unhappiest development for the King was a renewed outbreak of war between Denmark and Sweden. King Christian IV had made serious offers of naval help, but these were now withdrawn because he needed his fleet for his untimely clash with Sweden.

Depression came into the King's quarters with the autumn. The sickness, which had afflicted the army of Essex in the Thames valley during the summer, had spread by August to the King's troops and to the city of Oxford. The summer had been wet and hot, an unhealthy kind of weather for an overcrowded town; where the soldiers were sleeping on mattresses in the streets, the gentry in packed and stuffy garrets; where there were not enough laundresses or domestic labour generally; where drains and conduits were choked with offal. The epidemic was widespread rather than severe; few of the stricken died, though among them were William Cartwright, the poet, and Sir William Pennyman, the Governor of Oxford. Prince Maurice, in his camp before Plymouth, fell dangerously ill but the King sent the famous William Harvey in all haste to him and he presently recovered.[36]

The disappointing end of the victorious summer brought a harvest of recriminations between the Cavaliers. The King's army was not divided by any rivalry so evident as that between Essex and Waller on the Parliament side, but it was seamed with envy and corroded with intrigue. Since the Queen's return the old whispering plots and counter plots had broken out again in every corner. Almost immediately she became jealous of Rupert's ascendancy over the King.[37] On Falkland's death, George Digby had become Secretary of State and now, with the Queen's help, he resumed that dominance in the Royal councils which he had lost on Rupert's coming.

The tireless Prince was fortifying Towcester, recruiting in the Welsh marches, planning the reception and distribution of the forces from Ireland, organising a ceaseless and—to the Londoners—nerve-racking series of raids in the Chilterns and the Thames valley. Now and again he was in Oxford, attending a supper or dance given by the Queen, playing tennis with the King and the two young princes. But these were flying visits, brief interludes in his exacting duties with the army. He had no time to consolidate his position at Court and by temperament he was no match for Digby as a courtier or diplomat. His single-minded concentration on the duties and necessities of the war, regardless of the susceptibilities of others, made him enemies. The Duke of Richmond, who for the last year had smoothed out his difficulties with the Court circle, had been sent by the King on a mission to Paris, and Rupert, too honest himself to suspect or counteract Court intrigues, was left for two or three critical months without a friend in the Royal bedchamber.[38]

He did not hesitate to blame Wilmot for having let Essex and his relieving force get through to Gloucester, and Harry Percy for failing to supply Newport Pagnell, and thus made two bitter and insidious foes among the Queen's friends. Young courtiers, in trouble for military incompetence, sniped at him from the safety of privileged positions. Endymion Porter's son complained of " the frown Your Highness was pleased to cast upon me," but frowns did nothing to quell the insolent insubordination of these favoured courtiers.[39] Others who found the Prince too downright and self-willed for their liking, applied for garrison duty to escape him.[40] The cavalry, meanwhile, after the summer's raiding, was out of control, and he was assailed with complaints. The horse based on Newbury defied Colonel Boys, the commander of the neighbouring Donnington Castle and their officers encouraged them to molest the infantry. There had been confusion in the allotment of quarters between different regiments; clashes over lodgings and forage regularly occurred. One enterprising subaltern led his men at horse stealing and highway robbery for private profit and, in the general confusion of authority, evaded discipline by claiming to be under the command of a colonel who was too far off to interfere with him.[41] With some faithful support Rupert did what he could to maintain order but the problem was too large for one man to solve.

Confusion and dispute over the precedence of commanders was unceasing. In South Wales and the adjoining marches Sir William Vavasour was by far the ablest and most effective soldier. He had at first assisted the Marquis of Worcester and Lord Herbert in recruiting more troops after the loss of their first army at Highnam. Soon, to the great annoyance of Lord Herbert, the Council of War at Oxford sent orders direct to Vavasour. From this it was a short step for Vavasour to act independently of Herbert—who was, he hinted, unpopular in South Wales—and to imply that he ought to have command, if not in Wales, then at least on the English side of the border. Two others, unfortunately, hoped for this same command.[42] In North Wales, old Archbishop Williams after leaving York had fortified himself at Conway Castle and set up for the King's commander, a claim deeply resented by Sir Arthur Capel whom the King had appointed his general in those parts, and not popular with the more active Royalist gentry who found that the Archbishop's plans constantly interfered with their own.[43]

Disputes about the command multiplied with the King's victories, and radiated outwards from the intrigue-ridden Court. Showers of rewards, baronies and knighthoods, fell from the King's hands in return for money or in reward of valour; but the plentiful creations only increased the number of the unsatisfied. Byron, raised to the peerage after Newbury, wanted to be made governor to the Prince of Wales and tried to enlist Rupert's help. More reasonably he complained that he himself, and not some wealthy alderman of Chester, should be made governor of the town. Hertford, who had been honourably relieved of his military duties, still confidently interfered and his candidate for the governorship of Weymouth, a young gentleman of local influence, Anthony Ashley Cooper, was preferred to the soldier whom Prince Maurice wished to promote.[44] Within six months Ashley Cooper had gone over to Parliament but it was too late then for regrets.

III

The divisions in the King's quarters did not, however, seem so grave as those of the Parliamentary party. Essex and Waller were at open enmity; Lord Saye's son, Nat Fiennes, enraged by accusations of cowardice, had demanded an inquiry into his surrender at Bristol and, after an embittered trial, had been sentenced to death. It was widely and repeatedly rumoured that the Parliamentary leaders were shipping their goods to Holland, or even to New England, and while friends and foes to the Cause concurred in believing " all their last hope to be in their blessed brethren the Scots,"[45] the Scots themselves viewed warily the sectaries who abounded in London and in the armies.

Cromwell was accused of advancing Anabaptists. " They are

273

no Anabaptists," he wrote, " they are honest, sober Christians." [46]
But there were many besides the Scots who doubted that Cromwell's " honest sober Christians " might prove dangerous in the
end. He had made admirable soldiers of his humble East
Anglians; he had twice defeated the Royalist cavalry and he,
almost alone, had prevented total disaster in the Eastern Midlands
during the critical summer weeks of the Royalist advance. As
a soldier he was an indispensible bulwark of the Parliamentary
cause, but would he become dangerous when the war was
won? The question was already being asked. For the time
being his conduct was acceptable; he took the Covenant, as
did many others whose ideas of Church reform were known
not to be of the Presbyterian pattern. Some of them took it in
the cynical spirit of John Selden who held that it was better to
swallow such oaths like pills, without chewing. [47]

Pym sought to bridle Scottish criticism by emphasising the
points of agreement. The autumn and winter saw a further intensification of the persecution of the " prelatical " party. The
necessity for taking the Covenant caused a number of removals
and expulsions. About a third of the Fellows of Cambridge
colleges withdrew or were ejected and the University was
subjected to drastic reform. Choristers vanished from college
chapels, although Trinity, somewhat strangely, continued to
pay forty shillings a year to the organ-blower " for not blowing
the organ." [48] In Suffolk, a Parliamentary visitor, William
Dowsing, strenuously toured the parish churches and ordered
the destruction of painted screens, carved angels and other
abominations. At Ely Cathedral, Oliver Cromwell, if a classic
story is to be believed, put an end to the use of the Prayer Book by
interrupting the officiating priest with " Leave off your fooling
and come down." [49] The impeachment of Archbishop Laud,
long postponed for lack of evidence, was taken up once more,
though the Scots saw through this manœuvre intended to pacify
them. " He is a person now so contemptible that we take no
notice of his process," wrote Dr. Baillie, [50] the informative

Principal of Glasgow; he had come to England with the ministers who were to watch the interests of Scotland and the Covenant with their English allies, and for the next years his vivid and outspoken letters would illuminate the passing scene.

The Scottish divines were next invited to take part in the Westminster Assembly. Its sessions were, at least, properly heated by a good coal fire (Scots coal, at that) but, comfort apart, had little to commend them to the critical Covenanters. The religion of England was simply "in a most lamentable anarchy and confusion," which the long-winded and bookish arguments of many of the English divines seemed to increase. When the extirpation of Popery was under discussion, one of them held up the debate for an hour arguing about the meaning of the words: "it being a very nice business to know what Popery is, and what is meant by extirpation."[51] Of the lay members, John Selden applied textual criticism with blighting irony to arguments from the scriptures. "It may read so in your little pocket bibles with the gilt leaves," he said, "but the Hebrew reads thus—" The Scots wanted to see "the great Idol of England, the Service Book"[52] overthrown and replaced and were not to be entertained by displays of learning or dialectical skill. They were shocked to discover that the Assembly had no power to initiate ideas but only to discuss Church reform as Parliament directed—a typical English and Erastian plan, which they tried to circumvent by creating a mixed Committee of members of both Assembly and Parliament to plan out a programme of Church reform.[53]

In secular politics they had already taken action by adding to the prolific London press their own newspaper, *The Scottish Dove*. This weekly messenger from the ark carried in its beak an olive branch and a scroll inscribed "Holy Innocency is blessed." Within, the news was retailed from the Covenanters' point of view, but their power to dominate English politics would depend first and foremost on their military strength.

While the details of the military agreement were concluded

at Westminster, the Government in Edinburgh took measures to prevent any Royalist movement inside Scotland. The Solemn League and Covenant was to be taken throughout the land, signed by the men, solemnly sworn by illiterate women. In Stirling, where difficulties were anticipated, three troops of horse accompanied the documents. Noticeable protest occurred only in the Gordon country round Aberdeen; Huntly, the bewildered and bankrupt Gordon chief, did nothing, but Sir John Gordon of Haddo published the King's denunciation of the new Covenant and urged his clansmen to withhold their signatures. Argyll had, however, fatally divided the Gordons by winning to his party Huntly's popular eldest son, Lord Gordon. This young man, son of Argyll's sister, and no favourite with his own father, signed the Covenant himself and entered Aberdeen with a hundred horse; active, gracious and more beloved of the clan than his haughty father he brought over to the Covenant most of the neighbouring gentry.[54]

Hamilton made a last effort to rally the King's friends, but the Royalists had no confidence in his loyalty or his judgment. Their more daring leaders, Montrose and Ogilvie, had gone to Oxford; Huntly had shown himself useless against his Covenanting son. The Royalists decided that they could not rise, as things now stood, and Hamilton, in considerable perturbation of spirit, left to report his failure at Oxford, while the irrepressible Presbyterian matron, his mother, raised men from his lands for the Covenanting army.[55] A French envoy, despatched hurriedly to Scotland by Harcourt to see if he could prevent the war from spreading, came back with gloomy tidings. The Scots were no longer interested in the traditional friendship with France; they believed obstinately but wrongly that the French wished to help the King, and the veteran Protestant warrior Lord Leven, intoxicated by the prospect of a Protestant crusade, spoke of joining the French Huguenots, after the Papists had been quelled in England, and of overthrowing the Pope.[56]

It was typical of the Covenanting mind to combine this

soaring fanaticism with attention to practical details. Future plans were visionary but immediate arrangements were crystal clear. Towards the end of November the military bargain was concluded: the Scots would send into England eighteen thousand foot and two thousand horse, with a proportionate train of artillery. The English would pay this army for the duration of the war and make no peace that did not include the Scots.[57]

During all these negotiations, John Pym had been gravely ill; unable to eat he was wasting fast, slept little, and often fainted for weariness. He still attended Parliament, still worked with all his failing strength to create and cement the Scots alliance which was finally concluded in Edinburgh on November 23rd. On the same day a Parliamentary ship came into Leith with the first instalment of the promised pay—money which could not have been found but for Pym's untiring financial dexterity. A fortnight later, at seven in the evening of December 8th, 1643, he died.

The Cavaliers at once asserted that like King Herod he had been "eaten of worms"; the Parliamentarians, more plausibly, claimed that he died of overwork. But the post-mortem, signed by Theodore de Mayerne, the most famous doctor in London, and six others, makes it clear that his illness was cancer of the lower bowel.[58] After lying in state for two days he was buried with solemnity in Westminster Abbey. The Scots, who condemned funeral sermons as remnants of Popery, refused to attend.[59] Before the stricken Parliament men, Stephen Marshall preached with mournful eloquence on the passing of this " master workman, labouring to repair our ruinous house." His life, he said, had been spent in the public service; it was " his meat and drink, his work, his exercise, his recreation, his pleasure, his ambition, his all: what he was, was only to promote the public good: in and for this he lived; in and by this he died." [60]

John Pym died as reticently as he had lived, and Stephen Marshall's sermon remains the fullest personal account of him left to posterity. In the last three years of his life he effected, by his policy in Parliament, constitutional changes which permanently bridled the prerogative and altered the course of English history. In the last eighteen months of his life, by his management of Parliament, by his attention to the finances of the war and by his resolution to involve the Scots, he created the conditions for the King's ultimate defeat. But this man, one of the great architects of Parliamentary government, remains personally unknown to us. His private letters are too scanty to reveal his nature. An anonymous painter gives him an alert, smiling face which tells little; engravers endowed him with a crafty leer, which might be revealing if it did not in all likelihood arise from the clumsiness of the artist. His career shows him to have had phenomenal energy, persistence and political perspicacity, to have been a dexterous man of affairs and to have had unusual powers of persuasion and leadership. He wrote his political genius into the substance of English history; that is all that we can with certainty know about him.

When Pym died, the defeat of Parliament in the field might still have destroyed the constitutional changes that he had wrought. He had taken the measures, financial, military and Parliamentary, which made victory possible, but he left to his successors the task of winning it. Three of them for the next critical years carried on his work: Oliver St. John, Harry Vane, Oliver Cromwell.

St. John, the solicitor general, was generally regarded as Pym's successor in the Commons. He was also the friend and mouthpiece of Oliver Cromwell, who necessarily had to be absent from Westminster on the more urgent business of war. This able lawyer, who had first commanded public attention when he had defended Hampden in the Ship-money case, had worked with John Pym for three busy years in Parliament, and before that on the board of the Providence company. His interests and his family connections linked him to that group whose members, among whom Warwick and Saye were now the chief, combined Puritanism with ambition for the growth of English colonial power in the teeth of Spain. Only a few weeks before Pym died, amid all the troubles of war, a new committee had been set up to guard the interests of the English in the West Indies and especially in the Caribbean Sea where the earliest ventures of the Providence company had so recently ended in disaster, and where at this time Captain Jackson with three ships authorised by the Earl of Warwick was operating against the Spaniards. Vane and Cromwell were also on the Committee for the overseas ventures of the English; [61] differences might ultimately divide the successors of John Pym, but all were like him and like each other in the intensity of their belief in the righteousness and the value of colonial expansion against Spain.

St. John's legal knowledge and his acute, argumentative intellect served his party well, but he was not generally liked. " Of a dark and clouded countenance, very proud, and conversant with few but those of his own humour and inclination " he was not the man who could take over John Pym's persuasive tasks of leadership.[62] Very different was his principal colleague in the House, young Sir Harry Vane. He was to be called " young " for many years to distinguish him from his father, old Sir Harry. But at this time he was still young, being just thirty. Son of a court official and brought up in that elegant and knowing society, Vane retained throughout his life the graceful manners he had learnt as a youth, and in points where his heart was not deeply touched he was ingenious at finding expedients and managing men. But where his religious sensibilities were involved he could be uncompromising to the point of fanaticism, and when he saw, or thought he saw, some precious goal to be attained, he could be wonderfully unscrupulous about the means. As a child he had been gay and, as he put it, " given to good fellowship," but religion and reformation came upon him at the age of fifteen, and thereafter, to the dismay of his worldly family, he followed the inner light of the spirit into whatever embarrassing scrapes it might, and did, lead him. " I will never do anything, by God's good grace," he had written to his father during his early troubles, " which both with honour and a good conscience I may not justify or be content most willingly to suffer for." He continued in this frame of mind for the rest of his life. But he was more speculative, more intellectual, in many ways more tolerant than the generality of Puritans. A man of great reading with a restless, inquiring mind, tormented by doubt, open to new ideas, he seemed to his critics changeable and dishonest, but his friends knew him for a sincere seeker after a perpetually elusive truth. As a Parliamentary leader he had the social charm and persuasive manner that blunt Cromwell and forbidding St. John lacked, and he was an admirable speaker, cool, clear and rational. Though his irregular features, large nose and pale prominent eyes were not attractive, his face, when he was speaking, was transfigured by an earnest animation, and his fair, fashionably curled hair and well-groomed figure gave him a distinguished and pleasing presence.[63]

Vane had secured the Scots alliance although the Covenanters knew that his religious sympathies were not wholly with them. They knew that St. John and Cromwell were even less of their mind. But for the moment the essential, alike for Covenanters and for Parliamentarians, was to win the war.

IV

Victory seemed a long way off. The fleet, pulled in all directions by the operations of the West Country Royalists and the Dunkirkers, could neither protect London's merchant shipping nor prevent the transport of troops from Ireland. The Parliamentary forces in the Midlands were too weak to stop Lord Byron from marching towards Cheshire to clear a way for the Irish troops towards Oxford.[64] Not long after, elated with the divisions and despondency of the enemy, the Marquis of Newcastle tried to bribe Colonel Hutchinson to surrender

Nottingham Castle. "It had been an employment more be-seeming you," Hutchinson replied, "to come with ten thousand armed men to assault our well-defended walls, than with so many pieces of contemned gold, to lay your siege against an honest heart." The answer was crushing in its lofty nobility, but the very making of the offer indicated the weakness of the Parliamentary party.[65]

Early in December Hopton, advancing with some difficulty over muddy roads where his guns slipped and sank, had out-flanked Waller and reached Sussex. This was serious, not only because of the ultimate threat to London, but because Parliament drew the bulk of its armaments from the iron foundries of the Sussex Weald. Between Pym's death and funeral Hopton made himself master of the formidable fortress of Arundel. He had left a contingent under Lord Crawford to keep watch on Waller at Alton. Crawford, short of liquor, and also, it would seem, short of prudence, sent to Waller for a runlet of wine, promising a fat ox in return. Waller sent the wine but Crawford refused the ox, and challenged Waller to fetch it if he dared. Waller, who had used this exchange of pleasantries to take stock of Crawford's position, attacked at once. Crawford was crimin-ally unprepared and slipped off with the cavalry, leaving the infantry to fend for themselves. One young officer, Captain Bowles, and his men made a heroic stand in Alton Church, fight-ing from barricades across the nave until Bowles was killed under the Chancel arch and the survivors surrendered.[66] But the town and all within fell an easy prey. Waller took more than five hundred prisoners of whom at least a hundred re-enlisted in his forces. The rest were sent to London and marched through the streets in token of a much-needed and much-advertised victory.

The road to Sussex was now clear. Wilmot, sent off with some of the Oxford cavalry to hold Waller in play, failed to detain him, and the Parliamentarians, heartened by success and spoil, swept down into Sussex on Hopton's track. In a sea of mud and a downpour of rain, they drove the Cavaliers out of

Arundel town and penned them into the Castle. In the harbour at Arundel they stopped a Flemish vessel bound for Spain carrying among other cargo a painting of the marriage of Saint Ursula which had been commissioned for a church in Seville. This, in spite of the protests of more intelligent Parliamentarians, was for a time exhibited in London as a picture of King Charles and Queen Henrietta making a gift of England to the Pope.[67]

At Oxford, the King's further policy took shape. The Hamilton brothers arrived from Scotland in the third week of December and were instantly, to their great surprise, arrested. For Scottish advice the King now consulted Montrose, Ogilvie and Huntly's younger, loyalist son Aboyne. They had implored him to withdraw his confidence from Hamilton, and on inquiry had produced enough evidence to justify the arrest. Charles refused even to see Hamilton, though he could not unhappily reverse his elevation to a dukedom, an honour which he had given him early in the summer in the confident belief that he would prevent the Scots from entering the war. Hamilton was hurried away to safe-keeping at Bristol, but his younger brother escaped in disguise, fled to London and openly joined the Covenanters. " God did not only rescue him from the power of his enemies but from those ways also wherein he had walked all too long," said his new pious friends.[68]

The Earl of Antrim who arrived from Ireland, alight with enthusiasm, in the same week as the Hamiltons had a joyful welcome in Oxford. With his customary ingenuity and luck, he had escaped from his Scottish captors in Ulster, looked in on the Confederate Irish at Kilkenny, offered to command all the forces they sent to England, and now announced himself at Oxford as General in Chief of the Irish. Not until some months later did it become apparent that the Confederates had given him no such appointment.[69] Whatever additional powers he believed himself to possess, he was incontrovertibly chief of the Irish Macdonalds and in these winter weeks he had the King's encouragement to organise with Montrose the junction of his

people with their persecuted clansmen of the Islands and Highlands of Scotland for a general rising against Argyll, the Campbells
and the Covenant. In this movement Montrose hoped that the
discouraged Royalists from other parts of Scotland would
ultimately join and, in time perhaps, Huntly and the Gordons.

The King's military plans seemed ever more openly to
justify the accusation of his opponents that he employed Papists,
Irish and men of violence; but in his civil policy he stood forth
as the defender of national integrity and of the law.

He had not been successful in retaining the framework of the
law on his side. He had failed to have the law term adjourned
to Oxford although the Great Seal of the realm and its Keeper,
Edward Littleton, were with him. In November 1643, just
before Pym's death, Parliament after long debate had at last
decided to put a Great Seal of their own into use and to annul
all commissions under that other Seal which had been " secretly
and perfidiously conveyed away." [70] But the King, in December,
struck an answering blow. Profiting by Pym's death and the
dislike which he believed many of his original supporters felt
for the Scots alliance and the new Covenant, he issued a proclamation, suggested of course by the politic Edward Hyde, denouncing
the Scottish alliance and calling on all members of Parliament to
abandon the evil junto at Westminster who had sold England to
the Scots and to join him at Oxford in a free Parliament. To all
those who had offended him he offered a " free and general
pardon . . . that all the world may see how willing and desirous
we are to forget the injuries and indignities offered to us, and
by a Union of English hearts to prevent the lasting miseries,
which this foreign invasion must bring upon this Kingdom." [71]
Expulsion, desertion and absence had already thinned the House
of Commons to an average sitting of less than two hundred out
of the original six hundred members; the House of Lords was
in even more pitiable plight with an attendance of fifteen or a
score. The King could summon a better House of Lords from
his own following, and he could make shift to raise a House of

Commons not far inferior to that at Westminster. Such a rival
Parliament at Oxford might become a serious competitor to its
other half at Westminster. In theory, at least, Charles would
have brought the shattered sovereignty of King, Lords and
Commons together once more.

While preparations were made for the opening of Parliament
in Oxford, the King was playing once more with the idea of a
plot. It had started with the overtures of one Thomas Ogle,
made through Digby's father, the Earl of Bristol, who suggested
that the Independents might be won over to the King for fear
of the Scots and Presbyterians. He believed such men as Philip
Nye and the influential preacher Thomas Goodwin would agree
to the return of the Bishops and the triumph of the Church
provided only some measure of toleration for the sects was
allowed. Restive London, it was argued, only wanted peace,
and numerous influential city men would certainly support any
strong movement in that direction. Sir Basil Brook, ardent
Royalist and Roman Catholic, would assist, though as he was
in prison his help would be rather limited, and the goldsmith
Violet, an old go-between whom the Court had used, would
carry the King's letters to his city friends. There was hope of
support from the newly elected Lord Mayor, Sir John Wollaston.
The Governor of Aylesbury, Colonel Mosley, undertook to
surrender Aylesbury as soon as the time was ripe. Most helpful
of all, Parliament's scout-master general, Riley, joined the
conspirators, offering some hope of widespread desertion from
the Parliamentary armies. On the surface the conspiracy promised
even better than Waller's plot of the previous June. Beneath the
surface all was hollow, for Mosley was deceiving not Parliament,
but the King, and everything that went through his hands was
reported to Westminster.[72]

London, sunk in glum depression, seemed once again ripe
for trouble. No public plays, no bear baiting, scarcely even a
puppet-show; an occasional depressed procession of prisoners;
no Court, hardly any nobility; a hanging or so—another

Catholic priest, Father Bell, and a Royalist spy—to vary the usual diet of thieves; for economy's sake "no Lord Mayor's show, only a dinner"; a weekly fast imposed by Parliament every Wednesday, and another one kept by good Anglicans and defiant Royalists every Friday; to crown all, house to house searches for deserters from the army. Here the new Lord Mayor intervened, protesting that he would not be answerable for the good order of the City until this senseless pressure stopped, and the London deserters from Waller's forces were allowed to resume their useful civilian lives.[73]

With London in this unhappy mood, the first dispute arose between Parliament and the Scots Commissioners. They were shocked to discover that their English allies proposed to suspend business on Christmas Day. The Parliamentary leaders, anxious to preserve good relations, gave in at once and proclaimed that Christmas was to be regarded in the Presbyterian fashion as an ordinary working day. But the English divines of the West-minster Assembly, some of whom had already prepared their Christmas sermons, were not to be browbeaten. They deeply pained their Scottish colleagues by closing the session and preaching to their flocks in and about London as though no Godly Calvinist reformation had taken place.[74]

On January 3rd, 1644, the Covenanters were more profoundly disturbed by the action of several independent ministers. Led by Thomas Goodwin and Philip Nye they published and presented to Parliament an *Apologetical Narration* in which they gently repudiated the extravagances of the wilder sectaries and argued that their congregational churches were nearer to the practice of the early Christians, and more suited to the mutability of the times than the Presbyterian parochial system.[75] The Independents were a minority in the Westminster Assembly and this move was cleverly designed to bring their point of view before Parliament and the public, without risking a debate and vote in the Assembly itself where they would have been out-argued and out-numbered.

Unhappily for them, the publication of their plea coincided with the unmasking of the King's recent machinations to join with the Independents and the Royalists in the City for the overthrow of Parliament. The plot had been betrayed from within at the critical moment. Oliver St. John denounced the conspiracy as " a seditious and jesuitical practice and design, under the specious pretence of peace, to have rent the Parliament from the City, and the City from Parliament . . . thereby to have rendered up both Parliament and City to the designs of the enemy . . . the destruction and nulling of this present Parliament was intended, as likewise the engaging ourselves in a Treaty of Peace without the advice or consent of our brethren of Scotland." In plainer terms, the Royalist plot followed the design of Waller's earlier attempt: demands for peace in London were to coincide with the King's calling of Parliament to Oxford, the maturing of Ogle's plan for an agreement with the Independents, and the advance of Rupert through Aylesbury to London.[76]

The plot, generally called Brook's Plot, though Sir Basil Brook had hardly been its architect, ended with the arrest of the principals, and was chiefly notable for the suspicion it cast on the Independents. Very few had been personally involved, though the King, on Ogle's advice, had offered a royal chaplaincy to Philip Nye, and Ogle himself had approached Thomas Goodwin. It was not surprising, therefore, that when these two presented their *Apologetical Narration* to Parliament, the Covenanters saw their action as an integral part of Sir Basil Brook's " very wicked plot " to bring the war to an end with an understanding between the Prelatists and the Independents.[77]

Vane and St. John had much ado to quiet the suspicions and retain the friendship of the Scots Commissioners while the Lord Mayor, Sir John Wollaston, strove to smother the suspicions which his own conduct had aroused by offering a banquet— austere but dignified—to Parliament and the Scots Commissioners, adding as a suitable diversion for his guests a bonfire of idolatrous pictures, books and rosaries in Cheapside.[78] The Londoners bowed again to the expensive pressure of the war. Stephen Marshall tried to hearten the mulcted citizens to further efforts with praise for what had been done: " the Lord hath given thee great wealth and estate; grudge not to lay it out in His cause though there go pound after pound, and thousand after thousand, and regiment after regiment." [79]

By this time the army of the Solemn League and Covenant was ready to march. Old Lord Leven was in command; his cavalry general was David Leslie, another soldier trained in the Swedish service; the artillery—sixty cannon—was under Alexander Hamilton, commonly called " dear Sandy " and famous for having assisted the great Gustavus in his experiments with light artillery.[80] The minister and a lay elder from each regiment formed a council to care for the spiritual welfare of the troops and the tending of the sick. Swearing, plunder and the keeping of whores were forbidden; so were irreverent or impertinent references to the King (for these troops were not rebels but His Majesty's true subjects acting for his own good). The whole army " shall live together as friends and brethren, abstaining from words of disgrace, contempt or reproach, giving of lies, and all provocation by word or gesture."[81] The nobility of aspiration and unity of purpose of the Covenanting force compelled admiration.

Over roads choked with snow the Scots army marched from Dunbar to Berwick, which the Marquis of Newcastle had taken no steps to secure against them. Here Argyll joined it, as colonel of his own regiment, and composed a manifesto to the English Royalists in the North, urging them to join with the incoming Scots against the " popish and prelatical faction " and to rescue " His Majesty's person and honour so unhappily entangled in the counsels of those whose actions speak their ends to be little better than popery and tyranny." [82] The message was received with derision but it was composed with sincerity. Argyll, and most of those with him, truly believed that they were redeeming their misled King from error. Legally, too, their position was stronger than that of the Parliament men. The Council in Edinburgh which had authorised the alliance was in sober truth the Council appointed by the King, and the writs for raising the troops had, thanks to the extraordinary behaviour of Lanark, gone out under the King's official signet. Charles had not authorised his English subjects to rebel; but he had, by one accident after another, commissioned his Scots subjects to do so.

From Oxford, Prince Rupert immediately sent Sir Charles Lucas, the best cavalry officer he could spare, with two thousand men, to help the Marquis of Newcastle in the defence of the North. But Newcastle had wanted Byron to join him and was angry that so many of the Midland forces had been detached instead to fortify Chester and meet the new auxiliaries from Ireland.[83]

In the South, the Royalist advance into Sussex had ended in the rain and mud at Arundel. Cut off without enough food or water, the Royalists in the Castle repelled one severe assault from Waller's men, only to surrender a few days later. Waller took over all their arms and as many of their men as would re-enlist with him.[84]

Among his prisoners was William Chillingworth, the gentle and judicious author of The Religion of Protestants, that tolerant defence of the Church of England which in the tranquil days of peace had so much pleased the King. He was a dying man after the hardships of the siege, and a Puritan divine, Francis Cheynell, asked permission to look after him in Chichester, thus sparing him the long, cold journey to London. There followed a sinister little farce. Cheynell cared conscientiously for the bodily wants of the prisoner but was resolved to save his soul before he died. Day after day he harried him to deny the wicked statement made in his book, that Turks and Papists were not excluded from salvation. Chillingworth remained wearily firm in his generous beliefs; it was not for him, he said, to absolve or to condemn his fellow men. When death put an end to the relentless catechism, Cheynell paid for a seemly funeral, with cakes and wine and

CHARLES, PRINCE OF WALES
by William Dobson

The Pourtraicture of his Excellency Sr: Thomas Farfax Generall of all the English forces for the Seruice of ye: two houses of Parliament.

Guill. Faithorne Sculp.

SIR THOMAS FAIRFAX
from an engraving by William Faithorne

sprigs of rosemary for those who came and new gloves for the pall-bearers. But he refused to honour Chillingworth's wish to be buried in Chichester Cathedral, and had him laid " in the cloisters amongst the old shavelings, monks and priests of whom he had so good an opinion all his life." He stopped the reading of the Anglican service over the body, and as the coffin was lowered into the grave, he cast in with it a copy of *The Religion of Protestants* saying: " Get thee gone, thou corrupt, rotten book, earth to earth and dust to dust: get thee gone into the place of rottenness, that thou mayest rot with thy author and see corruption." This done, he marched into the Cathedral and delivered a sermon on the text " Let the dead bury their dead, but go thou and preach the Kingdom of God." [85]

The check at Alton and the fall of Arundel put an end to the Royalist advance in the south-east and saved the Sussex iron foundries for Parliament. Hopton fell back to Winchester and found himself in uneasy dispute with Rupert's cavalry over assignments for food and supply. But now the winter came down with bitter and prolonged fury. For a week in mid-January snow fell continuously over all England. The Scots could not cross the border and Fairfax, who had left Yorkshire to intercept the King's auxiliaries from Ireland in the Welsh marches, was held up at Manchester.[86]

Bad weather, and the intolerable difficulties of finding room to live in Oxford, reduced the expected numbers of King Charles's Parliament, but on January 22nd, 1644, he opened it formally in Christ Church Hall; he had for a beginning just over a hundred members of the House of Commons, and about thirty peers including some recent creations, Prince Rupert, whom he had made Duke of Cumberland, and several other commanders. The King spoke with dignity; he expressed his regret for the inevitable disorders of his troops, and accused the Westminster Parliament of inviting " a foreign power to invade this Kingdom." For the rest, he called on them to " vindicate and preserve " their true religion, to restore his

"Honour and Rights, which ye find to have an inseparable relation with your own interests," and to secure and confirm "your liberties, properties and privileges, without which I would not be King."[87]

While the King addressed one part of Parliament at Oxford, the other part at Westminster voted the formal expulsion of their renegade colleagues. The Oxford Parliament began by doing all that Charles could wish. They addressed a reproachful message to the Earl of Essex to lay down arms and dutifully attend the Oxford House of Lords, and they proclaimed the Scots to be invaders. In this they were supported by an eloquent repudiation of their "traitrous countrymen" signed by Montrose and the other Scots peers in Oxford.[88]

In the midst of this successful political manœuvre the King received bad news. Lord Byron had gone to meet the infantry sent from Ireland. With the first contingent of these he tried to clear Cheshire of the King's enemies, perpetrated an inexcusable atrocity at the village of Barthomley where he smoked out and killed a number of civilians in the church, and then laid siege to Nantwich. Profiting by a hard frost he invested Nantwich on both sides of the frozen river Weaver, but on news of the approach of Fairfax, fearing a thaw, he began to reassemble his divided army on the night of January 23rd. Fairfax and the thaw came together early in the morning of January 24th and Byron found himself with his forces divided and even the ramshackle bridge over the river swept away by the suddenly rising water. While Byron's stranded forces marched six miles to the nearest crossing, Fairfax, who had joined with the local troops of Brereton, had time to take up an advantageous position. Byron found himself compelled to fight in enclosed ground where his cavalry was nearly useless. His infantry, outnumbered, and attacked in the rear from the town, surrendered almost to a man. He made off with his cavalry to the safety of Chester.[89] The captured infantry, government troops from Ireland, joined the Parliamentary colours; only a few protested, among them Colonel

George Monk. He had seen the King in Oxford and having undertaken to serve him did not feel it to be consistent with honour and honesty to change sides. He was sent prisoner to London where for more than two years, in a penurious imprisonment, he chewed over the problem of a soldier's duty and loyalty.[90]

The victorious Fairfax was not intemperately joyful. The report of the victory which he sent to his wife (endorsed " for yourself, dear heart.") was more full of his anxieties about quarrels between the Parliamentary officers than of his own success. He had spent a large part of his private resources on equipping and clothing his troops for the campaign, he was ill with cold and worry and wretchedly uncertain about the future.[91] His unwillingness to be elated by victory, and his stubborn refusal to be cast down by defeat, were the great strength of Fairfax. Certainly, he had captured a large contingent of the infantry from Ireland but more were on their way and the Parliamentary fleet could not always intercept them. Fairfax did not underestimate the strength of the Royalists in the field or count too hopefully on the help of the Scots for his own side. They had by now crossed the snow-bound border, but the Royalists were strong in the North, as Fairfax knew to his cost from his experiences in the last year. The Scots might not advance so rapidly as Parliament hoped; they might even be recalled to their own country if trouble should break out in their rear.

In Oxford the King, with Antrim and Montrose, planned that trouble should indeed break out in Scotland. By the end of January their plans were far advanced. Montrose was to raise troops in the north of England in sufficient force to cross the border; Antrim was to go to Kilkenny and despatch to him ten thousand Irish (this was his lavish estimate). These would join with the Highlanders whom Montrose hoped to raise and the Royalists of the Lowlands, to make a general combustion in Scotland.[92]

This cheering project, together with the King's ever increasing hopes that the Confederate Irish would send him troops, enabled him to accept the disaster at Nantwich with equanimity. But he was aware that his policy was inconsistent, and that his repeated asseverations of respect for the laws and devotion to the Protestant religion did not match with his intention to let loose, alike upon Scotland and England, the largest possible number of fighting Irish clansmen. He resolved the contradiction, to his own satisfaction, by concealing one-half of his projects from those councillors who would not have endorsed them. Edward Hyde, concerned with the King's civil policy and the management of the Oxford Parliament, had only an indirect, partial and uneasy knowledge of the plans for bringing over the Irish. " There is very much in that transaction . . . that you and I were never thought wise enough to be advised with in," he lamented later to Secretary Nicholas.[93] The careful Nicholas attended to the daily business of a Secretary of State, but it was his colleague Lord Digby who handled the affairs of Ireland. One other stumbling block to his Irish plans the King had also removed. Parliament had appointed the Earl of Leicester Lord Lieutenant of Ireland in succession to Strafford, Charles not being at that time strong enough to insist that it should be Ormonde. Leicester, an anxious colourless man, had obeyed the King's order not to go to Ireland and had been for the past year at Oxford, torn between his loyalty to the King and his acute disapproval of his policy. Charles now forced him to resign his Lord Lieutenancy and appointed Ormonde.[94]

Members of the Oxford Parliament, meanwhile, were growing more critical. In the overcrowded town, lodgings were cramped and expensive and the ordinary business of living was harassing and uncomfortable. Most of them disliked the atmosphere of violence and reckless gaiety generated by the war. They took too seriously the oaths, the insults, the drunkenness that they saw and heard and against which the King's favourite chaplains preached in vain. They believed the loose talk of professional soldiers who cheerfully predicted " this war well managed will last twenty years." The contemporary civil wars in Germany had lasted for twenty-five years, as they well knew; the French civil wars of the last century for longer still; the war against Spain in the Low Countries was in its eighth decade. Members of Parliament in Oxford shuddered at the horrid possibility that war in England too might become endemic. One Oxford grievance, at least, they remedied. Provost Marshall Smith, the brutal warden of the prisoners in Oxford Castle, was removed at their request.[95] But one member, Edward Dering, found a fortnight in Oxford as much as he could endure and fled to Westminster, penitent and bewildered, saying that he found the King's quarters full of Irish and Papists.[96]

The bitter feelings of Edward Dering were shared by an Irish visitor who had also come to Oxford that winter. Murrough O'Brien, Lord Inchiquin, was the only important Irish chieftain who had unswervingly and actively supported the English from the outbreak of the revolt. On the death of his father-in-law, Sir William St. Leger, Lord President of Munster, he had taken over the protection of the settlers and had conducted the war on his own countrymen with efficient ruthlessness for the last eighteen months. Representations had been made almost from the moment of St. Leger's death that Inchiquin be raised to the Presidency of Munster. He was a young man, ambitious and high tempered, and he looked for no lesser reward.[97]

But in Oxford he was coolly received. He found that to be a Protestant and loyal to the English Government was no passport to the King's favour. Lord Antrim, claiming to come from Kilkenny with a commission from the Confederate Irish, was the darling of the Court. For all Inchiquin's loyalty, his privations, dangers and exertions, no return was to be expected. The Presidency of Munster had been promised elsewhere. He went back to Ireland, as an observer in Oxford all too lightly reported, "as full of anger as his buttons will endure."[98]

V

All the winter, in the Parliamentary quarters, the rivalry between Waller and Essex was a source of anxiety. Now that Hampden and Pym were both gone, Essex had more active enemies than active friends in the House of Commons. His most assured supporter was Denzil Holles, and Holles, though one of the dozen most prominent men in Parliament, had not succeeded to unofficial leadership when Pym died. He had been too frequently and too deeply concerned with the various movements towards a negotiated peace. Vane and St. John, working together, managed the Commons and guided policy. Cromwell and Haslerig, when not with their troops, strongly supported them. All these were critical of, or inimical to, Essex. But Waller, though his shaken reputation had grown since he had saved the Sussex iron foundries for Parliament, could hardly be intruded into the chief command, and Essex remained deaf to the hints that were given him to resign.[99]

For Vane and St. John the first objective was to work out an efficient means of co-operating with the Scots for the conduct of the war. The best way was clearly by means of a Parliamentary Committee on which the Scots Commissioners would also sit. For the composition and the powers of this new Committee of both Kingdoms the Scots put their trust in Vane. They were anxious above all that the friends of Essex, of whom Holles was still the most influential, should be kept under control, for they feared alike the inefficiency of Essex and his leanings towards accommodation with the King. He was known to have little love for the Scots. On the old Committee of Safety, Holles was prominent, but during the last months the more urgent work of prosecuting the war had been taken over by the Council of War organised in the crisis of the past summer. This Council was no ordinary Committee of Parliament because it had in it representatives of the army who were not necessarily members of either House. In the same way, the new Committee of Both Kingdoms would consist of the Scots Commissioners working with members of Parliament to organise the conduct of the war. Like the Council of War, this new Committee was to be an executive as well as an advisory body; it would give orders to the generals in the field. Parliament in fact delegated its responsibility to it.

The ordinance which bestowed so great an authority and which nominated the members of the Committee did not get through Parliament without some skilful manœuvring from Sir Harry Vane. It was drawn up and passed first by the Lords, Northumberland giving it strong support. As his lands in the North were now largely occupied by the Scots, it was natural that he should wish to be on good terms with them. The Lords further nominated to the Committee Vane, St. John, Cromwell and eleven others; they significantly omitted Denzil Holles, who was the only effective friend left to the Earl of Essex among the leaders of the Commons, and who still showed some inclination towards a negotiated peace.

In the Commons, however, Vane and his friends (like Pym before them) had only fluctuating support. The bill was rejected, partly because it came from the Lords, partly because of genuine doubts about the composition of the Committee. Vane and St. John therefore flattered the Commons with the initiation of a new bill to the same purpose which, after persuasion and argument had been applied, differed scarcely at all from the one that had been rejected. In the interim Essex had become aware that the new Committee as appointed would be hostile to him and had worked up a party in the Lords to oppose it. But it proved too illogical for the Lords to oppose a bill so like the one they had themselves drawn up only a few days earlier. They passed it and the Committee of Both Kingdoms came into being without Denzil Holles among its members.[100]

Of the Scots Commissioners on the new Committee by far the strongest personality was John, Lord Maitland. He was twenty-eight years old, but of that heavy physical type which settles fast into middle-age. His quickness of mind, ripe legal knowledge and good judgment made him such a spokesman as the Covenanters most needed in England and his Scots colleagues looked up to him with a wary respect.

Derby House was selected as the offices of the new Committee and was made ready for their sessions with hangings borrowed from one of the King's vacant palaces.[101] Its troubles in the management of the war began almost immediately. Waller had prevented the King from taking possession of Sussex, and Fairfax had stopped one large contingent from Ireland, but others poured in: seasoned troops with two years' experience in a dangerous war. Received at Chester by Byron, they were sent on to Shrewsbury to stiffen the new levies that Rupert was collecting there from Wales.[102] Fairfax, after his initial victory at Nantwich, could do no more to check them; he was needed in Yorkshire to hinder the Marquis of Newcastle in his operations against the invading Scots. The Committee of Both Kingdoms commanded him, on his way back, to take order against the Cavaliers in Lancashire. The godly garrison at Liverpool were apprehensive of Royalist vessels patrolling the northern Irish Sea. The Countess of Derby, whose husband had gone to the Isle of Man, which showed signs of revolt, had made the family stronghold of Lathom House a terror to the country round; her garrison raided, blackmailed and carried off for ransom those of the region whose loyalty they doubted.[103] Fairfax called on her to surrender, but behind her double ring of fortifications, with stores, arms and a devoted garrison, she defied him. Fairfax, entrusting further operations to Alexander Rigby, the Member of Parliament for Wigan, moved on into Yorkshire, while the massive, indomitable lady held her own, immobilising a large part of the Lancashire forces for several months to come.[104]

After the high hopes of January, a new run of disasters for

Parliament came in February and March. In the mud and floods which followed the January snowfall, the Scots reached New-castle confident of an easy capture and were repelled. A large part of their force was henceforward locked up in the siege, getting little or no help from the surrounding county, dependent on sea-borne supplies from Scotland and very short of fodder for the horses. Their quarters at Corbridge were successfully raided and many prisoners taken by Sir Marmaduke Langdale, the lean, hard, formidable Yorkshire Royalist whose flying cavalry next attacked the elder Fairfax at Pomfret and dis-comfited the troops he was gathering to join with the Coven-anters.[105] By the end of February it was clear that the Scots were at a standstill and the Londoners would get no Newcastle coal that winter.

In the Midlands, Sir John Meldrum had assembled the local forces for Parliament and gone against Newark with great preparations, intending to drive out the Royalists and break their line of communication with their forces in the North. The Royalist commander at Newark was Sir Richard Byron, younger brother of Lord Byron, who had already shown himself a faithful, active and capable soldier; but he had anxious work before him in heartening the garrison and steadying the towns-folk. Meldrum for his part, though troubled by the quarrels and insubordination of the local gentry under his command, was well supplied by the surrounding country, while the Committee of Both Kingdoms, to satisfy the Scots, supported his design and directed their other commanders to do so.[106]

At Westminster murmurs of discontent against the Scots grew even louder. Two months after their much advertised, much subsidised army had crossed the border, the town of Newcastle was still in the King's hands and the Royalists still dominant in the North. " Our friends are sad, our enemies speak and write contemptuously," wrote Dr. Baillie, and added " our eyes are towards the Lord."[107] The prolix debates of the Westminster Assembly bored and exasperated him, and the actions of the Independent ministers perturbed him almost as much as those of the enemy. Fearing the imposition of a Presbyterian system, they delayed agreement on every possible point. A group of them, nearly all New England men—bold spirits who had travelled farther and seen more than most of their colleagues—opposed barriers of argument to every decision. The "malapert rashness" of men like Hugh Peter was harmful, Dr. Baillie felt, in civil as well as in religious affairs. Philip Nye had the effrontery to declare that the Scottish plan for a National Assembly of the Church was a danger to the civil power. He was declared out of order, but the attack had been delivered, which was what chiefly mattered to Nye.[108] The Independents had a valuable ally in John Selden, who had no great interest in their views but delighted to score legal points "to humble the *jure divino*-ship of presbytery." He stung the Scots to fury by coolly announcing that certain practices they wished to reform were still an unrepealed part of the English law, and "we have sworn to protect the laws of the Kingdom."[109]

The fissure, as Scots and English both knew, was political as well as religious. The Covenanters believed in a monolithic state where civil and ecclesiastical power moved majestically as one; the Independents, whose views in and out of the Assembly, or in and out of Parliament, were increasingly popular, believed in a loosely articulated state where men would be free to follow their own choice in religion, and would (it was hoped) strive for godliness, without an organised Church. The Scots, as the astute Venetian secretary reported home, saw grave danger to themselves in this new "democratic force of a nation which has always been inimical to them."[110] The triumph of Independency in England might easily undermine the Presbyterian system in Scotland.

But on Sunday, March 24th, 1644, the disputes of the allies were hushed in a stunned silence before the appalling news that Meldrum, out-generalled before the walls of Newark, had sued for terms to Prince Rupert. He had given up all his firearms, four thousand muskets, as many pistols, all his ammunition, and thirty cannon. Many of his men had joined the Royalists. He himself with a bare two thousand "naked foot" had been allowed to retreat to Hull. So had ended the design of Parliament to make sure of Newark: their arms and money lost, their army disarmed, reduced, abashed and out of action, their supporters discouraged, and the Royalists entrenched triumphant across the road to the North.[111]

The Committee of Both Kingdoms met on the Sabbath day. This was no time for godly scruples. Troops and arms were diverted from Waller in the South to Essex who alone could keep open the northern approaches to London. The Lord Mayor was ordered to lay in stores and provide for rationing; shortage might soon become famine; a siege was possible. "It has much wakened the hearts of many to draw near to God"; poor Dr. Baillie tried to console himself with the thought, aware of the angry, reproachful disillusionment which surrounded him and his colleagues.[112]

An appeal from the King to save Newark had reached Rupert at Chester where he was alternately arranging for the reception of the Irish and recruiting troops from Wales. Pursued by further confused and contradictory messages from his uncle, he had left the city on March 12th, drawn a picked force of musketeers newly come from Ireland out of Shrewsbury, joined on his way with re-inforcements from the Midlands and the North, and was eight miles south of Newark at Bingham, by March 20th—an interval of time so short for the gathering of a large army that Meldrum dismissed the report of his approach as unworthy of belief until it was too late for him to make adequate dispositions.[113]

Rupert, who was anxious to damage Meldrum as well as to relieve Newark, marched on by moonlight, doubling the speed of his vanguard when his scouts reported that Meldrum was drawing off. But Meldrum was merely withdrawing his foot and guns into the strongly fortified husk of a burnt-out mansion just to the north of the town, called the Spittal. Behind the Spittal a bridge of boats over the Trent linked it to the large flat island which flanks the town on the north-west. Rupert kept well to the south of the town, then at the village of Balderton turned sharply to the north, thus putting himself between the town and Meldrum's probable line of retreat into Lincolnshire.

Just before nine o'clock on March 21st, 1644, from the brow of Beacon Hill, Rupert and his advance guard looked down on Newark, with Meldrum's guns and infantry in the Spittal, his cavalry massed before it. Rupert attacked at once, confident that the splendid cavalry he had with him could easily engage the opposing force until the rest of his army came up. Though Meldrum's cavalry counter-charged with formidable vigour, his confidence in his own men was justified, and soon Meldrum's broken horse were fleeing across the bridge of boats behind the Spittal into the island beyond. Meldrum was now surrounded on all three landward sides of the Spittal, though he still had egress by the bridge of boats to the island, and he had placed a guard at Muskham Bridge on the farther side of the island to ensure his communications with the outer world. But at this juncture the garrison from Newark sallied into the island and cut off, overpowered and scattered the guard at Muskham Bridge. By nine in the evening Meldrum found himself entirely surrounded, without room to manoeuvre and with food for two or three days at most. By speed, surprise and a rapid seizure of every advantage, Rupert had achieved a brilliant victory.

But he could not afford to linger, for the various contingents of his army, hurriedly drawn together, could not be spared for long and when Meldrum offered to treat he conceded that he might march away, leaving his arms and guns behind. More ruthless terms might have provoked the enemy to a delaying resistance which Rupert could not afford.

The terms were not so well respected as they should have been; the Royalist cavalry joyfully broke ranks and galloped to plunder the disarmed and retreating foe. Order was restored at least where Rupert himself was present; as he had done at Bristol he beat off his unruly men and with his own hand returned to one of the Parliamentary officers the colours which had been wrongfully snatched from him.[114]

The noise of the victory spread fast through the region. As Meldrum's men straggled towards Hull, the Parliamentary commanders rapidly evacuated Lincoln, Gainsborough and Sleaford. At Nottingham the austere Colonel Hutchinson strengthened his defences and stood resolute to defend the town to the last.[115]

At Oxford bells rang out and bonfires blazed for Prince Rupert's triumph. " The courtier, the scholar, indeed people of all ages, all sexes, all faculties (unite) in congratulating your happy success," wrote one of his agents in the city. King and Court " all on this side idolatry " with one voice praised his achievements and predicted that he would save the North, discomfit the Scots and carry his uncle's cause to a final and brilliant victory.[116] The relief of Newark was the most impressive feat of arms that he had yet performed; in thirty more years of arduous service, by sea and land, he would never again achieve a stroke so dexterous, so economical and so well-timed. It was his greatest hour, and he was fortunate because he did not know it.

CHAPTER THREE

THE NORTH AND THE WEST

March—October 1644

AT Oxford, hope soared. If the Cavaliers could break Waller in the South, as Meldrum had been broken in the Midlands, there would remain only the North and the war was as good as won.[1]

Waller's forces lay for the most part in Hampshire in the region south of the Winchester-London road. The Royalists who dominated the road itself from their garrisons at Winchester and Basing House now converged threateningly towards him. On March 27th, 1644, Lord Forth, bringing reinforcements from Oxford, joined Hopton near Alresford; with the cavalry, under Wilmot, last year's victor of Roundway Down, they had about five thousand foot and three thousand horse.[2]

Waller's anxieties during the past weeks had been increased by the desertion of one of his principal officers. Sir Richard Grenvile, younger brother of Sir Bevil, had been among the first of Ormonde's troops to be sent over from Ireland; captured at Liverpool, he had offered his sword to Parliament. Since he was an experienced professional soldier they had employed him, although his record as a wild fellow, whose wife had separated from him and who had been in trouble with the law on charges of libel and manslaughter, was no recommendation to the godly. Grenvile himself had no more laudable motive than that of securing arrears of pay owed to him for his Irish service. After campaigning with Waller through the winter in Hampshire and

Sussex, he rode to the King at Oxford early in March with thirty troopers, six hundred pounds of Parliament's money and a coach and six. He also brought information of Waller's strength and the details of a plot to betray Basing House. From Oxford he issued a statement cynically repudiating the masters he had betrayed; the Londoners replied by hanging him in effigy.[3]

Waller had to abandon further hope of taking Basing House and watch with concern the challenging movements of Hopton, Forth and Wilmot along Alresford ridge. His difficulties were threefold increased by an order he had just received to send most of his cavalry, under the veteran Balfour, to stiffen the army of Essex and secure the northern approaches to London. Once the cavalry was gone, he would be too weak to risk a general engagement and he hesitated between the advisability of fighting at once while he still had Balfour, or of not fighting at all.[4] On the night of Wednesday, March 27th, he had taken up a position near the village of Hinton Ampner which lies athwart a little river in a marshy bottom, overlooked by the long ridge of Alresford. The Royalists from the village of Alresford commanded the ridge and their advance posts, running down towards the valley under cover of hedges and scattered copses, were in some places within earshot of Waller's sentries.

On the morning of Friday, March 29th, a forlorn hope drawn from the London regiments advanced on the Royalist outpost in Cheriton wood, but were driven back by heavy firing. As they retreated, a part of the Royalist cavalry, without waiting for orders, charged down upon them. Haslerig, who had seen enough Royalist cavalry charges on Roundway Down to last him a lifetime, for a moment wavered, but bold Colonel Birch cheered him with a phrase from the bowling green: " Sir, this is but a rub; we shall yet win the cast." At this Haslerig led his men on, and broke in on the Royalist flank. Seeing their friends in difficulties with Haslerig's men, the rest of the Royalist cavalry came to their help and was soon dangerously involved in narrow lanes where they could not manœuvre. While the cavalry was thus entangled, Waller's infantry, with methodical resolution, fought their way uphill towards Alresford ridge, forcing back the King's men from hedge to hedge. Fearing for the stores in Alresford, Lord Forth ordered the evacuation of the little town, which he fired at both ends of its long straggling high street.

Balfour now supported Waller's action by a cavalry charge which finally routed the opposing horse and drove them in on their own retreating infantry. The disorder of the Cavaliers was complete; the horse scattered to the four points of the compass, and only the veteran skill of Hopton and Forth enabled them to get the baggage train away towards Winchester, leaving Waller to extinguish the fires in Alresford and occupy the town before nightfall. It was, in Sir William Balfour's phrase, " a great victory over our enemies beyond all expectation."[5]

The disaster to the Royalists was not, materially, so great as that suffered by Meldrum at Newark. The arms and baggage were nearly all safe and the scattered cavalry could reunite, although two of its best commanders had received mortal wounds—the King's young cousin Lord John Stuart, and Sir John Smith, whose valour had saved the standard at Edgehill.[6]

The battle of Alresford had, however, for the Parliamentary cause an importance that could not simply be calculated in terms of strategic gain or the capture of prisoners and arms. Since the beginning of the war, and in spite of lesser gains and conquests, Parliament's forces had been continually forced on to the defensive. The King had not won the war, but he had won all the major victories; Waller had been beaten at Roundway Down, Fairfax at Adwalton Moor. Cromwell and Manchester had stemmed the Royalist advance in the previous summer, and Essex at Newbury had prevented the King from advancing on London, but these were actions that staved off defeat and disaster: they were not victories which established the superiority of Parliament in the field. Alresford was an unquestioned and major triumph for the Parliamentary forces, the first in the war. The Royalists had sought battle (there was nothing accidental about this deliberately manœuvred engagement) and had been totally and ignominiously defeated. The event heartened the waverers, finally destroyed the peace-party in the Commons, and enabled Parliament, after rejoicings and thanksgivings which were for once wholly justified, to press for more money and more help from the Londoners.[7]

Waller's reputation rose again, and orders went out to recruit three thousand foot and seventeen hundred horses and dragoons for his army.[8] At this Essex, baulked even of his promised cavalry under Balfour, broke into angry protest. Had he been properly supported he could—so he said—have prevented Rupert's march to Newark, which was more than Manchester and all Parliament's cherished commanders of the Eastern Association had done. The victory won by Balfour and Waller—he put them carefully in that order—seemed very fine, but what if they had been defeated? His poor skeleton of an army would then have been expected, all alone, to save the Cause. The enemy, unopposed, " scour from the West to the North," he wrote: " Newark is not taken, Lincolnshire is lost, Gloucester is unsupplied and the last week there was but a step between us and death and (what is worse) slavery." The victory at Alresford, he contended, would be worthless if he had not the strength to take advantage of it and attack the Royalist forces round Oxford before they could recover.[9] Jealous though he was of his colleagues, some of what Essex said was true. A new appeal to London for gifts and volunteers was launched on his behalf at Guildhall at which the citizens were exhorted to " join their purses, their persons and their prayers together " for one last effort which would surely, after the victory at Alresford, win the war.[10]

Essex, in the complaint which had stimulated these fresh efforts, had uttered another dark warning. " The seas," he said, " have been and still are open to them out of Ireland."[11] In the last few weeks, however, a young man who had once been his page had deftly won for Parliament a number of key positions in the county of Pembroke, jutting out into the Irish Sea at the extreme south-west of Wales. Pembroke had been only of minor importance until the King's Irish plans made it imperative for him to control, and for Parliament to prevent him controlling, the coasts opposite Ireland. The Royalists had moved first. The sheriff of the adjoining county of Carmarthen, Sir Henry Vaughan, was for the King. With his kinsman Lord Carbery he occupied Tenby and Haverfordwest and, assisted by some of the King's ships from Bristol, threatened Pembroke and Milford Haven. Carbery, a violent man and a great talker, threatened fire and sword to all rebels and was said to have sworn to pack the Parliamentary Mayor of Pembroke into a barrel and roll him into the sea.[12]

Military leadership of the Parliamentary party was at this point assumed by Rowland Laugharne, the one-time page of Essex, who had had some training in the Low Countries. Cool, experienced and intrepid, Laugharne from the first out-generalled the noisier representatives of the King, and his operations on land were efficiently seconded at sea by Captain Swanley with a squadron of the fleet. Laugharne occupied the principal great houses round Tenby, and gradually moved in to block up the town, while Swanley first bombarded the Royalists out of Milford Haven, then penned the King's ships into a narrow creek near Tenby and threatened the little port from the sea. Carbery eluded the closing trap; Sir Henry Vaughan took fright and quitted Haverfordwest. Tenby alone, under a resolute commander, John Gwynne, held out until, in a three-day bombardment from land and sea, Laugharne battered his way in. " Had Tenby been saved the county had been easily commanded with horse," wrote an angry Royalist, " but now they have all the holds, Pembroke, Tenby and Haverford."[13] But Milford Haven was the most important gain because the possession of this valuable harbour gave Swanley and his squadron of the Parliamentary fleet a satisfactory base for patrolling the approaches to

Bristol and the Irish Sea. By the end of March Laugharne had secured the whole region and Swanley was ready to intercept the Irish transports.

The King's Irish plans became ever more complex. While his troops were fighting at Alresford, Charles in Oxford was receiving a deputation from the Confederate Irish led by Lord Muskerry. In return for their military help they asked for freedom to exercise their own religion and the suspension of the intolerable Poyning's Law, by which Acts of Parliament passed at Westminster were effective also in Ireland.[14]

The visit of the Confederate leaders stimulated in Charles's mind an impatience with Ormonde that turned into distrust when reports reached him that Ormonde was preventing Antrim from raising the troops he had promised. Ormonde confirmed the story by expressing in his despatches to the King his very reasonable doubts of Antrim's capacity and his fear that by giving a free hand to him the King would finally lose the support of the English in Ulster.[15]

The King had reason for wanting the Irish soon and at whatever cost, because his English fortunes, which had looked so hopeful in March, declined steeply in April. Spring had come late in the North, and a heavy snowfall immobilised Lord Leven and the Scots until the middle of March. But as the hold of winter relaxed they marched southwards, leaving a part of the army to continue the siege of Newcastle. In a series of sharp skirmishes on March 24th and 25th, they pushed the smaller Royalist forces back across the river Wear.[16] The Marquis of Newcastle from Durham appealed to Prince Rupert, his hyperbolic style hardly concealing his genuine anxiety: " In the first place I congratulate your huge and great victories, which indeed is fit for none but Your Highness . . . only this I must assure Your Highness that the Scots are as big again in foot as I am, and their horse, I doubt, much better than ours are, so that if Your Highness do not please to come hither, and that very soon too, the great game of your Uncle's will be endangered, if not lost: and with Your

Highness being near, certainly won: so I doubt not but Your Highness will come, and that very soon.

Your Highness' most passionate creature

W. Newcastle."[17]

His Highness's " most passionate creature " had found time even during these critical days to take offence at some message from Oxford and offer to resign, an intention from which he was deterred by a cajoling letter from the Queen.[18] When not in a pique he was, with the help of the professional soldier, James King, recently created Lord Eythin, energetic in his efforts to hold back the oncoming Scots. But on April 8th they were within two miles of Durham, and deploying to cut off his retreat. On the 12th he received the dismaying news that Sir John Bellasis, whom he had left in command in South Yorkshire, had been attacked by the two Fairfaxes at Selby; his guns, ammunition and most of his infantry had fallen to the Parliament forces, who now commanded most of southern Yorkshire and the main road to the south.[19]

The fall of Selby, and the consequent danger that both the Yorkshire forces and those of the Eastern Association might attack York, compelled the Marquis of Newcastle to fall back without delay before the advancing Scots and look to the defences of the northern capital. Leaving Durham in the small hours of April 13th, by way of Bishop Auckland, he sought refuge with his infantry and guns behind the solid walls of York. Sir Charles Lucas and the horse made their way through to Newark without loss, there to join with other Royalist cavalry, and do what they could to relieve pressure on York by scouring the country to the south.[20]

The Scots, following hard on Newcastle's heels, and the Fairfaxes advancing up the Ouse from Selby, met near Wetherby on April 20th. Within the next few days they had invested York on both sides of the Ouse; their two encampments were less than a mile from the wall, against which their " great battering

308

pieces " were trained. The two besieging armies numbered about sixteen thousand foot and four thousand horse; on the most optimistic calculation, a force of at least ten thousand would be needed to dislodge them.[21]

The Marquis of Newcastle, or more probably Lord Eythin, organised defence and rationing with exemplary care: civilians were reduced to one square meal a day; soldiers were issued with an ounce of butter, a penny loaf and a mutchkin of beans to which ale, meat and cheese were added as supplies allowed. On this system, with adequate ammunition and good artillery, York could hold out a long siege within the formidable circuit of its ancient walls.[22]

Prince Rupert was back at his post in Shrewsbury strenuously training recruits from Wales and Ireland when Newcastle's appeal reached him. The relief of York was henceforward his principal objective. Digby, who often took it upon himself to offer military advice, had urged him to stay in the Midlands after the relief of Newark and so remove the threat to York from the South.[23] It would have been good advice if the King had had a large enough army to attend at the same time to other necessities, but Rupert could not keep the forces he had gathered for the march on Newark for more than a few days away from the western Midlands and the Welsh border where their immediate duties were. If he had stayed longer at Newark he might have prevented the disaster at Selby, but there was no saying what other difficulties he might have caused elsewhere. The simple truth was that the war was dangerously extended and Prince Rupert, as the most active of the royal commanders, was in demand in too many places. He was urgently summoned to Oxford to discuss the defence of the city after the battle of Alresford which had laid it open to possible attack. He was summoned again to attend the Queen who was pregnant and wished to withdraw to Bath. Before he could obey, the ridiculous order was countermanded, but the threat to Oxford remained an alarming factor in his plans for the coming campaign.[24]

The army, scattered and shamed at Alresford, had been brought together again and the King reviewed six thousand foot and four thousand horse at Aldbourne on April 11th.[25] Returning to Oxford, he prorogued his Parliament there, to reduce the number of extra mouths to feed in a city already overcrowded.[26] On Holy Thursday, April 17th, with his two sons, he accompanied the Queen on her journey to Bath as far as Abingdon. There they parted; the Queen was haunted with the fear that she would die in her coming confinement;[27] but a more prolonged agony was to separate her from the husband whom she would never see again.

The King, to outward appearance, kept up his spirits. On returning to Oxford he received rather coldly envoys from Dublin whom Ormonde had sent to explain to him the complexities of the Irish situation. They made it clear to him that his loyal Protestant subjects of Ireland would accept no final treaty with the Confederate Irish which did not fully restore their property, re-establish the Protestant religion and bring the chief insurgents to trial.[28]

On Easter Day, with his two lively little boys, he strolled in Christ Church garden and was seen with admiration by John Taylor, the loyal ballad-monger, who had come to Oxford in search of copy. . . .

> In Christ Church garden then a gladsome sight was,
> My sovereign lord and many a peer and knight was,
> The hopeful Prince, and James Dux Eboracensis
> Whom God defend from rebels' false pretences.[29]

But the same day the King received intelligence of Newcastle's retreat to York.[30] Essex meanwhile had called a general rendezvous at Aylesbury; the opposing forces were closing in round Oxford. The King's commanders wanted to meet the threat with attack and to wipe out the disgrace of Alresford; they did not doubt their ability to do so. But Rupert, riding in from Shrewsbury to attend the Council of War, advised caution. It would be folly to risk a major engagement in the South while affairs in the North were still so uncertain. The Oxford army should act on the defensive only. Outlying garrisons—Reading, Banbury, Abingdon and Wallingford—should be strengthened with all the infantry that could be spared. A small force of cavalry would suffice to patrol the country nearest Oxford, and all the rest should be sent to join the forces under Prince Maurice which, since the winter, had been reducing the remaining strongholds in the West.[31] If the King thus drastically shortened his line, he could stand indefinitely on the defensive while Rupert marched to the relief of York. It was still early in the year; if all went well in the North there would be time to resume the offensive and settle with Essex and Waller before the summer's end.

The plan was accepted, though this, as Rupert must have feared, was no guarantee that it would be carried out, for the Council of War was a divided and unreliable body. Rupert, when he was there, could shout anyone down, even Wilmot, who usually disagreed with him and could shout nearly as loud; Lord Forth made diplomatic use of his deafness to quarrel with neither; Sir Jacob Astley was almost always several moves behind in any argument; the King took the advice of whichever of his advisers he favoured at the moment, and Lord Digby altered inconvenient decisions to suit himself afterwards.[32] In these disturbing circumstances the best that Rupert could do was to hope that his friend the Duke of Richmond now returned from France, would prevent any changes of plan after he left. Meantime, he rode back to Shrewsbury where his new-made army was almost ready to march for the North.

II

"The Scots are the predominant evil," Lord Digby had written, but while Rupert made ready at Shrewsbury for his march to the North, the Scottish Royalists were stirring against the Covenanters. They believed the time to be favourable. There had been much murmuring against the imposition of an Excise and the pressure put on the people to contribute to the support of the army. Discontent at being thus " pluckit and poyndit " was strongest in the regions where the Covenant had never been popular, strongest of all in Aberdeen, but the whole country felt the strain.[33]

The rigid religious policy of the government, which was made effective by the standing Commission of the Church, reached downwards through the regional Synods and local Presbyteries of elders and ministers into the lives of all. The smallest offences could lead to public reproof or penance—watering kale or bleaching cloth on the Sabbath, still more " stravaguing in the fields " at sermon time. Traditional feasts and superstitions were frowned on as offences against the moral law, and landmarks which had survived the iconoclasm of the Reformation, rude carvings and ancient stone crosses, were thrown down. Family feuds and private quarrels sometimes diverted and sometimes intensified the imposition of Presbyterian discipline. The nobility and gentry, especially, found it hard to accept interference with their privileges or their private lives and occasionally broke into defiance. " How be it you be compared to a dog you shall not bark here," said Dame Grizel Hamilton, barring an unpopular minister's way to his own pulpit.[34] Informers throve, prosecutions for witchcraft especially multiplied. But over a great part of Scotland the virtues of this harsh discipline were acknowledged even if their operation was often unwelcome. If it was irksome that the playing of the pipes and good fellowship in general should be discouraged, it was just as well that drunkenness, fornication and brawling should be put down and that sluts like " Hieland Mary, servitrix to James Balfour " who spent her idle moments " scandalously conversing " with the soldiers at Stirling, should be reprimanded and sent home.[35] In the Lowlands only a minority of the population, on account of religion, politics or personal interests, were deeply opposed to the rule of the Church. But anyone criticising the government was likely to get some covert sympathy from neighbours, because it was impossible for more than a rigid few to live up to the exacting standards now in force. Opponents of the Covenant deceived themselves when they took this passive and casual sympathy for an indication that the authority of the ministers was widely hated. It was not so: most of those who listened to the grievances of others and aired their own over a pot of ale, were in graver mood convinced of the righteousness or at least the usefulness of the new dispensation.[36]

Opposition to the Covenant was concentrated in certain regions of the Highlands. In order to eradicate the ancient Celtic customs and the Roman religion which still stubbornly lingered, the government was encouraging Gaelic-speaking students to enter the ministry, but it would be many years before the effects of this policy could be felt. Meanwhile the old antagonism between Celtic Highlands and Saxon Lowlands created, in the mountains, a natural resentment of the Covenanters' government particularly as the Synods tried to put down the lawlessness of the clans by using the weapon of excommunication.[37] But the divisions of politics and faith were often further confused by the rivalries or interests of individual chiefs.

The Campbells, who dominated the Western Highlands, stood in resolute devotion behind their chief, Argyll. This, however, served only to stimulate against the Covenant the numerous clans who were at enmity with the Campbells—the Macdonalds of the Isles and of the mainland, the Macleans of Ardgour and Duart, and such outlawed clans as the MacGregors and MacNabs. The animosity of the Camerons towards the Campbells was restrained by the fact that the young chief had been taken away by Argyll to educate at Inveraray,[38] but the Stuarts of Atholl, intimidated and resentful since Argyll's descent upon them in 1640,[39] were at best uncertain supporters of the government.

Farther north, the Earl of Seaforth, chief of the Mackenzies,

had been an active Covenanter in the earliest days but had later
been involved with Montrose in the attempt to undermine Argyll.
His present standing was doubtful, but the Earl of Sutherland,
his rival in dominating the region, had been the first to sign the
Covenant in 1638 and had never moved from it; his influence
could be relied on to keep most of the far north in obedience to
the government, although Lord Reay, in Strathnaver, was
Royalist, and there were disquieting rumours of the "malignancy" of Macleod of Assynt.[40] The greatest potential danger
was from the Gordons. Their chief, Huntly, remained unswervingly, if ineffectively, loyal to the King. Many of his
clansmen were Roman Catholic, and more were sympathetic to
the Episcopalian view, whose chief theological centre had been
at the nearby university of Aberdeen. The townsfolk, never
friendly to the Covenant, muttered at the heavy taxes and
resented their principal minister, the redoubtable Andrew Cant,
who had refused them access to the Lord's Supper for two years
after he came to them, saying that he could not, in a lesser time,
make them worthy to partake of it.[41]

Earlier in the century, as part of a general movement to
reconcile the interests of the greatest clans, Huntly had married
the sister of Argyll, and Argyll in recent years had acquired a
great influence over his eldest nephew, Huntly's heir. The
tension between father and son reached breaking point when
young Lord Gordon entered into a plan by which Huntly was
to evade his debts (the heaviest of which were to Argyll) by making over a great part of his lands to his heir. Agreement was never
reached and Huntly had parted from Gordon in evident
displeasure. His debts, however, made it difficult for him
to stir from home, and Lord Gordon, supported by a considerable faction in the clan, controlled the region for the
Covenanters, though he made no attempt to put into force an
order for his father's arrest made by the Committee of Estates
in January.[42]

Since Huntly would not move for the King it was left for

another of the Royalist Gordons to do so. On March 9th, 1644, at seven in the morning, Sir John Gordon of Haddo, rode into Aberdeen with a band of followers, seized the provost, with whom he had a personal feud, and three other supporters of the Covenant, and whisked out of the town again by ten o'clock, not forgetting to take up with him his two sons from school. The Aberdonians watched in mingled apprehension and pleasure. Haddo's precipitate action forced Huntly's hand. While Lord Gordon was trying to raise the neighbourhood to defend the Covenant, Huntly with trumpets sounding and two hundred horsemen at his back, occupied Aberdeen. The leading Covenanters fled; Huntly issued a proclamation in the King's name, seized all the arms he could find, called for recruits, and while these were drilled by handsome Nathaniel Gordon—at once the best professional soldier and the Don Juan of the clan—Huntly ordered the making of banners with the Royal Lion upon them, and black taffeta cockades for his men as a sign that they would fight to the death.[43]

At this news Argyll abruptly left the Scots army in England to stifle revolt at home. At Stirling, Royalist lords and gentry were already in surreptitious counsel, expecting soon to hear either from Montrose in England or from Antrim in Ireland.[44] By the middle of April Montrose, with thirteen hundred horse and foot recruited in Cumberland, crossed the Border near Gretna Green and was received with momentary enthusiasm at Dumfries.[45] For a few days it looked as though the Royalist revolt might spread across Scotland, if Montrose could reach Stirling and if Huntly would march from Aberdeen. But the government acted fast. Argyll was at Perth keeping watch on the Gordons, and a force of two thousand men was hurriedly despatched against Montrose.

Montrose had drawn up a manifesto calling on the people to join him for the defence of "true Protestant religion, His Majesty's just and sacred authority, the fundamental laws and privileges of Parliament, the peace and freedom of the oppressed and thralled subject."[46] His immediate hopes were fixed on the troops which Antrim had promised to despatch to Scotland early in April. There was no news of them; instead he heard of Covenanting forces marching against him, while his English troops threatened mutiny if they had to march on alone into unknown and evidently hostile country. His Scots friends in the South failed to support him. Between him and Stirling lay eighty miles of moor and moss, and already on the first day's march his advance parties clashed with Covenanting patrols. Distrustful of his guides and faced with the possible desertion of all his men, he fell back to Carlisle.[47]

The Royalists at Stirling went home, disheartened. Huntly, too, was disheartened for his divided clan had not risen as he hoped, the citizens of Aberdeen gave him very grudging support and Nat Gordon had left him after an ill-timed quarrel. His forces made a foray southwards and plundered the little seaport of Montrose, an action neither politic nor friendly. With Argyll fast approaching, Huntly left Haddo and his Royalist clansmen to their fate, collected money and clothes from his home, sent— with a gesture of surrender—his keys and his " stately saddle horses " to his Covenanting eldest son, and fled by sea to Strath- naver.[48]

At Aberdeen and Elgin, Argyll summoned delinquents and suspects to make their peace. " All men had entry, but none won out without a pass," though the less guilty often bought their freedom with generous contributions to the Covenanting cause, and the Aberdonians gave Argyll the freedom of the burgh. Argyll reproached the ministers for their slowness in resisting Huntly and commanded that the names of all faulty parishioners be handed in to him. Lord Gordon, now the nominal chief of his clan, was no more than a cypher. When his father was publicly pronounced excommunicate, he withdrew from the town, but came meekly back when the ceremony was over. He tried at least to save Haddo, who contemptuously rejected his intervention, fortified himself in his home and was shortly after handed over by his own people as the price of their pardon.[49]

Montrose, whom the King had now made a Marquis, returned to Carlisle to find that the citizens, enraged by the depredations of the Covenanting invaders, were unwilling to receive any Scot whatever his politics. Exercising his considerable persuasive talent he offered to subdue the Covenanters on the Border if they would take him in. He was as good as his word; with his small army he harassed the Covenanters besieging Newcastle, drove them out of Morpeth and South Shields, and penetrated their lines with timely supplies for the besieged, brought from Alnwick.[50] But the Royalist rising in Scotland which was to have caused the recall of the Covenanting forces had most dismally failed. Haddo was executed in Edinburgh; so was the hapless provost of Dumfries who had opened his gates to Montrose. Argyll took steps to strengthen the Covenanters of the North against further Highland outbreaks by organising bands of volunteers in Inverness and Elgin.[51] The government was more powerful, more feared and more respected than ever before; and nothing, meanwhile, was heard of Antrim and the ten thousand Irish with whom he was to have landed in Scotland for the King.

III

These Irish troops were the King's most fatal illusion. The more difficult the task of bringing them to his aid, the more ardently did he desire it. Ormonde, who to the King's impatient judgment seemed far too scrupulous in his conduct, had as yet concluded no agreement with the Confederates. Charles began to consider a secret and outrageous scheme put before him by his most ambitious and most incompetent servant. Lord Herbert, the Marquis of Worcester's son, who had already raised and lost an army from South Wales, now offered to go to Kilkenny, on the plea of private business, and enter into a treaty with the Confederate Irish without Ormonde's knowledge. As a devout Roman Catholic, with an Irish wife, he believed that he would command their trust, but his political projects had much the same ingenious extravagance as the inventions on which he spent his leisure time: a pocket engine for sinking ships, a floating garden, a combined hour-glass and fountain. He promised ten thousand men from Ireland and ten thousand more from his own and his father's lands in South Wales; he would procure from the Pope and other Roman Catholic princes a monthly subsidy of thirty thousand pounds with which he would also organise an invasion of East Anglia from the Spanish Netherlands. Antrim's promises were sober sense compared to the bright illusions of Lord Herbert who seems to have had, floating somewhere in his feverish brain, a vision of a Welsh-Irish empire over which he would bear his lofty sway.[52]

He fully understood that if his mission should be discovered before it had succeeded the King would deny all knowledge of it and leave him to his fate. For the exceptional risks he was to run, exceptional rewards were promised. He was to be unquestioned general of all the troops he raised; he was given a handful of peers' and baronets' patents to distribute among the Irish as occasion served; his father was to be made a Duke, and his son was to marry the King's younger daughter. He was himself to be made immediately Earl of Glamorgan.[53] The King, having thus unofficially sponsored an alliance with the Irish, the Pope and the Spanish Netherlands, issued an official statement in three languages to assure his Protestant subjects and the Protestant powers of Europe that he utterly repudiated the Roman Catholic religion and would remain unswervingly true to the Protestant faith of the Church of England.[54]

It did not apparently occur to the King that Glamorgan's interference with the Confederate Irish must of necessity reduce the chances of Ormonde's success. In other and more open ways he embarrassed the unfortunate Lord Lieutenant of Ireland, whose emissaries in Oxford were consistently slighted in favour of those who had come from the Confederate Irish. Court and Council followed the King's example, neglected and criticised Ormonde's representatives, caressed and flattered the Irish leaders, until the deputation from Dublin, exasperated into indiscretion, complained of the King's favours to the Papists. At this it was reported back to Ormonde that his envoys were thought to be little better than Roundheads.[55] Charles in his haste to win the Irish and the Catholics was in danger of alienating for ever the English and the Protestants in Ireland.

The loyalists in Ireland were doubly ill-used, for Parliament continued to describe all troops that came thence as " bloody, idolatrous rebels," although almost all that had come so far were from the government forces, and at least five hundred had already deserted to join what they took to be the Protestant side in the English war.[56] When Captain Swanley, cruising off the Pembroke coast, seized a transport from Dublin, he roped the captured soldiers together and threw them into the sea. While Swanley gloried in the destruction of the " Irish rebels," Ormonde mourned the loss of his men and protested that no more could be persuaded to embark when such hazards awaited them.[57]

IV

Rupert, at Shrewsbury, had the problem of Irish transport in mind, and was planning to march to York through Lancashire, capturing Liverpool by the way. The northern part of the Irish Channel, protected by the Royalist Isle of Man, would then be a safe crossing. But with every week the relief of York appeared more difficult. On May 6th, after two days of torrential rain, the forces of the Eastern Association under Manchester stormed and took the steep citadel of Lincoln and sacked the town.[58] In the last month the Royalists had lost control of Lincolnshire, and Manchester with six thousand infantry, a thousand cavalry and twelve cannon marched north unhindered to join in the siege of York.[59] Prince Rupert would now have three armies to settle with when he reached York—the Scots, the army of Fairfax and the army of Manchester. On May 16th, 1644, he marched from Shrewsbury with two thousand horse and six thousand foot; from Chester Byron's forces joined him; they now had fourteen thousand men.[60] Of all the generals in the field, on either side, Rupert's popular reputation stood highest, alike with friend and foe; " his very name is half a conquest ", a Royalist captain had written, and the Prince must in the last months have heard from every quarter of the King's war—from Newark, from Lancashire, from York, even from Pembroke the constant appeal for his presence, the reiterated belief that " the Prince alone can do it." [61] It was therefore with unshaken confidence in his own ability that he set out on the northern campaign, and his chief anxiety was not that his own plans might miscarry, but that the King in Oxford might act mistakenly.

His fear was justified. The King had at first accepted his advice to strengthen the garrisons round Oxford and stand on the defensive: he had second thoughts as soon as his masterful nephew had withdrawn. After a sequence of confused Councils of War it was decided to make the Oxford army more " nimble " in the field by withdrawing from Reading and Abingdon. Long before they could profit by their increased mobility, the enemy moved in to both towns and forced the King's cavalry wholly out of Berkshire, leaving the south side of Oxford naked to attack.[62]

Essex, astonished by this conduct into almost amiable co-operation with Waller, moved rapidly in on the eastern side and by the end of May had fixed his headquarters at Islip and his outposts at Cowley and Headington.[63] The King, to clear his head and keep up the spirits of his friends, took a day's hunting at Woodstock. While he successfully killed two fat buck, Waller, working round from Abingdon, put his men across the Thames at Newbridge, south-west of Oxford, on a causeway of boats, and began to move in on the west. The city was now threatened

OLIVER CROMWELL
after Robert Walker

GEORGE GORDON, MARQUIS OF HUNTLY
by an Unknown Artist

on three sides and Waller's forces would soon cut the lines of communication between the King and the West. In their now perilous plight, the King, advised probably by old Lord Forth, acted with ingenuity and daring. Leaving Oxford with most of the cavalry, he marched as though for Abingdon. To forestall attack on his garrison there, Waller fell back, leaving open the road to the west; the King and his party went through the gap, making first for Burford, then towards Worcester.[64] Oxford, they hoped, could hold out against a siege while they maintained themselves in the field till Rupert should return.

On their way, at Evesham, they heard that the Parliamentary forces at Gloucester had surprised and taken Tewkesbury. At Pershore the King's men destroyed the bridge, but in their clumsy haste lost some of their own troops by drowning. From Worcester on June 7th the King wrote to Rupert apologising handsomely for what had been done: "I confess the best had been to have followed your advice . . . the loss of Tewkesbury has put us to great hazards: yet we doubt not but to defend ourselves until you may have time to beat the Scots, but if you be too long in doing of it, I apprehend some great inconvenience." Digby wrote at the same time in a kind of cheerful despair: "Essex comes upon us one way, Waller likely to go about us on the Welsh side by Gloucester, Massey and the Lord Denbigh towards Kidderminster, both with considerable forces . . . Oxford is scarce victualled for a month . . . all the hopes of relief depend upon Your Highness's happy and timely success." The Duke of Richmond laconically summarised the King's condition: "We want money, men, conduct, diligence, provisions, time and good counsel."[65]

While the King and his advisers jeopardised the position at headquarters, Prince Rupert had achieved the first part of his northern campaign. He had thrust into the county of Lancashire, taken Stockport, and leaving the well-fortified town of Manchester alone, stormed Bolton on May 28th. Bolton, which prided itself on its austere religion, was flatteringly called "the

Geneva of the North," and fifteen hundred men from the country round had come in to help the garrison. But an unwalled town, however ardently defended, could not hold out against a well-organised attack. Two hours of fighting in steady, drenching rain sufficed for Bolton. The Cavaliers penetrated the narrow streets, trampling down citizens and soldiers until that " sweet godly place " was changed into " a nest of owls and a den of dragons." The commander of the Lancashire forces, Alexander Rigby, almost overwhelmed in the rout, played the Royalist, and shouting " the town is ours " managed to escape in the damp confusion. The victorious soldiers, given the plunder of the town to encourage them, took full advantage of the opportunity.[66]

George Goring, exchanged in the spring after nearly a year as a prisoner, had been active for the past month in Lancashire with his raiding cavalry, and a few days after the fall of Bolton he joined Rupert with five thousand men, " not so well appointed as was expected," but driving herds of stolen cattle with them. Lord Derby who, returning from the Isle of Man, had joined Rupert on his march, had beaten up some more infantry, mostly untried and almost unarmed men, from his own estates. The Puritans of Lancashire quailed before the storm and at Preston the burgesses nervously asked the Prince to a banquet. " Banquets are not for soldiers," said Rupert, and put the Mayor under arrest.[67]

On June 5th Rupert entered the little town of Wigan. Here the citizens who were Royalist rejoiced in the fate that had befallen their Puritan neighbours, and strewed flowers and green branches before him. At Lathom House nearby the besiegers had not waited for him, and the Countess of Derby, who had held them in check for over two months, clasped the all-victorious Prince to her ample bosom. He left her the banners he had captured and marched on to complete his work in Lancashire by taking Liverpool.[68]

Liverpool on its flat and muddy shore was not defensible for long against Rupert's artillery, but the garrison, composed of men who would meet in their leisure hours "to read the Scriptures, to confer of good things, and to pray together,"[69] were resolved to hold the town until they had shipped away as much of the arms and ammunition as they could. For five days while Rupert's batteries thundered against them with a great expenditure of powder the austere Colonel Moore and his men held out, until they had loaded their stores on to the ships in the haven. On the fifth day, the supplies and the principal officers having gone, Rupert entered the town, but although some cannon were left, the gunpowder on which he had counted to replenish his dwindling stores had all been taken.[70]

Rupert had, none the less, done the first part of what he set out to do—restored the domination of the Royalists in Lancashire and gained a port facing Ireland. So far, he cannot have been displeased with his progress: but the most difficult task was yet to come, and he needed more time to assure the success of his march on York than he had at first anticipated. He sent back for supplies of powder from the magazine at Oxford and announced his intention of completing the subjection of Lancashire so as to have the county solid behind him before he moved on York. The delay would also give him much needed time to put Lord Derby's ragged levies into better shape and to assemble from all the Northern counties the remaining scattered Royalist forces—those under Clavering in Cumberland and those with Montrose on the Border. With such a force fully assembled and equipped he could confidently challenge the three armies which blockaded York. His despatch to the King crossed with the stream of letters in which Charles and his advisers announced their misfortunes.[71]

Charles was disposed to blame Wilmot for the disastrous state of affairs. Rupert, far off in Lancashire, raged against the whole pack of councillors round the King: he knew Wilmot to be lazy and arrogant, and he had suffered from Harry Percy's obstruction whenever he wanted equipment or supplies: of the civilian advisers he disliked Culpeper and distrusted Digby. After the gloomy words of Richmond (" We want . . . provisions, time and good counsel ") and the King's touching plea (" the chief hope . . . is, under God, from you ") he realised that he might at any moment be called home. Digby, writing at the King's instructions, had urged him not to delay in bringing things in the north to a " quick upshot " that he might the sooner be free to come back to their help in the south.[72]

But it was not so easy to bring things to a " quick upshot " and Rupert hesitated at Liverpool, partly in anger, partly for lack of gunpowder and partly in a genuine dilemma, not knowing whether to call in all the troops in the north for an operation which he might have suddenly to abandon incomplete in order to rescue the King.[73]

V

While Rupert delayed, the situation in the south changed. Essex met Waller at Chipping Norton to discuss the best way of completing the King's discomfiture. He compelled the unwilling Waller to stay in the Midlands and follow the retreating King, while he himself struck through to the south-west to break up the siege of Lyme and, if possible, to capture the Queen, now hourly expecting her confinement at Exeter. This reversal of their usual parts and the intrusion of Essex into the western regions which had hitherto been Waller's allotted sphere was thought by Waller's friends in London to be a plot to undermine his authority.[74] But the Earl of Essex was not so subtle; it was simply that he had too low an opinion of Waller to believe him capable of relieving Lyme or cutting off the Queen at Exeter. The Earl of Warwick, his old friend, had taken a squadron of the fleet to the help of Lyme, and had found that he could do nothing effective without land forces to co-operate with him. It was natural for Essex to want to respond to this call in person, and to form a plan by which he and his cousin Warwick, in an amphibious operation, might together trap the King's forces in the west.[75]

Lyme had withstood the besieging army of Prince Maurice for nearly two months. The three thousand citizens and the garrison of five hundred, with the mayor as governor, united to hold the little seaport, but the effective organiser of the defence was Colonel Robert Blake, a merchant of Bridgwater, who had taken to soldiering in middle life and had seen hard service at Bristol. The town is tightly wedged into a cleft between high clay slopes which fall steeply towards the sea. On three sides it is thus walled in; on the fourth the sea washes. The hastily contrived defences were walls or rather barriers of turf strengthened at intervals by block-houses, also made of turf. They did not look very formidable and, weeks later, when all was over, the Earl of Warwick gave it as his opinion that " the courage and honesty of the officers and soldiers were in a manner their own defence."[76]

In the first major assault launched by Prince Maurice, the defenders had used almost all their small store of ammunition, but the noise of the firing was heard off Portland by three Parliamentary ships which crowded on sail and reached the town in time with fresh supplies. During the next fortnight Lyme was reinforced again, from Portsmouth. Owing to the steepness of the cliffs Maurice could not cover the harbour with his guns, and not until May 16th did he contrive a battery which threatened the Cobb, the long solid mole where most of the ships unloaded. For the next week his guns battered the Cobb and twice he sent raiding parties at night who temporarily seized it and burnt or sank all the small craft in the harbour. But without warships to co-operate with him he could do nothing against the squadron under the Earl of Warwick which appeared off Lyme on May 23rd and once more replenished the supplies of the besieged. Maurice grew reckless; he had locked up the best part of the Western army for over a month in this unlucky siege and could justify the expense of men and effort only by ultimate success. Three times between May 27th and 29th he stormed the town; but the defenders never slackened their resistance, the towns-women relieving the men at their posts. On the 30th Maurice tried in vain to set the town on fire with a bombardment of red-hot missiles. Still he would not raise the siege, convinced—as well he might be—that so small a place could not sustain so great an effort for much longer. Warwick had had to send away six of his eight ships on other business. Powder, shot and match were running short in the town, sickness had broken out, and Warwick's remaining ships were undermanned because he had landed more seamen than he could well spare to help the defenders. On June 5th, with only a few days' supply left, it seemed that the town must fall. There was still no news of relief.[77]

The Committee of Both Kingdoms, far from the scene of action, thought in political terms. Hardly had Essex set forward on his march to Lyme than angry letters came from Waller. With the help of Essex, he argued, he could settle with the King in a matter of days, but as it was he could do nothing, especially as Colonel Massey at Gloucester was refusing his men quarter and provisions in the surrounding country.[78] At once the Committee recalled Essex. He got their orders at Blandford on June 14th, refused to obey and marched on to Lyme. That night Prince Maurice, apprised of his approach, drew off towards Exeter.[79] By his misjudgment in forming the siege and his obstinacy in pursuing it, he had squandered eight weeks of valuable time, more than a thousand lives, huge supplies of ammunition and his own reputation.

Essex, still in defiance of his orders, advanced on Weymouth, whence the Royalists hurriedly withdrew. Thence, looping north and west again by Crewkerne and Chard, he moved on Exeter, where the Queen lay. On June 16th she had given birth to a daughter, attended by a midwife sent by the Queen of France and by Theodore de Mayerne, her usual physician, who had been dragged from his prosperous London practice by a personal appeal from the King—" *Mayerne, pour l'amour de moi, allez trouver ma femme.*" Exhausted with anxiety and pain, the poor Queen had thoughts only for her physical suffering: she had cramp in every limb, and a weight on her heart which nearly stifled her; her body was bent into a hoop, and she had lost the feeling of one arm and the sight of one eye. So she piteously declared to her husband, but Mayerne, who thought her symptoms hysterical, was not unduly anxious.[80]

The King, closely followed by the disgruntled Waller, was still moving hesitantly about Worcestershire. On the 14th June, after a Council of War at Bewdley, he wrote again to Rupert. " But now I must give you the true state of my affairs which . . . is such as enforces me to give you more peremptory commands than I would willingly do . . . If York be lost I shall esteem my crown little less . . . But if York be relieved and you beat the rebels' army of both Kingdoms which are before it, then (but otherwise not) I may possibly make a shift (upon the defensive) to spin out time until you come to assist me. Wherefore I command and conjure you by the duty and affection which I know you bear me that, all new enterprises laid aside, you immediately march according to your first intention with all your force to the relief of York. But if that be either lost, or have freed themselves from the besiegers, or that, for want of powder you cannot undertake that work, that you immediately march with your whole strength directly to Worcester to assist me and my army."

The King's letter left Rupert to judge whether he should proceed with the relief of York according to his original plan, or leave York to its fate and return to extricate the King. Culpeper, who had not been consulted on the wording of it, later took credit to himself for having said to the King, as soon as it was irretrievably despatched, " Before God, you are undone, for upon this peremptory order he will fight, whatever come on't."[81] The story sounds like a subsequent elaboration; there was no reason to suppose, when the letter was written, that if Rupert fought the results must necessarily be disastrous.

The letter had hardly been despatched when the King and his advisers took heart. They became suddenly aware that the two large armies which had closed in round Oxford a fortnight ago had thinned away; Essex and Waller were now a hundred miles apart. The King, therefore, evading Waller, who was at Stourbridge, turned eastward as though for Oxford, and marched across the Cotswolds by Broadway Down. Breaking all the bridges as they went, the Royalists drew in fresh contingents of foot from the garrisons by the way, and had gathered at Woodstock by June 21st about five thousand horse and six thousand foot as well as guns from Oxford.[82] With these forces they made a raid into enemy country and descended on the town of Buckingham. The King, from this advanced position, wrote to congratulate the Queen on the glad news of her daughter's birth, suggesting that she take this joyful occasion to offer the Earl of Essex, in her husband's name, a free pardon if he laid down arms and returned to his allegiance.[83]

The King's returning optimism was not groundless. His sudden invasion of Parliamentary territory and his conversion of a bewildered retreat into an aggressive advance caused alarm in London, where they feared a break through into the Eastern counties while Manchester and Cromwell were far off at York. In haste and fear they ordered Major-General Browne, whose cavalry patrolled the northern defences of London, to act with Waller to intercept the King.[84]

The King, not to be caught between two fires, rejected a wild suggestion of Wilmot's that they should march on London, and turned back to face Waller. On June 28th the Royalists were near Banbury, with Waller's army a few miles off on the farther side of the town. The King slept in a yeoman's house at Grymsbury, and next day marched north towards Daventry, keeping to the left bank of the little river Cherwell and hoping to draw Waller to fight at a disadvantage.

Presently the enemy came into view, marching the same way " within a coit's cast," with the gay little stream, sliding among willows, between them. Believing that Waller expected reinforcements of horse, the forward part of the King's army raced ahead to intercept these supposed auxiliaries, and a lengthening gap appeared between them and the rear, with the wagons and the guns. At Cropredy Bridge they placed a guard to prevent Waller from crossing the river, but he could clearly see from the farther bank that the Royalist forces were dangerously separated and was not deterred by the presence of so small an obstacle at the bridge. Waiting till the Royalist vanguard was out of the way, he attacked, took the bridge and put the bulk of his forces over it—fifteen hundred horse, two thousand foot, and a battery of light cannon. A smaller force he detached to wade across a ford a mile or so downstream and fall on the Royalist rear. Trusting to these to delay the rear of the King's army, he left his cannon and a small guard at Cropredy Bridge, and pursued the Royalist vanguard. They faced about, just where the road, on another narrow bridge, crossed a bend of the winding river. Making a barricade across the bridge with a wagon, they met Waller's oncoming forces in this narrow way with successive bursts of musketry fire.

While the Royalist vanguard held up the main body of Waller's army, Lord Cleveland, who commanded the King's cavalry in the rear, had seen the enemy forces cross the river and, without waiting for orders, had spurred his cavalry brigade forward, fallen upon the troops who had been stationed in front of Cropredy Bridge and scattered them utterly. Waller now found himself trapped between the two parts of the King's army, and his retreat cut off by the intervention of Cleveland's cavalry between him and the bridge. One of his most stalwart officers, Colonel Birch, still held the bridge itself. Otherwise his position would have been desperate. But his cavalry, by a series of flank charges, succeeded in drawing the Royalists away from the bridge. In an afternoon of violent and confused skirmishing he managed to get the bulk of his forces back to Cropredy Bridge and so, thanks to the steadfastness of Birch, to safety on the farther bank of the river. But his losses were heavy and included all his valuable light artillery. In the hot fighting Wilmot, in command of the King's vanguard, was slightly wounded, taken, and later rescued. One of Waller's officers was even luckier; unhorsed and surrounded, he was suddenly in the dust and confusion given a fresh horse by a Cavalier trooper, who urged him to " make haste and kill a Roundhead." For the rest of the long summer day and all the next the two armies faced each other across the river. The King knighted several valiant Cavaliers, attended an open-air thanksgiving before his whole army, hanged a Roundhead spy, and wrote to the Queen to arrange for the " christening of my youngest, and as they say prettiest daughter," in Exeter Cathedral.[85]

He also sent to Waller urging him to lay down arms. Later, Sir William Waller averred that the King's message had been accompanied by a note from an old flame of his (Waller had been a gay gallant in his time) pleading with " some soft passages " that he would accept the royal offer. But his memory seems to have played him false for at the time he refused to receive either message or messenger from the King. When Charles drew off towards Aynhoe, Waller, though too bruised to follow him, wrote triumphantly to the Committee of Both Kingdoms that he had certainly prevented the King from marching north to join Prince Rupert.[86]

The King's thoughts were with his wife in the West. It now seemed that he could leave the baffled Waller far in his rear while he dealt with the errant Earl of Essex. Essex had refused, a fortnight earlier, to help Waller: it was now Waller's turn to refuse to help Essex. In early July Essex was at Honiton in Devon, Waller at Towcester in Northamptonshire: the chances of their joining forces again that summer, even had they been willing to do so, were very slender if the King, and his western army, acted with even reasonable skill. Waller's men were deserting fast, and the countryfolk on whom they were quartered were sullen and inhospitable. The people of Hertfordshire petitioned against having to pay their own local levies; and the people of Bedfordshire bitterly complained when their horses were commandeered by Waller's captains. Waller's personal popularity was waning; others beside his senior colleague, Essex, disliked and resented him. Browne, though he obeyed Parliament's command to join him, made it very clear that he would take no orders from him. Colonel Massey, who at Gloucester held the most vital passage of the Severn, complained to Parliament that Waller had grossly increased his difficulties by taking away half his men and burdening him with the care of great numbers of prisoners. He, too, reported that his men were deserting because they had been too long absent from their families.[87]

With generals quarrelling and mutinous local levies, the war could never be won, and Waller summed the matter up in a letter to the Committee of Both Kingdoms. " Till you have an army merely your own that you may command, it is in a manner impossible to do anything of importance."[88] So he wrote on July 2nd, while he scoured the neighbourhood for horses to enable him to follow the Cavaliers. But he had lost his opportunity, and the King's path lay open to the West.

VI

For a short while in June it had looked as though the Prince's triumphant progress through Lancashire would divert at least one of the armies before York. The Committee of Both Kingdoms had suggested that help be sent, but the generals before York had wisely refused to budge. Soon the news of the King's retreat from Oxford had encouraged them to spread the rumour, intended to demoralise the defenders of the city, that Rupert would turn south again without coming any nearer.[89]

Rupert had received the King's commands on June 18th at

Liverpool. At much about the same time appeals reached him from a Royalist commander outside York, and from York itself. (Nine volunteers had been separately despatched to slip through the enemy lines; one only reached him.) The Prince sent out Goring to hasten the cavalry from Cumberland and began the march to York.[90]

The northern capital, after London the most splendid city in the Kingdom and incomparably the most beautiful, had been cut off for two months from the outside world. Its broad and solid walls, four miles in circuit, enclosed gardens and orchards, the crowded, overhanging medieval houses in narrow streets and the spacious modern mansions encircling the majestic Minster. Until the early days of June the besieged held the outer suburbs and outlying fields within an elaborate modern system of bastions and block-houses. But on June 3rd Manchester's army arrived with fresh supplies of ammunition and from June 5th for three days the besiegers attacked simultaneously on the south-east and the north, and Newcastle was compelled to shorten his line by abandoning and destroying the suburbs. On the North side, where his own headquarters were, the besiegers quenched the blaze, and under cover of the empty, half-burnt houses, came close enough to threaten the city wall with mining.

The defenders continued resolute, and set up their cannon in the streets ready for a house-to-house defence. They still held the ancient walls intact, with the small additional projection of the King's Manor, the great house completed by Strafford as a residence for the governors of the North. Two rivers, the Ouse and the Fosse, flow through York, and if the walls could not be held, an inner triangle of the city, with the Minster and the Castle, could still be defended behind the natural defence made by these two rivers. Newcastle destroyed the bridges over them, made all ready for defence to the uttermost, and, at a brief parley on June 14th, rejected all terms. On the 16th the besiegers mined Bootham Bar, the vulnerable northern gate and part of the Manor wall, but the defenders held the breach, counter-attacked and forced the besiegers to withdraw. They were, however, nearly exhausted by long watches and heavy fighting, and on short rations of bread and beans and beer.[91]

The three armies before York—the Scots, under Lord Leven, the northern army under Fairfax, the Eastern Association under Manchester—numbered an effective twenty-five thousand men. Rupert had been joined on the march by about a thousand cavalry from Cumberland; and he had sent for Montrose to join him with his troops from the Border, though it was unlikely that these additional forces would come up in time to help in the relief of York. Without them the advancing Royalist army numbered a little short of fifteen thousand.[92]

The Parliamentary generals outside York consulted, confidently enough; old Leven wrote blithely that they expected a visit from the Prince and were " making ready for his welcome."[93] On June 30th they heard he was at Knaresborough, fourteen miles due west of the city. Accordingly they withdrew their forces on the north side, crossed the Ouse on a bridge of boats and blocked the road from Knaresborough to York on the flat, heathy ground near Long Marston. While they massed on the Knaresborough road, Rupert, with unlooked-for rapidity, shot northwards, crossed the river at Boroughbridge early on July 1st and marched for the unguarded northern gate of York with the river between him and the enemy. He sent on a party to hold the bridge of boats against any attempt on their part to re-possess it, but it was not solid enough to be crossed in safety by a large army in a hurry, under threat of attack both from Rupert and from the garrison in York. At Newark he had surprised the Parliamentarians by his speed; at York he outwitted them by approaching from a direction they had not anticipated. With impotent mortification the Scots and English commanders watched Rupert's glancing banners and marching columns bear down towards York.[94]

The long siege was raised by a manœuvre more daringly conceived even than the relief of Newark. The liberated troops

333

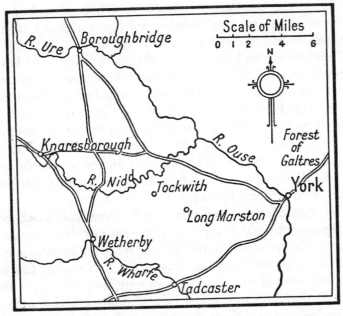

ENVIRONS OF YORK

poured out of the city to take what they could carry from the abandoned Parliamentary camp, where they found large supplies of ammunition and four thousand pairs of boots.[95] The Marquis of Newcastle composed an elegant letter of congratulation to the Prince:

" You are welcome, Sir, so many several ways, as it is beyond my arithmetic to number, but this I know, you are the Redeemer of the North and the Saviour of the Crown. Your name, Sir, hath terrified three great generals and they fly before it. It seems their design is not to meet Your Highness for I believe they have got a river between you and them but they are so newly gone as there is no certainty at all of them or their intentions, neither can I resolve anything since I am made of nothing but thankfulness and obedience to Your Highness's commands."[96]

The Prince, taking a letter of compliment for a military communication, gathered from this that Newcastle had nothing useful to tell him about the enemies' movements and was placing himself unreservedly at his disposal. He quartered for the night in the Forest of Galtres and sent Goring into York to tell the Marquis to be ready to march with him against the enemy at four o'clock next morning.[97] But at four next morning Newcastle and his troops were nowhere to be seen and Rupert, not wishing to lose the chance of attacking his opponents while they were still baffled by his movements, crossed the bridge of boats over the Ouse and marched towards the enemy at Long Marston without waiting for the forces in York. Believing the King's position still to be desperate (he knew nothing of the fight at Cropredy), he was anxious to strike instantly and conclude the campaign in the North.

The Parliamentary commanders, better informed, already knew that the King had rallied and feared that Rupert might strike southwards through Lincolnshire to join with his uncle's forces. Their fears were confirmed by a manœuvre of Rupert's, who sent out some parties of cavalry south of the city to confuse the enemy as to the direction of his march. In the small hours of July 2nd the assembled Parliamentary generals on Marston Moor decided to march for Tadcaster to bar the road to the south. The infantry had already gone when some of the Parliamentary patrols clashed with Rupert's advancing cavalry on the road to Marston. A trooper of the Eastern Association, taken and released, reported that he had seen the Prince himself who had eagerly asked if Cromwell was present and evidently intended to fight in that part of the front opposite him. " By God's grace, he shall have fighting enough," said Cromwell,[98] and meant what he said; but Rupert's approach, in the broadening daylight, was no matter for jesting. In haste they sent for their infantry back again, knowing that several hours must go by before their forces could be reassembled, and in that interval Rupert might attack.

He could not do so. He waited for the Marquis of Newcastle and the three thousand infantry in York, unaware that in his treatment of that nobleman he had made a mistake which, in its ultimate effects, was to undo all he had achieved in the relief of York. It was pardonable in him that he could not respond in kind to the complimentary missive of the Marquis. It was less pardonable that he took the older man's professions of service at their face value, making no allowance for the sensibilities of a commander twice his age, who had exercised unquestioned authority in the North for the past two years. It was unpardonable in him, a professional and by now experienced commander, to take no account of the state of the troops in York after their long, exacting and sometimes heroic service. Newcastle, his staff and his men had looked for a few days' rest and relief; they had justly hoped for congratulations, praise and even reward. They might have done without thanks, if they had been given rest and relief; they might have done without rest, if they had been encouraged by words of praise and heartened with hopes of reward. They got instead a peremptory command to march from a stranger who assumed authority over them all without even showing himself in the town. Even so, had Newcastle and his right-hand man, Lord Eythin, put their duty before their vanity and sought to redeem, rather than to increase, the Prince's error of judgment, the worst consequences would have been averted. Neither of them was capable of such a sacrifice.

Newcastle, on receiving Rupert's order, had—as always when he thought himself slighted—announced his intention of resigning.[99] The Scots professional, Lord Eythin, had personal reasons for disliking Rupert. Six years before, when the Prince had been taken prisoner in a skirmish at Vlotho on the Weser, Eythin had been in command and had been criticised for abandoning Rupert to his fate. Over the years his resentment of this criticism had grown; he ministered to Newcastle's anger and with culpable irresponsibility, stirred up the irritation of the soldiers in York which it should have been his business to allay. He said, in the hearing of many, that he did not think the men should be expected to march until they had at least received all their arrears of pay. The opinion soon became a general mutter in the camp; many of the men believed that Eythin had positively commanded them not to march. By two o'clock in the morning there was a general mutiny; they would not move a step.[100]

Leaving Eythin to bring them back to their obedience, Newcastle at length set out for the Moor, and joined Rupert, with a cortege of all the gentry in York at nine o'clock in the morning. " My lord, I wish you had come sooner with your forces," said Rupert, " but I hope we shall yet have a glorious day." Newcastle informed him that his men had been plundering the enemy's deserted camp, but Lord Eythin would no doubt soon bring them up. Rupert, aware of the present weakness of the opposing forces, suggested an immediate attack, without waiting for them. Newcastle objected and the Prince deferred to his judgment, thereby making his second unhappy error. The Parliamentarians were not yet present in force; they were hampered by standing corn and hedges, had too little room to manœuvre and their movements were slowed down by repeated showers of heavy summer rain. By the time that Eythin and the infantry from York reached the Moor at four in the afternoon, the opposing armies were fully reassembled and drawn up, and could be heard singing psalms in the damp heat of the afternoon.[101]

The Royalists were on the open Moor, the Parliamentary troops on slightly higher but much less convenient ground, partly in hedged fields and partly among furze and gorse bushes. Between the two armies ran a ditch sparsely fringed by hedges. The Parliamentary front extended for a mile and a half from the village of Marston on the extreme right to that of Tockwith on the left. Oliver Cromwell with the cavalry of the Eastern Association, about three thousand men, was on this left wing; Sir Thomas Fairfax with the Northern cavalry, about two thousand, on the right, in pitted and difficult ground. The Scots had agreed to divide their horse, providing a reserve of about eight hundred behind the English on each wing. David Leslie, their cavalry general, had chosen to be with Cromwell: "Europe hath no better cavalry," he declared, an astonishing testimonial from a Scottish professional soldier to the achievement of this English amateur. Both he and Cromwell knew that they would have Rupert to deal with, and the great testing moment of the Cromwellian method had come. The foot, Scots and English, was massed in the centre, under Lord Fairfax and the Earl of Leven.[102]

The Royalist front on the Moor was a little longer than that of their opponents. Rupert had wanted to know where Cromwell was stationed so that he could make dispositions to deal with this redoubtable leader of cavalry. His dispositions on the right wing, which faced Cromwell, indicated that he had given great thought to the matter. He had placed groups of musketeers between his squadrons of cavalry so that the force of Cromwell's charge would be broken by musketry fire—in the fashion evolved and effectively practised by Gustavus Adolphus. Rupert had stationed his men close to the ditch which divided the two forces so that Cromwell, should he attack, would not have space enough to recover from the disorder incident to traversing this obstacle. Rupert's dispositions strongly suggest that he intended to stay on his own favourable ground and provoke Cromwell into making the first charge, either by the harassing fire of his forward parties of musketeers in hedges between the two forces, or by some manœuvre on the flank. Both for his reputation and for Cromwell's the coming engagement was likely to be decisive and both were aware of it.

In the centre, in the foremost position, Rupert had put the best of his infantry, behind them the weaker forces from Lancashire. He was compelled to put the veteran infantry from York in the rear because of their late arrival on the field. In the extreme rear he had his own lifeguard and a small reserve of cavalry. On the left wing of the Royalist army opposite Fairfax was George Goring, Sir Charles Lucas and the Northern Horse.[103]

Lord Eythin, on looking at a draft plan of the position, dismissed it irritably: " By God, sir, it is very fine on paper but there is no such thing in the field."[104] His chief objection, it appeared, was that Rupert's forces were too near the enemy. (The enemy thought this also, having had great difficulty in drawing up their lines at all with the Cavaliers " close to our noses." But that was not what Eythin objected to.)[105] Rupert suggested a modification of the front, but Eythin would not co-operate. It was now about half-past four and Rupert, with rather more than three hours to sunset, suggested that they should begin operations. Eythin, supported by Newcastle, advised against any action which would provoke the battle. " Sir," he said, spitting out a grievance six years old, " your forwardness lost us the day in Germany where yourself were taken prisoner." Rupert again gave in.[106]

A general silence had now fallen on both armies. Neither wished to attack at a disadvantage and it began to look as if they might ultimately draw off without fighting and disappoint the crowd of curious spectators who from various safe distances were hoping to watch the combat.

At half-past seven, with about an hour of daylight left, Prince Rupert, deciding that nothing further would be done by either side that day, allowed the men to break ranks for supper and rode off to his quarters in the rear. By professional standards it was too late to begin a major engagement, though even so this decision of the usually vigilant and untiring Prince is hard to explain. Tired by the strain of the last forty-eight hours, discouraged by the hostility of his colleagues, he seems suddenly to have wavered in judgment, to have fatally allowed the unwillingness of Newcastle and Eythin to fight to blind him to the fact that the opposing army might, unprovoked, still take the initiative.

In every previous major engagement where he had been in command Rupert had attacked first. Was it hubris or weariness which made him act at Marston Moor as though his decision not to fight would prevent the enemy doing so? He had, to judge from his dispositions, intended to provoke Cromwell into charging first, so that he could take him at a disadvantage as he crossed the ditch. But what, except fatigue and discouragement, can have blinded him to the possibility of Cromwell's charging *without* provocation? This was exactly what Cromwell did. When the Royalists broke their ranks he saw, in the level rays of the declining sun, the only opportunity he would have that day of getting over the ditch while the Cavaliers were at a disadvantage. He charged.

Byron, in command of Rupert's first line, with remarkable speed got his men into action and bore down to meet him. But Cromwell was already over the ditch, and Byron by leading the first line out to attack prevented the musketeers from doing their part; they could not now check Cromwell's advancing horse-men because their own comrades were in their line of fire. Rupert, galloping up from the rear, met some of his own cavalry already in disorder. " Swounds, do you flee? " he shouted, " follow me," and led his second line into action. But the free movements of his cavalry were impeded by the now useless musketeers. David Leslie, with his Scots, had moved rapidly to the left-ward of Cromwell and, crossing the ditch beyond the extremity of Rupert's front, fell in with fury on his flank. This new attack came at a critical moment, for Cromwell, stunned by a blow on the back of the neck, was temporarily out of action, an accident which, but for the assistance of the Scots, might have discouraged his cavalry, locked in a sword-to-sword struggle with the best of Rupert's horse.

The Scots were fresh, but Rupert had no more reserves to bring up and his cavalry under the impact began to break and flee towards York, the panic communicating itself with horrible rapidity from squadron to squadron. In the fast gathering dusk he tried in vain, manfully seconded by Sir John Hurry, to keep some of them together. A Yorkshire officer, meeting the fugitives on the way to York, urged Hurry to lead them back to the field and got an oath in answer from the old soldier, who knew that cavalry once broken could not so easily be brought to fight again.[107]

In the centre during Cromwell's charge the remaining horse and all the foot of the Eastern Association had advanced upon the Royalist infantry and made short work of the Lancashire lads, who threw down their arms crying that they were pressed men with no heart in the fight. Only the stubborn Yorkshire men—the cause of all the trouble—now made a resolute stand although outnumbered and soon surrounded. It seemed to the men of the Eastern Association that the victory was complete. But on the farther side of the field disaster had come upon the Parliamentary cavalry under Sir Thomas Fairfax. Charged by Goring and the Northern horse, his men had been unable to repel the attack on the broken and enclosed ground where they stood. Except for Fairfax himself and a small body that he rallied, the rout had been complete and the fleeing horse, English and Scots alike, had cut through and spread alarm among the nearest of their own infantry. Here the generals had too quickly given all over for lost; Lord Fairfax rode for Hull and old Lord Leven for Leeds, starting the rumour of their defeat down the roads to the southward, to set the royalist bells ringing in Newark for a great victory.

On this side of the field the Royalist cavalry, careless and triumphant, were re-assembling on the very ground which the cavalry of Fairfax had occupied at the beginning of the battle, while just below them the Scottish foot, under General Baillie, prepared to make a last stand against them.

By this time the men of the Eastern Association had come full circle round the field and were now on the ground once occupied by Goring and the Royalist left wing. Apprised at last of the danger to the poor remnant of their northern cavalry and the Scots infantry, they formed for a final charge and the tired Royalist cavalry, far outnumbered and taken by surprise on disadvantageous ground, broke up before the onslaught. Some fled, more were killed, many, among them Sir Charles Lucas, were taken. Under the light of the rising moon, only the Yorkshire infantry were now left on the field. Some, with a desperate Yorkshire stubbornness fought on, while Fairfax, his face streaming blood from a sword cut, thrust his way among his men, beating up their weapons, and crying hoarsely, " Spare your countrymen." But it was midnight before the last shot was fired on Marston Moor and the last Royalist surrendered.[108]

Newcastle and Eythin had not fought it out with their doomed infantry though they had done what they could to hold the position until they saw that all was lost. They then withdrew to York. Rupert in the confused struggle to check the rout of his cavalry had been surrounded and at one time nearly taken. He cut his way out and reached York at about eleven that night, where his officers " came dropping in one by one."[109] Some time that night in the turmoil at York Rupert, Eythin and Newcastle were suddenly face to face. " What will you do? " asked Eythin. " I will rally my men," said Rupert, shortly. But Newcastle said, " I will go to Holland. I will not endure the laughter of the Court." After two days at Scarborough with Lord Eythin, where he flatly told the governor that all was lost, he set sail for Hamburg. He had behaved, he thought, " like an honest man, a gentleman and a loyal subject "; his conscience was clear and his self-esteem unimpaired.[110]

Cromwell, from a farmhouse among the wrecked fields, wrote on the night of the battle to his sister's husband: " Truly England and the Church of God hath had a great favour from the Lord, in this great victory given to us, such as the like never was since this war began . . . We never charged but we routed the enemy. The left wing, which I commanded, being our own horse, save a few Scots in our rear, beat all the Prince's horse, God made them as stubble to our swords . . . Sir, God hath taken away your eldest son by a cannonshot. It brake his leg. We were necessitated to have it cut off, whereof he died . . . There is your precious child full of glory, to know sin nor sorrow any more. He was a gallant young man, exceeding gracious. God give you His comfort."[111]

The Parliamentary losses were light, but of the King's men about four thousand were dead, the experienced officers of the Royalist army, the hardy Yorkshiremen who had followed the Royalist gentry and all that summer long defended their northern capital for the King. They found, for the most part, nameless graves, tumbled into shallow pits by the neighbouring villagers, becoming in the end a melancholy legend of the flat rural landscape. On the day after the battle Sir Charles Lucas, going over the moor with his captors to name the dead, could not conceal his anguish and with tears streaming down his cheeks sighed aloud, " Unhappy King Charles."[112]

The surrender of York was now only a matter of days. The Marquis of Newcastle's defection made every cautious or fair-weather Royalist in the North lay down arms. Leaders of more resolution would hold out for months to come, Richard Lowther at Pontefract and Hugh Cholmley at Scarborough; the garrison and citizens of Newcastle-on-Tyne still made good their long defence, but no northern army remained large enough to oppose the Scots and the Parliament forces. Rupert elevated Sir Thomas Glemham to the principal command in the North, with Goring to assist in the necessary and drastic re-organisation. Sir Marmaduke Langdale efficiently brought together the scattered squadrons of the northern cavalry and supported Rupert with all the weight of his austere authority. On July 4th they marched out of York with close on six thousand horse, and on the following night were joined at Richmond by Clavering with the men from Cumberland and Montrose from the Border. These fresh and undefeated troops formed a rearguard for Rupert's retreat into Lancashire, while George Goring scoured the country to bring in the rest of the broken cavalry.[113] In numbers at least the Royalists were still formidable, but they wanted equipment and made up in unruliness for what they now lacked in confidence. Goring, not a disciplinarian at the best of times, allowed his men to carry away geese and pullets, to raid and waste the contents of barns, and to drive off herds of cattle to supply them and their " leaguer ladies " (of whom there were many) with milk and meat.[114]

They fell back towards Liverpool but it was already clear that they could not hold Lancashire against the resurgent forces of the local Puritan gentry. Rupert reached Lathom House on July 22nd to find that the Earl of Derby had withdrawn to the Isle of Man, where a renewed threat of rebellion against his authority threatened to deliver this valuable base in the Irish Sea into Parliament's hands. In his absence Lathom House and some smaller residences of his remained as isolated outposts for the King in Puritan Lancashire.[115]

Langdale's cavalry and a dozen loyal garrisons would soon be all that remained to the King of his power in the North. Forty-eight standards, their drooping folds of crimson, yellow, blue and willow-green wrenched ragged by soldiers who had torn off strips for favours, were laid at the bar of the House of Commons, high among them Rupert's own great standard " near five yards long," blazoned with the arms of his house, the black and gold of the Palatinate, the blue and silver of Bavaria. The newly-arrived Ambassadors from the Dutch Estates, receiving their formal audience from Parliament, saw the piled, bedraggled trophies of the King's great army and drew their own conclusions.[116]

The first official news from Fairfax arrived in London on the evening of July 5th, after the House had spent a long and profitless day hearing evidence against Archbishop Laud.[117] The Scots Commissioners recognised the hand of God, and Dr. Baillie recorded that the wicked had suffered retribution: " Prince Rupert had done a glorious piece of service," he wrote, " but the blood of Bolton would not let him rest till all the glory he had got was lost in an hour."[118] Not the least cause for the thankfulness of the Scots Commissioners was for the part their own forces had played in the great conflict, vindicating their reputation and proving—after the disappointments of the spring —the value of their army in the field. They forgot Oliver Cromwell.

VII

Cromwell's thoughts were fixed on his own men and their actions—the men who now began to be called Ironsides, because Rupert, it was said, in the moment of his overthrow had called them by this name. " Our own horse, save a few Scots in our rear, beat all the Prince's horse," he had written to his bereaved brother-in-law, not intending to belittle the service of the Scots but speaking of what he had himself seen, the resolute charge of his own East Anglians. He was proud of his men and he identified himself with them, body and soul, especially soul. All the last year he had buffeted back angry complaints from Parliament, and from other commanders, that his men were Anabaptists, that his officers were " common men, poor and of mean parentage." These Anabaptists, these common fellows, had won a great victory. In all sincerity Cromwell was resolved that his " godly, precious men," should have the credit.[119] " Give Glory, all the glory to God," he had written, but he meant: to God and the Ironsides.

He despatched to London a messenger to report their triumph, Captain Thomas Harrison, a dark, flashing-eyed young man, son of a Staffordshire yeoman, once a lawyer's clerk. Harrison fought for the Kingdom of God on earth and believed, with entire conviction, that the thousand-year rule of the Saints would shortly come to pass. He also believed that God and the Independents had won the battle on Marston Moor, and said so with fervour and charm, to everyone he met, or, as Dr. Baillie complained, trumpeted over all the city the praise of the sectaries and their general, Cromwell.[120]

The Scots Commissioners saw with dismay the fruits of

victory, so long awaited and so hardly won, snatched from them by the Independents. The dangerous and despised sectaries were the heroes of the hour. It was on every tongue " with what courage undaunted Cromwell fought and all his honest blades."[121] The Independents were, in a moment, as strong in reputation as they had always been in fervour.

For the last three weeks the progress of the new Directory of Worship debated in the Assembly of Divines at Westminster had been obstructed by Philip Nye and his fellow sectaries who insisted that communicants should receive the sacrament in their places and not, in the Presbyterian manner, assembled round a table. If the ideas of the Independents had stopped short at the form of worship, the prospects for agreement would have been better. But their belief that every man had a right to his own interpretation of God's word and will was contrary to all Calvinist doctrine and struck, some thought, at the very foundation of righteousness.

A fortnight after the battle of Marston Moor a book slipped past the licensers to astound and dismay all who feared Independency. *The Bloudy Tenent of Persecution for Cause of Conscience* bore neither author's nor printer's name, but it was the work of Roger Williams, the gentle extremist from New England who had been expelled from the Calvinist colony of Massachusetts for his disturbing views and, with a band of followers, had founded the settlement of Rhode Island. He had come to England in the previous winter to obtain a charter for his colony, had got his charter and returned to America before his book was published. In its close-printed pages scandalised Presbyterians read " that the doctrine of persecution for cause of conscience is most evidently and lamentably contrary to the doctrine of Christ Jesus the Prince of Peace." Williams was not the first man to utter this belief; it had been put forward, also anonymously, some months before by the London citizen, Henry Robinson, but had attracted less attention than this second, similar plea.[122] Roger Williams " will have every man to serve God by himself alone, without any

Church at all," Dr. Baillie commented, more in amazement than in anger,[128] for the falsity of the opinion seemed to him self-evident.

The connection between authority in religion and authority in secular society was, to the majority of educated men, self-evident. The Anglican and the Presbyterian systems, each in its own way, established and sustained a form of social order. But the Anabaptists, and therefore it was believed most other sectaries, since they first broke out in Germany a century before, had preached equality, anarchy, and community of goods. The English preachings and prayings, callings to repentance, and public baptisms in Hackney Marshes were not yet so terrible as to threaten the social hierarchy or the sanctity of property. But, it was argued, if every man was to be free to choose and practise his own religion, if all doctrine was to be tolerated, there would in the end be no means of sustaining property or hierarchy against the prophets and messiahs who would surely arise.

The differences between the Divines in the Westminster Assembly, and the evident strain put on the Scots alliance were only the surface signs of a cleavage which penetrated to the roots of society. Young Hotham had predicted early in the war that if the present disorders should cause the common people " to cast their rider," there was no saying what would come to pass. The swelling power of the Independents made the common people every day more restive while the gentry's power to curb them every day grew less.

Oliver Cromwell, the " darling of the sectaries," had not himself any intention of destroying the social order; thinking chiefly of the necessity of winning the war, he did not at this time consider its possible consequences in other spheres. He had taken the Solemn League and Covenant because the military help of the Scots was essential; he advanced godly men, who happened to be sectaries, for their merit because he saw that, too, as essential to the winning of the war. But he fought the war to maintain the traditional society that he understood and valued against oppression from above or subversion from below, and he had not yet considered the explosive force of the religious and military instruments which he used.

On July 16th, 1644, York surrendered. Special provision was made for the preservation of the Minster, the many churches and their incomparable glass; Fairfax shared in the just Yorkshire pride in the monuments of a glorious past. The Royalists marched out with the honours of war and the terms with regard to the city were scrupulously kept, although there was some illicit plundering of the baggage wagons of the defeated. In the Minster, under the iridescent glow of the coloured windows, Robert Douglas, chaplain to Leven, preached on the text " The ungodly walk on every side; when they are exalted the children of men are put to rebuke."[124]

Two days later, on July 18th, Fairfax, Manchester and Leven sent a letter to Parliament requesting the speedy settlement of the reformed religion throughout the land. This might appear to be, on the part of the armies, a request for a Presbyterian settlement in accordance with the hopes of the Scots. But it would be difficult either for Parliament or the generals to leave Cromwell out of their calculations when the settlement came, ultimately, to be made, and the division of opinion was patent to all. Unity of council and concerted action were, however, still necessary to win the war. At Ferrybridge, a few days later, the three armies which had jointly defeated Rupert and taken York parted company. The Scots were to go north to reduce Newcastle-on-Tyne, Fairfax to deal with the last Royalist strongholds in Yorkshire, Manchester and Cromwell to clear the country to the south.[125]

Almost at once a difference began to appear between Manchester and Cromwell. Manchester who, since the King had attempted to arrest him with the Five Members in January 1642, had been so strong in the Parliament cause, seemed now to be assailed by doubt, and Cromwell, who only a year before had requested Parliament to appoint Manchester General, now with every passing week more bitterly resented his command. They were not temperamentally well matched; Manchester, in spite of his earnest piety, was a gentle, formal, well-mannered man, very much the aristocrat, fastidious and elegant in his dress, in tastes and manners very unlike the blunt and formidable Cromwell. But Manchester had real reason for the doubt and languor which seemed to overtake him when the siege of York was over. It is probable that he had been shaken by a brief visit paid to the camp of the besiegers in June by young Vane. Vane had come to consult with the principal commanders, both Scots and English so conveniently gathered before York, on a political question of high moment: nothing less than the deposition of the King. It seems possible that the name of Rupert's elder brother, the Elector Palatine, may have been put forward as a substitute. The Prince, now in Holland, had private ways of communicating with Vane whose younger brother and brother-in-law were in the immediate circle of his mother's household in The Hague. He had, by way of demonstrating his solidarity with Parliament and the Scots, recently taken the Covenant at a religious gathering in Delft. But Vane, whose private inclination was towards a republic, may not have reached the point of suggesting a new King, because Lord Leven, the Fairfaxes and Manchester had unanimously refused to entertain in any way the idea of deposing Charles.[126] If Cromwell was involved in the consultation, he can hardly have dissented from the unanimous view of his military superiors, but he was known to be friendly with Vane and to share many of his more extreme political ideas. Certainly, it was not long after the visit of Vane to York that Manchester became anxious about the future position of the King, suspicious of Cromwell, and languid in waging the war.

He lingered for ten days at Doncaster, and at Lincoln for nearly a month. He would not undertake the reduction of Newark, though it was an obvious objective. He was with difficulty persuaded to accept the surrender of Welbeck, where the Marquis of Newcastle's deserted household and children were only anxious to come to terms. When John Lilburne, supported by one of Cromwell's particular friends, Henry Ireton, captured the little stronghold of Tickhill, Manchester roundly abused him for his services and called him " base fellow " in front of many witnesses. All was far from well in the army of the Eastern Association, and Manchester's supporters noticed that Cromwell was building up a party for himself which split the once united force into two hostile factions.[127]

VIII

The Scots army, under Leven and David Leslie, were for their part very willing to transfer their activities nearer to their native borders, where they were, intermittently, apprehensive of trouble. In June they had briefly feared that Rupert himself, instead of marching on York, would make a diversion by invading Scotland.[128] That fear had evaporated but Montrose was still in action. The Scottish Estates, prorogued by the King in November 1641 until June 1644, had met according to this three-year-old decision in bland disregard of the changed circumstances and their now open rebellion against the King. The president of the meeting was Lord Maitland, now by his father's death Earl of Lauderdale; his dual character, as their principal Commissioner with the English Parliament and president of their own Parliament, made it clear that the purpose of this meeting was to strengthen the alliance and prosecute the war against their King. Their first action was to appoint the Earl of Callander to deal with Montrose's forces on the Border.[129]

The outlook seemed, on the whole, calm, and the chief work before them to send to the scaffold the Royalists captured in the spring.[130] But signs and omens were abroad and uneasy rumours. A whale had chased another up the Moray Firth and flung itself ashore at Tarradale; here and there springs were said to have spouted blood, and blood gouts had been seen floating in a well, though it was, in that case at least, "conjectured that some waggish person had cast such things in the water."[131]

In the second week of July news came from the West coast that a force of Irish had landed in Ardnamurchan.[132] The Earl of Antrim's army was not an illusion after all. The ten thousand he had promised to the King numbered about eleven hundred fighting men, some armed with muskets, but all of them much readier with dirk and claymore. They brought with them their wives, their children and their cattle, a tribe on the march. Ormonde, who was altogether doubtful of the King's wisdom in encouraging such an invasion and afraid of the effect their appearance as the King's soldiers might have on the settlers of the North, had refused them the use of an Ulster port. They had had to embark at Waterford, which partly accounted for their delay in coming.[133]. Their leader was Alaster M'Coll Keitach, the younger son of Coll the Left-handed who was a prisoner in one of Argyll's castles; for simplicity's sake his Saxon contemporaries called him Alexander Macdonald. He was twenty-five years old, stood six foot six in his brogues, and had already distinguished himself in the Irish fighting. A popular chieftain and a valiant warrior, Macdonald had with him his young wife and children and his attendant priests. Ruthless in war, he was well behaved in the necessary intervals, never sat down to meat without hearing a Latin grace or went into battle without first devoutly taking the Sacrament.[134]

The invaders advanced across the undefended country towards Badenoch, capturing two godly ministers as hostages, plundering crofts and driving off the cattle as they went. Rumour, within a week, made them four thousand carrying all before them.[135] In Edinburgh, Argyll undertook to put them down. Neither he, at this point, nor the Scots generals in England, imagined that this Irish irruption would be more than a temporary nuisance. The Estates concluded their meeting by sentencing the Royalist prisoners to death, decreeing the destruction of one of Montrose's castles, prohibiting (not for the first time) salmon fishing on the

Sabbath and the sale of intoxicants after ten o'clock at night, and rose after Loudoun, in a " pretty and eloquent " oration, had given thanks to God for preserving Scotland from the " general combustion."[136]

South of the Border, at Carlisle, Montrose too had news of the Irish landing, but he now had no troops with which to join them, for all that he had raised were needed by Rupert in England. He sent two friends, Lord Ogilvie and William Rollo, secretly into Scotland, but they brought back word that the Royalists had lost hope and would not rise again: the Irish had come three months too late. Montrose pondered the problem; obstinate in his conviction that the people of Scotland were " either fooled or forced " into obedience to the Covenanters, he began to think of returning alone to Scotland to raise the Highlands and lead the Irish.[137]

IX

While disaster overwhelmed the Royalists in the North, good fortune had not deserted them in the South. Waller still hovered about Oxford, but as he reported to the Committee of Both Kingdoms on July 20th, 1644, he had now much less chance of reducing the town. In the last six weeks it had been admirably fortified, properly provisioned and put into a state of defence by the energetic new deputy governor, Sir Henry Gage, the most distinguished English commander in the Spanish service who had newly returned from the Netherlands. It was no longer the ill-stocked, ill-guarded town that had so nearly been taken six weeks before.[138]

Waller withdrew sulkily to his old headquarters at Farnham and sent to Parliament for fresh equipment. Browne, only a little less dejected, strengthened the fortifications of Reading and Abingdon while respectfully informing the Committee of Both Kingdoms that he would not take orders from Waller, that his troops were in want of almost everything and were in consequence extremely unpopular in Berkshire, whose people had been afflicted for nearly two years with the quartering of both parties.[139]

For a few weeks longer the Earl of Essex continued his independent operations in the West. He had refused to come back to Waller's help after raising the siege of Lyme; he took Taunton early in July owing to the weakness of a Royalist officer who was subsequently tried and shot.[140] The war was growing more vindictive. At Dorchester, the Parliamentarians hanged seven Irish soldiers, in answer to which the Royalists hanged twelve prisoners recently taken in Wiltshire. Essex summarily executed a captured officer, alleged to have deserted from the Parliamentary forces; Prince Maurice retaliated by hanging a Parliamentary sea-captain who had recently fallen into his hands. It looked as though the damnable business of reprisals would have no end.[141]

But Essex failed in his principal objective, the capture of the Queen. At his advance, she recognised the danger and had, though desperately ill, the judgment to see that she should escape becoming a hostage in enemy hands. Leaving her new-born child she fled from Exeter, meaning to go to France. The Earl of Warwick patrolled the coast and should have stopped her leaving, but his attention was often diverted by the Dunkirk and Irish privateers, who swarmed in the Western approaches, so that she managed to slip away from Falmouth in a Dutch ship. A Parliament ship pursued and fired on her, but the Queen, though forced to crouch for safety in the stinking hold, had a flash of her old spirit and commanded the captain to sink his ship rather than surrender. When the rebel at length abandoned the pursuit she came on deck and stood looking after it, grinding her teeth. She reached Brest, ill, weary and disheartened, to be welcomed as a daughter of France with every kindness and honour, and to realise within a few weeks that the French Court would do anything in the world to content her except risk a man or a penny for her husband's cause.[142]

But her husband's cause was far from desperate. Essex, having

lost the Queen, stood at gaze in Devonshire. Before him lay the
narrowing West Country peninsula which the Royalists held.
Behind him, cutting him off from Waller and the London road,
were the King's advancing forces. He could not return the way
he had come without a battle. He was outnumbered, far from
home, and in hostile country; his plan had been, in that narrow,
sea-bound region, to cut off the King's Western forces with help
from the fleet. But Waller had failed him; he had let the King
and his forces come in pursuit to the West. His only hope now
was that Warwick would not fail him too.

The Queen had fled on July 14th. A week later her husband
was in Devonshire. Robert Herrick from his Dartmoor vicarage
at Dean Prior celebrated his coming:

> Welcome, most welcome, to our vows and us,
> Most great and universal genius!
> The drooping West, which hitherto has stood
> As one, in long lamented widowhood,
> Looks like a bride now or a bed of flowers,
> Newly refresh'd both by the sun and showers.
> War which before was horrid now appears
> Lovely in you brave prince of Cavaliers![143]

The King addressed a great gathering on Dartmoor; with him
was the Prince of Wales. "If I live not to reward you," he
promised them, "I hope this young man, my son and your
fellow soldier, will." But though the King was received with
enthusiasm, few enlisted.[144] On the 24th the King was at Chard,
on the 25th at Honiton, on the 26th he reached Exeter. Here he
saw his new daughter, reviewed Prince Maurice's troops and
received a small gift of cash from the town, while Essex retreated
westward down the peninsula and crossed the Tamar into Cornwall.[145] On the 29th the King advanced to Bow and slept in the
alehouse, and on August 1st he entered Cornwall, having
destroyed all the bridges over the Tamar to prevent any possible
outflanking move by Essex.[146]

Trying to keep in touch with Warwick's fleet, whatever else he might lose, Essex drew back to Lostwithiel along the Fowey estuary, and took up his position in a place defensible enough but too narrow for manœuvring against the King's forces which presently cut off all egress by land. Hence on August 4th he wrote with a great bluster of indignation and excuse to the Committee of Both Kingdoms for instant help by sea or land; Waller, who had not stopped the King from marching into the West, was in his opinion to blame for his present difficulties.[147]

All the summer the King's army had been divided by intrigue and mistrust and now, in the face of the enemy, the crisis came. Harry Wilmot, in command of the Oxford cavalry, had done good service at Roundway Down and more recently at Cropredy. He had been raised to the peerage in the spring as Lord Wilmot of Adderbury, a reward which did not assuage his ambitions or console him for certain miscalculations about the war; he had hoped for quick returns in money and power.[148] Failing these, he had recently married a rich widow with kinsmen of the opposing party. His humour all the summer had been sullen and difficult, and since discretion was never one of his virtues he had openly spoken of Prince Rupert's dangerous ascendancy over his uncle, and of his own belief that it would be better to make peace, if necessary by elevating the Prince of Wales against the King. It was not surprising in the circumstances that Charles was contemplating his removal.[149]

Harry Percy, the general of the Ordnance, supported him. Brother to the Earl of Northumberland, he had friends in London, and it was he who in 1641 had revealed the damaging details of the King's Army Plot.[150] He shared fully in Wilmot's dislike of Rupert, who had often accused him of mismanagement and delay at his critical task of keeping the forces in arms and ammunition. Both, in the course of the summer, had become hostile to Digby who, with an agile shift of his opinions, was now a Rupert man.

Digby's views reflected those of his master, the King. Charles had always shown a generous unwillingness to condemn his favourites for failure, and the defeat at Marston Moor increased rather than diminished the warmth of his feelings for his nephew. Against the resounding defeat, he weighed the numerous past successes and he knew that the Prince was working hard to save what could be saved. He probably shared with the optimistic Digby the belief that Rupert would shortly " renew the dispute on terms not unhopeful."[151] Rupert's best friend at Court, the gentle Richmond, was with the King again, and the Queen, whose jealousy had worked against him, was now abroad. For this reason Rupert, absent and defeated, exercised a greater influence over his uncle than he had done at any time in the last year when present and victorious. " Great fear some have of Prince Rupert, his success and greatness," wrote an observant informer.[152]

The crisis came in August when the King's army was camped at Boconnock above the trapped forces of the Earl of Essex. On August 6th Charles sent to Essex offering in noble and somewhat hazy terms to give peace to his suffering people if Essex would enter into an understanding with him. Wilmot contrived to add a secret personal message: namely that if Essex accepted the King's offer, Wilmot would organise support for him in the King's army which would enable them both to overthrow Digby and those who favoured war. Those who knew Wilmot well, understood him to have some idea of joining with Essex to take the King under their " protection " to London.[153]

It was clearly time for the King to act. On August 7th George Goring arrived hot foot from the North by agreement with Rupert,[154] and on the following day Wilmot was arrested at the head of his troops and Goring proclaimed general in his place.[155] Wilmot had been generally popular with his subordinates, to whom he was affable and free with entertainment, and immediately a number of them protested against their general's sudden disgrace. The King was able to answer with a formidable catalogue of Wilmot's indiscretions, culminating with his private message to Essex. Wilmot's only defence was the plea that he had too ardently desired peace and that he had intended no treason. He was wise enough to give no further encouragement to his followers, and was content soon after to go into exile in France where he strove to build up his position anew by earning the Queen's favour.[156]

Essex meanwhile rejected the King's overtures[157] and all thoughts of peace, according to the King's ideals or Wilmot's practical plots, were alike at an end. George Goring, bold, gay, and open-handed, rapidly ingratiated himself with the cavalry. Harry Percy, deprived of Wilmot's support, resigned, while Lord Hopton was put in charge of the Ordnance.[158] All this tended to but one end: Rupert, on his return from the North, would be made commander-in-chief. On August 15th, Digby wrote to him that the change would be effected as soon as Lord Forth, who had been recently created Earl of Brentford, could be given some honourable cover for his resignation.[159]

Rupert was on his way. For the first fortnight in August he was at Chester whither he had withdrawn with the remnant of his army at the end of July. He spent his time recruiting with considerable success but was hampered by lack of arms, for supplies of which he planned to send Sir John Hurry on a mission to the King of Denmark.[160] In Cumberland, Sir Thomas Glemham had re-assembled about three thousand men for action in the North. Lord Byron had rounded up at least two thousand more in Lancashire, but lost many of them again owing to his customary rashness, in a clash near Ormskirk, where the good service of Langdale alone prevented disaster.[161] Rupert was believed to have about two thousand, quartered on the Welsh side of the Dee. He immediately set about recruiting in North Wales and building up a new train of artillery. By the middle of August he was already despatching new contingents of horse and foot to be trained at Shrewsbury.[162] Very soon rumour credited him with five thousand. In London the Committee of Both Kingdoms speculated uneasily on his movements, wondering if he would break out towards the North to rejoin Byron and Langdale, or strike across the Midlands.[163] He did neither, but with a small guard of horse slipped down the Welsh border and by August 26th was in Bristol.[164] Here he was met by news which pulled him up short. His elder brother, the Elector Palatine, was in London with the King's enemies.

Rumour had predicted his coming for several weeks, and on August 18th he landed and proceeded immediately to the capital.[165] Parliament greeted him with less enthusiasm than he had expected but rooms were made ready for his use at Whitehall, and his request to attend the Westminster Assembly of Divines was willingly granted. It was widely believed that a party in Parliament favoured the idea of joining with the Scots to put him forward as a possible candidate for his uncle's throne,[166] and Charles himself wrote with asperity to enquire " upon what invitation you are come." To this the Elector piously replied that he wished nothing but " a happy concurrence " between King and Parliament, and would use his best endeavours to procure it. The King did not write again. Possibly to the Elector's disappointment, no one offered him his uncle's crown. Since the Scots were utterly opposed to such a thing, and Fairfax and Manchester had both rejected the idea, the Elector's presence was something of an embarrassment, but he was a thick-skinned young man and settled down to live at Whitehall for as long as Parliament would give him free board and lodging.[167]

The Elector's arrival called an immediate halt to the King's plans for making Rupert commander-in-chief. On August 30th he despatched to him a written protestation of his trust: " Concerning your generosity and particular fidelity and friendship to me, I have an implicit faith in you."[168] For the reason which prompted this sudden declaration Charles referred his nephew to what the bearer should relate. There can be little doubt what message came to Rupert by word of mouth; the King thus discreetly conveyed to him that he could hardly appoint him *generalissimo* when, at any moment, a party among the rebels might set up his elder brother for King. Until the Elector's prospects were either confirmed or dashed, the reorganisation of the army must wait.

Rupert digested his disappointment as best he could. He had other anxieties. The position on the Welsh border was disquieting. Oswestry had been lost in June and North Wales was full of discontent, with constant quarrels between Rupert's officers and old Archbishop Williams at Conway, who argued, sagely enough, that the inhabitants would turn against the King if their wool and cattle trade was disrupted. He protested in vain, and already the people, the drovers especially, were growing hostile. In South Wales Sir Charles Gerrard, another of Rupert's favoured cavalry commanders, had done extremely well, consolidating almost the whole of the region for the King and penning Rowland Laugharne and his Parliamentary forces into Pembrokeshire.[169] But Rupert was especially concerned for Montgomery Castle, possession of which was vital to his control of the northern Welsh marches and for the sending of the troops from Dublin, who still from time to time landed at Chester, to their headquarters at Shrewsbury. Lord Herbert of Cherbury, the owner, had refused to garrison it, and when Rupert sent for him he would not come on the frivolous excuse that he " was newly entered in a course of physic." On September 7th the learned and eccentric lord agreed to hand it over to the Parliamentary forces for a garrison, provided only that the soldiers did not cross the threshold of his library. A Royalist effort to recapture it was repelled with loss, and Rupert, with more distress, it was said, than he had felt for the loss of York, saw that a formidable obstacle now lay between his recruiting grounds in North Wales and the training place of his troops at Shrewsbury.[170]

But the King at Boconnock in Cornwall was too much delighted with his own good fortune to realise the potential dangers on the Welsh border. His forces under their new commanders had closed in on the baffled Earl of Essex, compelling him to withdraw farther down the peninsula towards Fowey.

Contrary winds prevented the Earl of Warwick from reaching him by sea, and by the time he did so the Royalists had occupied outposts above Fowey harbour so that he could not land to help his cousin. On August 26th Goring's cavalry occupied the out-lying villages of St. Blazey and St. Austell, while some of the King's infantry crept into the enemy camp and almost succeeded in blowing up the store of gunpowder. Essex, on the 27th, appealed once more to Parliament to send him help before it was too late. The Committee of Both Kingdoms acted fast in the face of this distress: they commanded the Earl of Manchester to march to the south-west and they ordered three thousand pounds' worth of food to be shipped to Fowey. But Essex had not waited. On August 31st he allowed his cavalry under the skilful Balfour to try to cut their way through the Royalist ring under cover of darkness. By a clever use of uneven ground they managed to outwit the Royalists and slip away, while Essex, abandoning his infantry and guns, was rowed out to one of Warwick's ships and escaped by sea.[171]

The infantry and the guns remained, penned into Fowey. Now that Essex had gone, the London veteran Philip Skippon was in command. At a Council of War he stubbornly argued that they could at least try to fight their way out, but officers and men were dejected by the events of the last month and out of heart since Essex had abandoned them. Overruled, Skippon had no choice but to sue for terms and on Sunday, September 1st, the infantry, after abandoning all arms, ammunition and cannon, was allowed to march away. The Royalists needed the ordnance—thirty-six cannon, ten thousand muskets and pistols, and several wagon loads of powder and match; they did not wish to be encumbered with prisoners, though they were willing enough to enlist any who showed a disposition to desert. The defeated army passed through the King's lines with no attempt at bravado or even dignity—" pressed all of a heap like sheep, though not so innocent; so dirty and so dejected as was rare to see," wrote a contemptuous Cavalier, and the Royalists from jeering soon fell to plundering. Philip Skippon, who alone retained a mournful dignity, rode over to the King and told him his men were breaking the terms. Charles received him coldly but restored order.[172]

X

Dismay spread among the Parliamentary leaders. " Since Pym died," lamented Dr. Baillie, " no' a wise head amongst them: many were good and able spirits, but not any of so great and comprehensive a brain. . . . If God did not sit at their helm . . . long ere this they had been gone."[173] But perhaps God no longer sat at the helm? The Presbyterians in the Westminster Assembly, all through August while Essex and his army were *in extremis,* had read the signs of God's anger and had denounced from their pulpits the " dangerous and licentious " doctrines which had offended God and brought punishment on his people. Preaching before Parliament (with the attentive Dr. Baillie also in the audience) Thomas Hill and Herbert Palmer " laid well about them " and did not scruple to " charge public and parliamentary sins strictly on the back of the guilty."[174] The guilty, in their opinion, were Roger Williams who " under pretence of liberty of conscience " had defended Jews, Turks and Papists in his *Bloudy Tenent of Persecution,* a book which should have been publicly burnt; John Milton for his *Doctrine and Discipline of Divorce*; and the anonymous author of *Man's Mortallitie,* which questioned the immortality of the soul. On August 26th, to assuage the wrath of God or that of the preachers, the House of Commons strengthened the Committee which controlled printing and issued an ineffective order to " inquire out " the authors of *The Doctrine and Discipline of Divorce* and of *Man's Mortallitie.*[175] God's wrath was not assuaged; a week later they heard in London that Essex had fled and his infantry surrendered at Fowey.

The hanging of two more Roman Catholic missionary priests, Ralph Corby and John Duckett, at Tyburn on September 7th barely diverted the attention of the people from the tidings of disaster.[176]   But in the religious situation which was now fast developing, the Independents were more troublesome than Papists and Prelatists.   The Presbyterian preachers redoubled their condemnations of them in sermons preached before Parliament, but John Goodwin, most eloquent and most popular of the sectarian divines, before his " gathered " flock in Coleman Street, denounced " the grand imprudence of men in suppressing any way, doctrine or practice, concerning which they know not certainly whether it be from God or no."   In his opinion the defeat of Essex might well be a judgment on the Presbyterian, not the Independent, party.   His sermon, printed soon after under the title *Theomachia*, became the doctrinal rallying point of the Independents, and swelled John Goodwin in the opinion of the Presbyterians from a genial and popular minister into " the Great Red Dragon of Coleman Street."[177]

The prosecution of the war could not wait until the divines had settled whether God was a Presbyterian or no.   On the news of the disaster in Cornwall, the Derby House Committee sent again to the Earl of Manchester to join Waller and proceed to the south-west.[178]   Their order found him in an irritable humour; he had refused to attack Newark, and Rupert had since sent reinforcements of cavalry to strengthen it.   Urged to reduce Chester, and so check the Prince's recruiting operations, he had said that the siege of such a town was no undertaking for " one month in the latter end of a summer," especially with Newark unreduced in his rear;   the majority of his officers had voted down the plan to the annoyance of Cromwell.[179]   On the first news that Essex was in trouble, Cromwell had tried to hasten the march southward, but Manchester had been openly rude to him, and when he heard, at Huntingdon, the full news of the disaster, he stopped the march altogether, threatened to hang any who tried to go on and muttered angrily that wars were easier to begin than to end, and this war was no way to serve religion.[180]

This indeed was a cause of his anxiety. By no wish of his, the sectaries had become the backbone of his army. Since the victory at Marston Moor had made Cromwell so great a man, Manchester was more appalled by the prospect of victory than by that of defeat. Cromwell and his faction might urge him to march at once to redeem the disaster in the West, but whatever their anxiety for the safety of London and Parliament they did not conceal their joy that Essex was now discredited and would, surely, be removed to make room for a general after their own hearts.[181] So violent was the disagreement that both generals came to London, Manchester supported by Lawrence Crawfurd, to lay their quarrels before the harassed Committee of Both Kingdoms.[182]

" Our labour to reconcile them was vain," wrote Dr. Baillie. " Cromwell was peremptor, notwithstanding the Kingdom's evident hazard, and the evident displeasure of our nation."[183] But the Scots commissioners and their friends in Parliament had, within a few days of the Cornish disaster, further cause for anxiety, and by the time Cromwell came to London their reputation had so far declined that their " evident displeasure" carried little weight. A new and fearful storm had broken in the heart of Scotland.

XI

Argyll had taken calmly the news of the Irish landing in July. He had the men, the resources and the experience to deal expeditiously with the intruders who had come, he confidently believed, too late to find any support among the cowed Royalists of Scotland. The leaders of the rising in the spring had been put to death. Huntly had fled to the far North; when his eldest son, Lord Gordon, found it difficult to hold down his clansmen and his neighbours in the name of the Covenant, Argyll had stationed Campbell troops at Turriff in the heart of the Gordon country.[184] Montrose was far off in England, without men or money, and with no hope of support for any Scottish venture from the broken Royalists of the northern counties. No wise man, in mid-August, would have given anything for the chances of Alaster Macdonald and his Irish as they pushed on into the heart of the Highlands looking in vain for Royalist allies.

Rumours of the Irish landing reached Montrose, forlorn and obstinate, at Carlisle and strengthened his purpose of returning into Scotland. Three men might slip through the Lowlands where an army could not pass. He chose two companions, secreted in the lining of a saddle the King's commission appointing him general in Scotland and his standard, and rode over the border disguised as the groom of two gentlemen travelling upon their peaceable occasions. Detected once at least, but not betrayed, he made his way to the house of a kinsman at Tullibelton, on the edge of the Highlands. Here he lay hidden while his companions scoured the country for news of the Macdonalds. They discovered them approaching the braes of Atholl. The Edinburgh government had called on the clans of the region, the Stuarts and the Robertsons, to resist the invaders, and when the Irish came into the open ground where the Tilt flows into the Garry at Blair Atholl, they found eight hundred men waiting to fight them. At this moment, and in the nick of time, Montrose walked into the Irish camp, and Macdonald's musketeers with a typical and lavish gesture, used the last of their powder in firing a salute to the King's general.[185]

Montrose had nothing to offer them except his leadership— neither money, nor arms, nor following, but a cool head, a persuasive tongue, some influence in that part of Scotland, a huntsman's knowledge of the hills and, as it was to turn out, a genius for guerilla warfare that was to be the marvel of the age. His first task was to persuade the Stuarts and the Robertsons that he, and not the Estates in Edinburgh, represented the rightful sovereign of Scotland whom the Irish also served; having made them friends with the Macdonalds, whom they had come to fight, he found himself in command of nearly two thousand men. In a meadow overlooking the river Tilt about half a mile from Blair Castle, whence a small Covenanting garrison watched him in helpless annoyance, he formally raised the royal standard.[186]

It was early August. The late summer and autumn lay ahead with golden weather for campaigning. With his small force he marched rapidly into the Tay valley, making for Perth and the country where he had most friends. As he emerged into the plain, he came upon other troops who had been called out against the Irish, mostly Grahams, his own people, whom he easily persuaded to join him.

Three miles outside Perth, on the breezy down of Tibbermore, Montrose and his army found the Covenanting troops from Perth, seven hundred professional cavalry, sent from the Lowlands, and six thousand infantry, " freshwater soldiers never before used to martial discipline," but stiffened by one regiment of trained men. Montrose's men, uncouthly clad, inadequately armed, with little ammunition and no cavalry, were outnumbered by at least two to one, a visible calculation which made Lord Elcho, in command of the Covenanters, over-confident of victory. Montrose, not greatly hoping this time to repeat his bloodless successes with the Stuarts, the Robertsons and the Grahams, sent to inform Elcho that he had the King's commission as lieutenant governor of Scotland, and to request his obedience, or at least a truce for discussion since the day was Sunday. Elcho, so far from recognising the King's commission, refused to Montrose's rabble the ordinary rights of war. He seized the messenger, swore to hang him when the battle was over, and sent back to say that in his opinion the Lord's Day was very fit for performing the Lord's work. He then gave his troops the word for the day, " Jesus and no quarter," and made ready to annihilate the foe.

Montrose had the advantage of slightly rising ground. The

greatest danger to his smaller force was that of being outflanked and surrounded; he drew them up therefore only three deep over a front considerably longer than Elcho's. In the middle he placed Macdonald and his Irish; on the right the Atholl contingent, " courageous, strong and tall-bodied men," eight hundred in all; on the left the Grahams.

Elcho began the battle by loosing a troop of his cavalry against the Irish infantry. Instantly a party of Macdonald's rushed forward with such bloodcurdling shrieks and brandishing of weapons as, with a little ragged musketry fire, served to bring Elcho's horsemen to a stand. Montrose seized on the moment of misgiving to advance. The Irish bore down with speed and clamour on the Lowland infantry and the local levies turned tail while the professional men wavered. Elcho's cavalry vainly tried to disorder the Irish by a flank charge, but the men of Atholl, who had no powder left, hurled stones at them until they wheeled and fled, overrunning some of their infantry. By this time Montrose's men had captured Elcho's cannon but there was no need to use them; the rout was already complete, and before sunset Montrose had entered Perth in triumph. The stores, the arms, the horses in Perth were his for the taking. Exactly a fortnight after crossing the border with two companions on a desperate venture, he had won a resounding victory and entered the third city of Scotland as a conqueror.[187]

Argyll hurried towards the scene of action and took comprehensive measures to deal with the rising.[188] Troops on the border were instantly ordered to the north. At Newcastle, the Scots leaders consulted. Lord Leven wrote urgent advice. At all costs, Montrose and the Irish must be prevented from gaining a hold in the Highlands where they would bring upon Scotland " the many miseries which the insolency of a barbarous enemy fastening himself in the heart of a nation " could inflict.[189]

He wrote too late. From all around, the Royalists came in to join Montrose, the Earl of Airlie and his younger sons, the Ogilvies and the Grahams from the land to the south of Perth, and from farther north Nathaniel Gordon rode in with thirty horse.[190] Thus strengthened, Montrose marched towards Aberdeen while Argyll assembled his forces for pursuit and sent the Chancellor Loudoun to England to contradict the wild rumours of Montrose's victory that were lowering the credit of the Covenanters in London. The tale of the " lamentable disaster " at Tibbermore was there before him, and on all sides bleak looks greeted the Scots from their despondent allies.[191]

XII

Against the background of this gloomy news, the Scots Commissioners and their English colleagues at Derby House tried to patch up the quarrel between Cromwell and Manchester. The Scots had been disappointing allies since the beginning of the year. They had failed to take Newcastle in six months of siege; their glory in the battle of Marston Moor had been filched by Cromwell; and now they had serious trouble in their own country. As their credit dropped that of their English friends dropped too. Everywhere, except in the Westminster Assembly of Divines, the sectaries were in the ascendant. In the Assembly they could delay but could not prevent the general acceptance of Presbyterian reforms planned by the majority. But in the House of Commons, when the Assembly propositions reached it, they could and did do more. On September 13th, 1644, Oliver St. John moved that a Committee should be appointed " to endeavour the finding out some way how far tender consciences, who cannot in all things submit to the common rule which shall be established, may be borne with according to the Word." The reasonable proposition passed without a division,[192] but when the Scots Commissioners heard of it they were appalled, for they saw muffled in this innocent-seeming motion the dreadful doctrine of toleration. No conscience, by their ruling, should be so tender as to object to the Presbyterian propositions; those who pretended such scruples were flouting the will of God, and therefore sinful or a cause of sin in others.

They suspected, probably with justice, the hand of Cromwell in St. John's motion; he was in London still, settling his quarrels with Manchester. They did not yet suspect that the third member of the dangerous triumvirate was their friend Harry Vane. Pleased by his civil tongue, his fervent piety and his numerous efforts over the last year to strengthen the alliance and understanding between Scots and English, they had apparently come to believe that Vane, in spite of the modifications he had made in the drafting of the Covenant, was on their side against the sectaries. They were wounded, and felt themselves wronged and betrayed, when in the long wranglings which now ensued Vane pleaded with eloquence that some toleration be allowed for tender consciences.[193]

The motion for the " Accommodation " of tender consciences, as it was usually called, was passed on September 13th, 1644, and on the same day the House voted their thanks to Oliver Cromwell for the great victory he had won at York over Prince Rupert and the Marquis of Newcastle. The meaning of such a vote was painfully clear to the Scots Commissioners. They contemplated with gloom their ungrateful and perfidious allies at Westminster, the malignant King at Oxford, their own country a prey to the murdering Irish: surrounded by so many evils they could only put their trust in God and pray for a better outcome.

The summer's campaigning was not quite over. The King, after leaving Prince Maurice to besiege Plymouth, was advancing eastward. Essex had landed at Southampton to take charge of what was left of his army—the infantry without arms and wretchedly clad, the cavalry exhausted with the retreat from Fowey and very short of horses.[194] Waller's troops at Farnham were mutinous, ragged and ill-equipped; Browne's troops at Abingdon could get no supplies from the country, defied their officers and fell to plunder.[195] Parliament's forces had failed to take Basing House and so reopen the road for London's wool trade. The Scots had still not taken Newcastle, the Fifeshire coal they sent to London could not meet the city's needs, and it looked as though there would be a third fireless winter. Manchester and Cromwell were with difficulty persuaded to shelve their grievances. From Scotland a stream of terrifying rumours came southward.

The glorious hopes that had risen in July when the battle at York was won were clouded with anxiety and doubt. The cleavage between Independent and Presbyterian threatened to create a second and more fearful struggle at Westminster, before the struggle with the King was over. In the early autumn of 1644 Parliament's victory was still uncertain, that of the King still possible. So it seemed to many of the Parliament party. So it seemed to Lord Digby; looking back over the agitations of the summer—the flight from Oxford, the disaster at York, the victory at Cropredy, the triumph at Fowey, the Royalist rising in Scotland, and the quarrels reported from Westminster—he felt his spirits rise. " God hath blessed his majesty's affairs even to miracle," he wrote to Ormonde. "We are now marching eastwards, victorious and strong . . . so that you may confidently esteem His Majesty's affairs here are in the best posture that they have been at any time since these unhappy wars."[190]

CHAPTER FOUR

THE REFORM OF THE ARMIES

October 1644—April 1645

THE optimism which so much endeared Lord Digby to the King was justified by the embarrassment of Parliament and the Scots, not by the strength of the Royalists. The King still had some garrisons and several forces of skirmishing cavalry in the north and eastern midlands, but his effective control of his kingdom was now limited to Wales, the south-western midlands and the south-west. Even his triumphant army in Cornwall had been reduced and exhausted by the efforts of the summer and was seriously short of horses.[1] The King needed the coming winter to recruit his forces, to secure the foreign help in arms, men and money that he hoped the Queen might send, and to bring into action the troops from Ireland on which he still so confidently counted.

In the year which had gone by since the Earl of Ormonde, at his command, made a truce with the Irish, several thousand men from Ormonde's own government forces had been sent into England. But, apart from the invasion of Scotland by the Macdonalds, no troops had been sent to his help from the ranks of the Irish insurgents, and Ormonde's negotiations with the Confederates at Kilkenny had been fruitless, chiefly because they continued to believe that it was his duty and interest, not to treat with them as Lord Lieutenant representing the interests of the settlers, but to put himself at their head as the leader of a united Catholic Ireland, and begin by driving the Scots from Ulster. Ormonde's refusal to do this created something like a deadlock.

Meanwhile the King's secret envoy, the Earl of Glamorgan, after receiving his commission in the royal bedchamber in the early spring of 1644, had been held back from setting out on his mission while the King reconsidered the wisdom of sending him. He was still in Oxford in the autumn.[2]

The King's useless attempts to mobilise the Irish to help him had already cost him more than he was willing to understand. Old Lord Blaney, the veteran soldier who, three years before, had brought the news of the Ulster rising to Dublin, spoke the opinion of most of the settlers when he declared that truce with the Irish was reprehensible to any man with " an English heart, a Protestant face and a Christian conscience."[3] Lord Inchiquin, the principal bulwark of the English in Munster, abhorred all thought of a truce with the Irish and denounced the policy which made allies of them against the King's Protestant subjects.[4]

Inchiquin was himself an Irishman and chief of the O'Briens; alone of the Irish chiefs, he had stood with the Protestants and the settlers from the outbreak of the troubles, and had received no reward for his loyalty. He had seen, on his visit to Oxford in the spring, that the King had not the means, even if he had the desire, to put down the Irish revolt. The royalist defeat at Marston Moor precipitated his defection with that of all the leading Protestants in Munster. It was not disloyalty but sheer necessity that made them turn henceforward to Parliament for help.[5] Inchiquin's first move was to seize on all the stores in the town of Cork and expel all Roman Catholic citizens. His defection gave the valuable ports of Southern Ireland to Parliament which immediately sent shiploads of arms to strengthen Cork, Youghal and Kinsale. Cheered at this demonstration of Parliament's efficiency and goodwill, Inchiquin implored Ormonde, in the best interests of all, to break off negotiations with the Confederates and to place himself at the head of the Protestants of Ireland.[6] It was an odd fate which pursued the loyalist Ormonde; that he was constantly called upon to lead one or other of the rebellious parties.

The harassed Ormonde would not listen to Inchiquin. With Ulster largely under the control of the Covenanters, and Munster allied with the English Parliament, the revenues of the Dublin government were sharply reduced. Import duties and a recently introduced Excise were the chief sources of ready money and as trade both by sea and land was almost at a standstill, they brought in far too little to the empty treasury.[7] The Lord Lieutenant was not greatly cheered by a visit from Antrim, full of the brave deeds of his clansmen in Scotland and much concerned to match himself a pair of dun-coloured coach horses. But he believed it his duty to remain loyal to his King and to represent him with fitting dignity and an air of confidence. At this low ebb of his fortunes a French traveller in Dublin noticed with admiration the Lord Lieutenant riding to Church in state on a Sunday, at the head of his guards, on his white Barbary horse.[8] In spite of his outward calm, he did not disguise from the King the " desperate and heartless condition " in which he found himself; " near eaten up of want, almost hopeless of relief, blocked up at sea, encompassed with powerful armies . . . with a very small, indigent, unsatisfied army, unfortified towns, unfaithful in-habitants . . . in addition to all these miseries, I am totally in the dark as to his Majesty's pleasure."[9] All that he knew for certain was that the King needed ever more and more help out of Ireland; accordingly, he prolonged the truce with the Con-federates until December, and in the early autumn received their representatives in Dublin in the hope of making the alliance for which Charles was waiting.

The King continued obstinately to underestimate the damage done to his cause by his relations with the Irish. Yet he had the evidence of it under his eyes in England. A trickle of desertions from the Royalist army during the whole of the last year had revealed the anger and disapproval felt by some of his adherents for the Irish entanglement. Anthony Ashley Cooper, governor of Poole, had shifted his allegiance from King to Parliament, and Inchiquin's younger brother, Royalist governor of Wareham in

Dorset, had handed the little port over to the Parliamentarians and sailed, with all his troops, for Munster.[10]

But the King's mind, as he advanced from Devonshire into Dorset in October, 1644 (" marching eastward, victorious and strong," in Digby's phrase), was once again confidently set on destroying the remaining Parliamentary forces in the south of England. Rupert joined him for a brief consultation and went back to Bristol to lead his newly-recruited troops to a rendezvous at Sherborne. He had scarcely gone before the King decided to hasten on, without waiting for him, to relieve the besieged garrisons at Basing House and Donnington Castle. He encouraged his men, in the wet and blustering weather, by sometimes marching with them himself on foot all day. He was cheered by another visit of the French resident, the Marquis de Sabran, friendly, well-informed, and fresh from London. Sabran, while admitting that Parliament had the greater resources, assured the King that time was on his side, for his enemies would soon mar all by quarrelling among themselves.[11] Thus heartened, the King on October 15th, 1644, entered Salisbury.

Waller, with a spurt of renewed confidence, had marched against him. " Destroy but this army and the work is ended," he had assured the Committee of Both Kingdoms, but he could not challenge the King's army alone; Essex and Manchester must be ordered to join him.[12] The French envoy's opinions were shown to be true; Manchester, protesting every mile of the way, angry with Cromwell and now jealous of Waller, held the march up for a week at St. Albans, then plodded on to Reading, and there stuck fast, though post after post reached him from London telling him to go on. " Still they would have me march westward, westward ho! but they specify no place . . . it may be to the West Indies or St. Michael's Mount," he grumbled, and muttered to himself that it would be best to make peace.[13] Essex, in Hampshire, had only reassembled a few hundred of his poor, battered cavalry and less than a thousand of the dejected, unarmed foot who had marched out of Fowey.[14] He was even less disposed than usual to join with Waller.

At Salisbury, though Rupert had not yet come with his additional forces and had sent word that his new army would not be ready to march for some days yet, the King continued confident and " a great gaiety possessed Goring," who, with a party of two hundred picked men, drove Waller from his quarters in Andover. " Our intention was to engage them," wrote a Cavalier, " but they disappointed our hopes by their heels."[15] The Cavaliers were enjoying themselves as their enemies stumbled and scattered before them under the lashing autumn rain. Manchester, who had at last agreed to move, joined Waller at Basingstoke on October 19th, where shortly after the poor remnant of cavalry from Cornwall under Balfour came in, to be followed forty-eight hours later by the Earl of Essex and his infantry. Manchester and Cromwell were now openly at odds; Essex claimed to be ill.[16] Though the junction had belatedly been made, the quarrels of the commanders and the poor spirits of their drenched troops augured very ill for their prospects.

Donnington Castle, an old square stronghold just to the north of Newbury, a Royalist outpost on the London road, had been besieged for nearly a month. As Waller's men fled from Andover, he called off the besiegers of Donnington whose governor, Colonel John Boys, flushed with the glory of a difficult and successful resistance, was knighted by Charles on October 21st. There was news of victory from near and far. The Royalists at Basing House, the massive and well-defended mansion of the Marquis of Winchester, which had been surrounded for over four months, successfully beat off a joint attack of Waller, Essex and Manchester, while the King, still expecting the arrival of Prince Rupert with forces from the west, occupied Newbury.[17]

II

While the King's men were thus employed in England, he received his first direct tidings from Montrose in Scotland.[18] After his victory outside Perth Montrose had marched on Dundee but made no attempt to take it, turning northwards towards Aberdeen. Lord Gordon failed to marshal his clansmen in defence of the Covenant, and stood mournfully aloof, watching this new incursion into his people's territory.[19] Montrose turned westwards up the Dee, gathering recruits as he went, crossed it at Drum, marched down the northern bank, evaded troops from Stonehaven sent to intercept him and appeared before Aberdeen on September 13th.[20]

In spite of two years' strenuous preaching by their famous minister, Andrew Cant, the Aberdonians were unwilling Covenanters, but they had a Covenanting provost and the town had been formidably garrisoned since the spring. Montrose gave warning that if they refused him entry he would take the town by assault and they had better send their women and children to safety. They refused him entry and as his messenger returned, an unknown soldier in the garrison wantonly fired on him and killed the drummer boy who accompanied him. This unprovoked barbarity " made Montrose mad "; he had warned the town of the fate which awaited them if they defied him, and things must now take their course.[21] The garrison, strengthened by the townsfolk who for months past had been armed and drilled, now drew out before the town confident that they could repel him. They had about two thousand infantry and five hundred cavalry. Montrose, rather better provided than at Tibbermore, had about fifty horsemen and fifteen hundred foot armed with muskets, dirks and bows, but no pikemen: it was a commonplace of military science that cavalry could be withstood best by pikemen. Montrose divided his troops into three, the centre to charge the enemy infantry, as at Tibbermore, with dirk and claymore. The two wings, each fringed with a score of horse, were to use their muskets to divert and hamper the enemy horsemen when they attacked.

The Covenanters, trusting to their superiority in cavalry, tried to outflank Montrose's forces and encircle them, but his musketeers on the wings coolly let them go by, then faced about and opened fire. Thus, instead of encircling Montrose's forces, the cavalry of the Covenanters found themselves cut off from their own infantry and with Montrose's forces between them and Aberdeen. In the meantime, the Irish in the centre hurled themselves against the Covenanting infantry and forced them back towards the gates of the town. The Covenanting cavalry, harassed by musketry fire, in disorder and cut off from the town, fled the field, taking most of the Covenanting leaders along with them. The defeated infantry pressed in flight through the city gates with Montrose's men on their heels.[22] The Irish took all that they could lay hands on. "The riches of that town hath made all our soldiers cavaliers," reported a gratified officer of Macdonald's. Montrose, turning his eyes away from the horrors of the sack which he had threatened and could not now prevent, remained outside the town until the following day, when he came to read the royal proclamation against the Covenant and tried, ineffectively, to restrain his troops. The citizens vainly protested their Royalism or stuck Montrose's emblem, a spray of oats, over their doors, but scarcely a house was left unplundered. More than a hundred perished in the capture and sack of Aberdeen, and it was a bare and battered city from which, after three days, Montrose and his army withdrew.[23]

He could not spare men to garrison the town; his plan was at first to startle the Edinburgh government by his raiding, and so to draw troops after him to the highlands until the lowlands were left demoralised and weak in men. Argyll with considerable forces, was already in pursuit of him. Entering Aberdeen, he established a new garrison, set the Aberdonians to their drilling again, proclaimed a reward of twenty thousand pounds for

Montrose, alive or dead, sent for Lord Gordon, and with the acquiescent young chief at his side ravaged the Gordon country to prevent any help reaching Montrose. He destroyed corn on the ground, drove off sheep and cattle, and requisitioned the horses for his baggage train, so that there was scarcely one left " to bring in a load of peats to the fire."[24]

As Argyll advanced, Montrose drew back into the hills, crossed into the Spey valley and marched south for Atholl, giving Argyll just so much reason to guess his movements as would make him follow. By the time King Charles, far down in the south of England, had news of his new champion's victories, Montrose had dragged Argyll and his army for the best part of two hundred miles after him—up the Spey valley, through the forest of Rothiemurchus, over the moors of Badenoch, through the mountains of Atholl, down the valleys of Tummell and Tay, and so "round about again into Angus and the Mearns." All this long, wild, exhausting march Argyll never brought Montrose to battle, never so much as sighted him. The Council in Edinburgh blamed him for delay, and his troops muttered at the hard going in the dangerous, roadless hills, while Montrose marched light and unhindered, his men hunting deer for food. Impertinent Royalists took heart to mock the Covenanters, and wondered aloud what had become, all this while, of Argyll and his great army.[25]

This good news from Scotland brought fresh joy to the Royalist army camped about Newbury. All the last weeks in London the hapless Scots Commissioners had been trying to conceal the extent of their trouble from their English allies, but they had no illusions about it themselves. Montrose's attack was " the greatest hurt our poor land got these fourscore years," wrote Dr. Baillie, and in England he saw with sorrow how the Independents rose in popular esteem and the Presbyterians sank as the reputation of their Scottish allies declined.[26]

In this dismal hour, and just in time to raise the spirits of the Parliamentary armies at Basingstoke, one long-expected victory came. The Scots took Newcastle-on-Tyne. It had been besieged since the early spring and had been cut off from all hope of relief since the collapse of the Royalist cause in the North. The governor, Sir John Marley, who was also the Mayor, was stubborn to the last and refused terms offered to him on October 17th although Leslie had mined the walls. The Scots fired the mines, breached the defences and launched a general assault. The garrison put up a brave fight against impossible odds, barricading the streets and fighting from house to house, but the town was occupied before nightfall on October 19th, and Marley, who had withdrawn with the surviving troops into the castle, capitulated at mercy three days later.[27]

Never was news more timely. The summer had been cold and wet; autumn had set in with early frost and biting wind. The Londoners were in no mood to face another winter without coal, and the fall of Newcastle brought them a hope of glowing hearths once more. It also restored the reputation of the Scots, and gave them a valuable bargaining counter against their critics; it would lie with them to hasten or withhold the supply of fuel to London.[28]

III

The Cavaliers at Newbury were in better heart than their enemies at Basingstoke, but they were fewer in number. Prince Rupert had still not come but the King was resolved, without waiting for him, to detach troops for the relief of Banbury, besieged for the past three months. Twice the enemy had penetrated the shattered walls and twice been driven out again, now ammunition was running low, water was short, all the horses except two had been eaten, and the walls, plugged with turf and mud, were becoming indefensible. The King could not delay in answering the appeal of its eighteen-year-old governor, William Compton, and his heroic garrison.[29]

The departure of fifteen hundred of the King's cavalry might have remained unknown to the Parliamentary commanders had it not been for the desertion of Sir John Hurry. He had left Parliament for the King with valuable information fifteen months earlier; now he turned his coat again and returned to Parliament, taking with him accurate information of the King's present strength and supplies.[30] Learning from him that the Royalists were fewer than they supposed, the Parliamentary generals moved cautiously towards Newbury from Basingstoke, meaning to cut off the King's road to Oxford and force him to fight before Rupert, and the troops who had gone to Banbury, could rejoin him.[31]

They reached Thatcham about noon on October 25th, and saw some of the King's army " drawn forth in a body upon a place of advantage " just to the north-east of Newbury. The Royalists were cautious; after repelling an attack on their position, they withdrew after dark, built up defences across the approaches to the town, left a strong detachment to the north-east at Shaw House, and drew up their main body on the rising ground at Speen Heath, north-west of Newbury, where they were partly under the protection of the guns of Donnington Castle. They meant to stand on the defensive until Rupert came up, or the Parliamentary armies, unable to find sustenance for their large force, had to withdraw.[32]

Next day, Saturday, October 26th, 1644, the Parliamentary generals took stock of the position. They decided that the defences between them and the town were too strong to be attempted, but they would force the King to fight by attacking him on Speen Heath. Essex, Waller and Cromwell with most of the Eastern Association cavalry were to march in a wide circuit to the north by Winterbourne and Boxford, and so fall upon Speen Heath from the west, while Manchester, with the rest of the Eastern Association army simultaneously attacked the King's outpost at Shaw House. The Royal troops, compelled to fight on two fronts with inferior forces, could hardly escape defeat.

The plan looked sound enough but the execution was mismanaged. Manchester, perhaps to divert attention from the lengthy manœuvres of his colleagues, attacked Shaw House before sunrise on October 27th and was thrown back with some damage. By the time he heard the prearranged signal—a cannon shot—by which his colleagues on the farther side of the field gave him warning that they were ready to attack, his men were already discouraged.

Essex, Waller and Cromwell had had a long march, and could not open the attack on Speen until nearly four o'clock in the afternoon. In the narrow muddy lanes their cavalry could not be used to the best effect, and after the initial onrush, in which they carried the village of Speen, they found themselves exposed to heavy musketry fire from the hedges as well as the guns of Donnington Castle; they were also harassed by the King's skirmishing cavalry. In spite of this the infantry of Essex, especially the regiment which had once been Hampden's, stubbornly fought to retrieve the honour lost at Fowey and retook, to their great joy, cannon which they recognised as their own, surrendered in Cornwall. But Cromwell's cavalry, of which much had been hoped, made little headway and it was some time before Manchester, on the farther side of the field, tried once more to draw off the Royalists by attacking their forces in and around Shaw House. By this time the autumn evening was closing in, and in the dusk two companies of his own infantry wasted time and lives fighting each other for a point whence the Royalists had already withdrawn. For the rest, the Royalists held their well-planned position at Shaw House with deadly determination, their leader, Sir George Lisle, throwing off his buff-coat so that the white glimmer of his shirt should be distinguishable to his men in the deepening twilight.

The unsatisfactory and unfinished conflict ended only an hour after nightfall. The King withdrew into Donnington Castle, whence all about he saw the flashing of muskets and heard sporadic firing from the darkened moor. After half an hour's consultation he left with the Prince of Wales and his personal guards to join Rupert's reinforcements coming up from the West. The main body of the army, after the cannon had been secured in Donnington Castle, drew off towards Oxford by way of Wallingford. The operation should have been hazardous, for the moon was now up and the enemy very close and well able to see their movements, but through exhaustion or negligence there was no pursuit that night. The active Colonel Birch aroused Manchester—poor Manchester was plagued with energetic subordinates—and wished to chase the enemy; the general only yawned and said it was too late. Birch, with a handful of volunteers went off by himself, but all he took for a prize was a coach containing the elderly German Baroness, who was wife to the Earl of Forth. [33]

At daybreak Waller and Cromwell went in pursuit, and Manchester, yielding to pressure, agreed to follow. They had delayed too long; the Royalists on their way to Oxford were already over the river at Wallingford, which they had strongly garrisoned. After a long day's pursuit into country which clearly could not, or would not, support so large an army, Manchester insisted on withdrawal,[34] and they fell back sullenly to secure, if they could, the surrender of Donnington Castle.

The King, after a fifty-mile march without a rest, had joined Rupert at Bath on the afternoon of October 28th.[35] Thence they returned to Oxford, meeting the Welsh forces brought up by Sir Charles Gerrard on their way. At Oxford the King knighted some of the heroes of that summer—Henry Gage for his relief of Basing House, William Compton for his endurance at Banbury.[36] On November 6th, on Bullingdon Green, he reviewed his reassembled army, fifteen thousand horse and foot, and proclaimed, at long last, the appointment of Prince Rupert as general. He elevated him at the same time to one of the most important places about the Royal household, that of Master of the Horse, left vacant since the disgrace of Hamilton.[37] It had become clear that the Elector Palatine would not have the effrontery to claim the Crown, and that no one in London had any intention of doing it for him. Prince Rupert was nonetheless anxious to prevent any rumours that he was arrogating too much power to himself, and he therefore persuaded the King to name the Prince of Wales commander-in-chief of the army and give to him the title of lieutenant general only.[38]

Much of the King's valuable artillery had been left in Donnington Castle, where Sir John Boys defied the discouraged Parliamentary forces. The King and Rupert with his refreshed army set out on November 9th to relieve the castle and get the guns away to Oxford. Apprised of their approach, Manchester called a council of war, but Cromwell strongly advised against any attempt to intercept him at this stage, arguing that the cavalry could not be brought together in time and was too exhausted to fight.[39] A half-hearted attempt was made to line the hedges in front of Donnington with musketeers and cover the King's approach with cannon. But this proved no serious hindrance, though the King's horse was shot in the foot as he rode at the head of his own regiment. The rest of the Royalist army came on boldly, " drums beating and colours flying, trumpets prattling their marches," and drew up to Donnington without any interference. Next morning, November 10th, they left again, with their rescued artillery and marched to Lamborne, all in the sight of the enemy, with no trouble except a half-hearted cavalry attack on their rear, which Rupert easily dispersed.[40]

IV

The Parliamentary commanders argued angrily together. Cromwell, at their first Council of War, had refused to venture his cavalry alone against the King's forces; at a second council of war, held before the King left Donnington, Cromwell changed his tune and urged that a concerted effort be made to prevent his slipping away from them yet again. Manchester, at long last, said openly what had been in his mind ever since the victory at Marston Moor. "Gentlemen," he pleaded, "I beseech you let's consider what we do. The King need not care how oft he fights, but it concerns us to be wary, for in fighting we venture all to nothing. If we fight a hundred times and beat him ninety-nine times, he will be King still. But if he beat us but once, or the last time, we shall be hanged, we shall lose our estates, and our posterities be undone." "My Lord, if this be so," answered Cromwell, "why did we take up arms at first? This is against fighting ever hereafter; if so let us make peace, be it never so base." But it was evident that Cromwell wanted no peace, for he went on to remind his colleagues that the Queen was in France, and they would therefore be wise to put the King out of action before help could be sent him from across the Channel. Manchester, with greater knowledge of foreign affairs, said flatly that the King would never get any help from France. His advice prevailed and no new battle was fought at Newbury to stop the King's return to Oxford with his cannon.[41]

The Parliamentary army, with its jealous and quarrelling commanders, was now in dismal plight. Even Cromwell admitted no further effort could be expected of men who were reduced by the marches and efforts of the summer to walking ghosts.[42] Waller declared that his men had been in constant service since the first battle of Newbury, more than a year ago, had fought through a bitter winter, a wet spring, a stormy summer, and now faced the winter again without rest or reward, and their pay in arrears.[43]

Bad news came in upon the Committee of Both Kingdoms from other regions. Disorder in the garrison at Windsor started a scare of another Royalist *coup* to seize London.[44] From Nottingham the reverberations of a quarrel between the Parliamentary governor and the local gentry spread to Westminster, and the Committee, in the midst of so many serious troubles, had to consider a dispute about the governor's dining arrangements which threatened to split their supporters in Nottinghamshire.[45]

From Gloucestershire, Colonel Massey complained that it was impossible to hold his troops together. As all these local forces were enlisted by the County Associations, they thought themselves free to leave the service of one county for another whenever better pay or prospects tempted them.[46] It was evident that something would have to be done to reorganise an army that was disintegrating.

Over the whole gloomy scene hung the threat of a serious breach with the Scots, and another fireless winter. The terms of the alliance had been broken on the English side; Parliament had failed to provide the money to keep the Scots soldiers in pay and they had repeatedly been denied food and fodder by the English among whom they quartered. After the capture of Newcastle they were at last in possession of a bargaining point; they refused to supply London with coal unless the revenues of the trade were secured to them to pay their army.[47] Although great efforts had been made all that summer to stock London with turf and firewood from all the country round,[48] the Parliamentary leaders were well aware that without coal they would hardly control London for another winter. The Scots exploited their new strength and pressed for an immediate settlement of the Church according to the Presbyterian model.[49]

Meanwhile, the long drawn out trial of Archbishop Laud had gratified his more vindictive enemies and served, though not very adequately, to keep before the public the knowledge that Presbyterians and sectaries alike abominated the episcopal church. But once again, as with Strafford, the prosecutors found that the law strictly interpreted could not be stretched to find the Archbishop guilty. What they were pleased to call " misdemeanours " in the administration of his office they could find in plenty but nothing that could be construed as treason. The prosecution lamely tried to show that so large a number of misdemeanours amounted to treason but the Archbishop's counsel made a mock of the attempt: " I never understood before this time that two hundred couple of black rabbits would make a black horse."[50]

By November they had decided that they would have to proceed with Laud as they had with Strafford, draw up a Bill of Attainder and send him to his death by a special decree made for that purpose. The bill passed its first reading in the House of Commons without difficulty.

It was a different matter when the Westminster Assembly recommended to the consideration of Parliament their new Directory of Worship, which contained in its preface the downright declaration that Presbyterianism was, by Divine Right, the only form of Church government. The supporters of the Bill produced it early in the morning, hoping that it would be passed by an empty House; but the lawyers John Glynne and Bulstrode Whitelocke, two of its opponents, delayed the proceedings with long speeches until the House filled up and the bill was voted down.[51]

The depressed forces of Parliament were all this while withdrawing from Newbury; they abandoned their works around Basing House, and fell back from Hampshire into the home counties to find winter quarters. It was a misty, damp autumn and on November 19th, the King's birthday, three suns were said to have been seen in the sky, and an inverted rainbow—heavenly omens betokening nobody quite knew what. The same day Parliament received a petition from the Eastern Association protesting with some justice that the army which they had spent so much to equip and pay was now constantly on service in other parts of England. They could not support so great a cost as this entailed. The Committee of Both Kingdoms listened to the Eastern Association as it might not have done to other complainants, and resolved that they must take steps to plan the army anew on a national basis.[52]

In the same week Parliament sent a delegation to the King to propose a new treaty. The inspiration had come from the House of Lords and had not been curbed by St. John and Vane in the Commons: they could afford to offer an olive-branch which they knew the King would ultimately reject. In the meantime the negotiations, as they had done two years before, would give them time to proceed with the major work of reorganising their army. In this they were very much wiser than their colleague, Denzil Holles, the leader of the Presbyterian sympathisers. He, with the secret help of the Scots Chancellor, Loudoun, of the fickle Lord Holland and the intriguing Lady Carlisle, was in touch with the French resident Sabran, who he believed could influence the King to consider the terms. Let a treaty once be set on foot, these hopeful conspirators calculated, and the Scots and Presbyterians would find means of joining with the King to overthrow the dangerous Independents. Only one concession was needful; that the King abandon the Anglican Church. The French resident, who knew Charles better after a few weeks than Lady Carlisle and Holles did after a lifetime, told them that they were asking the impossible.[53]

The Parliamentary messengers had a scathing welcome in Oxford. The sentries at the gate delayed them for two hours; they found poor, unfriendly lodgings in the town, and the King, who received them after dinner in the garden of Christ Church, was openly rude. When he heard that they came as messengers with no authority to argue the terms he refused to waste time, as he put it, on mere postillions, but gave them a sealed answer to carry back to Westminster. It was clear to all present at that interview, where the Princes Rupert and Maurice stood beside the King in open derision of the messengers, that he was confident of victory.[54]

Before the Parliamentary postillions could carry the King's letter home, the long approaching storm had broken at Westminster. The Committee of Both Kingdoms had been deeply perturbed by the quarrels between the generals, and some of its members, visiting the army on the eve of the fighting at Newbury, had seen for themselves how bitter was the disagreement. The Committee now asked for an explanation of the failure to stop the King at Donnington. In response, on Monday, November 25th, Cromwell placed before the House of Commons an account of the campaigning since the previous July, in which he condemned Manchester's " backwardness to all action, his averseness to engagement or what tends thereto, his neglecting of opportunities and declining to take or pursue advantages upon the enemy." He gave it as his opinion that if Manchester had more speedily joined Waller and Essex when commanded to do so by the Committee, " the King by this time had not had a foot on this side Salisbury, except Oxford, Winchester Castle and Wallingford."[55]

Immediately the opponents of the sectaries, in and out of Parliament, rallied to Manchester's support. Dr. Baillie believed the time was ripe for Cromwell's overthrow, and that his rashness in accusing Manchester would make an opportunity for destroying " that potent faction," the Independents. " This is our present difficile exercise," he wrote home to Scotland, " we have need of your prayers."[56]

On December 2nd Manchester offered his written answer to these charges, which proved to be a counter-attack on Cromwell as a defiant subordinate and a man of dangerous ideas; he had expressed a hope " to live to see never a nobleman in England "; he had said he would fight the Scots as willingly as the Cavaliers should they try to enforce Presbyterianism; he had accused the Westminster Assembly of persecuting " honester men than themselves," and he had deliberately filled the army with sectaries so that no peace should or could be made that did not suit them.[57]

The quarrel was now fairly launched into the stormy sea of politics. Cromwell was shown as the advocate of all those ideas most likely to " overturn " the state and to dismay not only the House of Lords but moderate men of all kinds. Other evidence came hissing up on the lips of Cromwell's enemies; his officers and those he favoured were not only " common men, poor and of mean parentage," but also very often New England men, returned wanderers, men who no longer had a stake in their native soil; moreover, he encouraged a " cluster of preaching officers and troopers," laymen who expounded the Scriptures without training or licence, and sometimes claimed to have seen visions; the troops in the Isle of Ely preached in every pulpit and, to add a grosser charge, Cromwell's Deputy Governor there, Henry Ireton, had raised fifteen thousand pounds locally and spent none of it on the defences.[58]

The Earl of Essex, Denzil Holles and Philip Stapleton, now the admitted leaders of the Presbyterian, or more truly the anti-Independent party, consulted with the Scots Commissioners; they, for their part, had received instructions from Edinburgh to demand action against Cromwell as an incendiary, for slandering the Scots and their friends and endangering the alliance. They abandoned the plan because expert lawyers doubted whether the charge could be effectively sustained, and Cromwell's support in the House of Commons, with Vane and St. John to organise it, was by now so strong that such an action could have led only to disaster.[59] There was also a growing fear of sectarian tumults in the city, tumults which almost broke forth at this time because it was thought the peers were trying to save Archbishop Laud from the scaffold. The angry recrudescence of this danger provoked the Earl of Essex to exclaim, " Is this the liberty which we claim to vindicate by shedding our blood? Our posterity will say that to deliver them from the yoke of the King we have subjected them to that of the common people."[60]

What indeed was the liberty for which the Parliament forces were fighting? Essex and Manchester had believed it to be the liberty of Lords and Commons against the power of the King. But there was coming up now, ever louder, a demand from the common people, associated inevitably with the revolt of the sectaries from the Presbyterians. The people, or those who claimed to speak for them, fixed their hopes on what they still called " Parliament," but they meant the House of Commons and specifically the Independents in it.

Suddenly a small single sheet without a printer's name was scattered in the streets during the night. "Alas pore Parliament," it began, " how art thou betrai'd!" and in a few strong phrases blasted the Earls of Essex and Manchester and demanded the prosecution of the war in Cromwell's fashion. The House of Lords protected its dignity and the reputation of Parliament by applying the recent ordinances against unlicensed printing and ordering that author and printer be found and punished. Neither could be traced, but the culprit was, very possibly, John Lilburne, making use of one of the secret presses which now operated in London.[61]

On the same day, December 9th, Cromwell in the House of Commons changed the nature of his demands. He implored his fellow members to " save a Nation out of a bleeding, nay almost dying, condition," and went on to suggest the means: " This I would recommend to your prudence, not to insist upon any complaint or oversight of any commander-in-chief upon any occasion whatsoever; for as I must acknowledge myself guilty of oversights, so I know they can rarely be avoided in military matters. Therefore waving a strict inquiry into the cause of these things, let us apply ourselves to the remedy; which is most necessary. And I hope we have such true English hearts and zealous affections towards the general weal of our Mother Country, as no Members of either House will scruple to deny themselves, and their own private interests, for the public good; nor account it to be a dishonour done to them, whatever the Parliament shall resolve upon them in this weighty matter."[62]

Zouch Tate, the member for Northampton, then moved that, as long as the war lasted, no member of the Lords or Commons should hold any military or naval command. On the face of it, this looked like an honest attempt to separate practical military questions from political and religious quarrels, and put an end to recriminations by relieving the most important officers of their commands. Essex, Manchester and Cromwell would all have to resign: offering a *quid pro quo*, Vane, who was Treasurer of the Navy, and some others who held offices of profit in the armed forces, avowed themselves willing to lay these down as the price of remaining in Parliament. It looked as though the army would be purged once and for all of political faction.

The apparent purpose of this sly and significant measure, which came to be called the Self-Denying Ordinance, was not the same as its real purpose. Parliament could, after all, make exceptions to its own decrees and while the majority in the Commons was controlled by Vane and St. John they were more than likely to find means of retaining Cromwell in the army. After all, as the French resident at once perceived, any member of the House of Commons could choose whether or not to retain his army command, for he had only to resign his seat legally to do so. No such action was possible to peers; for Essex and Manchester the Ordinance left no loopholes.[63] Under an appearance of equity which hardly admitted an argument, the new measure would cut short the quarrel with Manchester, ensure his withdrawal and that of Essex, and make room, in one way or another, for the domination of Cromwell.

This ultimate aim was not immediately grasped by the Scots, or by their English friends. " The House of Commons in one hour has ended all the quarrels which was betwixt Manchester and Cromwell," wrote Dr. Baillie. " This done on a sudden, in one session, with great unanimity, is still more and more admired by some as a most wise, necessary and heroic action; by others as the most rash, hazardous and unjust action that ever Parliament did." He added, with just foreboding, " the bottom of it is not yet understood."[64]

Who was behind this far-reaching measure? Whose brain had brought forth the ingenious scheme? Cromwell had heralded it in his speech and Zouch Tate had introduced it, but the subtlety of the scheme, its surface innocence and actual ingenuity, suggest that it had been born and brought to maturity in a more politic head than Cromwell's; he was still essentially the hand and not the brain of his party. The Self-Denying Ordinance had that about it which suggests the Parliamentary skill, the deceptive, smooth approach of Harry Vane.[65]

V

At Oxford, the bottom of it was not understood either. But it served to increase the optimism of the King and his friends. Their own army had triumphantly weathered a similar crisis in the past summer, but their enemies, quarrelling in Parliament, and mutinous in the ranks, were hardly likely to survive an operation more drastic than that which the King had performed when he dismissed Wilmot at Boconnock in August and gave Rupert the chief command at Oxford in November.

Filled with hope, the King dispatched the Duke of Richmond and the Earl of Southampton to Westminster to give, at greater length, his considered answer to the terms which Parliament had tentatively put forward. The outward part of their mission was to make clear the very limited framework within which he would discuss a treaty. Their concealed and more significant task was to find out what they could about the divisions of their opponents and to try to separate the Independents still further from the rest by indicating that the King would give them a measure of toleration if they would work towards peace. The hints and offers made by the Presbyterian sympathisers, even assisted by the charm of Lady Carlisle, left the King's messengers cold. If his enemies divided, the Independents, not the hateful and aggressive Presbyterians, were the party the King hoped to win. Whatever came of the treaty the disintegration and collapse of the Parliamentary cause was expected within a few weeks by the more sanguine Cavaliers.[66]

Although Oxford, shortly before the King's return, had been afflicted by a destructive fire, the atmosphere, as the Court prepared for Christmas, was generally cheerful. The great news of the season was of more victories in Scotland. A messenger, who reached the King's quarters a few days before Christmas, gave a full account of what had happened since Montrose, after the sack of Aberdeen, vanished into the highlands with Argyll in pursuit.

The Covenanting forces after following him " round about from Spey to Atholl " until they were tired out,[67] had hoped that they would stop him, with help from their troops now stationed in Aberdeen, when he emerged towards the coast. But he had marched for the second time that autumn through the Mearns, burning the barns and driving off the cattle of the Covenanters, and once again crossed the Dee at a place they had neglected to guard.

On October 15th the first snowfall in the north slowed down the marches of both armies, and before the end of the month Montrose decided to give battle to his pursuers before winter stopped their proceedings. He waited for them at Fyvie Castle, well entrenched in a steep orchard. Short of ammunition, he melted down for bullets all the suitable metal he could find in the house, pots, pans, trenchers, candlesticks and tankards, and was thus far better supplied than the attacking force had anticipated. They had been harried by skirmishing parties on the last days of their march, and after three useless attacks on his entrenchments at Fyvie, they gave up. Montrose fell back towards the mountains, beat off one last half-hearted attack as he went through the village of Huntly, and vanished into the mountains, undefeated, to recruit his forces for a fresh campaign.[68]

So much Montrose's messenger could report to the King, but long before he had told his tale and been rewarded with a knighthood among the festal lights of Oxford,[69] matters had gone further in Scotland. Montrose had expected some help from the Marquis of Huntly, who might, now that there was again a Royalist army on foot, have ventured out of his hiding-place in the far North. But Huntly did not stir, though he continued to convey to Montrose that he would do so if he received a commission from the King. Montrose had such a commission for him, and this he now dispatched.[70] Still Huntly did not move, and since the old chief would not come, the cunning Nathaniel Gordon went out from Montrose's camp to see if he could win the young chief for the King.

Lord Gordon was in Aberdeen with his uncle, Argyll, when Nat Gordon rode in, professed his sincere remorse for having joined Montrose, and did penance for adultery and for speaking despitefully of the ministers. When, some days later, Argyll went back to his own lands, leaving Lord Gordon in command at Aberdeen, Nat stayed with the young chief and used his influence to another purpose.[71]

Montrose had fallen back into the mountains, making for Blair Atholl once more. A heavy snowfall in November blocked the passes, and the Irish, unused to such mountains, cumbered by their women and children, and suspicious of their Scottish guides, grew mutinous. Somehow Montrose prevailed with them to push on, until they reached at last the blessed shelter of Blair. Here smaller and larger bands of men daily came in, for the news of the rising had spread throughout Scotland. Under the King's banner now were ranged men from Galloway and the Border, from Orkney and the Hebrides; the widely scattered Macdonalds came in to join their Irish clansmen, from Glengarry, from Lochaber, from the Isle of Skye.[72] The Macdonalds now made up the greater part of Montrose's army, and when the bitter weather of November was succeeded by a mild December, they grew restive for an immediate attack on the lands of the Campbells, their hereditary foes. Montrose and his more sober colleagues vainly argued the dangers of a campaign in mid-winter in country that could be reached only by crossing passes as high and dangerous as those in which they had so recently been lost. If the weather changed while they were still in the Campbell country, they might never get out again. But the Macdonalds would not be gain-said, and Montrose, who responded easily to the challenge of the impossible, was not unwilling to be overruled.[73]

The decision was taken on St. Francis Xavier's day; a blessed omen, said the Irish priests, that this great apostle to the heathen should stand patron over a crusade against the heretic Campbells.[74] This time the Irish left their women and children behind; they set out in mild weather, marched to Killin at the head of Loch Tay, where the MacNabs joined them, then along Glen Dochert under the rugged flank of Ben More, then struck north-west by Tyndrum and the head of Glenorchy and had reached Loch Awe, before, at that dead season of the year, the Campbells were aware of their coming. Startled fugitives from the hamlets on Loch Awe fled before them over the hills, down the wild and steep Glen Aray to the head of Loch Fyne, that deep inlet of the sea on which stood Argyll's principal seat and fortress, at Inveraray.[75]

The place had long been thought inaccessible to enemies, and Argyll would not at first believe that Montrose was upon him. When he realised his mistake, he acted with his usual judgment. His death or capture would be a disaster for the Covenant; putting his duty to the cause before the selfish thought of personal honour, he left immediately by sea. His clansmen took refuge in the hills or within the walls of the castle which Montrose, without artillery, did not attempt to take. But his men burnt and plundered the surrounding village and all the farmsteads of the region. "We left neither house nor hold unburned, nor corn, nor cattle that belonged to the whole name of Campbell," an officer of the Macdonalds exulted.[76] From time to time their priests called them to holier occupations. Sheaves from the plundered barns were piled up to support an altar stone, the men held up their plaids for a screen against the wind, and after fifty years' intermission, the Mass was celebrated again in Campbell country.[77]

It could not be long concealed from the rest of Scotland, or from the English, that Argyll's stronghold had been penetrated and his people exposed, defenceless, to the raiders. The destruction of crops and stores and houses and the seizure of cattle would for years impoverish the clan and throw additional burdens on its chiefs; the wound to Argyll's reputation would in time be healed, but Montrose had gravely shaken the confidence of the Covenanters in their hitherto invincible champion.

In London, the Scots Commissioners did their utmost to discredit the rumours that came from the North, but they were
assailed now by complaints even from their friends, " that a
cursed crew of barbarous rebels should so overrun the land."[78]
Even their successes had proved unblessed, for with the news of
the surrender of Newcastle " the pest came to Edinburgh " and
by the winter was raging there.[79] But at Westminster Parliament had received ambassadors from the young Queen of
Sweden and, to the great annoyance of the Scots Commissioners,
was discussing with them the possibility of obtaining help from
thence. They need not have feared that Parliament would gain
a new and rival ally; the true purpose of the Swedes was only
to enlist the help of the English fleet in their war on Denmark,
and when they found they would not succeed in this, they lost
interest in the alliance.[80]

VI

In spite of the troubles in Scotland and the cleavage in their
own ranks, the Parliamentarian leaders seemed with the coming
of winter to have regained confidence. Sabran noticed their
buoyancy with surprise. He heard loose talk of European conquests—" vast designs abroad "—and this at a time when they
should have had their hands fully occupied at home. There were
clashes between Dutch ships and English patrols at sea; the
English came off worst, but were not cast down. Soon, it
seemed, they intended to re-assert their sway over the seas. The
time was approaching faster than Sabran could guess. On the
eve of the war, the Earl of Warwick had authorised Captain
William Jackson to sail on a marauding expedition to the West
Indies. Now, two and a half years later, he was on his way home,
and would soon report to those that had sent him the extraordinary, if minor, successes that his raiding parties had achieved.
The power of Spain, in his belief, was at an end: " The veil is

now drawn aside and their weakness detected by a handful of men . . . who hath dared them at their own doors and hath beat them out of many strongholds."[81] The war would prevent a renewal of the conflict with Spain for some years to come, but the reconnoitring was done and the ultimate intention was not forgotten.

Meanwhile the divided Parliament at Westminster still had the war to win. The leadership of the Commons was split between Harry Vane and Denzil Holles, who had with him a party in the Lords, all the Presbyterians in the Westminster Assembly, an increasing group of moderate men in the Commons, and, of course, the Scots. His chief weakness at this time was that he had no seat on the Committee of Both Kingdoms, which really transacted the urgent business of the nation. Vane and Holles, though they bitterly disagreed on religion and on policy in the war, held certain ideas in common; both believed in the greatness and mission of their country. It was a phenomenon of the time that, in spite of divisions, set-backs and apparent disintegration, the ultimate goal of many Puritan Parliament men and the leading Puritan soldiers was the greatness of England, betrayed as they felt it had been during its years of home-keeping neutrality under King Charles. In the autumn of that year John Milton, provoked by a sermon attacking his pamphlet on divorce, wrote his great appeal for the freedom of the press. *Areopagitica* attracted very little attention. But it contained a splendid vision of England: " Methinks I see in my mind a noble and puissant nation rousing herself like a strong man after sleep, and shaking her invincible locks. Methinks I see her as an eagle mewing her mighty youth, and kindling her undazzled eyes at the full midday beam." Thoughts like these, vague but deep and powerful, were common among Parliament's supporters and the Puritans. No one on the King's side was inspired by this same afflatus.

The Self-Denying Ordinance was now before the House, and the new Directory of Worship, to replace the Prayer Book, had been presented to Parliament by the Westminster Assembly. The Committee of Both Kingdoms at Derby House, meantime, discussed the reorganisation of the army on a "new model" and placed before the House measures for the reform and reorganisation of recruiting, supply and payment. In the next weeks the Independents in Parliament and in the Army must either win or lose the game. Vane had a narrow and unreliable majority in the Commons; the Lords, though two or three of their now pitiful number led by Lord Saye supported the Independents, were on the whole opposed to them. But one thing Vane must have known; if the Independents gained control of the Army, all the rest would follow. Defeat on the religious question could be redeemed; defeat on the new modelling of the Army, or defeat over the Self-Denying Ordinance, would be final.

On December 19th, 1644, the Self-Denying Ordinance passed the Commons. When Parliament re-assembled after Christmas, which had been kept as a fast,[82] they gave order that the new Directory of Worship, agreed on by the Westminster Assembly, should be generally issued in place of the prelatical Prayer Book, with its "unprofitable and burdensome ceremonies." The Directory contained a simple framework of church services with room for the extempore prayers on which the Puritans set so much store.[83] This was the Calvinist method, but there was little in the new Directory that could not be adapted to the use of the "dissenting brethren." For them the crux of the matter was not so much the manner of worship as the parish system, which created artificial boundaries to the pastor's flock and prevented the people from placing themselves freely under a shepherd of their own choice. The Presbyterian method of election, though it gave the people a say in the naming of their minister, allowed no freedom of movement from one flock to another, and held the congregation as rigidly within the authorised boundaries of a parish as the old unreformed Church had done. Moreover, by a Parliamentary ordinance of the autumn they still had to pay tithes, an imposition for the upkeep of the parish clergy which the Independents, who were usually also paying for another minister of their own, greatly resented.[84] The small Independent minority in the Assembly, aware that their grievances would always be shelved or voted down, had already laid their objections to the parish system before the Commons, who had authorised a limited printing of their opinions for distribution, and there the matter apparently rested.[85]

While members of both Houses thought over the implications of Church reform, the Self-Denying Ordinance hung fire in the House of Lords, in spite of repeated hints from below that they should consider it with all speed. Most of the Lords saw very clearly that its first effect would be to deprive two of their number, Essex and Manchester, of their commands, and diminish further the already much diminished powers of the peers in the land, even if (as then seemed inevitable) Cromwell was also forced to resign, the price seemed a high one to pay. They retaliated on the chivvying Commons by asking with asperity why no action had been taken on the Earl of Manchester's allegations against Cromwell. On January 13th, 1645, after more than three weeks' delay, they rejected the Ordinance.[86]

This looked like a victory for the Lords and the Presbyterians, but Vane was not so easily defeated. He turned the complaints of the Lords into an instrument against them, referred their demand for the further enquiry into Manchester's accusation of Cromwell to a Committee, and secured a report from that Committee which made a constitutional issue out of the matter. Accusations levelled at a member of their House, the Commons pointed out, were a breach of privilege and further procedure in the matter could not be countenanced.[87]

This adroit manœuvre demonstrated to the Lords the inconveniences which arose when officers in the army were also members of Parliament and could not therefore be brought to book. How could army discipline and privilege of Parliament both be be maintained? Clearly by no other means than that embodied in the Self-Denying Ordinance: by separating the two functions.

It followed therefore that the only way out of this deadlock was for the Lords to reconsider, in one form or another, the very ordinance that they had rejected.

After this ingenious piece of political strategy, victory was once again within the grasp of the Independents. A few days later, on January 23rd, the parochial system of Church government was resolved on by the Commons without a division; it was policy on the part of the Independents to let the Presbyterians win this empty victory, intended no doubt to satisfy the Scots and maintain the alliance. But if the New Model Army and the Self-Denying Ordinance worked out according to their hopes, no religious settlement voted in Parliament was likely to prevail against the real power of armed dissent.

VII

While the bloodless conflict at Westminster proceeded, the Londoners had been edified with a series of bloody object lessons. Three traitors to the Parliamentary cause were executed at the turn of the year. Sir Alexander Carew, a West Country baronet, as second in command of the Plymouth garrison, had tried to deliver it up to Prince Maurice. Guilty of confused politics rather than of baser motives, he met his death on Tower Hill with courage and dignity. He was followed on the first two days of January, 1645, by the unfortunate Hothams, first the son, then the father, condemned for their attempt to deliver Hull to the King. Their guilt, long in doubt, had been damningly proved when the correspondence of the Marquis of Newcastle was captured after Marston Moor. No one believed Sir John Hotham's contention that he had corresponded with Newcastle simply to gain time when his garrison was in difficulty—a trick he averred that had been commonly practised by professional soldiers in Germany. It had, in fact, also been practised by Edward Massey, the Governor of Gloucester. But too much in Hotham's past contradicted his protestations of innocence and he died, the day after his unfortunate son, on Tower Hill.[88]

Another intended victim was Roger Lestrange, who had made an unsuccessful attempt to raise King's Lynn for the Royalists. But Rupert wrote in person to Essex, pointing out that Lestrange, a known Royalist with a commission from the King, must be regarded as a prisoner of war, exempt from trial as a traitor or a spy. The military argument worked: Essex protested and Lestrange was let off.[89]

A fourth victim went to the block on January 10th, 1645. ("*Je ne vis jamais tant de sang,*" wrote the Marquis de Sabran.)[90] It was Archbishop Laud, against whom the Bill of Attainder had passed the Lords on January 4th, the very day on which the Prayer Book was abolished and the new Directory of Worship authorised. The King had sent to the Archbishop during the summer a pardon drafted to cover all possible charges; it was the least he could do to help his old servant. But when Laud showed it, Lords and Commons alike put it by, as of no effect against the decision of Parliament.[91]

The old Archbishop had been hounded and harried at his trial to make a Presbyterian holiday. William Prynne led for the prosecution and exacted, with unlimited interest, payment for all that Laud had once made him suffer in the Star Chamber. The broken Archbishop, fumbling with his notes, deprived of the books and papers from which, with a scholar's method, he had always been accustomed to work, still defended himself with consistency and skill. One thing he clung to throughout, because it was the simple truth: he had never wittingly assisted the Vatican or considered any re-union between the Church of England and the Church of Rome; furthermore, he had repeatedly used his strongest endeavours, and often with success, to prevent young Protestants from falling under the fashionable spell of the Roman Church. "Ever since I came in place," he said, "I laboured nothing more than that the external public worship of God might be preserved and that with as much decency and uniformity as might; being still of the opinion that Unity cannot long continue in the Church, when Uniformity is shut out at the Church door. And I evidently saw that the public neglect of God's service in the outward face of it, and the nasty lying of many places dedicated to that service, had almost cast a damp upon the true and inward Worship of God; which, while we live in the body, needs external helps, and all little enough to keep it in any vigour."[92]

At about noon on January 10th, 1645, William Laud came from the Tower on foot through the crowd to Tower Hill. In his hand he carried a sheaf of notes for his last sermon: "I am an old man and my memory is short," he said to the people from the scaffold and added with a wry simplicity, "This is a very uncomfortable place to preach in." He was the fifth Archbishop of Canterbury to die by violence, but of his martyred predecessors in the primacy of all England he spoke only of St. Alphege, murdered by the Danes, and of Simon Sudbury whom Wat Tyler's peasant rabble had brought, like him, from the Tower to the Hill and there beheaded. He said nothing of Becket, who had died to maintain the power of Rome, or of Cranmer, who had been burnt for rejecting it. He declared himself undeserving of death "by any known law of this Kingdom" and added, "I hope my cause in Heaven will look for another dye than the colour that is put upon it here." But his chief concern was to vindicate his master and himself from the aspersion of Popery. The King, he declared, was "as sound a Protestant . . . as any man in the Kingdom," and for himself, "I have always lived in the Protestant religion as established in England and in that I come now to die." When he had finished, he gave his notes to his chaplain, but seeing a busy Puritan minister close by, and knowing how quickly his words might be changed or twisted, he pleaded, "Let me have no wrong done me."

When he turned towards the block, he found his way barred by a crowd of spectators: "I did think . . . that I might have had room to die," he said as he pushed his way through them, and when he reached the block he saw, through the slats of wood on which he knelt, the upturned faces of those whom curiosity had prompted to crouch underneath the scaffold itself. Suddenly at his side appeared Sir John Clotworthy, the notorious bully and speculator in Irish land who had been the first and most vicious mouthpiece of the Commons against Laud's friend and fellow sufferer, the Earl of Strafford. Clotworthy, hoping to startle some Popish admission from him at the last, plagued him with questions until Laud turned from him to the executioner—" the gentler of the two "—who alone could put an end to the argument.[93]

To the unconcealed disappointment of his enemies Laud had died protesting his repugnance to the Church of Rome. His speech, reported with malicious glosses and interpolations, was the subject of more than one defamatory sermon. Old Dr. Burton, in his popular pulpit, danced a vindictive war-dance, shouting that the Archbishop, " Satan's second child," ought to have been sown up alive in a sack and thrown into the Thames.[94]

At the Court of Oxford, among the alarums of war, the Archbishop received less tribute than his past greatness or the nature of his death would have justified. The King, in a conversation with Digby reached the conclusion that the murder of the Archbishop by Parliament might well be held in Heaven to wipe out his own guilt for having consented to the death of Strafford;[95] a strangely egotistical comment on the judicial murder of his poor old servant. But some university poets broke into elegiac grief. Laud's most lasting monument would be the Persian and Greek manuscripts which his agents had so diligently searched out and rescued from the Ottoman dominions:

> Those Attic manuscripts, so rare a piece,
> They tell the Turk he hath not conquered Greece[96]

Gratefully remembered by scholars, Laud has found apologists among the clergy of the Church for which he died, but he is not generally loved. If his methods had been mistaken, his diagnosis of the ills of the Anglican Church had been right and his vision for its improvement had been lofty. In his defence, at his trial, he had pleaded that he had tried only to make the worship of God in England more seemly. He had in fact done a great deal more in trying to reform the manners of the clergy, to recruit better men into the ministry, and to restore the finances of a church which had been progressively plundered and disendowed for nearly a century. Had he succeeded in what he meant to do, he would be one of the great architects of the English Church.[97] He failed, and sealed his failure with his blood. He stands with Archbishop Cranmer an imperfect and much criticised man, but in the final record a faithful servant and a martyr whose blood has been the seed of the Church.

The furious disputes between the Presbyterians and the Independents which were pursued in the pulpits of London churches, in the assembly places of the sectaries, and fell, licensed or unlicensed, from the London printing presses, fulfilled the old Archbishop's frequent warning against allowing too much liberty in spiritual matters. Men who in the time of his power had been friends and fellow-sufferers for conscience sake were now mercilessly clawing each other. Henry Burton vindicated the Independents, William Prynne at enormous length supported the Presbyterians, but John Lilburne, in an open letter to him, accused him of waging war on God: " for Sir, let me tell you, it is the incommunicable prerogative of Jesus Christ alone to be King of his Saints, and Law-giver to his Church and people and to reign in the souls and consciences of his chosen ones." [98]

The martyrs of the last decade were now free to dispute with each other and for the time being at least to preach and practise their various doctrines. The present government found its martyrs elsewhere, and a fortnight after the death of Laud another Catholic priest went to the gallows with a cartload of common criminals. Henry Morse was a priest of some local renown, a Jesuit who had worked in England for many years and had been famous for his devoted attendance on the sick in the terrible plague of 1636. The number of his conversions had given rise to indignant complaints in the suburbs of the City. He was accompanied to Tyburn by the French and Portuguese envoys with five or six coachloads of the faithful, and there ended a life of patient devotion and self-sacrifice by a death of exalted fortitude.[99]

Sabran, the French resident who attended the execution, was shocked at the increasing ruthlessness and growing confidence of the Parliamentary government. When the King's emissaries were at Westminster, he had frankly advised the Duke of Richmond that no weakening or moderation was to be expected from Parliament, and the King, if he agreed to treat, must " show his teeth while asking for peace " and make ready to renew the war.[100]

VIII

The King did not need to be told, and Rupert, as Lieutenant General, was vigorously preparing for the Spring offensive. He had placed a garrison at Chipping Campden to cut off Gloucester from its trade in Cotswold wool, much as Basing House interrupted the wool trade of London. Colonel Massey, still holding Gloucester for Parliament, was now harassed by three neighbouring garrisons: the Cavaliers at Worcester and Cirencester ate up the provisions his own troops needed, and the new outpost at Campden strangled the livelihood of the citizens.[101]

Rupert next planned to regain Abingdon, lost by the folly of Wilmot in the previous summer. The Parliamentary governor was " faggot-monger Browne," as the Cavaliers called him, because he had tried to supply London with firewood shipped in barges down the Thames. He was known to be in difficulties; his men, mutinous and short of pay, were deserting to rival Parliamentary garrisons, chiefly to Aylesbury.[102] Digby, with his usual optimism, had tried to seduce Browne from his loyalty to

Parliament;[103] when he failed in this, Rupert, with the able assistance of Henry Gage, planned a surprise attack. It was made in the small hours of January 11th, 1645, from the south side of the town, over Culham bridge; an advance party penetrated into Abingdon by way of the ruined abbey before they were detected. But General Browne counter-attacked across the river; regardless of the bitter cold his men waded the icy water and fell on the exposed flank of the advancing Royalists. Disordered by the unexpected onslaught, the Cavaliers failed to support their vanguard in the town, and at daybreak had to withdraw, with heavy losses. The veteran Sir Henry Gage had been mortally wounded.[104]

Among the prisoners taken by Browne were five officers who had served in Ireland. Rupert, acting fast but not quite fast enough, sent to suspend all exchanges of prisoners until arrangements were made for their release. But already Browne had hanged them in Abingdon Market Place.[105]

The King suffered other checks. Sir Richard Grenvile, who had blockaded Plymouth since the autumn, tried in vain to carry it by assault, but was thrown back with serious loss because the garrison had been strongly reinforced from the sea.[106] George Goring, who had received a somewhat fanciful commission as Lieutenant General for Hampshire, Sussex, Surrey and Kent, pushed forward through the southern counties and reached Farnham, to the momentary dismay of Parliament, on January 9th. He could not maintain himself in this advanced position, and after an abortive attack on Christchurch in Hampshire he fell back to Salisbury, leaving a very evil reputation behind him in the county through which he had passed.[107] While he and Grenvile were thus occupied, there had been no troops to spare to watch the approaches to Taunton, the chief Puritan stronghold in Somerset, which was plentifully relieved with stores of all kinds by the efficient young renegade Anthony Ashley Cooper.[108]

In spite of these failures, the King thought of nothing less than defeat. He regarded the peace negotiations almost openly as a mere device to pass the winter and pursued them, as he wrote to the Queen, chiefly to quiet the members of what he widely called his " mongrel Parliament "—the poor loyalist members who had returned to Oxford for a second uncomfortable session.[109] In spite of their presence, the face of Oxford was wholly turned towards war. Civilian households were told to lay in six months' stores or leave the city; all able-bodied citizens were called to work on the defences; the King in person went the rounds of the fortifications twice every week, and his men rehearsed on the Isis the transport of heavy guns across rivers on rafts.[110]

Rupert continued his policy of promoting men of whose capacities and of whose loyalty to his own ideas he was certain. In succession to Henry Gage, he made William Legge governor of Oxford, and his principal engineer, Bernard de Gomme, Quartermaster General. Both were good appointments, if capacity alone was the criterion; but Gomme was very young, a foreigner and a dependent of Rupert's and Legge was a close personal friend. It looked like the building up of a private faction. Sir Arthur Aston, who had been invalided out of the governorship of Oxford on account of a broken leg got when he was " curvetting on horseback before certain ladies," had done everything in his power to undermine his successor, Sir Henry Gage, and now that Gage was dead had confidently hoped to be made governor again.[111] This gave Rupert another waspish enemy in the army. In the court circle he had also to reckon with the Earl of Southampton's resentment, because he had hoped for the Mastership of the Horse which the King had bestowed on his nephew.[112]

The Prince was plagued by other criticisms: trouble in the West where Edmund Wyndham did not wish to serve under Hopton " who has disobliged me "; annoyance at Newark, where Sir Richard Byron was advised by his mother to object to having one Rhodes, an upstart, associated with him in the government of the town;[113] and other complaints, just or unjust, serious or trivial. If the reorganisation of the Royalist army brought victory, all criticism would be silenced, but Rupert was formidably increasing the number of enemies who would turn on him if he should be again defeated. The Queen was a long way off, but she had with her in Paris by now his two most bitter enemies, the Marquis of Newcastle and Lord Wilmot, who seem at one time to have contemplated making up accusations against Rupert to be put forward in the Oxford Parliament by the Marquis of Hertford and Lord Glamorgan, two noblemen whose military capacities Rupert had signally failed to appreciate.[114] Nothing came of this plot, but such things made an uneasy background for the Prince's efforts to reorganise the royal armies.

At times, the King found even his closest friends, Digby always excepted, " strangely impatient for peace," as he put it to the Queen. But one group, led by Harry Percy, Wilmot's friend, he thought might be dangerous and had them arrested. Report credited them with a plot to kidnap the Prince of Wales and take him to London, and with having given warning to General Browne of Prince Rupert's attack on Abingdon.[115] But the undoubted reason was their interest in that scheme, not unknown to Denzil Holles, whispered from London by Percy's sister, Lady Carlisle, that the King should make peace with the Presbyterians and the Scots and so destroy the sectaries: a scheme to which Charles would not listen. " Be confident," he had written to the Queen, " that I will neither quit Episcopacy nor that sword which God hath given into my hands."[116]

Henrietta Maria, after weeks of serious illness, was now herself again and wrote him a stream of loving-chiding letters. Why had he allowed the rebels to be styled " Parliament " in a recent message to them, she asked. There was an appearance of irresolution in all he did and his reputation for infirmity of purpose was the greatest difficulty she experienced in trying to raise help for him abroad. The rebels, too, were more successful than he was in advertising their victories to all.[117] She painted tempting visions of foreign help for his cause. The Duke of Lorraine, an ambitious soldier with an unlimited capacity for making promises, had offered about ten thousand men who, allowing for some little trouble in finding transport, could be brought to England at any time.[118] She had herself approached the Prince of Orange, through her Anglican chaplain Stephen Goffe, asking for ships for Lorraine's troops, to which three thousand Dutch infantry could well be added, together with a declaration of war on the English rebels: if he would comply with these demands, she promised to reward him by the marriage of his daughter to the Prince of Wales, provided he could give her a large enough dowry.[119] The Prince of Orange, who thought the Duke of Lorraine's troops imaginary and was not anxious to marry any more of his children into the House of Stuart, was courteous but unresponsive.

The King in Oxford hoped for a higher bid for his son from Portugal and the Portuguese resident, Antonio de Sousa, was once again well received when he came on a visit from London. It was conveyed to him that a dowry of a million ducats would marry the Infanta Catherine of Braganza to the Prince of Wales.[120]

Though he agreed to the Queen's numerous plans,[121] the King's hopes of money and troops from abroad were not so vivid as his ever-present expectation that the Confederate Irish would agree to send him thousands of fierce and valiant men. For month after month, the negotiations in Ireland had hung fire, because the Confederates demanded more than Charles felt he could openly give to them. The Cessation, the armistice signed in the autumn of 1643 for a limited period, had been extended several times, but no permanent treaty had yet been concluded. Meanwhile Ormonde and the troops under his control respected the truce, but the Covenanting Scots in the North continued the war and the English and Anglo-Irish commanders in Munster, led by Inchiquin, had repudiated the King, Ormonde and the Cessation, and were now fighting the Irish in the name of Parliament. The Irish Confederate government at Kilkenny, aware alike of Ormonde's weakness and of the King's desperate need for help, believed that they had only to wait a little longer to dictate what terms they pleased. In vain the Queen herself had written to them imploring them, as a fellow Catholic, to accept Ormonde's terms of limited toleration. Already a great number in the Confederate Assembly, encouraged by the Papal agent Scarampi, would consider nothing short of the restoration of the Catholic Church throughout all Ireland.[122]

Ormonde vainly implored Digby to procure him more definite advice of the King's wishes. " It is of necessity that I receive clear instructions," he wrote, " or else it is odds but that, through my ignorance, or by a sudden change ... I shall unwillingly fall into some pernicious error." By the autumn of 1644 he was asking to be relieved of his charge as Lord Lieutenant because of the evident impossibility of achieving what the King wanted. Charles assured him of his continued confidence, and commanded him to conclude the treaty on what terms he could so as to send the troops to England during the winter months, while the seas were comparatively free of Parliamentary patrols. At the same time he renewed his commission to Glamorgan and made ready to send him to treat secretly with the Irish should Ormonde fail.[123]

With these hopes in mind, the King despatched his Commissioners, led by the Duke of Richmond, to meet those appointed by Parliament and the Scots at Uxbridge. The prospects for the treaty were very dark. The King had been extremely unwilling to refer to his opponents by the name of " Parliament," and had given in only because a majority in his Council voted for the use of the term. For their part Parliament had made great difficulty about admitting the titles of some of the Royalist Commissioners because they had been granted under the King's Great Seal after they had authorised a new Great Seal of their own. Of their own Commissioners, Vane and St. John were generally believed to be watch dogs set to guard their more moderate colleagues lest they should grow too friendly with the Royalists. Christopher Love, one of the Parliamentary chaplains, preached a sermon at the outset of the negotiations calculated to insult the King's

Commissioners and discourage any serious attempt to make peace. On his side the King was resolved to discuss nothing connected with Scotland without consulting Montrose, who was very far off and whose name was anathema to the Scots Commissioners; he had also instructed his delegates to lose no opportunity of telling the Parliamentary representatives in private " that they were arrant rebels, and that their end must be damnation, ruin and infamy except they repent." Such kind of talk, he believed, " might do good."[124] Even those with no private information of Court and Parliamentary politics could see that nothing was likely to come of the meeting at Uxbridge. "Peace," wrote the London barrister John Greene, " is wonderful improbable and scarce to be hoped for."[125]

The Commissioners decided to allow three days' discussion in rotation to each of the three principal points at issue: the reform of the Church, the control of the armed forces, and the future settlement of Ireland. On the religious question it was evident to the Royalists that several of the Parliamentary Commissioners were at odds with the Scots. Chancellor Loudoun, the leading Scots Commissioner, came privately to Edward Hyde and exercised his very considerable persuasive powers to get him to commit the King to Presbytery. Loudoun's attempt followed on his action in entering into the plans for peace secretly sponsored by Holles and Lady Carlisle, and foreshadowed what was soon to become the guiding star of Covenanting policy: the hope of winning Charles for Presbytery and so dividing the English against themselves and crushing the Independents. He failed utterly. In the verbal exchanges of the next days, the Royalists could not exploit the division of their enemies because they could not abate anything of their master's resolution to preserve the Episcopal Church entire. The Scots, who had most to gain and most to lose, were throughout the most vocal. Lauderdale, " having no gracious pronunciation and full of passion," wrote Hyde, " made everything much more difficult than it was before." Loudoun, disappointed at an obstinacy he had not expected, vehemently attacked Hyde and was as vehemently answered, and the commissioners by the last day at midnight had reached an angry deadlock.[126] This concluded their debates on the Church.

The days spent arguing over the control of the armed forces were equally fruitless, as both King and Parliament insisted on exercising effective power over these and neither side would abate a jot of its demands. The discussions of the settlement of Ireland followed the same tedious and useless course. Only, in the intervals of the public meetings, some of the Lords on the Parliament side spoke gloomily to the King's Commissioners. If peace was not made at Uxbridge, they argued, there would be no holding the extremists in Parliament. With their New Model Army and other plots and projects, they would get rid of Essex, overthrow the nobility, perhaps establish a republic—who could tell?[127] This kind of talk from the Earl of Pembroke and others may have been sincere; the older nobility who had let themselves be drawn on to Parliament's side were by this time deeply perturbed. The most judicious of them, Northumberland, maintained an outward air of calm authority and was vigilant to preserve his own power and dignity, but not one of these baffled men had by now any clear idea of what the future might hold. The French envoy in his reports wrote of " the servitude in which the House of Commons holds the House of Lords."[128] He did not exaggerate. By skilful management, almost by sleight of hand, the leaders of the Commons had outwitted the Lords in every disagreement for the last three years. The whole government of the country was now concentrated in the hands of the Committee of both Kingdoms which the Commons dominated. John Selden had his jest at the Lords' expense: " The House of Commons is called the Lower House in twenty acts of Parliament but what are twenty acts of Parliament amongst friends? "[129] There was no question which was in practice the upper, and which the lower House by 1645.

If the Earl of Pembroke and others who poured their

anxieties into the ears of Edward Hyde thought their worries would move the King to make peace, they greatly misjudged him. Report of fear and division among the rebels only stimulated the King's natural optimism and gave him confidence in his power to destroy them all.

IX

While the Uxbridge negotiations ran their depressing course rumours trickled through from Scotland—" untruths and uncertainties," the Scots Commissioners hoped—which could not but raise the too mercurial spirits of the King.[130] Already a contingent of the Scots army in England had been sent home under William Baillie, an officer of some reputation trained in Dutch and Swedish service. He met Argyll and the Covenanting Lords at Dumbarton in deep gloom, for Montrose was then in the heart of the Campbell country. Baillie did not conceal his low opinion of the noble generals who had been for the last six months outwitted by Montrose and a handful of Irish. He refused to serve unless he was independent of orders from Argyll, an arrangement to which Argyll agreed with unconcealed resentment.[131] Their joint plan was now to trap Montrose between their two forces as he tried to get away from Inveraray; Baillie with his lowland troops was to go to Perth to keep watch on the highlands from the eastern side, while Argyll, transporting his cannon and some at least of his men by sea, occupied Inverlochy at the head of Loch Linnhe and patrolled the Great Glen to block Montrose's egress in the north and west.

In mid-January Montrose and his army withdrew from the Campbell country, skirting the head of Loch Awe, turning up the strait pass of Brander, the black rock sheer on the right hand, the black river on the left. On the shore of Loch Etive, near Dunstaffnage, they found one large and three small boats. Crossing and re-crossing, by daylight, moonlight and starlight, Mon-

trose put all his men across to the farther bank and struck north-
east, then west along Glencoe. The weather was warm for the
time of the year and wet, with heavy rain and lightning on the
hills, and the streams in spate. On the shores of Loch Leven
Montrose showed for the first time a tremor of disquiet. His
scouts reported Argyll's forces gathering at Inverlochy, which
some of them had reached by sea. Should they try to stop him
as he emerged from Glencoe he might have to fight at a serious
disadvantage, with no place of retreat. He would not be safe
until he had crossed Loch Leven to the barren heights of Lochaber,
but in the murky winter night he could find no boats. Argyll
failed to take the opportunity, and at daybreak some boats were
discovered and the crossing made without interruption. A few
stragglers were cut off and killed by Argyll's patrols, but the
main body of the army vanished into the mountains. On January
25th Montrose was believed to be " betwixt the head of Loch
Ness and Lochaber."

Baillie, from his Perth headquarters, was irritable at the news;
no one had expected Montrose in mid-winter to go to ground
in the terrible and trackless heights of Lochaber. Baillie considered marching up the coast road to Aberdeen, then striking
westward into the mountains, but it was no time of year for such
ventures and in the end he stayed at Perth.[132] If Montrose remained where he was his men must surely perish of cold and
hunger; if he came out by Inverness the garrison there, strengthened by the Mackenzies and Frasers, should be able to deal with
him; and the plain of Moray was Gordon country where young
Lord Gordon was still, for anything Argyll or Baillie knew to
the contrary, loyal to the Covenant. Argyll waited at Inverlochy,
ready to pursue Montrose if he ventured down into the Great
Glen and fall on his rear while the Inverness garrison attacked him
in front.

None of this happened, although Montrose was now reported
at Kilcummin, near the head of Loch Ness, in the midst of the
Great Glen. He and his men were in wonderfully good heart.

All through his march he had despatched elegant letters to the highland chiefs calling them to arms in the King's name. He had now with him Maclean of Duart and Maclean of Lochbuie, the chiefs, or acting chiefs, of the Macdonalds of Keppoch, Glengarry and Clanranald, the Stuarts of Appin, the Macphersons, the outlawed MacGregors, the Camerons, and the Robertsons. To strengthen and confirm their loyalty to the King's cause and to each other, a necessary precaution in a land so rent with feuds, Montrose at Kilcummin drew up a bond which they solemnly subscribed vowing to maintain " the power and authority of our sacred and native sovereign, contrary to this present perverse and infamous faction of desperate rebels now in fury against him " and " mutually to assist one another herein as we shall be desired or the occasion arise."[133]

Lost in the wilds, his enemies thought him, but Montrose, who knew very well what he was about, was uniting the Highland clans with considerable skill before considering what move he should next make against the opposing forces. If he marched on to Inverness he realised that he would be attacked simultaneously by the Inverness garrison in front and by Argyll in the rear. It would be wiser, therefore, to settle first with Argyll. As Montrose was soon to report to the King: " I was willing to let the world see that Argyll was not the man his Highlandmen believed him to be, and that it was possible to beat him in his own Highlands."[134] He did therefore what Argyll had least expected; he turned in his course, and while Argyll's scouts patrolled the Glen to report on his progress to Inverness, he recrossed the mountains of Lochaber. It had now turned bitterly cold and the march was one which only the hardiest troops could endure. Sometimes on the heights they were " in knee-deep snow; " sometimes they waded " brooks and rivers up to their girdle " and the shepherds who guided them were not always certain of the way. They marched by night and day, with brief halts only because of the cold, and on the second day " about the shutting in of the night " they came round the shoulder of

Ben Nevis and saw below them Inverlochy and the long, cold arm of Loch Linnhe. Some of their foremost men clashed with a patrol of Argyll's, which fled into the gathering dusk to give the alarm.[135]

Below, at Inverlochy, Argyll took counsel. The effective commander of his forces was Duncan Campbell of Auchinbreck, a young man whom his chief had sent for from Ulster, where he had greatly distinguished himself.[136] Argyll had about fifteen hundred lowland infantry which Baillie had rather grudgingly allowed to go with him, and two thousand of his own Campbells. He had one or two cannon, transported by sea; and in the loch he had his own galley. He seems to have thought that the force on the mountainside above him could be only some small remnant, so strong was his conviction that Montrose's army could never emerge alive from the frozen hills. This conviction, added to the pain that he was suffering from a dislocated shoulder, was perhaps the reason for his decision to retire to his galley on the loch and leave Auchinbreck in sole command.

Auchinbreck, however, thought the force on the hill was one to be reckoned with, for he drew up his army with great care, the Campbells in the centre with the cannon, flanked by the Lowlanders; Inverlochy castle, with a further small reserve of Highlanders, was in his immediate rear. All night his men were kept awake by sporadic musketry fire from small wandering groups of Irish approaching and withdrawing by favour of the moonlight and the uneven ground. The main body of Montrose's troops stood to arms all the long winter night, and neither he nor they had anything to break their fast but oatmeal sodden in snow and eaten off the point of a dirk. Before dawn—it was Sunday, February 2nd, 1645, Candlemas Day—the Irish took the sacrament and committed themselves and their fortunes to the care of Saint Patrick and Saint Bridget.[137]

Montrose had massed the Scottish Highlanders, mostly in small contingents, in the centre—Stuarts of Appin and Atholl, Macdonalds of Glencoe, Clanranald and Glengarry, and Macleans—perhaps five or six hundred in all. He had divided the Irish, placing Macdonald on the right wing and his very able lieutenant, Magnus O'Cahan, on the left. He had a score of horse belonging to his Graham and Ogilvie kinsmen, and these he held back to use as occasion served.

All was made ready in the darkness, and at the first streak of sunrise the waiting Campbells heard, from the mountainside, the trumpet sounding the onset. Before Auchinbreck could take stock of the situation by daylight, the Irish had charged. They fell upon the Lowlanders on both wings of the Covenanting forces, " leaping in amongst them with their swords " and throwing them immediately into disorder. Auchinbreck ordered his Campbells to charge against Montrose's centre, but Montrose's Highlanders charged almost at the same moment and the two forces met in full career. Ogilvie with his troop of horse meanwhile outflanked the Campbells, dispersed their reserve and blocked their retreat to the Castle. Assailed simultaneously in front, flank and rear, the Campbells fought valiantly but in vain. Some were forced into the loch, a few broke away to the hills, Auchinbreck, mortally wounded, was taken prisoner, with some other gentry of name, but fifteen hundred of the Campbells were killed; it was such a disaster as would cripple the fighting force of the clan for years to come. Their chief had not waited to see the end, and his galley was far down the loch before the last of his clansmen fell.[138]

That night in Montrose's camp, by the rugged walls of Inverlochy castle, the Irish sang a Te Deum, and Montrose, exalted by victory, wrote with fervour to his King protesting against any project of peace until the war should be won: " The success of your arms in Scotland does not more rejoice my heart, as that news from England (i.e. of the Uxbridge treaty) is like to break it. . . . The more your Majesty grants, the more will be asked; and I have too much reason to know that they will not rest satisfied with less than making your Majesty a King of straw. . . . Forgive me, sacred Sovereign, to tell your Majesty that, in my poor opinion, it is unworthy of a King to treat with rebel subjects, while they have the sword in their hands. And though God forbid I should stint your Majesty's mercy, yet I must declare the horror I am in when I think of a treaty, while your Majesty and they are in the field with two armies, unless they disband, and submit themselves entirely to your Majesty's goodness and pardon. . . . Through God's blessing I am in the fairest hopes of reducing this Kingdom to your Majesty's obedience, and, if the measures I have concerted with your other loyal subjects fail me not . . . I doubt not before the end of this summer I shall be able to come to your Majesty's assistance with a brave army."[139]

Montrose marched now, with banners flying, north-east towards the plain of Moray while from all the mountains round the chiefs came in to him. The chief of the Grants brought three hundred men; Seaforth, the chief of the Mackenzies, first fled before him, then turned about and came to join him. Best of all, Nathaniel Gordon came, bringing with him Lord Gordon; the young chief, rising in sudden belated defiance of his uncle, Argyll, " leapt quickly on his horse " and rode to join Montrose, " who made him heartily welcome and supped joyfully together." Later he would bring five hundred infantry and eight-score horse of the Gordon clan to swell the victorious army.[140]

In Edinburgh Argyll, with his dislocated arm still in a sling, reported to the Estates that he had pursued Montrose far into the North, with one small skirmish in which he had unhappily lost a number of men.[141] The Estates thanked him for his good services, voted Montrose a traitor, degraded him from the nobility, condemned him to be hanged and quartered when taken, and conferred a part of his lands on Argyll to defray his expenses; the Assembly of the Church called sternly on the King to repent for having loosed the Irish upon them. With a saving touch of realism they also agreed that negotiations should be opened with the condemned traitor, James Graham, for an exchange of prisoners.[142] Neither the practical move nor the empty gestures were of any avail against the danger which, with every passing week, grew more menacing in the Highlands and must, within a little while, break forth into the Lowlands and the heart of the Covenanting country.

X

All this while, far south at Uxbridge, the peace negotiations ground slowly to a standstill. It was clear that peace was even less welcome to the King than to the extremists among his enemies. " That which has been the great snare to the King," wrote Dr. Baillie, " is the unhappy success of Montrose in Scotland."[143] But long before Charles received Montrose's sanguine letter his faith in his ultimate victory had been wholly restored. While the negotiations continued, the Parliamentary delegation had been put out of countenance by the news that Sir Lewis Dyve had taken Weymouth for the King.[144] Some ships laden with Spanish bullion had recently surrendered themselves at Bristol, seeking shelter from piracy and storm; their cargoes, worth £200,000, were a welcome help to the King for the pay and equipment of his army.[145] The despatch from Montrose reached Oxford on February 19th, 1645, and by that time the commissioners at Uxbridge had come to a deadlock on every subject under discussion. The armistice agreed on during the negotiations was to end at midnight on the 22nd. No move was made to extend it any further, and the commissioners parted in mutual dissatisfaction, each side equally convinced that the other had had no true intention of making peace.[146]

The sufferers were the moderate party in the Commons, and the House of Lords. The hints they had dropped to the Royalist Commissioners had clearly revealed their fears of the Independents, whom the reorganisation of the army and the continuance of the war would inevitably bring into power. They returned to London to see their fears fulfilled as the plans for the New Model went forward. The Scots, too, would have been glad enough to make peace if the King would have accepted the Presbyterian form of Church government but, unlike the Presbyterian English, they had an army of their own which could not be affected by the changes in the English army and which, if the Independents ultimately gained control, could be used to restrain them. But for the English opponents of the sectaries, in Parliament or in the army, it was a black day when the treaty failed. The King's intransigence gave them no choice but to support the plans for continuing the war against him.

Was it a black day, also, for the King? Later many were to think so. He had had an opportunity of making peace and he had rejected it, for had he agreed to the Scottish and Presbyterian plan, the Independents would have been hard put to it to break the treaty. But he could not truly be said to have considered and rejected terms that he had never contemplated accepting. As he had written to the Queen, he would not quit Episcopacy or the Sword that God had put in his hands. Defending both, he was to lose both, for Uxbridge was his last chance of making a treaty that was not a surrender.

The ordinance for the New Model Army had been passed while the negotiations were in progress. The collapse of the Treaty was followed by yet another meeting at Guildhall where Vane, in sober and fervent words, explained the failure of the peace treaty and appealed to the City for another loan, eighty thousand pounds this time, to carry on the war. The comprehensive plan embodied in the new ordinance was to establish the Parliamentary army on a national basis. The money to support it was still to be raised by the County Committees but they were to render their accounts to Parliament, and no longer to be responsible only for locally raised troops. Rates of pay were standardised and commanders were no longer to tempt men from other forces by offers of higher reward. For all this, ready money was needed, since the county assessments were never very prompt in coming in, so that London's help was urgently needed if the re-modelling was to proceed smoothly. Existing regiments were to be re-modelled and new recruiting set on foot, to create a unified national army of twenty-two thousand men, in eleven regiments of horse, twelve regiments of foot and ten companies of dragoons. Argument arose with the House of Lords on the question of the appointment of officers; the Peers demanded and ultimately obtained a clause by which the names chosen by the commanders-in-chief must come before Parliament for approval.

Philip Skippon was unanimously designated as Major General of the new forces.[147] The choice of a commander-in-chief was more difficult, and the Lords, for the moment, still holding by Essex and Manchester, would make no decision. But the Commons had sent for Sir Thomas Fairfax. No objections could seriously be raised against him. He was a professional soldier of unimpeachable breeding; his religious views were unobtrusive and he had never played any part in Parliamentary politics; his tact in keeping the peace between difficult allies had been apparent at the siege of York, and he had shown throughout the war courage, endurance and military judgment which commanded general respect. On February 19th, 1645, he appeared before the Commons. Hailed by Speaker Lenthall as a new Agamemnon, he answered modestly (his slight stammer made him no great orator); out of respect for Parliament he refused the offer of a chair and remained standing, a spare, upright figure with one arm in a sling from a recent wound in the shoulder.[148]

Lords and Commons, Presbyterians and Independents, still had some hopes and hatreds in common. They still regarded the Irish rebels as the most pestilential of their enemies, and while the revolt in Ireland remained unsuppressed and the King sought for peace and alliance with the Confederates, all his English opponents could unite to exact vengeance on any Irish who fell into their hands. It was no accident that through the whole of that quarrelsome winter in London the trial and fate of two Irish chieftains, alleged leaders of the Ulster rising, had, from time to time, created a certain solidarity of hate between the parties at Westminster.

Hugh MacMahon and Connor M'Guire had been arrested in Dublin in October, 1641, on the eve of the Ulster rising,[149] and sent over to London some months later. Their joint escape from the Tower in the autumn of 1644 had fatally reminded their captors of their almost forgotten existence. Hiding in a London house, M'Guire had foolishly purchased oysters from a street vendor, leaning from his window and addressing her in a rich Irish brogue. Recaptured, the two unfortunate young men had, at long last, faced their trials for treason. MacMahon had been hurriedly despatched in November. M'Guire was tried during the Uxbridge Treaty and defended himself with intelligence and dignity.[150] It was, of course, in vain, and he was sentenced to a traitor's death for having countenanced the revolt of his people against a government which persecuted their religion and stole their land. The House of Lords refused to recognise his Irish chieftainship as giving him a claim to the more merciful death reserved for noblemen, and every effort that a rigid inhumanity could devise was made to prevent his gaining absolution or receiving the sacrament from a Catholic priest. This was partly circumvented, for a priest stationed in the crowd at Tyburn had arranged silently to pronounce absolution at a given sign from the victim when he was ready to receive it. All the way to Tyburn one of the sheriffs of London rode alongside him, demanding further details of the Irish rising and the names of his associates. M'Guire had thought at least that he might pray in quiet, but until the moment when the rope was fixed about his neck, the sheriff's voice cut across his devotions, confusing him in the midst of the best-remembered phrases. "Jesus, Jesus, Jesus," he repeated at last, and clung against all interruptions to the single name of his Redeemer, until the cart drove off and he was left hanging. The sheriff instantly cut the rope so that the rest of the barbarous sentence could be performed while he was fully conscious, but the executioner foiled the sheriff's brutality by slitting the victim's throat.[151]

News of the war was various, and some of it disheartening.

Waller had been delayed in going to the help of Weymouth by the lack of arms, knapsacks and stockings for his men. Cromwell's regiment, sent to support him in this western march, had mutinied at Portsmouth, whence seven hundred of them marched back to their old quarters, so that Cromwell was hurriedly ordered to leave Westminster and try what a thousand pounds of pay would do to restore order.[152] From Gloucester, Colonel Massey complained of the uncontrollable depredations of the Royalists from the Forest of Dean and protested vigorously against the elevation of sectaries to commands in the army. Nearer London, mutiny broke out among the troops at Henley.[153]

Two major triumphs marked the end of February. The Royalists had taken Weymouth, but could not dislodge the Parliamentarians from Melcombe, at the opposite side of the bay, so that the harbour remained useless to them. A Royalist night attack on Melcombe nearly succeeded owing to the treachery of some citizens who let in the Cavaliers, but the Parliamentary garrison resisted manfully and ultimately counter-attacked, driving back the intruders with loss. Their position was further strengthened when Captain Batten landed a detachment of seamen, and the Royalists, disheartened, withdrew to Dorchester.[154]

Far more serious for the King was the loss of Shrewsbury. It had always been the recruiting centre for Wales, had been so used by Rupert all the Spring of 1644, and was now being used by Maurice for the same purpose. "I wish your brother had some experienced commander by him," wrote one of Rupert's candid friends, anxious at the worsening situation in Shrewsbury.[155] The governor, Sir Michael Ernle, was a sick man and neglected his duties; the troops were undisciplined and the townsfolk by this time hostile to them. The walls were slackly guarded and the scouting was bad, for, when Maurice was called away to Chester for consultation, Colonel Mytton, the Parliamentary commander for Shropshire, brought up twelve hundred men under cover of darkness without any alarm being given. With a small advance party he was rowed across the Severn, and was led by two traitors to an unguarded point in the defences, through which a few of his men penetrated. These surprised and overpowered the guards at the bridge, where, under cover of darkness, the rest of Mytton's forces were waiting to rush the town as soon as their comrades let them in. Shrewsbury was entered before the Royalist commanders were aware of what had happened. It was four o'clock on a February morning and pitch dark. The governor staggered out from his sick-bed and was killed as he tried to rally his men. Few of the other officers did as much. Before daylight, and after only a little ill-managed street fighting, the Royalists were penned into the castle. They surrendered at once, on disgraceful terms; the Welsh and English withdrew to Ludlow with their arms, leaving behind the entire magazine and stores, fifteen cannon, and all soldiers who had come out of Ireland. Colonel Mytton hanged thirteen of these on the following day.[156]

The outrage provoked Rupert to make a personal appeal to Essex against this barbarous conduct in a letter drafted for the purpose by Edward Hyde: " I have taken prisoner of those who have taken arms against His Majesty of all nations, English, Scottish, Irish, French, Dutch, Wallons, of all religions and opinions that are avowed by Christians," he wrote, " and have always allowed them quarter and equal exchange . . . and shall do so still."[157] Was it still too much to expect the like conduct of Parliament? It was indeed too much. They had issued an ordinance in the previous autumn condemning to death any Irishman, or any Roman Catholic Englishman born in Ireland, who should be found in arms against them.[158] Rupert's protest, and the hangings in reprisal which duly took place about a fortnight later,[159] were alike powerless to stem the vindictive treatment of all Irish prisoners. The Parliamentarians had become the victims of their own propaganda, believed every atrocity against the Irish and were ready to inflict the same in return.

They had entered upon the horrible and disastrous course from which nothing was now to deflect them.

The King was, for some days, deeply cast down by the disaster at Shrewsbury, but he considered how he might improve his fortunes in war, and never contemplated re-opening the treaty. On the penultimate day of February he wrote privately to Ormonde commanding him to offer to suspend the Penal Laws against the Roman Catholics and to conclude a peace with the Confederate Irish " whatever it cost."[160] The only essential was to have more troops quickly.

For several weeks, as quarrels rent the Parliamentary army, as Lords and Commons disagreed, as the Scots alliance creaked under the strain and the Independent ministers disrupted the Westminster Assembly, the King's prospects for winning the war had seemed reasonably good. During those weeks Prince Rupert and George Digby had been equal in the King's favour, and had worked together for the prosecution of the war. The fall of Shrewsbury brought about a change. Its loss removed the clearing centre and training ground on which Rupert had for so long relied on the Welsh border; it dangerously threatened the line of communication between Oxford and Chester—the vital port for Ireland and the gathering centre for supplies from North Wales; and it exposed Hereford and Worcester to attack. The Royalist hold on the Welsh marches had never been absolute, but Rupert and Maurice had contrived with their flying cavalry to keep open the ways from the recruiting grounds of North and South Wales to the King's headquarters. Now the position was extremely precarious. Massey had moreover suddenly reasserted himself at Gloucester, sallied out into the Forest of Dean and in a sharp skirmish defeated Sir John Winter and scattered his men, thus freeing himself of at least one troublesome enemy.[161]

Rupert, at Ludlow, surveying the threat to all his hopes, feared the disruption of supplies from Wales and possibly a rising of those disaffected from the King in the heart of Wales itself.[162] The country was impoverished and the disturbances of war had

brought the trade in cattle almost to a standstill. Archbishop
Williams from Conway tried to protect the people and pleaded
that some consideration be shown to " our poor drovers, the
Spanish fleet of North Wales, which brings hither what little
silver we have." But garrison commanders up and down the
country pressed home their demands for food and fodder by
indiscriminate raiding, and Rupert had recently authorised
cavalry patrols to exact contribution from those who were back-
ward in payment. Added to this there was quarrelling between
rival commanders, disregard of Welsh sensibilities by the English,
resentment of the English by the Welsh, and a whole complex
of regional feuds. The "nursery of the King's infantry," was now
a place of division, strife and poverty.[163]

At Oxford a suggestion seems to have been made that the
Court should move to Exeter or Bristol to give greater coherence
to the King's position. It was never even discussed in Council—
Hyde believed, because the ladies were against it—[164] but so
emphatic a withdrawal would have discouraged all the King's
supporters at home and abroad.

Rupert, depressed about the prospects of victory, found himself increasingly opposed to Digby, whose sanguine temperament
was proof against disasters and who strenuously objected to any
suggestion that negotiations be resumed. Charles had recently
taken back into his favour Lord Cottington, once his easy-going
Chancellor of the Exchequer, who had let him go to war with
the Scots in 1639 with no money to pay his troops. These two
restored the King to his natural optimism, so that when Sabran,
the French envoy, visited him in Oxford in March he found him
resolute against all accommodation, although his confidence in
his English army was no longer what it had been. He trusted
instead to Montrose in Scotland and hoped still more from the
quarrels and divisions of his enemies at Westminster.[165]

" The distraction of the rebels among themselves is very
great and increaseth daily," wrote Digby to Ormonde, with
satisfaction,[166] but he regarded the distraction of the King's com-

manders among themselves without much anxiety and in that he was wrong. Sabran had pointed out to the King that he ought to take advantage of the disorders and disputes of his enemies to bring up troops to threaten London.[167] But the Royalist forces were operating only in the West, on the Welsh border, and in the northern midlands. It was already apparent that the reorganisation of the King's army had failed. Rupert, in spite of his energy, intelligence and devotion, had neither the experience nor the temperament for this kind of task. By March, 1645, the extent of his failure to unite and co-ordinate the armies was becoming apparent. From Lord Loughborough in Leicestershire, from Sir Richard Byron at Newark, from Lord Byron at Chester, and louder and louder from the West, complaints reached Oxford. Goring arrived late in February and left after high words with Rupert. Byron followed him in March, threatening to resign unless more attention was given to his needs at Chester.[168]

The worst trouble was in the West. There, the King had decided to set up the Prince of Wales with a Council and Court of his own.[169] Although he was not yet fifteen, and would be only a figurehead, Rupert foresaw that troubles must arise if the Prince of Wales, who was in any case nominally commander-in-chief, had a Court and Council separate from his father. Such an arrangement would make continual opportunities for intrigue between ambitious officers who would play off one Court against the other and both against Rupert. Charles paid no attention to his nephew's annoyance; true to his ancient custom of taking away with one hand the power he had given with the other, he probably thought that a new Court in the West, and the confusions arising therefrom, would be a useful drag on Rupert's power.

The Prince of Wales, escorted by Sir Edward Hyde and Lord Culpeper, left Oxford on March 4th, 1645, to take up his quarters at Bristol.[170] Much had been promised by the Western gentry during the winter, and much had been boasted by the Western generals, but the Prince and his Council found nothing but disorder on their arrival. The gentry had raised neither money nor men in preparation for the Spring and now made excuses and blamed each other.[171] Grenvile, who had been left in the autumn to besiege Plymouth, had seized on the neighbouring estates of his wife (who had separated from him long since), was living in high style, holding rich citizens and gentry up to ransom, and every so often terrorising the country folk by hanging out of hand those who displeased him, a habit he had picked up in Ireland.[172] He had not reduced Plymouth. For this failure he blamed Sir John Berkeley, the governor of Exeter, who had, he said, out of jealousy made difficulties about quarters and intrigued to get him removed into Somerset.[173] Neither Grenvile nor Berkeley would accept orders from the other. Both claimed to be independent of Goring and in this they may have been justified. Goring held no command in the West; his commission had been made out for Hampshire eastwards, but after an astonishing thrust forward to Farnham in Surrey, which he reached on January 9th, he had failed to consolidate this advanced position and had fallen back with his army into the West. He was now ineffectively besieging Taunton, and exasperating Grenvile by a claim that his commission gave him superiority throughout the West.[174]

The troops of all three generals were undisciplined but those of Goring had the worst reputation. His drinking bouts were becoming notorious; " dear General," wrote George Digby, " beware of debauches."[175] But Goring, drunk or sober, had a deservedly high reputation as a soldier, and was undoubtedly more impressive to the enemy for his capacities and his quality than any other general in the West. " God's blessing be on your heart, you are the jolliest neighbour I ever met with," wrote Waller to him, pretending to take lightly a series of harassing raids on his quarters on the Wiltshire-Somerset border. The two gallant professionals met at Shaftesbury to discuss an exchange of prisoners with such display of splendour and good fellowship on both sides that the country people thought this could be nothing less than the peace treaty to end the war.[176] But Goring flouted the Prince of Wales's Council, disregarded their orders, mislaid their cyphers, and was dangerously indiscreet about everything that he was told,[177] but he could still on occasion act with skill, and his friends were slow to believe that drink and disease were destroying his courage and his judgment, leaving only a boundless and hollow ambition. " My Lord," Sir Arthur Capel cheerfully entreated him, " if you give the rebels a good bang, I'll be content to lose a month's pay to you at piquet."[178]

In an evil hour for the Cavaliers, Cromwell had left his Parliamentary duties at Westminster, re-joined his mutinous regiment, restored order and marched towards the West. Joining with Waller, he surprised the Royalist sheriff of Wiltshire at Devizes and made him prisoner with three hundred of his men. Thence he pushed on to Dorset to hamper the supplies and the recruiting of the King's Western army. Though Goring, in one of his bursts of energy, drove the Ironsides out of Dorchester, the Royalist position in the Western counties was now gravely threatened.[179]

" I expect nothing but ill from the West," Rupert wrote to his confidant, Colonel Legge, at Oxford on March 20th,[180] and some days later he repeated his complaints: the western generals undoubtedly regarded the coming of the Prince of Wales as freeing them from any dependence on his orders. In the best interests of the King, he wondered whether a solution would be to take charge of the Prince of Wales himself and so prevent, by one high-handed act, the dangers of a divided command.[181] The speculation was idle; he was at heart too deeply loyal to the King to carry out such a stroke. But his letter showed how utterly the attempt to unify the King's forces under a single command had failed.

In spite of his efforts, the Royalist army was more divided by intrigue and rivalry than it had ever been before. This was the more regrettable because occasional successes showed that

the spirit and dexterity of the Royalists had not flagged. Sir
Marmaduke Langdale and his cavalry had been successful in
re-entering Yorkshire, and raising the long siege of Pomfret,
which set Fairfax speculating on the chances of a Royalist revival
in the North, and caused momentary consternation in London.[182]
In the Welsh marches Rupert and Maurice by defeating Edward
Massey at Ledbury put a stop to his raiding and strengthened the
position of the Royalist garrison at Hereford, which still successfully guarded the southern marches for the King.[183]

XI

In the counties of Worcester, Hereford and Dorset the last
months had brought a new element into the war. Plagued by
the exactions of the armies, the assessments, the foraging and the
billeting of troops, the country people—mostly yeomen and
their sons, with some of the smaller gentry and a few of the clergy
—were banding together against both parties. These "clubmen," as they were commonly called, for the rank and file had
no better arms, provided a warning signal alike for Royalists
and Parliamentarians. In spite of violence, plunder and indiscipline, the policy of both parties was to conciliate rather than
intimidate the country folk. Assessments in cash and kind could
only be raised if men could till, sow and reap, tend their livestock
and sell their produce with as little disturbance as possible. The
ruin of the country brought with it, inevitably, the ruin of the
armies; from all over the country commanders complained that
contributions were short because supplies in cash and kind could
not be raised from people who had nothing to spare. The dis-
location of the cattle markets in North Wales or of the cloth
industry in the West Riding re-acted instantly on the armies. All
over the country, in a greater or lesser degree, both sides faced
the same problem. Both had failed in maintaining discipline in
their armies, and although the normal circulation of the country

was not absolutely blocked, the pulse beat irregularly and weakly. The "clubmen" confronted the armies with the outcome of their failure: a widespread and growing movement to counter force by force, and to refuse further subsistence to the troops.

Colonel Massey, at Gloucester, tried to gain the support of the clubmen against the Hereford cavaliers, whom he represented as their real oppressors,[184] but though a persuasive commander might temporarily win them to his purposes, such manœuvres would not for long neutralise the danger. The only answer was the imposition of a new and effective discipline on the troops, which would give to a people exasperated but far from crushed, security against unbridled robbery and the means to reap their harvests, milk their cows, herd their cattle, shear their sheep and market their corn, cheese, meat, hides and fleeces with reasonable convenience.

It was possible that Parliament's planned New Model Army, with its reformed organisation and discipline, might be Parliament's solution of the problem. The King had no solution. The discipline of his army had long declined from the ideal he had once fixed for it, and even his most experienced commanders could not maintain it when pay was short, quarters and provisions inadequate, and many of the principal officers resented any restraint on their own power, pleasure and profit.

At Westminster, both parties and both nations, Presbyterians and Independents, Scots and English, recognised the absolute necessity of making the new organisation of the army work efficiently. They had already the framework of a national organisation in the Committees of local gentry appointed to collect the assessments levied on the counties. Members of Parliament had always been concerned to communicate the anxieties and wishes of the Commons to the boroughs and counties that they represented, while their friends at home communicated to them likewise their local difficulties and discontents. The ordinance passed in February, 1645, for the improved security and maintenance of the army strengthened a system which was already in existence and needed only to be more vigorously used.[185]

The King had no such framework within which to work. He too had appointed County Committees but means of controlling these from the centre were haphazard and incompetent. The Parliament which he had called to Oxford and which was now in its second session was a generally despised body, so that if its members did indeed take the trouble to keep in touch with their counties and boroughs, what they said or advised was likely to be of little effect. The King's Council which, in peace, had been unequal to the task of maintaining contact with the regional government of the country, was even less capable of doing so in war. Parliament at Westminster, acting now chiefly through the Committee of Both Kingdoms, performed a definite task of government and maintained the war by ordinances controlling the civil, economic and diplomatic life of the nation. Almost by accident they had invented a form of government—a Cabinet, linked closely to the House of Commons, and relying on a nation-wide executive of local authorities, which later generations were to adopt and develop but not fundamentally to alter.

The King, since the outbreak of the war, had abandoned the task of government altogether; in the effort which he, his principal councillors and his generals made to wage the war successfully, they made little (if any) attempt to solve the administrative problems on which in the long run success depended. Rupert shared a common error with others of the King's advisers in believing that the solution lay in promoting the right men. This was something, but it was surface work; centralisation and co-ordination of a much deeper and more thorough kind was also needed. And this was never attempted by the Royalists, or even seen to be necessary. The lack of political insight which had precipitated the King into the war was reflected in his management of it. He never saw, and few of his councillors did, that the effectiveness of any political theory depends on the skill with which it can be integrated into the practice of government. He failed in war, as he had failed in peace, because he never fully understood what one of his secretaries had once said: " There goes more to it, than bidding it be done." For the King a thing wished for, a thing bidden, was a thing done. But closing the gap between bidding and doing is the whole craft of government. That craft Charles, King by the Grace of God and Divine Right, never mastered, never even saw that he needed to master it.

At Westminster they built on surer foundations. The organisation was there. They needed only to put the right men at the top. Fairfax, the new commander-in-chief, was not an Independent, but as a judicious professional soldier he had no intention of waging the war without Cromwell to command the cavalry and other good officers, whatever their religion. His list of army appointments went through the Commons without difficulty; the Lords objected to more than forty names and tried to strike them out. Lord Saye, the constant friend to the Independents, was on the alert. The voting was even when he announced that he held a proxy for Lord Mulgrave, and would use this vote in favour of the list. Making a stand, the Earl of Essex claimed that he too held a proxy for his half brother, Lord Clanricarde. It was a futile throw; Lord Clanricarde was a Roman Catholic, living in Ireland, and his vote was not allowed.[186] Did Essex in that moment of defeat remember the time, four years ago, when he and some of his own colleagues were glad enough to hear the rabble cry out " No Popish Lords " and so to secure the majority which sent Strafford to his death?

A few days later the Commons sent up the new commission for Fairfax to prosecute the war; the conservative Lords protested that it did not contain, as their earlier Commission to the Earl of Essex had done, a clause for the preservation of the King's person. This omission, they rightly saw, changed the character of the war. There was no longer any pretence of fighting for the better safety and honour of the sovereign. Nothing now preserved him from the threat of deposition by force. Again, by a single vote, the moderate Lords were overruled and the commission was passed as the Commons had drafted it.[187]

The Lords had rejected in January the measure by which no member of either House could hold a commission in the army or navy. They had since been made to see that their rejection had drawbacks, because no army could be properly organised if its officers were in a position to plead privilege of Parliament when questioned for their actions. With minor alterations, this dangerous bill now came up again for their decision. All fight had gone out of them. On April 2nd, the day after the new list of officers was passed, Essex and Manchester resigned.[188] On April 3rd the Lords passed the unwelcome measure which received from the press on April 4th the name by which history knows it, the Self-Denying Ordinance.[189] The only immediate unhappy loss to Parliament's forces was the Admiral, the Earl of Warwick. Caught in the same trap as Essex and Manchester, he handed over his authority to William Batten, and diverted the energies that he had spent on the naval war to the more dubious task of stamping out witchcraft in the Eastern Counties.[190]

Cromwell was on active service and evidently could not be removed at once, especially as Fairfax was determined to retain him. He was continued, at first temporarily, then permanently, in the army, and was within a few weeks to be made General of the Horse.[191]

The immediate problem concerned the troops of Essex and Manchester, especially the infantry. Would they accept without demur the change in command and drastic reorganisation to which they were to be submitted? The number of regiments was to be reduced almost by half with, inevitably, unwelcome changes for many, loss of face and, in theory, of pay. But recent disorders, and shortages had been such that the hope of greater security might well outweigh with the majority the reduction in power and place.

On Saturday, April 5th, 1645, Philip Skippon, the universally respected commander of the London Trained Bands, who was now Major General under Fairfax, reviewed the infantry at Reading. "Gentlemen and fellow soldiers all," he began, and informed them of the change in the command and the plans for a better organised army, in which they could be sure of food, clothing and regular pay, and must absolutely and under pain of death abstain from plunder. They were to have immediately, in earnest of Parliament's good faith, fourteen days' pay, shoes and clothes. To a man they agreed to re-enlist under the new dispensation.[192] At St. Albans on April 6th, Easter Day, Fairfax addressed the cavalry, some old, some newly recruited, with equal success.[193] The New Model Army had come into being.

This army would win the war. During the months when it was being created there had been open and secret quarrelling, cunning manoeuvres in the House of Commons and arguments in the Committee of both Kingdoms; there had been a month of futile negotiation with the King when half the Parliamentary Commissioners spied on the other half and the Presbyterians tried to outwit the Independents at Uxbridge, just as the Independents were trying to outwit the Presbyterians at Westminster. But in spite of the ever widening cleavage between the King's opponents, the Scots and the English, the Presbyterians and the Independents, they did not doubt their approaching victory.

Sabran noticed this aggressive confidence, and knew, for he was a careful observer, that it was well founded. Controlling London and the sea, having larger and better organised forces in the field, they would need to be very unlucky indeed if they were now to lose the war. Discontents in London and mutinies in the army were surface troubles only, fit to arouse the unquenchable optimism of the King, but giving him no real grounds for hope.

The King did not face certain defeat, but defeat was probable unless he could gain substantial help out of Ireland or from foreign allies. But the events of the winter had made clear once again that the King pursued his objectives regardless of his prospects of success. In war it is not uncommon for the course of the fighting to modify the aspirations of the combatants. In Germany at about this time, after twenty-six years of fighting, French, Spanish, Swedish, Danish, and German diplomats were gathering at Munster to negotiate a peace which had remarkably little to do with the Protestant revolt in Bohemia, the original cause of the German war. The course of the fighting had gradually changed the nature of the conflict. This had not happened in England and was not to happen. The disheartening deadlocks reached at Oxford in 1643 and at Uxbridge in 1645 were a tribute to the steadfastness with which the King stood by his principal claims: that he would maintain the Church, and that he would suffer no restraint on his power over the armed forces. Parliament for their part stood with equal tenacity to their demands: that the King resign his leadership in Church and army to them.

Had the King won in the field, this intransigence of both parties would have presented no problem, for once the King had power to do as he pleased, no one could effectively have questioned his right to do so. He would have re-established the Church, compelled a dissolution of Parliament, tried and executed his more dangerous enemies as traitors, and maintained his prerogative in future by the use of force when necessary. But if Parliament won, a wholly new problem would face them. They had been fighting in the tacit conviction that the King, when defeated, would agree to their demands. But if the King, *whatever his circumstances*, refused to do so, there was no means by which they could compel him; no means, therefore, short of deposing him, by which they could attain their objectives, and no means at all by which they could make their actions appear constitutional and just to the majority of Englishmen or to foreign nations. Victory was almost within their grasp, but what the nature of that victory would be and what its outcome were questions time alone would answer.

CHAPTER FIVE

THE END OF THE CAVALIERS

April—October 1645

ON Easter Tuesday, April 8th, 1645, Prince Rupert, temporarily abandoning the Welsh marches, appeared in Oxford for a rapid consultation. He was under no delusion about the prospect before him. He respected the generalship of Sir Thomas Fairfax, distrusted the rumours of unrest in the Parliamentary forces and had never put any faith in the armies which his uncle expected from Ireland or from abroad. The King, in his opinion, was strong enough to win a negotiated peace but hardly strong enough to win the war. For the first time he found himself in sympathy with older and more disillusioned councillors, with the Marquis of Hertford and the Earl of Southampton, and all those who cautiously and vainly pleaded for a renewal of the negotiations at the first possible opportunity. Against him, smilingly in favour with the King, was the confident Lord Digby.[1]

The King's optimism was not absolutely unfounded. He had lost Shrewsbury; he had never taken Gloucester; he had failed to hold Weymouth or to take Plymouth; Taunton defied him. But on the whole he still dominated the South-West. He had valuable ports for trade and communication in Bristol, Exeter and the Cornish towns. In spite of the troubles in North Wales he could draw on the Welsh highlands to recruit his armies. He controlled Cornish tin and the iron in the Forest of Dean; he was effectively holding up the wool trade of London and Gloucester.

436

With so much, he could have treated favourably. With so little, he could not—without extreme good fortune—win the war. Rupert, and others of his advisers, clearly saw this, but Charles himself could not believe that God would abandon him. One of his officers, already fearing the worst, wrote at about this time: "We have a just cause, and the resolution of desperate lovers to defend it to the last man."[2] The King was not unlike a desperate lover, if it be remembered that no lover is ever truly desperate, because it is the nature of love to hope always for a miracle. So now he would not listen to counsels of caution, but was convinced that the material help of which he stood in need would reach him—somehow, from somewhere—before it was too late.

He appealed to Venice for a loan of a million ducats, a quarter of it in cash. The Venetians declined. He authorised Sir Kenelm Digby discreetly to ask the Vatican for help.[3] The Queen continued to press the Duke of Lorraine to send troops to her husband, while she approached the Duke of Courland for supplies to help Montrose.[4] She appealed to the Dutch to sell arms and ammunition to the King and refuse them to Parliament, to take her husband's merchant shipping under the protection of their navy, and to allow vessels carrying the King's commission to sell their prizes and their cargoes freely in Dutch ports. For all these advantages she could only offer in return the Prince of Wales as bridegroom to the Prince of Orange's daughter. But this could hardly be regarded as an argument to move the hard-headed Dutch Estates, who were restive under the influence of the House of Orange, while the Prince himself preferred a less glorious and less dangerous match for his daughter with a German prince.[5]

Three days after his rapid consultation at Oxford, on April 11th, 1645, Rupert was at a council of war in the West with the Prince of Wales and his advisers. They ordered the obstreperous Goring, who had made another successful raid on Waller's quarters in Wiltshire, to pursue this advantage by thrusting forward towards Salisbury with his cavalry, while sending his guns and infantry to help Grenvile reduce the obstinate enemy at Taunton. Goring obeyed the second part of the command, but instead of following Waller left his cavalry idle and, on the plea of ill-health, repaired to Bath to take the waters.[6]

The King let himself be cheered by the disorders which, after the surprisingly calm beginning, now broke out in the Parliamentary New Model Army. Many of the recruits were pressed men, doubtfully willing to fight; those from Kent were mutinous; in Hertfordshire they began at once to plunder. The veterans of the army of Essex soon began to resent the new officers appointed by Fairfax, and at Abingdon Colonel Pickering, an Independent, provoked a mutiny by preaching to the troops.[7]

In London bad news from Ireland and Scotland spread gloom. The Confederate Irish in the South had taken the important fortress and harbour of Duncannon in spite of the troops whom Parliament had sent, or tried to send, to the Protestant forces of Munster. It was reported, too, that the Marquis of Ormonde had nearly concluded his negotiations with the Irish for sending help to the King.[8] At the Committee of Both Kingdoms Sir Harry Vane now openly taunted the Scots Commissioners with the poor achievement of their vaunted armies and the expense of their alliance.[9] They, for their part, unable to report the extinction of Montrose, managed so far to disguise the effects of his warfare as to have a thanksgiving in London for his alleged defeat at Dundee.[10] But the King's friends, neither then nor later, regarded the happenings at Dundee in that light.

II

Montrose had successfully foiled the efforts of the Covenanters to bring him to fight, but he was hindered from making a descent into the Lowlands by the uncertain friendship of the Gordons; their young chief remained loyal to his new friend but many of his clansmen, confused by a supposed command from Huntly

himself, suddenly abandoned Montrose at Dunkeld, on the edge
of the Highlands, just as he intended to advance towards the
Forth and invade the Lowlands. In this predicament Montrose
could only withdraw. But to give a different colour to his
necessary retreat, he planned, with a picked force of six hundred
musketeers and his few cavalry, to raid the town of Dundee
before he retired into the mountains.

He marched from Dunkeld at midnight and by noon on April
4th, 1645, was master of Dundee. His men were busy at their
plunder when General Baillie with three thousand foot and eight
hundred horse was reported scarcely more than a mile away.
Montrose's captains urged upon him different counsels of agitation
or despair, but with a well-simulated appearance of calm he asked
them each to do his duty, to leave the issue to God and the
management to him.[11] Drawing his disordered troops together
with astonishing speed and making the cavalry serve as rearguard
to the infantry, he left the town on the eastern side just as Baillie
approached it from the west, but he had to leave by the only way
open to him, the coast road to Arbroath, and was therefore with
every step increasing the distance between his fugitive army and
the safety of the hills. Baillie struck inland and marched through
the night to cut him off when he turned, as he must, from
Arbroath back to the mountains.

Montrose assumed that Baillie would move in exactly this
way and evaded him by doing the unexpected. As soon as his
scouts were sure that Baillie had turned inland to outflank him
and cut off his retreat, he made his tired troops face about and
march back the way they had come. All that night both armies
marched; pursuers and pursued passed each other by within a
few dark miles. Baillie, heading for Brechin, was vigilant all
the way for any signs of Montrose's men striking inland for the
mountains. They did indeed strike inland, but *behind* the rear of
Baillie's army, while he looked for them in front. By daylight
Montrose's six hundred, who had marched two successive nights
and had stormed and taken a town, could go no farther. Within

reach of the mountains they halted for a rest, dropped down and slept where they lay. Baillie's vanguard, who had found the scent again, nearly surprised them, but Montrose's officers, alerted in time, forced their tired men to their feet, and staggered the last three miles into the sheltering hills before Baillie came up with them.[12]

This was the victory celebrated in London, the triumph of General Baillie over Montrose at Dundee. But everyone in Scotland, and a fair number in London, saw the matter differently. Montrose had raided Dundee with complete impunity. If he could do this to Dundee in despite of General Baillie, and get away unscathed, no town in Scotland would henceforward feel secure against him.

III

At Westminster, the Committee of Both Kingdoms was fully occupied with the English war. On April 20th, 1645, a fortnight after the reorganisation of their New Model Army, they ordered Oliver Cromwell to advance west of Oxford and cut, if he could, the line of communication between the King and Prince Rupert on the Welsh border.[13]

On April 23rd Cromwell was at Watlington; on the 24th, moving northwards, he beat his way across the Cherwell at Islip, driving back the Queen's regiment and taking the lovely standard strewn with the golden lilies of France.[14] That night he summoned the outlying garrison at Bletchingdon House. Frank Windebank was in command, a brave young spark, but lacking in vigilance. Expecting no attack he had allowed his wife to invite a number of her friends on a visit. Roused in the small hours, surrounded by frightened girls, he remembered the manners of the drawing-room rather than the camp, and immediately gave up the house to preserve his guests from the horrors of a storm. Next afternoon when he got back to

Oxford he was tried by court martial, condemned to death, and shot.[15]

Cromwell continued on his way, leaving Oxford to the south, then he turned west. At Bampton, on the edge of the Cotswolds, he intercepted a body of troops marching to the King's head-quarters from Wales under Sir Richard Vaughan. These he scattered, taking some prisoners. " The enemy is in high fear," he reported to Westminster, " God docs terrify them."[16] He was thinking of Windebank's surrender and some timorous state-ments made by the prisoners he had taken at Bampton. But the King, who had had to postpone a plan for joining Rupert because Cromwell had driven off most of the draft horses in the Oxford region, was not in the least afraid. Digby summoned Rupert instead to march to Oxford sweeping up the necessary draft horses as he came, and Goring was ordered up from the West with the troops he had there.[17] Cromwell meanwhile met with a check at Faringdon. He summoned the garrison peremptorily on April 29th, threatening to put all to the sword if they did not surrender; but they rejected the bullying summons and repelled the attack which followed.[18]

In London, the Scots Commissioners urged that Fairfax should return to the North, where the Royalist skirmishing cavalry was increasingly active and dangerous. But West Country members in the House of Commons were insistent that he must first relieve Taunton, where Colonel Blake, with splendid resolution, short of food and short of fodder, still defied the Western army of the King. The West Country gentlemen had their way and Fairfax set out on the long march, summoning Cromwell to meet for consultation at Newbury. Cromwell, abandoning the attack on Faringdon, hastened to meet him, narrowly avoiding a clash with Goring, who was on his way to Oxford.[19]

Suddenly, the King's armies were on the move, with no signs of the " high fear " which Cromwell had attributed to them. On May 3rd Rupert and Maurice marched from Broadway by Stow on the Wold to Oxford which they reached on the evening of the 5th.[20] Two days later the King left with them for the summer campaign, day by day marching or riding at the head of his troops.[21] On May 8th, at Stow on the Wold, he held the general rendezvous. His army consisted of five thousand foot and six thousand horse. This, with the troops already in the west or to be raised there, seemed an impressive number. The two armies, wrote Digby, who had seen only one of them, are " equal to any the rebels have at this time." He added " we have great unanimity among ourselves and the rebels great distractions."[22]

Digby wrote with his customary optimism, but the generals at the King's Council of War at Stow on the Wold had bitterly disagreed on the plan of campaign. The majority wanted to march into the West and, with the help of the Western army, cut off Fairfax, who was known to be on his way to Taunton, as Essex had been cut off in the previous summer when he had gone to the relief of Lyme. Rupert was opposed to this. In the first place he argued that the relief of Chester, hard pressed by the Parliamentary forces in Cheshire and North Wales, was essential to keep open the principal sea-route to Ireland whence the King expected help. But he had another and a far stronger reason for urging a northward march: Fairfax was now in the south, the Scots army, unpaid, unsupplied, at odds with the English, and in constant anxiety because of the trouble at home, was in no state to control the North. Langdale had recently inflicted a serious defeat on the elder Fairfax, and his men were in good heart for more campaigning in their own county, but they would be unwilling and intractable if compelled to march into the unfamiliar West. Pomfret and Carlisle still held out for the King, making two important centres of support on the way to Scotland, and relief had been promised to the garrison at Carlisle not later than May.[23] In Scotland itself Montrose was active. If the King advanced that way he might well regain the North; he could then send Montrose the cavalry he badly needed, defeat the Covenanters both in England and in Scotland, force them out of the war and so once again confront the Parliamentary army from a consolidated position, with no enemy in his rear.[24]

Rupert gained his point, not without much murmuring from his opponents. The Prince had grown, during the last months, altogether to distrust the prospect in the West. The disputes between the Western generals made the creation of a joint effective army impossible. Berkeley at Exeter had refused Grenvile any share in the supplies he drew from Devon; Grenvile in return took for himself all that could be got from Cornwall and trespassed on Berkeley's ground whenever occasion offered. They had agreed to co-operate in the siege of Taunton but when Grenvile was disabled by a wound he encouraged his officers to refuse obedience to Berkeley. Meanwhile Goring arrogated the chief command to himself by virtue of his commission for the Southern counties, which had not, in fact, been intended to cover the West—an intrusion of authority bitterly resented by Hopton.[25]

Relying on the Northern Horse and his own for the coming campaign, Rupert agreed to Goring's return to the West and gave him, probably with some idea of stilling the ceaseless dispute about precedence, a more extensive commission.[26] The effects of this were not immediately felt, for before the King's Council of War was concluded, on May 8th at Stow on the Wold, the situation had already altered. Fairfax, marching into the West, was overtaken at Blandford by a peremptory command from Parliament: on hearing that the Royalist army had moved from Oxford, they now believed the danger to be greatest in the Midlands, and called him back to keep watch on the King's movements.[27] He detached a small relieving force for Taunton and turned obediently towards Oxford.

In the orchards round Taunton, among the blossoming fruit trees, the Royalists, six thousand strong, were trying to carry the town by storm. Within, Robert Blake unthatched the houses to feed the gaunt horses of the garrison, and improvised match from bedcord for his musketeers. On May 6th the Royalists, attacking on the east side, drove the defenders back from their outpost beyond the East Gate, but failed to force the passage of the Gate itself. Twenty-four hours later, at seven in the evening on May 8th, they stormed the East Gate and this time forced an entrance, but the long East Street which runs uphill from the gate is narrow enough to be held against numbers by a few, and they could make no further headway. Next day at noon they renewed the assault on two sides of the town; the weight of their numbers, their heavy guns, their unspent ammunition told hard against Blake's now almost exhausted men, and this time the Royalists battered their way up East Street firing the wooden cottages. (On their left hand the new almshouses, built in 1635 by Robert Gray, handsome in solid brick, defied the flames.) Blake's men now withdrew from the outer defences to an inner triangle of bulwarks round Taunton's stately, elegant church tower, and the substantial castle. Here, by nightfall, Blake and his garrison still held out, surrounded by homeless people from the smoking suburbs. Summoned to surrender at dawn, Blake sent back the curt message that he would eat his boots first. The Royalists were tired and angry, with nothing to show for all their efforts but an unconquered citadel and smouldering town. They attacked again, but were startled by news of a relieving force at hand. They had made no attempt to intercept them earlier, believing them to be auxiliaries of their own sent by Goring. Now they mistook again, thinking the new army much larger than it was. They hurriedly blocked the approaches to Taunton by felling the orchard trees, and, with only this rude obstruction to protect their rear, drew off as fast as they could march. The soldiers and citizens of Taunton joyfully welcomed their friends, and for a second time Robert Blake was acclaimed the godly hero of the Parliamentary cause in the West.[28]

Rupert, on his march to the North, heard that Fairfax was on his way back towards the Midlands. He was disappointed that neither the Western army nor Goring had held him in play, for his return changed the face of things. Rupert sent to Goring to bring his cavalry with all speed to a Midlands rendezvous at Market Harborough.[29] Otherwise the news was good. In South Wales Sir Charles Gerrard, terrorising the country with his flying cavalry, had fallen upon Rowland Laugharne at Newcastle Emlyn and compelled him to headlong retreat into Pembrokeshire; he had evacuated Haverfordwest and Cardigan, retaining only Pembroke and Tenby for Parliament.[30] This set free most of Gerrard's forces to join with the King in the Midlands.

Fairfax was still new to his task and confused by the different orders from his masters at Westminster. If he could be tempted to give battle, and made to confront the united forces of Rupert, Goring and Gerrard before he himself could make a junction with Cromwell, his defeat was almost a certainty. With Fairfax defeated, the northern campaign would be an easy matter. Rupert and Digby were, for the moment, at one. " On my conscience," wrote Digby to Goring, " it will be the last blow in the business."[31]

Good news had come from Chester, where the Parliamentary commander, Sir William Brereton, had abandoned the siege,[32] but from Oxford the King's friends reported anxiously that Fairfax and Cromwell were converging on the city with about thirteen thousand men and sixteen cannon.[33] Rupert, who had absolute faith in his governor of Oxford, the experienced Colonel Legge, was not perturbed. He advised the King to march rapidly into the eastern Midlands, and so draw the enemy away from Oxford by threatening their fattest counties. With all speed the King's army headed for Leicestershire.[34]

Langdale and the Northern Horse joined them at Ashby de la Zouch,[35] but Gerrard and the Welsh could not reach them so fast and there was no news of Goring's three thousand, ordered to Market Harborough. Goring was having one of his bad spells. He had bungled an attempt to intercept Fairfax on his return from the West; his high-spirited forces converging from opposite directions on what they took to be the retreating enemy, had fought each other for two hours before the mistake could be disentangled: "the most fantastical accident since the war began," reported Goring impenitently.[36] A few days later he was in his favourite Bath again, whither the councillors of the Prince of Wales had moved their young charge owing to the prevalence of plague in Bristol. Here Goring, supported by Lord Culpeper, took exception to Rupert's orders: they argued that the King should return to Oxford, they themselves and the Western army would meet them there and quickly make an end of Fairfax and "this new raw army." With a tactful gesture to Rupert, they compared this project to his own brilliant defeat of Meldrum before Newark in the previous year.[37] But it was in fact a barefaced effort to reverse his decision for a northern campaign and shift the axis of war back to the south-west.

Long before their untimely objections reached the King's quarters, Rupert's new plan had begun to take effect. Parliament had recalled Cromwell to defend the Eastern Association and deceived by a mischievous and groundless report that Oxford would be betrayed by the governor, had left Fairfax alone to the siege. Sir Edward Nicholas wrote anxiously to the King from the beleaguered city but was bidden to be patient and bear the stringencies of a siege, even if the Duke of York had to go on short rations.[38] "For God's sake give us all the time you can," wrote Digby in tearing spirits; the King would soon have all his forces gathered to fight "a battle of all, for all." Things could not be going better: "we never had more cause to thank God since this war began."[39]

The King's forces were strengthened by local troops under Lord Loughborough, who, as Henry Hastings, had from the outset of the war maintained the Royalist cause with vigour and ferocity, in Leicestershire. Rupert's foraging parties scoured far afield to the Puritan villages of Nottinghamshire, and exacted supplies for man and beast, threatening that otherwise the people would be "exposed to the plunder of the hungry soldiers."[40]

On May 29th the King's army advanced on Leicester, well garrisoned by Parliament and lying, comfortable and falsely secure, within its stout medieval walls. The Royalists took the garrison fairly by surprise; a reconnoitring party, three or four miles beyond the gates, had so little expected to meet an enemy that they had their greyhounds with them and were varying their military duties by coursing a hare or two. Startled, but not dismayed, they retreated into Leicester in good order.[41]

On the following morning Rupert drew up his forces outside the town, fired two of his cannon to alarm the inhabitants, and then sent a herald to offer pardon to the citizens if they opened their gates to the King. They refused the offer and detained the herald. Rupert, who all the previous night had directed his engineers in the setting up of a battery on the south side of the town,[42] opened fire at three in the afternoon and by six o'clock had blasted a wide breach in the wall. The defenders, nothing daunted, covered the gap with cannon drawn up five yards behind the wall. At midnight Rupert, having carefully made his dispositions, gave the signal for a general assault. The Royalists stormed the city on three sides at once, the main force attacking the breach on the south side, while two smaller forces, with scaling ladders, assailed the town on the north and east. The cavalry meanwhile stood ready to force a way in as soon as their infantry should penetrate the town and open the gates. The defenders fought valiantly but in vain. Within an hour the Prince's " great black standard " was triumphantly planted on their silenced battery inside the walls; by one in the morning on May 31st the Royalist infantry had overpowered the guards at the city gates and let in their cavalry who " scoured the town."

Leicester paid very dear for its defiance of the King. No attempt was made by Charles or any of his officers to control the violence of their men. Mercifully the lust to kill soon gave way to the greed of plunder. The King's infantry, mostly Welsh boys newly come from their barren mountains, fell joyfully on the good things of Leicester, rummaged through houses and cottages, shops and cellars, stuffing their knapsacks with gear and their pockets with good English coin. By daylight there was "not a cottage unplundered" and the men staggered to their waggons heavy with spoil and well pleased with the King's service.[43]

At the Council of War which met after the capture of the city the momentary agreement of the King's advisers was broken, and Rupert was again in opposition. No news yet suggested that Fairfax had withdrawn from Oxford, and the King's councillors, anxious for the headquarters which contained so much of their property, wished to turn back. Rupert still believed that they would draw Fairfax away simply by continuing their progress in the Midlands.[44] As Cromwell had been drawn off when the King's army headed eastward, so Fairfax, the Yorkshire general, would be drawn if they headed northwards. The northward march still had all the advantages that he had demonstrated three weeks before to the Council at Stow on the Wold. Montrose, in a despatch recently received, had implored the King to spare him five hundred horse, were it only for a month; with these he was confident he could bring a Scots army into England before the end of the summer.[45] This was yet another strong argument for continuing the march to the North. If Fairfax followed, they could turn and fight him when they chose and at his disadvantage.

Rupert had also a more compelling reason. The Northern Horse were unwilling to march southwards. Their unwillingness proved decisive, for although Rupert was overruled in the Council and all was set in train for the march to Oxford, the Northern Horse, whatever Langdale or the King said to them, stubbornly faced about and took the road for their old quarters in Newark.[46] This brought the King's plans to a stand for the time being, but Rupert proved to be wise in his hopes as well as his fears. The day after the mutiny of Langdale's cavalry, Fairfax abandoned the siege of Oxford. The King heard the news at Daventry with joy. "My affairs were never in so fair and hopeful way," he wrote to his queen,[47] and to Secretary

LEICESTER AND NASEBY

Nicholas he gaily predicted: "If we peripatetics get no more mischance than you Oxfordians are like to have this summer, we may all expect probably a merry winter."[48]

As the King's spirits rose, Rupert's sank. He was perturbed by his uncle's preference for the views of his other councillors,[49] and by the continued absence of Goring, in despite of all orders to hasten his forces. Fantastic rumours of quarrels in the opposing army deceived others, but not Rupert. The King and the gay young men in his Lifeguard might believe that Fairfax had boxed the ears of General Browne,[50] but the Prince did not underestimate the strength or the unity of the enemy. He knew that only the utmost vigilance and skill would draw Fairfax to fight at a disadvantage, and it was no part of his plan of campaign that the King was hunting in Fawsley Park near Daventry, and the whole army enjoying its ease on Thursday, June 12th, when Fairfax was reported five miles away. He had come by way of Newport Pagnell and Stony Stratford, had about eight thousand men and was hoping that Cromwell would receive Parliament's order to join him and would act on it in time. He feared, from what he had learnt from prisoners, that Goring's forces would soon be added to those of the King [51]; his best hope, as he saw it, was to force the King to fight before this junction could be made.

That night the King's army, without undue haste, evacuated Daventry and withdrew to Harborough. Here the Council of War met and here Rupert once again put forward his plan for continuing the march northward. They had a long enough start of Fairfax to be able to slip quietly away to Newark, and he did not judge the present moment favourable for the battle " of all, for all," on which Digby was counting. Goring and his cavalry had not come; neither had Gerrard yet joined them; Fairfax even without Cromwell, who was known to be on his way, outnumbered the King's army. Rupert was not in favour of accepting the battle which Fairfax was evidently seeking, and would prefer to postpone this very serious and perhaps final engagement until the enemy was more evidently at a disadvantage and the King had a better choice of time and ground. But now to Digby's cheerful voice was added that of John Ashburnham, a favourite Gentleman of the King's Bedchamber. The two hopeful and inexperienced civilians saw both their objectives combined in one movement and had no patience with Rupert's obstructive military arguments. They wished to go back to Oxford and Fairfax was in the way: it was the heaven-sent moment to win the great victory they all wanted and return in triumph to Oxford. Besides, they argued, it would be ignominious to march northwards with Fairfax at their heels; this would look like a retreat; it was better to be the pursuer

450

than the pursued. Their ignorant arguments prevailed once more against those of the highest commander in the army.[52] In the short June night Rupert, who must now make the best of a battle he had not advised, led a party to reconnoitre the enemy's position, while the King's army marched southwards from Harborough in search of the battle which was to end the war.

Earlier in that same night Cromwell and his forces had joined Fairfax, at which all the Parliamentary army " gave a mighty shout for joy of his coming."[53] Fairfax now had about fourteen thousand men under officers who had in the past three years abundantly proved their capacity: Philip Skippon commanded the infantry, Oliver Cromwell the cavalry with, under him, the dour and resolute Henry Ireton. Fairfax had in his hands on this critical night an intercepted letter from Goring to Rupert, the letter which announced Goring's objection to the summons he had received.[54] Then Goring was not coming, and was nowhere near. Fairfax saw his opportunity and took it. He marched warily towards the royal army, halting in the small hours at Guilsborough, six miles south of Market Harborough.

South of Market Harborough rises an abrupt ridge of country, the watershed between the Avon and the Welland, crowned by the village of Naseby. Between Naseby and Harborough the ground slopes away in a series of lessening ridges, making a broken sequence of small hills and valleys, watered by numerous streams. It had been a wet spring and the ground in the hollows was marshy. The generals of both armies, under cover of the dark, sought the best dry, high ground on which to face the enemy. In the early summer dawn reconnoitring parties sighted each other; and as each commander calculated to the best of his ability what the other would do, and moved accordingly, they found themselves between seven and eight o'clock in the morning drawn up on two opposing grassy ridges with a shallow dip between them. A blustering north-west wind was more troublesome to the Parliament forces, who faced almost due north, than to the Royalists, but it could not truly be said that either side had markedly gained any advantage of ground, or wind, or sun.

The King's forces in the windy summer morning looked magnificent, with bright fluttering banners of every colour and fantasy, as the light flashed from polished breastplates, glowed on damask banners, taffeta scarves and velvet cloaks. Oliver Cromwell was moved to prayer: "When I saw the enemy draw up and march in gallant order towards us, and we a company of poor ignorant men, to seek how to order our battle—the General having commanded me to order all the horse—I could not (riding alone about my business) but smile out to God in praises, in assurance of victory, because God would, by things that are not, bring to naught things that are. Of which I had great assurance: and God did it." John Okey, a godly colonel of dragoons, had much the same thoughts, and called on the Almighty to remember " a poor handful of despised men whom they thought to have swallowed up before them."[55] The " poor handful," the " things that are not," the Parliamentary forces, outnumbered the " things that are," the King's men, by two to one, as Cromwell, with the careful calculation of an experienced soldier, very well knew. The predominance was greatest in cavalry; it was this which ensured the victory.

Oliver Cromwell was on the right wing. Opposite him, on the King's left, he had the gaunt Sir Marmaduke Langdale and his obstinate Northern Horse. In the centre Philip Skippon commanded the infantry, a plebeian opponent to the gay and gallant band of courtier-soldiers who surrounded the King, riding at the head of his army, all in gilt armour, on his beautiful Flemish horse. On the Parliamentary left Henry Ireton, who had that morning been elevated to the rank of Commissary General, faced the redoubtable Rupert. A long double hedge, marking a parish boundary, here ran at right angles to Ireton's line almost as far as Rupert's position. Realising that this was the side which would need strengthening, Cromwell had put Colonel Okey with his regiment of dragoons along the hedge, ready to pour an oblique fire into Rupert's ranks as he charged. Both parties completed their dispositions at about the same time, towards eleven in the morning. Fairfax gave his men the word for the day: " God is our strength." The King, wishing the glorious event to be for ever linked with his beloved wife, had given the word: " Queen Mary."

Rupert began the battle, not risking this time the delay which had been disastrous at Marston Moor. His horsemen swept down, then up, the slope with undiminished force and broke full on Ireton's front line. The musketry fire from the hedge failed to break their impact. Ireton, himself wounded, could not rally his men. Two regiments, those on the inside nearest to the infantry, broke completely. Not a few " went clear away to Northampton and could never be stopped."[56] The King's foot almost immediately pressed forward, crossed the shallow ditch between the lines and closed with the Parliamentary foot, some of whom had already been thrown into disorder by the dispersal and flight of the cavalry nearest to them. In that first clash Philip Skippon was shot in the right side under the short ribs, the bullet penetrating coat and armour. He managed to keep his horse and continue directing his men, but the news that he was hurt spread discouragement and the Parliamentary infantry gave ground.

At this moment Cromwell led the first line of his cavalry against Langdale's Northern Horse on the left of the King's position. Langdale's horse did not break and scatter, but they gave ground and their retreat dismayed some of the infantry in the centre. The King, with his usual courage and more than usual presence of mind, hoped to hearten his infantry by himself advancing among them, but as he tried to go forward a Scottish professional soldier among his attendants put his hand on his bridle and crying, " Would you go upon your death? " turned his horse's head. This movement of the King was mistaken for a command. Someone shouted " March to the right hand," and part of the Royalist foot wheeled away, carrying the King along with them. In the general disorder, they had fallen back some way before he could again get them to stand.

By this time the greater numbers of the Parliamentary cavalry were beginning to tell. On the Parliamentary right Cromwell had charged with less than half his forces; the rest were still fresh. On the disordered left wing of the Parliamentary army, Rupert's cavalry had only come into direct contact with about half Ireton's horse; the rest had fallen back, dismayed, as their comrades fled before the Cavaliers, but they were uninjured, still in good order, and could be brought back into action. Rupert, returning to the help of the infantry with troops victorious but no longer fresh, found his men exposed to a flank attack from this uninjured enemy cavalry.

On the farther side of the battle, Langdale's uncertain forces, pounded by recurrent waves of Cromwell's horse, gave ground again and finally broke, some galloping for Leicester, others seeking refuge as far off as their old headquarters in Newark. The King's infantry was now naked of cavalry cover on the left wing, and open to the punishing onslaught of Cromwell's Ironsides. The Welsh levies, mostly new to the wars, had fought manfully until this moment but they, seeing no hope of victory, refused to obey their officers, and mindful of the booty they had taken surrendered in whole companies provided they might keep their spoil. The officers, seeing the game lost, mostly saved themselves by flight. For Rupert's cavalry nothing was now left but to cover the King's retreat from the lost field. By one o'clock in the afternoon there was " not a horse or man of the King's army to be seen except the prisoners."[57]

In the desperate flight of the King's cavalry, by way of Leicester to Ashby de la Zouch, which the King reached in the small hours, no care had been taken for the wagons and coaches which accompanied the army. George Digby kept his wits about him enough to preserve his own coach and possessions, but had little reason to congratulate himself as Secretary of State, for the King's entire correspondence fell into the hands of the enemy. In many coaches ladies and officers' wives were taken, and some women, " full of money and rich apparel," who were neither ladies nor wives. Many of these wealthier camp followers bought mercy from their victors; the pillage of that day was reckoned at a hundred thousand pounds in gold, silver and jewels.[58] But mercy was denied to the common camp followers, the drabs and drudges, many of whom the soldiers killed. Afterwards, shame-faced at this massacre of women, they said that they were " Irish women of cruel countenances," armed with long knives; it seems more likely that they were Welsh, crying out in a strange language, and defending themselves with the cutlery they carried to dress and cook meat for their menfolk.[59]

The King lost on Naseby field all his infantry, all his guns and most of his baggage train. When, three days later, his garrison at Leicester surrendered, they handed over to Fairfax the remaining magazine of arms and five hundred horses. The disaster was total.[60]

IV

Fairfax, in a laconic despatch, announced to the two Houses the greatest victory God had yet vouchsafed to the Cause.[61] Cromwell was more eloquent, both in his praises of the Almighty and his own men. After an account of the battle somewhat more explicit than that of Fairfax, he concluded: " This is none other but the hand of God; and to him alone belongs the glory, where-in none are to share with him. . . . Honest men served you faith-fully in this action. Sir, they are trusty. I beseech you in the name of God not to discourage them. . . . He that ventures his life for the liberty of his country, I wish he trust God for the liberty of his conscience, and you for the liberty he fights for."[62]

The House of Commons had the letter printed, cautiously omitting the last sentence. They had trouble enough on their hands with the Scots and the sectaries vehemently disputing, without adding lieutenant general Cromwell's views on liberty of conscience to the uproar. The House of Lords, however, in a moment of inattention gave the whole text to their printer and revealed the attempted suppression to the indignation alike of Presbyterians and sectaries.[63]

At Marston Moor Cromwell had boldly claimed the victory for his troops. He did so, with more right, at Naseby. After Marston he had proudly vindicated his men against those who scorned them as sectaries and men of low birth. After Naseby, his letter implied a threat. His men were fighting for liberty of conscience; let not narrow-hearted divines or meddling Scots deny it to them.

The warning was doubly apposite. That week John Lilburne had been called before the Committee of Examinations at the instance of William Prynne and reproved for his recent attack on Prynne's religious views and on the " Egyptian bondage " of the Presbyterian system. The Committee let him off with a caution which was not likely to stem his eloquence, and the angry Prynne went home to write another venomous pamphlet against free-speakers.[64]

The smouldering hatred between Presbyterians and Independents ever and again erupted in flame. Robert Baillie, in a moment of indiscretion, had openly doubted the loyalty of the Independents to the common cause, not without reason, as the King had more than once indicated his willingness to help them against the Presbyterians, and an intrigue conducted by Lord Savile, whom Charles had released for the purpose, had newly come to light. Baillie's ill-judged words reached the ears of the Commons[65] almost simultaneously with the news of Naseby, which was brought to London, as Baillie himself and the Presbyterians complained, by one of the New Model officers, " ane horrible Anti-triastrian "—a disbeliever in the Trinity. But " horrible Anti-triastrians " were among those who had won the recent great victory; it was no moment to be accusing the sectaries of disloyalty and poor Baillie had to apologise at the bar of the House for his insinuations against the Independents.[66]

The mood of London had changed from the gloom which

followed the King's capture of Leicester to general jubilation. The dismal train of sick and wounded soldiers whose coming had signalised the distress of the Parliamentary forces now gave place to godly efficient young horsemen from the New Model Army, coming every day with fresh tidings of victory. The army, of which a month before the most discouraging prophecies had been made, was now acclaimed as the saviour of the Commonweal. With the popularity of the Army the position of the Independents, inside and outside Parliament, grew always more secure.[67] On June 21st the prisoners from Naseby marched in, more than four thousand men, with more than fifty captured standards going before. The French resident, looking down on them from his window, was amazed; they were hale and sturdy, with few wounded, not like soldiers whose hearts had been in their cause and who had fought to the last.[68] In Tothill Fields, where they camped, they were preached at in Welsh. Some re-enlisted in the Parliament forces; some swore never to fight again and were sent home. But Alonso de Cardeñas, the Spanish resident, who like his French rival had noticed the good quality of the men, asked leave to recruit some for his master's service. The response was good enough to alarm Sabran into procuring permission to do the same.[69] The Portuguese resident was less happily placed, because the King's letters taken at Naseby revealed that he had abused his diplomatic privileges to convey letters from the King's quarters to the Queen.

The King's correspondence now in the hands of Parliament went back over more than two years. It consisted largely of his letters to and from the Queen. These revealed his attempts to get money and men from the King of Denmark, the King of France, the Prince of Orange and the Duke of Lorraine; they put beyond all doubt his intention of bringing Irish Confederate forces to England. No more damaging weapon could have been forged for his enemies to use against him. They did not hesitate. Within a month of their victory at Naseby the publication of *The King's Cabinet Opened* placed before shocked and excited readers the most intimate and indiscreet discussions of policy between the King and Queen.[70]

The Royalists professed horror at this violation of the King's private life. The Athenians, they said, had returned unopened the captured letters of Philip of Macedon to his wife because they thought it " shameful and dishonest " to pry into conjugal secrets. But there were recent examples of this kind of conduct. In 1620 at the Battle of the White Hill outside Prague the principal councillor of the Protestant King of Bohemia (King Charles's brother-in-law and Prince Rupert's father) had lost his private papers in the rout; published by the victorious Emperor, these documents had shown the intrigues and dubious manœuvres by which the election of the King had been secured. The revelation had proved a heavy blow to the Protestant Cause in Europe, not least because wary monarchs and cautious diplomatists were henceforward unwilling to commit to paper secrets of policy which might hereafter be publicly exposed. In the smaller and more compact circle of King Charles's friends and potential allies the publication of The King's Cabinet Opened had the same effect. It destroyed goodwill and deepened distrust just at the moment when the King's serious defeat gave him most need of help. In Paris the exiled Queen put a brave face on disaster and assured everyone that her husband needed only a little help soon to win the war, but his cause was henceforward given over for lost by every intelligent European statesman.

V

The King, with his cavalry, had by way of Lichfield, Wolverhampton and Bewdley, reached the safety of loyal Hereford. The barely concealed dislike of Rupert for Digby had come violently to the surface. It was the irony of the situation that Rupert, who had advised against the battle, had to carry all the odium of the defeat while Digby, at whose instance it had been fought, was in no way blamed for the outcome. Rupert was for immediately linking up what remained of the cavalry with the still intact Western army, before Fairfax and Cromwell, pursuing their immense advantage, swept down in force into the Southwest. But the King, undiscouraged by the surrender of almost the whole of his Welsh infantry, was for raising more Welsh to take their place, in conjunction with Gerrard's Welsh forces, regardless of the delays that this must cause. Rupert was anxious, short of sleep, irritable, and fatiguingly active. The King preferred Digby's smiling calm.

Announcing to Ormonde, five days after Naseby, "the unfortunate loss of a most hopeful battle," Digby went on to say that the King's forces joined with those of Goring in the West would, with the help of the troops expected from Ireland, soon repair the damage. "The consequences of this disaster will have no great extent. . . . We all take it for granted here that the peace of Ireland is concluded."[71] The peace of Ireland, by which the Confederates were to help the King, was not within sight of conclusion but the King still counted on it and took the occasion to urge his secret agent for Ireland, the laggard Earl of Glamorgan, to hurry on his journey. As to his own prospects, wrote the King, "I am nowise disheartened by our late misfortune . . . I hope shortly to recover my late loss with advantage if such succours come to me from that Kingdom (Ireland) which I have reason to expect."[72] While Rupert, seconded by the gloomy hardworking Langdale—"a creature of Prince Rupert's," wrote Digby disparagingly[73]—did what he could to repair the disaster and to bring home its magnitude to the King, Charles neglected his advice and preferred Digby's soothing counsels.[74] All was not lost. The Irish in their thousands would soon be with him, and from Scotland Montrose sent word of his continued success during the last weeks.

Montrose had withdrawn to Speyside after the raid on Dundee. General Baillie, chivvied by the angry government in Edinburgh, tried to draw him by cautiously advancing into

Atholl, but Montrose turned north down the Spey towards the coast. Baillie sent his second in command in pursuit; he was no other than the renegade Sir John Hurry, who had now entered Scottish service. On May 9th, not far from the sea, between Nairn and Auldearn, Hurry under cover of a thick mist overtook Montrose. Within a few minutes of his unsuspecting quarry, he had his men fire off their muskets to clear any clotted powder from the barrels so that they should be ready to attack. The muffled detonation apprised Montrose of his danger less than ten minutes before Hurry was upon him.

At Montrose's back was the little township of Auldearn, high on a green ridge, round its grey stone church, its approaches deceptively masked by a series of steep hillocks. Montrose profited by these to conceal the smallness of his numbers: he had about fifteen hundred foot and three hundred Gordon cavalry recently returned to him. This cavalry he stationed some way in front and to the south of the ridge, hidden from Hurry's advancing troops by the contour of the hill. The Irish infantry under Macdonald were in the cultivated and partly enclosed ground immediately before the town, well to the right of the Gordons and some way behind them. In the gap between these two main bodies, he raised his own standard to deceive Hurry into taking this, the weakest place, for the real centre of his battle. If Hurry took the bait and attacked this almost non-existent centre, his men would be exposed to Macdonald's attack on the one side and to the concealed Gordon cavalry on the other.

The ingenious plan miscarried. Macdonald, " better with his hands than his head," would not wait tamely until the enemy came up, but charged out with his men, and so attracted Hurry's main attack to himself. But for the extraordinary valour of the Irish and the cover they got from the stone walls and enclosures among which they fought, they would have been overwhelmed. Montrose, who saw that they could not sustain the attack they had invited, galloped to Lord Gordon with a deceptively cheerful countenance and the words: " Will you let the Macdonalds have all the glory of the day?" Heartened by the suggestion of a victory all but won, and jealous for the honour of their clan, the Gordon cavalry swept down the hill towards Hurry's exposed flank. The startling appearance of an unexpected force caused one of Hurry's captains, in too great haste to get his men to face about, to give the order to wheel in the wrong direction. The three hundred Gordon cavalry broke with full force into the disordered lines and drove the Lowland cavalry off the field. Hurry's infantry was now exposed to a flank attack from the Gordons, while the Irish, relieved and revived, still held them in front. The Covenanters could not long withstand the double onslaught; it proved, as Montrose reported to the King, " a very absolute victory."[75]

That night in Auldearn Montrose banqueted with what good fare the little town could provide—a hero among heroes, in a northern epic of hard fights, deep draughts and bardic eloquence. At Inverness, Hurry court-martialled and shot the officer who had given the faulty order; then, with his broken remnant, fell back to join General Baillie at Cromar.[76]

While such news came from the North it was impossible to make the King accept the cruel truth of his situation nearer home —all his Welsh infantry gone, his cannon, wagons, powder magazines, his draft horses, and all his secret correspondence. He would not understand the meaning of the disaster, and scarcely even seemed to realise that Fairfax and Cromwell were marching, unhindered, towards the West as fast as they could go. Yet he was not wholly blind to his personal danger and wrote with dignity and calm to the Prince of Wales to warn him, if his father were taken prisoner, on no account to agree to dishonourable terms with the rebels, even if they threatened the King's life.[77] But when he turned from such ultimate contingencies to consider immediate plans, he preferred to dwell on the happy news from Scotland and to calculate with pleasure and confidence the size of his imaginary army in Ireland.

After three long days in Hereford, assembling recent recruits from Wales and assessing the possible strength to be gathered either by new recruiting or from garrisons, Rupert took his leave of the King, rode to Cardiff, and crossed by boat to Barnstaple, where he met the Prince of Wales on June 26th to agree on measures for the defence of the West.[78]

The King, released from his nephew's disturbing presence, moved into South Wales and on July 3rd was warmly received at Raglan Castle by the loyal Marquis of Worcester, proud father to the Earl of Glamorgan on whose Irish troops he so fervently counted. He had his favourite attendants with him, his gentle cousin Richmond with his young brother, Lord Bernard Stuart, the poet-courtier Earl of Lindsey, the gay and voluble Digby. At Raglan, where the Marquis of Worcester lived with comfort and ceremony, the King resumed the broken thread of his normal life. He kept regular hours, played bowls daily, drove in his coach to a mid-weekly service at the village church with all his retinue, had interesting conversations with his friends, discussed religion and politics with his didactic, good-natured host, and borrowed from him the works of Gower, the old English poet. " We were there all lulled asleep with sports and entertainments," wrote Sir Edward Walker, " as if no crown had been at stake or in danger to be lost."[79]

The King had some reason to imagine that it was policy to appear confident. This, at least, he conveyed to Secretary Nicholas, who had been left to manage his civil affairs in Oxford. Charles feared that his more judicious councillors would be distressed to learn from the letters now published that he and his Queen had had no better opinion of the self-sacrificing loyalists who had risked their estates and reputations by attending Parliament in Oxford than to call them a " mongrel Parliament." Nicholas was bidden to explain away the opprobrious phrase, and to hearten them with the news that the losses at Naseby had been made good by fresh levies from Wales. So much for public consumption: but privately to Nicholas Charles wrote that he would tolerate no " melancholy men " about him, and that the Welsh levies, when completed, would indeed repair his recent losses. These last hopes were soon to be disappointed. Parliamentary propaganda, in the form of *The King's Cabinet Opened*, soon reached the gentry of Wales who, reading of his projected alliances with foreign powers and with the Confederate Irish, grew suspicious and cold.[80]

Digby in the meantime wrote cheerfully to the Queen: " We have had many little successes," he assured her, since the black day at Naseby: the forces of Parliament and the Scots were melting away while the King's grew strong again; the country folk were rising against the enemy forces, and " every day may beget alterations for the better."[81] His letter was dated from the halcyon calm of Raglan on July 10th, 1645, a day which begot an alteration very much for the worse in the King's fortunes in the West.

Rupert had joined the Prince of Wales at Barnstaple to find the state of the King's army in the West worse than it had ever been. George Goring, who had argued that he could not join the King's forces before Naseby because of the necessity of defeating the enemy in the West and re-forming the siege of Taunton, had allowed provisions for the garrison at Taunton to pass through his lines unquestioned. Sometimes he made himself popular with the local gentry with convincing offers to improve the discipline of the troops and requests " that solemn prayers might be said in all churches for him " that God might bless his enterprises. At other times he was sunk in debauch for days together with his brother-in-law and lieutenant general, George Porter.[82]

Desertion steadily thinned Goring's ranks, while the projected increase of the Western army came to nothing because of the rivalry of Grenvile and Berkeley, neither of whom would concede to the other any right to forage or contributions save what he could himself seize. Efforts to reconcile them were made in vain. Grenvile had seized on the estate of his wife (who had long since divorced him) and stocked it plentifully with stolen cattle. Both he and Goring made a practice of seizing and holding civilian prisoners for ransom, until the local Justices of the Peace directed the people to defend themselves against Grenvile and his men as common breakers of the peace.[83]

Even without this encouragement the country folk were already in arms, and the " clubmen " were becoming a serious problem to the King's troops. The Prince of Wales met a party of them at Castle Cary and spoke them fair, an art in which he already showed some skill.[84] Goring, roused into exercising his natural charm, half persuaded others to join the King's army, and lent them arms and officers. Thus stiffened, they grew dangerous, and had a sharp brush with Parliament's troops under Massey at Sturminster Newton. With this perturbing news Massey met Fairfax and his advancing army at Blandford. Fairfax who had already seen something of the clubmen on his way, received a very civil deputation from them and returned a civil answer. He promised to keep good order and to trouble the countryside as little as possible. For the rest, he told them of the King's letters taken at Naseby, and warned them that a foreign invasion was to be feared if Parliament did not win a speedy and final victory. His honest and serious manner, his fine presence and business-like treatment of their protests, most of all the good discipline of his troops, made the necessary effect. The clubmen, for the moment, seemed satisfied.[85]

This interview was on July 3rd, 1645, on the highway between Blandford and Crewkerne. The New Model Army was close upon the King's Western forces, to whose divided ranks all Prince Rupert's efforts had brought neither order nor union. Torn in too many directions, he was forced to leave the defence of Somerset to Goring, whom he briefly interviewed before Taunton; then he rode to Bristol, which was now the lifeline of the King's cause, his gateway to the world outside, his chief remaining source of income.[86]

At Crewkerne on July 5th the advance guard of Fairfax came

into collision with some of Goring's troops, who made off almost without resistance. The men of the New Model had marched over eighty miles in five days, which was strenuous enough for heavily equipped men in high summer over unknown and ill-made roads, but at Crewkerne, where Fairfax ordered a halt to rest, they shouted to go on, all night if need be, to relieve the garrison at Taunton.[87] But Goring had again broken up the siege and Taunton no longer stood in need of relief; there was no hurry; they rested for a long Sabbath day at Crewkerne. Then they turned northward in search of Goring.

Goring was not without a plan. He saw the necessity of pre-venting Fairfax from swinging round to reach the Bristol Channel and so cutting off the Western army from the rest of the King's forces. Greatly outnumbered, especially in cavalry, Goring's problem was to puzzle Fairfax as to his movements and so get him to divide his army. In this he was successful. He made a feint in the direction of Taunton, which deceived Fairfax into sending Massey with about four thousand cavalry to see what was happening. Midway Massey took Goring's brother-in-law, George Porter, entirely off his guard, his troops dismounted, bathing, or basking on the river bank at Ilminster. But though Massey dispersed and captured Porter's men, he was now ten miles from Fairfax with three rivers in between.

Meanwhile Goring, sending his guns and baggage back to Bridgwater, had made himself strong at Langport, where Fair-fax would have to fight him (not waiting for Massey's return) if he was to prevent his withdrawal with all his equipment to the safety of Bridgwater. The country was broken and hilly; every road was a deep trench in the soft, red soil, waterlogged by the heavy summer rain, and, in this leafy season, arched over by hazel, hawthorn and willow almost into tunnels. "The country," wrote Fairfax's chaplain, "is so full of strait passages that it is very hard to engage an unwilling enemy." Such a "strait passage," a hollowed lane between thorn hedges knee deep in water and so narrow that no more than two could ride abreast, ran down from Goring's quarters at Langport across a stream and up again to where Fairfax lay at Long Sutton.

On the morning of July 10th, 1645, the Parliamentary scouts reported that Goring was moving. He had placed two cannon at the top of the lane and lined the hedges with his musketeers, reckoning that if Fairfax was drawn to attack, he would have to deal first with this tunnel of death. The discipline and resolution of the New Model Army made even this possible. Picked bands of musketeers fought their way up the hedges, engaging and dislodging the Royalists, while the cavalry, after forcing the passage of the stream, pressed up the lane and, although greatly outnumbered and with little room to form for a charge, flung themselves on Goring's well-placed cavalry. They were thrown back after a tussle at the sword's point, but their attack had given their comrades time to emerge into the open and form for an effective charge on the enemy's flank. The Royalist cavalry began to break, and soon overtook the infantry in its hitherto orderly retreat to Bridgwater and " set them all running." In a last effort to stem the advance of Fairfax, Goring fired Langport, but Cromwell's Ironsides " followed the victory through the fire." He himself led his men on," the fire flaming on both sides of him," till they reached the farther end of the village and chased the Royalist cavalry half-way to Bridgwater.

At this battle of Langport Cromwell reckoned they took two thousand prisoners, with at least fifteen hundred good horses. The Royalist guns were safe in Bridgwater and the infantry for the most part escaped, but stragglers were mercilessly harried and cut down by the " clubmen "—ironically the very bands whom Goring had provided with arms and officers. Goring, with his demoralised remnant, made no further effort to hold open the line of communication with Bristol, but leaving the garrison at Bridgwater to fend for themselves, fell back as far as Barnstaple, announcing that his men were not at present in a condition to fight again. The victorious officers of the New Model looked upon each other in wonder and amazement. Colonel Harrison in the midst of battle had been rapt into ecstasy, praising God like a man inspired, and Cromwell reported that day in a voice of wonder: " To see this, is it not to see the face of God? "[88]

VI

News of the disaster at Langport broke untimely upon the happy circle at Raglan. Startled, the King visited Cardiff to see how his new Welsh levies were shaping, then, on Tuesday, July 22nd, had a rapid consultation with Rupert, who had crossed the Bristol Channel to meet him at Crick. The Prince had had a busy week. On the previous Wednesday, to raise the sinking spirits of the western troops, he had led his cavalry in a successful night raid on the enemy quarters at Wells. On Friday he had seen representatives of the Somerset clubmen outside Bristol and tried, in vain, to enlist them in the King's forces. On Monday he had parleyed with another gathering of country folk on Lansdowne hill, had then attempted to reorganise the depressed garrison of Bath, had crossed the Severn that night, spoken with the King on the Tuesday, and so back to Bristol the same day to complete the provisioning and fortifying of the town which the King proposed to make his headquarters.[89]

Rupert was thankful at least for this belated decision of his uncle to come nearer to the West and so to consolidate his position there.[90] But immediately on his return to Bristol he learnt that Bridgwater had surrendered to Fairfax after a brief bombardment. Its fall, with considerable stores, provisions and valuables, taken there for safety from all the region round, was another heavy blow to the Royalists in the West,[91] but the more serious effect was the cutting of the line between Bristol and the Western Army in Devon and Cornwall, so that Bristol could no longer be regarded as a safe headquarters for the King. He had made his decision to consolidate in the West when it was already too late to do so. It was evident that he must now change his plan, though he did not, for some time, give Rupert any intimation of his revised projects.

For the time he was at Cardiff busy with the new Welsh levies. These refused to serve him unless he would dismiss Sir Charles Gerrard, who during the eighteen months that he had commanded in South Wales had provoked the resentment of the inhabitants by the violence and indiscipline of his men. The King, attempting to please everyone, pleased no one: he allowed Gerrard to answer the charges of the Welsh gentry in arrogant words, and then removed him from his command. The Welsh, angered by what had been said, were not appeased by what had been done; the gentry and their tenantry dispersed, unwilling to serve the King.[92] Gerrard, also offended, had to be rewarded with a barony, by the granting of which the King gave offence to another loyal servant, Sir Thomas Glemham, who had just arrived from Carlisle, where he and his garrison had held out for many months in dire distress, constantly promised relief and always disappointed.[93]

The fall of Carlisle was followed before the end of July by the surrender of Pomfret and Scarborough, both also hopeless of relief from the defeated King. In these conditions the good news which Charles still received from Montrose in Scotland raised his hopes in vain, since not only the Scottish lowlands, but the whole of England now separated him from his champion in the North. But Charles was in pursuit of another dangerous illusion. All that summer the relations between the Covenanters and their allies had deteriorated; in London their Commissioners wrangled, unhappily and continuously, with Parliament about the shipping of Newcastle coal and their right to the profits, about the pay and quarters of their ill-used and neglected army. Certain of the Scots Lords in the army contrived to send a message to the King hinting at an alliance against the Independents who now controlled the Parliamentary Army. Charles, failing to see that any alliance with the Covenanting Scots must be founded on his toleration, if not his acceptance of Presbytery, began to dream of a grand alliance in his interest between Montrose and the Covenanters against the rebel English; let these two parties join together with the ten thousand men he confidently expected from Ireland, and he would be strong enough to win the war.[94]

In this vain hope he secretly resolved to go to Scotland. The intention, like all his secrets, was soon a matter of general rumour. Rupert got wind of it before any official message reached him and wrote in distraction to the Duke of Richmond, his truest friend in the King's immediate circle. "It is now in everybody's mouth that the King is going for Scotland. I must confess it to be a strange resolution, considering not only in what condition he will leave all behind him, but what probability there is for him to get thither. If I were desired to deliver my opinion, which your Lordship may declare to the King, His Majesty hath now no way left to preserve his posterity, kingdom and nobility, but by a treaty. I believe it a more prudent way to retain something than to lose all." As for the army that Charles expected from the Confederate Irish, Rupert spoke his mind: "It is apparent they will cheat the King, having not five thousand men."[95]

The King's answer was a document in which noble resignation to the worst was shot through with unalterable hope for the best. "As for your opinion of my business and your counsel thereupon," he wrote, "if I had any other quarrel but the defence of my religion, crown and friends, you had full reason for your advice; for I confess that speaking either as a mere soldier or statesman, I must say there is no probability but of my ruin. Yet as a Christian I must tell you, that God will not suffer rebels and traitors to prosper, nor this cause to be overthrown. And whatever personal punishment it shall please him to inflict upon me must not make me repine, much less give over this quarrel. And there is as little question that a composition with them at this time is nothing else but a submission, which, by the grace of God, I am resolved against, whatever it cost me, for I know my obligation to be, both in conscience and honour, neither to abandon God's cause, injure my successors, nor forsake my friends. . . . He that will stay with me at this time must expect and resolve either to die for a good cause or (which is worse) to live as miserable in maintaining it as the violence of insulting rebels can make him . . . Believe me, the very imagination that you are desirous of a treaty will lose me so much the sooner. As for the Irish, I assure you, they shall not cheat me but it is possible they may cozen themselves."[96]

The King wrote with the serenity of one who had been educated for succession to an assured throne, and nourished in the religious conviction of his rights under God. Rupert, the son of a dispossessed King, educated in the pretentious poverty of an exiled Court, ardently desired to save his uncle from a fate he knew too well. Knowing what it meant to lose all, he thought it more prudent " to retain something " even by submission. Charles, who had neither the knowledge nor the imagination to understand the worst possibilities before him, thought it better to face total disaster than to make any compromise. The King and the Prince were divided not only by temperament but by the experience of a lifetime.

In one point the King was right. If he intended to fight to the end, then it was in the highest degree undesirable that Rupert should appear to wish for a treaty. But Charles still failed to realise that he must do more than proclaim his resolution not to surrender; he must cease counting on the impossible and take practical steps to preserve what was left of his army. The situation in Wales was only a degree less serious than that in the West. In the South the Welsh " began to be saucy; "[97] General Laugharne re-assembling his forces in Pembrokeshire, scattered the Royalists at Colby Moor on August 1st, drove them out of Haverfordwest and advanced on Carew Castle.[98] In North Wales, Archbishop Williams at Conway was as usual at loggerheads with Sir John Owen and Lord Byron about the assessing and garrisoning of the region, and the King's attempts to reconcile them were fruitless.[99] Meanwhile Charles and his lifeguard

moved cautiously northward up the Welsh border on the opening
stretch of the projected march to Scotland.

The pastoral simplicity of their progress pleased the King,
recalling as it did the hunting parties that he so greatly enjoyed,
with alfresco meals in the summer warmth, or farmhouse fare
under some humble roof. His wonted formality was sometimes
sacrificed. At Radnor, at the best house to be found, he dined
on cheese and a pullet in the parlour while his attendants sat
hungrily round the kitchen fire until the good wife, innocent of
protocol, put her head round the parlour door " and very soberly
asks if the King had done with the cheese for the gentlemen
without desired it."[100]

From Brecon the King wrote to the Prince of Wales instruct-
ing him to leave for France if he should find himself " in apparent
danger of falling into the rebels' hands," and to obey his mother
in all things except religion.[101] He sent once again to Ormonde
in Ireland, asking him to come over in person with every man
that he could raise. Digby, who had been instructed to draw
up a frank account of their present desperate plight for Ormonde's
information, faithfully catalogued all the disasters but could not
prevent cheerfulness from breaking in at the last: Hopton, in
Cornwall, he said, had six thousand men and would shortly
drive Fairfax into the sea, as Essex had been driven the year
before.[102]

The Earl of Ormonde had not underestimated the King's need
of help even in the spring. After Naseby he knew without
prompting that the need was desperate. But try as he would,
neither he, nor his principal agent, the Roman Catholic loyalist
Clanricarde, could come to any conclusion with the Confederate
Irish. For nearly five months the treaty had stuck upon a single
issue: the King had given Ormonde permission to offer toleration to the Roman Catholics; but the Confederate Irish, inspired
by the Papal agent Scarampi and the general Assembly of their
clergy which met during the summer, demanded the open
exercise of their faith and the retention of the cathedrals and

churches that they had taken in the course of the war.[103] In the
meantime the Earl of Antrim, regardless of the King's interests
or Ormonde's treaty, was offering several thousand of his clansmen to the King of Spain for the war in the Netherlands.[104]

The Earl of Glamorgan, delayed first by his own affairs in
Wales, then by an inopportune shipwreck, reached Dublin at last
in July, 1645. He was well received by Ormonde, who knew
nothing of his secret commission and welcomed his offer to
represent to the priestly Assembly at Kilkenny the wisdom and
necessity of co-operating with the King. But the days went by
and, as far as Ormonde could tell, Glamorgan got no nearer to
a treaty than Clanricarde had done. Glamorgan had in fact
promised the Irish that the King would satisfy all their demands
by a secret agreement only to be published at a later date, but as
the Confederate Irish made no haste to fulfil their part of the
bargain and send troops to the King, or to accept, as a necessary
façade, the terms offered by Ormonde, Glamorgan's intervention was hardly as successful as he had hoped. The Irish were
themselves divided: a few trusted Glamorgan's secret offers
entirely, but the dominant lords of the Anglo-Irish party believed that only an open treaty with Ormonde would ultimately
prove valid. In the meantime neither the open nor the secret
negotiation prospered.[105]

In England, as Charles moved northwards, God continued to
favour the " rebels and traitors " in the south. Rupert had tried
in vain to reorganise and strengthen the garrison at Bath; his
intervention merely provoked a mutinous discontent among
soldiers and citizens and when Fairfax appeared before the town,
it surrendered at once.[106]

Fairfax now moved on Sherborne Castle, where on August
2nd George Digby's half-brother, Sir Lewis Dyve, bade him
defiance. For the time being Fairfax, for lack of ammunition,
could do nothing but encamp before the walls and wait until a
fresh supply reached him. The " malignant clubmen " of the
region, as Cromwell called them, were active once again and the

King's officers were known to be in touch with them. Colonel Fleetwood, sent by Cromwell with a troop of horse, surprised some of the leaders at Shaftesbury in consultation with messengers from the Royalists and carried them off as prisoners to the camp at Sherborne. Next day the clubmen were reported mustering in great force to attack the Parliamentary camp and release their leaders. Cromwell marched out against them and talked over one party who dispersed and went home. A second and larger body rejected all overtures, rashly opened fire with their fowling pieces and shouted that they were waiting for Hopton to enrol them for the King. At this Cromwell ordered a party of his dragoons to charge them. They broke up at once but for the laggards, who were taken prisoner and brought back to Sherborne.[107]

In anxious London the menace of the clubmen had been exaggerated; something like a new Peasants Revolt was feared, and the defeat of Fairfax was gloomily, and groundlessly, reported.[108] The check inflicted on them by Cromwell prevented the movement from growing, and as the good discipline of the New Model Army became apparent in the countryside, the clubmen gradually dispersed. With the extinction of the King's disorderly army, the cause for their protest was taken away. In some districts, until late that summer, a few vindictive gangs lay in wait to inflict vengeance on the defeated Cavaliers, but as a third force that could seriously help or injure either party they vanished from the changing scene.

Parliament at Westminster faced more serious troubles. Victory was to be the beginning, not the end, of their difficulties. London was noisy with the discontents of Presbyterians and sectaries. Prynne poured forth his learned comminations against Lilburne, and Henry Burton banged out his Independent doctrines in the pulpit of St. Mary Aldermary. A nobler, finer, more influential voice was that of John Goodwin, preaching at St. Stephen's Coleman Street. There were links between Goodwin's congregation and John Lilburne, who had been twice apprehended and twice released during the summer for libelling Prynne. A new attack, this time on Speaker Lenthall, ended with his incarceration in Newgate, but Goodwin's flock supported him in his troubles, prayers were raised—"Lord, bring thy servant Lilburne out of prison"—and a petition for his release was organised by William Walwyn, a substantial merchant, whose fortune and whose intelligence were alike to be valuable to the sectaries.[109]

With such storms gathering, the Westminster Assembly, once the impressive centre from which all reformation was to come, seemed inept, if not irrelevant. The Windmill Tavern, where the liveliest of the sectaries commonly met, might come to be more important in the end, and the Tavern had already during the summer of 1645 challenged the Assembly, when at a meeting at which Walwyn and Lilburne were both present, a group of sectaries drafted a petition that the divines at Westminster should go home to their preaching duties—a thinly disguised demand for the dissolution of the Assembly.[110]

As old conservatives had long predicted, not the King's power alone but all authority in Church and State was now the object of attack. Parliament, which had nourished the rebellion, vainly strove to restrain its effects. Few in the Commons were not shocked when *Mercurius Britanicus* published an advertisement for a wanted man named Charles, a traitor and a runagate, who might be recognised by a stammer and an inability to speak the truth. The French envoy protested. The House of Lords took action, brought home the offensive paragraph to its authors and had them shut up in prison. They were two officers of the New Model Army, Mervyn Audley and Robert White.[111]

VII

Meanwhile the King, in his northern march, had safely reached Lichfield. Here he placed Lord Loughborough under arrest. Loughborough, who had sustained the Royal cause in the Midlands from the very outset of the war with ardour and no small success, had been made governor of Leicester at its capture and had surrendered it immediately after Naseby. He could hardly have done anything else, but the King was in a mood to treat every capitulation as a crime.[112] Besides, Loughborough, like Rupert, may have doubted the possibility of ultimate victory and the King had very firmly declared that he would have no " melancholy men " about him. Digby, who was ever more convinced that the King had only to hold out the winter and then, with plentiful Irish and foreign help, win the war in the spring, was seriously worried because few, if any, of the soldiers now agreed with him, and he had difficulty in preventing them from discouraging the King.[113]

At Lichfield despatches came in from North and South, from Montrose and Goring, which greatly supported Digby's optimism. Goring wrote that he had plans for new levies in the West which would soon make the King's army in that region as strong as it had ever been.[114] Montrose reported a victory over the Covenanters which had brought them, he confidently believed, *ad Triarios*—to their last stand.[115]

For six weeks of the stormy Scottish summer Montrose and his band, living on oatmeal and the plentiful game they shot, had moved lightly in and out of the Grampian passes, joined now by one clan, now by another in the raiding they understood so well. He was reported in Badenoch, on Speyside, even as far south as Coupar Angus. Baillie, unable to fight in the mountains, unable to keep his troops properly supplied if he left the foothills, lumbered angrily in pursuit but found no trace of his enemy except

trampled heather where his army had gone by.[116] Towards the
end of June Montrose thought it time to make Baillie fight, and
came down to where the Spey runs out towards the sea. Baillie
was at Keith in a strong position. Montrose sent a message to
know if he would come into the open and try a fall. Baillie not
unnaturally answered that he would fight "when it pleased
himself."[117] At this Montrose and his men disappeared again
into the mountains. This, after a little hesitation, drew Baillie
forth. He could not afford to let Montrose get over the passes
and down again to Aberdeen, or whatever other city he might
take into his head to visit. Baillie marched rapidly up Strathbogie meaning to cut Montrose off if he tried to strike eastwards
down the valley of the Don. Montrose, informed of this pursuit,
out-marched Baillie to Alford, where the Don runs in a wide
marshy valley through a series of fords. Here, concealing his
army behind the shoulder of a hill, he waited for Baillie's
approach.

Baillie, left to himself, might not have fought. He had cut off
Montrose's march to Aberdeen which was his principal objective.
But Balcarres, who commanded the cavalry, and was exasperated
at Baillie's caution in the face of so nimble and dangerous a foe,
forced him to act by putting the cavalry over the ford so that
Baillie had to follow. The whole Covenanting army was now
drawn up on the broad, boggy, gently rising bank of the Don,
with Montrose above them on the brow of a low hill.
Balcarres appears to have thought that Montrose was retreating,
would not dare to abandon the height, and could be attacked
either as he attempted to withdraw, or else driven from his
position.

Baillie was far less confident and his doubts grew when he
saw the length of Montrose's front on the brow of the hill. Both
armies had about two thousand foot; Baillie had six hundred
cavalry, Montrose less than half that number. But Montrose had
drawn up his men on a long front and, as so often before, gave
his opponent the impression of a much larger force. On the

wings was the Gordon cavalry, flanked by companies of Irish foot. In the centre were the rest of the infantry, Macdonalds of Glengarry, Gordons, Grahams and Stuarts of Atholl, with a small reserve in the rear.

As at Tippermuir, Aberdeen and Inverlochy, Montrose relied on the irresistible force of his men in attack and gave the order for a general advance. Baillie's troops, both horse and foot, stubbornly stood their ground, and it was not until the Irish infantry fell to slashing the horses' legs with their dirks that the Covenanting cavalry broke, leaving Baillie's infantry alone. At that moment Montrose called up his reserve, and Baillie's men, seeing this new enemy appear over the brow of the hill, fled towards the swollen fords of the Don. The Irish and the Highlanders were upon them before they could cross, and about fifteen hundred of the Covenanting infantry were left dead on the field or in the river. A part of the cavalry alone got over the Don and away, and these only escaped because of an accident which, for Montrose and his army, robbed the victory of all joy. At the moment of victory the young chief of the Gordons had been killed. After Auldearn, Montrose's men had waked the echoes all night with feasting, but the night of Alford was a night of tears. Lord Gordon, in his brief life, had played a doubtful part; he had acquiesced in the harrying of his clan by Argyll and more than one Royalist Gordon had had cause to curse him. But since he had joined Montrose his doubts had been at rest and he had followed him with a rapt devotion which was to make him a part of the Montrose legend: " Never two of so short acquaintance did ever love more dearly."[118]

Baillie fled to Perth. A general fast was proclaimed throughout Scotland, with deep searching of all consciences to discover wherein the Almighty had been offended. In London the general's cousin, Dr. Robert Baillie, almost questioned the ways of Providence: " We are amazed that it should be the pleasure of God to make us fall thus the fifth time before a company of the worst men in the earth."[119] His fellow Commissioners in London shared his distress: "We pray the Lord to discover the cause of his great wrath, manifested by the continued heavy judgments of pestilence and sword, and why our forces there have received defeat upon defeat even these five times from a despicable and inconsiderable enemy, while the forces of this nation obtain victory upon victory."[120] That was the bitterest cup of all: in England the Independent army prospered while in Scotland Presbyterian soldiers fell before the sword of the excommunicate James Graham.

It was a black year for the Covenanters. The plague, raging in Edinburgh, spread to Stirling, where the Estates were in session. They removed to Perth and fixed a general rendezvous of new forces to be raised against Montrose.[121] Dr. David Dickson preached on a text from Isaiah: "Who gave Jacob for a spoil and Israel to the robbers? did not the Lord, he against whom we have sinned? for they would not walk in his ways, neither were they obedient to his law."[122] General Baillie was called in question and argument grew bitter. He resigned his command. The Estates, having no other general, prevailed on him to stay but appointed a Committee of War from among their number to guide his actions. In doubt and fear they quarrelled over small points, abused and accused each other—had not the representative from Aberdeen once drunk a health to Montrose? Over them all hung the heavy knowledge that the English needed their help no longer, had challenged their right to occupy Carlisle, kept their troops in England short of all necessities and then censoriously complained because they were ill-equipped and disorderly in comparison with the well-supplied, well-cherished New Model Army. The Scots considered asking Argyll to go South again to argue with the English, yet they dared not let him go (so deeply did they rely on him in time of crisis) until James Graham was destroyed.[123]

While they talked at Perth, and their troops assembled to protect them in the meadows by the Tay, Montrose appeared close above the town on the fringe of Methven wood, too weak in numbers to attack but well able to keep them in constant alarm.[124] After three or four days of this sport he withdrew, to make a series of forays into Fife to impede his enemies' recruiting. Then he struck south, through the country where his own lands lay and turned up the valley of the Forth towards Stirling, welcomed and feasted by his friends as he went. The Covenanting army from Perth came fast on his tracks; south of the Forth in Clydesdale, the Earl of Lanark, Hamilton's younger brother, raised a second army for the Covenant in the broad Hamilton lands. It looked as though Montrose had ventured too far and would be trapped between two forces each greater than his own.

His pursuers thought that the passage of the Forth must hold him up, because the only bridge was at Stirling, a town strongly garrisoned. But Montrose's lightly-armed men, without artillery and almost without baggage, forded the river ten miles above the town and were away over the hills to the south before Baillie knew of it. The Committee of War, chief among them Argyll, urged an instant pursuit, and Baillie's men started on the exhausting march over the steep Campsie hills in the sultry August weather. Baillie knew Montrose well enough to be sure that he would turn and fight them long before he was in any danger of being trapped by the approach of Lanark's army from Clydesdale. He was right. In the airless heat of the August noon, as the Covenanters slogged over the rough ground, they sighted the enemy. Montrose had halted in a strong position on the curved lip of a hollow in the hills, where the outlying cultivated patches of the little village of Kilsyth made a series of defensible trenches and breastworks. Baillie was not in favour of fighting, but the Committee of War were resolved to do so and argued that by taking possession of a small hill between Montrose's position and their own they would have a great advantage over him. In vain Baillie pointed out that the ground was very uneven, broken by stone walls and strips of cultivation, interspersed with furze and bent; they could not cross it in any order of battle, and yet would be exposed during the whole of their march to a possible attack from Montrose's nimble and deadly Highlanders. Balcarres, though he had been rash at Alford, was the best soldier on the Committee and supported Baillie's arguments. The rest poured scorn on the idea that Montrose's troops would leave their entrenched position and challenge in the open a force so much larger and better armed; in the sweltering heat they could see that the Irish and Highlanders had stripped to their shirts and would not believe that in this half-naked state they meant to fight. Baillie was out-voted and early in the afternoon of August 16th, 1645, the Covenanters began the fatal march.

As their army, with the cavalry leading and the foot in the rear, came heavily over the uneven ground, Baillie was aware of a party of Macdonalds making up towards them under cover of the furze bushes. His musketeers fired without waiting for a command and misjudged the distance; their bullets fell short and the Macdonalds, leaping forward, attacked them before they could re-load. Meanwhile, a few of the Gordon cavalry had attacked another part of the line. The double impact disordered the Covenanters but they might still have extricated themselves, for both attacks were slight in themselves, and both were premature, the outcome—as so often in Montrose's battles—of the independent impulses of the Highlanders. But Montrose, to support and extricate his friends, now launched a general attack. The old stalwart Airlie led on the rest of the cavalry and he himself, stripped like his men for easier movement in the heat, charged with his infantry. The Covenanting cavalry, already in disorder and unable to manœuvre on the rough ground, turned tail before Airlie and rode down their own infantry, who were, at the same time, attacked in flank by Montrose's Highlanders. A few Covenanting officers managed here and there to rally scattered groups of their sweating, confused and startled men, but their army was without a centre, without a plan, without even a rallying cry, for no watchword had been given that day.[125]

Argyll, Lothian and the other Lords of the Committee, fled among the first. At Queensferry, twenty miles away, they took

SIR HENRY VANE THE YOUNGER
after Peter Lely

ÆTAT. SVÆ 23. Aᵒ 1641. IOHN LILBURNE

G: Glo: fecit.

Gaze not vpon this shaddow that is vaine,
But rather raise thy thoughts a higher straine,
To GOD (I meane) who, set this young-man free,
And in like straits can eke deliuer thee.

JOHN LILBURNE
from an engraving by George Glover

ship to Berwick, where Lanark joined them. At the news of the
battle he had abandoned his newly raised troops and fled from
his own lands. Hence they appealed for instant help to their
generals in England, and sent Loudoun to Westminster, where
he appeared, all in tears, to implore assistance for his distressed
country.[126] In all Scotland no army remained in the field against
Montrose. Poor Dr. Baillie turned in reproachful bewilderment
to his God. " What means the Lord, so far against the expectation
of the most clear-sighted to humble us so low, and by his own
immediate hand, I confess I know not. . . . The particulars of this
sixth victory I yet have not fully heard: the slaughter, captivity
and flight was most shameful. Glasgow came out and componed,
as some say, for eighteen thousand pounds. . . . I long much to
know what is become of my wife and children. . . . After Glasgow, the most of Clydesdale and Lithgowshire componed.
Edinburgh sent him out all the prisoners and, they say, thirty
thousand pounds."[127]

Edinburgh had little choice. Half the garrison had deserted
because of the raging plague, and the dead lay unburied in the
empty streets. Montrose threatened fire and sword if his friends
were not released from the Tolbooth, but no threat was needed.
The keeper of the prison himself boldly averred that " Montrose
was a worthy nobleman . . . there was none like him in the
Kingdom," but that the lords who had run away, Lanark,
Loudoun, and especially Argyll, were base men and oppressors.[128]
Later he would have cause to regret this indiscretion, but in that
latter half of August, 1645, all the Royalists in Scotland were
speaking out, and all the doubtful or timorous in the Lowlands
were making their peace with Montrose. It was said that Lady
Loudoun herself, the Chancellor's wife, had greeted the handsome
Macdonald with a kiss.[129]

Such romantic libels apart, the country was at his feet, and
the arrival of Sir Robert Spottiswoode, the King's Secretary of
State, who by devious ways had reached him from the King with
his commission as Lieutenant-governor of Scotland, could not

have been more timely. On August 18th he entered Glasgow to a resounding welcome, was feasted by the citizens and that day issued a proclamation summoning a new Parliament in the King's name.[130] To prevent his wild forces from damaging the city he fixed his headquarters outside at Hamilton's great palace of Bothwell, and here on a shining August day reviewed his victorious army and in the King's name knighted Alaster Macdonald for his services.[131]

VIII

Some part of this fantastic news, travelling fast on the wings of victory, reached the King eight days only after the battle of Kilsyth. His campaigning had taken on a kind of madness, for while Montrose was at Glasgow, the King at the head of his forces was entering the town of Huntingdon in the heart of the Eastern Association. He had pursued his plan of going northward only as far as Doncaster, though he had by this time scraped up about two thousand cavalry and described his condition as " miraculously good." [132] But near Rotherham he had news of the Scots approaching in force and " retreated with more than ordinary haste." [133] Changing course in a south-easterly direction, he profited by the absence of almost all the Parliament forces in the West and struck right at the heart of the Eastern Association. At Stilton he scattered a small force which tried to resist him, but the garrison at Huntingdon fled. The King's men helped themselves to their excellent equipment—" back, breast, headpiece and brace of pistols " to each man:[134] not for a long time had they been so complete. The oppressed Royalists of Huntingdon, and others who suddenly rediscovered their Royalist sympathies, came out " with much compliment, all hatting and bowing," and Charles was received with acclamation as he rode through the streets. But soon his men were drinking in the taverns " by pailfuls " and the plundering began. They seized all the horses.

They drove off seven hundred head of cattle and sold them back to their owners for ready cash. The King had issued orders that his men were to take nothing from any who were not known to be rebels, but his cavalry " made all men delinquents where they quartered thereabouts." In the Puritan county of Huntingdon they were probably not far wrong. The King, to show his good intentions at least, hanged a soldier for plundering a tradesman and another for stealing from a church.[135]

All this while, far off on the borders of Wales, the town of Hereford was still hard pressed by the main body of the Scots army under Lord Leven. Elated with their victories, the King and his roving force turned westwards to relieve it. All across the Midlands scattered Parliamentary bands hurried out of his path; at Thame a party of schoolboys enjoyed the venison pasties left cooking in the oven for a dinner the soldiers did not stay to eat.[136] By way of Oxford and Worcester the King reached Hereford on September 4th, but Leven had not waited for his coming. Short of food and pay, hated and obstructed by the English villagers, the Scots before Hereford were worse off than the besieged garrison; the shocking news of Montrose's last victory cast them into despair, and on the King's approach they withdrew towards Gloucester.[137] Charles entered Hereford among a rejoicing people and Digby wrote in high spirits to Jermyn in Paris that Montrose was master of Scotland and would devour David Leslie if he ventured thither; that Prince Rupert would shortly make an end of Fairfax before Bristol, and—of course—that large forces would soon come from Ireland.[138]

Digby deceived himself about the West, as about so much else. Except for Goring's promise of fresh levies no good news had come out of the West since the disaster at Langport. Goring, so far from redeeming his promise, had sunk into drunken indolence while the remnants of his army disintegrated. He roused himself enough from time to time to renew his quarrel with Grenvile and both continued to slander Berkeley and criticise the Prince of Wales's Council, until those in charge of the young prince seriously feared that one or other of the head-strong generals might seize him, either to betray him to the enemy or to hold him as a hostage.[139]

For the first fortnight of August Fairfax had been delayed by the siege of Sherborne Castle, the last place in Dorset to be held for the King. Sir Lewis Dyve, Digby's half-brother, held the fortress with defiant valour, much assisted by a couple of game-keepers in his garrison, excellent shots, who made a practice of picking off the Parliamentary officers with their fowling pieces. But Fairfax was waiting only for his heavy guns, against which Sherborne could never stand; they came by sea and were in place by August 14th. He gave Dyve one more chance to sur-render, which he scornfully rejected, and carried the castle by storm that night. Dyve was sent prisoner to London; the arms and ammunition in the castle enriched the Parliamentary maga-zine and the plentiful booty of household goods, which the soldiers were allowed to take as their reward, they sold next day in open market at Sherborne to buyers from all the country round.[140]

The only danger which Fairfax feared was that Rupert, from Bristol, might raise the country behind him if he went farther into the West. He decided therefore to move against Bristol as soon as Sherborne had fallen.[141] Rupert was fairly strong in cavalry and in guns but his infantry was weak. The loss of Bath left Bristol dangerously exposed, and the clubmen of the region hampered him in getting supplies. The strong hand of Fairfax over the Dorset clubmen and the good discipline of the New Model had done their work; the country folk round Bristol were already the auxiliaries of Parliament.

For more than a month Rupert had been strengthening Bristol against a possible siege. He had large stores of powder and nearly a hundred cannon. He had brought in corn from South Wales and cattle from the surrounding country; all citizens had orders to stock their houses with food for six months. But for the most part the substantial citizens had left, and there was in consequence little order or authority among the civilian population. Plague had broken out and the town was dismally depressed by the perpetual interruptions of its trade. Neither the Bristol Trained Bands nor the recent recruits from Wales had much enthusiasm or experience as soldiers, and the garrison of about fifteen hundred was too small adequately to man defences nearly five miles in length. The hedges, hollow lanes and ditches in the approaches to the town provided cover for an advancing enemy which Rupert, in the time at his disposal, had not been able to destroy.[142]

As Fairfax advanced Rupert called a Council of War. In the absence of any clear news from the King or any certainty that Goring could or would relieve the city, it seemed best to rely on the strength of the artillery to hold the walls, while Rupert and his cavalry harrassed the besiegers by sallying against them. Over-confident in his artillery, Rupert had assured both the King and the Prince of Wales that he could hold Bristol for several months; his stores and his guns should have made a long resistance possible, always supposing the circuit of the walls remained intact.[143]

Fairfax formed the siege on August 21st, 1645, and during the next days Rupert's horsemen harried him without mercy. The redoubtable Colonel Okey, whose dragoons had done good work at Naseby, was captured. Rupert's successes, reported as far as London, perturbed Parliament and, coupled with the King's recent raid on Huntingdon, caused the Royalists with their customary optimism to predict the approaching defeat of Fairfax, trapped between the victorious King and the victorious Rupert.[144]

But Rupert's luck did not hold. Sir Richard Crane, the colonel of his guards, was killed in a sally; Fairfax counter-attacked and took one of the outlying forts in the defences. Beating rain prevented Fairfax from launching a general assault, but it also stopped Rupert's cavalry raids, because the ground became too slippery. The Parliamentary army, about twelve thousand strong, encircled the town on both sides of the Avon and built a bridge over the river without further Royalist interference. Treachery within the town was discovered and punished, but it showed how little the Royalists could depend on the citizens. Meanwhile a squadron of Parliamentary ships landed reinforcements for Fairfax and kept watch in Bristol roads against any attempt to assist the town from the sea.[145] During the sieges of Hull and Plymouth the Parliamentary commanders had constantly been relieved from the waterside, but the Royalists at Bristol were blockaded by sea as well as land.

On September 3rd the wind and rain of the last week changed to fair weather and Fairfax sent a summons to the Prince. Fairfax had learnt his profession fighting for the Protestant Cause in Europe; to him therefore Rupert, who had also fought for the Protestant Cause and suffered long imprisonment in an imperial fortress, was an honourable young man grievously misled. He urged him respectfully to reconsider his present conduct. " I take into consideration your royal birth," he wrote, " and relation to the Crown of England, your honour, courage and the virtue of your person. . . . Sir, the Crown of England is and will be where it ought to be, we fight to maintain it there; but the King, misled by evil counsellors . . . hath left his Parliament and his people. . . . Sir, if God makes this clear to you, as he has to us, I doubt not but he will give you a heart to deliver this place. . . . And if, upon such conviction you should surrender it . . . it would be an occasion glorious in itself and joyful to us, for the restoring of you to the endeared affection of the Parliament and people of England—the truest friends to your family it hath in the world."[146]

Rupert, unmoved by this appeal, asked leave to send to the King, and when this was refused, offered to negotiate, a well-known subterfuge for gaining a few days' delay during which he might hear something either from the Prince of Wales's Council or from the errant and uncommunicative King. By an evil chance, while he treated with Fairfax at Bristol the question of his mother's pension and his elder brother's income was being discussed in London and the Elector Palatine was voted £8,000 a year by Parliament. This irrelevant fact was soon to acquire a sinister and damning relevance.[147]

On September 9th Fairfax realised that Rupert was playing for time, broke off the treaty, organised his forces for the general assault and, at two o'clock in the morning of September 10th, gave the signal by firing four of his great siege pieces at Prior's Hill Fort, the most formidable strongpoint in the circuit of Bristol defences. Rupert's guns gave answer. They were many and well placed and they made the assault on the long and thinly manned wall more costly and more dangerous than Fairfax had anticipated. But his men showed the same fanatic resolution that had distinguished them at Langport. Within an hour they had broken through the defences in two places on the Avon side of the town. On the side towards the river Frome (assaulted with such fearful loss by the Cornish two years before) the men at Prior's Hill Fort long held out against a furious onslaught. Here it was, as Cromwell afterwards reported, that Colonel Henry Bowen contested with the Royalists " two hours at push of pike, standing upon the palisades "—the attackers and the defenders alike heroic in resolution. But the Royalists were overwhelmingly outnumbered and their line was already penetrated. By five in the morning Prior's Hill Fort was taken and all the defenders killed. Abandoning the outer defences (as poor Fiennes had had to do in the face of Rupert's attack two years before), Rupert withdrew his forces towards the castle. But the inrush of Cromwell's cavalry (even so had Rupert's men rushed the breach against Fiennes) separated those who fell back to the citadel from those who still maintained an isolated resistance in the forts on the outer defences. At eight in the morning of September 10th Rupert appealed to Fairfax for terms.[148]

Two considerations had weighed with him: he saw some of his best troops cut off in the strong points along the wall and condemned, if he continued the fight, to the pitiless destruction that had fallen on the gallant men at Prior's Hill Fort; more immediately fatal, the well in the citadel in which he and his cavalry must take refuge had been damaged. and resistance without water could at best be brief. Faced by the certainty of utter destruction if he fought on, he hoped to save at least a part of his army by treating in time. Most of his officers agreed with him, and the dissident minority who still believed something might be done to prolong resistance seem to have said little. It was evident that Rupert himself, though he had sufficient military reasons for what he did, was no longer in a frame of mind to inspire his men to a heroic and probably desperate last stand.[149]

By the terms of surrender Fairfax let him march out with his troops and have safe convoy to Oxford. The soldiers took with them their colours, pikes and drums, bag and baggage, the cavalry their horses and each man his sword; Rupert tried in vain to have their firearms also included, but this concession he obtained only for his own guards. He saved an army of a thousand horse and fifteen hundred foot; he lost the town, the stores of corn and cheese, the cattle, the well-stocked magazine and more than a hundred cannon.[150]

Fairfax behaved with his customary generosity, "all fair respects" passing between him and his defeated enemy. He escorted the Prince through his lines, placing him on his right hand, and at his final parting from the victors, Rupert, who among soldiers was never behindhand in civility, said to the fanatic Colonel Harrison that "he never received such satisfaction in such unhappiness" and would recompense it should it ever lie in his power.[151]

Cromwell wrote a lengthy despatch to Speaker Lenthall, and again, as he had done after Naseby, exhorted the House to remember that his men fought and died for freedom of conscience: "Sir, they that have been employed in this service know that faith and prayer obtained this city for you. . . . Presbyterians, Independents, all had here the same spirit of faith and prayer; they agree here, know no names of difference; pity it is if it should be otherwise anywhere . . . from brethren, in things of the mind we look for no compulsion, but that of light and reason."[152]

The House of Commons exercised its usual discretion and published Cromwell's account of the taking of Bristol with the signature of Fairfax and the last paragraph excised. Once more their foolish censorship failed of its purpose. One of the secret printing presses worked by the Independents procured an unaltered transcript of the letter, printed off hundreds of copies and scattered them about in the streets.[153] Henry Burton uttered a flaming sermon against the Presbyterians from the pulpit of St. Mary Aldermary, where he had licence to preach, and the vicar, Edward Calamy, an orthodox Calvinist divine, locked the church door in his face when his next day for preaching came.[154]

The King had moved from Hereford to Raglan, where he was busy with " a very plausible design on paper " for the relief of Bristol with the help of Goring's largely imaginary forces.[155] The news that Rupert had surrendered Bristol shook him from his customary equanimity. For once he did not underestimate the loss. Bristol was his only valuable seaport, his most precious possession for diplomacy, for revenue and for war: and Rupert, only a few weeks before, had promised to hold it. Suddenly things which Digby had hinted to him took dreadful shape in his mind.

No reconciliation had occurred between Rupert and Digby since the retreat from Naseby, and to Digby it had seemed that Rupert and the professional soldiers had conspired to discourage the King. Naturally (he argued) they wanted a negotiated peace so that they might save whatever profits they had made out of the war; they would desert the King to save their own fortunes.[156] No higher morality was to be expected from mere mercenaries. As the schism grew between Digby and Rupert, time-servers and gossip-mongers had widened the gap. Digby's secretary in Oxford distilled venom against Rupert for his master's private ear: he wrote that William Legge, the governor, and the rest of the Prince's junto, "the Cumberlanders," as he called them, were resolved at all costs to get Digby removed from the King's council, and were themselves about to make private overtures to the rebels.[157] As early as May there had been groundless rumours, which deceived Fairfax, that Legge was ready to betray his trust. One obvious and terrible argument there was against Rupert—the constant presence at Westminster of his elder brother, the Elector Palatine, as the guest and pensioner of Parliament. Further reports from this poison pen in Oxford described Rupert on his return from Bristol walking in Christ Church garden deep in sinister talk with Colonel Legge while nobles and courtiers stood by bare-headed as if he were the King: "The House of Palatine do think themselves assured of the Crown."[158]

The sequence of events became deceptively clear to the King. While Rupert and Fairfax exchanged civilities at Bristol, Parliament had voted eight thousand pounds to the Elector Palatine. Immediately afterwards Rupert had handed over Bristol, retaining command of his troops (known to be devoted to him) and marching with them direct to Oxford. In that city, where lay the King's younger son and most of his remaining treasure, Rupert had a creature of his own, Colonel Legge, in command. Unless the King acted quickly the game was in Rupert's hands: he would deliver Oxford to the enemy, turn his army against the King and, with his elder brother's assistance, compel his uncle to a base surrender, if indeed no worse.[159]

Believing himself betrayed, the King acted with pitiless resolution. He publicly revoked Prince Rupert's commission; he dismissed Colonel Legge from the governorship of Oxford, and he ordered his nephew in a letter of bitter reproof to leave the country immediately. "Though the loss of Bristol be a great blow to me," he wrote, "yet your surrendering it as you did is of so much affliction to me, that it makes me forget not only the consideration of that place, but is likewise the greatest trial of my constancy that hath yet befallen me; for what is to be done, after one that is so near to me as you are both in blood and friendship, submits himself to so mean an action (I give it the easiest term) . . . you assured me that, if no mutiny happened, you would keep Bristol for four months. Did you keep it four days? Was there anything like a mutiny? More questions might be asked, but now I confess to little purpose. My conclusion is, to desire you to seek your subsistence (until it shall please God to determine of my condition) somewhere beyond the seas, to which end I send you herewith a pass."[160] He took no risk of Rupert's disobedience to this command, for he sent orders to his Secretary of State in Oxford, Sir Edward Nicholas, to arrest the Prince and Colonel Legge.[161]

Nicholas, a friend of Rupert, who had all that summer impotently watched the machinations of the cabal against him, knew the extent of the King's error but could not disobey. He found Rupert at dinner with Legge; there was nothing left for the Prince to do but demonstrate his loyalty by submission to the King's wish.[162] He wrote, however, asking that at least he might be heard in his own defence; the letter, a little incoherent, for he was no great master of the pen, ended on a note of such genuine distress that a man less blinded than the King must have been moved: "Wherever I am, or how unhappy so ever, and by your will made so, yet I shall ever retain that duty to Your Majesty which I have ever entertained as your Majesty's most obedient nephew and faithful, humble servant, Rupert."[163] Nicholas, who sent on the letter, added that to his knowledge the Prince had not fifty pounds in the world to maintain himself while under duress at Oxford, or to transport himself abroad.[164] So much for the great sums of money which, it was now freely rumoured,[165] he had taken for betraying Bristol.

IX

Digby was triumphant. The loss of Bristol he digested rapidly, like all other losses. Within a week of it he informed Nicholas that he had two other projects and " if either succeed we shall not think our condition much impaired."[166] Now that the King had got rid of Rupert, " the conduct of our military affairs will perhaps fall into more fortunate hands," he wrote to Lord Jermyn, and added the reassuring news that Montrose would shortly enter England with twenty thousand men. His cheerful news fell on ears apt to receive it, for Lord Jermyn, in Paris with the Queen, was equally sure that thousands of foreign troops would sail before the spring.[167]

Digby's two projects were, of course, the Irish treaty and help from Scotland. For Scotland, indeed, his hopes were high. Since the Covenanters in the Lowlands were making their peace with Montrose, why not the Covenanters in England too ? Some of them, embittered by their treatment by Parliament, had already made tentative overtures to the King, and Digby now wrote hopefully suggesting that the Scots commanders in England should embrace this happy occasion of joining forces with the King.[168]

The King and his advisers once again showed their inability to understand that their adversaries had principles as strong as their own. Stubbornly convinced that the rebellion had no cause except greed for profit, power and place, Charles was not for months to realise that the Covenanters would no more unite with Montrose than Montrose with them. It was true that a few weeks before some of the Covenanters had indeed made overtures to the King; it was true that they had tried to find a solution with him at the Treaty of Uxbridge, but they had done so merely because they believed a defeated monarch might be more amenable to their policies than the arrogantly victorious Parliament. But now, appalled by Montrose's conquest of their country, the Scots Commissioners had thrown themselves wholly on the mercy of Parliament, imploring help against the imminent triumph of the malignants in Scotland, and taking measures to stifle the ill-advised movement that some of their discontented soldiers had previously made towards the King. Only the strong alliance of the two countries could now prevent the " utter devastation " of Scotland which they feared; if their poor battered army " once so honourable and terrible," was to survive at all, it could do so only by maintaining friendship with the English: " It is better that our weakness be known than that our faithfulness be suspected."[169]

It was widely rumoured, across the Midlands and as far as London, that Montrose, carrying all before him, had entered England.[170] The Royalists firmly believed it. His invading force was reported at Penrith, then at Kendal.[171] From Cornwall, even the disheartened councillors of the Prince of Wales believed in his coming and urged the King to join him.[172]

The King could stay no longer at Raglan. The fall of Bristol made South Wales unsafe for him. The coast was watched from Swansea eastwards by the ships of Parliament, and by land the victorious Rowland Laugharne was fast advancing from Pembroke.[173] Charles once more turned North in the vain quest for Montrose; in four days of weary marching with his remaining cavalry he crossed " the vast and rude mountains of North Wales," hearing by the way from Lord Byron that the suburbs of Chester had been betrayed to the enemy and the city was likely to fall at any moment. Chester was his last important outlet to the sea, and the nearest port for Ireland; it must be held so that the Irish troops, when they came, would have a landing-place. The King deflected his course to relieve the city and on September 23rd his cavalry " tired and overmarched " entered Chester on the Welsh side, where there was still no blockade.[174]

On the following day, the cavalry under Langdale drew out towards Rowton Heath to drive the besiegers from their works.

Their coming was, however, known to the enemy and a strong party of horse under General Poyntz was on its way from Whitechurch. This unexpected reinforcement proved too strong for Langdale, who was driven back into the town with heavy loss. Among the dead was the King's cousin, Lord Bernard Stuart, the commander of his lifeguard, the third and youngest brother of the Duke of Richmond to be killed in the war. Even Digby was distressed. This young man's death, he wrote to Ormonde, " was such a loss as a victory would scarce repair," although the battle, he more cheerfully reported, had not been in any sense a defeat: it had given the defenders of Chester time to repair their walls and, since the city was not yet blocked up on the Welsh side, they could certainly hold it for some time to come.[175] In this at least he proved right.

The King, who had watched the horrible rout of his cavalry from the walls, was deeply cast down. He told the mayor that if he could not bring relief to their city within reasonable time he would not blame them for abandoning his cause. " O Lord, O Lord," he sighed in tragic bewilderment, " what have I done that should cause my people to deal thus with me ? "[176] Leaving Lord Byron to hold Chester for as long as he could, he withdrew to Denbigh, mustered his discouraged troops and tried to reanimate them with a rumour that Montrose had defeated Leslie and would soon be with them.[177] Even Digby's spirits were a little damped. He wrote to Ormonde suggesting that the Irish (of whom there was still no sign) ought perhaps to land in Scotland; as no one had yet been appointed to replace Rupert, he ventured the opinion that Ormonde might come over to undertake the task.[178]

The immediate problem was to find a safe garrison to which the King could go, for in the absence of definite news he had decided that the northward march was too hazardous. Worcester seemed at first the obvious place; it had been elaborately fortified since the battle of Naseby as a possible headquarters for the King should Oxford prove untenable.[179] But Prince Maurice was the governor and when he came to see the King at Denbigh he made it clear that he did not accept the justice of his brother's disgrace and believed Digby to be responsible for it. If the King went to Worcester, Digby feared alike the personal animosity of Maurice and his influence on the King: furthermore, Worcester was near enough to Oxford for Rupert himself to come there in the hope of defending himself to the King, an opportunity which had hitherto been denied him. Digby's politic desire to keep Charles away from Worcester was reinforced by other arguments. On September 26th Berkeley Castle surrendered to Fairfax, a loss which made Worcester very much less safe. On Digby's advice the King decided to go to Newark, where he would be in a well defended garrison and, Digby calculated, well out of Rupert's reach.[180] Leaving Wales by way of Bridgnorth, the King got safely to Lichfield and thence " by unknown ways and passages with many dark and late marches " to Newark,[181] still waiting and hoping for news of Montrose.

The rumours were now all of defeat and no hint of success anywhere started even a flicker of false hope. Outside the walls of Chester, General Poyntz and his cavalry had joined the besiegers and shouted to the garrison that Montrose had been defeated. Within Lord Byron wondered darkly: " I do not like this return of Poyntz's horse; I fear something is amiss with my Lord of Montrose."[182]

While the King traversed the Midlands, Cromwell reduced the Royalist garrisons in Wiltshire and Hampshire. He took Devizes before the end of September. Winchester, much battered, capitulated on October 5th. All the Cavaliers of the region and several fugitives from Oxford had by this time taken refuge within the formidable ramparts which surrounded the two great mansions, old and new, commonly called Basing House. Here the Marquis of Winchester declared his intention of holding out for ever; his house's other name, he said, was " Loyalty."[183] Fine words, but the Marquis and his garrison, who had manfully resisted the attacks of Waller and Essex, knew nothing of the New Model Army, and had not reckoned on the fanatic zeal of the soldiers or the power of their artillery. Cromwell laid siege to Basing House on October 8th; by the seventh day of the siege his cannon had gravely breached the outer walls and in a general assault of incredible ferocity his men overwhelmed the defenders and rushed the house in less than an hour.

It was a mansion, wrote Cromwell's chaplain, Hugh Peter, " fit to make an Emperor's Court," but a " nest of idolatry." In the heat of conquest the victors killed civilian refugees as well as soldiers. The fanatic Colonel Harrison with his own hand slew " Robbins the player," a comedian who had once delighted London audiences, and a young woman, a clergyman's daughter, was run through as she tried to protect her father. But the soldiers were soon more taken with the splendour of the place than the ungodliness of its inhabitants, gave over killing for plunder and seized upon everything they could carry, stripping the walls of hangings and the prisoners of their rich clothes: poor Inigo Jones was left with only a blanket. Idolatrous pictures, rosaries and Popish books were loaded into a wagon to make a public bonfire in London. All the rest the men were allowed to sell, as they had done before at Sherborne: plate, hangings, jewels, furniture, the iron bars from the windows, and the lead from the gutters. The spoils and the sale lasted for days, and dealers came from London to bargain for the riches of Basing House.[184]

During the disorders of the conquest, Hugh Peter, the arrogant voluble chaplain of the Ironsides, spied the Marquis of Winchester, standing forlorn without hat or cloak, and set upon him at once to argue him out of his misguided loyalty: he found the old man unequal to him in debate. " He was very soon silenced," wrote Peter, " only hoping that the King might have a day again."[185]

The fall of Basing opened up once more the choked arteries of commerce; woolpacks could now move freely down the road to London and the highway from the capital to the West was safe once more. Cromwell advised the destruction of the house to save the expense of holding it. The garrison at New-bury, he argued, would suffice to keep watch on the last strong-holds of the Cavaliers at Wallingford and Faringdon.[186]

The worst news for the Royalists came from the North. No further despatches had come from Montrose, but in all the Parlia-mentary quarters his defeat was given out for sure before the end of September, and in London they had already celebrated a thanksgiving.[187] The King would not believe it, but it was the truth. The Scottish Royalist army never crossed the Border.

X

Montrose had been confident that the Lowlands would rise. In the dismay caused by his victory at Kilsyth many Covenanters had come in to him. Almost, Argyll himself had wavered.[188] But some of the weather-cock allies who had joined him at Glasgow were enemies in disguise, who worked on the credulous, quarrelsome Highlanders to divide them from their leader. Before Montrose moved southward Lord Aboyne, Huntly's younger son, who now led the Gordons, " took a caprice and, on a fancied slight, retired to the north with all his men."[89] Alaster Mac-donald, impatient of playing a secondary part, however glorious, withdrew half his Irish on a raiding expedition to Galloway, leaving Montrose only seven hundred. Urged on by the King's command to come South, and relying on promises of help from the Earls of Roxburgh, Home and Traquair, Montrose began his march to the Border on September 5th. Before he reached Kelso he learnt that Roxburgh and Home had failed him, that David Leslie had crossed the border with his cavalry from England and was marching to cut off his retreat to the Highlands. Montrose with his seven hundred Irish turned about and made for Selkirk, meaning to out-distance Leslie, regain the hills, and fight him in country of their own choosing. His movements were discovered or betrayed, possibly by Traquair's son, who deserted that same night.

Leslie, changing course, and advancing under cover of a dense autumn mist, surprised the Irish at Philiphaugh on the Yarrow early on the morning of September 13th. Montrose and his cavalry, about two hundred in all, were quartered at Selkirk a mile away. Apprised too late, Montrose came up with his small force of cavalry to find the Irish infantry locked in desperate conflict. They were out-numbered by more than three to one and already surrounded. Montrose was for hurling himself into the hopeless tumult to die with his men, but his friends overpowered and compelled him to flee. They galloped to Lord Traquair's house but the wily turncoat would not open his door. Scattering for safety, by devious paths most of them made their way over the Pentland hills, across the Forth, and so by Strathearn back to the braes of Atholl.

At Philiphaugh the Irish infantry surrendered. Leslie gave them quarter for their lives and on this understanding they laid down their arms. But the ministers who attended his army protested, and Leslie, weakly conceding that he had given quarter only to the commanders, allowed his men to slaughter first the camp followers, the women and boys, and later, on the march, little by little to hang and drown the men.[190]

The Estates voted Leslie a gold chain and a handsome reward.[191] But though the victory at Philiphaugh was trumpeted far and wide, neither the Committee of Estates at home nor the Scots Commissioners in London could easily throw off their fear of some new and terrible visitation from Montrose. They quaked when they heard that he was recruiting in Atholl and had proclaimed a rendezvous at Dunkeld.[192] He had been defeated but not destroyed and none could yet be certain that he would not start again on a fresh career of victory.

XI

Montrose's defeat was hardly reported for certain before rumours of his growing strength again reached England. The bewildered King, turning this way and that, vainly pursued his plan of making a separate peace with the Scots, but the Earl of Leven, to whom Digby made overtures as commander of the Covenanting force in England, merely reported the matter to Parliament.[193] At Welbeck, just north of Newark, on October 13th Charles called a Council of War. Here Digby was vehement for an immediate march to Scotland to seek out Montrose. He had reasons other than those of military expediency. The Princes Rupert and Maurice were on their way to Newark, and the situation in the garrison there, where the governor was a fervent supporter of the Prince, was disquieting.

During his few days at Newark the King had taken steps to solve a troublesome problem. At every fresh defeat or surrender the common soldiers of the Royalist army were apt to desert, or to enlist in the opposing forces; the officers, whose code of honour was more rigid and who had more to lose, remained in the King's service. The phenomenon of officers without men was frequent enough in all the wars of this epoch: these " reformados," as they were called, usually formed themselves into troops or companies and fought as private soldiers until some renewed expansion of the army gave them better employment. A large number of " reformado " units in an army was almost always a source of trouble.

The King's army had disintegrated so rapidly in the last months that no effective rearrangement had been possible. Moreover, while junior officers could be " reformadoed," officers of higher ranks could not, so that the King's dwindling army came to be scandalously over-officered. At Newark, with only two thousand men under arms, twenty-four officers claimed the titles, privileges, pay and other rights belonging to the rank of colonel or higher.[194]   Contributions in cash and kind levied on the countryside were reckoned in relation to the number of these officers, and the King's army was in consequence extremely unpopular round Newark because of the sum exacted for this top-heavy garrison.

The problem might have been solved by a general capable of gaining the confidence of the army.   No such commander was at hand.   Although he could inspire devotion to his person, the King had never earned much respect for his military judgment. Digby, who was now all-powerful with him, had always been despised by the soldiers and was now hated by all supporters of Prince Rupert.   The King's attempts to control the pretensions of the four and twenty colonels in Newark provoked angry mutterings, and Digby was already wondering whether it would be diplomatic for him to go away for a short while, when the news of Rupert's approach made it almost imperative for him to do so.

On these grounds, therefore, he was strong for the march to Scotland when the Council of War met at Welbeck.   But the King had hardly decided to go north when a messenger came from Montrose.   He had been captured and detained on his journey but was able now, belatedly, to tell them the dismal truth: the Covenanters were masters of the Lowlands, Montrose had retreated north of Stirling and could do nothing effective unless the King could send him at least one regiment of cavalry. In the circumstances the King could not venture in person on so perilous a quest, but Digby, supported, to his surprise as he later averred, by Marmaduke Langdale and received with the acclamation of the men, or so he said, agreed to lead the Northern Horse to make a junction with Montrose.   " At half an hour's warning, having (I protest to God) not dreamt of the matter before, I marched off from the rendezvous "—so far Digby's version, though there is little doubt that Langdale's request that Digby should command, and the cheering of the men, had been prearranged, with the King's knowledge, to make Digby's somewhat irregular appointment seem a response to spontaneous demand. The King gave him, for this expedition, a commission as Lieutenant General of all the forces north of the Trent.[195] It was the first important appointment to be made after Rupert's fall, and when Charles rode back into Newark, the discontented soldiers there cannot have failed to notice that the man who had broken the Prince had now been given a great part of his command.

Rupert and Maurice, with about a hundred horse, were by this time at Belvoir Castle. They had repelled one enemy attack, but most of the way they followed by-roads and avoided the enemy, and once they came across country on a route that Rupert remembered from a time when he had hunted there as a boy eight years before.[196] Rupert's first impulse of submission had given place to a bitter sense of injustice when the King would not even hear his defence. In London, in Paris, in the Low Countries and all over England the slander that he had taken money to betray Bristol was repeated and enlarged: it was given out that he and Legge had planned the surrender of Oxford, even that he and Maurice had connived at the taking of Shrewsbury in the previous February.[197] His friends rallied to him, indignant to hear him traduced, enraged at the squandering of the King's remaining military resources now that all pretence of professional guidance had gone. Encouraged by his friends, and defying the King's order of arrest, he set out with Prince Maurice, a score of his officers and his own troop of horse to confront his accusers and demand an enquiry into the surrender of Bristol.

Charles interpreted his action differently. He believed that his rebellious nephew intended to force him, at the sword's point, to make peace with Parliament, and sent a cold command to him to return at once to Oxford if he came with any talk of treating.[198] This Rupert disregarded, and on October 16th, as he approached Newark, once the scene of his greatest triumph, he was met with every honour by Sir Richard Willis, the governor, and the newly ennobled Lord Gerrard, both acting in defiance of the King's wishes.[199]

Arrived in the town, Rupert "comes straight into the presence, and without any usual ceremony, tells his Majesty that he was come to render an account of the loss of Bristol."[200] The King gave no answer but went in to supper, during which he spoke to Maurice but not a word to Rupert. Next day he agreed that a Council of War should consider Rupert's case. On hearing his nephew's account of what had happened at Bristol the King gave it as his opinion that he had not been wanting in "courage or fidelity to us" but that he might none the less have held the castle some time longer in expectation of relief. To this Rupert replied that his Council of War at Bristol had agreed with him that relief was not to be expected, no intimation of that sort having been received from the King, and that he had surrendered to save the men who had "so long and faithfully" served the royal cause. At a second hearing the Council of War at Newark unanimously agreed that Rupert was not guilty of any failure in courage or fidelity, and passed over in silence the King's allegation that Bristol could have been held longer.[201]

The verdict was satisfactory to Rupert and his friends, but it was not pleasing to the King. He was justly perturbed by the indiscipline of the Newark garrison and the complaints of the countryside and he did not easily forgive the disobedience of Rupert and his friends. As in South Wales he had removed Lord Gerrard to please the Welsh gentry and tried (unavailingly as it was to appear) to appease him with a peerage, so now he planned to remove Willis and appease him with an apparently more important command. Newark was already threatened by the approach of the enemy and Charles himself was planning an immediate departure for Oxford; before he went he resolved to bestow the governorship of Newark on Lord Bellasis, who was locally well known and well liked, and take Willis back to Oxford with him as commander of all his horse-guards, the post held until his recent death by his young cousin, Lord Bernard Stuart.[202]

The plan did not work. However honourable the post which the King offered to Willis, his removal from Newark was bound to be interpreted as a mark of the King's disapproval, which it was. On the late afternoon of Sunday, October 26th, a few hours before the King should have left the endangered city, both the Princes, with Willis, Gerrard and a dozen more, again strode into the room where he sat at dinner. Willis broke silence and etiquette with angry words: the whole town knew that he had been dismissed from his place as governor, he protested; he had been publicly affronted and demanded a public explanation. " It is because he is my friend," broke in Rupert, and Gerrard, releasing the pent-up resentment of all the weeks since his dismissal in South Wales, shouted that Digby was behind this, and Digby was a traitor.

The King ordered them out of the room. Before evening a petition demanding justice for Sir Richard Willis and signed by Rupert, Maurice, Gerrard and twenty more was clamorously brought to him. One of the petitioners, with belated caution, hoped that the King would not call this action mutiny. " I shall not christen it," said the King, " but it looks very like."[203]

That night, undeterred, he proclaimed Bellasis governor. The town was in uproar; Rupert's friends beat the drums to call the men to arms and the principal cavalry officers made ready to leave. Next morning the mutinous cavalry filled the market-place with Rupert at their head. The King rode out to face them, cold and calm. Those who were discontented with his service, he said, could withdraw to Belvoir Castle and make what arrangements they would for disbanding. He would not prevent them: neither would he yield to them.

There was no more to be said. The protest had failed, and neither Rupert nor any of the others, would—in the last resort— use force against the King or those who still had his confidence. Shamefacedly, almost meekly, they rode away to Belvoir. The best of them by now recognised that, whatever wrongs they had suffered, their mutiny was inexcusable, something which, later, Rupert and others would try to expiate. By midday the town was quiet, but the King had lost his best cavalry officers and his army was broken beyond all hope of recovery.[204]

While this final clash of will between the King and his nephew destroyed the army at Newark, Digby had found simpler means to lose the Northern Horse. At Sherborne in Yorkshire he surprised an infantry regiment of Parliament and with some dexterity took most of them prisoners and gained possession of all their arms and baggage. When a small force of cavalry came to their rescue, Digby, by his own account, won a complete victory over them too, but it was marred by an unfortunate accident: while he was chasing the fleeing enemy through the town, Langdale's men mistook the fugitives for their own fellows, thought they had been defeated and took to flight, leaving all the spoil of their previous victory behind them. They left also—and even Digby thought this unfortunate—the whole of his private correspondence on the King's affairs.[205]

Digby and Langdale now made for Lancashire, but here they were hindered by the active Parliamentary levies. On a false rumour that Montrose had rallied and was in Glasgow, they pressed on into Scotland as far as Dumfries, where they learnt the truth and turned back again, planning to winter in the inaccessible region round Cartmel, between the mountains and the sea and await (as always) the coming of the Irish. But the active enemy found them out before they could entrench themselves as they had planned. Their troops, lacking all confidence in them, deserted by the hundred and Digby, with a few of his officers, took ship for the Isle of Man. From this delightful place, where he greatly enjoyed the hospitality of the Earl and Countess of Derby, Digby reported with unabashed good humour his catalogue of disasters, and announced his intention of proceeding to Ireland to find out what had become of the promised help from the Confederates.[206]

In England the tale of Royalist disaster continued. In South Wales, Rowland Laugharne took Carmarthen, Thomas Morgan battered his way into Chepstow, and a fortnight later rushed the town of Monmouth and reduced the castle by mining. Raglan Castle was now laid open to attack and the Marquis of Worcester made powerless to help the King.[207]

The Prince of Wales and his council withdrew into Cornwall, as Fairfax compelled the surrender of Tiverton and continued his western march.[208] The only places of consequence now left to the King were Oxford, with a few outlying garrisons, Newark, Worcester, Hereford, Exeter, the county of Cornwall, part of North Wales and, most valuable of all, the hard-pressed town of Chester, where (if he could hold out through the winter) the King still believed that the Irish might land.

Parliament tried to finish the war immediately. The Committee of Both Kingdoms ordered the Scots under Leven and the northern army under Poyntz to march on Newark. The King, it was confidently predicted, could not escape the closing net.[209] He deceived their expectation. He left Newark at ten o'clock at night on November 3rd; protected by what was left of his devoted life-guard, moving fast, across country and over by-roads, he completed the dangerous journey to Oxford by the afternoon of November 5th.[210] The new governor of Oxford was Sir Thomas Glemham; he had commanded already in two doomed cities, York and Carlisle, and was expert at prolonging a defence when all hope of relief had gone. Deprived of the two young men who had for the last three years inspired his counsels, the sanguine Digby and the dynamic Rupert, the King in his sad and straitened Court at Oxford faced the winter almost without illusion, almost without hope.

BOOK THREE

BETWEEN WAR AND PEACE

October 1645—January 1647

CHAPTER ONE

PRESBYTERIANS AND INDEPENDENTS

October 1645—April 1646

THE war in England was almost at an end. All danger that the King would enter his conquered capital to fasten the yoke of prelacy and prerogative on the nation had now gone. But the stable government by means of King, Lords and Commons and a uniform Protestant church, which the King's opponents had legislated to protect in 1641 and which they had fought to preserve, had been destroyed in the course of the fighting.

In the autumn of 1645 the King's power was in abeyance; the House of Lords, attended by a score of members, was without authority and nearly without influence; the direction of power and the control of policy lay, not with the Commons, but with that small group of men who formed the Committee of both Kingdoms. The Church, laid waste by sequestration and persecution, had not as yet been reformed by the dilatory efforts of the Westminster Assembly, and there was no longer any generally recognised spiritual order.

The attack on " scandalous ministers," which had begun before the war, had increased in scope and effect as the war proceeded and the Parliamentary armies extended their hold; but neither side would tolerate opponents in the pulpit, though the ministers persecuted or ejected by the Royalists were fewer in number. Parliament combined in the care of a single Committee the plight of these " plundered ministers " and the punishment of those whom it characterised as "scandalous," so that places could usually be found for clergy expelled by the King's party in parishes from which Parliament had ejected the incumbent.[1]

The visitations conducted in Archbishop Laud's time had revealed illiteracy, drunkenness and dereliction of duty among the English clergy, and some of those ejected by Parliament were in fact "scandalous ministers." But to the catalogue of human frailties Parliament had added other crimes. Every clergyman and schoolmaster was required to take the Covenant and not all had consciences elastic enough to enable them to do so. Since the introduction of the new Directory of Worship, the use of the Prayer Book was no longer permitted, and any minister who would not discard his surplice, substitute extempore prayer and long preaching for the regulated catechism and formal services of old was in danger of expulsion. Even if he committed no serious crime against the new order, ill-wishing parishioners might turn informers and a man might be slandered out of his living for a private grudge. Signatures and support for groundless complaints could be got easily enough in the ale-house from unsteady hands and fuddled heads.

Since it was not desirable to precipitate too many people into penury, some provision was made out of the tithes for the wives and children of expelled clergy, but the single man could expect nothing, and even the wretched relief allotted to the others was difficult to secure. The wife of the Dean of Bristol was reduced to hawking bunches of rosemary in the street; a learned cleric in Norfolk was found by a friend supporting life on a diet of cold oatmeal dumplings, having no fire to boil a pot or warm his hands.[2]

Schoolmasters and scholars who failed to take the Covenant were liable to the same penalties. The Cambridge colleges had been ruthlessly purged early in the war. The headmaster of the Charterhouse School in London, a notoriously Royalist establishment, was removed from his post. But even Parliamentary

authority quailed before the redoubtable Dr. Busby of Westminster, who continued to direct the secular and religious
education of his boys without the least concession to the rogues
and rebels who sat in power three minutes' walk away from his
desk.[3]   Richard Busby was a remarkable exception.   Other
scholars and clerics who had defied the orders of Parliament were
imprisoned in Ely House and Lambeth Palace, where in spite of
cramped quarters several of them contrived to hold classes for
pupils sent to them by Royalist parents.

The persecution left the church disordered and desolate and
caused intense suffering to many innocent, and some guilty, men.
For the older clergy, death was often hastened by the shock and
hardship of ejection. While Puritan pamphleteers magnified the
crimes of the evicted, Royalist writers listed their undeserved
sufferings—how one was "molested, silenced, dead," another
"vexed to death," others "assaulted in church," "reviled,
abused and dead."[4]

It was easier to disrupt the Church than to reform it. The
members of the Westminster Assembly interminably argued;
their Directory of Worship had been accepted by Parliament,
but their more significant Directory for Admonition, Excommunication and Absolution was still under discussion. This latter
instrument, closely modelled on the system now current in
Scotland, would have turned England into a theocratic state with
almost unchecked powers for punishment, discipline and, ultimately, blackmail in the hands of the clergy. The same system,
in Scotland, suited the party in power, who contrived, through
the political influence and the genuine religious fervour of Argyll,
to dominate the ministry. It would not have suited England,
where no great nobleman, and certainly no commoner, united in
himself the attributes of worldly power and spiritual zeal which
gave Argyll his unique authority.

The Independents naturally fought this rigid theocracy based
on the artificial framework of the parish and not, as they would
have wished, on a free association between the minister and his

flock; but they were strongly supported in their objections by the majority of legal-minded Parliament men. It was a truism of English historical and legal thinking that the civil power should, in the last resort, be superior to the spiritual; Henry II had fought Becket on this issue, and Henry VIII had repudiated the Pope. To many, who did not greatly care about the details of ceremony, the chief crime of King Charles had been to give too much power to the Church. What would they have gained by abolishing the High Commission and all ecclesiastical jurisdiction if immediately they set it up again in another form? The majority of educated Englishmen had objected not to bishops exercising judicial power, but to the Church in any form exercising too much power.

The Scots were brought up suddenly against a difference not only of religion but of outlook. In their country religion had been, over the centuries, a means of curbing, controlling and bringing under the law a fierce, high-spirited and much divided people; but in England the civilising influence of the secular law had been separate from that of the Church and equally strong. The English looked to the civil magistracy as the effective instrument of order and government and distrusted the interference of the spiritual power. In the Westminster Assembly itself, and more strongly still in the House of Commons, the Scots found the projected new discipline attacked and modified; if it came to be accepted at all in England, those excommunicated by the ministers were to have a right of appeal to Parliament. Parliament, too, was to have control in the last instance over the choice and ordination of ministers, and the selection of elders.

While the Scots heard with irritation the arguments of their English brethren in favour of secular power, the small Independent minority in the Westminster Assembly astutely out-manoeuvred the Presbyterian majority. They had been asked some months before to submit to their fellow divines a declaration of their tenets, but they foresaw that they would obtain no advantage by doing so because their views would be out-argued and out-voted

CHARLES I
by Peter Lely

ALEXANDER HENDERSON
by an Unknown Artist

by the others, and they would appear thus merely as an obstinate and eccentric minority unwilling to accept the views of the august Assembly. Knowing full well that they enjoyed far greater support in Parliament, they delayed for seven months and finally presented to the Assembly (and published to the world) a statement accusing the Presbyterians of systematically shelving or stifling their arguments: since experience had taught them to expect no fair hearing from their colleagues, they declined to make any further statement of their tenets.[5]

The anger of the Presbyterians, and more especially the Scots Commissioners, reflected their dismay at what had happened. The Independents had, in effect, withdrawn support from the Assembly and thereby, in the eyes of all but the most zealous Presbyterians, destroyed its claim to synthesise and unite the best of Puritan theology. Penned within the Assembly, the Independents could be held in check; but now they had freed themselves to act as they chose with the help of their friends in Parliament, the support of their growing congregations and the New Model Army. The Army had been only six months in existence but already the strong personalities of some of its officers had given it, in the eyes of perceptive observers, a political direction and coherence that had been lacking in all previous armies, and that was most dismally lacking in the unpaid, demoralised army of the Presbyterian Scots. Certain names were beginning to be known, besides that of Lieutenant General Cromwell—Ireton, Harrison, Okey, Rainsborough. These men represented something to be reckoned with.[6]

The growth of Independency was a threat to the social as well as to the religious order. Its opponents understood this in a blundering imprecise way when they persistently styled the Independents "Anabaptists" and accused them (wrongly) of holding the beliefs in community of goods and of women which for a time had distinguished the Anabaptists of Munster in the previous century. But what really aroused their anger was the claim of humble and uneducated people to interpret the Word of

God. Dr. Baillie was perturbed lest the " silly, simple lads " in the Scots army should come into contact with opinions which might corrupt them.[7] His anxiety for the welfare of their souls was genuine, but it arose, however innocently, from the conviction that such as he must always know, under God's guidance, what was best for " silly, simple lads." They were not to be encouraged to think for themselves.

But, dismayingly, they were thinking for themselves. They might be heard—they were indeed heard—haggling over a stall not about the price of the wares, but about the seventh verse of the fifth chapter of the first epistle of St. John. One of the participants in this particular argument, asked if he was an Anabaptist, cried: " No, but I am a downright separatist and will, by the Grace and power of God, seal it with my blood."[8]

When ordinary men and women got it into their heads that it was a fine thing, by the grace and power of God, to be " downright separatists," the secular as well as the spiritual order was threatened. The " gathered Churches " of the separatists were democratic institutions. The congregation came together of its own will, chose its own minister by free election, supported him by contributions freely organised and given. Now that all authority was shaken and every speculation possible, the " gathered Churches " would soon be taken by some as the pattern for a reformed secular order, a society which came together by free consent of the governed, by agreement of the people.

It needed only an accident of personalities, the fusion of these religious ideas with the political preoccupations of two remarkable men to make Independency, in the next years, a driving force towards social revolution. In the autumn of 1645, the social outcry was still muffled and confused by the religious dispute and the last cannonades of the war; but it had begun.

John Lilburne's was the voice crying in the wilderness of discontent. He had left the Army because he would not subscribe to the Covenant, such forcible oath-taking being against his conscience. Since then he had wrangled, in and out of Newgate, before Committees of the Commons and before Committees of the Lords, with the vindictive, indefatigable Prynne, whose views on the supreme authority of Parliament he fiercely contested. Above the authority of Parliament, Lilburne raised, exultant, " the incommunicable prerogative of Jesus Christ," by which Kings, Prelates, Parliament and even Prynne were to be overruled. It was the prerogative of Jesus Christ " to reign in the souls and consciences of his chosen ones."[9] Obedient to the supreme authority of Christ which he felt within him, Lilburne spoke out against William Prynne and Speaker Lenthall, denounced the Presbyterian dispensation, the mismanagement of the war and the government of the City of London.

For his attack on Speaker Lenthall he found himself in Newgate, whence he smuggled out to a clandestine press his pamphlet, *England's Birthright*.[10] It appeared anonymously in print on October 10th, 1645, a vigorous, confused, lively document in which he triumphantly equated liberty of conscience with the civil liberties of the true-born Englishman. *England's Birthright* was, like most of Lilburne's pamphlets, drawn from his own experience. After leaving the army, he had tried to set up in the cloth trade, only to discover that the purchase, sale and export of cloth in London was controlled by the ancient and privileged company of Merchant Adventurers. The company had advanced large sums of money to Parliament during the war, and its privileged position was not therefore something into which the House of Commons felt impelled to enquire. Lilburne's attack was all the more embarrassing because it was true. He claimed that the Merchant Adventurers were nothing but a vile, illegal monopoly, an offence against the free-born subject and, in these present times of shortage a great cause of want and suffering to sheep farmers, clothiers, and merchant seamen, not to mention honest fellows like himself trying to set up in trade.[11]

Living in London, Lilburne had also discovered that he and his like were excluded from any control of the government of the City. On the eve of the war a sudden, inspired outcry had caused a change in the Common Council, but it had been only the substitution of a predominantly Puritan group of aldermen for a predominantly Royalist one; nothing had been done to give the generality of the citizens any share of power, or to permit any below the rank of alderman to vote in the election of the Mayor. In April, 1645, a petition for wider representation had reached the Lord Mayor, but little notice had been taken of it. Lilburne, who had probably had something to do with it, printed it in *England's Birthright* and repeated the demand for more democratic government of the city.

The checks he had received in his trading ventures during the last year, the censorship imposed on the press, the claims of the Presbyterian ministers, and the bitter struggle with Prynne caused him to include ministers, censors, merchants and the whole gang of lawyers in the forces of evil who must be brought down to make way for the rule of Christ. What were lawyers, he asked with blistering scorn, but " thieves *cum privilegio* " who used the intricacies of their knowledge to uphold the rich, the powerful and the privileged against the humble and meek?

In *England's Birthright* the cry for liberty for conscience's sake is secularised. It becomes the cry for liberty for the sake of a just society. Lilburne believed that he was continuing the struggle that he had waged against the prelates in the days when the Star Chamber had had him whipped through the streets. In a sense he was right, for he was still fighting against authority. But the authority he had now challenged was not that of any church: it was the authority of law and property and privilege.[12]

The day after the appearance of *England's Birthright* a more restrained and judicious pamphlet appeared in support of it. This was *England's Lamentable Slavery*, the work of William Walwyn, a citizen and merchant of London who was none the less an exponent of the new doctrines. Walwyn had an original and questioning mind, was a very wide reader, especially of Seneca, Plutarch and Montaigne, and loved to entertain and argue with his friends in the library and garden of his house in Moor-fields. The piercing logic of his arguments, the clarity of his intellect, together with the genial eloquence and good nature which distinguished all that he said or wrote, had won for him a limited but by no means negligible influence. In his anonymous pamphlet, *The Compassionate Samaritane*, published in 1644, he had protested, as others were now on all sides protesting, against the exclusive right which Presbyterian ministers claimed to interpret the Word of God. This, he suggested, was the old pre-latical tyranny under another name for it was ultimately not to be endured that men should be forced " against their mind and judgment to believe what other men conclude to be true." His doctrine, although it was inspired by Christian feeling, was also derived from his wide reading in the humanities. He held that men could achieve a just society by the cultivation of reason guided by love, and freed from the authority of divines or lawyers, whose motives were too often and too obviously affected by causes other than the respect for truth and justice.[13]

Walwyn admired the courage and fervour of Lilburne, if he sometimes questioned the logic of his arguments. It is uncertain when they met, but they had been brought together during the long wranglings of that summer with the Presbyterians and Prynne. Out of their alliance was to grow the most remarkable political movement of the century.[14]

Lilburne had a vocation for martyrdom. He deliberately provoked persecution and endured it heroically, though never in silence. He saw himself, in a manner so unabashed that it defies the name of vanity, as the central figure and the hero of the conflicts which he aroused. But in spite of this innocent and passionate egoism, or perhaps because of it, he was not only admired, but greatly loved. He was no austere and repellent fanatic, but a lively well-groomed young man. In the heat of argument his thrusts and parries and counter-thrusts were an entertainment to watch. The London populace, short of plays and bear-baitings, took something of the same pleasure in the controversies now raging, and watched the performers, preachers and pamphleteers, with the zest they had once brought to more brutal sports. Lilburne was by far the most daring performer and for that alone would have been popular with the Londoners. He was also the first man to voice their special grievances. In his protests against Merchant Adventurers, aldermen and lawyers, thousands of inarticulate small tradesmen and artisans heard the words that they most passionately wanted to hear. Lilburne enjoyed and responded to the notice that was taken of him; but if he was a demagogue, he was also a saint. The core of his character and the core of his doctrine was concern for his fellow men. By fighting for himself he fought for them, and during the twenty years of his adult life he repeatedly and painfully demonstrated the terrible penalties that outraged authority will inflict on those who refuse to compromise with truth or to submit in silence to injustice.[15]

His friend and helper, William Walwyn, was one of the first men in English politics to understand that ideas can best be translated into action if those who hold them are organised, linked and directed from above. In little more than a year Walwyn would create, behind Lilburne, in London and in the Army, the Leveller party. By the autumn of 1645 the word, which was so soon to be one of menace, had not been applied to Lilburne and his friends, and meant no more than it had done for the last forty years—namely, a rioter who threw down the fences of new enclosures.

But to anyone watching the political scene in that autumn of 1645, the sharpest division still seemed to be that between Presbyterians and Independents, the gravest problem the reform of religion and the future of the monarchy. No one yet foresaw that the Independents would be split from end to end by the ferment of their own ideas, and few could guess how profoundly property and hierarchy had been shaken by the war, or what intoxicating glimpses of a better world the common people of England had seen through the cracks.

II

The unquenchable hopes of the King sprang afresh from these divisions of his enemies, though he was no more percipient than his principal opponents in recognising the depth and significance of the movements which were now beginning to stir among his people. Still, for him, politics was a matter of surface diplomacy, of winning help from his fellow sovereigns abroad, of dividing Presbyterians from Independents, or Scots from English, by bribes of power and favour, and the winter was passed in a labyrinth of abortive negotiations and imaginary plots.[16] The overtures made by the Scots army in the late summer had been in themselves abortive, but knowledge of them had reached Parliament and further increased the distrust between the allies:[17] that at least was a potential gain to the King. Intermittently he played also with the idea of winning the Independents by promises of toleration. By thus attempting to seduce one group or the other, he increased the doubts and fears of each, but he did not break their strained alliance. He had too little to offer, and neither his word nor his judgment commanded respect.

It was the same with the foreign powers to whom, either directly or through his wife, he appealed for help. They were interested in his fate only in so far as they could draw advantage from it to themselves. In these years King Charles reaped the tares he had sown in his days of power. It mattered little that his foreign policy had been selfish, opportunist and directed only to material ends: gratitude and generosity had never been virtues widely practised in international diplomacy. But his policy had also been feeble, vapouring and deceitful. His fellow-rulers knew him as a monarch who rarely had the strength of purpose to carry out his intended designs and whose ablest envoys had constantly been checked by the vacillations of his judgment. Now, therefore, that he was defeated by his own people, those who for one reason or another thought it wise to intervene would do it only on their own terms and in their own way, setting aside the suggestions and demands of a King in whom they placed no faith.

Parliament had had from the outset the advantage in foreign policy because they controlled the navy, and the King's attempt to counteract this by using the Dunkirk pirates had caused the Dutch to overlook for the time being their increasing commercial rivalry with the English and co-operate with the Parliamentary navy against the common enemy. Admiral Tromp and the Earl of Warwick had been during the most critical years of the war efficient partners against the Dunkirkers and their allies, the Irish sea rovers who carried or claimed the King's commission.[18]

For the rest Parliament had in Sir Harry Vane a diplomatist of considerable ability who managed, even at the worst of times, to convince the various foreign Residents—the French, the Spanish, the Venetian, the Portuguese—that it would be in the interests of their masters to keep on good terms with Parliament. Even the most Royalist of them, the Portuguese Antonio de Sousa, had done little more for the King than smuggle his letters for him. The Spaniard had early seen that the neutrality of the English navy against Spanish ships and the right to recruit for his master among Royalist prisoners of war were advantages worth pursuing. It was ironical that the King of Spain, whom Charles had done so much to help in the days of his power, was the first European sovereign to give official recognition to Parliament as the government of England.

The French government, for whose help since the death of the inimical Richelieu the King had vainly hoped, wrangled from time to time with Parliament about the seizure of French vessels bound for Royalist ports but had no intention of going to war about what was at worst merely an inconvenience. The infant King Louis XIV and his mother the Regent had in fact signed a formal treaty of friendship with King Charles in the summer of 1644, but this was a mere gesture of politeness, with no meaning whatsoever.[19]

It was lucky for Parliament, and for England, that the civil war coincided with a European struggle which allowed neither France nor Spain to consider seriously the idea of anything but diplomatic intervention. It might have been worth while for either of these great rivals for European dominance to re-establish Charles by force of arms and thus secure a puppet government and the control of the English Channel. But such an action in the 1640's was beyond the resources of either, and both fell back on the alternative of neutrality with an anxious eye on the movements of the navy, thus allowing the English to work out their insular fate alone.

But the defeat of the King involved at least a question of prestige for the French Crown, and in the late autumn of 1645 Mazarin thought it wise to send over a new representative with the special mission of discovering what could be done to restore the King to his throne with at least some semblance of dignity and power. At the same time the King's plight had stirred the Pope to action, not indeed to help the King, but to make certain that the Irish, or rather the Church in Ireland, should gain the utmost advantage from his appeal for their troops. The King's extremity was Ireland's opportunity; it must not be lost.

So at last in the autumn of 1645 the royal appeals for foreign intervention were answered, though not in the way that Charles had hoped. It would be hard to say which of these two diplomatic forays was the more fatal to him.

The Pope's intervention in Ireland was not unprovoked. Sir Kenelm Digby, scientist, dilettante, philosopher, and cousin to George Digby had, with the King's knowledge and the Queen's support, gone on a secret mission to Rome. On his way thither he represented his King's dire need to several of the Italian princes, but found them "a frugal generation." In Rome he learnt the contempt in which his master was held when he was refused an audience by the Spanish ambassador and told to wait his turn with the crowd in the ante-room. Sir Kenelm's chief project was to persuade the Pope to contribute arms and money to the Irish army which the Earl of Glamorgan was raising to help the King. To this plea Innocent X answered that he would assist the King only if he first proclaimed his submission to Rome.[20]

This was, unhappily for Charles, not the end but only the beginning of Papal interference. For two years the Vatican had had a representative, Pier Francesco Scarampi, among the Confederates, but they themselves had already asked that they might have with them nothing less than a Papal Nuncio. Innocent X, who had succeeded Urban VIII in 1644, adopted a more active policy towards the Irish, and in the summer of 1645 granted their desire. His choice fell on Giovanni Battista Rinuccini, Archbishop of Fermo, an elderly, distinguished Florentine, honest, devoted and industrious, with some legal training, little political judgment and no knowledge of Ireland. Ill-equipped by nature for his difficult mission, Rinuccini was further handicapped by his instructions from the Pope.

The Vatican would be content with nothing less than the extinction of Protestantism in Ireland. No compromise settlement was to be tolerated. Queen Henrietta Maria was sourly condemned because during the last months she had urged the Irish to accept the Ormonde treaty. This, in the eyes of the Pope, was to put her husband's interests before those of Holy Church. Rinuccini was instructed to accept no settlement put forward by the Protestant Ormonde, and to authorise no agreement between the Irish and the King that did not fully restore the Church in Ireland and bind the King in future to appoint a Roman Catholic Lord Lieutenant. So far, therefore, from hastening the Irish treaty and encouraging the Confederates to succour the King, Rinuccini was to prevent the signing of the Ormonde treaty at any price. He was, furthermore, charged with the thorough reformation of the Church in Ireland. The oppression under which the Irish had lived for so long had created abuses which must be checked. Priests had acquired dangerous habits of independence; monks and nuns, who had lived dispersed and secretly in the private houses of the faithful, had become recalcitrant to conventual discipline. The people, used to hearing mass secretly without stirring from their houses, found it troublesome to attend churches and continued the hugger-mugger practices of the years of oppression. Such laxity the Nuncio was charged to put down.[21]

Thus instructed, Rinuccini set out from Italy. On his way, in Paris, he confirmed his unfriendly opinion of Queen Henrietta Maria as a half-hearted Catholic surrounded by advisers who wanted to help from the Vatican, but were not prepared to accept the Vatican policy.[22] Here too he met Richard Bellings, the secretary of the Supreme Council, who had for the last six months been in Europe trying to secure financial help for the Irish Confederates. " All men wished well to the Cause," Bellings later wrote, " but no man was in condition to assist us." The disillusioned realism of the Secretary and his association with the Irish peers of the Ormondist party, made a bad impression on Rinuccini, who was resolved to trust only those who were whole-heartedly for the Vatican and the clerical party in Ireland.

At La Rochelle, waiting for shipping, Rinuccini received a letter from the Earl of Glamorgan which, in respectful terms, welcomed him on his way with the information that his advice and assistance was alone wanting for the successful conclusion of a secret treaty between the King and the Confederates.[23] Heartened by this knowledge and determined at all points to cross the schemes of Ormonde, the Nuncio set sail in early October in a vessel fitly named the *Saint Peter*. The protection of the saint was invoked and was needed, for the *Saint Peter* ran into fog off Waterford and was then chased far to the westward by a pirate. She anchored at last off the wretched hamlet of Kenmare on the coast of Kerry and the Nuncio spent the night in a shepherd's hovel, couched among beasts of burden, a predicament which, he piously reflected, resembled that of his infant Saviour.[24]

The supplies of ammunition which he had brought to assist

the Confederates in their holy war were safely landed at a more convenient haven some days later. The Nuncio meanwhile traversed the damp, green, unfamiliar land towards Limerick, where he was formally met by Scarampi with disquieting news. The Confederates under Castlehaven had signally failed to reduce the port of Youghal on the south coast. The failure made some suspect the Anglo-Irish Castlehaven of being half-hearted or even treacherous, but the real reason for this failure may well have been the inability of Irish-Dunkirk vessels to prevent Parliamentary ships reaching Youghal with arms and victuals from Lyme Regis and Liverpool. The Protestant enemy therefore still held a vital stretch of the coast from Cork eastwards, and under the leadership of Inchiquin was growing stronger. The Scots, under Monro, were still powerful in the North, and in a recent small skirmish had killed the Archbishop of Tuam and captured all his papers. Rinuccini could not know that the loss of the Archbishop's papers was, within a few weeks, to have certain disastrous repercussions, but he grieved for the loss of an energetic prelate on whom he had been told he could rely for whole-hearted support of the Vatican policy.[25] A little discouraged, but still serenely confident of ultimate success, he went on to Kilkenny, where he made his solemn entry on November 12th through a steady downpour of rain.[26]

The Nuncio found that the Marquis of Ormonde had by this time persuaded a considerable part of the Supreme Council, led by his brother-in-law, Lord Muskerry, seriously to consider making a treaty which would ensure to the Irish nothing more than the removal of the worst disabilities to which the Catholics were subjected and a measure of independence of the English Parliament. Privately, the Earl of Glamorgan offered to the Irish the return of the churches and church land which they held, and the open practice of their faith. He convinced Rinuccini that these offers were genuine by handing to him a personal letter from the King in which Charles adjured the Nuncio to put his faith wholly in Glamorgan by whose arrangements, whatever they were, he promised to abide.[27] The confusion between the secret and the open treaty had hitherto prevented the signing of either. This suited Rinuccini, for he disliked them both. The Ormonde Treaty he regarded as insupportable, and Glamorgan's terms as insufficiently favourable. He kept before his eyes with single-minded idealism the vision of a united Catholic Ireland, in which the rights and property of the Church would be fully and freely restored. If the King of England would grant, in effect, the total restoration of everything in lands or rights, let alone in religious practice, that had been lost at the Reformation, then—and only then—he could count on help from the Vatican.

Rinuccini thus set himself, as he sincerely believed, to "unite" the dissident parties in the Assembly and on the Supreme Council in support of demands more extreme than any that had hitherto been made. The great majority of the Irish lords and landowners knew that Rinuccini's ideal was as impossible of achievement as it would have been economically ruinous to them; his efforts to unite all parties in this policy therefore had the immediate effect of sharpening divisions, increasing suspicion and postponing the sending of help to the King. The first effect of his intervention was to put off indefinitely the signing of a treaty with either the Marquis of Ormonde or the Earl of Glamorgan. While the King in Oxford still hoped that he would see an Irish army by the spring, the Nuncio at Kilkenny, with all the prestige of his great position, relentlessly destroyed all prospect of a treaty, mistakenly believing that he acted in the best interests of Ireland and the Church. The Lords of the Supreme Council, more realist in their views, vainly pointed out to him the strength of the Protestant forces that they would have to contend with if once they allowed the King to lose the war. Sure of himself, and of his mission, Rinuccini continued to work up among the clergy a protest against the Ormonde treaty and made ready himself to fight it at all points and at whatever cost.[28]

While the Vatican thus fatally interfered with the King's Irish affairs, the French government wished him to reorient his

Scottish policy. Mazarin's plan for restoring peace in the warring Kingdoms of the British Isles was founded in part on the time-honoured French tradition of allying with Scotland, and in part on the mistaken belief that the combatants would abandon their ideals to promote their interests. He therefore sent over towards the end of the summer an envoy to Scotland, Jean de Montreuil, an ingenious young diplomat with some experience of King Charles's affairs as he had been in London a few years before. Montreuil was to see first the Scots Commissioners in London, then to go to Edinburgh and Oxford, and by persuasive arguments to build up the old understanding between France and Scotland and so guide the King and his Scots subjects into alliance against the English rebels. The balance of power would thus be re-established between King and Parliament, and a satisfactory compromise solution could then no doubt be reached. While the war lasted, Mazarin calculated that many works of art were probably being sold to defray expenses, and he added a private instruction to Montreuil to look out for any tapestries or manuscripts which might come into the market.[29]

For some weeks after his arrival in London, the tension between the Covenanters and the English flattered Montreuil's hopes of breaking down their alliance. The English complained that the Scots army had never done anything except take Newcastle, and that it had exhausted the country with plunder. The Scots Commissioners answered that no money had been paid to them for seven months, and that Parliament was stinting them of set purpose to compel them to live on the country and so become hateful to the people. By the autumn their whole army was in need of shoes and clothes, and incidents between the hungry ill-used soldiers and the people among whom they quartered were frequent.[30] When Parliament finally sent money, boots and firearms, it added a request for the evacuation of Carlisle and Newcastle, Scots garrisons in these towns being altogether offensive to English pride.[31] Only the very considerable tact and charm of the Scots Chancellor Loudoun, then in London, prevented a breach and maintained reasonably smooth relations with the Parliamentary leaders.

While he was firm and tactful with Sir Harry Vane and Oliver St. John, Loudoun was friendly to Montreuil, for he well understood how to maintain two or three policies until he saw which would best answer to the unfolding situation. The negotiation was in the main left to another Commissioner, Lord Balmerino, while Sir Robert Moray was despatched to France to win over Queen Henrietta Maria to a project which would involve abandoning the gallant Montrose and his Highland Catholic allies and favouring the heretic Presbyterians. In London, the malcontent Earl of Holland and the mischievous Countess of Carlisle gave Montreuil the benefit of their advice, indicating how bitter the antagonism to the sectaries had now become, and how, with a little good fortune, not only the Scots but the City of London and the English Presbyterians might be drawn into alliance with the King. Montreuil, a clever, reasonable man, saw the pattern clearly take shape, and did not doubt that if the King and the Covenanters came together the war would be satisfactorily concluded with a compromise settlement.[32]

Montreuil's rational outlook contributed to his misapprehension, for the quarrel which he hoped to settle was beyond the reach of reason. Loudoun and Balmerino spoke him fair, but behind the fair words the deeds of the Covenanters were not those of men anxious to be reconciled to their King on any but their own terms. Some moderation in the treatment of Montrose's men, taken at Philiphaugh, would have indicated a desire for compromise more clearly than words. There was no moderation. Argyll and Warristoun kept a firm hand over the Estates which met at St. Andrews in the winter, and foiled an attempt by Sir John Smyth, the commissioner for Edinburgh, to create a milder climate with the help of those waverers who, having submitted to Montrose in the panic after Kilsyth, were now anxious to avoid the consequences.[33] The dominating party hastened, in Warristoun's phrase, to expel " the unclean beasts " from the

Ark, voted to death all the most eminent of Montrose's "wicked crew," and condemned the lesser men to fines and obloquy. They revealed their rigid anger with the King by executing his Secretary of State for Scotland, Sir Robert Spottiswoode, whose crime was that he had carried to Montrose the Commission appointing him Lieutenant Governor of Scotland. This was a calculated defiance, to the meaning of which Montreuil should not have been blind. The condemned royalists were executed, some at Glasgow, some at St. Andrews, so that examples of the Lord's vengeance might be witnessed by as many as possible. Among them were the lame Sir William Rollo, who had crossed the Border with Montrose in disguise; Nat Gordon, whose presence of mind at Auldearn had dispersed the Covenanting cavalry; Magnus O'Cahan, the ablest soldier among the Irish; two boys of eighteen, and one wounded man who had to be carried in a chair to the scaffold. Of this judicial massacre of prisoners of war one of the ministers was commonly reported to have said: "The work goes bonnily on."[34]

III

The King's perennial optimism was blighted by the disasters of the winter. Everywhere his last strongholds were yielding. Sydnam Poyntz, the German-trained professional who had destroyed the King's guards at Rowton Heath, scoured the Northern Midlands threatening the isolated garrisons at Skipton, Welbeck and Bolsover. Repulsed at Belvoir, he ordered the killing of all the prisoners taken in the unsuccessful assault.[35] Beeston Castle on the Welsh border was starved out, the conquerors finding when they entered it no food left but a piece of turkey pie, some biscuits and a live peacock.[36] Lathom House, after its long history of resistance, capitulated in December.[37]

In the West, Fairfax continued his advance. At Tiverton Castle his men, with a lucky shot, shattered the drawbridge chain and rushed the bridge before the defenders could pull it up again.[38] The Prince of Wales's councillors took their precious charge back to Truro while Fairfax sent very civilly to ask him to disband his troops and trust himself to Parliament. "Rogues and rebels," cried the high-spirited boy on hearing the message, "are they not content to be rebels themselves but they must have me of their number?"[39] The King's Western Army was disintegrating. Goring, after pleading illness for a month, left for France, and Grenvile, when required to assist at least in the defence of the Prince, advised him to appeal to Parliament for a treaty with or without his father's consent.[40] From France meanwhile, Goring's father, the Earl of Norwich, requested to be made Governor of Pendennis and cheerfully declared that he had prepared himself for the hopeless heroic task by reading a great number of romances.[41]

In North Wales, Sir William Vaughan raised a force for the relief of Chester, where Lord Byron still held out, but he was intercepted and defeated by Brereton near Denbigh.[42] If troops were ever to come from Ireland, Chester must be held for their reception, but the town was now in desperate plight. The suburbs had been burnt and their hungry inhabitants camped in the city, mutinous and resentful. After Sir William Vaughan's defeat, no further help came from North Wales, which had been drained of arms and men in the two previous summers, where the people were now openly hostile and Archbishop Williams at Conway was bickering with the military commanders. Famine was imminent in Chester, and the long suffering people pursued Lord Byron with tears and threats; he appealed to Oxford for help, sending as his messenger the lovely young woman whom he had recently married; she touched all hearts, but help she could not get.[43]

Only one event caused a flicker of anxiety in London—the return of Prince Rupert to the King. He had applied for a pass to go abroad but Parliament would grant it only if he undertook never again to fight for his uncle and to this he would not agree.

After lingering unhappily at Worcester, where Lord Astley, his one-time tutor, was governor, he rode for Oxford early in December taking Maurice with him. His letters to the King were at first rejected as insufficiently penitent, but from Woodstock he sent an apology and an acknowledgment of his errors so humble and so complete that the King softened at last and welcomed him back to Oxford. But Parliament need have felt no anxiety; the jealousies of his other councillors prevented the King from giving his best soldier any military command, not even that of his own life-guard.[44]

The winter had come down with exceptional severity. For nearly seven weeks from December 8th an iron frost gripped the land. Roads became impassable, rivers froze.[45] In the second week of the frost, Colonel Birch, collecting volunteers from the Parliamentary garrisons of Bath, Bristol and Gloucester, pushed through the snow to make a surprise attack on Hereford. The Royalist governor, Sir Barnabas Scudamore, knighted by the King for his defence of the town against the Scots, was troubled by the discontent of the citizens and indiscipline of the troops. Early on the morning of December 18th, 1645, after a long night on duty, he was roused from brief sleep to hear that the enemy were within the walls. Birch had marched through the winter darkness and concealed his troops in a hollow near the east gate of the town. At daybreak, a dozen of his men disguised as labourers, tried to enter the town on the pretence that they had come to work there; while they held the guards in talk, their comrades rushed the gate. The dispirited royalists hardly contested the attack, and Scudamore with about fifty followers escaped over the frozen Wye, leaving the town to its fate.[46]

The Parliamentary soldiers were rewarded for their cold night march by a day of plunder, though afterwards Birch maintained good discipline. The Dean of Hereford Cathedral was Herbert Croft, one of the King's chaplains, who had been preferred to the deanery a few months earlier as a reward for his courage in carrying despatches across enemy country; now, from the pulpit of his cathedral, he condemned the image-breaking of the Puritan soldiery, and but for the intervention of Birch himself would have been fired on by a fanatical captain.[47]

The fall of Hereford left the King little to call his own in the Welsh marches, and gravely hampered the efforts of Lord Astley to recruit men from Wales for one last army. During Astley's recruiting journeys the command at Worcester fell to Colonel Washington, a soldier of equal courage and ferocity, who in the triumphant days of the Cavaliers had been the first to enter the breach at Bristol. In these last months at Worcester he and his subalterns, drunken, blaspheming and reckless, plagued the countryside for horses and money. Later, as the enemy closed in, they fought them with tigerish energy, raided their quarters, beat them up, took prisoners, horses, standards. The furious tenacity of Henry Washington was to give Worcester its proud title of " *civitas fidelis*," " the first of the cities that declared for the Crown and the last which held out in defence thereof."[48]

The last attempts at discipline on the King's side were everywhere breaking down. His captains were now nearly all desperate men, some nobly so, in their loyalty to a ruined cause, others ignobly anxious only to seize what pleasure and what profit was still to be had. A kind of policy might be detected in this Royalist delirium; their troops scouring the country on plundering expeditions, proved to their enemies that the febrile pulse of the cause had not ceased to beat. So in this winter when the war seemed won, even Puritan Bedfordshire felt the wrath of their raiding parties.

Troops from Raglan, which alone held out in South Wales, from time to time alerted the region and attempted, vainly, to re-take both Monmouth and Chepstow.[49] From Ludlow, Lichfield, Worcester, Woodstock, Banbury, Borstall, Oxford, Wallingford and Ashby de la Zouche the King's flying horsemen still intimidated the land. In the West, above all, their name was held in execration. " If they would fight more and plunder less," wrote Culpeper from the Prince of Wales's council, they might be thought very good cavalry indeed. Outcast young ruffians joined them for the sport; the godly in the West country had it for sure than the devil had been seen not far from Crediton, disguised as a carrier, and had struck three cavaliers dead with a terrible stink of brimstone.[50]

These troubles at least had the colour of warfare and would stop with the war. But the general disorder of the countryside would not end so quickly. There had been, even from the beginning, some resolute adventurers who used one cause or the other —but most frequently the King's—to cover their private crimes. Horse-stealing was easy for the enterprising robber who invaded a lonely farmstead with half a dozen fellows at his heels, claimed to be a Captain from the nearest garrison and took away all the horses and money he could find. The King's generals had struggled in vain to check these abuses.[51]

With the collapse of the Royalist armies many young men, uprooted from their homes, unskilled in any trade, with the taste for adventure and the habit of plunder, were loosed upon the countryside. Some went abroad, recruited for foreign wars by the agents of France, Spain and Venice. Many came to London to live by their wits until the authorities, half in fear of Cavalier disturbances and half in anxiety for the good name of the capital, organised special patrols to round up the vagrants and tried, not very effectively, to enforce the laws by which the destitute were compelled to return to their native parishes.[52] The bolder of the drifting soldiers swelled the ranks of thieves and gave a new air to an old profession. They drew round them bands of followers, promoted themselves to the rank of Captain —and came perhaps to believe that they had indeed been officers and gentlemen in the palmy days of the King's war—and held up the coaches on the roads. The footpad, mounted, became the aristocrat of the underworld; he aspired to wit and good manners, aped the appearance of the fashionable blades, took purses with a jest and was gallant with the ladies. Jemmy Hinde, a saddler's son from Chipping Norton, was the first to be famous, as

" Captain Hinde," a gentleman of the road. He was only the most notorious of many. From the wreck of the Cavaliers came the English highwayman, who was to enliven the news sheets and the stage for a century to come.[53]

The defeated King wavered from one design to another. He wrote repeatedly to Ormonde to hasten the help from Ireland, and offered to send his younger son, the Duke of York, as a pledge of his good faith;[54] he also wrote to the Pope assuring him that he would stand by whatever treaty his agent Glamorgan should make with the Nuncio.[55] He ordered the councillors of the Prince of Wales to get him safely away to France or Denmark—advice which they disregarded, believing that the boy's departure would be fatal to what was left of the King's party in the West.[56] He was cheered at receiving an intimation from David Leslie that the Scots army would be willing to receive him,[57] but he continued to make surreptitious approaches to the Independent leaders, and he was cast down when Parliament, to which he had sent for a safe-conduct for messengers to discuss terms, refused to grant any passes, " former treaties having been made use of for other ends under pretence of peace." [58] Hoping still to gain time by negotiating, Charles wrote again, this time offering to come to Westminster in person to discuss a settlement if Parliament would assure him that he might come in freedom and safety.[59]

When Montreuil, the new French envoy, reached Oxford on January 2nd, 1646, to urge the King to set aside other projects and make the Covenanters his friends, he found Charles intransigent. He would not in any circumstances recognise Presbyterianism in England: he would rather lose his Crown than his soul. As for abandoning Montrose, which Montreuil saw to be necessary, it was not to be thought of; with overflowing tenderness towards his Scottish champion, he declared that Montrose was like one of his children and he would make no agreement with the Covenanters unless Montrose was accepted too, as he put it, " hand in hand in open daylight."[60] All that Montreuil could get from him after long argument was an undertaking to consider toleration for Presbyterians in England, and to treat with the Covenanters if they would promise safety and honour to Montrose. Montreuil returned to London to find the Scots Commissioners restive, and rumours of the King's secret approaches to them now so widespread that Parliament had increased the forces between Oxford and Newark lest the King try to join the Scots forces besieging that town. The dealings between Charles and the Covenanters were known to the Independent leaders through a correspondent who was privy to all that went on at the Queen's Court in France, while Montreuil's two principal advisers in London, Lord Holland and Lady Carlisle, had never been famous for discretion. His own colleague too, the French resident Sabran, perhaps out of jealousy, made a habit of dropping hints to his English friends, indicating sometimes that the King was coming to London and sometimes that he was joining the Scots.[61]

Since the principal effect of these tales and rumours was to increase the animosity between Parliament and the Scots, they were not altogether harmful: they might even help the King. But hardly had Montreuil returned to London when unexpected disaster from another quarter struck the King's affairs into confusion and destroyed all confidence in his offers. On January 16th, 1646, a draft of the secret treaty with the Irish Confederates reached Westminster.[62] Fate had caught up with the Earl of Glamorgan.

The draft had been found among the papers of the Archbishop of Tuam, killed near Sligo in the previous October, but it had been a little while before the nature of the document was recognised, and longer still before a copy of it reached London. The Marquis of Ormonde in Dublin had been informed of it three weeks earlier, on Christmas Eve. Appalled to discover what Glamorgan had been doing all this while in the King's name, he consulted at once with Digby. Even Digby was shocked at the discovery, though neither he nor Ormonde had any illusions. They both knew the King's handiwork when they saw it. What they had to decide was whether—now the secret was out—he would acknowledge it himself.[63] They rightly decided that he would not, and that the best they could do to save his good name with his Protestant subjects would be immediately to take action against Glamorgan.

The Earl of Glamorgan, all unknowing of the discovery, was still at Kilkenny, where in a daze of reverence for the Nuncio he had involved himself still further in the labyrinth of deception. Under Rinuccini's influence he had made the secret treaty still more favourable to the Irish and had included a clause by which the Lord Lieutenant should in future be a Roman Catholic. The plan was now that the Confederates should publicly accept the Ormonde Treaty, but send privately to the King making it clear that no troops would be sent from Ireland until he ratified not the open Ormonde Treaty, but the secret Glamorgan Treaty on the terms of which alone they would act. To ensure that this blackmail worked, Glamorgan himself was to be in command of the Irish forces intended for England.[64] Well pleased with his success he hurried to Dublin, only to be denounced at the Council table for acting without warrant and placed under arrest.[65]

Ormonde had done what he could to preserve the King's honour but Glamorgan's projected treaty was known in London beforehand. The House of Commons, outraged by this new proof of the King's relations with the Irish, therefore received his urgent appeals for a personal treaty in suspicious silence. Privately, some of the Independent leaders were discussing a project for deposing him in favour of the little Duke of Gloucester under the regency of their friend the Earl of Northumberland.[66] Reports from Paris, received at much the same time as the Irish news, revealed the Queen's attempts to raise money there from the Catholic clergy and the mission of Sir Kenelm Digby to the Vatican. They also revealed, to the great embarrassment of the Scots Commissioners, some of their own recent conspiratorial colloquies with the French envoy. The Scots met the situation as best they could with an emphatic statement that there was no truth whatever in the allegations against them.[67]

The King strove a little longer to redeem the situation, and somehow to maintain at one and the same time his interest with the Independents, the Presbyterians, and the Confederate Irish. On January 29th, 1646, he formally denounced Glamorgan in an official message to Parliament;[68] but he wrote to Ormonde in a milder tone. " Upon the word of a Christian," Charles declared, he had never meant anything to be done without Ormonde's knowledge and consent; yet Glamorgan, he believed, had acted not out of treachery but from excess of zeal and should be handled gently. The King advised that proceedings be opened against him for the look of things, but brought to no conclusion.[69] To Glamorgan himself he wrote in mild reproof of his indiscretion and advised him in future to seek the advice of George Digby in anything he undertook.[70]

Letters from Oxford to Dublin had to be carried across miles of occupied country and over seas patrolled by Scots and Parliamentarian ships. News came intermittently and Ormonde had to act as he thought best, in ignorance of the King's immediate wishes. One thing was clear to him: without troops from Ireland the King was irretrievably lost. But when he tried to resume negotiations with the Irish he found that, influenced by the Nuncio, they would discuss nothing further until Glamorgan was released. Indeed the clerical party had considered marching on Dublin as soon as they heard of Glamorgan's arrest and had been restrained only by the still dominant influence of the more politic lords whom Rinuccini called the " Ormondists."[71] The Confederates were by now deeply divided. Rinuccini had brought over the greater number of the clergy to his point of view, and had created an intransigent block who would not accept in any circumstances the " ignominious and infamous " peace offered by the Marquis of Ormonde.[72] But the Nuncio went further, for when the released Glamorgan reappeared at Kilkenny, he was told that the King's envoy in Rome, Sir

Kenelm Digby, had offered still more advantageous terms, not only freedom of worship and an independent Irish Parliament, but all the strong places of Ireland to be put into Irish hands. Rinuccini was therefore against the conclusion of any treaty until Kenelm Digby should come from Rome.[73]

At a surface view, there seemed much to be said for the Nuncio's resolution to force King Charles to accept a restored Roman Catholic Ireland. Though they were short of money and experiencing some difficulties now in Ulster and Munster, the Confederates held the greater part of the country and were only asking the King to recognise a situation which they had already brought about by force of arms. How indeed, after more than four years of freedom and self-government at Kilkenny, could they be expected to rest satisfied with concessions so meagre as those offered by the Ormonde Treaty?

But the Nuncio and the intransigents who supported him argued as though Ireland were an isolated country in which England had no interest. They forgot that the defeat of the King of England would release the formidable army of Parliament to fight against them. A tentative suggestion had already been made that, when his work in England was done, Lieutenant General Cromwell should proceed to Ireland.[74] Whatever general was chosen, the chances of a Confederate Irish victory would be gravely diminished if they allowed the King to be overthrown in England; the forces which had conquered him would then be released to destroy them also.

Many of the nobility, Irish and Anglo-Irish alike, saw the danger and were supported by the relatively small group of lawyers and professional men among the Confederates. They saw that by postponing the treaty and by striving to get too much, they might lose all. But their opinions were tainted by a too evident self-interest: many of them had acquired land from the spoils of the Church and had, from the first, opposed any settlement which involved the restoration of this plundered property. This element in their opposition made them morally weak against the influence which Rinuccini exercised over the priests and the people.

The influence of these lords, chief among them Lord Muskerry, was for the moment bent upon sending troops to the King, without further delay. With this urgent need in view they reached a complicated interim agreement by which neither the Ormonde nor the Glamorgan treaty was to be accepted pending news from the Vatican, but preparations to help the King were to be made at once. By February, 1646, three thousand men were ready to sail as soon as shipping could be found. Glamorgan attributed this achievement to his own influence and wrote to the Prince of Wales's Council that he had six thousand men (the exaggeration came easily) ready to sail for England. It was fortunate, he added, that Chester was still in the King's hands, ready to receive them.[75]

His information was out of date. Chester had fallen. Lord Byron, unable longer to resist in a starving, hostile town, without fodder or ammunition, had surrendered to Sir William Brereton on February 3rd, 1646.[76] Glamorgan's promises of speedy help came as a mockery to men defeated: his letter was given to the Prince of Wales and his Council as they embarked from Pendennis for the Scilly Isles.[77] The West had been lost to the King.

IV

In the New Year, as soon as the frost relaxed, Fairfax had moved again. The King's Western forces were incapable of resisting. On Goring's departure for France his command of the cavalry had fallen to Lord Wentworth, one of the wildest of the " wild boys." He inherited the feud with Grenvile and their troops ferociously fought each other for the best quarters while Fairfax advanced.[78] " There is so great a fear through the hand of God upon them," wrote Fairfax to his father, " as three of

our men did chase a hundred of them."[79]   On January 15th, 1646,
the Prince's Council in despair called on Hopton to take command of the "dissolute, undisciplined, wicked, beaten army."
Grenvile, with rage in his heart and a cold in his head, refused
obedience, pleaded illness and resigned his command.   Fearing
what thwarted ambition might make him do, the Prince of
Wales had him arrested.   Hopton, resolute in despair, took stock
of his position: he had a little less than two thousand infantry
and about eight hundred cavalry, valiant men, but in great disorder.   Only the Prince of Wales's own horse-guard were still
"very exact upon duty."[80]   The first plan was to advance into
Devon for the relief of Exeter, where Sir John Berkeley still
held out, but four days after Hopton took command, Fairfax
stormed and took Dartmouth. He gave every man of the defeated
garrison half a crown to go in peace to his own home, or three
shillings if he preferred to enlist in the New Model Army.[81]
After Dartmouth, Royalist deserters daily joined his advancing
forces.

The fall of Dartmouth was marked by a miraculous haul of
fishes in the bay, most welcome to the hungry soldiers.[82]   It was
also marked by the capture of a ship with letters from the Queen;
the Captain threw the packet overboard but it was rescued, only
a little blotted, and sent to London. From its contents the Committee of Both Kingdoms learnt further details of the Queen's
projects for raising troops in France—which cannot have perturbed them much for no foreign army was now likely to land
in time to help the King. They also learnt more details of
the intrigue between the Scots Commissioners and the French
envoy on the King's behalf, evidence which embarrassingly contradicted the Commissioners' recent categorical statement that they
were innocent of all dealings with the King.[83]   But confident
in the imminent victory of the New Model, the English leaders
believed they could afford to postpone the reckoning with the
Scots.

The fall of Dartmouth put an end to any immediate hope of

relieving Exeter; Hopton advanced instead into North Devon, hoping to turn the enemy's flank. He fortified himself at Torrington, where on February 16th Fairfax attacked, and fought his way into the town. Hopton himself was wounded in the face and his horse killed: " Had his officers followed his example it would have been a difficult matter for us to enter the town," wrote a judicious professional in the Parliamentary army. Fairfax, no less than Hopton, fought at the head of his men, and nearly perished when, in a thunderclap and a sheet of fire, the roof of Torrington Church went skywards, and came down in an avalanche of burning timber, masonry and lead. It was the Royalist arsenal, eighty-four barrels of gunpowder, fired by Hopton's command. In the resulting disorder, pursuit through the narrow roads beyond Torrington was abandoned and Hopton got his defeated remnant with no baggage, no guns, and very few standards over the Cornish border to Stratton. Here a messenger from France reached him with the empty news that five thousand men were being raised with all speed for the King's help.[84]

In Torrington market-place, when day came, Hugh Peter preached among the wreckage to a people who were by now ready to welcome Fairfax as their deliverer. He marched into Cornwall, entered Launceston, turned along the north Cornish coast, Hopton retreating before him, took Bodmin and seized in Padstow harbour a ship from Ireland with letters from George Digby and Glamorgan. The Irish crew were hanged; the letters were read aloud by Hugh Peter to a large crowd on Bodmin Moor, to whom he explained with his customary eloquence, that the King would have sold them all to murdering Irish Papists, had not the army of Parliament saved them in the nick of time.[85]

Hopton fell back to Truro; the Prince of Wales and his civilian attendants had already escaped by sea. The cavalry officers had turned mutinous and clamoured for surrender before all was lost. Hopton strove for two or three more days to hold them loyal while he got his few remaining guns into Pendennis Castle.[86]   Fairfax, fast approaching, beat up some of the cavalry and, rich in prisoners, sent to him to surrender.[87]   Hopton could do no more: his soldiers would no longer fight, but as the Parliamentarians came in to the outposts beyond Truro, cheerfully welcomed them, saying there was a truce.   At midnight on March 9th Hopton sent an offer to negotiate.   Fairfax, announcing his intention of occupying Truro, asked him to appoint commissioners.   Hopton pulled out of Truro as best he could, leaving hundreds of his men to give a good-natured, drunken reception to the conquerors.   In three days of negotiation, during which his men deserted by dozens to the enemy, officers and all, Hopton agreed to disband his forces and go abroad; the wretched terms were signed on March 13th, 1646, and confirmed over a tactfully mournful supper offered by Fairfax to the vanquished.[88]

Fairfax now summoned Pendennis Castle and was answered by the commander, the aged John Arundel, with rhapsodical defiance.[89]   Leaving " Jack-for-the-King " in this last stronghold of Cornish royalism to be reduced later, Fairfax marched back to Exeter, where Sir John Berkeley still held out, with the King's youngest child, Princess Henrietta, in his care.

All this while the King at Oxford, surrounded by his loyal few, hesitated between alternative courses of despair.   He entertained a wild plan for striking suddenly south-eastwards and capturing one of the Cinque Ports—Hastings, perhaps, the *locus classicus* of invasion—which he would hold until the Queen sent him (" for God's sake as thou lovest me ") five thousand men from France.[90]   Bad news came by every courier.   Belvoir Castle had surrendered and Ashby de la Zouch and Lichfield.   Corfe Castle, defended for months by the widow of Lord Chief Justice Bankes and her squadron of daughters, was lost by treachery. In South Wales the Raglan garrison was penned in by the triumphant forces of General Laugharne who occupied Cardiff and sealed up the coast of South Wales.[91]

At Oxford still from time to time the old gaiety and gallantry

flickered. Mary, daughter of the courtier-poet Aurelian Towns-
end, was the " admired beauty " of the declining Court and the
King himself gave her away at her winter wedding in Christ
Church Cathedral.[92] But the calls of military duty interfered
even with the ordering of the royal Bedchamber. It was Lord
Lindsey's month to attend, and Charles, looking forward to his
cultivated conversation, wrote to hasten his coming and teased
him with the tale of " two fair ladies " impatient to see him.
But Lindsey, in command at Woodstock, could not leave the
garrison for fear of mutiny in his absence.[93]

The King's hopes moved inconstantly from one point to
another as he had news—from London, from Paris, from Scotland and Ireland—of the rifts between his enemies and the plans
of his friends. In the House of Commons the Independents were
in the ascendant, but in the Assembly of Divines and in the City
of London the Presbyterians were strongest, and the animosity
between the two grew daily more bitter. The Presbyterian
divine Thomas Edwards (the " shallow Edwards " of Milton's
contemptuous sonnet) had published late in February a sheaf of
anecdotes about the wilder doings and sayings of the sectaries
under the offensive title of *Gangraena*: it was very good reading,
and very much read. The Covenanters and their friends quoted
it everywhere; the Independents, collectively and individually,
were outraged.

These divisions were cheering to Montreuil as he worked
away at his project for uniting the King, the Covenanters and the
Presbyterians in general. But Charles in Oxford followed the
desires and devices of his own heart. He saw no harm in approaching the Independents as well as the Presbyterians, and on March
2nd he instructed Secretary Nicholas to write to the younger
Vane offering concessions to the sectaries if they would assist
him against their rivals:

" If Presbytery shall be so strongly insisted upon as that there
can be no peace without it, you shall certainly have all the power
my master can make to join with you in rooting out of this

Kingdom that tyrannical government; with this condition that my master may not have his conscience disturbed (yours being free) when that easy work is finished. Lose not this fair opportunity."[94]

Charles wrote to the Queen on the following day assuring her that the monarchy should lose nothing by any concession that he made, nor would he enter into any agreement with the Scots if it meant abandoning the English Church. " The nature of Presbyterian government is to steal or force the Crown from the King's head," he told her, and therefore she must not expect him to yield anything vital to them.[95]

While the King wrote in these terms to his Queen, Vane received with suspicion his message of friendship to the Independents. He knew from his informants in Paris that a grand alliance between the Covenanters and the King was to be engineered from France, and he returned no answer to the royal overtures. In the House of Commons on March 5th the ordinance governing excommunication and the moral jurisdiction of elders and ministers was passed after lengthy debate.[96] It was not wholly satisfactory to many of the English Presbyterians, and not at all to the Scots, because it left the final judgment of moral offences not with ministers and elders but with Parliament, putting the State very emphatically higher than the Church. The Lord Mayor stimulated a petition to Parliament against this reversal of the usual Presbyterian practice, but the Commons would not consider it. The Scots Commissioners noted the resentment of the City and believed that they could count on their friendship if it should come to a break with Parliament.[97]

But while matters seemed to work so well towards a union of Scots and English Presbyterians against the Independents, Charles in Oxford pursued his wilder policies. On March 4th he sent to the Earl of Glamorgan, whom he had publicly repudiated five weeks earlier, a patent secretly creating him Duke of Somerset with the clear indication that he should go on with the Irish treaty.[98] On March 12th he wrote to the Queen expressing the hope that he could destroy Presbyterians and Independents with the help of the Roman Catholics, urging her to hasten the tardy help of the Vatican, and offer to the Pope with the utmost secrecy the abolition of the penal laws in England if he would "heartily and visibly" assist in restoring him to his throne.[99]

One of the King's few remaining commanders, Lord Astley, had got together about two thousand infantry in Wales and was at Worcester, ready to come to Oxford. With this small army the King might make a shift to postpone surrender until French troops were ready, until the Vatican subsidies materialised, until Montrose conquered Scotland again, until the Irish somehow made a landing.

Astley was an experienced soldier and he had the capable Charles Lucas to second him but he had to get from Worcester to Oxford avoiding the attention of Parliamentary garrisons at Gloucester, Evesham and Warwick. Colonel Morgan, governor of Gloucester, had not forces enough to guard all the crossings of the Avon, and Astley and his men got over the river without damage. But Morgan sent in haste to Brereton to help him with cavalry and until Brereton came he delayed Astley's progress by skirmishing on his flanks so that he was still some miles short of Stow on the Wold when night fell on March 20th. At nine that evening Brereton and his cavalry joined Morgan. During the night Astley took up a strong position on the steep flank of the hill below Stow on the Wold, and here, half an hour before day, on March 21st, 1646, Morgan and Brereton attacked him. The Welsh levies, new to the business, put up little fight. Sixteen hundred surrendered with all the arms and ammunition. The cavalry fled towards Oxford. Astley himself, unhorsed and surrounded, gave up his sword to one of Colonel Birch's men. "You have done your work, boys," said the old cavalier, "you may go play, unless you fall out among yourselves."[100]

Next day the King wrote to the Queen that he had "neither force enough to resist, nor sufficient to escape to any secure place." But he had several possibilities still in mind: he asked the Queen to continue her appeals to the Vatican, while he himself wrote once more to Parliament offering to come in person to make peace if they would respect his honour and his person. Alternatively he could still go to the Scots.[101] Montreuil, who had returned to Oxford, pressed this last plan, but in his dejected state the King listened to him without either trust or hope. He knew his own countrymen better than Montreuil could do and was not deceived by the persuasive words of the Scots Commissioners in London, who had made Montreuil believe that a little yielding over the religious question would secure their alliance. Montreuil could not see why Charles so resolutely objected to Presbyterianism and was so unwilling to allow Montrose to be, in his euphemistic phrase, " *eloigné pour quelque temps*."[102]

The King's hope of making a separate peace with the Independents had, however, been quenched by Vane's refusal to reply. His offers to come to London in person were received by Parliament with frigid suspicion. They respectfully informed him that they could not receive him. They thought, probably with justice, that he planned to make himself master of the City by some stroke of policy. The place was choked with distinguished Royalists, some in prison after capture, others at liberty seeking to make their formal peace with Parliament. A sudden movement of these Cavaliers, perhaps helped by the City Presbyterians, and the House of Commons might be overpowered. Parliament ordered the Royalists to leave London and called out the Trained Bands to secure the King's person from danger should he approach.[103] That put an end to his hopes of entering London as a free man. As the alternatives narrowed, he gave in wearily to Montreuil's proposals in favour of the Covenanters. He agreed to listen to their arguments on religion, even to accept anything that was not wholly against his conscience; he would consider the plan of sending Montrose as ambassador to France if they were opposed to reconciliation, and he would order the surrender of his garrison at Newark into their hands, if Montreuil for his part could persuade Leslie's army to receive him with full assurance of his " safety and honour."[104] On April 2nd Montreuil left Oxford for the Scots' camp before Newark, promising to send word for the King to follow as soon as he had arranged for his reception.[105]

Hardly had Montreuil departed when the King's unsteady optimism returned. Perhaps, after all, it would be possible to weave together the disparate parties whose interest it was to support him, to combine the Covenanters, Montrose, and the Confederate Irish in a single alliance. He decided to leave for Newark without waiting for Montreuil's message and only Rupert's unwillingness to escort him on so dubious a venture made him change his mind.[106] He sent off in close succession messages to his remaining champions. He assured Glamorgan that he would ratify all his promises to the Nuncio in return for troops.[107] He informed Ormonde that he was about to join the Scots army who, he trusted, would co-operate with Montrose to help him against his enemies.[108] He wrote to Montrose urging him to march towards the Covenanters' headquarters in England and " take them by the hand."[109]

Politically, if political expediency had been all, this last astonishing suggestion was not wholly unreasonable. The Covenanters had been grossly abused by their English allies: they had been brought into the war when Parliament was *in extremis* but as soon as the danger was over their men had been cheated of their pay, harassed by complaints, forced into poor and inadequate quarters, while their religious views and their political needs had been neglected at Westminster.

For the last two months Lords and Commons had been working out propositions of peace that might ultimately be offered to the King, but the Scots were not consulted until the terms were drawn up and were then told that alterations could not be made. The control of the militia was, as it always had been, the most important of Parliament's demands; but they

wanted this control for themselves alone. The Scots were to
have no share in it. Since England and Scotland were separate
countries, there was of course no argument whatever for allowing the Scots any say in the control of the English army. But it
was none the less disquieting for the Scots to see this hostile and
aggressive English Parliament, with a large army already at its
disposal, officered largely by Independents, resolving to seize
for itself unquestioned control of the armed forces.[110] On this
and on other points the Scots and the House of Commons were
at loggerheads, and the ill-feeling blazed into anger when the
Scots Commissioners on April 11th published an account of
their disagreement on the proposed settlement which was little
less than a denunciation of their Parliamentary allies. Lords and
Commons united to condemn this document and ordered it to
be burnt by the hangman. At the same time they published an
answer in which they accused the Scots of gross indiscipline,
mismanagement of their forces and unwillingness to co-operate
with the English in the prosecution of the war.[111] Short of an
open breach, animosity could go no farther.

The Independent majority in the House of Commons
followed up this insult to the Scots by a more subtle insult to the
Assembly of Divines. The Assembly had petitioned against the
new Ordinance which gave Parliament power over the elders
and ministers of the Church; righteously they argued that elders
and ministers exerted their moral authority *iure divino*, by the
will and appointment of Jesus Christ. The Commons delayed a
fortnight before answering; then they voted the petition a
breach of privilege. After delaying another fortnight they confronted the Divines with a set of questions in which the reasonable,
ironical spirit of John Selden could be clearly detected. The
House of Commons very solemnly asked to be shown those
places in the Scriptures which set forth that the authority
of ministers, elders, national and provincial synods were all
" by the will and appointment of Jesus Christ"; and, in the
event of disagreement between these bodies, it asked which

of the dissidents could be shown to act *iure divino*? Parliament in fact was learnedly and legally fooling the Presbyterian divines.[112]

Thus, if political expediency alone had been considered, the Covenanters might well at this eleventh hour have abandoned their ungrateful allies. That they should, in the King's phrase, "take Montrose by the hand," would have meant too great a sacrifice of pride and principle for them as well as for him. But they might have made concessions which would have enabled the King and the remaining English Royalists to join with them against the Independents and their army. Political expediency, however, played only a small part in their calculations, as the hapless Montreuil was finding to his cost. Between the perfidious English Parliament and the sinful King and his Irish-Popish accomplices, they trod the difficult path that their religious duty dictated. They would be glad enough to get the King into their power, but they made not the least concession to tempt him.

The King, as he saw disaster close in upon him, followed with equal fortitude the dictates of his conscience. Privately at this time he committed a vow to writing, and gave it to the safe-keeping of a trusted servant. He swore solemnly that he would never permit Presbyterianism in England and that, when he should be restored again to his just authority, he would give back to the Church all the property that had been seized by the Crown since the Reformation.[113]

Meanwhile, the April days passed and Montreuil did not return from Newark. The King sent a messenger after him, Michael Hudson, one of his chaplains, a man of ingenuity and daring whom he had used before on dangerous errands. But still no word from Montreuil.[114]

All other news was bad. Sir John Berkeley had sued for terms at Exeter and on April 13th his garrison marched out. "The Western war, I trust in the Lord, is finished," wrote Fairfax.[115] Princess Henrietta and her governess became the prisoners of Parliament. The only disappointment in the campaign had been the escape of the Prince of Wales to Scilly, and his capture seemed certain when a Parliamentary fleet of twenty sail bore down on his place of refuge. For once the Royalists were fortunate; a sudden storm dispersed the Parliamentary ships, and in the welcome interval the Prince and his company put off in one of the King's pirate ships, the *Proud Black Eagle*, and ran before the wind to Jersey.[116] The Prince, pleased with these new adventures, took the helm for two hours under the guidance of Henry Mainwaring, a grizzled sea-rover with the skill of a lifetime in his hands and head.[117] For the time being the Prince was safe and his anxious, exhausted followers could enjoy an Arcadian calm pacing the shady avenues and looking on the green pastures of Jersey, at ease among a " cheerful, good-natured people." The Prince had a small yacht built for him at St. Malo and spent his time learning the art of navigation.[118] The governor of Jersey, Sir George Carteret, was virtually dictator of his small domain by the strength of his fortified castle and the piratical ships which he had at his disposal.[119] But even in the Channel Islands personal quarrels divided the King's friends, and Sir George Carteret would give no help at all to the Royalist governor of Guernsey, Sir Peter Osborne, whom he had left to fend for himself as best he might.[120]

For the time being the Prince was safe, but the King's plight grew hourly more desperate. Within a week of Exeter's fall, Barnstaple, Dunster and St. Michael's Mount surrendered. Leaving the isolated fortress of Pendennis still holding out for the King, Fairfax marched for Oxford. If the King was to escape the closing trap he had no time to lose. His troops in Oxford were demoralised, his garrisons at Woodstock, Banbury, Faringdon and Borstall were unable any longer to get food for man or beast from the sullen country folk; enemy patrols chased them home when they came out to forage. " We had gallant hunting of them from place to place over the hills," wrote a Parliamentary officer.[121]

A more insidious undermining of the King's last supporters had gone on all the winter. Parliament had offered a piece-meal settlement to Royalists by allowing them to compound for their estates—to buy peace and pardon by an outright payment reckoned on the value of their lands. Specially favourable treatment was promised to those who came in to compound before May 1st, 1646. In the spring the King's poor and anxious supporters, by twos and threes, and—in April—by the score bowed to the miserable necessity of saving what could yet be saved.

Not until April 21st did the King have word from Montreuil. The French envoy was utterly cast down. The Scots at Newark had shown themselves " abominable relapsed rogues " and had utterly rejected the terms which their Commissioners in London had suggested. If the King came to them they would promise nothing; they would not protect his servants against seizure by Parliament; they insisted that he accept without reservation and immediately the Presbyterian dispensation. As for Montrose, he was outside all pardon. Montreuil suggested that if he must go into exile, this might be given an honourable colour by sending him as ambassador to France. They scorned the thought. Montreuil humbly admitted now that Charles knew the Scots better than he did and had been right in his doubts. His mission had failed. He could no longer in the circumstances advise the King to go to Newark.[122]

Next day, April 22nd, the King once more appealed to the Independents. He sent to the commanders nearest Oxford, first to Commissary General Ireton, then to the even more extreme Colonel Rainsborough, offering to disband his forces if they could get him an assurance from Fairfax and from Parliament that he could " live and continue King still," and keep his own particular friends in his service.[123] But even while he made the offer he entertained a new and wilder plan of slipping away in disguise to King's Lynn, where he knew there were loyalists who might help him to a ship. Once on the sea, he could sail to join

Montrose in Scotland, or failing that, to Ireland, to Denmark, or to France.[124]

Henry Ireton, baffled by the King's message, communicated it to Cromwell, who was that week at Westminster, and Cromwell was too wary to let his Independent following involve themselves in such an intrigue. The Scots had aroused angry criticism by their disingenuous dealings with the King; the Independents during the winter had been under the same cloud, but here was a chance to demonstrate their plain-dealing loyalty to the common cause. In the House of Commons on April 25th, Cromwell declared the content of the King's message and handsomely apologised for the incorrect behaviour of his friend Henry Ireton in sending it to him rather than directly to Parliament. There had of course been no question of Ireton's making any answer to it or entertaining any thought of a private accommodation.[125]

As far as those at Westminster could see, the King was trapped. Whatever the busy French envoy had planned for him with the Scots had apparently come to nothing. The Independents denied all intention of responding to him. Oxford was shut in by the army and the King's surrender to his Parliament was a matter of time. After so much anxiety, so many changes of fortune, so many losses, so much effort, the long war was at an end.

Already Hugh Peter had preached a sermon of thanksgiving for the peace that (but for the few last strongholds of war) once again lapped the countryside. " Oh, the blessed change we see, that can travel now from Edinburgh to the land's end in Cornwall, who not long since were blockt up at our doors. To see the highways occupied again; to heare the Carter whistling to his toiling team; to see the weekly Carrier attend his constant mart; to see the hills rejoycing, the valleys laughing."[126]

Four days after Cromwell's announcement in the House of Commons, on April 29th, the King's escape was reported in Parliament.[127] Whither he had gone, where he now was, no one knew. At once the momentary calm dissolved; Presbyterians and Independents, English and Scots looked upon each other with angry alarm. Someone had betrayed the common cause; someone was concealing the King. At first it was generally thought that he must have reached London. For fear of some sudden rising, a review of the City Trained Bands was postponed, and it was proclaimed throughout the City that anyone concealing the King was guilty of a capital crime.[128] Not a stir, not a ruffle greeted this proclamation; no informer moved; not a household behaved mysteriously. The King was not in the City.

For a week the angry tension mounted; then on Wednesday, May 6th, 1646, the House of Commons learned, in a letter from their army before Newark, that the King, early on the morning of May 5th, had ridden into the Scottish quarters at Southwell and given himself up. The Scots themselves announced the event twenty-four hours later. The King's coming was, they said, " matter of much astonishment " to them, and they assured their English brethren that they would not " make use of this seeming advantage for promoting any other ends than are expressed in the Covenant."[129]

Parliament peremptorily requested the Scots to transfer the King to the custody of the English garrison at Warwick, broke open the letters of the Scots Commissioners in London and arrested their principal secretary.[130] This was without effect, for presently they received word from Newark that the King had commanded his garrison there to surrender to the Scots who were now marching triumphantly northwards, bearing their prisoner with them. In vain the English protested against the removal of their King: they were paying dearly for their neglect of the Scots army and disparagement of the Scots alliance. Leslie's troops, with the King in their midst, had gone two days on their northward march before Parliament's message of protest had left London, and they were secure, with their royal prize, within the city of Newcastle long before the messengers caught up with them.

The English did not deceive themselves. The King was still the King, the essential piece in the game without whom no final settlement could be made. The Scots, in gaining power over his person, had won the war more truly than if they had been victorious, unaided, in every battle. The rise of the New Model Army, the battles of Naseby and Langport and Stow on the Wold, so many mercies from the hand of God—and all to give the victory to the Scots.

CHAPTER TWO

THE KING AND THE SCOTS

THE Scots were speaking the bare truth when they declared that the King's coming had taken them by surprise. Their negotiations with Montreuil had ended in deadlock, and Charles himself had not known, when he left Oxford, what he intended to do. On April 26th, 1646, he had told his Council—the last he was ever to call—that he would probably go to London. He left with two companions only, the chaplain Michael Hudson, and John Ashburnham, one of the grooms of the Bedchamber, resourceful men who knew the country well. Late at night the King had his hair cut short and put on a false beard and a suit of drab clothes. For this belittlement the Cavalier poet John Cleveland would find a startling image:

> Oh the accursed stenography of fate!
> Our Princely eagle turned into a bat.[1]

At three in the morning of April 27th the governor of Oxford, Sir Thomas Glemham, opened the East Gate to let Hudson and Ashburnham out of the beleaguered town. " Farewell, Harry ! " he said to the serving man who at a little distance respectfully followed them, with their luggage strapped to his saddle.[2]

The little party made first towards London, passing the enemy outposts without arousing suspicion. The King hoped vainly for some sign from London and lingered along the ridge from Harrow to Hillingdon looking towards Westminster. Then he changed his mind and made north by St. Albans to Market

Harborough, where he hoped that Montreuil would send him word that the Scots had softened their demands. Finding no news at Market Harborough he advanced cautiously to Stamford, then, sending Michael Hudson to seek Montreuil, he turned east with Ashburnham, following his third and wildest plan, that for embarking at King's Lynn. The news of his escape was by this time public and he did not travel by day in case of discovery. At Downham in Norfolk he and Ashburnham waited four days at the Swan Inn for news from Hudson, asked for a fire in their room, and to the great curiosity of the innkeeper burnt a number of papers. A barber, called in to attend them, noticed that they had been trying to cut their hair with knives. Fortunately Hudson returned and hurried them away before questions were asked.

According to Hudson, Montreuil could get nothing in writing from the Scots, but he had noted down their verbal promises which seemed a little better than before: they said they would receive the King with safety and honour, would not wrong his conscience and would let him keep Hudson and Ashburnham with him. On this assurance the King made for Newark; he had no alternative, for he was being looked for everywhere and could never have escaped by sea.

They travelled at night and deviously, paused for brief refreshment at Little Gidding but dared not stay long in this haven of Anglican peace. They spent a night in an ale-house at Copingford, where they shared the hearth with the innkeeper, his wife and children. At six in the morning of May 5th they reached Montreuil's quarters at the Saracen's Head at Southwell. He had gone out to look for them and missed them by the way. Until his return the King lay down on his bed and slept.[3]

Montreuil had made his last arrangements about the King with the elderly Earl of Dunfermline,[4] who carried little weight with his fellow Covenanters. But the principal Commissioner whom the King found at Southwell was the Earl of Lothian. A cosmopolitan young man, bred at Court, where his father had long been a prominent figure, he knew the world, was a dilettante of the arts and had been sent ambassador to France by the Covenanters in 1643; on his return he had been arrested in Oxford, an action which he did not forgive. He greeted his sovereign with hard good manners, making very sure that he should feel the punitive iron hand within the glove of ceremony. The Covenanters saw immediately what they had to do: first, to get their prize out of reach of the English, then to compel him to repudiate Montrose, accept the Covenant, and give his sovereign authority to the making of such a religious settlement in both countries as they desired to see. The King, they argued, " would never have come hither if he had not resolved to give us satisfaction in our just desires." They denied any formal agreement with Montreuil and at once assailed the King about his religion. Charles, hoping to mollify them, ordered the governor of Newark to surrender without delay, and by the evening of May 6th the terms were signed.[5] Three days later the Scots started for Newcastle, taking the King with them. On the journey one of their ministers preached before him on a text from the second book of Samuel:

> And the men of Israel answered the men of Judah, and said, " We have ten parts in the King, and we have also more right in David than ye; why then did ye despise us, that our advice should not be first had in bringing back our King? "[6]

Such words augured well for the love between the Scots and the King, but he found within a few days that they expected him to sign the Covenant. They had agreed not to force his conscience, but preaching at him, harrying him, arguing with him was not the same as forcing. Charles endured all with studied equanimity.[7] Meanwhile Lothian and his colleagues demanded that Montrose be compelled to submit to the Estates, who had already sentenced him to death by hanging. As an afterthought they asked the King to admit to a debt of thirty-six thousand pounds for the property destroyed by his so-called Lieutenant Governor of

Scotland. Montreuil intervened to suggest that Montrose and Alaster Macdonald be allowed to go with their troops to the French King. Lothian, with a sneer, answered that he honoured the King of France too much to thrust a gang of brigands on him.[8]

The King had not been three days in Newcastle before the Earl of Callander warned Ashburnham that he and Hudson should escape before they were handed over as prisoners to the English. On the hint they fled, Ashburnham carrying with him the first letter Charles had been able to write to the Queen.[9]

The King ventured now to hope that Parliament, to prevent a Scots triumph, would come to an agreement with him. As a gesture of appeasement he ordered the garrison of Oxford to surrender, and wrote to Parliament protesting his ardent desire for a general peace and the reformation of religion, his unwillingness to make division between them and the Scots, and his readiness to accept the terms he had rejected at Uxbridge, more especially that the control of all military appointments would be, for the next seven years, in Parliament's hands. At Westminster the Lords and the City were favourable, but the Commons, still dominated by the Independents, remained immovable, and would not agree to treat.[10]

The King's persistent optimism withered in the barren soil of the North. Throughout his troubles he had always been surrounded by respectful attendants, and in the last months of disaster their loyalty had lapped him in an atmosphere of melancholy but soothing devotion. Now, suddenly, he was with men who openly blamed and accused him, few of whom he liked, none of whom he trusted. Through the good offices of Montreuil he could still write to the Queen, and to her he poured out his despair. This was what had come of the French plan for making him go to the Scots: he was now alone, without a friend, "barbarously baited" by the Covenanters, who would clearly do nothing to make him King again. He implored her to have the Prince of Wales fetched away from Jersey and brought to her in safety: would that she could do as much for him.[11]

In these conditions even the Earl of Lanark, Hamilton's younger brother and tool, was welcome to him. Lanark, once his Secretary of State in Scotland, had joined the Covenanters in 1644 and had been responsible for handing over his successor in office, the Royalist Sir Robert Spottiswoode, to execution.[12] But at least the King had known Lanark from his youth, and found him respectful and well-mannered. A timid hope struck root: he might make himself a party in Scotland with the help of the Hamiltons. He sent word by Lanark that he would be glad to receive his elder brother once more into his favour.[13]

In Scotland the King's champions Montrose and Macdonald still fought on. Macdonald was raiding the outlying territories of Argyll and Hamilton, the Isles of Arran and Bute, and the peninsula of Kintyre. The Campbells, weakened by their losses at Inverlochy, could not hold their own. The Macdonalds levied toll on the fishing villages and settled in to stay as long as food and tribute were forthcoming.[14] Argyll, who depended on this country for the supply of oatmeal and herrings, which he regularly sent to the Scots forces under Monro in Ulster, was perturbed enough to set out for Ireland to see what should and could be done. On his way from Edinburgh to the west he found at Stirling a regiment of Campbells who had got the worst of a brush with the Atholl men, under Montrose's cousin Inchbrakie, at Callander.[15] The Royalists were still very active in Scotland.

They were active and they were numerous, but they were not united. Montrose had tried in vain to persuade Huntly to join in active co-operation with him, but Huntly claimed an independent command and conducted an ineffectual war of his own, while his younger son, the ruffianly Lord Lewis Gordon, wasted the country from Speyside to Inverness in defiance of Montrose.[16] But Seaforth, chief of the Mackenzies, after long wavering, declared for the King. Montrose went north to consult with him and for a brief moment it looked as though the country beyond Inverness might rise. Seaforth issued a manifesto against the party of Argyll and was rumoured to have five thousand men under arms, but the putative five thousand had dwindled considerably before Montrose got them as far as Inverness to lay siege to it. For the first time in his campaigns he had a train of artillery—guns shipped by the Queen—which " battered hot " upon the town.[17] But he could not stand against the well-equipped force sent by the Covenanters to relieve Inverness. The heart was no longer in him for the risks and miracles of the previous year and he took refuge in the Grampians.[18]

The immediate outlook for the Scottish Royalists was not hopeful, but so long as Montrose was at liberty in the mountains the Covenanters did not feel secure. Should new Irish forces, whose coming was rumoured, land in Kintyre and join with Macdonald: should this Irish army push through into Atholl and join with the Royalists there: should Montrose resume his shaken authority over them all, the Covenanters might again find themselves in grave distress. Hence, therefore, the pressure they put on the King at Newcastle to make his champion lay down arms.

As the King's fortunes darkened, he brooded on his betrayal of Strafford: believing that God was punishing him for this atrocious fault,[19] he would not repeat it in a different form by ordering Montrose to make an unconditional surrender and go meekly to the gallows. Lanark, who understood this scruple, persuaded his colleagues to alter their demand. Let them agree that the " excommunicate traitor James Graham " might go into exile and ask the King only to order him to disband his army. This satisfied Charles and on May 19th he sent the necessary order to Montrose. In Edinburgh they rang bells and lit bonfires while, unaware as yet of what the King had done, Montrose and Seaforth mustered their Highlanders for the summer's war.[20]

Argyll, by this time, was back from Ireland, and before the

end of May had joined the King at Newcastle. The crisis of his career had come, and he knew it. In his seven years' guidance of Covenanting policy he had been sometimes unfortunate but rarely mistaken. He had out-manœuvred the King in 1641 and secured for the Covenanters all the key positions in the state. He had skilfully prevented the growth of a moderate, or a Royalist, party by destroying confidence in the King. He had sustained the Scots army in Ulster and thus staked out for his countrymen a substantial claim on the spoils of re-conquered Ireland. He had husbanded the resources of the Covenanters by remaining neutral in the English war for more than a year, and had entered the war only on condition that the English paid the Scots army in the field, and made a peace which extended and confirmed the doctrine and discipline of the Presbyterian Church.

From that moment things had gone less smoothly. The Scots had not been successful enough in war to hold the English true to the alliance. The successes of the New Model Army in England and of Montrose in Scotland had each in a different way destroyed the reputation of the Covenanting soldiers. Argyll himself had been unfortunate. A conscientious chief, he was deeply distressed by the torrent of trouble that had come down on clan Campbell in the last two years. But the King's surrender should mark a change of fortune: all might yet go well. If Argyll handled the new situation with his usual skill the Covenant should triumph throughout the three Kingdoms, and the great work of reform be completed to the lasting credit of Scotland and the glory of God.

Power and position were not indifferent to Argyll, but he believed—like the King in another sphere—that he was the instrument of Heaven, predestined to wield such power, and under obligation to wield it well. He did what he could to discover and carry out the will of God, and, like the King, rarely spent less than two hours a day at his devotions. " Very civil and cunning," the King described him to the Queen;[21] but there was between these two men who deeply and rightly distrusted each other a certain similarity of temperament. Both had oblique and complicated minds, matched with great sincerity of spirit. Both were prepared to deceive and prevaricate in the good cause, just so far and no farther. But Argyll, unlike the King, was a clever man.

The immediate objective was to compel or persuade the King to accept the Presbyterian system. The veteran Alexander Henderson was sent for to accomplish this great work, assisted by four other ministers. Every two or three days the King exchanged written arguments with Henderson, and took part in verbal debates with the whole team, until he found some of them so offensive that he would speak no more with any except Henderson and Robert Blair. These two were always civil and would from time to time fall on their knees and beseech him not to harden his heart.[22] But he had hardened his heart, and although he bore with Henderson and tolerated Blair, he hated the unfamiliar pressure of argument and had no intention of yielding. " I never knew what it was to be barbarously baited before," he wrote to the Queen, " all I can do is, but delaying of ill. . . . All the comfort I have is in thy love and a clear conscience."[23]

" Delaying of ill " was now his best hope until something happened to save him. Montreuil went back to the French Court with news of the disaster their policy had brought on the King. Charles played for time, spinning out the argument on Church government, carefully annotating and answering the memoranda submitted to him by Henderson. On ecclesiastical points he could indefinitely prolong the debate. On points of policy, delay was not so easy. A crisis arose over Ireland in the second week in June.

In that brief moment of illusion when the King had believed he could persuade the Covenanters to join with Montrose and the Irish against the English, he had written to the Marquis of Ormonde to explain the plan. Ormonde, who did not know for some weeks that this project had been abandoned, communicated it to Monro, the general of the Scots forces in Ulster. Monro, ignorant of the negotiations between Montreuil and his country-men, and righteously indignant that the King should wish the Covenanting troops to join hands with the excommunicate James Graham and his Irish butchers, sent the letter on to Parlia-ment, where it was read on June 6th, 1646. The Scots Com-missioners, embarrassed at yet more evidence of their past deal-ings with the King, asserted that Monro's delivery of the letter to Parliament was proof enough that they had never entertained so monstrous a plan.[24] To remove all doubt of their complicity with the Irish they compelled the King to write commanding Ormonde to cease treating with the Confederates, and to re-iterate to Montrose the order to disband which had not yet been obeyed. Charles had no means of conveying to either of these loyal servants that he was acting under duress.[25]

He strove none the less to snatch a small advantage from the evil moment by widening the rift between Parliament and the Scots. He wrote to Westminster freely offering once more to treat with the English on whatever terms they chose to present, and enclosing a general order of surrender to be sent to his few remaining garrisons in England and Wales.[26]

While Parliament brooded over Monro's revelation, a disaster had fallen on him in Ulster which suddenly and gravely changed the face of affairs in Ireland. Owen Roe O'Neill, who had been quiescent in Ulster for some time, moved into action. Exhorted by the Nuncio and strengthened by some of the supplies he had brought, O'Neill marshalled his men for attack. Monro, pinched for lack of fodder, marched from Belfast to try what " victuals or cattle " he could wrest from the Irish. On June 5th O'Neill barred his way across the Blackwater at Benburb; evasion might have been possible, but Monro's men, though weak through the shortages they had long endured, were determined to fight. O'Neill, experienced veteran of many European campaigns, had drawn up his troops, almost all infantry, where rough ground and furze bushes would hamper the attackers. It was late afternoon, about six, before the battle started, and O'Neill's men withstood the Scottish onslaught for over two hours. At sunset, when the failing light robbed Monro of the advantage of his firearms, O'Neill ordered his infantry to charge. The tired cavalry of the Scots retreated before this new attack and, in the thickening dusk, fell foul of their infantry, converting retreat into rout. They left six cannon on the field, almost all their muskets and baggage, twenty-two standards, and many dead.

" The Lord of Hosts had a controversy with us to rub shame on our faces, till once we shall be humbled," wrote Monro, while at Kilkenny the Nuncio celebrated a *Te Deum* in the reasonable belief that the Scots were driven out of Ulster, and in the less reasonable hope that the Confederate Irish would now be able to win the war for themselves without signing any peace with the Protestant Ormonde. His hope that the final liberation of Catholic Ireland was at hand was echoed afar off in Rome, where a *Te Deum* was sung for the victory of the great O'Neill in the basilica of Santa Maria Maggiore.[27]

The Scottish defeat at Benburb brought home to the much divided English Parliament the realisation that, whatever their differences with the Covenanters, they could not break with them while the Irish danger lasted. After five years, it was high time to make a settlement at home and send an effective army to Ircland to quell the rebellion and re-establish Anglo-Scottish property rights and the Protestant religion. They gave orders to several officers of the Army to start recruiting volunteers for Ireland now that the English war was over.[28] The recriminations of the last months were silenced before this reminder of the Irish danger, and when, in the latter half of June, Argyll appeared at Westminster, he was received without hostility. English and Scots set to work drafting the terms they would jointly offer to the King.

Since the King had given himself into the power of the Scots, his remaining garrisons had one by one surrendered—Woodstock before the end of April, Borstall House and Banbury,

Ludlow, Carnarvon, Anglesey and Beaumaris in May and June. Fairfax, with the besieging army round Oxford, heralded negotiations with the governor by presenting venison, veal, lamb, capons and butter to the young Duke of York, who was still within the town.[29] Cromwell, while the siege dragged on, sent for his eldest daughter Bridget, a large, plain, serious girl who took after her father, and married her, on June 15th, to the equally earnest and formidable Henry Ireton. His paternal advice on marriage was of a kind sympathetic to these devout young people: " Let not husband, let not anything, cool thy affections after Christ. I hope he will be an occasion to inflame them. That which is best worthy of love in thy husband is that of the image of Christ that he bears. Look on that, and love it best, and all the rest for that."[30]

Ten days later the terms of the surrender of Oxford were concluded. The Duke of York was to join his brother and sister in honourable captivity at St. James's. The Princes Rupert and Maurice were to leave the country. The garrison marched out with the honours of war, preceded by sad coachloads of ladies and gentlemen, the major and minor officials, the attendants and aspirants to favour, all that were left of the King's war-time Court.[31]

A few garrisons still held out. Sir Thomas Tyldesley defended Lichfield Cathedral and close; Henry Washington bade the rebels defiance at Worcester; alone of the strong places which had once ringed Oxford, Wallingford under Thomas Blagge remained unreduced. Sir John Owen held Conway in despite of the persuasions of Archbishop Williams who, seeing that all was now useless, was trying to make the best peace he could in the interests of his poor countrymen of North Wales; in the Welsh marches Sir Henry Lingen at Goodrich and the Marquis of Worcester at Raglan vainly maintained their castles for the King; John Arundel and his long-enduring garrison at Pendennis held grimly on to this last landing-place in Cornwall lest troops should come from abroad, but they were desperate for lack of food; the Channel Islands and the Scilly Isles were still for the King; on the lone rock of Lundy Sir Thomas Bushell postponed surrender and the Earl and Countess of Derby were in undisturbed possession of the Isle of Man.

II

The war was over and the King's party beyond all hope defeated. It seemed that nothing more remained to him but to accept whatever settlement his Scots and English opponents agreed to offer him. In the third week of June, Parliament completed a final draft of its terms. They demanded that he accept the Covenant, abolish the Episcopal church and consent to such reform in religion as the Scots and English should agree upon. They asked that restrictions, fines and penalties be imposed upon Roman Catholics in England and Scotland, which, together with the compulsory education of their children by approved Protestants, would within a short while extinguish their religion altogether. The King was, further, to surrender all control over the armed forces into the hands of Parliament for twenty years. (At Uxbridge the term had been seven years only.) Finally, they made void all titles created since January, 1642, and added a list of Royalists totally or partially exempted from pardon which included by name or definition all his principal supporters in the two Kingdoms.[32]

The projected treaty was the hybrid production of two different ideas. The clause that the King should sign the Covenant was inserted to please the Scots; to have the King in person Covenant-bound was to gain the greatest possible security for the Presbyterian Church of Scotland. As for the religious settlement of England, that, as the relevant clause made clear, had yet to be decided. If the religious terms were not wholly satisfactory to the Scots, they were not unsatisfactory either. But the military clause still deeply disturbed them;[33] neither the past history of the two nations, nor their experience of the last five years, gave them any certainty that an English Parliament in absolute control of the armed forces might not use its military power to coerce Scotland. From their point of view, it would be at least very much safer to have the armed forces of England controlled by a King whom they had bound by the Covenant.

The insistence of the Scots on the control of the King's religion and of the English on the curtailment of his military power reflected the different political needs of the two nations. The military problem was the essential problem in England, as Pym had seen in 1641. At the end of the war, as at the beginning, what mattered to Parliament was to take out of the King's hands the means which he might use to re-establish and extend his authority. The war itself had shown the reality of the danger; the King's opponents did not forget how near they had been to defeat in the terrible summer of 1643, or how ruthlessly the King had marshalled and used his military power against them, or for that matter the frank statements of the intention to control his people by force of arms that he and his Queen had made in their letters. The Scots, on the other hand, had no need to take away from the King a power he had never in Scotland been able to exercise. Effective military power, as Scotland's history of armed rebellion clearly showed, lay not with the King but with nobles, chiefs and landowners. What mattered in Scotland was to bind the King *morally* so that he could not, as Scots Kings had commonly done, appeal to one faction against another, but would be docile to the party in power.

The new terms reflected a genuine attempt on the part of the English Parliament to reach agreement with allies who had once again grown powerful. The Scots Commissioners were no less anxious than the English to achieve at least the appearance of unity, partly because of the Irish danger, and partly because they recognised in the King's actions a familiar pattern of policy. So long as they were at odds with the English Parliament the King could indeed play the traditional game of encouraging one party against the other, creating a division and yielding to the demands of neither. Within forty-eight hours of receiving the terms from Parliament, they approved and sent them back.

Argyll in person carried them to the House of Lords, where, on June 25th, 1646, he made a speech impressive alike for its frankness and forbearance. Certainly, he admitted, there were details in these propositions that were not wholly to the liking of the Scots, but this was no time to delay the making of peace, and they were willing, therefore, to let the propositions go forward. He gave thanks to God that, in alliance, the two nations had achieved so much. Had the English, in the time of the Bishops' Wars, deserted the religious cause of Scotland, questionless the Scots would have been in great trouble; had the Scots, in the darkest time of the late war, deserted the English, " your Lordships all know what might have been the danger." Therefore, he urged them, " let us hold fast that union which is happily established between us; and let nothing make us again two, who are so many ways one; all of one language, in one island, all under one King, one in Religion, yea, one in Covenant." As for the aspersions recently cast upon the Scots for taking the King's part, he assured them that their " natural affection to his Majesty " made them hope that he might be " rather reformed than ruined," and the monarchy " rather regulated than destroyed." In such hopes as these, he trusted the English were of the same mind. For the rest, he pointed out with modesty and tact, that the indiscipline of the Scots army so much complained of in England could best be cured if Parliament would assure to them adequate quarters and supplies for the rest of their short stay.[34]

The promptitude of the Scots in accepting the terms and the good sense of this admirable speech from the acknowledged leader of the Covenanters went far to heal the breach between the allies. Argyll had a firm grasp of the disparate elements in the situation. He knew the King well enough to realise that he would be as unwilling to divest himself of his military power as to sign the Covenant: there was no need to haggle over this question with the English, when the King would do it for them. Meanwhile the Scots possessed the King. The English could put little pressure on him to accept their terms, but the Scots could work on him, day and night, to sign the Covenant. When he had done so, they might break with the English: not before.

III

Those who drew up the terms in London calculated that the King had lost the war and knew that he had lost it. But Charles, forewarned of the character of the terms which were to be put before him, cast about for means to renew the conflict. During July he wrote to the Queen and Ashburnham urging them to contrive means for his escape to France;[35] to the Governor of Worcester, Colonel Washington, asking him to hold out for another month;[36] and to Glamorgan in Ireland offering once more to put himself wholly in his hands and those of the Papal Nuncio[37]—a hint that he would accept any treaty they should decide upon.

At Worcester, Colonel Washington had surrendered on the day that the King wrote his letter,[38] but from Ireland the desolate King might still extract some cause for hope. The faithful Ormonde was working towards a treaty with the Confederate Irish, with Lord Digby to encourage and advise him, while Glamorgan continued his manœuvres with the Nuncio, planned journeys to Italy or France for further help and promised twenty warships, ten thousand muskets and forty thousand pounds by midsummer. The estimate was ludicrous, because ever since Charles had been compelled in January officially to repudiate Glamorgan, the Nuncio, while using him to cross Ormonde's schemes, had quietly exerted his influence to prevent any Irish soldiers being sent to the inconstant King. Even the sanguine George Digby doubted Glamorgan's powers of performance and greeted his promises with an ironical prayer: " Lord, increase our faith."[39]

Immediately on his coming to Dublin, Digby had appointed himself the principal architect of the King's Irish policy. He turned his dazzling charm alternately on Ormonde's council, on the Confederate leaders at Kilkenny and, less successfully, on the suspicious Nuncio. He managed, to Glamorgan's annoyance, to secure money, ships and a body of three hundred men from the Confederates, with whom he sailed away to fetch the Prince of Wales from Jersey. Arrived in Jersey, Digby found the Prince's councillors unwilling to let him go to Ireland. After scandalising Edward Hyde by the suggestion that they allow him to kidnap the Prince, he sailed on to France to consult the Queen, leaving his Irish troops behind in Jersey without a penny to support them.[40]

During his short stay in Paris he irradiated the Queen's Court with the sunshine of his hopes. He assured her that the treaty with the Confederate Irish was concluded, and that they would shortly send twelve thousand men to join Montrose in Scotland, while Argyll would not delay to add his Campbells to this new Highland-Irish army. Believing these chimeras, Digby was able to tell Cardinal Mazarin with great conviction that the French Crown had nothing to lose by supporting King Charles, who was in a fair way to regain his throne through the joint help of the Catholic Irish and the Covenanting Scots.[41] Mazarin was not deceived. He knew from the gloomy reports of the French envoy how ill the Scots had received the King, but he was growing anxious lest the total destruction of the King and the establishment of an aggressive English Republic should be damaging to France and he saw a useful possibility of gaining a strategic foothold on the coast of Ireland. He agreed therefore to help the King if the Lord Lieutenant, Ormonde, could made an effective alliance with the Confederates. Digby completed his work by seeing the Papal

Nuncio in Paris and asking him to use his influence to have Rinuccini recalled because his intervention did only harm to the King's, and so to the Irish, cause.[42]

On his way back to Ireland Digby landed again on Jersey bearing the Queen's request that her son be sent to her. This occasioned an argument so violent in the Prince's Council, that the meeting was suspended by the Prince himself. He was now sixteen years old, and took decision into his own hands; acting on the authority of a letter privately received from his father eleven months previously, he resolved to re-join the Queen. He left on June 25th for France, while his disapproving councillors stayed behind in Jersey, where Edward Hyde was already beginning work on his History of the Rebellion.[43]

Lord Digby, early in July, was back in Dublin, where he conveyed to Ormonde that, since the King was now in captivity, the Queen was henceforward to be considered as exercising his authority in all questions of policy. More important still for the harassed Lord Lieutenant was the knowledge that France had promised help if he could but conclude his treaty with the Confederates. This promise, which was explicitly confirmed by the French envoy at Kilkenny, swayed the greater number of the Confederate leaders towards the Ormonde Treaty.[44]

Unhappily, Glamorgan at the same time received the King's promise to place himself unreservedly in the hands of the Nuncio, and interpreted this as a direct incitement to overthrow the Ormonde Treaty and replace it by that very treaty of his own which had previously been repudiated. Charles was thus himself instrumental in destroying the alliance with the Irish Confederation which after nearly three years of laborious work Ormonde had brought into being. On July 30th Lord Muskerry and his colleagues, having ratified the treaty in defiance of the Nuncio, Ormonde had it formally proclaimed in Dublin. At long last it seemed that the Irish army was ready to come into England, and since the port of Conway under Sir John Owen still held out for the King, they had a landing-place assured to them. But Rinuccini had been working on the Irish clergy since the winter to prevent the acceptance of the Treaty by the people, and he had with no little skill played on the quarrels and divisions of the Supreme Council. Ormonde was soon to learn that the acceptance of his terms by Muskerry was no guarantee that they could be enforced on the Confederates.[45]

All this while the King at Newcastle, playing for time, pursued his desultory religious argument with Henderson. On a sullen day in July the Duke of Hamilton came to him. Their reconciliation after Hamilton's long imprisonment was awkward. Both were at a loss, blushed, faltered and fell silent, but the initial embarrassment once over, Charles called Hamilton to him and in half an hour's talk seemed to have repaired their broken friendship. Hamilton added his diplomatic persuasion to the arguments of the ministers: let the King but accept the Presbyterian way of church government and the Scots would help him to gain better terms, on all other matters, from the victorious English Parliament.[46]

The advice of Hamilton was not unexpected; the King was more oppressed by the entreaties of his wife and the pressure of the French government. Mazarin was perturbed at the ill-success of Montreuil's mission; he had imagined that a wholesome respect for France would have induced the Covenanters to follow the course he indicated to them and join wholeheartedly with the King. Their conduct he partly attributed to Montreuil's inexperience and he now sent an older man, Jean de Bellièvre, as ambassador extraordinary with instructions to tell the Scots in no uncertain language that they had greatly offended France and would have the hostility of their one-time ally to reckon with unless they lowered their demands on the unhappy King. For the rest, Mazarin instructed Bellièvre to work assiduously towards making a breach between Presbyterians and Independents. The King's salvation was, he believed, to be found only with the former and the King must be saved. An English Republic, which would in all probability be strong enough to tax its subjects for a maritime war, would be a much more uncomfortable neighbour than the chastened and impoverished English King was ever likely to be.[47]

Mazarin, though he over-estimated the influence and coercive power of France, wrote otherwise as a practical statesman, weighing and considering real dangers and real possibilities. Queen Henrietta Maria was, however, allowed to add her advice to that given to Bellièvre. She, poor woman, following Digby, declared that if Charles would but declare for Presbytery, he could easily unite the Covenanters, the Irish and Montrose to fight for him. Or if this failed, then the Independents should be made to break with the Presbyterians and to join with the Irish and Highlanders.[48] Her ideas were as remote from reality as her husband's. Neither appeared capable of understanding that the Covenanters and the Irish could not by any compulsion be brought into the same alliance. The only difference between the Queen and her husband was that the King, though he did not credit his adversaries with any scruples of conscience, had an active conscience himself. The Queen credited neither the Scots nor the King with such troubles—were they not all heretics? did it matter what they swore?—and was distracted by her husband's obstinacy in refusing the Covenant.

When, in July, the Prince of Wales joined her in Paris a new anxiety assailed the King; it was possible that his wife and her headstrong councillors would try to save him against his will, by making those very concessions, in the name of her son, that he refused to make himself. He wrote therefore to those about the Prince, to Lord Culpeper, who attended him, Jack Ashburnham and the Queen's trusted servant Jermyn such a command as he believed they could not disregard. "I conjure you by your unspotted faithfulness, by all that you love, by all that is good, that no threatenings, no apprehensions of danger to my person, make you stir one jot from any foundation, in relation to that authority which (my Son) is born to. I have already cast up what I am like to suffer, which I shall meet, by the Grace of God, with that constancy that befits me. Only I desire that consolation, that assurance from you, as I may justly hope that my cause shall not end with my misfortune, by assuring me that misplaced pity to me do not prejudice my Son's right." The two principal points on which the King would never yield were the control of the militia and the government of the Church—and of the two the Church was the more vital " for people are governed by pulpits more than the sword."[49]

His determination not to yield one jot to the Presbyterians was no mere whim, no capricious preference of one doctrine to another. He firmly and justly believed that the Presbyterian way of church government was incompatible with the sacred authority which God had vested in the King. But at Newcastle, with the Scots, he was for the first time in his life surrounded by men as fanatical as himself, without escape or respite from their company. For the first time he saw, undaunted and with dreadful clarity, what could happen to the anointed King alone among enemies. He did not yet expect or foresee that he would pay for his convictions with his life; he was by nature too changeable and too sanguine to allow such an idea to gain a deep hold on him. But henceforward he reckoned it among the possibilities.

On July 30th, 1646, a week after he had carefully coded this message and smuggled it out, the Commissioners from Parliament reached Newcastle headed by the Earl of Pembroke. Charles listened to the terms, which he had long since decided to reject, and asked if the Commissioners had power to discuss them. They answered that they had power only to carry back his answer. " An honest trumpeter might have done as much," said the King, looking with hostility at the turncoat Pembroke and his pompous deputation.[50]

The Scots, as in honour bound to their allies, urged him to accept, and the Chancellor Loudoun used the outspoken language to which the King was now accustomed. If he refused the terms, Loudoun assured him, " you will lose all your friends in the

Houses, lose the City and all the country; England will join against you as one man; they will . . . depose you and set up another government; *they will charge us to deliver your Majesty to them.*" Here was the real threat, for, Loudoun went on, " if you lose England by your wilfulness you will not be permitted to come and reign in Scotland." Changing from menaces to persuasion, he told the King that there were indeed elements in the proposed treaty that the Scots did not like, but in the interests of peace men must sink their differences.[51]

Charles knew well that the Scots did not like all the terms of the treaty. The mistake he made was in believing that they disliked it so much that, in the last resort, they would break with Parliament and side with him. He took Loudoun's threat to surrender him to the English as empty bluster designed to frighten him into taking the Covenant as the price of Scots help. He answered Parliament's propositions with a refusal, thinly disguised as a request for delay, and when the Scots Commissioners in London, after his answer had been given, declared their willingness to withdraw their army and surrender the King,[52] he remained convinced (not entirely without reason) that this was only a deliberate policy of blackmail to make him yield in everything to their wishes. He had his own plans; he sent messages to his friends in Paris to stimulate the Irish project and perhaps contrive some plan for his escape. He charged Argyll and Loudoun to go to Westminster to reason with the English to modify their terms; and he sent Hamilton to Edinburgh to see if he could induce in the Scottish Estates a willingness to accept from him a partial instead of a total agreement to the Covenant.[53] All these were mere subterfuges to spin out the time.

Relieved for the moment of those who had chiefly plagued him in argument, the King appeared calm. He played chess with his attendants, a game of which he was always fond, and accepted cheerfully a bulletin of news from London, sent by the Scots permanent Commissioner there, the Earl of Lauderdale, who reported increasing hostility to the Presbyterian party.[54] The King was not displeased; if the hostility increased but a little more he believed the Scots would have to take his part against the Independents whether or not he accepted their Covenant.

The King's implied rejection of the terms had indeed been met at Westminster with mixed feelings, which were summed up in an anecdote current a few years later. A Presbyterian member was supposed to have exclaimed in dismay to an Independent colleague: " What will become of us now the King has refused ? " To which the other answered: " Nay, what would have become of *us* had he accepted ? "[55] All the summer long in London the tension between Independents and Presbyterians had increased. The bitterest division in England was no longer that between King and Parliament, Cavalier and Roundhead, but that between the sectaries and their opponents.

IV

The sectaries, as Dr. Baillie had already observed, were anxious to further and preserve their own ideal of what seemed to Baillie and the Scots " a horrible liberty "; in pursuit of this they would be as willing, or more willing, to " settle themselves in a new kind of popular government"[56] as to seek a just peace with the King.

All that spring and summer London had been disturbed by their activities and Parliament torn between their sympathisers, led by Vane and Cromwell, and the more conservative faction dominated by Denzil Holles. Holles was the same age as Cromwell and had a long Parliamentary career behind him. His father, the Earl of Clare, had bought his nobility from King James I for fifteen thousand pounds. Denzil, a younger son, inherited something of the business acumen and rapacious energy that had made the family fortunes in the previous century. He was high-spirited, quarrelsome, obstinate and impulsive, with great political courage but no subtlety. He was a man of the world, had been bred at Court and had danced in a masque with King Charles in his youth. His favourite sister had married Strafford and for her memory's sake he had tried, agonisingly and ineffectively, to save Strafford's life. But for this deviation, he had been a consistent opponent of the King for the last twenty years. It was he who, in March 1629, had thrown himself bodily on the Speaker when he tried at the King's command to adjourn the Commons, swearing " By God's wounds, you shall sit till we please to rise." At the beginning of the war he had been among the first to raise a regiment and had been prominent on the earliest Committees for the conduct of the war, but he had from time to time considered the possibility of a negotiated peace, he had resented the rise of the Independents, he had been excluded from the Committee of Both Kingdoms, and had come in the last months to be regarded as the principal opponent of Vane and Cromwell, and the leader of what was commonly called the " Presbyterian " party.

The name was convenient and has stuck to Holles and his supporters from that day to this, but it was not strictly accurate. The " Presbyterians " in Parliament were not necessarily and certainly not fanatically Presbyterian in religion. They supported the Directory of Worship which had been voted in the predominantly Presbyterian Westminster Assembly, and they wished to see the church organised within a parochial framework. But this was in the interests of order and civil government rather than from purely religious motives. The great weakness of the English Presbyterians, as Baillie saw it, was their lack of spiritual conviction, which constantly put them at a disadvantage with the sectaries. At the present time, fear of the Independents united their interests with those of the Scots. But their principal desire was to gain possession of the King's person, to send the Scots army home, disband the New Model, and re-establish peace and Parliamentary government.

Holles had sometimes disagreed with Pym about methods of prosecuting the war, but in the summer of 1646 he and his supporters were very close in their hopes and ideals to the hopes and ideals for which the fighting had begun. They were against the sectaries and their wild ideas of liberty; they were against further upheaval and the menace of popular government. They believed in the privileges of Parliament and of the gentry who composed it, and they viewed with hatred and contempt, but not yet with fear, the preachers, the soldiers, and those of their Parliamentary colleagues who yearned towards new doctrine and dangerous licence. As Holles was himself to write, in bitterness of heart, three years later, he and his honest friends desired " nothing but the settlement of the Kingdom in the honour of the King and the happiness and safety of the people: and whensoever that could be obtained to lay down the Sword, and submit again to the King's sceptre of peace more willingly than ever they resisted his force and power." But their enemies, the Independents, vipers in the bosom of Parliament, designed to " ruin the King and as many of the nobility and gentry as they could, alter the government, have no order in the Church, nor power in the State over them."[57]

On one issue only the Presbyterians and Independents were united. Both wished to see the last of the Scots army—Holles and his friends because its presence on English soil made the Presbyterian cause unpopular, and the Independents because they rightly saw in it the only force which, if it came to a trial of strength, could be opposed to their own New Model. On this one question the whole House of Commons was united. Otherwise the two hundred and sixty members, or thereabouts, who now attended the House were divided (as they had always been) by their professional and regional interests into groups which would be associated now in one way, now in another. The support on which Vane or Holles could rely fluctuated uncertainly with the nature of the question discussed. The lawyers were for the Independents, when Presbyterian measures threatened to subject the State to the Church, but might swing against the Independents on neutral measures. The City men were not so much strongly Presbyterian as strongly anti-Episcopal; the large loans that London had raised were in part on the security of the Bishops' goods and lands, and it was therefore of great importance to them that Parliament should retain its hold over this plundered property of the Church.

The Yorkshire members were most of them willing to accept the leadership of Sir Philip Stapleton, a sharp little terrier of a man with great local influence and a reputation much enhanced by his gallant conduct in the war. He was the wholehearted henchman of Denzil Holles. Important also was Sir John Clotworthy, a great landowner in Ireland, whose support of Holles drew with it the votes of many of those who, having Irish interests, were accustomed to follow Clotworthy's masterful lead. Sir Philip Stapleton was prominent on the Committee of Both Kingdoms which enabled him to keep Holles informed of what went on there, but so long as the war lasted, his exclusion from this body, where policy was discussed and initiated, had gravely hampered him. With the war at an end, it became possible once again for policy to be initiated from the floor of the House and for the power of the inner junto on the Committee to be challenged without endangering the fortunes of the armies in the field. Holles emerged therefore in the summer of 1646 as the inheritor of the constitutional policies of Pym, the true House of Commons man against the cabinet influence and popular claims alternately exercised or put forward by Vane, Cromwell and the Independents.

The shrivelled House of Lords, which rarely now mustered more than twenty-five members, was on the whole for the Presbyterian group. The Earl of Manchester had good reason to hate the sectaries and so had the disgruntled Earl of Essex, but some of the strongest personalities in the Lords were of the opposite way of thinking—the subtle, sharp-witted Saye, and the quietly powerful Northumberland whose appearance of lofty unconcern concealed the swift and accurate observation which had enabled him, unobtrusively and unfailingly, since the days when he had been Strafford's friend, to move to the winning side before anyone else perceived that it would win.

It was typical of Holles and his fellow conservatives that they had been unwilling to agree to new elections to fill up the gaps in the Commons made by the death, withdrawal or expulsion of nearly two hundred members since the beginning of the war. They feared that new men, upstarts and soldiers, would swell the ranks of the Independents in the House. But they had had to yield to an evident necessity as county after county was cleared of the King's troops. Their fears were not realised; the elections which had taken place since the late summer of 1645 produced very little change in the size of the groups in the House. Polling had been on the whole free from any but the usual pressure exercised by local patrons and men of influence. The House had forbidden any officer or soldier to interrupt or molest electors and though some undoubtedly used their influence, the voters were not necessarily intimidated. At Stafford the conduct of Captain Foxall, who brought in his company of soldiers, unarmed however, to support the candidate he favoured was later raised before the Committee of Privileges.[58] A good number of officers in the Parliamentary armies were returned, several of them for seats with which they already had family connections: Colonel Hutchinson for Nottingham county, which was his own, Colonel Robert Blake for his home town of Bridgwater.

Some had feared that since the Royalist half of the gentry were ruled out, the dearth of " the better sort " would bring low-born men into the House. But the " recruiters," as the new members were called, came of the same kind of families, and often of the same families as their predecessors:[59] the elections of 1645-6 scarcely at all reflected the social disturbances which were taking place. Certain strong personalities were added to the Independent strength in the House, but the Presbyterians also had their share. The Independents gained Commissary-general Henry Ireton,

Cromwell's son-in-law, Colonel Harrison, Colonel Bingham, Colonel Fleetwood, as well as Hutchinson and Blake. On the extreme wing of their party, they had Colonel Rainsborough, who was soon to be associated with the Levellers, and the less well-known Major Thomas Scott. But other officers hostile to the Independents were returned to Parliament: Colonel Massey, the defender of Gloucester; Colonel Birch, the governor of Hereford; General Browne, a Londoner and a moderate; and for Wells in Somerset the new member was Clement Walker, one of the most bitter and virulent foes whom the Independents were to encounter on their rise to power.

In Parliament, Holles and his friends narrowly held their own. But in spite of the help of the Lord Mayor, a strong opponent of the sects, they were not able to control the increasingly sectarian sympathies of the London populace. The Lord Mayor organised a Remonstrance from the Common Council demanding the suppression of the congregational churches and vigorous proceedings against all sectaries. Before it could reach the House William Walwyn had written a moderate and persuasive answer to it; John Goodwin's flock put up the money to print ten thousand copies and John Lilburne and others distributed them round the streets of Westminster. Holles in the House of Commons mustered all his strength and out-voted the Independents on a motion to receive the Lord Mayor's Remonstrance by a hundred and fifty-one votes to a hundred and eight. In the House of Lords it fared worse, for though the majority received it with thanks, of the five and twenty Lords present, nine, led by Northumberland and Saye, registered a strong protest against it.[60]

A week later, on June 2nd, 1646, the Independents of the city presented a petition to the House setting forth their case. They had worked more discreetly than their opponents: Holles and his party were evidently taken by surprise and the Independents, by the narrow majority of four, passed a vote of thanks to the sectarian petitioners.[61] But the Independents in Parliament, though they encouraged the protests of their friends in the City, made no attempt to prevent the various ordinances for Church government from going through the House, and a week after the incident of the sectaries' petition, the House without a division gave order for the election of elders in the London parishes. Without some outward compliance with the views of the Scots in religion the Independent leaders were well aware they would never get rid of the Scots army.[62] Besides, they knew that while the Independents predominated in the New Model, concessions to the Presbyterians in Parliament would be temporary and harmless. Neither Holles nor the Scots fully realised that the fight had already been transferred from the floor of the House to the street and the camp. The Presbyterian party in Parliament and the City would be powerless in the end against the new forces which the war had created.

John Lilburne, by the burning advocacy of his own personal cause, was transforming the sectarian cry for religious freedom into the more searching and more dangerous cry for popular rights in civil government. He was not capable of abandoning a righteous cause. More than a year ago Cromwell had encouraged him to bear witness against the Earl of Manchester and some of his officers for their half-hearted conduct in the war. The purpose of Lilburne's evidence, as Cromwell saw it, had been to get rid of Manchester from the army. But this purpose was in the end achieved by the Self-Denying Ordinance, and Cromwell, after its passing, had abandoned all further attack on Manchester. Lilburne was not so easily satisfied; if men did wrong they should suffer for it, and he continued to ask for justice on Manchester and other half-hearted soldiers until one of them sued him for libel and was awarded two thousand pounds damages. Lilburne had not the money and would not have paid if he had. Instead, he put out a pamphlet, *The Just Man's Justification*, in which he repeated all his accusations. At this Manchester lost patience. Lilburne was summoned before the House of Lords, but he asserted his inalienable right as an Englishman to be tried only by his fellow commoners and refused to answer any questions. The Lords committed him to Newgate whence he published, on June 11th, 1646, *The Freeman's Freedom Vindicated*, holding the Lords up to obloquy as oppressors of the common people. The Lords again sent for him. He denied their jurisdiction, barricaded himself into his room in Newgate, had to be dragged to Westminster by force, kept his hat on before the peers, would not kneel, stopped his ears when they spoke to him, and finally trounced them for their tyranny in a loud, challenging speech. They ordered his last two pamphlets to be burned, fined him another two thousand pounds, and sent him to the Tower for seven years, with the futile order that he be kept *incommunicado*. Lilburne's aggressive resistance made him the most popular man in London; the citizens would have rushed the Tower and stormed the House of Lords if he had indeed been held *incommunicado*. His wife Elizabeth, a faithful imitator of her husband's methods, found new means to embarrass the Lords by accusing them of putting man and wife asunder, clean contrary to God's known law. They gave in and let her visit him freely.[63]

In the Tower Lilburne made new friends. The Royalist soldier, Sir Lewis Dyve, Lord Digby's half-brother, quickly saw that a trouble-maker of Lilburne's capacity ought to be encouraged, and lent a sympathetic ear to his opinions. More useful to Lilburne was the friendship of Sir David Jenkins, the Welsh Royalist Judge, who had been taken at Hereford and was now awaiting trial for having condemned several Parliamentarians for high treason. Jenkins, who greatly appreciated Lilburne's spirited baiting of the Lords, strengthened him for future contest with his expert legal advice. Lilburne, with his shrewd, acquisitive mind, learnt rapidly. He also found out and assiduously studied the numerous records stored in the Tower. He was to come forth from his imprisonment very much better equipped to fight for the Englishman's birthright than he had been when he went in.[64]

Lilburne, for all his vitality and courage, was not physically strong; he was anxious for the fate of his wife and children, left without support, and he resented the preferential treatment accorded to prisoners richer and better born than he. His sufferings, none the less, had an air of triumph. Thanks to the angry House of Lords, he was now centrally and heroically situated in the Tower, whence he could exhort the humbler citizens of London to throw off the yoke of their oppressors, the Lords, the rich, the privileged. He had become, in the second cycle of persecution upon which he was now entering, Freeborn John, the recognised champion of the common people.

Outside the Tower the sage William Walwyn echoed and expanded the ideas of which Lilburne had made himself the visible embodiment. In his anonymous *Pearl in a Dunghill* Walwyn justified Lilburne's defiance, and warned Parliament that, now the war was over, they had duties towards the men who had won it and the people who had so loyally endured and supported the struggle. The people were neither slaves nor children. They had seen, suffered and thought much during the four years of conflict. They were " a knowing and judicious people; affliction hath made them wise, now oppression maketh wise men mad."[65]

Neither Lilburne nor Walwyn was blinded by veils of inherited tradition which made it almost impossible for many of those in Parliament to see clearly what was happening. Holles was no fool, but he could not conceive of any society not supported by the hierarchic framework that he knew, and he did not believe that the authority of men of education, birth and property could be effectively challenged. Later he would explain everything as the outcome of a sinister Independent plot, a conspiracy of a few clever unscrupulous men—Cromwell, St. John, Vane. He did not realise that the Independent leaders were, as he was himself, the victims of forces they barely understood. Men trained to the exercise of power in a stable society are often unable, on account of the authority they have possessed for so long, to recognise the danger, the value, or even the existence of forces outside their previous experience.

The change that had happened in England in the last four years was simple and obvious but it was overlooked or misunderstood by those in power. The war had affected every county and every town in the land. The sufferings it had caused had been mild, by the standards of contemporary European conflict, but most of the population had endured fluctuations of fortune and some had suffered real distress. Only in Essex out of reach of the quartered troops did the price of bread remain stable throughout the war.[66] Artificial shortage was created wherever the armies lodged by their needs in food and fodder. The demands made by the soldiers, in cash or kind, had been a burden on all, if for a few there were compensating advantages, for some of the money collected by the County Committees stuck to the hands of those who handled it. The contractors who supplied the saddles, boots and belts, shirts, coats and breeches of the soldiers made their profit; so did gunsmiths, swordsmiths, blacksmiths, the owners of powder mills and cannon foundries, and all those who could supply what the armies needed and were strong enough to bargain over prices and delivery. The casual labourer, with little to lose, stood to gain additional work fetching and carrying for the passing troops and repairing the damage when they had gone—digging out the trampled ditch, mending the broken hedge, and on occasion burying the slain at so much a head and estimating the numbers at the highest plausible figure. The very poor were not those who suffered most.

Those who suffered most were the yeomen and the small tradesmen, the weavers of the West Riding with all their mechanism of sale and distribution dislocated, the cattle-drovers of North Wales and the Herefordshire marches, the sheep farmers of the Wiltshire Downs, the hard-working yeomen up and down the country whose horses had been confiscated, whose cattle and sheep had been driven off. There was distress in the country and discontent, but there was no widespread destitution. A famine had been often predicted but during the war it did not come. By a cynical trick of fate, it was the first peace-time harvest, that of 1646, which failed utterly, projecting its consequences on to the following year.

Throughout the war King and Parliament had tried to meet expenses as far as possible by mulcting those of the opposing party whose property came into the power of their armies. In the closing months of the war the systematic plucking of the Royalists began. Those who had borne arms for the King bought out their sequestrated estates for sums which varied from a twentieth to a half their value. This process of compounding temporarily impoverished many of the gentry, and caused some improvident felling of timber and alienation of property to raise money quickly; but it ruined only a few and, while it gave work to lawyers and enriched money-lenders, it caused no widespread change in the pattern of land tenure or even the occupation of land. But it induced an atmosphere of instability and disquiet, a widespread sense of grievance and injustice. More-over, this division of the country into sheep and goats, this penalisation of one half of the gentry by the other half, in-evitably shook the respect of the humbler sort for the gentry as a whole.

The war had been fought, on both sides, by young men drawn from ordinary people of town and country whose ultimate intention was to return to the life whence they had come. None of the armies in the field, not even the Scots, contained a majority of professional soldiers whose outlook and interests made them a separate society from the civilian population. Apart from the adventurous spirits who took to crime and vagabondage, the King's troops had gone back rapidly to their civilian life though some, if the moment of defeat found them too far from home, had enlisted in the Parliamentary forces. They returned to the plough and the workshop enriched by experiences which could not always be reconciled with the social order in which they had grown up and in which they had to take their places once again.

The hierarchy of rank had been marked by social conventions, by details of dress and behaviour, trivial in themselves but of great symbolic significance. For a nobleman to be compelled to appear with his head uncovered before persons of lower rank was a real humiliation, imposed and felt as such. The strictest rules, generally known and respected, had governed forms of address, who gave place to whom in a crowd, who stood in presence of whom, and who gave leave to sit. In the extremity of war all these conventions had naturally been broken. In fear and danger and distress, in moments of endurance and of heroism, men and women act under the imperious necessity of the moment and see each other stripped of all pretences; from this shock the social conventions cannot immediately recover. In the taking of a fortress, in the confusion of a defeat, in the storming and sack of great houses the " meaner sort "—as they were usually called—had seen their betters in unguarded, undignified and pitiful postures. The soldiers of the King's army had been encouraged to despise their opponents as rogues and there had been ceaseless and quite untruthful propaganda to make out that all their officers were vulgar upstarts. In the same way the soldiers of the Parliamentary army had learnt to think of the King's men as all alike " malignants," the greatest of whom God, in his time, would put down. Soldiers of both sides had lived in a topsy-turvy world where military rank no longer marched in step with gentility, and a poor labourer's son might be doing no more than his duty by knocking a brace of gentlemen on the head. Besides which, what with casual plunder, licensed foraging, and the seizure of the rents and property of the opposing party, everything in the country from a hatband to the revenues of an estate had, temporarily at least, become seizable by the strongest.

It would have taken more than four years of such disturbance to destroy a pattern of society which had grown over centuries, and in practice the courtesies and conventions of the social hierarchy had been generally respected by both sides except in the heat of action. But an atmosphere of challenging discontent inevitably grew from the experiences and propaganda of the war, an atmosphere in which it was natural for other kinds of complaint—at economic loss or commercial depression—to be linked with an angry questioning of the social order.

This mood was diffused throughout the country, partly by disbanded soldiers, partly because many of the civilian population had themselves shared in the same kind of experiences. Lilburne's demand for justice to the small man came therefore at a moment when it was bound to arouse a sympathetic response. In the New Model Army this feeling was at its strongest. The soldiers, mostly young men, had been inspired by talk of freedom of conscience; they had been told that they were doing God's work in pulling down princes and prelates; and though the majority of their officers were drawn from the gentry, some of them were not. Colonel Harrison was the son of a Staffordshire butcher; Colonel Berry and Colonel Pride, of obscure parentage, had worked respectively in an iron-mill and a brewery.

With the war at an end, the soldiers of the New Model waited restlessly for peace and pay. Sometimes they blamed the county committees for their discomforts, and at Nantwich incarcerated the committee-men in the common gaol and would not release them till money came for their wants. This was a new way to treat the gentry. Those nearer London read the pamphlets of Walwyn and Lilburne, or listened to others reading them, and their animosity grew against the great ones in Parliament who made no haste either to pay them or to establish a just peace in accordance with the needs and wishes of honest, God-fearing Englishmen. In their enforced idleness they thought and debated much on religion and politics—they had little else with which to divert or exercise their minds; they listened to the eloquence of their sectarian chaplains, Peter, Dell, Saltmarsh, who taught a broader, more luminous, more tolerant faith than that of prelatists and Presbyterians, and gave them the inspiration and the right to think for themselves. Dell, that summer, had urged the Army at the siege of Oxford to remember that " the power is in you, the people; keep it, part not with it."[67]

The troops were alive to rumour, responsive to every breath of suspicion. In the spring many of them had believed that Holles and his friends in Parliament had themselves contrived the King's flight to the Scots, so that the Independents and the Army should be robbed of the fruits of victory.[68] In the summer another and better founded rumour went round: that Holles and the dominant party at Westminster were plotting to get rid of them by shipping them for service in Ireland.

The war in England had, after all, begun over a dispute with the King about putting down the Irish rebellion. It was therefore only reasonable that the first call on the Army, after the defeat of the King, should be for the re-establishment of English control in Ireland. Some officers, mostly with family interests in Ireland, had already volunteered to take over regiments to fight there, but one of them, Colonel Michael Jones, found himself faced by the threat of mutiny when he tried to muster his troops for the journey. They would not budge until they were paid.[69]

The desire of Parliament to ship soldiers to Ireland was reasonable enough. The Scots had been grievously defeated in Ulster; the Ormonde government was making peace with the rebels; the latest disaster was the capitulation of the great fortress of Bunratty near Limerick, in spite of an expensive and resolute effort of the Parliamentary navy to strengthen it from the sea.[70] Since Monro's defeat in Ulster, Lord Inchiquin in Munster alone had an effective army in action to protect the settlers, and help from England was many years overdue. But the suspicions entertained by the soldiers of the New Model were not groundless, for if it was the evident duty of the victorious Parliament to put down the Irish rebellion, it was also very much to the interest of Holles and the Presbyterian group to break up and ship away an Independent Army whose existence was a menace to their authority.

On July 31st, 1646, in a thin house, Holles inspired a motion that six regiments be ordered to Ireland. He had miscalculated his moment, and the motion was defeated by a single vote.[71] It was, perhaps, a merciful defeat for the attempt to move six regiments might easily have precipitated a general mutiny, and Parliament had troubles enough on their hands without that.

V

The tension between Scots and English steadily grew, but the Covenanters did not want a breach with Parliament until they were sure of bending the King to their will, and Holles with the majority in Parliament did not want a breach with the Scots until he had recovered possession of the King. To conservatives bent on preserving the ancient rule of law, the King was still of the highest importance, for his consent alone would give authority to any settlement which was to be made. They utterly condemned the loose and violent talk sometimes uttered by the Independents of deposing the King and replacing him by the Duke of Gloucester (a merry little six-year-old very popular with the Londoners)[72] or by a republican government. It was significant that no one now spoke of Prince Rupert's brother, the Elector Palatine, who had tacitly presented himself as a candidate for the throne two years before. As a Calvinist prince he had been (and had probably seen himself to be) the Presbyterian candidate, should the Presbyterians want one. But now that the removal of the King had become associated with the Independents, neither the Covenanters, nor the party of Denzil Holles, thought it safe to meddle with ideas of deposition any more. The Elector Palatine, content to put his convenience before his dignity, made himself comfortable in one or other of his uncle's unoccupied palaces on an allowance paid him by Parliament out of the sequestrated estates of Cavaliers. His amours, which were plentiful, entertained the more scandalous news-sheets, but his patronage of men of learning and especially scientists during these years was always intelligent and sometimes generous.[73]

Since the dominant group in Parliament did not want a breach with the Scots until they had regained possession of the King, they did what they could to restrain the animosity between Covenanters and Independents. In mid-August they put before the Commons an ordinance against those who wrote or published libels on the Scots; this brought about a verbal duel between Holles and Cromwell. Cromwell vigorously defended the freedom of the press and Holles tried to quell him by asking with scorn how he could take up the cause of " base libellers." Holles had his following well organised for this occasion and his restrictive ordinance was passed by a majority of thirty votes.[74]

As peace spread over the land during the summer of 1646 Cromwell, no longer needed in the field, assumed the leadership of the Independents in Parliament as well as in the Army. Working with Haslerig as his right hand, he was gradually eclipsing Vane in the active guidance of Independent policy. He was no longer the distant presence, thundering from afar, but present and active day by day at Westminster, bringing with him the fame that he had acquired in the field as the creator of the Ironsides, the man who had staved off disaster in the terrible summer of 1643, and had vanquished at Marston Moor the invincible Rupert. He brought also to his work in Parliament the authority and decision which he had learnt during his years as a soldier.

While Cromwell and Holles strove for domination the Scottish tragedy ran its course. The Covenanters, in the words of Argyll, had wanted to see their King " reformed not ruined," and they had staked everything on his reformation. But he could not be reformed without his own consent and if he proved obdurate to all their entreaties, if he would not sign the Covenant and accept the Presbyterian dispensation once and for all, they faced irreparable disaster.

Alexander Henderson, to whom the conversion of the King had been entrusted, had already recognised defeat. He had been a sick man before he came to Newcastle; after two months wrestling with the King he retired to Edinburgh to die, " most of heartbreak " wrote his friend Robert Baillie. Henderson, who had been the greatest architect of the Covenant, had retained the power to see virtue even in those who opposed it. Others—the harsher Warriston or the simpler Baillie—might condemn the King as " a man obstinate beyond induration . . . a wilful and an unadvised prince."[75] Henderson recognised in him a faith, mistaken no doubt, but as settled, clear and earnest as his own. The revelation of the King's integrity confronted him with a problem he could not solve. The Covenant was righteous; yet the King, a righteous man, would not accept it. God might solve this enigma of right conflicting with right; but Henderson could not. Worn out with seeking for an answer, he died in Edinburgh on August 19th, 1646, exhorting his countrymen in his last hours to perform the impossible and remain true to their Covenant and to their King.[76]

Argyll and the leaders of the party still hoped that Charles might yield. He was preached at with ruthless zeal by the reverend Andrew Cant, who had browbeaten Royalist Aberdeen into submission and had a great reputation as a converter.[77] Hamilton brought all his influence to bear. So did the new French ambassador Bellièvre, so did the Queen and the King's most trusted servants and councillors in Paris. Ashburnham, Culpeper and Jermyn, the very three to whom he had written in terms so explicit of his immovable resolution never to abandon the Church, now in ciphered letters entreated him to be a " King of Presbytery " rather than no King at all.[78]

The Covenanters, growing desperate, sent the Commissioners of the Estates to argue him into yielding. Surely he could see that he had no other hope of regaining his Crown? The Independents, Lauderdale vehemently argued, were not to be trusted; if he made it impossible for the Presbyterians to help him, he would find no truth and no help in the sectaries. But Lauderdale overreached himself. The King must have known that already the Scots were talking of handing him over to the English; he did not believe they meant it but took all such rumours, and Lauderdale's arguments, as threats designed to force his conscience by fear. He retorted to Lauderdale with an argument equally true: if they abandoned him merely because he would not sign the Covenant, the Independents alone would gain by it. Was it in their interest to give the Independents so great an advantage? King and Covenanters both alike erred, for he thought that they, in the last resort, would be governed by self-interest and not by conscience; and they thought the same of him.[79]

The Earl of Callander, indeed, tried at one point to cut through the argument and bluntly accused the King of having some concealed source from which he still expected help. Charles denied the imputation: he could not yield, he said, on a point of conscience.[80]

He was truthful in saying that he could not yield on a point of conscience, but he also believed that he had other sources of help. He had heard that Ormonde had concluded peace with the Confederate Irish and on September 16th, 1646, he managed to write to him secretly. The port and town of Conway had surrendered in August but the Castle still held out so that something could be done to assist an Irish landing there, or some other port might be seized on the Lancashire coast.[81]

But unknown to the King all his hopes in Ireland had already vanished. His earlier letter to Glamorgan, offering to place himself unreservedly in the hands of the Nuncio, had been delivered to Rinuccini in July.[82] Strong in the conviction that the defeated King could be compelled to grant full restitution of the property of the Church, which Ormonde had denied, the Nuncio spared no effort to make void the Ormonde Treaty. The Irish clergy, gathered at Waterford, conformed to his will and denounced it.[83] He threatened with a papal interdict any town in Ireland where it should be proclaimed. Waterford,

Wexford and Clonmel shut their gates on Ormonde's heralds. At Limerick the rabble, incited by a friar, stoned the mayor who tried to proclaim the treaty, then tumultuously elected another in his place and plundered all the Protestants in the town. " The wicked designs of worldly neuters or cold Catholics were dashed and blasted in an hour to God's honour and glory," wrote an Irish chaplain of the Nuncio.[84]

Glamorgan, who was constantly at Rinuccini's side, played the innocent and wrote to Ormonde protesting that he had nothing to do with these " most unfortunate and newly occasioned distractions." But the terms of his secret treaty were now openly put forward as the only basis on which good Catholics could accept a peace, and the Nuncio clearly intended to make him Lord Lieutenant in Ormonde's place.[85]

Ormonde hastened to Kilkenny and found the leaders of the Supreme Council who had signed the Treaty helpless against this new turn of events. Digby, never at a loss, appealed to Lord Inchiquin in Munster to abandon his alliance with Parliament and, at this of all moments, to declare for the King. Inchiquin was unmoved.[86] Still hoping to rally his supporters Ormonde advanced to Cashel and was turned back at the gates, while the Nuncio called on Owen Roe O'Neill to take arms against him. O'Neill, setting aside the approaches which had been made to him at Digby's instance in the last months, responded to the call. " All pacts are broken, and we are at open war," Rinuccini reported with joy to the Vatican. Ormonde, narrowly escaping capture, slipped back into Dublin, while O'Neill entered Kilkenny with the Nuncio in triumph on September 18th, 1646.[87]

The military occupation of Kilkenny was followed at once by a revolution in the Supreme Council. The dominating party, the Irish and Norman-Irish lords and the lawyers who had seen in the Ormonde treaty the best hope for their country, were overthrown. The aged President of the Council, Lord Mont-garret, veteran of the Elizabethan rising of 1598, fled; so did the

Earl of Muskerry, who had principally negotiated the Ormonde treaty. Richard Bellings, secretary to the Council and son-in-law of Mountgarret, was thrown into prison. The clergy triumphed, supported by the clamorous townsfolk who believed too easily the fervent prophecies of preaching friars. The Ormonde Treaty was repudiated by the new Confederate government, and the Nuncio indulged in a glorious vision of a free, Roman Catholic, united Ireland, which, under the Lieutenancy of Glamorgan, would launch upon the shores of England an army capable of restoring the King and exterminating the heretics.[88] He treated with easy scorn the anxiety of the Queen's agent in Kilkenny, who saw at once that French help, which had been offered to Ormonde, would not be forthcoming to support the Nuncio's wilder plans.[89]

In Dublin Ormonde looked with the resignation of despair on his shattered plans and deluded countrymen, doomed as he now justly feared to the " most certain ruin that ever people were betrayed into."[90] The Irish disaster was beyond redemption. It had been clear to Ormonde, as it had been to the Confederate leaders, the nobility and gentry, who had signed his treaty, that the future of Ireland depended on the restoration of the King to some semblance of power. The victory of his opponents, whether Scots or English, Presbyterian or Independent, would be equally disastrous to the Irish. It would matter little whether a Covenanting army or the New Model Army was ultimately loosed upon them: but one or the other would certainly invade unless the King could be restored to a position of enough authority to make and maintain his own terms with the Irish.

The present success of the Confederates was illusory; they had maintained their revolt because the government at Westminster had been otherwise occupied. The Nuncio mistook good fortune for good management and seems really to have believed that the Irish forces with help from the Vatican could maintain themselves against the English government and even conquer England. To him King Charles was an untrustworthy

heretic and he had no interest in preserving his Crown; he had
even given it as his opinion that Ireland might manage better
when the King was defeated and the need to help him was
removed.[91] But all he had achieved by breaking the Ormonde
treaty was the postponement of Irish help for the King at a time
when postponement must be fatal. He had done worse, for the
acceptance, followed by the repudiation, of the Ormonde treaty
created an absolute distrust of the Irish in the only Roman Catholic
power which could and would have sent help: Cardinal Mazarin
would not now risk men or cash or credit on this crazy venture.
The sole help of the Vatican, even if it came, would not be
enough to save Ireland, and the Nuncio himself admitted that
he had not for months heard another word about the treaty that
Sir Kenelm Digby was supposed to be negotiating with the
Pope.[92]

The fissures between Irish, Norman-Irish and English-Irish
which had hampered the Confederates from the start, the
divergence of interest between the landed and the landless, were
now past reconciliation. The cry of " *Hiberni unanimes* " raised
in 1642 was rendered void by the violence with which the Nuncio
and O'Neill's army had taken control of the Supreme Council.
They had their way, but they did not carry all Ireland with them;
the clergy and the townsfolk supported the Nuncio, but the
lawyers and the small gentry furiously distrusted him because of
his open desire to take away from them the spoils of the Church.
Outside the towns the Irish stood by their tribal leaders, as they
had always done. If the O'Neills were sound for the Nuncio, the
MacCarthies were for Muskerry, who had signed the Ormonde
treaty; the Macdonnells were for Antrim, who was now only
interested in hiring troops to foreign princes; the Butlers were
for Mountgarret, Ormonde's kinsman and a supporter of the
Ormonde treaty; the Burkes were for their loyalist chief,
Clanricarde; the O'Briens were for Inchiquin and Parliament,
against all the rest of the Irish. So little did the Nuncio understand Ireland that he had assumed that he and the friars and their

flocks in a few Irish towns could dominate the country against the power of the landed men and the rooted influence of the chiefs. So little did he know Ireland that he discovered only now, when he had gone too far to retract, that the Anglo-Welsh Earl of Glamorgan was unacceptable to the Irish as Lord Lieutenant. Not until this moment did it apparently occur to the Florentine Rinuccini that his white-headed boy was not of the right race.[93]

The Confederate army was rent by the new conflict of loyalties. Owen O'Neill had declared for the Nuncio, but Castlehaven, one of the ablest of the commanders in the South, had resigned; the Nuncio took it easily; he had always thought the man a lukewarm Catholic and probably a spy of Ormonde.[94] Muskerry and Mountgarret had withdrawn their support and that of their people. Thomas Preston, the general of the southern Irish forces, had temporarily agreed to obey the Nuncio, but no one who knew his past history of rivalry with O'Neill thought that their co-operation would last.[95]

The Marquis of Ormonde, Lord Lieutenant for a captive King, responsible for the lives and property of the remaining Protestant settlers and the loyalist Irish, faced at the end of September, 1646, the hardest problem he had yet had to meet. The Nuncio had shattered his peace and conjured up a new war against him; if he yielded to the Nuncio he would commit himself and his King to a policy that went deeply against his own religion and that of his master, a policy in the ultimate success of which he did not believe; he would betray those very people, the settlers and the loyalists, who had endured most for him. In the present temper of the Irish Confederate forces he did not know what danger to these people an ill-timed surrender might bring. The only alternative was to appeal for help to those who could send it: the English Parliament. He could not as he put it in a letter to the King, " draw upon our heads the blood of so many Protestants as without seasonable succour will be shed by the rebels' sword, or drunk up by famine." At whatever cost (and the cost to him was likely to be high) he must apply for relief to the English Parliament.[96]

The last of the King's loyal officers bowed to the logic of events.

VI

The King was unaware for some weeks longer of what had happened in Ireland. In the meantime he derived new hope from the rivalry of the Presbyterians and Independents in London. In mid-September the House of Lords and the Presbyterian party both suffered another blow in the death of the Earl of Essex. He had never regained the brief popularity he had enjoyed in the early days of the war, but he wielded considerable influence through his riches, his lands and his commercial interests and he made a bond between the House of Lords and the rich Presbyterians of the City of London.[97] He died unexpectedly, after being "four days aguishly distempered, then fiercely assaulted with a lethargy," and was buried in Westminster Abbey. If the doggerel pamphleteer can be trusted he retained to the end his incapacity for being impressive:

> A gawdy herald and a velvet hearse,
> A tattered anagram with grievous verse,
> And a sad sermon to conclude withal,
> Shall this be styled great Essex' funeral?

His effigy and escutcheon in the Abbey were torn down and defaced a few days later, for no political reason, by a deranged iconoclast.[98]

The arguments between Presbyterians and Independents in the House of Commons were echoed in the pulpits and taverns of London. A new crisis had been provoked by the unfortunate Paul Best, an inoffensive man who was unsatisfied as to the divinity of Christ; he had never published his views or attempted to convert anyone, but he had indiscreetly shown a paper of opinions to a friend, who informed against him. He had been in prison for over a year when in the spring of 1646 the House of Commons, appalled at the blasphemy, voted him to death by hanging. On second thoughts they were uncertain whether, strictly speaking, they had the power to inflict this penalty and in September, therefore, the more rabid opponents of the sectaries put forward an ordinance to make heresy and blasphemy capital offences.[99] Independent opposition was tough and continuous: by the end of the month the atrocious bill lay becalmed in committee. Paul Best tranquilly awaited the worst in his prison, but in the streets and the pulpit the war for spiritual freedom went on, linked ever more closely with the new emerging claim for the rights of all freeborn Englishmen.

Richard Overton, one of the Windmill Tavern group associated with John Lilburne and William Walwyn, worked a secret press in a house in Bishopsgate. Hence in the course of the summer he had issued a number of pamphlets in favour of " that famous and worthy sufferer for his country's freedom, Lieutenant-Colonel John Lilburne." In one of these he had declared in forthright fashion that the Commons had, or ought to have, no power except as the agents of the people who, he claimed, should have " free choice of a Parliament once every year." This unvarnished demand for the establishment of a true democracy had got him into prison and hence, undeterred, he fitted to his polemical bow *An arrow against all Tyrants shot from the prison of Newgate into the Prerogative Bowels of the Arbitrary House of Lords.* In this he eloquently asserted the natural right of every man to be " King, Priest and Prophet in his own natural circuit and compass." God bestowed power and judgment on individuals; they—and not God—delegated authority to those whom they chose to govern them. Any attempt by Parliament, therefore, to check the views and beliefs of ordinary people was an offence against the " just rights and prerogative of mankind."[100]

The government mistakenly tried to deal with Overton as

they had with Lilburne, and found that he, too, would defend his rights with his person. He would not submit to arrest, had to be dragged through the streets with his legs dangling " like a couple of farthing candles " till the officers lost patience and carried him by head and heels to Newgate, where he arrived clutching a volume of Coke's *Institutes* to his belly, and lecturing the crowds who followed him on the legal, inalienable rights of Englishmen.[101]

Lilburne continued to be the unofficial leader of the campaign for the birthright of all Englishmen. From his imprisonment in the Tower he instigated a demonstration at Guildhall when the new Lord Mayor was elected on September 29th, 1646. A group of humble citizens, headed by a watchmaker from Cornhill who had fought in the war, asserted their right to vote; this was refused in an angry scene, whereupon they lodged a protest in the name of the free-men, citizens and commonalty of London. Lilburne, after speedy consultation of all the records on which he could lay hands, wrote and published within a week or two *London's Liberty in Chains*, claiming that every freeman's right to vote had been a principle of government in Saxon times and that a charter of King John had given to all London citizens the right to elect the mayor.[102]

The Lord Mayor was none the less elected for the coming year as he had been elected in the past, but if the result was displeasing to Lilburne it was not satisfactory to Parliament either. Not since Pennington's tenure of office in 1643 had they had a Lord Mayor wholly after their own heart. The Royalist sympathies of the City were steadily reasserting themselves and Sir John Gayer, chosen Lord Mayor in the autumn of 1646, was notoriously Royalist: he had even collected Ship-money for the King ten years before.[103]

VII

The Presbyterians, in England and in Scotland, were beginning with incredulous anxiety to perceive that the shape of
things was no longer what they had anticipated. While the sectaries quietly increased their power in London and at Westminster, the King at Newcastle continued, against all advice, to
refuse to buy the help of the Scots at the price of signing the
Covenant.

With useless ingenuity Charles worked out a plan with the
help of Will Murray for suspending a Church settlement for
three years, authorising for that space the system as it now stood
in England, and submitting the future of the Church to further
discussion, with the full intention on the King's part of getting
a decision in favour of the Bishops. Pleased with this delaying
action he wrote to William Juxon, the upright Bishop of London,
to know whether in his view it would be permissible to yield to
necessity and temporarily abandon the Church of England, with
the determination " to recover and maintain " it as soon as he
had power to do so.[104] Juxon consulted with Brian Duppa, the
expelled Bishop of Salisbury, before reaching a not very helpful
conclusion: the King might accept the situation as he now found
it in England and Scotland, but should not authorise or guarantee
its continuance.[105] The answer was of no consequence for the
King's plan found no favour with anyone.

The King had come to the Covenanters on a misunderstanding
that could not now be set right. He had believed that in the last
resort they would fight for him, their native sovereign, alongside
such friends as he still had in the field. They had believed that
he would not have come unless he were ready to give his consent
to the great work of reformation on which their hearts were set.
Few of them believed that his upholding of the Bishops was truly
a matter of conscience; they thought that his coming to them

had indicated his willingness to accept their religion and that his subsequent refusal to do so arose from a deliberate and evil change of mind.[106]

The predicament of the King, who was alone, in danger, baited by his enemies and firm in his resolution to resist, was more evidently dreadful than the predicament of those who baited him. But the Scots leaders, though less immediately to be pitied, were in the more tragic dilemma. They were, in their own fashion, loyal to their King. His Stuart predecessors over the last two centuries had held the Scottish crown by a dangerous tenure amid the factions of a powerful nobility; but the Scots though apt to rebellion were possessively attached to their monarch with an arrogant and critical devotion. The King in Scotland was the head of the household and the father of the family; his people might speak ill of him, but they were privileged to do so and would defend him against the attack and criticism of any outside their circle. This possessive attitude to the sovereign was now modified by ideas taken from the Old Testament. The power which Samuel had wielded over Jewish Kings was reflected in the freedom with which the ministers and those of the godly party corrected the faults of King Charles, and the idea of Kingship which prevailed among the Covenanters was not the less genuine for being Biblical. They hoped to make of Charles a godly monarch who would give the full support of the secular power to the Presbyterian Church and who, being mortal, would admit also to being sinful, and would, like David of old, repent of his sins. A King who humbled himself before the ministers of God might also be a great and glorious King; they had abundant proof of this in the Scriptures, and why should King Charles object to behaving as the greatest kings of Judah had done?

This conception of Kingship had had time to develop, in Scotland, during the long generation since 1603 when there had been no active and present King in Scotland against whose behaviour its plausibility could be checked. It was the extraordinary product of extraordinary circumstances, and could only have been created by a people whose devotion to the idea of a King was as strong as their religious faith, but who were deprived of his physical presence.

In the autumn of 1646 the Covenanters, who had for eight years lived in the faith that such a monarch and such a monarchy might indeed exist, faced the extinction of their hope. The frank and voluble Baillie made it the theme of his letters: " the King's madness has confounded us all."[107] Argyll and Warriston were more tight-lipped but their sense of defeat was no less, for both had lived and worked with this vision before them, and were aware that the King's refusal to be a King of Presbytery made an end of their hopes of preserving him as King at all. If they could not preserve him as King, " reformed not ruined," in Argyll's phrase, their whole conception of Church and State was threatened.

Ever since the King's refusal of the peace propositions the Scots Commissioners in London had been anxious about the future of their prisoner. If Charles would not sign the Covenant he became not merely useless but dangerous to them, and would be a focus for dissatisfaction if they took him back to Scotland; but they deeply feared the dangers he might run if he fell into the hands of the English, and the Independents with their strong talk of deposition should come into power. What then could they do, now that the war was over and their army would have to withdraw across the border within the next few months? The English suspected them of planning to let the King escape, and the Commons discussed and in the end rejected a motion demanding that he be instantly delivered up.[108] But letting the King escape seems to have been the only solution that did not occur to the Covenanters. Had he escaped it would have been to join his Popish Queen in France and involve himself, since he could make no alliance with the Covenanters, with Montrose, the Irish rebels, and no doubt the Vatican. They could not in conscience minister to such wickedness.

The Covenanters could not withdraw until some of the money owing to their army was paid over to satisfy their men. This caused at least a delay and gave them time to think over their predicament. The Scots estimated the debt at six hundred thousand pounds; the House of Commons made a counter-offer of one hundred thousand pounds.[109] The upper and lower limit being thus fixed, the Scots Commissioners and the Commons proceeded to bargain cautiously towards agreement midway. The transaction was separate from any plans they also had about the disposal of the King. But they were not blind to the implications of what they were doing and indeed they perceived that the money and the evacuation could be used to compel the English to treat their King respectfully; they discussed at one time the advisability of imposing on the English a guarantee not to depose the King as a condition of their withdrawal. Later, they saw the possibility that their motives would be misrepresented if the King's name was brought in at all. Argyll, Loudoun, Lauderdale and Warriston declared that it was " unseasonable " to raise the question of the King in connection with a money treaty.[110] But no wise precautions and no good intentions were in the end to prevail against the persistent, incorrect, but plausible slander that in the autumn of 1646 the Scots undertook to sell their King.

Their Commissioners in London pressed for a joint agreement with Parliament about the King's future, an agreement that would secure his " honour and safety."[111] But on September 18th without consultation or even warning, the House of Commons declared that the King's person should be disposed of as both Houses thought fit. The aggressive statement was challenged by Loudoun in three persuasive speeches showing that " the King being King of Both Kingdoms and his person indivisible," his fate was a matter for the two nations to decide between them.[112]

The House of Commons, supported in this by the Lords, were firm in their resolve to have the King delivered to them with no conditions at all and no obligation further to consult the Scots.

To hasten this happy hour they ordered the sale of lands confiscated from the Bishops so as to raise the money to pay off the Covenanting army.[113]

Once the pay came for the Scottish army, the Covenanters must decide whether to take the King with them into Scotland, to leave him behind as the unconditional prisoner of the English, or to stay in England and risk an armed clash when their quondam allies came to drive them out and seize the King.[114] The last alternative was abandoned as soon as thought of; it was too risky and too wearisome. That left them with the bare alternative: to take the King with them, or to leave him behind.

Charles believed that his compatriots, in the last resort, would not desert him. Incredibly, he still thought he could win over the most rabid of his opponents with gifts of power and place. When the aged Sir Thomas Hope, Lord Advocate, died that autumn, Charles without prompting bestowed the influential office thus vacated on the most bitter and consistent of his enemies, the fanatic Warriston. He was surprised and deeply wounded when Warriston, in return, failed to exert a moderating influence on his colleagues. He relied with equal optimism on Hamilton to save him from being delivered to the English, and wrote to him as though confident that the Scots would not yield him up if they realised the danger. The English, he said, " think to get me into their hands, by telling our countrymen that they do not intend to make me a prisoner. Oh no—by no means, but only to give me an honourable guard forsooth, to attend me continually for the security of my person. Wherefore I must tell you . . . that I will not be left in England when this army retires."[115]

He forgot that there were grave objections to bringing him into Scotland if he would not take the Covenant and proclaim himself of their party. Montrose, obedient to his command, had disbanded his forces in July and when, in August, the King had changed his mind and urged him to continue the struggle, it was already too late. But in the north Huntly was still in arms.

He had always been jealous of Montrose and had deliberately refused to consult with him when the King's order for disbandment came. By this hostile and secretive policy he had achieved his own extraordinary goal, for once Montrose withdrew he could (and did) claim to be the King's principal champion in Scotland. Besides the captious Huntly, Alaster Macdonald was at large in Kintyre, and since the defeat of Monro at Benburb he might even be reinforced from Ulster.[116]

The defection of many gentry in the Lowlands after the battle at Kilsyth, only a year ago, had revealed the real weakness of the Covenanters. They had done nothing to reconcile and convert their foes: their procedure had been too questionable, their methods too harsh. Afterwards one of the greatest among them, Samuel Rutherford, was to regret the error: " Our work in public was too much in sequestration of estates, fining and imprisoning, more than in a compassionate mournfulness of spirit towards those whom we saw to oppose the work. . . . It had been better had there been more days of humiliation and fasting . . . and far less adjourning commissions, new peremptory summons, and new drawn-up processes. And if the meekness and gentleness of our Master had got so much place in our hearts, that we might have waited on gainsayers and parties contrary-minded; and we might have driven gently, as our Master Christ, who loves not to over-drive, but carries the lambs in his bosom."[117] But they had followed different and less Christ-like methods and were piling up against themselves already the hatred of a growing minority. If the King came among the Scots without accepting the Covenant, his presence would encourage every opponent of the party in power, open or secret, throughout the land.

The only way out of the dilemma which appeared to the Covenanting leaders was the eleventh hour conversion of the King and towards this they still strenuously worked, not without help from the Queen and her friends. She was still convinced that if he would yield on the religious question, he would, with

the help of Scots, French and Irish, soon regain all he had lost.
" My hopes are great; provided you are constant and resolute,
we shall be the masters yet, and we shall meet again with greater
joy than ever before. Good bye, my dear heart."[118]

In October the French took Dunkirk, the port from which
the King's pirate ships had operated during the war. At once it
was rumoured that Prince Rupert would be made governor. He
had recently joined the Queen in Paris and had been appointed
by the King of France general of all the English troops then in
French service. Some grounds for this rumour may have existed,
because the Spanish ambassador in England, the ingenious Don
Alonso de Cardeñas, perceiving how suspect the French had
become to the Independent party because of their intrigue with
the Scots, had thought of approaching them to send men from
the New Model to help in the defence of Dunkirk. It may have
been the answering echo to this abortive plan of Cardeñas that
the French thought of placing one of King Charles's commanders
in the strategic port that faced England across the narrow seas.
But nothing came of it.[119]

The King found better grounds for hope in the mounting
discontents of England. Rumours of mutiny in the Army
multiplied; it could not be disbanded without great danger, for,
with the difficulty of paying the Scots, Parliament had let the
pay of the English army fall badly into arrears. On October 7th
the New Model was voted to continue for another six months.
Meanwhile the men did little except read the pamphlets of Lilburne and listen to their sectarian preachers. At Amersham
Richard Baxter, the learned Presbyterian divine, staged a public
debate with the sectaries before a large congregation of soldiers,
but came off the loser.[120] At York, the unpaid troops mutinied
against the authority of General Poyntz, who had not the religious
knack.[121] Fairfax, on November 12th, was formally received in
London with great rejoicings and official thanks from Parliament,
but it was generally known that Cromwell had the greater
influence in the Army, and that he meant no good to the Pres-

byterian party. Oliver Cromwell had indeed two strong reasons for resenting Denzil Holles and his followers in Parliament. As a commander he had always demanded recognition for the services of his men, who were now kept short even of their due pay. As a seeker after God he believed in and required for himself and others that liberty of conscience which the Presbyterians denied. Cromwell and the sectarian officers he had elevated represented a graver and more immediate threat to the Presbyterians than that from Lilburne and his pamphleteering friends.[122] So at least it appeared.

The Royalists took heart; here and there from all over the country reports came in of their attempts to tamper with servants of Parliament whom they believed discontented, with Rowland Laugharne in South Wales, with Batten, the tough sea-captain now Admiral of the Fleet. Michael Hudson, a ubiquitous conspirator, managed to re-join the King with the outline of a plan for a general Royalist rising to be led by the Prince of Wales; but Charles for once was unconvinced.[123] Too many failures had disillusioned him. He had thoughts of escaping, and a ship sent by the Prince of Orange lingered long in the harbour of Newcastle " under pretence of being careened." But he did not move; he seemed strangely apathetic—" sullen " was the unflattering word used by an observer—as though indifferent to " the very paroxysm of his affairs."[124]

The Covenanters speculated on the cause of his silence. Some believed he had already a secret treaty with the Independents, and was therefore unperturbed. Meanwhile the time for the Scots withdrawal was close at hand. On December 4th it was reported in Newcastle that " the two hundred thousand pounds is all told three days ago."[125] Frantically now the Covenanters strove to convert the King. Lanark implored him to yield;[126] the ministers preached at him with redoubled fury. On Sunday, December 6th, before a large congregation, the preacher called for the 52nd Psalm: " Why boastest thou thyself, thou tyrant: that thou canst do mischief? Thy tongue imagineth wickedness: and with lies thou cuttest like a sharp razor." Charles was too quick for him; with the voice of authority that was his in time of crisis, he made the congregation join in the 56th Psalm instead: " Be merciful unto me, O God, for man goeth about to devour me."[127]

Bellièvre and Montreuil together exhorted him to sign the Covenant and go into Scotland. It was Mazarin's price for French help.[128] Briefly he contemplated the idea of abdicating, allowing his son to make the necessary concessions, and then resuming his Crown and repudiating them; but it seemed too risky and when the Queen and her councillors all too enthusiastically took up the idea, he dismissed it with indignation. " Good God," he wrote, " what things are these to try my patience! And is it possible that having not been able to convince my reason, that you can believe I will submit to yours, or anybody else's, against my conscience? . . . In what security do you think I can be, when it shall be believed, that my son will grant what I deny? . . . I conjure you, as you are Christians, no more thus to torture me. . . . For remember a good cause is no more to be abandoned than one's friends."[129]

Argyll was in deep distress. He feared for the King the violence of the Independents, and though he consoled himself with the thought that they were not yet in undisputed power,[130] he must have known how uncertain was the control of Denzil Holles over Parliament. But he could see no way of taking the King into Scotland without imperilling the sacred cause of the Covenant. Speaking to the French envoy, half thinking aloud, he considered whether the King could be safely brought to Scotland as a close prisoner—behind bolts and bars, but waited on as befitted a King on bended knee.[131]

On December 16th, in Edinburgh, the Estates considered whether or not they could receive the King in Scotland, and by a great majority voted that they could not do so. Hamilton and Lanark protested, but although both were genuinely distressed, neither had any alternative solution to offer.[132] The King himself, when he heard at Newcastle that Scotland had rejected him, continued quietly with a game of chess.[133]

On December 20th he appealed to Parliament to let him come freely to London to arrange a personal treaty. He would " make no other demands but such as he believes confidently to be just, and much conducing to the tranquillity of the people." A King, he wrote, who would not hear a subject would be thought a tyrant: how could they his subjects refuse to hear their King ?[134]

They could. At Westminster they were arranging for the place of his confinement—his residence they called it—in England. They chose Holmby House, a country mansion in Northampton-shire, remote from any large town, which could be kept well guarded. On December 23rd they concluded their financial treaty for the withdrawal of the Scots.[135]

On Christmas Eve the King attempted to escape and was immediately intercepted. The guard round his quarters was doubled and he was informed that he must henceforward con-sider himself a prisoner.[136] The French envoy tried to contrive another escape in spite of all; Huntly was at Elgin with his clansmen in arms[137] and if Charles, by sea, could reach the coasts of the Gordon country a new Royalist rising in Scotland might be achieved. Bellièvre approached David Leslie to connive at the King's escape; in return he would be made Earl of Orkney and a Knight of the Garter. The bribe should have sufficed for a cadet of a poor Scots family; so thought Bellièvre, but he forgot that Leslie had a stubborn conscience. The offer was refused.[138]

No more could be done. Escape was cut off. The Scots troops, from their further garrisons, were systematically evacuating England. Argyll had withdrawn from the scene of his defeat.

Charles was outwardly calm. Attended at a respectful dis-tance by General Leslie, he played golf. He twitted the Scots on their commercial stupidity: they had sold him, he said, far too cheap.[139] In cypher he smuggled out letters to Ormonde by way of the French envoy. He told him to " re-piece the Irish peace,"[140] because a very faint new hope, the merest marshlight, had begun to flicker above the Irish bog. Ormonde had not, after all, surrendered to the English Parliament; the garrison of Dublin had refused to serve under any other commander than himself and the immediate Confederate threat to the city had been removed because O'Neill and Preston, in despite of the Nuncio, quarrelled, doubted and delayed.[141] What would come of this troubled situation time would show, but the indefatigable George Digby had immediately seized upon the opportunity to approach both the Nuncio and O'Neill in the King's interest.[142]

On December 31st, 1646, the King composed a message which he sent by Bellièvre to the two Queens—his wife and the Queen-regent of France. It was like the last signal of distress from a sinking ship before impenetrable night should cut him off. He was now, he wrote, held rigidly as a prisoner, and his condition in the hands of his English foes would be the same. He adjured these two great ladies (each of whom was in some sort the guardian of a throne) to remember that his cause was " the cause of every King in Christendom." If he perished, sovereignty itself was threatened. He had now done all that he could to save himself; henceforward he could be saved only by his fellow monarchs. His hope was set on the treaties now being made by the assembled European powers at Munster to conclude at long last the dividing religious wars of Christendom. When peace was made in Germany, when the long struggle between the Spaniards and the Dutch ended, when France, Sweden and their allies were satisfied, he exhorted them to remember him, and his poor loyal subjects (of whom he still had many) and to come to his help against the wicked and much-divided rebels who now had power over him.[143]

On January 2nd, 1647, the Commissioners from Parliament arrived at Newcastle, led by the Earls of Northumberland and Pembroke. After some friendly conversation about his children in London the King agreed to go to Holmby, knowing that he had no choice. The appointment of the servants who were to wait on him was supervised by Parliament and he agreed at length to the attendance of James Harrington, whose family had long been associated with the Court, but who was himself a philosopher of experimental and even republican views, and to Thomas Herbert, a pompous kinsman of the Earl of Pembroke who had distinguished himself in youth by travelling to Persia. Both these gentlemen were of unimpeachable loyalty to Parliament. He was allowed none of his own chaplains and, to their great chagrin, he refused to hear the preaching of the now fashionable divines who accompanied the Commissioners, Stephen Marshall and Joseph Caryl. Only with reluctance did he permit them to say grace at dinner.[144]

On January 21st, 1647, he contrived to send a letter to Montrose, who had escaped to Norway, entreating him to go to the Queen.[145] Now that his alliance with the Covenanters had foundered and his escape to the Highlands to join Huntly had failed, he hoped again for a miracle from this faithful servant if he united himself to the little Court near Paris where Henrietta Maria spun the frail, far-stretched webs of intrigue between Dublin, Dunkirk and Rome.

On Thursday, January 28th, 1647, the Scots Commissioners took their leave of the King. He was calm but quietly reproachful: " I came to your army at Southwell for protection," he said, " and it was granted me."[146] They had no answer; most of them realised already with helpless gloom that the clumsy confusion over the payment of their troops had started the cry of " traitor Scots who sold their King " that would not soon be silenced. They were innocent of the intention, if not of the deed, but they could never prove it. On January 30th, 1647, they marched out, passing under the King's window with colours flying and drums beating " as though to flaunt their infamy," wrote Montreuil, whose ingenious and unwise diplomacy had brought this thing to pass. The fishwives of Newcastle pursued them with brickbats and cries of " Judas."[147]

A political poet was soon to apply the same comparison,

unfairly but understandably enough, to Hamilton's wretched fumblings in these disastrous months:

> Rather than he his ends would miss
> Betrayed his Master with a kiss. . . .[148]

As the Scots marched out, the English under Philip Skippon marched in. There was no formal change in the treatment of the King. Some time in the course of the day he must have heard outside his rooms the familiar clanking and stamping of the changing of the guard, as the Scots sentinels appointed by David Leslie gave place to the English troops appointed by Philip Skippon.[149]

VIII

The year 1646, the last of war and the first of peace, had been a bad year, a year of frustration and misunderstanding in politics, of sickness and shortage. The mortality from plague in London had been higher than at any time since the black months of 1636. Over the whole country the harvest was poor. No smiling peace had come back to England, but an uncertain and discontented truce. The Scots had packed up and gone home to a country no less disturbed and ill at ease than England was.

By candlelight on December 31st, the day on which the King composed his appeal to the sovereigns of Christendom, the House of Commons passed an ordinance forbidding all preaching by laymen. A modifying amendment from the Independents was defeated by a hundred and five votes to fifty-seven, Cromwell and Haslerig acting as tellers for their party. Hopelessly outnumbered in a thin house, the Independents let the ordinance itself go through without a division. Within the walls of Parliament the Presbyterians and their sympathisers still prevailed, with, behind them, some of the influential men of the City who had recently petitioned for the speedy disbanding of the Army.[150]

Cromwell commended all to God and awaited events. Outside Parliament the sectaries continued to spread their opinions. From their house in Bishopsgate the wife and brother of Richard Overton were still printing his pamphlets but early in January, 1647, the law caught up with them for their unlicensed activity. Brought before the House of Lords, Mrs. Overton emulated the conduct of Lilburne and her husband, refused to move a step when ordered to prison, and allowed herself, with her baby in her arms, to be dragged through the streets as he had been, denying and defying the authority by which she had been arrested.[151]

"Toleration is the cause of many evils, and renders diseases or distempers in the State more strong and powerful than any remedies,"[152] reflected the Marquis of Argyll, and certainly in Scotland the rigid Presbyterian discipline prevented those rash opinions from spreading which now infected the body politic of England. The only evils still affecting Scotland were the Marquis of Huntly lurking in the North with an infinitesimal following, and Alaster Macdonald with his Irish still lording it in the peninsula of Kintyre. The kingless kingdom of the Scots was otherwise in peace and order, in austere contrast to the troubled realm of England. But the Covenanters had lost what they fought for, and faced without the King an empty future.

The future of England, disordered and uncertain though it seemed, was bright with hope. Among the sectaries there was talk of a coming millennium and the Rule of the Saints. Sometimes it was conceived in terms practical enough; Hugh Peter held up before the eyes of his countrymen the living example of New England. In seven years in that land of promise he would boast " I never saw beggar, nor heard an oath, nor looked upon a drunkard."[153] If such things could be achieved across the Atlantic, why not at home? The moment was at hand for building the New Jerusalem. If this, for Hugh Peter, meant an industrious, temperate and innocent society, it meant for Lilburne, Walwyn and Overton a society where men were free and equal before the law, could speak their minds on all subjects, and were tied down by no unjust prohibitions and unfairly maintained privileges.

John Pym, John Hampden and the rest of those who had made the Parliamentary opposition to the King had believed that the rights of the subject were protected by the rights of Parliament; for them the provisions of Magna Carta and the Common Law were the bulwarks of liberty. But Overton dismissed Magna Carta as a " beggarly thing,"[154] and Walwyn had stigmatised it as the work of a Norman conqueror inadequate to the rights of freeborn Englishmen.[155]

More, much more, was needed to make Englishmen equal and free. As for the law and lawyers they had come in the last months to assume a foremost place among the enemies of the people because they stood, inevitably, on the side of those who were trying to bring under control the exuberance of action and opinion that the war had bred. They came forward as the interpreters and defenders of existing laws and privileges. That lawyers, some of them at least, were time-serving and corrupt, had always been admitted. Selden could jest dryly at the majesty of the law: " The judges, they interpret the law, and what judges can be made to do, we know."[156] The rascally lawyer who showed the wicked man how to enrich himself through the loopholes in the law had been a common figure on the stage before the playhouses were closed. But in general the attitude of ordinary men and women to the law had been familiar and possessive, if sometimes cynical and sometimes critical. Of late years the lawyers, remote from the armies, arguing in Westminster Hall, drawing fees for protecting, as it seemed, the rich against the poor, upholding privilege as by law established, snubbing the aspirations of religious and political innovators, and exploiting the elastic law of libel to trip up Lilburne and his friends, had provoked bitter and growing animosity.

From the beginning of the century the Common Law had been the chief protection of the subjects' rights against the Crown. The Inns of Court had been the nurseries of the legalist opposition to the King. In the first years of the Long Parliament the advice and skill of the lawyers—Glynne, Maynard, Whitelocke —had done much to shape and guide Parliamentary policy. In the opening struggle between the Crown and the subject, the influence of Sir Edward Coke, the greatest lawyer of his time, had been paramount. In the autumn of 1642 those who then led the fight against King Charles were defending what they believed to be the law. "Law and liberties," was their cry; "ancient privileges fixed by law"; "the accepted law of the land."

The men of the New Model Army knew nothing about that; John Lilburne and his friends dismissed the law as mumbo-jumbo written down in "Pedlar's French" for the express purpose of deceiving simple folk and enriching lawyers. They asked not for liberty according to the law, but simply and directly for liberty. They had not fought to preserve the law but to restore a lost freedom, which the lawyers no less than the King had wickedly curtailed.[157]

In the new situation which had come into being the defeated King was merely a piece in the game to be used or set aside in the struggle between authority (Parliament or Presbytery, Church or Law) and the people. The war between King and Parliament had brought no solution, but had created a new and far more dangerous conflict.

Pamphleteers of every creed from Royalist to Republican were apt to write of their country's "bleeding, dying condition." But they exaggerated. The war had strained the national resources, interrupted trade and manufacture, created a heavy burden of public debt, caused great wastage in agriculture, loss of timber and live-stock. But there was no damage that an active people could not remedy. Discontent and disorder were signs of energy and hope, not of despair. The powerful cry now was not for a return to the old ways, but for strenuous change and new solutions. Here was no weary resignation, but new demands and bold ideas. Milton's description, written three years before, was true to what he heard and saw; " a Nation not slow and dull, but of a quick, ingenious, and piercing spirit, acute to invent, subtle and sinewy to discourse, not beneath the reach of any point the highest that human capacity can soar to." Nothing in the intervening years had dulled the wits of his compatriots or made them instruments less fit for the great work to which many now believed themselves called, first for the liberation and reform of their own country, then for the enlightenment of the world.

THE END

MAPS

MAP I. THE BRITISH ISLES SHOWING CITIES
AND PORTS OF STRATEGIC SIGNIFICANCE

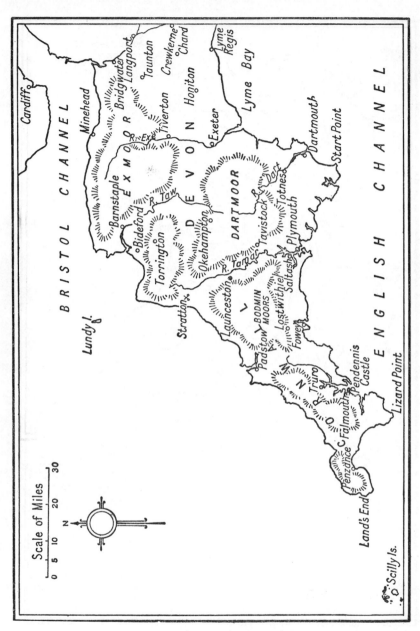

MAP 2. THE WEST COUNTRY

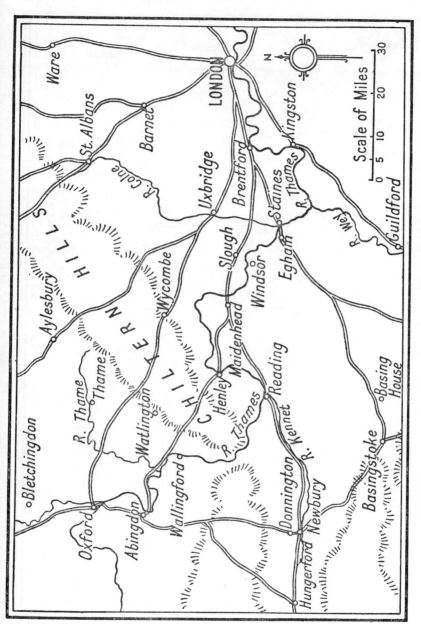

MAP 3. OXFORD AND LONDON

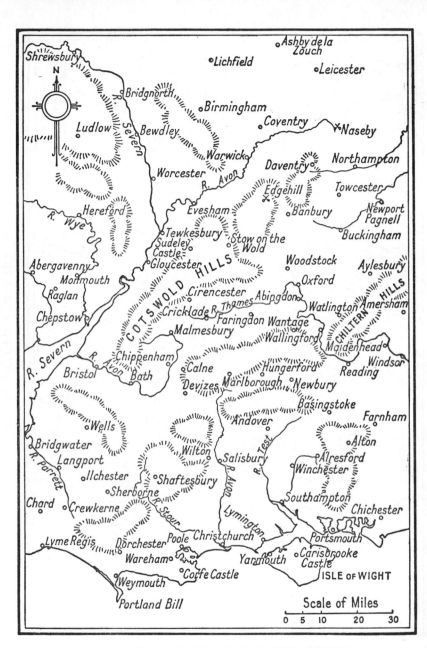

MAP 4. THE MIDLANDS AND THE SOUTH

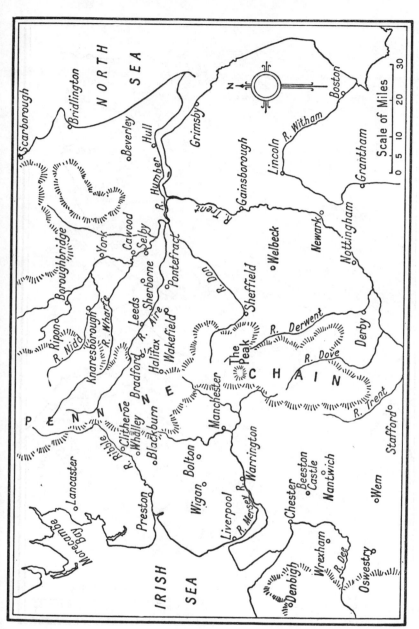

MAP 5. THE MIDLANDS AND THE NORTH

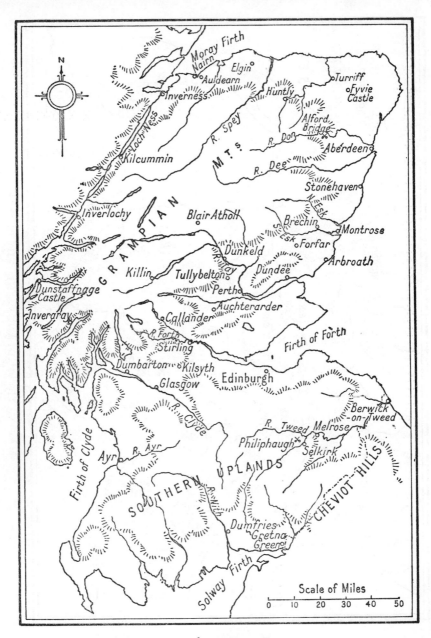

MAP 6. SCOTLAND

BIBLIOGRAPHICAL NOTE

BIBLIOGRAPHICAL NOTE

The references to each chapter indicate the principal sources used. The material for this period is limitless but time, unfortunately, is not. Much detail on the administration and financing of the war still needs to be investigated, though the recent work that has been done on the papers of two of the County Committees (Staffordshire and Bedfordshire) casts some light on this side of affairs. I have relied in general on the very numerous contemporary sources which are available in print and confined my MS research to a few essentials.

The MSS of Prince Rupert's Correspondence and the Despatches of Sabran, both in the British Museum, have been worked over by many other scholars but the Rupert Correspondence is extremely rich and various, and Sabran's week-by-week reportage is so lively, that both repay further study. The MSS of the City of London—the Minutes and Journal of the Common Council—throw light on the politics of the corporation. Valuable work on the politics and administrations of London in the early years of the Long Parliament has been done by Valerie Pearl who most generously allowed me to consult her manuscript thesis.

For other MS sources that I have used, I would like to thank the Keeper of the Records for Scotland Sir James Fergusson for many helpful suggestions, Lord Leconfield for very kindly putting at my disposal some useful papers in connection with the fleet, and Professor Wallace Notestein of Yale for allowing me to consult his seventeenth century pamphlets. For other suggestions and loans I have expressed my gratitude at the appropriate places in the references. I would like also to thank the directors and staff of the numerous libraries where I have worked, either as a " regular " or as that more troublesome thing a transient visitor clamouring for quick attention: these include the Public Record Office, London; H.M. Register House, Edinburgh; The British Museum; the National Library of Scotland; the Bodleian Library; the University Library, Glasgow; the Library of Trinity College, Dublin; the Folger Shakespeare

Library, Washington; the Library of the Institute for Advanced Study, Princeton; the Huntington Library; the libraries of the Universities of Harvard, Yale, Princeton and Columbia; and the ever-welcoming London Library which has given inestimable service to scholars for the last century.

In giving my references I have followed the usual custom of citing the title of the book in full the first time and citing it on later occasions by the author's name or by an abbreviated title. All references to Clarendon are of course to Macray's edition, and the numbers refer to the *Book* and the *paragraph* unless otherwise stated. For brevity's sake I have made use of certain stock abbreviations, and, occasionally, of a very much abbreviated title. A list of these is given below.

Abbott: *Writings and Speeches of Oliver Cromwell*, edited by Wilbur Cortez Abbott, Volume I, 1599-1649, Cambridge, Mass., 1937.

Acts and Ordinances: Acts and Ordinances of the Interregnum 1642-1660, ed. C. H. Firth and R. S. Rait, London, 1911.

B.M. Add. MSS: British Museum, Additional Manuscripts.

Burnet, *Lives:* Gilbert Burnet, *Memoirs of the Lives and Actions of James and William, Dukes of Hamilton*, London, 1677.

C.J.: Commons Journals.

C.S.P.D.: Calendar of State Papers, Domestic Series.

C.S.P.I.: Calendar of State Papers, Irish Series.

C.S.P.Ven: Calendar of State Papers, Venetian Series.

Cal.Clar.S.P.: Calendar of the Clarendon State Papers, ed. Ogle, Bliss, Macray and Routledge, Oxford, 1869 seq.

Clarendon State Papers: State Papers collected by Edward Earl of Clarendon commencing from the year 1621, ed. R. Scrope and T. Monkhouse, Oxford, 1767-86.

Collins, *Sydney Papers: Letters and Memorials of State . . . from the originals at Penshurst*, ed. A. Collins, London, 1746.

Commentarius: Barnabas O'Ferrall, Daniel O'Connell, *Commentarius Rinuccinianus de Sedis Apostolicae Legatione*, ed. Stanislaus Kavanagh, *Irish Manuscripts Commission*, Dublin, 1932-49.

H.M.C.: Historical Manuscripts Commission.

Hopton, *Bellum Civile: Hopton's narrative of his campaign in the West and other papers*, ed. C. E. H. Chadwyck-Healey, Volume XVIII of the *Somersetshire Record Society Publications*, London, 1902.

L.J.: Lords Journals.

Lancashire Civil War Tracts: Tracts relating to military proceedings in Lancashire during the Civil War, ed. G. Ormerod, *Chetham Society,* London, 1844.

Manchester's Quarrel : Documents relating to the quarrel between the Earl of Manchester and Oliver Cromwell, ed. J. B. Bruce and D. Masson, *Camden Society,* London, 1875.

Maseres Tracts: Select Tracts relating to the Civil Wars in England, ed. Francis Baron Maseres, London, 1815-26.

Montreuil: The diplomatic correspondence of Jean de Montreuil and the brothers de Bellièvre, ed. J. G. Fotheringham, *Scottish History Society,* Edinburgh, 1898-9.

N.S.: New Series.

P.R.O.: Public Record Office, London.

Reg. P.C.Scot.: Register of the Privy Council of Scotland.

T.T.: Thomason Tracts, King's Library, British Museum. (The most important collection of civil war tracts. I give the number by which each volume may be identified when referring to a pamphlet in this collection.)

Wardlaw MS.: Chronicles of the Frasers, ed. W. Mackay, from the so-called *Wardlaw MS., Scottish History Society,* Edinburgh, 1905.

REFERENCES

REFERENCES

BOOK I: CHAPTER I

1. *Somers Tracts*, 2nd edition, London, 1809-15, IV, pp. 141-7; Lawrence Price, *Great Britain's Time of Triumph*, London, 1641; J. H., *King Charles his Entertainment*, London, 1641; H.M.C., *Buccleuch MSS.*, I, p. 286; H.M.C., *Cowper MSS.*, II, p. 295; see H. Reynold, *Le Baron de Lisola*, *Revue Historique*, XXVII, p. 330 for two interesting dispatches of the imperial ambassador.

2. H. Finch, *Nomotechnia*, English edition, London, 1627, p. 81

3. *Journal of Sir R. Twysden, Transactions of the Kent Archaeological Society*, I, 1858, pp. 188-190.

4. Calybute Downing, *A Discourse upon the reasons that produce a desired event of the present troubles of Great Britain*, London, 1641. I have to thank Mr. Christopher Hill for kindly drawing my attention to this pamphlet and lending me his copy.

5. Evelyn, *Diary and Correspondence*, ed. Bray, London, 1859, IV, pp. 95, 119; D'Ewes, *Journal from the first recess of the Long Parliament to the withdrawal of King Charles*, ed. W. H. Coates, New Haven, 1942, p. 140n; *L.J.*, IV, p. 438.

6. Clarendon, Bk. IV, 127-8.

7. *Ibid.*, 128; Evelyn, ed. Bray, IV, p. 116. For a full elucidation of this policy see B. H. G. Wormald, *Clarendon*, Cambridge, 1951, Pt. I, i.

8. *Clarendon*, Bk. IV, 74.

9. *C.S.P.D.*, 1641-3, pp. 201-2; Ludlow, *Memoirs*, ed. C. H. Firth, London, 1894, pp. 21-2; D'Ewes, p. 219; *A Declaration of the Commons, concerning the rebellion in Ireland*, London, 1643; Nalson, *An impartial collection of the Great Affairs of State*, London, 1682-3, II, p. 638; R. Dunlop, *The Forged Commission of 1641*, *English Historical Review*, II, p. 527; see also p. 93 of this book for what I believe to be the most likely interpretation of this confused business.

10. Clarendon, Bk. IV, 121; H. Ferrero, *Lettres de Henriette Marie . . . à sa soeur Christine, Duchesse de Savoie*, Turin, 1881, p. 50.

11. Clarendon, Bk. IV, 77; *C.S.P. Ven.*, December, 1641, passim.

12. A. P. Newton, *The Colonising Activities of the English Puritans*, New Haven, 1914, pp. 301-3, 308; this very accusation, in respect of Warwick, occurs in the Royalist newssheet, *Mercurius Pragmaticus*, in December, 1647.

13. D'Ewes, pp. 198-9.

14. Richard Ward, *The Principal Duty of Parliament Men*, London, 1641.

15. See *The King's Peace*, p. 191.

16. D'Ewes, pp. 212, 221, 233-4.

17. *Ibid.*, p. 200; Clarendon, Bk. IV, 108-9; *C.S.P.D.*, 1641-3, p. 188.

18. D'Ewes, p. 216n.

19. *Ibid.*, p. 211.

20. *Ibid.*, pp. 213-6, 216n; Clarendon, I, p. 455.

21. H.M.C., *Buccleuch MSS.*, I, p. 286.

22. *C.S.P.D.*, 1641-3, pp. 186, 192; *C.S.P. Ven.*, 1640-2, p. 261; H.M.C., *Buccleuch MSS.*, I, p. 288.

23. D'Ewes, pp. 219-220; Rushworth, *Historical Collections*, London, 1659-1701, IV, pp. 436-7.

24. *C.J.*, II, p. 332; *L.J.*, IV, pp. 459-60.

25. *Somers Tracts*, IV, pp. 148-50.

26. Rushworth, IV, p. 233; Clarendon

denies that there was a depression in London in 1641-42; it was no doubt exaggerated by the King's enemies, but it is evident that there was considerable unemployment, and numerous sources point to, at least, a recession in trade.

27. Clarendon, Bk. IV, 17.

28. W. Notestein, *Commons Debates for 1629*, Minneapolis, 1921, pp. xlii-lv; *C.J.*, II, pp. 319-234; D'Ewes, pp. xx-xxi.

29. Spalding, *Memorials of the Troubles in Scotland*, ed. J. Stuart, *Spalding Club*, Aberdeen, 1850-51, II, p. 97; W. J. Couper, *The Edinburgh Periodical Press*, Stirling, 1908, p. 56.

30. Hall, *Works*, London, 1837-9, I, p. xlii.

31. R. Day, *Two Looks over Lincoln*, London, 1641.

32. *C.S.P.D.*, 1641-43, pp. 193, 197, 202; Butler, *Hudibras*; D'Ewes, pp. 270-71.

33. There had been an earlier casualty among the King's painters when A. van Dort, the keeper of his pictures, committed suicide in May 1640.

34. D'Ewes, p. 244-8

35. *C.S.P.D.*, 1641-3, p. 202; Nalson, II, p. 736.

36. D'Ewes, pp. 258-9, 261.

37. *Ibid.*, pp. 263, 268-9; *H.M.C., Buccleuch MSS.*, I, p. 289.

38. Nalson, II, pp. 720-2, 726-7, 758-9; D'Ewes, p. 290; *H.M.C. Report IV, MSS of the House of Lords*, pp. 107, 108. Mr. Willson Coates, after studying the MSS in the House of Lords concluded that many signatures had been written in by local clergy, and, even allowing for the illiteracy of some of their parishioners, are unlikely all to be genuine.

39. Giles Calfine, *A Mess of Pottage*, London, 1642. (*T.T.*, E. 179.19).

40. *C.S.P.D.*, 1641-3, pp. 202, 207; see *The King's Peace*, p. 291.

41. *The Discovery of a Swarm of Separatists*, London, 1641. (*T.T.*, E. 180.25).

42. *C.S.P.D.*, 1641-3, p. 201; *C.S.P. Ven.*, 1640-2, p. 265; *His Majesty's Special Command . . . with a relation of the uproars*, London, 1641. (*T.T.*, E. 179.19).

43. *L.J.*, IV, pp. 473-74.

44. *C.S.P.I.*, 1642, pp. 347, 350-1.

45. *Ibid.*, p. 352; Carte, *Life of James Duke of Ormonde*, Oxford, 1851, V, pp. 266-7; *H.M.C., Ormonde MSS*, New Series, II, p. 271; *H.M.C., MSS, of the Earl of Eglinton*, pp. 48-50; *Lismore Papers*, ed. Grosart, London, 1886, Second Series, IV, p. 228.

46. Clanricarde, *Memoirs and Letters*, London, 1757, pp. 29-33.

47. Carte, *Ormonde*, V, p. 272; *H.M.C., Egmont MSS*, I, p. 53; *C.S.P.D.*, 1641-3, p. 198; *C.S.P.I.*, p. 350.

48. *C.S.P.I.*, p. 350; D'Ewes, p. 252; *A Declaration of the Commons*, (*T.T.*, E. 61.23), p. 10.

49. D'Ewes, p. 288; Clarendon, Bk. IV, 91-2.

50. D'Ewes, pp. 294-5.

51. *Ibid.*, pp. 296-8, 305.

52. *C.S.P.Ven.*, 1640-2, p. 265.

53. *Ibid.*, pp. 323-4; *C.S.P.D.*, 1641-3, p. 208; *L.J.*, IV, p. 483.

54. D'Ewes, p. 319; J. Bond, *Downfall of Old Common Counselmen*, London, 1642; *Somers Tracts*, IV, pp. 588-9; Clarendon, Bk. IV, 181-2.

55. D'Ewes, pp. 335, 340.

56. Nalson, pp. 742-50; Rushworth, IV, pp. 452-3; Clarendon, I, p. 493; see also Wormald, pp. 34ff.

57. D'Ewes, p. 347; *L.J.*, IV, p. 490.

58. D'Ewes, pp. 350, 355; see *The King's Peace*, p. 467.

59. Clarendon, Bk. IV, 102.

60. D'Ewes, pp. 350-1.

61. *Ibid.*, pp. 352-3; *C.S.P.D.*, 1641-3, p. 214; *H.M.C., Montagu of Beaulieu MSS*, p. 138.

62. *C.S.P.Ven.*, 1640-2, p. 271; *C.S.P.D.*, 1641-3, pp. 214, 216, 217; Hall, *Works*, I, pp. xlv-xlvi; *H.M.C., Montagu of Beaulieu MSS*, p. 138; Clarendon, Bk. IV, 139

63. *C.S.P.D.*, 1641-3, p. 214; *Archives de la Maison d'Orange-Nassau*, ed. Groen van Prinsterer, Utrecht, 1857-61, Second Series, III, p. 495; *A True Relation of the Most Wise Speech made by Captain Venn*, London, 1641 (*T.T.*, E. 181.21); *P.R.O. Transcripts*, 31.3.73, *Despatch of La Ferté Imbault*, folio 5.

64. Clarendon, Bk. IV, 139-40; Hall, *Works*, I, p. xlvi; Nalson, II, pp. 794-5; *Archives de la Maison d'-Orange-Nassau*, Second Series, III, p. 498; Gardiner, *History of England*, London, 1899, X, p. 122-3.

65. *C.J.*, II, p. 362-3; *L.J.*, IV, pp. 498-9; D'Ewes, p. 365-7; Hall, *Works*, I, p. xlvii; *Archives de la Maison d'-Orange-Nassau*, Second Series, III, p. 496; Clarendon, Bk. IV, 142.

66. Rushworth, IV, p. 466; D'Ewes, p. 373; *MSS of the City of London, Minutes of the Common Council*, December 31, 1641.

67. D'Ewes, p. 373.

68. *Archives de la Maison d'Orange-Nassau*, Second Series, III, p. 496; Clarendon, Bk. IV, 280. Clarendon implies that Lady Carlisle was the agent used; both he and Heenvliet suggest that the threat to the queen precipitated the king's personal participation in the attempted arrest of the Five Members.

69. *C.S.P.D.*, 1641-3, p. 243.

70. Carte, *Ormonde*, V, pp. 281-2; Rushworth, IV, pp. 472-3.

71. Clarendon, Bk. IV, 122.

72. *C.J.*, II, pp. 366-7; *L.J.*, IV, pp. 500-1; D'Ewes, pp. 377-8; Clarendon, Bk. IV, 150, 154.

73. *L.J.*, IV, p. 501.

74. *Archives de la Maison d'Orange-Nassau*, Second Series, III, pp. 494-5.

75. *C.S.P.D.*, 1641-3, pp. 235, 287.

76. D'Ewes, p. 378.

77. *Ibid.*, pp. 383-4; *C.S.P. Ven.*, 1640-2, p. 276.

78. D'Ewes, pp. 381-4; Verney, *Notes on the Long Parliament*, ed. Bruce,

Camden Society, London, 1845, pp. 138-9, *C.J.*, II, p. 368; Rushworth, IV, p. 477-8; *P.R.O. Transcripts*, 31.3.73, *Despatch of La Ferté Imbault*, folio 10.

79. Clarendon, Bk. IV, 155; *C.S.P.D.*, 1641-3, pp. 238, 252; *Somers Tracts*, IV, p. 589.

80. *C.S.P.D.*, 1641-3, pp. 241, 242-3; *Somers Tracts*, IV, pp. 348-9; *H.M.C.*, *Montagu of Beaulieu*, *MSS*, p. 141; *Archives de la Maison d'Orange-Nassau*, Second Series, III, pp. 501-2.

81. D'Ewes, pp. 388-391; *C.S.P.D.*, 1641-3, p. 245; Dugdale, *Short View of the late Troubles in England*, London, 1681, p. 82; Clarendon, Bk. IV, 156, 162.

82. *The Dramatic Records of Sir Henry Herbert*, ed. J. Q. Adams, New Haven, 1917, p. 58.

83. *C.S.P.D.*, 1641-3, pp. 248-9; Clarendon, Bk. IV, 198; *MSS of the City of London, Minutes of the Common Council*, January 8th, 1642.

84. *C.S.P.D.*, 1641-3, pp. 239, 249; Clarendon, Bk. IV, 124, 158, 192.

85. Clarendon, I, p. 509n; *Archives de la Maison d'Orange-Nassau*, Second Series, III, p. 502.

86. *C.S.P. Ven.*, 1641-2, p. 281; *H.M.C.*, *Montagu of Beaulieu MSS*, p. 141; Eachard, *History of England*, London, 1707-18, II, p. 280; *Memoires de Madame de Motteville*, ed. Petitot, Paris, 1824, p. 109; *C.S.P.D.*, 1641-3, p.256.

87. *C.S.P. Ven.*, 1641-2, p. 281, *C.S.P.D.*, 1641-3, p. 252.

BOOK I: CHAPTER II

1. *C.S.P.D.*, 1641-3, p. 254; *B.M.*, Harleian MSS, 164, *D'Ewes Diary*, folio 321a; *C.J.*, II, pp. 370, 372-3.

2. *H.M.C.*, *Portland MSS*, I, pp. 31-2; III, p. 83; *C.S.P.D.*, 1641-3, pp. 253, 259-60.

3. Rushworth, IV, p. 496; Verney, pp. 144f.

4. *Archives de la Maison d'Orange-Nassau*, Second Series, IV, pp. 7ff.

5. *Surrey Archaeological Society Transactions*, XXII, H. E. Malden, *Civil War in Surrey*, p. 105; *ibid.*, XXXVI, The Earl of Onslow, *Sir Richard Onslow*.

6. *MSS of the City of London, Journal of the Common Council*, January 19, 1642.

7. *L.J.*, IV, pp. 523-4.

8. *C.S.P.D.*, 1641-3, pp. 253, 263-4; *Somers Tracts*, IV, pp. 357-8; Clarendon, Bk. IV, 216.

9. Rushworth, IV, p. 501; *H.M.C. Report II*, p. 170; Burnet, *Lives*, pp. 189-91; Cox, *Hibernia Anglicana*, London, 1689, p. 211.

10. *Archives de la Maison d'Orange-Nassau*, Second Series, IV, p. 15; *C.S.P.D.*, 1641-3; p. 254; *Oxinden Letters*, p. 272.

11. *C.S.P.D.*, 1641-3, p. 265; *The Douai College Diaries*, 1598-1654, ed. E. H. Burton and T. L. Williams, *Catholic Record Society*, 1911, II, p. 432. Alban Roe and Thomas Greene were beatified in 1929.

12. Clarendon, Bk. IV, 244; *C.S.P.D.*, 1641-3, pp. 255, 265, 269.

13. *C.J.*, II, p. 390.

14. *L.J.*, IV, pp. 540-3; *Oxinden Letters*, p. 271.

15. *C.J.*, II, p. 400; *L.J.*, IV, pp. 543, 550; Clarendon, Bk. IV, 255-61; Verney, p. 149.

16. *C.J.*, II, p. 404.

17. Clarendon, Bk. IV, 239-43; *L.J.*, IV, p. 557-8; *C.J.*, II, p. 407; D'Ewes MS, folio 362b.

18. *L.J.*, IV, p. 566.

19. *Archives de la Maison d'Orange-Nassau*, Second Series, IV, p. 22; *C.S.P.D.*, 1641-3, p. 276; *C.S.P. Ven.*, 1642, p. 296.

20. *C.S.P.D.*, 1641-3, pp. 286, 290.

21. *Archives de la Maison d'Orange-Nassau*, Second Series, III, p. 496; *C.S.P.D.*, 1641-3, pp. 276, 289;

J. Forster, *Biographical Essay on Cromwell*, London, 1860, p. 74.

22. *C.S.P.D.*, 1641-3, pp. 198, 288.

23. *Reg. P. C. Scot.*, VII, pp. 198, 211.

24. *C.S.P.D.*, 1641-3, p. 277; *C.J.*, II, pp. 430-3, 442; Clarendon, Bk. IV, 302-10.

25. *C.S.P. Ven.*, 1640-2, p. 296; 1642-3, p. 5; Mme. de Motteville, p. 111.

26. Clarendon, Bk. VI, 40; Haller, *Liberty and Reformation in the Puritan Revolution*, New York, 1955, p. 69; Stephen Marshall, *Meroz Cursed*, London, 1642.

27. Carte, *Ormonde*, V, pp. 335-6; *L.J.*, IV, pp. 593-5.

28. *Ibid.*, pp. 617-8; Clarendon, Bk. IV, 317-21.

29. Clarendon, Bk. IV, 340; *The Petition of the Citizens of London, Feb. 26th, 1642 (T.T., E. 140.12)*.

30. *C.J.*, II, p. 461; Clarendon, Bk. IV, 322.

31. *L.J.*, IV, pp. 621-2; Clarendon, Bk. IV, 326-8.

32. *Acts and Ordinances*, I, pp. 1-5; see also J. Allen, *Enquiry into the Growth of the Prerogative*, London, 1849, and Haskins, *English Representative Government*, Oxford, 1948.

33. *C.J.*, II, 467, 478-9, 484; Clarendon, Bk. IV, 388.

34. *C.J.*, II, pp. 471, 473, 478, 486; Clarendon, Bk. IV, 340; Verney, p. 163; *MSS of the City of London, Journal of the Common Council*, January 19 and March 2; *Oxinden Letters*, p. 272.

35. Clarendon, Bk. IV, 343-4.

36. *H.M.C., Franciscan MSS*, p. 118.

37. *A Contemporary history of affairs in Ireland . . . entitled an "Aphorismical discovery of treasonable faction,"* ed. J. T. Gilbert, Dublin, 1879, pp. 33-4.

38. Hogan, *Letters and Papers relating to the Irish Rebellion between 1642 and 1646*, Dublin, 1936, pp. 12-13; *Rawdon Papers*, ed. E. Berwick, London, 1819, pp. 86-92.

39. *A collection of the state letters of . . .*

the Earl of Orrery, ed. T. Morice, London, 1742, pp. 2-4; *C.S.P.I.*, p. 357.

40. *Lismore Papers*, Second Series, IV, p. 18, 150-1, 259, V, pp. 99-107; *H.M.C., Report VIII*, Appendix III, p. 437.

41. Clanricarde, pp. 22, 26-7, 84-109 *passim*; Hogan, pp. 81-2; Carte, *Ormonde*, V, pp. 285-6; Clanricarde's mother was Frances Walsingham who had been married to Sir Philip Sidney and to the great Earl of Essex, before she became his father's wife.

42. *Narratives illustrative of the contests in Ireland*, ed. T. C. Croker, *Camden Society*, London, 1841, pp. 7, 11, 14ff; Frost, *History of County Clare*, 1893, pp. 359-60.

43. Clanricarde, pp. 21, 72-4.

44. *H.M.C., Egmont MSS*, I, I, p. 74; *Lismore Papers*, II, IV, p. 265.

45. *H.M.C., Montagu of Beaulieu MSS*, p. 146; *Reg. P. C. Scot*, pp. 190, 209.

46. See J. M. Read, *Atrocity Propaganda and the Irish Rebellion, Public Opinion Quarterly*, Princeton, 1938; Henry Jones, *A Remonstrance*, Dublin and London, 1642 (*T.T.*, E.141. 30); see also Barnabas O'Ferrall and Daniel O'Connell. *Commentarius Rinuccinianus*, ed. Fr. Stanislaus, Dublin, 1932-49, I, pp. 252, 364.

47. Rushworth, III, I, pp. 405-21; Henry Jones, *A Remonstrance; Records of Elgin*, II, p. 245.

48. *Memoirs of James, Earl of Castlehaven*, 3rd edition, London, 1684, p. 62; Clanricarde, pp. 72, 77, 80; see also Bagwell, *Ireland under the Stuarts*, London, 1909, I, pp. 342-4.

49. James Turner, *Memoirs of his own Life and Times*, ed. L. Thomson, Edinburgh, 1829, p. 20; Carte, *Ormonde*, V, pp. 294-5.

50. *Lismore Papers*, Second Series, IV, p. 264; V, p. 55; Castlehaven, pp. 43 seq.

51. *Two Biographies of William Bedell*, ed.

Shuckburgh, Cambridge, 1902, pp. 62, 205.

52. *H.M.C., Egmont MSS*, I, I, p. 166; Carte, *Ormonde*, V, pp. 294-5.

53. *Ibid.*, pp. 292-3.

54. *Ibid.*, pp. 266-7; *Somers Tracts*, IV, pp. 588-9.

55. N. Bernard, *The whole proceedings of the siege of Drogheda in Ireland*, London, 1642; see also Hogan, p. 165.

56. Whitelocke, p. 54.

57. *L.J.*, IV, pp. 647, 650; Clarendon, Bk. IV, pp. 346-51.

58. John Worthington, *Diary and Correspondence*, ed. J. Crossley, Chetham Society, 1847, p. 11.

59. J. E. B. Mayor, ed. *Two Lives of Nicholas Ferrar*, Cambridge, 1855, pp. 152-4.

60. The best analysis of Hyde's point of view at this time is to be found in B. H. G. Wormald, *Clarendon, Politics, History and Religion*, Cambridge, 1951, Part I, section 2, especially pp. 80-1.

61. *Clarendon State Papers*, II, p. 139.

62. *C.S.P.D.*, 1641-3, p. 300.

63. Clarendon, Bk. V, 2-10; cf Wormald, p. 77.

64. Heylyn, *Aerius Redivivus*, Oxford, 1670, p. 447.

65. *Clarendon State Papers*, II, p. 141.

66. *C.J.*, II, p. 463.

67. Abbott, I, p. 163.

68. *C.S.P.D.*, 1641-3, p. 314.

69. Baillon, *Henriette Marie de France, étude historique . . . suivi de ses lettres inédites*, Paris, 1877, pp. 366-76. References to the letters of Henrietta Maria are given from Baillon's work in preference to the edition by Mrs. Everett Green (London, 1857) when Baillon gives the original French and Mrs. Green supplies only a translation.

70. *C.S.P.D.*, 1641-3, p. 304.

71. *Ibid.*, p. 312; Clarendon, Bk. VI, 35.

72. *Rural Economy in Yorkshire in 1641, being the farming and account books of Henry Best*, ed. C. B. Robinson,

Surtees Society, 1857, p. 102; *H.M.C.*, *Report*, VI, Appendix III, p. 439.

73. *Autobiography of Joseph Lister of Bradford*, ed. T. Wright, London, 1842, pp. 7-8.

74. *The Fairfax Correspondence*, ed. G. W. Johnson, London, 1848, II, pp. 299, 367-75, 393, 419; *Camden Miscellany*, VIII, p. 4.

75. *Douai College Diaries*, II, p. 433.

76. *Cal. Clar. S.P.*, I, p. 228; *C.J.*, II, 525, 527; *Reg. P. C. Scot*, pp. 241, 249.

77. *H.M.C.*, *Report*, X, *Appendix VI*, p. 145.

78. Carte, *Ormonde*, V, p. 309; Castlehaven, p. 39.

79. Baillon, p. 378; *H.M.C.*, *Franciscan MSS*, pp. 138-9.

80. *C.S.P. Ven.*, 1642-3, p. 41.

81. *C.S.P.D.*, 1641-3, pp. 306, 307, 308, 312.

82. *C.J.*, II, 542; *C.S.P.D.*, 1641-3, p. 329; see also A. M. W. Stirling, *The Hothams*, London, 1917, pp. 53-60, and Basil N. Reckitt, *Charles I and Hull*, London, 1952, Chapter IV. Mr. Reckitt comments on the strange inaction of the Royalists in the town; in the absence of any evidence in his favour, I shall continue to entertain the gravest suspicions of the Elector Palatine in this connection.

83. D'Ewes, *Autobiography and Correspondence*, ed. Halliwell, London, 1845, II, pp. 291-2; Hauck, *Briefe der kinder des Winterkönigs*, Heidelberg, 1908, p. 21; see also *H.M.C.*, *Report*, XII, *Appendix VIII*, MSS of the Duke of Atholl, p. 29 where the prince mentioned is undoubtedly the Elector and not, as stated, the Prince of Orange.

84. *C.S.P.D.*, 1641-3, p. 316; Baillon, pp. 380-3.

85. *C.S.P. Ven.*, 1642-3, p. 52.

86. N. Wallington, *Historical Notices*, ed. R. Webb, London, 1869, p. 9; *C.J.*, II, pp. 549-50; Verney, p. 175; *C.S.P.D.*, 1641-3, pp. 3, 6.

87. *Letters of Lady Brilliana Harley*, ed. T. T. Lewis, Camden Society, 1854, pp. 166-7, 170-1; *Reliquiae Baxterianae*, London, 1696, pp. 40-1; *H.M.C. Various*, I, p. 320; *H.M.C.*, *MSS of Wells Cathedral*, II, p. 427; *H.M.C.*, *Montagu of Beaulieu*, p. 147; *True Newes from Norwich written by T.L.* (*T.T.*, E. 140.17).

88. *The Knyvett Letters*, 1620-44, ed. Bertram Schofield, London, 1950, p. 107.

89. *H.M.C.*, *Ormonde MSS*, New Series, II, p. 372; *Captain Yarner's Relation*, London, 1642.

90. *H.M.C.*, *Ormonde MSS*, New Series, II, p. 6; Castlehaven, p. 42; *Clarendon State Papers*, II, p. 143; *Captain Yarner's Relation*.

91. Cox. *Hibernia Anglicana*, pp. 206-8; Cox and others reject Antrim's story, partly because some of the details can be shown to be inaccurate chronologically, partly because—as Cox argued—it would have been simpler for the King to make Ormonde Lord Lieutenant straight away, instead of asking him to assume the government by a *coup d'état*. Cox prints on pp. 210-11 three highly suspicious letters from Charles to Ormonde, dated June and October 1641, and February, 1642. In fact, Charles—who had appointed the Earl of Leicester Lord Lieutenant to satisfy Parliament—could not have substituted Ormonde without provoking the gravest suspicion. I am inclined to think that Antrim's story is basically true, that Ormonde—who can hardly have liked the scheme—was in no hurry to act on it; that the premature rising did in fact throw out all plans. I have been driven to this conclusion by the repeated evidence that the Irish had expected Ormonde to lead them and regarded his failure to do so as a betrayal. This could hardly have been so unless there had been

some grounds for believing him involved in the rising.

92. *Castlehaven*, pp. 43, 58; Gilbert, *Contemporary History*, I, p. 31.

93. *Clarendon State Papers*, II, p. 143.

94. Carte, *Ormonde*, V, pp. 309-10.

95. James Wilson, *History of Scots affairs*, 1654, pp. 18-19.

96. *Reg. P. C. Scot*, p. 165.

97. Spalding, *Memorialls of the troubles in Scotland*, ed. J. Stuart, *Spalding Club*, Aberdeen, 1850-1, II, pp. 142, 125.

98. *Minutes of the Synod of Argyll*, ed. Duncan C. MacTavish, *Scottish History Society*, Third Series, XXXVII, Edinburgh, 1943, pp. 59, 61.

99. Hogan, p. 47; Turner, *Memoirs*, pp. 20-22; Robert Monro, *A True Relation of the Proceedings of the Scottish Army in Ireland*, London, 1642.

100. *L.J.*, IV, pp. 567-8; *Memoirs of Henry Guthry, Bishop of Dunkeld*, ed. G. Crawford, Glasgow, 1747, p. 114.

101. Spalding, II, p. 141.

102. *C.S.P. Ven.*, 1642-3, p. 54; *Reg. P. C. Scot*, pp. 256-7.

103. *Ibid.*, pp. 256-9, 261, 284-5; Spalding, II, pp. 141, 147-50, 160; Guthry, p. 116; *H.M.C., Buccleuch MSS*, I, p. 298; *Letters and Journals of Robert Baillie*, ed. Laing, *Bannatyne Club*, Edinburgh, 1841, II, pp. 43-4.

104. *C.S.P.D.*, 1641-3, p. 329.

105. *Ibid.*, pp. 320-5.

106. *C.S.P. Ven.*, 1642-3, pp. 22, 109.

107. *C.S.P.D.*, 1641-3, pp. 316, 322-3; *L.J.*, V, p. 61.

108. Clarendon, Bk. VI, 139.

109. *C.S.P. Ven.*, 1642-3, p. 70; *H.M.C., Buccleuch MSS*, I, p. 302; Clarendon, Bk. VI, pp. 156, 212-3; Rushworth, IV, pp. 718-9.

110. *Oxinden Letters*, p. 301; *L.J.*, V, pp. 87-8; see also C. H. McIlwain, *The High Court of Parliament*, 2nd edition, New Haven, 1934, pp. 161, 352.

111. Clarendon, Bk. VI, 320-2.

112. *C.S.P.D.*, 1641-3, p. 336; *Yorkshire Diaries*, Surtees Society, 1877, p. 135; *C.S.P. Ven.*, 164-3, p. 78; *H.M.C., Cowper MSS*, p. 318.

113. *Acts and Ordinances*, pp. 6-9; Clarendon, Bk. VI, 336-8; *Trevelyan Papers*, ed. Collier, Camden Society, 1872, III, p. 227; *The Diary of the Rev. Ralph Josselin*, ed. Hockliffe, *Camden Society*, 1908, p. 13; *H.M.C., Portland MSS*, III, p. 94; Brilliana Harley, pp. 181-2, 187; Clarendon, Bk. VI, 39-42.

114. *Knyvett Letters*, p. 102.

115. Clarendon, Bk. VI, 316, 326-32.

116. *Knyvett Letters*, p. 105.

117. *Ibid.*, 365; Burnet, pp. 194, 196; *Somers Tracts*, IV, p. 363; Clarendon, Bk. VI, 375; *L.J.*, V, p. 369; *The Last News from York and Hull*, London, July 1642.

118. *L.J.*, V, p. 280.

119. R. Bell, *Memorials of the Civil War* (usually called Volumes III and IV of *The Fairfax Correspondence*) London, 1849, I, p. 441; *A Letter concerning the Lord Chandos*, London, 1642; *Terrible News from Leicester*, London, 1642; (*T.T.*, E. 113.6 and E. 108.26); *L.J.*, V, 145, 148, 191.

120. *H.M.C., Buccleuch MSS*, I, p. 305; *H.M.C., Cowper MSS*, p. 319.

121. Brilliana Harley, pp. 177, 181-2.

122. *C.S.P.D.*, 1641-3, pp. 342, 343, 361.

123. Dircks, *Life and Times of the Second Marquis of Worcester*, London, 1865, p. 330. See A. H. Dodd, *Studies in Stuart Wales*, Cardiff, 1952, pp. 64 seq. for the rivalry between Lloyd and Lord Herbert and the internal rivalries in Wales.

124. G. Penn, *Memorials of William Penn*, London, 1833, I, p. 19.

125. Bankes, *Story of Corfe Castle*, pp. 122, 129, 139.

126. *The Voyages of Captain William Jackson*, ed. V. T. Harlow, *Camden Miscellany*, XIII, 1924, p. 1.

127. Clarendon, Bk. VI, 39-44, 377-81; *L.J.*, V, p. 185; *Acts and Ordinances*, I, p. 12.

128. Clarendon, Bk. VI, 374; the Providence, according to a list in the *Petworth MSS*, No. 40, was of 304 tons, with a crew of 110, carrying 14 guns.

129. *Ibid* Bk. VI, 437; *Fairfax Correspondence*, III, p. 12; *L.J.*, V, p. 217; see also E. Broxap, *Sieges of Hull, English Historical Review*, XXXII, 1917.

130. Clarendon, Bk. VI, 388-90.

131. Carte, *Letters*, I, p. 16.

132. *Yorkshire Diaries*, p. 137.

133. *Lancashire Civil War Tracts*, pp. 30ff, 112-3.

134. *C.J.*, II, p. 769; Clarendon, Bk. VI, p. 67.

BOOK I: CHAPTER III

1. Spalding, II, p. 210; Guthry, pp. 118-9.

2. See *The King's Peace*, pp. 224-5.

3. *H.M.C., Hamilton MSS, Supplementary Report*, p. 68.

4. *Reg. P. C. Scot*, VII, pp. 288-96.

5. Patrick Adair, *A true narrative of the rise and progress of the Presbyterian Church in Ireland*, Belfast, 1866, p. 97.

6. *The Letters and Journals of Robert Baillie, Principal of the University of Glasgow, 1637-1662*, ed. D. Laing, Bannatyne Club, Edinburgh, 1841-2, II, pp. 45-54; Peterkin, *Records of the Kirk of Scotland, containing the acts and proceedings of the several assemblies from the year 1638 downwards*, Edinburgh, 1838, p. 330; Spalding, II, pp. 172-3.

7. *Reg. P. C. Scot.*, VII, pp. 314, 318-9.

8. Gordon Albion, *Charles I and Rome*, p. 375; Hogan, pp. 82ff.

9. Gilbert, *Contemporary History*, p. 43; Turner, *Memoirs*, p. 26; *Commentarius* I, pp. 332, 337-8; Hogan, pp. 119-20.

10. *H.M.C., Ormonde MSS*, N.S., II, pp. 168-9.

11. *Good Newes from Ireland*, London,

1642; *A True Copie of Two Letters brought by Mr. Peters*, London, 1642; H. Peter, *A True Relation of the passages of God's Providence in Ireland*, London, 1642. (*T.T.*, E. 109.4, E. 121.44 and E. 242.15.) See also Clanricarde, pp. 219, 231, 286; Carte, *Ormonde*, V, pp. 348-50; Hogan, pp. 90, 103-11. For an account which does what can be done to explain the behaviour of Forbes, see R. S. Stearns, *The Strenuous Puritan*, University of Illinois, 1954, pp. 188-97.

12. Carte, *Ormonde*, V, p. 357.

13. Abbott, I, pp. 188, 191; Ryves, *Querela Cantabrigiensis*, London, 1647, pp. 4-5.

14. *H.M.C., Portland MSS*, I, pp. 56-7.

15. *A letter sent from Mr. Sergeant Wilde and Humphrey Salway*, London, 1642; *Joyfull Newes from Wells*, London, 1642; *A Perfect Relation of the Proceedings of the Marquesse Hartford . . . in Wells*, London, 1642; *A letter . . . concerning the Lord Shandois*, London, 1642. (*T.T.*, E. 107.14; E. 111, 4-5; E. 113.6); *Memoirs of Edmund Ludlow*, ed. C. H. Firth, Oxford, 1844, I, p. 34; Whitelocke, p. 59; *C.S.P.D.*, August 1642 passim; Clarendon, Bk. VI, 3-7; Hopton, *Bellum Civile*. Somerset Record Society, XVIII, London, 1902, pp. 6ff.

16. *Douai Diaries*, p. 437.

17. Malbon, *Memorials of the Civil War in Cheshire*. Cheshire Record Society, 1889, pp. 24-5; R. H. Morris, *Siege of Chester*, Chester, 1924, p. 315.

18. *H.M.C., Portland MSS*, I, p. 52; *The Proceedings at Banbury*, London, 1642. (*T.T.*, E. 111.11).

19. *H.M.C., Portland MSS*, I, p. 50; *C.S.P.D.*, 1644, pp. 179, 180.

20. *Acts and Ordinances*, I, pp. 16-20.

21. Eliot Warburton, *Memoirs of Prince Rupert and the Cavaliers*, London, 1849, I, pp. 109-110, 460-2.

22. Malbon, pp. 31-4; Woolrych *Yorkshire's Treaty of Neutrality, His-*

tory Today, V, pp. 696-794; Clarendon, VI, 254-5, 257-9; *True Intelligence from Lincolnshire*, London, 1642 (*T.T.*, E. 113.7); J. R. Phillips, *Civil War in Wales*, London, 1874, II, pp. 44-8; Pennington and Roots, *The Committee at Stafford*, 1643-5, Manchester, 1957, p. xx.

23. Godfrey Davies, *Parliamentary Army under Essex, English Historical Review*, XLIX, pp. 33, 35; Abbott, I, p. 191; *Letters of Nehemiah Wharton*, ed. H. Ellis, *Archaeologia*, XXXV, pp. 312-5; H. Ross Williamson, *John Hampden*, London, 1933, pp. 300-8; *Joyful Newes from the Isle of Ely*, London, 1642; *A True and Perfect relation of the seizing of the House of Mr. Barnes*, London, 1642 (*T.T.*, E. 115.9 and 13).

24. Ludlow, I, p. 39.

25. *Acts and Ordinances*, I, pp. 14-16; *C.S.P.D.*, 1644, pp. 313-4.

26. *C.J.*, II, p. 651.

27. *C.S.P. Ven.*, 1642-3, pp. 130, 135; *C.S.P.D.*, 1641-3, p. 374; *A Perfect Diurnal of the proceedings in Hartfordshire*, London, 1642; *A True Relation of the late expedition into Kent*, London, 1642 (*T.T.*, E. 115.7, 10).

28. Clarendon, Bk. V, 446; Bulstrode, *Memoirs and reflections upon the reign of King Charles I*, London, 1721, p. 72.

29. *H.M.C., Report XII*, Appendix IX, p. 10; Clarendon, V, p. 418.

30. Wood, *Civil War in Nottingham*, p. 21; see T. S. Willan, *River Navigation in England*, London, for an excellent map showing the navigable stretches of English rivers at this time.

31. Wood, *Civil War in Nottingham*, p. 5.

32. Nehemiah Wharton, pp. 316, 318, 320.

33. Clarendon, Bk. V, 447-9; *A True Relation of . . . His Majesty setting up his standard*, London, 1642 (*T.T.*, E. 115.4); Wood, *Civil War in Nottingham*, pp. 21-2.

34. Clarendon, Bk. V, 8-18, pp. 301n; *C.S.P. Ven.*, 1642-3, p. 153.

35. *Ibid.*, p. 160; Wood, *Civil War in Nottingham*, p. 25; *Records of the Borough of Leicester*, ed. H. Stocks and W. H. Stevenson, Cambridge, 1925, IV, pp. 317-9, 327.

36. Clarendon, Bk. VI, 58-61.

37. *A true relation of a brave exploit . . . in taking of the Castle of Dover* (*T.T.*, E. 115.8).

38. *A true relation of how the Isle of Wight was secured* (*T.T.*, E. 116.40); *H.M.C., Portland MSS*, I. pp. 54-6.

39. *Articles exhibited against Sir Philip Carteret*; *The remonstrance of the . . . Common Council of Jersey* (*T.T.*, E. 110.15; E. 114.9).

40. *H.M.C., Portland MSS*, I, p. 61; Lismore Papers, II, V, p. 109; *A Declaration of all the passages at the taking of Portsmouth* and *A true relation of the town of Portsmouth at the late siege* (*T.T.*, E. 117.10 and E. 118.22). Clarendon's account (II, p. 315n) is unduly hard on Goring whose reputation suffered owing to his behaviour later in the war. Until drink and disease undermined him, Goring enjoyed and deserved a high reputation as a soldier, and even to the end of his career he was capable of flashes of brilliance.

41. *H.M.C., Portland MSS*, I, pp. 57-8; *A true relation of the taking of 46 Cavaliers at Brackley* and *True Newes from Oxford* (*T.T.*, E. 117.11, E. 114.31); Wood, pp. 56-7.

42. *H.M.C. Report X, Appendix VI*, pp. 147-8; *A most Excellent Relation of the Proceedings at Sherborne* and *The Newest Relation of . . . the late occurrence at Sherborne* (*T.T.*, E. 117.12 and 4).

43. *C.S.P.D.*, 1641-3, p. 389.

44. Clarendon, Bk. VI, 22-3.

45. Warburton, I, p. 396; *Several Occurrences that have lately happened in the taking of Dudley Castle*; Clarendon, Bk. VI, 29.

46. Clarendon, Bk. VI, 49.
47. *C.S.P.D.*, 1641-3, p. 309; *A Copy of a letter sent from Robert, Earl of Essex* (*T.T.*, E. 118.26); Anthony Wood, *Life and Times*, I., pp. 59-60.
48. *C.S.P.D.*, *loc. cit.;* Ellis, *Original Letters, Second Series*, II, pp. 297-301.
49. Ludlow, p. 40; N. Fiennes, *A Most true Relation* (*T.T.*, E. 126, 38 and 39); Clarendon, Bk. VI, 44-6; Bulstrode, *Memoirs*, pp. 73-4; Willis-Bund, *Civil War in Worcestershire*, pp. 35-45.
50. Godfrey Davies, *Parliamentary Army Under Essex*, p. 36.
51. Clarendon, Bk. VI, 43; Nehemiah Wharton, pp. 326, 330; Carte, *Letters*, I, p. 15; for the fame of the organ see Wickham Legg, *Seven Weeks Journey*, p. 79.
52. Bruno Ryves, *Mercurius Rusticus*, London, 1647, pp. 1-3, 13-15; *H.M.C., Report X, Appendix VI*, pp. 86, 146-7; *C.S.P. Ven.*, 1642-3, p. 142; Peck, *Desiderata Curiosa*, London, 1779, II, p. 474.
53. Heylyn, *Aerius Redivivus*, Oxford, 1670, p. 452; *A true relation of the late expedition into Kent* and *A copy of a letter sent by Dr. Paske* (*T.T.*, E. 116.22; E. 115.10); *Mercurius Rusticus*, pp. 6-11; *Catholic Record Society*, XXIV, p. 259; other interesting details about Fr. Bullaker in F. de Marsys, *Histoire de la persécution des Catholiques en Angleterre*, Paris, 1646, pp. 6off.
54. E. Robinson, *A Discourse of the Civil War in Lancashire*, Chetham Society, LXII, 1864, pp. 12-14.
55. *H.M.C., Montagu of Beaulieu*, p. 146; Clarendon, VI, 64; I am indebted to Mr. Dore, who is working on a life of Sir William Brereton, for much useful information about the connections between Cheshire families and settlers in Ireland.
56. *Cheshire Civil War Tracts*, Chetham Society, 1908, I, pp. 60-3; Malbon, pp, 26-7.
57. J. Harland, *Lancashire Lieutenancy under the Tudors and Stuarts*, Chetham Society, 1859, p. 293.
58. Robinson, *Civil War in Lancashire*, pp. 7-11; *Military Proceedings in Lancashire*, ed. G. Ormerod, Chetham Society, 1844; E. Broxap, *Civil War in Lancashire*, Manchester, 1910, Chapter III.
59. *Maseres Tracts*, I, p. 417; *H.M.C., Portland MSS*, I, p. 67.
60. Hacket, *Scrinia Reserata*, London, 1693, II, p. 186-7.
61. See *The King's Peace*, pp. 210, 271.
62. Margaret, Duchess of Newcastle, *Life of the Duke of Newcastle*, ed. C. H. Firth, London, 1886, p. 25.
63. *C.J.*, II, p. 794; *C.S.P. Ven.*, 1642-3, p. 178; *A true relation of the taking of a great ship at Yarmouth* (*T.T.*, E. 121.21).
64. T. Mendenhall, *The Shrewsbury Drapers and the Welsh Wool Trade in the XVI and XVII Centuries*, Oxford, 1953, p. 202; for Charles's residence in Shrewsbury see also the article by H. Beaumont in *Transactions of the Shrewsbury Archaeological Society*, LI, Shrewsbury, 1941.
65. *H.M.C., Report XII Appendix IX*, pp. 11-12; *A loving and loyal speech spoken at Raglan Castle* (*T.T.*, E. 122.14); J. Phillips, *Civil War in Wales*, II, pp. 26-9.
66. *Ibid.*, pp. 31-2; *C.S.P. Ven.*, 1642-3, pp. 181, 186; Clarendon, Bk. VI, 69; J. W. Gough, *The Superlative Prodigal*, Bristol, 1932, p. 60.
67. Collins, *Sydney Papers*, II, p. 667-8.
68. Baillon, p. 445.
69. Collins, *Sydney Papers*, II, p. 667.
70. *Oxinden Letters*, p. 282.
71. *H.M.C., Report VII*, p. 441.
72. *Rump Songs*, London, 1662.
73. Hyder E. Rollins, *Cavalier and Puritan*, New York, 1923, p. 138.
74. *Autobiography of Captain John Hodgson*, Edinburgh, 1806, p. 89.
75. Clarendon, Bk. VI, 76.

76. G. Davies, *Battle of Edgehill, English Historical Review*, XXXVI, p. 41.

77. *C.S.P. Ven.*, 1642-3, p. 186; Clarendon, Bk. VI, 73, 95.

78. Clarendon, Bk. VI, 76.

79. The movements of Essex are from the account by Denzil Holles, *An Exact and True Relation of the fight near Kineton* (*T.T.*, E. 124.26), pp. 3-4; those of Rupert and the King from *Prince Rupert's Journal in England*, ed. C. H. Firth, *English Historical Review*, XIII, p. 731; from Bulstrode, p. 76, and Warburton, II, pp. 10, 12.

80. Holles's account, as above, p. 4; Godfrey Davies, *Edgehill*, pp. 30-2.

81. Clarendon, Bk. VI, 78, 83; Carte, *Letters*, I, p. 9.

82. Clarendon, II, p. 365n; Colonel Peter Young has published, in the *Journal for the Society of Army Historical Research*, XXXIII, 1955, the plan of "Etch-hill" drawn by Rupert's chief engineer Bernard de Gomme some months later and now in the Royal Library at Windsor. This plan clearly shows the Swedish formation which must have been Rupert's idea as Lindsey would hardly have been familiar with it.

83. *Somers Tracts*, IV, p. 476; Bulstrode, pp. 77-8.

84. Bulstrode, p. 78.

85. Ellis, *Original Letters*, Second Series, III, p. 303.

86. Hinton, *Memoirs*, pp. 11-13.

87. I prefer the account of this incident given by Edward Walsingham in his short Life of Smith (*Brittanicæ Virtutis Imago*, Oxford, 1644), to the highly improbable alternative story which credits Smith—an active cavalry officer during a hot fight—with disguising himself as a Parliamentarian and retrieving the standard from behind Essex's lines. Lord Bernard Stuart asserts that the standard was only out of the Royalists' hands for about six minutes.

88. Edgehill was described by a great number of eye-witnesses, among the Parliamentarians Denzil Holles (E. 124.26), Nathaniel Fiennes (E. 126.38 and 39) and Lord Wharton, *Eight Speeches spoken in Guildhall* (E. 124.32); also a Parliamentarian officer Edward Kightley, *A Full and True Relation* (E. 126.13). For the Royalist side, there is the anonymous *Relation of the Battaile fought between Keynton and Edgehill*, Oxford, 1642 (E. 126.24). Lord Bernard Stuart's account and two others printed by Godfrey Davies in *English Historical Review* XXXVI, pp. 30-44, Bulstrode, Clarendon, and the excellent account in Carte, *Letters*, I pp. 9-14; Colonel Burne in his *British Battlefields*, p. 193, draws attention to the evidence of King James II, who as a child of nine was present at the battle. Of modern writers, I am most indebted to the two articles by Godfrey Davies which I have frequently cited.

89. Ward, *Diary*, p. 92.

90. Abbott, I, p. 204.

91. *Acts and Ordinances*, I, p. 37; *MSS of the City of London, Minutes of the Common Council*, 18th October 1642.

92. Ludlow, p. 45

93. Warburton, I, p. 465; Clarendon, Bk. VI, 98 and p. 354n.

94. Edward Kightley, *A Full and True Relation* (*T.T.*, E. 126.13).

95. *Somers Tracts*, IV, p. 487; Anthony Wood, *Life and Times*, I, p. 68.

96. *C.S.P. Ven.*, 1642-3, pp. 192-3; "over seventy" is the Venetian resident's figure but a list published on November 7th (*T.T.*, 669.f.6/86) gives only fifty-six names.

97. *Reg. P. C. Scot.*, p. 359f; *C.J.*, II, pp. 832, 854; *L.J.*, V, pp. 430-1, 437; Clarendon, Bk. VI, 104-7.

98. Warburton, II, p. 68; *Abington's and Alisburie's present miseries*, London, 1642 (*T.T.*, E 128.33).

99. Ellis, *op. cit.*, III, IV, p. 216; *C.J.*, II, p. 838.

100. Clarendon, Bk. VI, 130-133; White-locke, *Memorials*, pp. 65-6.
101. Lilburne, *Innocency and Truth Justified*, London, 1645; M. A. Gibb, *John Lilburne*, London, 1947, pp. 91-2.
102. Godfrey Davies, *Parliamentary Army under Essex*, p. 37; *A True and Perfect relation of . . . the King's army at Old Brainceford*, London, 1642 (*T.T.*, E. 128.17).
103. John Rous, *Diary*, p. 129.
104. *C.J.*, II, p. 846; *Special Passages*, 8-15, November, 1642 (*T.T.*, E. 127.12); John Gwynne, *Military Memoirs*, Edinburgh, 1822, pp. 4-5.
105. *H.M.C.*, *Report XII*, Appendix II, p. 327; Godfrey Davies, *Battle of Edgehill*, p. 43.
106. Clarendon, Bk. VI, 137; Gwynne, Chapter I.
107. Gwynne, *loc. cit.*
108. Clarendon, Bk. VI, 149-53; *L.J.*, V, pp. 456 ff; *C.J.*, II, Nov. 20-30, 1642, *passim*.
109. *C.S.P.D.*, 1641-3, pp. 408, 459.
110. *Proceedings in Kent*, Camden *Miscellany*, III, p. 5.
111. *Acts and Ordinances*, I, pp. 33-6, 43-4; *C.J.*, II, pp. 859, 860.
112. *C.S.P. Ven*, 1642-3, p. 210; Warburton, II, p. 68.
113. Rushworth, V, pp. 65-6, 67-8.
114. *Ibid.*, V, pp. 69-70.
115. *Acts and Ordinances*, I, pp. 40-1; on the Parliamentary management of this assessment, see J. H. Hexter, *Reign of King Pym*, Cambridge, Mass., 1942, p. 17.

BOOK I: CHAPTER IV

1. See Prestage, *O Doutor Antonio de Sousa de Macedo, Residente de Portugal em Londres*, 1642-6.
2. *Diary of John Evelyn*, ed. Bray, IV, pp. 333-4.
3. *Archives de la Maison d'Orange-Nassau*, Series II, IV, pp. 64-71; Clarendon, Bk. VI, 173-6.
4. *Journal of Thomas Cunningham, Scottish History Society*, Third Series, XI, pp. 64-8.
5. Baillon, p. 447; Knuttel, *Catalogus van der pamfletten verzameling in de Koninklijke bibliotheek*. Hague, 1889-1920, I, ii, Nos. 4869, 4981.
6. Warburton, II, p. 6; Clarendon, Bk. VI, 170; Rushworth, III, I, p. 83.
7. Gough, *Superlative Prodigal*, pp. 62-3; see also Forrer, *Biographical Dictionary of Medallists*, London, 1904 seq, articles on Briot and Rawlins.
8. *Reg. P. C. Scot.*, VII, pp. 359-63; Burnet, *Lives*, pp. 204-6.
9. *H.M.C.*, *Hamilton Papers, Supplementary Report*, 1932, p. 64; Baillie, II, pp. 58-9; Spalding, II, 219-21; *Reg. P. C. Scot.*, VII, p. 373.
10. *Hamilton Papers, loc. cit.*; *Reg. P. C. Scot.*, VII, pp. 374-9, 381, 430; Spalding, II, pp. 222-5; Baillie, II, pp. 59-60, 104; Burnet, *op. cit.*, pp. 206-9.
11. On the Assembly of the Confederation and the Constitution, see Coonan, *The Irish Catholic Confederacy and the Puritan Revolution*, Dublin, 1954, pp. 139ff; Bellings *Irish Confederation*, ed. Gilbert, Dublin, 1882, pp. 111ff.
12. Castlehaven, pp. 59-60; *H.M.C.*, *Franciscan MSS*, p. 218; Hynes, *The Mission of Rinuccini*, Louvain, 1932, pp. 9-10.
13. *Letters of Queen Henrietta Maria*, ed. M. A. Everett-Green, London, 1857, p. 149.
14. Clarendon, Bk. VI, p. 310.
15. *H.M.C.*, *Portland MSS*, I, pp. 69-70.
16. *Farington Papers, Chetham Society*, 1856, pp. 89-91; *Autobiography of Adam Martindale, Chetham Society*, 1845, pp. 30ff.
17. *Fairfax Memorials*, ed. Firth, pp. 366, 368; *Fairfax Correspondence*, III, pp. 25, 27-9.
18. Webb, *Memorials of the Civil War* in Herefordshire, London, 1879, I, pp. 205-6.

19. *B.M., Add. MSS* 18980, *Prince Rupert's Correspondence*, folio 6.

20. *Marlborough's Miseries*, London, 1642 (*T.T.*, E. 245.8); Clarendon, Bk. VI, 156-7.

21. *A Complaint to the House of Commons*, London, 1642 (*T.T.*, E. 245.5); Pennington belonged to the Fishmongers Company, but his numerous interests have been traced by Mary Frear Keeler, *Members of the Long Parliament*, Philadelphia, 1954, p. 302.

22. *Sea-coal, charcoal and small coal*, London, 1643 (*T.T.*, E. 86.20); *The Midwives just Petition*, London, 1643 (*T.T.*, E. 86.14).

23. *Oxinden and Peyton Letters*, ed. Dorothy Gardiner, London, 1937, p. 11.

24. *Acts and Ordinances*, I, p. 47.

25. *The Image of the Malignant's Peace*, London, 1642 (*T.T.*, E. 244.12); *An Exact and True Relation of that tumultous behaviour at Guildhall*, London, 1642 (*T.T.*, E. 130.15); *MSS of the City of London, Minutes of the Common Council*.

26. Clarendon, Bk. VI, 196-206.

27. *H.M.C., Portland MSS*, I, p. 79; *H.M.C., Ancaster MSS*, p. 411; *Documents relating to the history of Winchester Cathedral*, ed. W. R. W. Stephens and F. T. Madge, *Hampshire Record Society*, London, 1897, pp. 47-8; Heylyn, *Aerius Redivivus*, pp. 450-1.

28. *C.S.P. Ven.*, 1642-3, p. 222.

29. Anthony Wood, *Life and Times*, I, pp. 60, 71-4, 83-4.

30. *Ibid.*, p. 68.

31. *Ibid.*, p. 59; *Beau MSS*.

32. *C.S.P.D.*, 1641-3, p. 427.

33. Atkyns, *Vindication*, p. 47; Anthony Wood, pp. 80-1; Samuel Luke, *Journal*, ed. I. G. Philip, *Oxfordshire Record Society*, 1950-3, I, pp. 4-5.

34. *A Guide to the Exhibition of Historical Medals in the British Museum*, London, 1924, pp. 34-8; Ellis, *Original Letters*, Second Series, III, p. 309.

35. Philip Warwick, *Memoirs*, London, 1701, p. 231; *Diary of the Reverend John Ward*, ed. C. Severn, London, 1839, p. 162; *C.S.P. Ven.*, 1642-3, p. 237.

36. *Somers Tracts*, IV, p. 486.

37. *A Speech by Prince Rupert*, Oxford, 1642 (*T.T.*, E. 83.28); Madan, *Oxford Books*, Oxford, 1912, II, p. 198; the speech has been considered a forgery but I can see no good reason for doubting that it is substantially authentic.

38. E. Walsingham, *Alter Brittaniae Heros*, Oxford, 1645, p. 9.

39. *The Petition of the Palsgrave and the Queen his mother*, London, 1642 (*T.T.*, E. 122.12).

40. *True Newes from our Navie*, London, 1642, (*T.T.*, E. 128.4); *C.S.P.I.*, 1643, p. 376; *H.M.C., Report X, Appendix VI*, p. 941; *Commentarius*, I, p. 519.

41. Most of the relevant sources for the Chichester incident are given in Thomas-Stanford, *Sussex in the Great Civil War*, London, 1910, pp. 42-54; Clarendon, Bk. VI, 235-6.

42. *Journal de Jean Chevalier, Société Jersiaise*, p. 21; Hoskins, *Charles II in the Channel Islands*, I, pp. 61ff. For naval information I am much indebted to Mr. J. R. Powell who has most generously allowed me to consult before publication his naval history of the Civil War.

43. Clarendon, Bk. VI, 171.

44. Burnet, *Lives*, p. 203.

45. In the interpretation of Pym's handling of Parliament I have followed J. H. Hexter's *Reign of King Pym*; Pym has left us no evidence of his policy except that which can be derived by the most meticulous and dispassionate examination of what actually happened in the House and what was actually achieved. Historians of this period will long remain indebted to Professor Hexter for the minute analysis

of the evidence which has enabled him to restore reality to this confused stretch of Parliamentary history.

46. *H.M.C., Portland MSS*, I, p. 85; Anthony Wood, *Life and Times*, I, p. 80; Rushworth, III, ii, pp. 110-113; Clarendon, Bk. VI, 214.

47. J. B. Williams, *History of British Journalism*, London, 1908, pp. 41ff; see also the excellent abridgement of *Mercurius Aulicus* with introduction by F. J. Varley, Oxford, 1949.

48. Aubrey, *Brief Lives*, ed. Powell, London, 1949, p. 99.

49. *Mercurius Aulicus, October* 1-7, 1643; Madan, II, p. 295.

50. *Rump Songs*, I, pp. 149-51.

51. *Somers Tracts*, IV, p. 479.

52. See numerous pamphlets and broadsheets in the Thomason collection, more especially 669, f. 6 (94); 669, f. 4 (73); E. 150.12.

53. Hyder E. Rollins, *Martin Parker, ballad-monger*, in *Modern Philology*, XVI; the tune of " When the King enjoys his own again " is in Chappell, *Popular Music*, II, pp. 434-9.

54. J. B. Williams, pp. 41-59.

55. *A Complaint to the House of Commons*, Oxford, 1642.

56. *C.S.P. Ven.*, 1642-3, p. 231.

57. *C.S.P.D.*, 1641-3, p. 439; Rushworth, III, ii, pp. 113-6; Sir Charles Firth believed Garraway's speech to be a forgery; in its final form it was probably much embellished, but I can see no reason why he may not have said something of this kind.

58. *C.J.*, II, pp. 935, 937-8.

59. Clarendon, Bk. VI, 230-1.

60. Rushworth, III, ii, pp. 125-6; Hexter, *Reign of King Pym*, p. 29.

61. Carte, *Ormonde*, V, pp. 1-3, 380.

62. Clarendon, Bk. VI, 232-4; *Cal. Clar. S.P.*, I, p. 237.

63. Clarendon, Bk. VI, 33, 288.

64. *H.M.C., Portland MSS*, I, p. 92; Hopton, *Bellum Civile*, p. 30; Mary Coate, *Cornwall in the Great Civil War*, Oxford, 1933, pp. 42-4.

65. Clarendon, Bk. VI, 270.

66. Clarendon, Bk. VI, 269; Malbon, pp. 35-6; *Cheshire's Successes*, London, 1643 (*T.T.*, E. 94.6).

67. Martindale, pp. 31-2; Robinson, *Civil War in Lancashire*, p. 25; *Lancashire Civil War Tracts*, pp. 128-30.

68. Hodgson, *Autobiography*, p. 94; *Fairfax Memorials, Maseres Tracts*, I, p. 414.

69. *A Relation of the taking of Leeds*, and Crompton, *A true and Plenary Relation*, London, 1643 (*T.T.*, E.88. 19 and 23); *Fairfax Memorials*, I, 419; Rushworth, III, II, p. 150.

70. *Military Memoirs of Colonel John Birch*, ed. Webb, *Camden Society*, 1873, p. 203.

71. *Fairfax Correspondence*, III, p. 33; see Heaton, *Yorkshire Woollen and Worsted Industry*, Oxford, 1920, pp. 208f.

72. *H.M.C., Portland MSS*, I, p. 87

73. *H.M.C., Report VII*, p. 441.

74. *H.M.C., Portland MSS*, I, p. 90.

75. *C.S.P. Ven.*, 1642-3, p. 236; Savile's own account of the affair is in *Camden Miscellany*, VIII.

76. The Queen had raised 1,250,000 Dutch florins and a gift from Amsterdam of an additional 40,000 florins; also a sum of about nineteen thousand pounds in the Spanish Netherlands. *Archives de la Maison d'Orange-Nassau*, Second Series, IV, p. 52; *C.S.P. Ven.*, 1642-3, p. 194; *C.S.P.D.*, 1641-3, p. 516.

77. *A True Relation of the Queen's Majesties Return out of Holland*, York, and Oxford, 1643 (Bodleian Library); *C.S.P. Ven.*, 1642-3, p. 239; Baillon, p. 455; Madame de Motteville, p. 210.

78. Madan, p. 222; *B.M., Add. MSS*, 18980, *Prince Rupert's Correspondence*, folio 19; Whitelocke, *Memorials*, p. 64.

79. Phillips, *Civil War in Wales*, I, p. 147; *Prince Rupert's Journal*, p. 732.

80. Clarendon, VI, 237-8; Warburton, II, pp. 107-8, 115; *A Relation of the taking of Cirencester*, London, 1643 (*T.T.*, E. 90.7); *B.M., Add. MSS*, 18980, folios, 17-19; Nehemiah Wallington, *Historical Notes*, pp. 144, 147; *A Particular Relation of the action before Cyrencester*, no place, 1643. This pamphlet, not in Thomason, of which a copy is in the library of Yale, is the most vivid account.

81. Hexter, pp. 14, 21-2.

82. *East Riding County Archives, Hotham MSS*, No. 10, Pym to Hotham, Feb. 20, 1643.

83. *Acts and Ordinances*, I, pp. 79, 85-100.

84. Baillon, pp. 456-8; Madame de Motteville, p. 211; Heylyn, *A Briefe Relation of . . . the landing of the Queen's Majesty*; *A True Relation of the Queen's Majesties Return*. The last named pamphlet is not in the Thomason collection; I have to thank Mr. J.R. Powell for drawing my attention to it and lending me his photostat of the copy in the Bodleian.

85. Slingsby, *Memoirs*, pp. 91-2; *Fairfax Memorials, Maseres Tracts*, II, pp. 420-1.

86. *Clarendon State Papers*, II, p. 183; *H.M.C., Portland MSS*, I, p. 123; Baillon, p. 448; Spalding, II, pp. 229-30.

87. *H.M.C., Portland MSS*, I, p. 701.

88. Warwick, p. 235.

89. F. H. Sunderland, in a biography of Langdale (London, 1926), credits him with having been a soldier under Vere in the Palatinate. No reference is given. The Dictionary of National Biography mentions no military exploits earlier than the Civil War, but it is, I think, safe to assume that Langdale had previous experience.

90. *Lancashire Civil War Tracts*, p. 130; Martindale, pp. 31-2; Robinson, *Civil War in Lancashire*, pp. 25-30; *A Letter from Sir John Seton*, Chetham Miscellany, III, 1862; Warburton, II, p. 143; Broxap, pp. 63-4, 76-7.

91. Warburton, II, p. 150; Baillon, p. 470-1.

92. *King's Cabinet Opened*, London, 1645, p. 28.

93. Clarendon, VII, 274, 276.

94. *Ibid.*, 279-82, 284; *The Battaile of Hopton Heath*, Oxford, 1643 (*T.T.*, E. 99.18); Warburton, II, p. 138; for a full account listing all known sources see Peter Young, *Battle of Hopton Heath, Journal of the Society for Army Historical Research*, XXXIII, No. 133.

95. *A brief relation of a bloody plot against Bristol* (*T.T.*, E. 93.3); *Prince Rupert's Journal*, p. 732; Phillips, *Civil War in Wales*, II, p. 63.

96. *H.M.C., Report XII, Appendix II*, p. 332; Clarendon, VI, 292; Washbourne, *Bibliotheca Gloucestrensis*, Gloucester, 1825, pp. XXXVI, 269.

97. Abbott, I, pp. 218-21; *Knyvett Letters*, pp. 32-4; Worthington, *Diary and Correspondence*, Chetham Society, 1847, I, p. 18; Ryves, *Mercurius Rusticus*; Kingston, *East Anglia in the Great Civil War*, London, 1897, pp. 93-5; for the Lowestoft incident see also Ketton Cremer, *A Norfolk Gallery*, London, 1950, pp. 61-3.

98. *C.S.P. Ven.*, 1642-3, pp. 242, 248.

99. Anthony Wood, *Life and Times*, I, p. 87.

100. Warburton, II, pp. 161f.

101. Baillon, p. 465.

102. Whitelocke, p. 65; *B.M., Add. MSS*, 18980, *Prince Rupert's Correspondence*, folio, 31.

103. *C.J.*, I, pp. 997-8; Everett Green, pp. 174-175.

104. Carte, *Ormonde*, V, pp. 380, 390-1, 393, 394, 432.

105. Hexter, *Reign of King Pym*, pp. 23-4.

106. *Acts and Ordinances*, I pp. 106-117; Christopher Hill, *Agrarian Legislation of the Interregnum, English Historical Review*, 1940, pp. 224-5.

107. Clarendon, V, 125.

108. Rushworth, V, 125.

109. Clarendon, Bk. VI, 359.

110. Burnet, *Lives*, p. 210; Clarendon, Bk. VI, 335, 349; Baillie, II, pp. 161f.

111. Burnet, *Lives*, p. 212; Carte, *Letters*, I, p. 19. Hamilton's policy proved to be so mistaken as to look either imbecile or treacherous, but if the war in England had ended in the King's victory before the end of 1643, his advice would in fact have been perfectly sensible. It is important to remember that both Charles and Hamilton calculated (or gambled) on a quick victory. The mistake lay in following a line of conduct which was not only useless, but actively harmful in the event of the King's *not* winning the war before the Covenanters came in. Hamilton had no hedge against this eventuality.

112. P. L. Ralph, *Sir Henry Mildmay, royalist gentleman*, New Brunswick, 1947, p. 164.

113. Robinson, *War in Lancashire*, pp. 32-4; *Lancashire Civil War Tracts*, pp. 95 seq.; Broxap, pp. 82-4 gives a useful map.

114. *Prince Rupert's burning love to England Discovered in Birmingham's flames*, London, 1643 (*T.T.*, E. 100.8); *Prince Rupert's Journal*, p. 733; *Joyful Newes from Lichfield*, London, 1643 (*T.T.*, E. 99.13).

115. *Joyful Newes from Lichfield*; *Valour Crowned*; J. Randolph, *Honour Advanced* (*T.T.*, E. 99.13, 25, 28).

116. Spalding, II, pp. 240-1; Burnet, *Lives*, p. 216.

117. Clarendon, VII, 20; *C.J.*, II, 40.

118. Rushworth, III, ii, pp. 148-50.

119. Edward Whirley, *The Prisoner's Report*, London, 1643 (*T.T.*, E. 93.23).

120. *Reg. P. C. Scot.*, VII, pp. 429-33.

121. M. Wood, *Edinburgh Burgh Records*, Edinburgh, 1938, II, pp. 28-9.

122. Carte, *Ormonde*, II, pp. 445-6.

123. Aitzema, *Saken van Staet en Oorlogh*, Hague, 1669-72, II, p. 880.

BOOK II: CHAPTER I

1. *Prince Rupert's Journal*, p. 733; John Randolph, *Honour Advanced, and Valour Crowned*, London, 1648 (*T.T.*, E. 99.25 and 28).

2. Gwynne, Chapter III; Atkyns. *Vindication*, pp. 21-3; Clarendon, Bk. VII, 35-6; *L.J.*, VI, p. 17; *Victory Proclaimed . . . before Reading; The Last Joyful Intelligence from Reading; Mercurius Bellicus; An Exact Relating of the Delivery of Reading* (*T.T.*, E. 100.4, 5, 7 and 11).

3. Clarendon, Bk. VII, 41-4; Gardiner, I, p. 130.

4. *The Victorious and Fortunate Proceedings of Sir William Waller; Mercurius Bellicus*, London, 1643 (*T.T.*, E. 97, 2 and E. 100, 7); Ludlow, I, p. 51.

5. Chudleigh's account of this extraordinary affair is in *Special Passages and Certain Information*, April 25-May 2 (*T.T.*, E. 100, 17). Other accounts are in *Portland MSS*, I, p. 706 and Hopton, *Bellum Civile*, pp. 38-9. Mary Coate, *Cornwall in the Great Civil War*, pp. 60-5 gives the fullest summary of all contemporary sources.

6. *Rump Songs*, I, pp. 134-5.

7. Hexter, p. 9; *H.M.C., Cowper MSS*, I, p. 314.

8. Godfrey Davies, *Parliamentary Army under Essex*, p. 40.

9. *C.S.P. Ven.*, 1642-3, p. 269; *Acts and Ordinances*, Nov. 1642-April 1643. passim; Nef, *Coal Industry*, II, pp. 81-2.

10. Clarendon, Bk. VII, 22; *C.S.P. Ven.*, 1642-3, pp. 258, 262, 269; Prestage, *Antonio de Sousa*, pp. 44-5; Challoner, *Memoirs of Missionary Priests*, London, 1924, p. 445.

11. *C.S.P. Ven.*, 1642-3, p. 272; *Oxinden and Peyton Letters*, p. 17; *Diary and Correspondence of John Evelyn*, ed. E. de Beer, Oxford, 1955, II, p. 55; *Cheapside Cross censured and condemned*, London, 1643 (*T.T.*, E. 100.2).

12. *C.J.*, III, pp. 51-2; *L.J.*, VI, p. 11;. *Lismore Papers*, Second Series, V. p. 122.

13. Godfrey Davies, *Parliamentary Army under Essex*, p. 38.

14. Hexter, pp. 91, 116; Clarendon, VII, p. 84.

15. Warburton, II, p. 161; *C.S.P. Ven.*, 1642-3, p. 252; see also W. O. Scroggs, *Finances under the Long Parliament*, *Quarterly Journal of Economics*, 1907.

16. John Greene, *Diary*, *English Historical Review*, XLIII, p. 391.

17. *Acts and Ordinances*, I, pp. 85-100.

18. *H.M.C.*, *Report VIII*, *Verney MSS*, p. 439.

19. T. Bayly, *The Marquis of Worcester's Apothegms*, pp. 99-100.

20. A. M. Everitt, *The County Committee of Kent in the Civil War*, Leicester, 1957, p. 37. For an admirable summary of Civil War taxation see Hughes, *Studies in Administration and Finance*, London, 1934, pp. 119ff.

21. *Civil War Papers of Sir William Boteler*, *Bedfordshire Record Society Publications*, XVIII, 1936, pp. 2, 38.

22. *Acts and Ordinances*, I, pp. 87-8.

23. For an example of this see Guttery, *The Civil War in Midland Parishes*, p. 61.

24. *Cal. Clar. S.P.*, I, p. 239.

25. D. Pennington and I. Roots, *The Staffordshire County Committees*, *Staffordshire Record Society*, 1957, pp. 43-4.

26. *H.M.C.*, *Report VIII*, *Verney MSS*, p. 441.

27. Everitt, p. 42; *Twysden's Journal*, II, p. 209; Malbon, pp. 240-253 has a series of letters revealing the technique of petty persecution as practised on a Royalist in Cheshire.

28. Jenkins, *Edward Benlowes*, London, 1952, pp. 137-8.

29. Ketton Cremer, *Norfolk Gallery*, p. 29; *Norfolk Assembly*, London, 1957, pp. 32-3.

30. *Fairfax Correspondence*, III, pp. 133-5, 176-7.

31. *Farrington Papers*, *Chetham Society*. XXXIX, 1856, pp. 97-100.

32. Thomas-Stanford, *Civil War in Sussex*, p. 193.

33. Memorial Inscription in Oxford Cathedral.

34. Ellis, *Original Letters*, Second Series, III, p. 311-2; Gough, *Superlative Prodigal*, p. 65; *A True Abstract of a List . . . with some few special orders ordained in His Majesty's Army*, London, 1643 (*T.T.*, E. 129.28).

35. Guttery, *passim*.

36. Washbourne, *Bibliographia Glocestrensis*, p. 39; Phillips, *Civil War in Wales*, II, p. 220; *Archaeologia Cambrensis*, Third Series, XV, p. 334.

37. *H.M.C.*, *Rawdon MSS*, II, p. 110.

38. Warburton, II, pp. 74, 82.

39. *H.M.C.*, *Report VII*, p. 557.

40. Atkyns, *Vindication*, pp. 20, 23; Warburton, II, p. 191.

41. Lord Herbert was in a peculiar position because, in spite of his raising of forces in South Wales the King hesitated to give him command in the region because of his religion. See J. F. Rees, *Studies in Welsh History*. Cardiff, 1947.

42. Bayly, *Worcester's Apothegms*, pp. 93-6.

43. *B.M.*, *Add. MSS*, 18980, *Prince Rupert's Correspondence*, folios, 91, 97.

44. H. E. Bell, *Court of Wards and Liveries*, Cambridge, 1953, pp. 150, 152ff.

45. Warburton, II, pp. 77, 85

46. *Ibid.*, pp. 103, 104; *B.M.*, *Add. MSS*, 18980, folios, 5, 91, 97.

47. Warburton, II, p. 187.

48. See *T.T.*, E. 129.28, for one such Royalist order.

49. *Journal of Sir Samuel Luke*, pp. 206-7.
50. V.C.H., *Warwick*, II, p. 195.
51. Coate, *Cornwall*, pp. 38-9; Clarendon, Bk. VI, p. 253.
52. For the contempt of the Cornish for the other Royalist troops see Atkyns, *Vindication*, pp. 24, 35.
53. See *The King's Peace*, p. 85.
54. Haller, *Liberty and Reformation* p. 259.
55. Leo F. Solt, Typescript Thesis, Columbia University Library.
56. William Foster, *Charles I and the East India Company*, English Historical Review, XIX, 1904, pp. 456-63.
57. Baillon, p. 487.
58. Prestage, *Antonio de Sousa*, p. 15.
59. Baillon, p. 477; *Reg. P. C. Scot.*, VII, pp. 442-444.
60. *A Declaration of the Commons with some papers of the Earl of Antrim*, pp. 53ff (*T.T.*, E. 61.23); *H.M.C.*, *Portland MSS*, I, p. 121; Baillie, II, pp. 67, 74-5.
61. Baillon, p. 481.
62. *York Depositions, Surtees Society*, XL, p. 40; *Fairfax Memorials*, ed. C. H. Firth, pp. 376-7.
63. *Fairfax Memorials, Maseres Tracts*, I, pp. 423-4; *L.J.*, II, p. 67.
64. Baillon, pp. 474-5, 484; *C.J.* II, p. 98.
65. Hopton, *Bellum Civile*, pp. 43-4; Coate, pp. 66-70; Clarendon, Bk. VII, 88-9.
66. *Joyfull Newes from Plimouth*, London, 1643 (*T.T.*, E. 102.9); Clarendon, Bk. VI, 91-2.
67. *H.M.C.*, *Portland MSS*, I, p. 710.
68. Abbott, I, p. 230.
69. Abbott, I, pp. 96-7; Warwick in his *Memoires* (p. 249) tells how he heard of Cromwell's fancies from Dr. Symcotts. This evidence, which used to be regarded sceptically as mere gossip has become more respectable with the discovery and publication of Dr. Symcott's notes on his patients which make it clear that he was an observant and intelligent man who long attended the Cromwell family. He says nothing in his notes of Cromwell's " fancies " but there are clear indications of Cromwell's hypochondria. See *A Seventeenth Century Doctor and his Patients, John Symcotts, Bedfordshire Historical Society Publications*, XXXI, 1951, p. 76.
70. Abbott, I, p. 231.
71. Whitelocke, *Memorials*, p. 72; Firth, *The Raising of the Ironsides*, *Transactions of the Royal Historical Society*, XIII.
72. Abbott, I, pp. 236-7; *H.M.C.*, *Rawdon MSS*, II, p. 103.
73. *C.J.*, III, p. 41.
74. *Lismore Papers, Second Series*, V, p. 143.
75. Ludlow, I, p. 68; *C.S.P. Ven.*, 1642-3, p. 286; Sanford, *Studies and Illustrations of the Great Rebellion*, London, 1858, pp. 563-4; the confessions of Challoner and Tompkins, the two principal victims, are in the *T.T.*, E. 57, 7 and 9; see also Rushworth, V, pp. 322-30.
76. *C.J.*, II, pp. 117-8; *Acts and Ordinances*, I, pp. 175-6, 180-4.
77. Laud, *History of the Troubles and Trial*, pp. 205-6.
78. *Acts and ordinances*, I, pp. 186-7.
79. *H.M.C.*, *Portland MSS*, I, p. 704.
80. Abbott, I, p. 237; *A True Relation of the Discovery of a most desperate Plot*, London, 1643 (*T.T.*, E. 59.2).
81. Hopton, *Bellum Civile*, pp. 49-50; Atkyns, *Vindication*, pp. 25ff.
82. *H.M.C.*, *Report VII*, pp. 551-2.
83. Clarendon, Bk. VII, p. 75.
84. By far the best account is *His Highness Prince Rupert's late beating up of the Rebel's quarters at Post-Comb and Chinnor . . . his Victory in Chalgrove Field*, Oxford, 1643 (Bodleian Library); see also Warburton, II, pp. 203-9; Clarendon, Bk. 75-7; *Two Letters from Robert, Earl of Essex* (*T.T.*, E. 55-19). The Parliamentary accounts make much of the failure to intercept the convoy, but from the

Royalist account it is clear that intercepting the convoy was an afterthought; the real purpose of the expedition was to demoralise the army of Essex. At Watlington an annual distribution of blankets to the poor was made out of a charitable fund said to have been created from the money left behind by the startled treasurer of the Parliamentary forces; this distribution has continued into the present century.

85. *H.M.C., Report VII*, pp. 551-2.
86. Clarendon, Bk. VII, p. 82-4; *Elegies on the death of Colonel Hampden*, London, 1643 (*T.T.*, E. 71.4).
87. *C.S.P. Ven.*, 1642-3, pp. 292, 295, 297; *H.M.C., Portland MSS*, I, p. 715; *L.J.*, VI, p. 116. Hexter, p. 133.
88. *H.M.C., Portland MSS*, I, pp. 717-9.
89. *Fairfax Memorials*, ed. Firth, pp. 385-6; *Maseres Tracts*, pp. 427-31; Hodgson, *Memoirs*, p. 99; Lister, *Autobiography*, p. 23.
90. *Fairfax Memorials*, ed. Firth, p. 388.
91. *The King's Cabinet Opened*, London, 1645, p. 33.
92. Coate, p. 77. I have modernised the spelling of this letter. Miss Coate, who discovered the original of this famous and moving document (known before only in a rough draft) prints it in full in her book, with a photograph of the MS at Prideaux Place, Padstow.
93. Hopton, *Bellum Civile*, pp. 84-5; Clarendon, Bk. VII, 104.
94. Contemporary accounts of the battle from the Parliamentary side are in *The Parliament Scout*, July, 6-13, 1643, and in *Thomason Tracts*, E. 60, 8, 9 and 12. Royalist accounts are in the *Mercurius Aulicus*, July 6-13, 1643; Atkyns, *Vindication*, pp. 30-34, and Hopton's and Slingsby's narratives in *Somersetshire Record Society Publications*, XVIII, pp. 53-5, 94-7. The sources are all brought together in Coate, *Cornwall*, pp. 78-81. A. H. Burne, *More Battlefields of England*,

pp. 161-171 is helpful. The poem quoted is Cartwright's elegy on Sir Bevil Grenvile.
95. Atkyns, *Vindication*, pp. 34-5; *Slingsby's Narrative*, p. 97.
96. Atkyns, *Vindication*, pp. 36-7; *B.M., Add. MSS*, 18980, *Prince Rupert's Correspondence*, folio 83.
97. *H.M.C., Various*, I, p. 111; Clarendon, Bk. VII, 113-5.
98. For the Parliamentary side I have used *A True Relation of the late fight between Sir William Waller and those sent from Oxford*, London, 1643 (*T.T.*, E. 61.6); for the Royalist side the narratives of Hopton, Slingsby and Atkyns, *Vindication*, pp. 36-8; and above all *Sir John Byron's Relation*, York, 1643, which is not in the Thomason Tracts though the British Museum possesses a copy. I have to thank Colonel Peter Young for drawing my attention to this and for lending me his transcript. The time of the arrival and departure of the Cavaliers in Oxford is given in *Add. MSS*, 18980, folio 83. There is a full account with maps and photographs by J. M. Prest in *Wiltshire Archaeological and Natural History Magazine*, LVIII, and an important map and elucidation of this extraordinary Royalist victory by Colonel Young in the *Journal of the Society for Army Historical Research*, Vol., XXXI, No. 127.
99. *H.M.C., Portland MSS*, III, p. 113.
100. Warburton, II, p. 229.
101. *Musarum Oxoniensium*, ʼἐπιβατηρια Oxford, 1643.
102. *H.M.C., Ormonde MSS, New Series*, II, pp. 305-6.
103. *Fiennes Relation*, p. 12; *Bernard de Gomme's Narrative, Journal for Army Historical Research*, IV, pp. 182-3; *A Remonstrance to Vindicate Essex*, London, 1643 (*T.T.*, E. 71.7).
104. For the information supplied by Fiennes at the time of his trial see *T.T.*, E. 64.12 and E. 255.1; Rupert's

chief engineer, Bernard de Gomme left an account which is printed in Warburton, II, pp. 236-64 and more fully in the *Journal of Army Historical Research*, IV; see also the accounts by Hopton and Slingsby in *Publications of the Somersetshire Record Society*, XVIII, pp. 58, 92-3.

105. Coate, p. 100; Clarendon, Bk. VII, 132.

106. Clarendon's account of this incident (VII, 144-8) should be accepted with caution. No one would contend that Rupert and Maurice were a tactful pair, but Clarendon believed and recorded everything he could to their discredit. Hertford's complaint that the surrender of Bristol was taken without consulting him does not tally with the printed terms where his name appears beside that of Rupert and Maurice's name does not. Atkyns, admittedly a great admirer of Maurice, gives the impression in his *Vindication* that Maurice behaved with modesty and civility to Hertford. As for the trouble over the governorship it is fairly clear that Hertford was trying to steal a march on Rupert just as much as Rupert was doing so on Hertford. Both were equally to blame for the confusion.

107. *Mercurius Aulicus*, July 30—August 5, 1643; Warburton, II, p. 268.

108. See Mary Frear Keeler, *Members of the Long Parliament* for details of the interests and possessions of Humphrey Hooke and Walter Long, the Bristol members.

109. J. Latimer, *Records Relating to the Society of Merchant Adventurers of the City of Bristol*, Bristol Record Society, 1952, pp. 106-7, 121-2, 160-3.

110. Atkyns, *Vindication*, p. 44.

111. *A Declaration of the Commons Concerning the Rebellion in Ireland*, London, 1643 (*T.T.*, E. 61.23), pp. 44-5; *C.S.P. Ven.*, 1643-7, p. 6; *C.S.P.D.*, 1641-3, pp. 472-3; *Cal. Clar. S.P.*,

I, p. 243; Gough, *Superlative Prodigal*, pp. 68ff; Clarendon, Bk. VII, 138-43.

112. *H.M.C.*, *Report VII*, pp. 555-6; *Camden Miscellany*, III, *Proceedings in Kent*, pp. 26-34; *MSS of the City of London, Journal of the Common Council for* July 18th.

113. Dugdale, p. 123; *Acts and Ordinances*, pp. 202-14.

114. *Ibid.*, pp. 215-9.

115. *C.J.*, III, p. 191; Hexter, p. 144.

116. *L.J.*, VI, p. 127.

117. *Knyvett Letters*, pp. 119, 121; *C.J.*, III, p. 183; Hexter, pp. 124-5.

118. *L.J.*, VI, p. 160; *H.M.C.*, *Portland MSS*, I, p. 715; see also *A Remonstrance to Vindicate the Earl of Essex*, London, 1643 (*T.T.*, E. 71.7).

119. Hexter, pp. 141-3; Clarendon, Bk. VII, 187; *H.M.C.*, *Report V, Appendix*, I, pp. 98-9.

120. *C.J.*, III, p. 183.

121. *Reg. P. C. Scot.*, VII, pp. 442-4; *H.M.C.*, *Portland MSS*, I, pp. 121-2; *C.J.*, III, pp. 146-7.

122. Baillie, II, pp. 74-5; Guthry, pp. 130-1; Spalding II, pp. 252-3; Carte, *Letters*, I, pp. 19-20; Robert Montet de Salmonet, *Histoire des Troubles*, Paris, 1661, pp. 200f.

123. Baillie, II, pp. 79; Burnet, *Lives*, pp. 233-4.

124. Abbott, I, p. 251; Firth, *Raising of the Ironsides*, pp. 68-73.

125. *A Remonstrance to vindicate . . . Essex*; *L.J.*, VI, p. 160.

126. *Mercurius Aulicus*, Aug. 6-12, 1643; *Knyvett Letters*, p. 126; *C.J.*, III, p. 197; *H.M.C.*, *Report VII*, pp. 557-8; Clarendon, Bk. VII, 168-70; Hexter, pp. 137-48.

127. *C.S.P. Ven.*, 1643-7, p. 8; *H.M.C.*, *Report XII*, II, pp. 335-6; Gardiner, I, p. 187n.

128. Collins, *Sydney Papers*, II, p. 669; Whitelocke, p. 69; Clarendon, Bk. VII, pp. 157-8, 176 and note.

129. *H.M.C.*, *Report VII*, p. 561; *Acts and Ordinances*, I, pp. 251-4; 260-1.

130. C.J., III, p. 206; Hexter, 148, 151.
131. H.M.C., *Ormonde MSS, New Series*, II, pp. 306-7; see also C.J., III, p. 290.
132. Henry Foster, *A True Relation of the Marchings of the Trained Bands of the City of London; A True Relation of the several passages which happened to our army*, London, 1643 (*T.T.*, E. 69.15; E. 67.13).
133. *Trial of Nathaniel Fiennes* (*T.T.*, E. 255.1).
134. *Pythouse Papers*, p. 58; Warburton, II, p. 282.
135. Wraxall, *Historical Memoirs*, ed. Wheatley, II, p. 288; Collins, *Sydney Papers*, II, p. 669.
136. *Prince Rupert's Journal*, p. 734; Salmonet, *Histoire des Troubles*, pp. 202-3.
137. Clarendon, Bk. VII, 187-9; Warburton, II, p. 272.
138. The siege of Gloucester from the point of view of the besieged is well described by the town clerk John Dorney in *A Brief and Exact Relation of the Siege of Gloucester*, London, 1643 (*T.T.*, E. 67.31.), also in Corbet, *Military Government of the City of Gloucester*, 1645, reprinted in Washbourne, *Bibliotheca Glocestrensis*. The march of the London Trained Bands is described in Henry Foster's pamphlet cited above and also in *A True Relation of Robert, Earl of Essex*, London, 1643 (*T.T.*, E. 70.10); Warburton, II, pp. 279ff; Gwynne, p. 35.
139. *Archaeologia Cambrensis*, IV, VI, p. 206.
140. Warburton, II, p. 286n.
141. Gardiner, I, p. 206.
142. C.S.P.D., 1641-3, p. 484.
143. Penn, I, p. 69; Clarendon, Bk. VII, pp. 193, 198.
144. Carte, *Ormonde*, V, p. 465-7.
145. Baillie, II, p. 90; Spalding, II, p. 145.
146. C.J., III, pp. 219-20, 223, 224, 226, 230; Rushworth, III, ii, p. 482.
147. C.S.P. Ven, 1643-7, p. 24; Henry Foster, *True Relation; A True Relation of the late expedition of Robert, Earl of Essex;* Gwynne, pp. 36-7; Warburton, II, pp. 289-90nn.
148. *Prince Rupert's Journal*, p. 734; *Pythouse Papers*, p. 17; Foster, *True Relation;* Clarendon, Bk. VII, 208-9.
149. Warburton, II, p. 292; Warburton's source is the so-called *Diary* of Prince Rupert compiled by one of his household, a document which appears totally to have vanished between Warburton's time and Gardiner's, and which I have been unable to trace. It is extremely favourable to Rupert, but the style and character of the excerpts quoted by Warburton have nothing in them to suggest that it is inauthentic, and Gardiner used them with apparent confidence.
150. The first battle of Newbury is the most confused and controversial battle of the entire Civil War. Mr. Money, a hundred years ago, seems to have spent a happy life-time accumulating facts and drawing plans for his monumentally bewildering book on *The Battles of Newbury*. The late S. R. Gardiner tramped with him over the terrain and no doubt greatly enjoyed himself while arriving at slightly different conclusions. Colonel Burne (*Battlefields of England*, pp. 201-12) points out some of Money's probable errors and is thorough and ingenious. Contemporary Parliamentary accounts are *Perfect Diurnal*, Sept. 23, *A True Relation of the late Battell near Newbery*, London, 1643 (*T.T.*, E. 69.2) and Foster, *True Relation*; Royalist accounts are *A True and Impartial Relation*, Oxford, 1643 (probably by Digby), *T.T.*, E. 69.10; also *Mercurius Aulicus* for the relevant week; and two *MS* accounts, *B.M., Add. MSS*, 18980, folio 120; and Byron's account *Bodleian Library, Clarendon MSS*, 1738 (5).

151. Clarendon, Bk. VII, 231-4.
152. Defoe, *Memoirs of a Cavalier, Works,* Boston, 1903, V, p. 241; the origins of this book are obscure and critics are uncertain how much is the work of Defoe, and how much (all, some or none?) is a genuine document of the Civil War period.
153. *Prince Rupert's Journal,* p. 735.
154. Whitelocke, p. 71; *A True Relation of the late Expedition of Robert, Earl of Essex; A True Relation of the late Battle near Newbury* (T.T., E. 70.10; E. 69.10).
155. Whitelocke, p. 71; *C.S.P. Ven.,* 1643-7, p. 27; *L.J.,* VI, p. 230.
156. Sanford, p. 648.
157. Whitelocke, p. 71.

BOOK II: CHAPTER II

1. Rushworth, V, pp. 475-7; *The Covenant with a narrative of the manner of taking it,* London, 1643 (T.T., E. 70.22).
2. Baillie, II, pp. 90ff; Ludlow, I, p. 65; Guthry, p. 137; Burnet, *Lives,* p. 240; text of the Covenant, Rushworth, V. pp. 478-9.
3. Spalding, II, p. 261.
4. Baillie, II, pp. 98-100; Spalding, II, pp. 266-70, 278; *Reg. P. C. Scot.,* VIII, p. 84; Peterkin, *Records,* p. 355; *Edinburgh Burgh Records,* 1642-55, pp. 33-5.
5. H.M.C., *Portland MSS,* I, p. 115.
6. Baillie, II, p. 103.
7. Gilbert, *Irish Confederation,* II, pp. 252ff.
8. *Lismore Papers,* Second Series, V, pp. 230-1.
9. Turner, *Memoirs,* pp. 26-7.
10. Castlehaven, pp. 83, 85, 90.
11. *Horrid and Strange News from Ireland,* London, 1643 (T.T., E. 78.1); Rushworth, V, p. 531.
12. Hogan, pp. 157-61.
13. *Commentarius,* I, p. 392; Albion, *Charles I and Rome,* p. 376.

14. Rushworth, V, pp. 548-53; *Commentarius,* I, pp. 401-2, 424f.
15. Rushworth, V, pp. 555-8.
16. H.M.C., *Portland MSS,* I, p. 133; H.M.C., *Egmont MSS,* I, pp. 282, 297; C.S.P.I., I, p. 386; Turner, *Memoirs,* p. 29; Crawford, *Ireland's Ingratitude,* London, 1643 (T.T., E. 33.28); Carte, *Ormonde,* V, pp. 481ff.
17. Warburton, II, p. 320; Gardiner, I, p. 249; Gilbert, *Irish Confederation,* II, pp. 378-9.
18. Carte, *Ormonde,* V, p. 303; Carte, *Letters,* I, p. 36; *A Declaration of the Commons,* London, 1643 (T.T., E. 61.23); Phillips, *Civil War in Wales,* II, p. 101; Ludlow, I, p. 64; *Mercurius Civicus,* Oct. 26 to Nov. 2, 1643; *A True Copy of a Letter . . . from Bridgewater,* London, 1643 (T.T., E. 74.14 and 20).
19. Carte, *Ormonde,* III, pp. 37, 96, 104; V, pp. 504, 525; Crawford, *op. cit.;* H.M.C., *Ormonde MSS,* New Series, II, pp. 343-4; Gumble, *Life of Monk,* London, 1671, pp. 15-17.
20. C.S.P. Ven., 1643-7, pp. 32, 36; Davies, *Parliamentary Army Under Essex,* p. 42.
21. Zachary Gray, *Impartial Examination of the Third Volume of Neal's History of the Puritans,* London, 1737, Appendix p. 3.
22. C.S.P. Ven., 1643-7, pp. 25, 30; Whitelocke, p. 71; Nef. *The Rise of the British Coal Industry,* I, pp. 158-9.
23. H.M.C., *Portland MSS,* I, pp. 135, 141-3.
24. *Proceedings in Kent,* pp. 37, 42-4.
25. Rushworth, V, pp. 283-4; *A Brief and True Relation of the siege of King's Lynn,* London, 1643 (T.T., E. 67.28); Ketton Cremer, *Norfolk Gallery,* pp. 67-71; Clarendon, Bk. VII, 177; H.M.C., *Report VII,* pp. 559, 562-3; Slingsby, *Memoirs,* p. 103.
26. Abbott, I, pp. 260-1.

27. Manchester's account of the Battle of Winceby is in *L.J.*, VI, pp. 255-6; other accounts are in *Fairfax Correspondence*, IV, pp. 62-5; Ludlow, *Memoirs*, I, p. 58; *H.M.C., Rawdon MSS*, II, p. 105; there are two *True Relations* in (*T.T.*, E. 71, 5 and 22); *Parliament Scout*, Oct. 13-20, 1643.

28. *H.M.C., Portland MSS*, I, p. 138; Broxap, *Sieges of Hull*, p. 473; Warwick, *Memoirs*, p. 210; *C.S.P. Ven.*, 1643-7, pp. 28, 34; *A True Relation of the Victories*, London, 1643 (*T.T.*, E. 71.22).

29. Warburton, II, p. 322; *H.M.C., Portland MSS*, I, 144; H. G. Tibbutt, *Sir Lewis Dyve, Bedfordshire Historical Record Society*, 1948, pp. 42-5; *Prince Rupert's Journal*, p. 735.

30. *Pythouse Papers*, p. 2; *Letter-book of Sir Samuel Luke*, pp. 196-201.

31. *H.M.C., Portland MSS*, I, pp. 154-5, 159-60; *C.S.P. Ven.*, 1643-7, p. 46.

32. *H.M.C., Portland MSS*, I, pp. 151-2; Carte, *Ormonde*, V, p. 521.

33. *Parliament Scout*, Nov. 10, 1643; *C.S.P. Ven.*, 1643-7, pp. 26, 30, 41.

34. Clarendon, Bk. VII, 299, 303, 307; *C.S.P. Ven.*, 1643-7, pp. 40, 67; *Pythouse Papers*, p. 2; *C.S.P.D.*, 1641-3, p. 502.

35. Prestage, *Antonio de Sousa*, pp. 17-8.

36. Warburton, II, p. 307; Lady Fanshawe, *Memoirs*, pp. 24-5; *B.M., Add. MSS*, 18980, folio 125; E. Greaves, *Morbus Epidemius*, London, 1643 (*T.T.*, E. 79.22).

37. For the Queen's jealousy see Clarendon, Bk. VII, p. 182, and for various typical intrigues, Bk. VII, 239-40, 278-85.

38. *Pythouse Papers*, pp. 17, 55; *C.S.P.D.*, 1641-3, p. 510; *Letterbook of Sir Samuel Luke*, pp. 196, 201.

39. *Pythouse Papers*, p. 54; *B.M., Add. MSS*, 18980, *Prince Rupert's Correspondence*, folio 164.

40. Carte, *Ormonde*, V, p. 521.

41. *B.M. Add. MSS*, 18981, *Prince Rupert's Correspondence*, folio 15; Warburton, II, pp. 358-9.

42. *Ibid.*, folios 4, 16; Warburton, II, p. 332; *Pythouse Papers*, p. 15.

43. Carte, *Ormonde*, V, pp. 506-8; see also *Correspondence of Archbishop Williams with Ormonde*, ed. Beedham. London, 1869; B. Dew Roberts, *Mitre and Musket*, 1938, and Dodd, *Studies*, p. 89.

44. *B.M., Add. MSS*, 18980, folio 147; 18981, folio 13; Clarendon, Bk. VII, pp. 199-200.

45. *Rawdon MSS*, II, p. 105; Baillie, II, pp. 114-5.

46. Abbott, I, pp. 258-9.

47. Selden, *Table Talk*, ed. Reynolds, London, 1892, p. 123.

48. *Acts and Ordinances*, I, p. 371; Tatham, *The Puritans in Power*, Cambridge, 1913, p. 124.

49. Abbott, I, p. 270.

50. Baillie, II, p. 139.

51. Lightfoot, *Works*, ed. J. R. Pitman, XIII, p. 11.

52. Baillie, II, pp. 107-10, 117; Lightfoot, pp. 165-6.

53. W. A. Shaw, *A History of the English Church during the Civil Wars*, London, 1900, I. pp. 150ff. See also S. W. Carruthers, *Everyday Work of the Westminster Assembly*, Philadelphia, 1943.

54. Baillie, II, pp. 102-3; Spalding, II, pp. 286-93, 295, 298-9, 303.

55. *Ibid.*, pp. 274, 292, 295.

56. *Ibid.*, p. 282; *Correspondence of Montereul*, Scottish History Society, XXX, Edinburgh, 1899, II, p. 550.

57. Rushworth, V, pp. 485-7.

58. *A Narrative of the Disease and Death of John Pym*, London, 1643 (*T.T.*, E. 79.27).

59. Baillie, II, p. 118.

60. Stephen Marshall, *Threnodia*, London, 1643 (*T.T.*, E. 80.1) pp. 34-5.

61. *Acts and Ordinances*, I, pp. 331-3.

62. Keeler, *The Long Parliament*, p. 331.

63. G. Sikes, *Life and Death of Sir Harry*

Vane, London, 1662, p. 9; *Proceedings of the Historical Society of Massachusetts*, XII, pp. 245-6.

64. H.M.C., *Portland MSS*, I, p. 153; Carte, Ormonde, V, p. 521.

65. Lucy Hutchinson, *Memoirs of Colonel Hutchinson*, ed. Firth, London, 1905, pp. 198f; *A Discovery of the Treacherous Attempts of the Cavaliers*, London 1643 (*T.T.*, E. 79.30).

66. *A Narrative of the Great Victory at Alton*, London, 1643 (*T.T.*, E. 78.22); Hopton, *Bellum Civile*, pp. 70-1; there is a brass to Edward Bowles in Alton Church near the place where he fell.

67. C.S.P. *Ven.*, 1643-7, pp. 51, 57; C.S.P.D., 1641-3, p. 506; Birch, *Memoirs*, p. 5; Wilmot to Rupert, Dec. 24, 1643, *B.M. Add. MSS*, 18980, folio 167; *A Narrative of the Great Victory at Alton; The Seagull or the New Apparition*, London, 1644, (*T.T.*, E. 54.4); *Portland MSS*, I, p. 78. The picture, apparently from the workshop of Rubens and ascribed to Gerard de la Valle, showed also the martyrdom of Saint Ursula and her eleven thousand virgins in the background. This was claimed by some to be a representation of the Queen's landing at Bridlington, but a saner pamphleteer pointed out that no such disaster had befallen Her Majesty, God be thanked, at Bridlington, nor had she a suite of eleven thousand.

68. Clarendon, Bk. VII, 405-6, 408; C.S.P.D., 1641-3, p. 510; Dugdale, *Diary*, p. 60; Baillie, II, p. 138; H. W. Meikle, *Correspondence of the Scots Commissioners in London*, London, 1917, p. 6; L.J., VI, p. 388. Even Bishop Burnet finds Lanark's behaviour at this point beyond his considerable whitewashing powers.

69. Carte, *Ormonde*, V, p. 539; VI, p. 39.

70. *Acts and Ordinances*, I, pp. 340-2.

71. L.J., VI, p. 361.

72. *Camden Miscellany*, VIII, pp. 1-12; Baillie, II, p. 137.

73. *Greene's Diary*, p. 393; Marsys, pp. 129ff; *Mildmay's Diary*, pp. 166, 168; C.S.P. *Ven.*, 1643-7, p. 46.

74. Baillie, II, p. 120.

75. The *Apologeticall Narration* is reprinted in Haller *Tracts on Liberty*, II, pp. 305ff; see also Haller, *Liberty and Reformation*, p. 116ff.

76. Rushworth, V, pp. 379-81; Baillie, II, pp. 118, 130; *A Cunning Plot*, London, 1644 (*T.T.*, E. 29.3).

77. *Camden Miscellany*, VIII, pp. 27-8, 33-4; Baillie, II, p. 130.

78. Baillie, II, p. 134; C.S.P. *Ven.*, 1643-7, p. 67.

79. Stephen Marshall, *A Sacred Panegyrick*, London, 1644 (*T.T.*, E. 30.2).

80. *Papers Relating to the Army of the Solemn League and Covenant, Scottish History Society*, New Series, XVI, Edinburgh, 1917, p. 25.

81. *Ibid.*, pp. 6-9.

82. C.S.P.D., 1644, p. 31.

83. Warburton, II, pp. 356, 371, 483.

84. C. Thomas-Stanford, *Civil War in Sussex*, Chapter VI; *A Full Relation of the late Victory obtained by Sir William Waller; An Exact and True Relation of the taking of Arundel Castle*, London, 1644 (*T.T.*, E. 81.10 and 12).

85. Cheynell, *Chillingworth Novissima*, London, 1644.

86. *B.M. Add. MSS*, 18981, *Prince Rupert's Correspondence*, folio 7; C.S.P. *Ven.*, 1643-7, p. 66; *Fairfax Memorials*, ed. Firth, p. 392.

87. H.M.C. *Rawdon MSS*, pp. 117-9; *His Majesty's Speech delivered at Oxford*, Oxford, 1644 (*T.T.*, E. 30.6).

88. Carte, *Letters*, I, pp. 43-4; Clarendon, Bk. VII, 370-2; 398; Rushworth, V, pp. 502-3.

89. Rushworth, V, p. 302; *Mercurius Civicus* (*T.T.*, E. 30.7); Carte, *Letters*, I, pp. 36, 40-1; *Cheshire Civil War Tracts*, p. 110; *Fairfax*

Memorials, p. 392; *Magnalia Dei*, London, 1644 (*T.T.*, E. 141.13); Malbon, pp. 94-5, 110-1.

90. Gumble, pp. 18-21.

91. *Fairfax Memorials*, loc. cit.; *Fairfax Correspondence*, III, pp. 74-5.

92. Carte, *Ormonde*, V, p. 531; *H.M.C.*, *Report II*, p. 172; *C.S.P.I.*, 1633-47, p. 292.

93. *Clarendon State Papers*, II, p. 337.

94. Carte, *Ormonde*, V, p. 510; VI, pp. 104-113; Collins *Sydney Papers*, II, pp. 673-4.

95. Whitelocke, p. 80; Ludlow, I, p. 89; *C.S.P.D.*, 1644, p. 57; Madan, II. 320.

96. Whitelocke, p. 77; *C.S.P.D.*, 1644, pp. 85-6; *A Declaration concerning Sir E. Deering*, London, 1644 (*T.T.*, E. 33.4).

97. Hogan, pp. 62-4, 163.

98. Carte, *Ormonde*, VI, pp. 36, 38, 39; *B.M. Add. MSS*, 18981, *Prince Rupert's Correspondence*, folio 57.

99. *C.S.P. Ven.*, 1643-7, p. 78.

100. *Acts and Ordinances*, I, pp. 381-2; Baillie, II, p. 81, 118-19, 141. Notestein, *The Establishment of the Committee of Both Kingdoms*, American *Historical Review*, 1912, pp. 477-95. J. H. Hexter, *Reign of King Pym*, p. 103n suggests that Notestein's views should be modified on one point. The appointments to this Committee do not represent essentially the triumph of the Independents over the " Presbyterian " party, but the triumph of the opponents of Essex over his friends, of the active war party over the half-hearted. Among other confusions of terminology it is worth noting that at this period Baillie considers Vane and his following as the " good " party, and regards Holles, later to be the leader of the loosely named English " Presbyterian " party, as the very reverse of " good " because he was too pacific in his views.

101. *C.S.P. Ven.*, 1643-7, p. 76.

102. Warburton, II, pp. 373, 376.

103. Robinson, *Civil War in Lancashire*, pp. 45-6.

104. *Fairfax Correspondence*, III, pp. 85-6; Warburton, II, pp. 363-4; Robinson. loc. cit.

105. Warburton, II, p. 482; Napier, II, p. 24; *C.S.P.D.*, 1644, pp. 42-3; *H.M.C.*, *Report X*, *Appendix I*, p. 52; C. S. Terry, *Alexander Leslie*, London, 1898, pp. 192-4.

106. *C.S.P.D.*, 1644, pp. 23, 60-1.

107. Baillie, II, p. 156

108. *Ibid.*, II, pp. 145-6, 165, 168.

109. Lightfoot, p. 121.

110. *C.S.P. Ven.*, 1643-7, p. 83.

111. Baillie, II, p. 153; Carte, *Ormonde*, VI, pp. 85, 87-8; *C.S.P.D.*, 1644, p. 71.

112. *Acts and Ordinances*, I, pp. 398-405; *C.S.P. Ven.*, 1643-7, p. 88; *C.S.P.D.*, 1644, p. 74; Baillie, II, p. 153.

113. *Prince Rupert's Journal*, p. 735; *Pythouse Papers*, p. 4; *Prince Rupert's Raising of the Siege of Newark*, London, 1644 (*T.T.*, E. 38.10).

114. Alfred C. Wood, *Nottinghamshire in the Civil War*, pp. 72-82 gives an excellent and full account with detailed references to contemporary sources. Col. Peter Young adds to and modifies Wood's account at some points (particularly in one estimate of the numbers engaged) in *The Royalist Army at the Relief of Newark*, *Journal of Army Historical Research*, XXX, No. 124. I have myself used chiefly *Prince Rupert's Raising the Siege of Newark* (cited above), *Mercurius Aulicus*, March 17-23; and *The Siege of Newark as delivered to the Council of State* (*T.T.*, E. 39.8). Warburton gives some of the relevant correspondence but is weak on the operation itself. Clarendon, for whom Rupert can do no right, sourly comments " so great success doth often attend bold and resolute attempts, though without reason or advice, which would never have

approved this enterprise." No doubt he would have found something equally disparaging to say had Rupert waited for the sage approval which, it seems, he lacked, and left Newark to its fate. The poem on the siege ascribed to Davenant and quoted by Eva Scott in her *Rupert Prince Palatine* bears no resemblance to the work of Davenant, and I can find no trace of it earlier than the beginning of the nineteenth century. It would seem to be late and spurious.

115. *Memoirs of Colonel Hutchinson*, pp. 223-4.

116. B.M., *Add. MSS*, 18981, *Prince Rupert's Correspondence*, folio 105.

BOOK II: CHAPTER III

1. *C.S.P. Ven.*, 1643-7, p. 89.
2. Walker, p. 7.
3. *C.S.P. Ven.*, 1643-7, pp. 81, 84, 86; Rushworth, V, pp. 384-5; Coate, pp. 132-3.
4. Clarendon, Bk. VIII, 12; Birch, pp. 9-11.
5. Walker, pp. 7ff; Clarendon, Bk. VIII, 13-16; *Mercurius Aulicus*, March 24-30; *Somersetshire Record Society*, XVIII, for the narratives of Hopton pp. 78-84 and Slingsby pp. 100-3; *Sir William Balfour's Letter, A Fuller Relation of the Victory Obtained at Alsford*, London, 1644 (*T.T.*, E. 40.1 and 13), see also *H.M.C., Portland MSS*, III, pp. 107-10, and *The Kingdom's Weekly Intelligencer*, pp. 2-10, April 1644, (*T.T.*, E. 42.4). Of the more recent accounts G. N. Godwin, *Civil War in Hampshire*, London, 1882, pp. 129-32 is not very helpful; Colonel Burn's reconstruction in *More Battlefields in England*, pp. 183-91 disentangles the topography of what was certainly on the Royalist side one of the most ill-managed actions of the war.
6. Walsingham, *Brittaniae Virtutis Imago*.

7. *C.S.P. Ven.*, 1643-7, p. 89; Baillie, II, p. 154.
8. *Acts and Ordinances*, I, pp. 413-8.
9. *L.J.*, VI, p. 505.
10. *C.S.P.D.*, 1644, pp. 104-5; Rushworth, V, p. 662.
11. *L.J.*, VI, p. 505.
12. W. Smith, *A True Relation of the success of . . . Captain Swanley*, London, 1644 (*T.T.*, E. 42.14).
13. *Ibid.*, *A True Relation of the Routing of His Majesty's Forces in Pembroke*, London, 1644 (*T.T.*, E. 42.13); *A True Relation of the Proceedings of Col. Langhorne* (sic), London, 1644 (*T.T.*, E. 42.19); see also Phillips, *Civil War in Wales*, II, pp. 140-53; A. W. Leach, *Civil War in Pembroke*, London, 1937, pp. 64-82.
14. Carte, *Ormonde*, VI, p. 74.
15. *Ibid.*, pp. 43-6, 58, 61.
16. Robert Douglas, *Diary*, pp. 54-5.
17. Warburton, II, p. 397.
18. Baillon, pp. 505-6.
19. *Fairfax Memorials* (Maseres Tracts), I, pp. 436-7; Warburton, II, p. 434; Rushworth, V, p. 68.
20. Douglas, *Diary*, pp. 55-6; *Monckton Papers, Philobiblon Society Miscellany*, XV, pp. 16-17.
21. Douglas, *Diary*, pp. 56-7; *The Kingdom's Weekly Intelligence*, April 30-May 7.
22. *H.M.C. Report X, Appendix I*, p. 54.
23. B.M., *Add. MSS*, 18981, *Prince Rupert's Correspondence*, folio 99-101.
24. Warburton, II, pp. 404-5; Clarendon, Bk. VIII, 21; *Pythouse Papers*, p. 69.
25. Walker, p. 8; Symonds, p. 3.
26. Clarendon, Bk. VIII, 23; *C.S.P. Ven.*, 1643-7, pp. 98-9.
27. Baillon, p. 510.
28. Rushworth, V, p. 953; Gilbert, *Irish Confederation*, III, pp. 143-8.
29. John Taylor, *Mad Verse, Sad Verse, Glad Verse, Bad Verse*, Oxford, 1644
30. *C.S.P.D.*, 1644, p. 131.
31. Walker, p. 13; Clarendon, Bk. VIII, p. 26.
32. Clarendon, Bk. VIII, p. 27-33.

33. Spalding, II, pp. 311-3, 317, 321.
34. *Reg. P. C. Scot.*, VIII, pp. 29-30, 128-9; Baillie, II, pp. 91-3; *Presbytery Book of Strathbogie, Spalding Club*, Edinburgh, 1843, pp. 33, 40-41.
35. *Maitland Club Miscellany*, I, p. 480; *Inverness and Dingwall Presbytery Records, Scottish History Society*, XXIV, p. 1; *Reg. P.C. Scot.*, VIII, 1643-4 *passim.*
36. It is difficult to gauge the popularity even of a modern regime as predictions of election results not infrequently show. It is impossible to hazard more than a guess at the true nature of popular feelings three hundred years ago. Writers sympathetic to the Covenant believe the Presbyterian dispensation to have been widely and firmly supported, while writers of Catholic or Episcopalian sympathies follow the evidence of Spalding, Bishop Guthry and others to show that it was generally disliked. The best narrative and descriptive accounts by contemporaries are nearly all by Royalists who naturally record everything in the government's disfavour; but the significant failure of the King's friends ever to create an effective opposition to the Covenant, except in the Highlands and round Aberdeen, is very strong evidence that the government rested, on the whole, on the consent and co-operation of the majority.
37. Peterkin, p. 351; *Minutes of the Synod of Argyll*, p. 81.
38. J. Drummond, *Memoirs of Sir Ewen Cameron of Lochiel, Abbotsford and Maitland Clubs*, Edinburgh, 1842, p. 58.
39. See *The King's Peace*, p. 341.
40. W. Fraser, *The Sutherland Book*, III, pp. 171-2; also the *Memorials of the family of Wemyss*, Edinburgh, 1888, III, p. 88. The Macleod of Assynt whose name is associated with the capture of Montrose in 1650, was at

this time a minor; the Assynt whose "malignancy" perturbed Sutherland was probably his guardian.
41. For details of Cant's ministry in Aberdeen see Spalding, II, *passim.*
42. *Ibid.*, II, pp. 91, 207-8, 306.
43. *Diary of Alexander Jaffray*, ed. J. Barclay, London, 1833, p. 21; Spalding, II, pp. 324-5, 330-3, 343. Nat Gordon's exploits as a gay, reckless and irresistible lover are celebrated in contemporary ballads.
44. Turner, *Memoirs*, pp. 36-8.
45. Wishart, *Memoirs of Montrose*, ed. Murdock and Simpson, London, 1893, pp. 45, 362; *True Relations of the Happy Success of the Marquis of Montrose*, Oxford, 1645, pp. 1-2.
46. Napier, *Memorials of Montrose, Maitland Club*, Edinburgh, 1850, II, pp. 146-7.
47. Napier, II, p. 144; Salmonet, *Histoire des Troubles*, pp. 226-8; *H.M.C., Laing MSS*, I, p. 215; *A True Relation of the Happy Success of the Marquis of Montrose*, pp. 2-3.
48. Spalding, II, pp. 340-1, 345-53, 367.
49. Spalding, II, pp. 357-8, 363-4, 370; *New Spalding Club Miscellany*, I, p. 390; *Transactions of the Royal Historical Society*, V, pp. 375-7; *Transactions of the Buchan Field Club*, p. 7.
50. *A True Relation of ... Montrose*, p. 3; Baillie, II, p. 196; *Thurloe State Papers*, I, pp. 55-6.
51. *Records of Elgin*, I, pp. 281-2; *Records of Inverness*, II, pp. 181-3.
52. *Clarendon State Papers*, II. p. 201; for Glamorgan's character and ambitions see A. H. Dodd, *Stuart Wales*, pp. 64-5, 91.
53. Collins, *Peerage*, London, 1779, I, pp. 206-7; *Clarendon State Papers*, II, pp. 201-3.
54. See Madan, II, p. 358.
55. Carte, *Ormonde*, VI, pp. 130, 146, 147; *H.M.C., Egmont MSS*, I, i, pp. 281-2.
56. Warburton, II, p. 371.
57. Carte, *Letters*, I, p. 48; Carte,

Ormonde, VI, p. 137; Beedham, p. 10; Kingdom's Weekly Intelligence (T.T., E. 46.4); Archaeologia Cambrensis, Third Series, XV, pp. 314-8.

58. Baillie, II, p. 178; A True Relation of the taking of . . . Lincoln (T.T., E. 47.2).

59. An Exact Relation of the Siege before York, London, 1644 (T.T., E. 50.30).

60. Firth, Marston Moor. Transactions of the Royal Historical Society, New Series, XII, p. 89. Prince Rupert's Journal p. 736; Archaeologia Cambrensis, First Series, I, p. 37.

61. Atkyns, Vindication, p. 43; Warburton, II, pp. 381-4; Phillips, Civil War in Wales, II, pp. 155.

62. C.S.P.D., 1644, pp. 156, 161; Walker, pp. 13-15.

63. C.S.P.D., 1644, p. 195; Walker, p. 16.

64. Walker, pp. 18-21; Symonds, pp. 7-9; Warburton, II, p. 417. Gardiner attributes this skilful move to Lord Forth, and it is difficult to see who else would have had the skill to advise it.

65. Warburton, II, pp. 415-8.

66. C.S.P.D., 1644, p. 206; Firth, Marston Moor, p. 70; An Exact Relation of the Massacre at Bolton, London, 1644 (T.T., E. 7.1).

67. Firth, Marston Moor, p. 70; Robinson, Civil War in Lancashire, p. 51.

68. History and Antiquities of Man, Chatham Society, pp. 450-1. The Countess of Derby, Charlotte de la Tremouille, was first cousin to Rupert's father.

69. Martindale, Autobiography, p. 37.

70. Ibid., p. 41; Robinson, Civil War in Lancashire, p. 52; Carte, Ormonde, VI, p. 151; H.M.C., Report X, Appendix IV, pp. 102-3; Firth, Marston Moor, p. 70.

71. Warburton, II, pp. 427-8; The contents of Rupert's dispatches from Lancashire can be pretty accurately deduced from the King's replies to them on June 14th.

72. Carte, Ormonde, VI, p. 151; Warburton, II, pp. 416-8.

73. It is clear from the King's letter of June 14 that Rupert had announced his intention of postponing his march to York on military grounds before he heard of the situation in the South.

74. C.S.P.D., 1644, p. 214; Baillie, II, p. 193.

75. C.S.P.D., 1644, p. 555.

76. H.M.C., Report X, Appendix VI, pp. 152-3; Rushworth, V, pp. 677-82.

77. H.M.C., Report X, Appendix VI, loc. sit.; L.J., VI, p. 595; C.S.P.D., 1644, pp. 205, 227; Jesop, A More Exact and Full Relation, London, 1644 (T.T., E. 51.15); Edward Drake's Diary of the Siege, in Bayly, Civil War in Dorset, p. 147f. The coastline has very much altered, owing to erosion and the famous "landslip"; J. R. Powell in Blake and the Defence of Lyme Regis, Mariner's Mirror, XX, summarises the sources and gives a very useful conjectural map of the defences.

78. C.S.P.D., 1644, pp. 238-9.

79. Ibid., pp. 233-4.

80. Madame de Motteville, Memoirs, I, p. 184; Hinton, Memoirs, pp. 18-19; Baillon, p. 512.

81. Warburton, II, pp. 437-9; Bray, Evelyn IV, pp. 140-2.

82. Symonds, pp. 14-18; Clarendon, Bk. VIII, 55-7.

83. C.S.P.D., 1644, pp. 313-4.

84. Ibid., p. 272.

85. C.S.P.D., 1644, pp. 293, 313; Walker, pp. 31-3; Symonds, pp. 23-4; Birch, p. 13; Gwynne, p. 42; Digby's account to Prince Rupert is in Warburton, II, pp. 472-3; An Exact and Full Relation of the Last Fight Between the King's Forces and Sir William Waller, London, 1644 (T.T., E. 53.18); Clarendon, Bk. VIII, 64-70.

86. Recollections of Sir William Waller,

London, 1788, p. 107; *C.S.P.D.,*
1644, pp. 293-4; Walker, p. 34.

87. *C.S.P.D.,* 1644, pp. 301, 323, 325,
344, 382; *H.M.C., Report VIII,* p. 3a.

88. *C.S.P.D.,* 1644, p. 301.

89. *C.S.P.D.,* 1644, pp. 223-5; Warburton, pp. 434-5.

90. Warburton, II, *loc. cit.;* Douglas,
Diary, p. 59; *H.M.C., Portland MSS,*
I, p. 179.

91. *News from the Siege before York* and
An Exact Relation of the Siege before
York, London, 1644 (*T.T.,* E. 52.9
and C. 59. G. 20); Douglas, *Diary,*
pp. 59-60; *C.S.P.D.,* 1644, p. 246.

92. *Fairfax Memorials, Maseres Tracts,* I,
p. 437 estimates the army as about
twenty-nine thousand. Sir Charles
Firth, *Marston Moor, Transactions of*
the Royal Historical Society, New
Series, XII, pp. 23-30 estimates the
Parliamentary and Scots armies at
twenty-five thousand, Rupert at
rather less than fifteen thousand, the
troops in York at about three
thousand.

93. *H.M. Register House,* Edinburgh,
Committee of Estates Papers, Leven to
Lauderdale, 21 June, 1644.

94. *C.S.P.D.,* 1644, p. 311; Firth,
Marston Moor, p. 73.

95. Firth, *Marston Moor,* p. 71.

96. *Pythouse Papers,* p. 19.

97. *Prince Rupert's Journal,* p. 737. Sir
Hugh Cholmley's narrative in English *Historical Review,* V, p. 347;
the importance of Newcastle's letter
in determining Rupert's action is
often overlooked.

98. *Parliamentary Scout,* July 4-11, 1644.

99. Cholmley's narrative, p. 349.

100. *Ibid.,* p. 347.

101. *Ibid.,* p. 348; Slingsby, p. 112;
Simeon Ash, *A Continuation of The*
Intelligence, London, 1644 (*T.T.,* E.
2.1).

102. Firth, *Marston Moor,* pp. 31-5.

103. The dispositions of the Royalists are
clear from Bernard de Gomme's
plan (*B.M. Add. MSS,* 16370, folio

64—reproduced in Firth's *Marston*
Moor). The explanation of Rupert's
peculiar formation is my own de-
duction; Rupert must have had
some purpose in thus departing from
his usual tactics and his position (too
near the ditch in the opinion of
Eythin) suggests that however he
meant to begin the battle, he did
not intend to begin it as at Edgehill
with a charge. Cromwell in fact
did exactly what Rupert wanted him
to do, but unhappily for Rupert at
a moment when he was not expecting
it.

104. *Bodleian Library, Clarendon MSS,* No.
1805; Clarendon, III, p. 376n.

105. Leonard Watson, *A More Exact*
Relation, London, 1644 (*T.T.,* E.
2.14), p. 4.

106. Cholmley's narrative, p. 348.

107. *Monckton Papers,* p. 18.

108. The most comprehensive modern
account of Marston Moor at the
time of writing is still that given by
Sir Charles Firth in *Transactions of*
the Royal Historical Society, New
Series, XII. This includes a list of
the principal contemporary authorities with reflections on their respective
value. The reconstruction by Colonel
A. H. Burne, in *British Battlefields,*
suggests several points of interest.
I have in general followed Firth in
making most use of the following
accounts: Cholmley's Narrative
(English Historical Review, V, pp.
347-51); Leonard Watson, *A More*
Exact Relation, London, 1644 (*T.T.,*
E. 2.14); Simeon Ash, *A Continua-*
tion of True Intelligence, 16 June to
10 July, 1644 (*T.T.,* E. 2.1); *A Full*
Relation of the late Victory (by a
Scot), London, 1644 (*T.T.,* E. 54.19);
Fairfax Memorials in Maseres Tracts,
I, pp. 437-8; Douglas, *Diary,* pp.
61-4. Warburton gives Byron's untimely charge from *Rupert's Diary*
but is otherwise inaccurate about this
battle. Clarendon is wholly mislead-

ing, and so is the account given by the Duchess of Newcastle many years later in her *Life* of her husband, although this besotted lady's rendering of her husband's smug exculpations are sometimes cited as an authority. Fuller's *Worthies* (p. 639) on the other hand gives some interesting details, including the suggestion that Hurry was responsible for dividing Rupert's cavalry with musketeers. I am indebted to Mr. Daniel George for having drawn my attention to this account.

109. Firth, *Marston Moor*, p. 71.
110. Warburton, II, p. 468; Collins, *Sydney Papers*, pp. 33-4; *C.S.P.D.*, 1644, p. 386. Clarendon, III, p. 376n; Cholmley, *Memoirs*, London, 1870, p. 69.
111. Abbott, I, pp. 287-8.
112. Sanford, *Studies*, p. 610.
113. Digby to Rupert, July 17, *B.M.*, *Add. MSS*, 18981, folio 205-6; Warburton, II, p. 470; *Prince Rupert's Journal*, p. 737; *A True Relation of . . . Montrose*, pp. 3-4.
114. *C.S.P.D.*, 1644, p. 376; Robinson, *Civil War in Lancashire*, p. 57.
115. *Prince Rupert's Journal*, p. 737; *History and Antiquities of Man*, pp. 4, 9-10.
116. Whitelocke, p. 90; *A Full Relation of the Late Victory*.
117. *C.S.P. Ven.*, 1643-7, pp. 117; *L.J.*, VI, p. 616.
118. Baillie, II, p. 203.
119. *Manchester's Quarrel*, pp. 72, 73.
120. Baillie, II, pp. 208-9, 218.
121. *A True Relation of the late Fight between the Parliament forces and Prince Rupert*, London, 1644 (*T.T.*, E. 54.7).
122. Roger Williams, *Bloody Tenent of Persecution*, London, 1644, p. 247; Haller, *Tracts on Liberty*, III, pp. 105-73.
123. Baillie, II, p. 191.
124. Slingsby, p. 116; Douglas, *Diary*, p. 66; the text is Ps. xiii, 9.

125. *Manchester's Quarrel*, p. 1.
126. *C.S.P. Ven.*, 1643-7, pp. 110, 135-6; *B.M.*, *Add. MSS*, 5460, *Sabran's Dispatches*, folio 232; Meikle, *Correspondence of Scots Commissioners*, p. 9. The association of Vane with the Elector's family was very close; his younger brother, Walter Vane, was a soldier in the Netherlands and well known at the Queen of Bohemia's Court while his sister, Frances, was wife to the Queen's steward, Sir Robert Honeywood, whose strong influence over the Queen is noticed by Sabran, folio 243.
127. *Manchester's Quarrel*, pp. 59ff, 80-1; *C.S.P.D.*, 1644-5, p. 149.
128. *H.M. Register House*, Edinburgh, *Committee of Estates Papers*, Leven to the Estates, 21 June, 1644.
129. Balfour, III, pp. 165, 170, 174.
130. *Ibid.*, p. 177.
131. *Chronicles of the Frasers, The Wardlaw MS*, ed. W. Mackay, *Scottish History Society*, Edinburgh, 1905, pp. 390-1.
132. Balfour, III, pp. 215, 217; P. Gordon, *A Short Abridgment of Britane's Distemper*, Spalding Club, Aberdeen, 1844, pp. 62-3.
133. Cregan, *Daniel O'Neill, Royalist Agent*, Irish Historical Studies, II, p. 401.
134. W. Forbes Leith, *Memoirs of Scottish Catholics during the XVIIth and XVIIIth Centuries*, London, 1909, I, pp. 302-3; *Britane's Distemper*, p. 66.
135. Balfour, III, pp. 209, 215, 217.
136. *Ibid.*, pp. 231, 232, 245.
137. *A True Relation of . . . Montrose*, p. 4; Napier, II, p. 145.
138. *C.S.P.D.*, 1644, p. 363; Walsingham, *Alter Britannicae Heros*, Oxford, 1645.
139. *C.S.P.D.*, 1644, p. 382, 485, August *passim*.
140. *Ibid.*, p. 335; Walker, p. 42.
141. Rushworth, V, p. 686; Ludlow, I, pp. 95-6; *C.S.P.D.*, 1644, p. 351; *C.S.P. Ven.*, 1643-7, p. 126.

142. *Archives de la Maison d'Orange-Nassau*, II, IV, pp. 106-10; Motteville, pp. 213, 222; Baillon, p. 514ff; *C.S.P.D.*, 1644, p. 356f.
143. Herrick, *Poems*.
144. Walker, pp. 43, 45; Rushworth, V, pp. 688-90.
145. *H.M.C., Records of the City of Exeter*, p. 325.
146. Symonds, pp. 41-2.
147. *C.S.P.D.*, 1644, p. 399.
148. See Chapter II, p. 102.
149. Warburton, II, p. 416; Clarendon, Bk. VIII, p. 96. G.E.C.'s Peerage gives the marriage of Wilmot to Anne St. John, widow of Sir Henry Lee of Ditchling, as probably 1644. Biographers of their famous son, the poet Rochester, generally agree that his parents were married in 1644. This does, indeed, seem probable as Wilmot left the country in the autumn of that year and his wife is not known to have left it at all. Some future biographer of Rochester might, however, trace Wilmot's subsequent movements to find out how this exile in France became the father of a son in Oxfordshire in April, 1647.
150. See *The King's Peace*, p. 440.
151. Digby to Rupert, July 17, *B.M., Add. MSS*, 18981, folio 205-6.
152. Carte, *Ormonde*, VI, p. 167.
153. *Ibid.*, p. 190; Symonds, pp. 108-9.
154. *B.M. Add. MSS*, 18981, *Prince Rupert's Correspondence*, folio 208; Carte, *Ormonde*, VI, p. 190.
155. Clarendon, Bk. VIII, p. 98; Bulstrode, pp. 106ff; *B.M. Add. MSS*, 18981, folio 00.
156. Rushworth, V, pp. 693-8; Symonds, pp. 106-10; Clarendon, Bk. VIII, pp. 96, 105-6; Carte, *Ormonde*, VI, p. 203.
157. Rushworth, V, p. 693; Walker, pp. 57-8.
158. Walker, p. 56; Clarendon, Bk VIII, p. 97.
159. *B.M., Add. MSS*, 18981, folio 220.

160. *Archaeologia Cambrensis*, Third Series, XV, p. 322.
161. Warburton, III, pp. 21-2.
162. Beedham, *Unpublished Correspondence of Archbishop Williams*, p. 18.
163. *C.S.P.D.*, 1644, pp. 392, 423, 428, 440.
164. *Prince Rupert's Journal*, p. 737.
165. Baillie, II, p. 221.
166. *C.S.P. Ven.*, 1643-7, p. 130.
167. Hauck, *Briefe der kinder des Winterkonigs*, pp. 25ff; *B.M. Add. MSS*, 5460, *Sabran's Dispatches*, folio 207.
168. Warburton, III, p. 23.
169. *C.S.P.D.*, 1644, p. 332; *Archaeologia Cambrensis*, Third Series, XV, p. 317; First Series, I, p. 37; Phillips, *Civil War in Wales*, II, pp. 188, 189-92.
170. Warburton, III, p. 22; *H.M.C., Rawdon MSS*, II, pp. 132-3; Beedham, p. 22; Phillips, *Civil War in Wales*, II, pp. 201-91; *Autobiography of Lord Herbert of Cherbury*, ed. Sidney Lee, London, 1886, pp. 279-85.
171. Walker, pp. 76-80; Symonds, pp. 65-7; *C.S.P. Ven.*, 1643-7, p. 138; Clarendon, Bk. VIII, 109, 116; Rushworth, V. pp. 704-5; Bulstrode, p. 109.
172. Symonds, p. 67; Whitelocke, p. 98; Warburton, III, p. 4; *C.S.P.D.*, 1644, Sept. 14; Bulstrode, pp. 110-1.
173. Baillie, II, p. 216.
174. *Ibid.*, pp. 220, 221.
175. *C.J.*, III, 606.
176. Marsys, pp. 141ff; *B.M. Add. MSS,*, 5460, *Sabran's Dispatches*, folio 257-9.
177. Haller, *Liberty and Reformation*, pp. 146-7.
178. *C.S.P.D.*, 1644, pp. 490-1.
179. *Manchester's Quarrel*, pp. 8-9.
180. *Ibid.*, pp. 389, 417; 1644-5, pp. 150-2, 158.
181. *Manchester's Quarrel*, pp. 11-12, 76.
182. *Manchester's Quarrel*, p. 61.
183. Baillie, II, p. 230.
184. Spalding, II, p. 399; Forbes Leith, I, pp. 271f.
185. Spalding, II, p. 402 Guthry, p. 162;

Wishart, pp. 55-7, 367-8; *Britane's Distemper*, pp. 68-73.
186. *A True Relation of* . . . *Montrose*, p. 5.
187. *Ibid.*, pp. 6-8; Wishart, pp. 61, 370; Spalding, II, p. 403; *Britane's Distemper*, pp. 73-4; Carte, *Letters*, I, p. 73.
188. *H.M. Register House*, Edinburgh, *Breadalbane MSS*, contains details of Argyll's measures.
189. *Thurloe State Papers*, I, pp. 47-8; *H.M. Register House*, Edinburgh, *Committee of Estates Papers*, Leven to the Committee, 10 Sept., 1644.
190. Spalding, II, p. 404.
191. Baillie, II, pp. 225, 227.
192. *C.J.*, III, p. 626.
193. Baillie, II, pp. 230, 235.
194. *C.S.P.D.*, 1644, p. 502; *C.S.P. Ven.*, 1643-7, p. 140.
195. *C.S.P.D.*, 1644, pp. 469, 527.
196. Carte, *Ormonde*, VI, p. 199.

BOOK II: CHAPTER IV

1. Clarendon, Bk. VIII, 145.
2. Gilbert, *Irish Confederation*, III, pp. 41ff, 151ff.
3. *C.S.P.I.*, 1643-7, p. 395.
4. Carte, *Ormonde*, VI, p. 181.
5. *Ibid.*, pp. 171-2; Rushworth, V, pp. 974-8.
6. *C.S.P.I.*, 1643-7, p. 435; *Clarendon State Papers*, II, pp. 171-2; *Cal. Clar. S. P.*, I, p. 252; *H.M.C.*, *Egmont MSS*, I, I, pp. 235-6.
7. *Ibid.*, VI, p. 209; *C.S.P.I.*, 1643-7, p. 395; H. Hazlett, *Financing of British Armies in Ireland*, 1641-9, *Irish Historical Studies*, I, p. 23.
8. La Boullay le Gouz, *Voyages et Observations*, Paris, 1653, pp. 436-7.
9. Carte, *Ormonde*, VI, p. 153.
10. *Ibid.*, p. 198; *Memoirs, Letters and Speeches of Shaftesbury*, ed. W. D. Christie, London, 1859, pp. 104-6.
11. Carte, *Ormonde*, VI, p. 223; Walker, pp. 106-7; Symonds, pp. 128-9, 141; *H.M.C.*, *Portland MSS*, I, p.

188; Warburton, III, pp. 26-7; *B.M.*, *Add. MSS*, 5460. *Sabran's Dispatches*, I, folios 331-2. Clarendon, Bk. VIII, p. 148-9 gives the impression of a disillusioned and defeated march, but this is not confirmed by other sources.
12. *C.S.P.D.*, 1644-5, p. 12.
13. *C.S.P.D.*, 1644-5, pp. 151-6, 158; *C.S.P. Ven.*, 1643-7, p. 144; *Manchester's Quarrel*, p. 84.
14. *C.S.P.D.*, 1644-5, p. 502.
15. Clarendon, Bk. VIII, p. 149-150; Walker, pp. 106-7; Symonds, p. 121; *H.M.C.*, *Portland MSS*, I, p. 188.
16. *C.S.P.D.*, 1644-5, pp. 60, 62, 65; *Manchester's Quarrel*, pp. 47-8.
17. Symonds, p. 142; Walker, p. 108.
18. Symonds, p. 142.
19. *Britane's Distemper*, p. 80; Spalding, II, p. 405.
20. Spalding, *loc. cit.;* Napier, II, pp. 162-3; *H.M. Register House*, Edinburgh, *State Papers*, 166.
21. Spalding, II, p. 406.
22. *Ibid.*, p. 407; *Britane's Distemper*, pp. 81-4; *True Relation . . . of Montrose*, pp. 9-11.
23. Carte, *Letters*, I, p. 74; Spalding, II, pp. 407-12; Napier, II, pp. 160-70; *Diary of Alexander Jaffray*, p. 25. It is not easy to decide just how much damage was done at Aberdeen. Spalding, a Royalist, lists 118 citizens killed, all men. It is possible that Jaffray, the provost who ran away, exaggerates the extent of the massacre. In the *New Spalding Club Miscellany*, II, Edinburgh, 1900, pp. 391-2 are a number of compensation claims made by Aberdonians at the end of the war; it is significant that quite as many (if not more) of these are for damage done by Covenanting troops as for damage done by Montrose's men.
24. Spalding, II, pp. 414, 416-7; *Records of Old Aberdeen*, New Spalding Club, Edinburgh, 1899, I, p. 75.

25. *True Relation*, p. 12; Napier, II, pp. 168-9; Spalding, II, pp. 419-20; *Correspondence of Sir Robert Kerr, first Earl of Ancram and his son William, third Earl of Lothian*, Edinburgh, 1875, pp. 173-4.

26. Baillie, II, pp. 230-1, 234.

27. Douglas, pp. 78-9; Rushworth, V, pp. 645-52. Most of the sources are assembled in C. S. Terry, *Life of Alexander Leslie*, Chapter VIII.

28. Baillie, II, pp. 238, 262-3; *C.S.P. Ven.*, 1643-7, p. 150; Meikle, pp. 47, 54; *Lothian-Ancram Letters*, I, pp. 176-7.

29. Gwynne, p. 50; Walker, p. 110; Clarendon, Bk. VIII, 152.

30. Walker, p. 110; Clarendon, Bk. VIII, 153.

31. Clarendon, *loc. cit.*

32. Walker, p. 111.

33. The second battle of Newbury, a rather confused engagement in itself, is further confused by the quarrel of Cromwell and Manchester and the attempts of their friends to defend each at the other's expense. The chief Royalist accounts are *Mercurius Aulicus*, Oct. 27-Nov. 3; Walker, pp. 110-114; Bulstrode, pp. 117-9. Clarendon, Bk. VIII, pp. 154-60 adds little to these, but there are some interesting details in Gwynne, *Memoirs*, Chapter XI-XIV, and in Symonds, pp. 145-6. Simeon Ash, *A True Relation of the Battel at Newbury*, London, 1644 (*T.T.*, E. 22.10) is chiefly a defence of Manchester. Other accounts in connection with the quarrel between Manchester and Cromwell are in *C.S.P.D.*, 1644-5, pp. 150, 152-3, 156ff, and *Manchester's Quarrel*, pp. 48-50, 85-7. Ludlow *Memoirs*, I, pp. 102-5 is limited to one part of the battle but is straightforward. See Hinton, *Memoirs*, p. 18 for some details of the Royalist retreat and Birch, *Memoirs*, pp. 18-21 for his part in the pursuit.

34. *C.S.P.D.*, 1644-5, pp. 149-50, 157; Ash, *True Relation*, p. 6.

35. Symonds, p. 146; *Prince Rupert's Journal*, p. 737.

36. Symonds, p. 147.

37. *Prince Rupert's Journal*, p. 737.

38. Symonds, p. 147; Walker, p. 117; Clarendon, Bk. VIII, 258.

39. Ash, *True Relations*, p. 6.

40. Symonds, pp. 148-9.

41. *C.S.P.D.*, 1644-5, pp. 148, 150-1, 155, 159-60; *Manchester's Quarrel*. pp. 92-3.

42. *C.S.P.D.*, 1644-5, p. 148.

43. *Ibid.*, p. 114.

44. *Ibid.*, p. 126.

45. *Ibid.*, p. 115, see also Lucy Hutchinson, *Life of Colonel Hutchinson*.

46. *C.S.P.D.*, 1644-5, p. 131.

47. *C.S.P. Ven.*, 1643-7, pp. 153-4.

48. *Mercurius Civicus*, July 11-17, 1644; *An Ordinance for Provision of Turf*, London, 1644 (*T.T.*, E. 2, 16 and 23).

49. *C.S.P. Ven.*, 1643-7, p. 154.

50. State Trials, IV, p. 586.

51. Whitelocke, p. 106; Baillie, II, p. 240.

52. *C.J.*, III, pp. 699, 703.

53. *B.M.*, *Add. MSS*, 5460, *Sabran's Dispatches*, I, folio, 349.

54. Whitelocke, pp. 109-10; *C.S.P. Ven.*, 1643-7, pp. 160-1; *C.S.P.D.*, 1644-5, p. 143.

55. *Manchester's Quarrel*, pp. 78-95.

56. Baillie, II, pp. 244-5.

57. *Camden Miscellany*, VIII, *A Letter from the Earl of Manchester*.

58. *Manchester's Quarrel*, pp. 72, 73.

59. Whitelocke, pp. 111-2; Abbott, I, pp. 312-3; Meikle, pp. 51-2.

60. *C.S.P. Ven.*, 1643-7, p. 162.

61. Haller, pp. 136, 369 and n 58; *Alas, Pore Parliament*, London, 1644 (*T.T.*, E. 21.9).

62. Abbott, I, pp. 314-5.

63. Clarendon, Bk. VIII, 192-7; *B.M.*, *Add. MSS*, 5460, *Sabran's Dispatches*, I, folios 408-9; *C.J.*, III, pp. 718, 726, 728.

64. Baillie, II, p. 247.

65. This point of view is argued from circumstantial evidence most convincingly in a typescript thesis *The Rise of the Independent Party* (Harvard, 1936) by J. H. Hexter. One half of this thesis was enlarged and published as *The Reign of King Pym*. The second half which analyses Vane's leadership of the Commons has unhappily not been published.

66. *Clarendon State Papers*, II, p. 280; Clarendon, Bk. VIII, 203; *Trelawny Papers*, Camden Miscellany II, p. 9.

67. Baillie, II, p. 262.

68. Spalding, II, pp. 421, 423f; *Britane's Distemper*, pp. 91-3; Wishart, pp. 74-5, 376-7.

69. Symonds, p. 161; the messenger was William Rollo, the lame soldier who was one of the two to cross the border with Montrose. I suspect him of being the anonymous author of the *True Relation* which breaks off short at the moment when he would have left Scotland, and which was published in Oxford a few weeks after his arrival.

70. *Britane's Distemper*, pp. 89, 92. Montrose had been blamed for not sending Huntly his commission earlier, but it can have been no easy matter to find a messenger to carry so important a document to Huntly at Tongue. It was natural enough to wait in the hope that Huntly might emerge from his remote hiding place.

71. Spalding, II, p. 432.

72. Forbes-Leith, I, pp. 300-2.

73. *Ibid.*, p. 304; *Britane's Distemper*, pp. 94-5.

74. Forbes-Leith, I, p. 304.

75. *Ibid.*, I, p. 308-9; *Britane's Distemper*, p. 97.

76. Carte, *Letters*, I, p. 75; Wishart, pp. 80-1, 380.

77. Forbes-Leith, I, p. 310.

78. *C.S.P.D.*, 1644-5, p. 310; Meikle, p. 53.

79. Spalding, II, p. 425.

80. *C.S.P. Ven.*, 1643-7, pp. 169, 171.

81. *B.M., Add. MSS*, 5461, *Sabran's Dispatches*, II, folios 10, 12; *Camden Miscellany*, XIII, *Voyages of Captain William Jackson*, p. 35.

82. *Minutes of the Westminster Assembly*, ed. Struthers and Mitchell, London, 1874, p. 21.

83. *Acts and Ordinances*, I, pp. 582-608.

84. *Ibid.*, pp. 567-9.

85. Haller, p. 374; *C.J.*, III, p. 733. See also Struthers and Mitchell, p. 19; Lightfoot, p. 342.

86. *L.J.*, VII, p. 135.

87. Carte, *Ormonde*, VI, pp. 233-4; *C.S.P.D.*, 1644-5, p. 263; *C.J.*, IV, p. 25.

88. Reckitt, *Charles I and Hull*, pp. 119-28; Whitelocke, p. 91.

89. Rushworth, V, pp. 807-8; for an excellent sketch of the whole incident see Ketton Cremer, *Norfolk Gallery*, pp. 79-80.

90. *B.M., Add. MSS*, 5461, *Sabran's Dispatches*, II, folio 29.

91. Clarendon, Bk. VII, 206, 208; *Acts and Ordinances*, I, pp. 608-9.

92. *State Trials*, IV, p. 359.

93. Rushworth, V, pp. 835-40. See also *Brief Relation of the Death of the Archbishop*, Oxford, 1645 (*T.T.*, E. 269.20) and *The Archbishop of Canterbury's Speech*, London, 1645 (*T.T.*, E. 24.15).

94. Burton, *The Grand Impostor Unmasked*, London, 1645 (*T.T.*, E. 26.4).

95. *The King's Cabinet Opened*, p. 24.

96. *An Elegie on . . . William Laud*, Oxford, 1645 (*T.T.*, E. 271.8).

97. See *The King's Peace*, pp. 98ff; the case which I tried to make out for Laud in that volume would have been fuller and stronger had Christopher Hill's *Economic Problems of the English Church*, Oxford, 1956, been available at the time. This most interesting study of the finances of the English Church reveals the magnitude of the problem which defeated Laud and

others. For a recent view of Laud by one more competent than most historians to judge his position and achievement see the late Archbishop Garbett's lively little character sketch in his *Church and State in England*, London, 1950. Professor Trevor-Roper's biography (revised edition, 1962) remains the standard work.

98. *A copie of a letter written by John Lilburne*, London, 1645 (*T.T.*, E. 24.22).

99. B.M., *Add.MSS*, 5461, *Sabran's Dispatches* II, folios 83-9; see also the recent full and interesting biography of Henry Morse: Philip Caraman, *Priest of the Plague*, London, 1957.

100. *Sabran's Dispatches*, II, folio 2.

101. *C.S.P.D.*, 1644-5, pp. 237-8, 248, 253.

102. *Ibid.*, p. 233.

103. Whitelocke, pp. 115-6.

104. *C.S.P.D.*, 1644-5, pp. 246-7; *A Full Relation of the Victory Obtained by our Forces at Abingdon*, London, 1645, (*T.T.*, E. 24.14); *A letter sent to Major General Browne*, London, 1645 (*T.T.*, E. 24.20).

105. *C.S.P.D.*, 1644-5, pp. 247, 249.

106. *Ibid.*, p. 251; Birch, *Memoirs*, p. 15. The bringing of troops to Plymouth by sea is well described in John Syms, *Journal of the Civil War*. B.M., *Add. MSS*, 35, 297, folio 47.

107. Whitelocke, p. 121; Clarendon, Bk. IX, p. 7.

108. Clarendon, *loc. cit.*; Shaftesbury, *Memoirs*, pp. 104-6.

109. *King's Cabinet Opened*, p. 13.

110. *C.S.P.D.*, 1644-5, p. 301; Slingsby, *Diary*, pp. 139-42.

111. Anthony Wood, *Life and Times*, I, p. 110; Clarendon, Bk. VIII, p. 65.

112. *King's Cabinet Opened*, p. 4.

113. Warburton, III, pp. 47-50.

114. Carte, *Ormonde*, VI, p. 206.

115. *King's Cabinet Opened*, p. 11; B.M., *Add. MSS*, 5461, *Sabran's Dispatches* II, folio 45; *Perfect Passages*, Jan. 8-22, 1645 (*T.T.*, E. 25.17).

116. *King's Cabinet Opened*, p. 1.

117. Baillon, pp. 526, 529.

118. *The King's Cabinet Opened*, p. 31; *Archives de la Maison d'Orange-Nassau, Second Series*, IV, p. 129.

119. *Ibid.*, p. 133.

120. *C.S.P.D.*, 1644-5, pp. 261-2; B.M., *Add. MSS*, 5461, *Sabran's Dispatches*, II, folio 60; Prestage, *Antonio de Sousa*, pp. 23-4.

121. *King's Cabinet Opened*, p. 2.

122. *Commentarius*, I, pp. 496-7.

123. Carte, *Ormonde*, III, p. 139; V, pp. 8-9; VI, pp. 209, 225-6, *Clarendon State Papers*, I, p. 264.

124. Clarendon, Bk. VIII, 213, 219; *Thurloe State Papers*, I, p. 64-65; *Evelyn's Diary*, ed. Bray, IV, pp. 135, 137, 138.

125. *Greene's Diary, English Historical Review*, XLIII, p. 602.

126. Clarendon, Bk. VIII, 222-3, 224, 230-1; see also *Thurloe State Papers*, p. 65; Meikle, p. 60.

127. Clarendon, Bk. VIII, pp. 243-7.

128. B.M., *Add. MSS*, 5461, *Sabran's Dispatches*, II, folio 77.

129. Selden, *Table Talk*, ed. Reynolds, p. 47.

130. *C.S.P.D.*, 1644-5, p. 329.

131. Baillie, II, p. 417.

132. Montrose's movements are best given by the Jesuit father who accompanied the Irish, in Forbes-Leith, I, pp. 311-20; for Argyll and Baillie, *Thurloe State Papers*, II, pp. 60-1; there is a series of letters from Baillie during these days among the *Committee of Estates Papers* in H.M. Register House, Edinburgh; all are dated from Perth.

133. Napier, II, pp. 172-3.

134. Spalding, II, p. 443; Napier, II, p. 176.

135. *Britane's Distemper*, p. 100; Spalding, II, p. 444; Wishart, pp. 83-4, 381; Napier, II, 176.

136. James Burns, *Memoirs*, p. 8.

137. Forbes-Leith, I, p. 321.

138. *Britane's Distemper*, pp. 101-2; Spalding, II, pp. 444-5; Wishart, pp. 84-5, 381-2; Forbes-Leith, I, pp. 321-3.

139. Napier, II, pp. 177-8.
140. Forbes-Leith, I, pp. 322-3, 327; Spalding, II, pp. 446-451.
141. Balfour, III, p. 273; Guthry, p. 180.
142. Balfour, III, p. 270; James Burns, *Memoirs*, p. 9; *Acts of Parliament of Scotland*; *The Remonstrances of the General Assembly*, 13 Feb. 1645 (*T.T.*, E. 292.7).
143. Baillie, II, p. 231; his opinion is echoed by Burnet, *History of his own Time*, London, 1839, p. 23, who learnt it from Lauderdale.
144. Clarendon, VIII, 239.
145. *B.M.*, *Add. MSS*, 5461, *Sabran's Dispatches*, II, folios 66, 74.
146. Clarendon, VIII, 351; Meikle, pp. 60-2.
147. *L.J.*, VII, pp. 204-9; *Acts and Ordinances*, I, pp. 614-26.
148. Whitelocke, p. 127; *C.J.*, IV, p. 54; *Fairfax Memorials* (*Maseres Tracts*) pp. 440, 443.
149. See *The King's Peace*, pp. 468, 469-70.
150. *B.M.*, *Add. MSS*, 5461, *Sabran's Dispatches* II, folio 99.
151. *The Last Speeches . . . of the Lord Maguire*, London, 1645, (*T.T.*, E. 270.19); *H.M.C.*, *Franciscan MSS*, p. 245.
152. Firth, *Raising of the Ironsides*, pp. 60-1; *C.S.P.D.*, 1644-5, p. 282.
153. *Ibid.*, pp. 301-2, 314.
154. The sources on the Royalist defeat at Weymouth are collected in H. G. Tibbutt, *Life and Letters of Sir Lewis Dyve*, pp. 60-64 but the causes of the precipitate Royalist withdrawal still remain mysterious.
155. *B.M.*, *Add. MSS*, 18981, *Rupert's Correspondence*, folio 40; *Cave to Rupert*, Feb. 15th, 1645; Warburton, III, p. 59.
156. *Shrewsbury Taken, A Copy of Sir William Brereton's Letter*, London, 1645 (*T.T.*, E. 270.26); Clarendon, VIII, 239; *Archaeologia Cambrensis, First Series*, I, p. 38.
157. Clarendon, VIII, p. 531n.
158. *Acts and Ordinances*, I, pp. 544-5.

159. Malbon, p. 168: the apparently gratuitous hangings which occurred in Cheshire in the middle of March were, I have little doubt, the reprisals for what had happened at Shrewsbury.
160. *Cal. Clar. S.P.*, I, pp. 258, 264; Carte, *Ormonde*, V, p. 13; VI, p. 258.
161. *C.S.P.D.*, 1644-5, p. 332.
162. Clarendon, Bk. VIII, 239; Warburton, III, p. 63; Whitelocke, p. 129.
163. *National Library of Wales, Calendar of Wynn Papers*, Aberystwith, 1926, pp. 285-7; *Archaelogia Cambrensis, Fourth Series*, VI, 1875, *Correspondence During the Great Rebellion*, p. 309; see also A. W. Dodd. *The Pattern of Politics in Stuart Wales, Transactions of the Honorable Society of Cymmrodorian*, 1948, pp. 56-7; see also his *Studies in Stuart Wales*, pp. 88-9; Warburton, III, p. 56.
164. Clarendon, Bk. VIII, p. 279.
165. *B.M.*, *Add. MSS*, 5461, *Sabran's Dispatches*, II, folio, 146-7.
166. Carte, *Ormonde*, VI, p. 264.
167. *Sabran's Dispatches*, loc. cit.
168. Warburton, III, pp. 67, 70; Carte, *Ormonde*, VI, p. 272; Clarendon, Bk. IX, p. 25n; Symonds, p. 152.
169. Clarendon, Bk. IX, p. 9n.
170. *Ibid.*, Bk. VIII, 279, 286.
171. *Ibid.*, Bk. IX, p. 10.
172. *Ibid.*, Bk. VIII, pp. 140-1.
173. Carte, *Letters*, I, p. 97.
174. Sandford, p. 619; Clarendon, Bk. IX, p. 10.
175. Sandford, pp. 620-1.
176. Bulstrode, pp. 120-2.
177. *Cal. Clar. S.P.*, I. p. 261; Clarendon, Bk. IX, pp. 10-15; Sandford, pp. 619-20.
178. Sandford, p. 621. Goring had been badly wounded some years before and was evidently troubled by recurrent bouts of pain which may explain his behaviour.
179. Clarendon, Bk. IX. p. 9; *Cal. Clar.*

S.P., I. p. 262; Sanford, pp. 616-7.

180. Warburton, III, p. 70.
181. Ibid, pp. 73-4.
182. Ibid., pp. 67-8; Fairfax Correspondence, III, pp. 182-3; B.M., Add. MSS, 5461, Sabran's Dispatches, II, folio 138; Meikle, p. 61.
183. Carte, Ormonde, VI, p. 271; the account in Mercurius Aulicus is printed in Webb, Civil War in Herefordshire, II, pp. 178-9.
184. Whitelocke, p. 133.
185. Acts and Ordinances, I, pp. 614-26.
186. B.M., Add. MSS, 5461, Sabran's Dispatches, II, folio 27, March-April; L.J., VII, p. 277.
187. L.J., VII, 298.
188. L.J., VII, 299.
189. Acts and Ordinances, I, pp. 664-5; L.J., VII, p. 302.
190. L.J., VII, p. 313.
191. C.J., IV, pp. 138, 169.
192. Rushworth, VI, p. 17.
193. C.S.P.D., 1644-5, p. 358.

BOOK II: CHAPTER V

1. Carte, Letters, I, pp. 80, 82.
2. Carte, Ormonde, VI, p. 276.
3. C.S.P. Ven., 1643-7, pp. 181-2, 187.
4. C.S.P.D., 1644-5, p. 387.
5. Lord George Digby's Cabinet Opened, p. 24; C.S.P.D., 1644-5, p. 388-9.
6. Clarendon, Bk. IX, 13; Sanford, p. 623; Cal. Clar. S.P.I. p. 263.
7. C.S.P.D., 1644-5, pp. 407, 411; B.M., Add. MSS, 5461, Sabran's Dispatches, II, folio 174; Carte, Letters, I, p. 130; Gardiner, II, p. 193.
8. Meikle, p. 66.
9. B.M., Add. MSS, 5461, Sabran's Dispatches, II, folio 176.
10. Whitelocke, p. 137.
11. Wishart's original Latin reads: "Hortatus denique ut munera sua fortiter capesserant, eventum Deo, caeteraque suae curae permitterent." English translations of Wishart, from 1647 to 1893, have various renderings of this

magnificent display of religious faith, self-confidence and sang froid.

12. Wishart, pp. 93-5, 386-7.
13. C.S.P.D., 1644-5, p. 419.
14. Abbott, I, pp. 341-2.
15. Ibid., pp. 340, 342; Symonds, p. 163; see The King's Peace, p. 339 for Frank Windebank's earlier exploits.
16. Abbott, I, p. 344.
17. Warburton, III, pp. 77-8; Cal. Clar. S.P.I., p. 264; Gardiner, II, pp. 204-5n.
18. Abbott, I, pp. 344-5.
19. Meikle, p. 74; Walker, p. 104; Clarendon, Bk. IX, 28.
20. Symonds, p. 164.
21. Slingsby, p. 146.
22. Walker, pp. 125-6; Carte, Ormonde, VI, p. 287.
23. Isaac Tullie, Siege of Carlisle, p. 23.
24. Clarendon, Bk. IX, 29, and Walker, pp. 125-6 give Rupert's insistence on the northern march, but the soundness of Rupert's reasoning touched on in Clarendon, becomes clear from the anxiety expressed by the Scots Commissioners in London when the King's intention for the North became known to them. Meikle, pp. 74, 77-8.
25. Clarendon, Bk. IX, 15, 20, 21, 22; C.S.P.D., 1644-5, p. 511.
26. Clarendon, Bk. IX, 31, 43.
27. C.S.P.D., 1644-5, p. 459.
28. Sandford, p. 624; C.S.P.D., 1644-5. p. 479; Two Letters, the one from Sir Thomas Fairfax, the other from Colonel Ralph Weldon; A Great Victorie . . . at the raising of the siege from before Taunton; A Narration of the Expedition to Taunton, London, 1645 (T.T., E. 284, 9, 11; 285.10).
29. Clarendon, Bk. IX, 44.
30. Warburton, III, pp. 79; Phillips, Civil War in Wales, II, pp. 248-54.
31. H.M.C., Portland MSS, I, pp. 224-5.
32. Walker, p. 127.
33. Warburton, III, pp. 97-8.
34. Walker, p. 127.
35. C.S.P.D., 1644-5, p. 521.

36. *Ibid.*, p. 506; but see also *P.R.O., S. P. Dom*, 1645, DVII, No. 79.
37. *Ibid.*, p. 520; Clarendon, Bk. IX, 47.
38. *Evelyn*, ed. Bray, IV, p. 148; Baillie, II, p. 487; *L.J.*, VII, pp. 431-2.
39. *C.S.P.D.*, 1644-5, p. 522.
40. *Perfect Passages*, May 28-June 4, 1645 (*T.T.*, E. 262.2); for the behaviour of the armies in the midland villages see also Guttery, *Civil War in Midland Parishes* and F. H. West: *Rude Forefathers*, London, 1949, especially pages 67-8.
41. Slingsby, *Diary*, p. 146.
42. *Prince Rupert's Journal*, p. 739.
43. Symonds, pp. 179-80; Slingsby, pp. 146-8.
44. Walker, p. 129; Warburton, III, p. 100.
45. *The King's Cabinet Opened*, p. 10.
46. Slingsby, p. 149.
47. *The King's Cabinet Opened*, p. 14; *Prince Rupert's Journal*, p. 739.
48. *Evelyn*, ed. Bray, IV, pp. 149-50.
49. Warburton, III, p. 100.
50. Symonds, p. 190; *The King's Cabinet Opened*, p. 14.
51. Symonds, p. 193; *A more exact Relation of the great victory . . . in Naisby Field*, London, 1645 (*T.T.*, E. 288.28), Nathaniel Wetham, *Life*, 1907, p. 96.
52. Walker, p. 129.
53. *A more exact Relation*.
54. H. Peter, *God's Doing, Man's Duty*, p. 21; Bulstrode, p. 125.
55. Abbott, I, p. 365; *A More Particular Relation*, London, 1645 (*T.T.*, E. 288.38).
56. Wogan's account in Carte, *Letters*, I, pp. 128-9.
57. The accounts of Naseby which I have principally used are that by Wogan in Carte, *Letters*, I, pp. 128-9; the letters of Fairfax (*L.J.*, VII, 433-4) and Cromwell (Abbott, I, p. 359); *A More Exact Relation* (*T.T.*, E. 288.28); Colonel Okey's account (*T.T.*, E. 288.38) and two other Thomason Tracts, E. 288, 28 and 33; Walker, pp. 129-31; Sprigge, pp. 33-40 Colonel Burne's reconstruction in *British Battlefields* is useful to anyone studying the battle on the ground because of his vivid little sketches of the terrain as it is to-day.
58. *Hull Letters*, p. 89.
59. *A More Exact Relation*; The barbarous massacre of the women has never been fully explained and remains an indelibile blot on the New Model Army. The Royalists, though their discipline was often deplorable, never did anything as bad as this. An effort has been ingeniously made to link the massacre with the coeval witch trials in Essex, and to suggest that the East Anglian soldiers regarded these women as witches. A woman had been lynched by the Parliamentary troops just after the relief of Lyme and another on the march to Newbury on suspicion of witchcraft. But there is a considerable difference between the killing of one victim and a mass attack. The likeliest answer would seem to be that the women, finding themselves surrounded by the enemy, and understanding nothing of war, fought with what weapons they had to protect their belongings, and the soldiers, angry at resistance when the battle was over, beat them down with their swords. In such a scuffle the casualties among women, unprotected by buffcoats, helmets, or armour, would be very high.
60. *A More Exact Relation*.
61. *L.J.*, VII, p. 433.
62. Abbott, I, p. 360.
63. *Ibid.*, p. 360n.
64. Lilburne, *Innocency and Truth Justified*.
65. *C. J.*, IV, p, 207.
66. Baillie, pp. 279-80, 282-6.
67. *B.M., Add. MSS*, 5461, *Sabran's Dispatches*, II, folios 240-70 *passim*.
68. Whitelocke, p. 147; *Sabran's Dis-*

patches, II, folio 271; *H.M.C., Report VII*, p. 451.

69. Ludlow, I, p. 123; *C.S.P. Ven.*, 1643-7, p. 211; *B.M., Add. MSS*, 5461, *Sabran's Dispatches*, II, folios 307-8, 338; the Spanish ambassador never missed an opportunity; during the treaty of Uxbridge he had been thinking of engaging Rupert and his cavalry for his master's service if the English war ended. See Lonchez et Cuvelier, III, p. 526.

70. Clarendon, Bk. IX, 41.

71. Carte, *Ormonde*, VI, p. 301.

72. Ellis, *Original Letters, First Series*, III, pp. 310-11.

73. Carte, *Ormonde*, VI, p. 303.

74. Warburton, III, pp. 120-1.

75. Wishart, pp. 98-103, 389-91; Napier, II, p. 203, *Britane's Distemper*, pp. 122-6. John Buchan in his *Montrose*, gives an admirable account of this battle which is difficult to describe but easy enough to understand on the field itself.

76. Baillie, II, p. 418.

77. *Cal. Clar. S.P.*, I., p. 268.

78. *Prince Rupert's Journal*, p. 739; Warburton, III, pp. 120-1.

79. Slingsby, pp. 155-6; Walker, p. 132; Bayly, *The Marquis of Worcester's Apothegms*, pp. 13-21.

80. *Evelyn*, ed. Bray, IV, pp. 153, 156-7; Dodd, *Studies*, pp. 95-7.

81. *C.S.P.D.*, 1645-7, pp. 13-14.

82. Carte, *Letters*, I, pp. 97ff; Clarendon, Bk. X, 24-28; Bulstrode, pp. 142-6.

83. Clarendon, Bk. IX, 24, 54; *H.M.C., Portland MSS*, I, pp. 227-8.

84. *Cal. Clar. S.P.*, I, p. 267.

85. *The Proceedings of the Army . . . containing the story of the Clubmen; A Letter sent to William Lenthall; The Desires and Resolutions of the Clubmen; The Kingdoms Weekly Intelligencer*, 10-17 June, 1645; (*T.T.*, E. 292.16, 22 and 24; E. 288.31).

86. Clarendon, Bk. IX, p. 66.

87. *Proceedings of the Army;* Sprigge, p. 57.

88. Sanford, pp. 626-8 reprints the most important of the pamphlets on the Battle of Langport; Cromwell's account is in Abbott, I, pp. 364-6; there is also Sprigge, pp. 64-6, and for the Royalists, Bulstrode, pp. 138-40 and Clarendon, Bk. IX, pp. 50, 51, 57. Colonel Burne in *More British Battlefields*, pp. 195-201 gives the explanation of Goring's on the whole skilful handling of his troops, which I have followed.

89. *Prince Rupert's Journal*, p. 739; Symonds, p. 210.

90. Clarendon, Bk. IX, 68.

91. Sprigge, p. 67ff; Symonds, pp. 210-211; Walker, p. 117.

92. Clarendon, Bk. IX, 71; Walker, pp. 117-8.; see also A. H. Dodd, *Studies in Stuart Wales*, pp. 93-4.

93. Clarendon, Bk. IX, 72; *C.S.P.D.*, 1644-5, pp. 618-9; see Isaac Tullie, *Siege of Carlisle*, for some idea of the sufferings of Glemham.

94. *H.M.C., Portland MSS*, I, p. 334; Meikle, pp. 68-72; *L.J.*, VII, p. 514; Zachary Gray, Appendix I, pp. 92-4; *The Late Proceedings of the Scottish Army*, London, 1645 (*T.T.*, E. 294.2).

95. Warburton, III, p. 149.

96. The best version of this letter which appears in several sources is probably Rushworth, VI, p. 132.

97. Carte, *Ormonde*, VI, p. 313.

98. *A True Relation of the late successes . . . in Pembrokeshire* (*T.T.*, E. 298.6); Leach, *Civil War in Pembroke*, pp. 110-2; Phillips, *Civil War in Wales*, II, pp. 266-7.

99. *Archaeologia Cambrensis*, IV, vi. pp. 310-11.

100. Slingsby, pp. 167-8.

101. Clarendon, IX, 74.

102. Carte, *Ormonde*, VI, pp. 305-9; *C.S.P.I.*, 1633-47, p. 408.

103. Carte, *Ormonde*, VI, pp. 292-3, 297; *C.S.P.D.*, 1645-7, pp. 20-7; *C.S.P.I.*, 1633-47, p. 404; *Commentarius*, I, p.

529; Gilbert, *Irish Confederation*, IV, pp. 278-9.

104. Lonchez et Cuvelier, III, p. 527.

105. Rushworth, IV, p. 242.

106. Sprigge, p. 76-7; *A Full Relation of the taking of Bath*, London, 1645; (*T.T.*, E. 294.21).

107. Abbott, I, pp. 368-9; *Two Great Victories*, London, 1645 (*T.T.*, E. 296.6).

108. *B.M.*, *Add. MSS*, 5461, *Sabran's Dispatches*, II, folio 334.

109. Haller, *Liberty and Reformation*, p. 145; Whitelocke, p. 154; Edwards, *Gangraena*, p. 40; Frank, *The Levellers*, New York, 1956, pp. 55, 60, 300.

110. Haller, *Liberty and Reformation*, p. 277.

111. *C.S.P. Ven.*, 1643-7, p. 208; *B.M.*, *Add. MSS*, 5461, *Sabran's Dispatches*, II, folio, 322; *L.J.* VII, p. 525

112. Whitelocke, p. 153; *Huntington Library*, Hastings MSS.

113. *Lord George Digby's Cabinet*, p. 54.

114. *Cal. Clar. S.P.*, I, p. 272; *H.M.C.*, *Portland MSS*, I, p. 245.

115. *Ibid.*, p. 246.

116. Baillie, p. 418.

117. *Britane's Distemper*, p. 129.

118. *Ibid.*, pp. 128-30, 133; Wishart, pp. 115-6, 398; Baillie, p. 419.

119. Baillie, II, p. 304.

120. Meikle, p. 97.

121. Balfour, III, p. 293.

122. *Ibid.*, p. 303 (Isaiah, 42, 24).

123. *Ibid.*, II, p. 307; Meikle, pp. 70, 122; *L.J.*, IV, pp. 479-82.

124. Wishart, pp. 45-6; *Britane's Distemper*, pp. 136-7.

125. The only eye-witness account of Kilsyth is that by General Baillie himself in Baillie, II, pp. 420-3. It differs in some respects from those in Wishart, pp. 122-5, 402-3 and *Britane's Distemper*, pp. 139ff. John Buchan has made a careful and eloquent reconstruction in his *Montrose*.

126. Meikle, p. 107; *B.M.*, *Add. MSS*, 5461, *Sabran's Dispatches*, II, folio

374; he describes Loudoun as "*fort esploré.*"

127. Baillie, II, p. 310.

128. Meikle, p. 107; *Edinburgh Burgh Records*, 1642-55, ed. Marguerite Wood, pp. 74-6, 404-6.

129. Guthry, p. 195.

130. *Thurloe State Papers*, I, pp. 70-1; Napier, II, pp. 223, 230; Salmonet, p. 308.

131. Wishart, pp. 139-40, 411.

132. *Evelyn*, ed. Bray, IV, p. 159.

133. Clarendon, Bk. IX, 86; Zachary Gray, III, *Appendix*, p. 90.

134. Symonds, p. 231.

135. Walker, p. 136; *The Royall Entertainment of the King's Army by the Royalists of Huntingdon*, London, 1645 (*T.T.*, E. 298.26).

136. Anthony Wood, *Life and Times*, I, p. 123.

137. Webb, *Civil War in Herefordshire*, II, pp. 391-7; *A Declaration of the Earl of Leven*, 14th Sept., 1645 (*T.T.*, E. 301.8); *H.M.C.*, *Portland MSS*, I, p. 234.

138. Walker, p. 137; Slingsby, p. 162; *C.S.P.D.*, 1645-7, p. 112.

139. *Ibid.*, pp. 46-7; Carte, *Ormonde*, VI, p. 312; Clarendon, IX, 58, 60.

140. An admirably full account of the operations at Sherborne and its fall is in H. G. Tibbutt, *Life and Letters of Sir Lewis Dyve*, pp. 70-77 where full references are given to all contemporary sources; *H.M.C.*, *Portland MSS*, I, pp. 242-3.

141. *Fairfax Correspondence*, II, p. 268 (or 248).

142. Warburton, III, pp. 168-9.

143. Clarendon, Bk. IX, 81.

144. *B.M.*, *Add. MSS*, 5461, *Sabran's Dispatches*, II, folio 375.

145. Warburton, III, pp. 171-2; Abbott, I, pp. 374-5.

146. Warburton, III, pp. 172-3.

147. *C.S.P.D.*, 1645-7, p. 126; *C.J.*, IV, p. 265.

148. Abbott, I, pp. 375-7; Warburton, III, pp. 175-6; *L.J.* VII, pp. 584ff.

149. See the rather double-edged testimony of Slingsby, one of the dissident minority, in *Somersetshire Record Society*, XVIII, p. 103.
150. Warburton, pp. 176-7.
151. Warburton, III, p. 183; *Moderate Intelligencer*, Friday, Sept. 18, 1645.
152. Abbott, I, p. 377.
153. See *Catalogue of the Thomason Tracts*, I, p. 397.
154. Henry Burton, *Truth shut out of Doors*, London, 1645 (*T.T.*, E. 311.1).
155. Walker, p. 129.
156. Warburton, III, pp. 190, 192.
157. *C.S.P.D.*, 1645-7, pp. 58-9, 72-3, 99; see also *Lord George Digby's Cabinet*.
158. *C.S.P.D.*, 1645-7, pp. 116ff, 136-7, 141-2. I regret that this poisonous scandalmonger should have been no other than Edward Walsingham whose brief biographies of John Smith and Henry Gage are among the most inspiring pamphlets issued during the war.
159. The thought behind the King's dismissal of Rupert is necessarily a matter of conjecture, but he hints in a letter to Prince Maurice (Warburton, III, p. 189) that his fears are not of a kind he can commit to paper. In view of the rumours current about Rupert during these weeks and the reports of Digby's informant in Oxford, the King's reasons can, however, be assumed with tolerable certainty. It was freely rumoured in London that Rupert and Fairfax had made peace and that Rupert would compel the King to accept it. Montreuil, I, p. 10.
160. Clarendon, Bk. IX, 90.
161. *Evelyn*, ed. Bray, IV, pp. 163-5.
162. *C.S.P.D.*, 1645-7, p. 144.
163. *Ibid.*, p. 143.
164. *Ibid.*, p. 144.
165. *B.M., Add. MSS*, 5461, *Sabran's Dispatches*, II, folios 389-90.
166. *Nicholas Papers*, ed. G. F. Warner,

Camden Society, London, 1886, I, p. 64.
167. *H.M.C., Report VIII*, Appendix, p. 212b; *Lord George Digby's Cabinet*, p. 59.
168. *Cal. Clar. S.P.*, I, p. 278.
169. *B.M., Add. MSS*, 5461, *Sabran's Dispatches*, II, folio 391; Meikle, pp. 82-3.
170. Josselin, p. 28.
171. Carte, *Letters*, I, pp. 94, 95.
172. *Clarendon State Papers*, II, pp. 188-9.
173. *C.S.P.D.*, 1645-7, p. 96; Symonds, p. 239.
174. Carte, *Letters*, I, p. 91.
175. Slingsby, pp. 168-9; Symonds, p. 242-3; Clarendon, IX, p. 119; Carte, *Letters*, I, pp. 91-2. See also R. H. Morris, *The Siege of Chester*, Chester, 1923, pp. 110-21; Malbon, *Civil War in Cheshire*, pp. 182-4.
176. Morris, *Siege of Chester*, p. 226.
177. Carte, *Letters*, I, pp. 91-3; Symonds, p. 244.
178. *C.S.P.D.*, 1645-7, pp. 161-2; *Lord George Digby's Cabinet*, p. 55.
179. *Diary of Henry Townshend*, ed. Willis Bund, *Worcestershire History Society*, London, 1920, III, p. 235.
180. Walker, p. 42; Clarendon, Bk. IX, 120-1.
181. Slingsby, pp. 170-1.
182. *C.S.P.D.*, 1645-7, pp. 164-5.
183. Abbott, I, pp. 381-3; *Peters' Relation*, London, 1645 (*T.T.*, E. 305.8).
184. Abbott, I, pp. 384-5; *Peters' Relation*; see also *The Weekly Account*, 8-15 Oct., 1645; *The Moderate Intelligencer*, 9-16 Oct., 1645 (*T.T.*, E. 304.27; E. 305.3).
185. *Peters' Relation*.
186. Abbott, I, p. 386.
187. *Josselin*, 29; *C.S.P.Ven.*, 1643-7, p. 215; Meikle, p. 119.
188. At his trial Argyll made the astonishing assertion that, in 1645, he had tried to make peace with Montrose and had been overruled by the Committee of Estates. It is possible that this incident, if genuine, occurred

some weeks earlier though after Kilsyth seems the likeliest time. *State Trials*, pp. 1427, 1449.

189. Napier, II, 233.

190. Guthry, pp. 200-3; Wishart, pp. 143-5, 413-4; *Britane's Distemper*, p. 150; Salmonet, pp. 310ff. The records of Melrose in Maidment's *Analecta Scotica*, I, pp. 108-10 indicate that a few Highlanders from Montrose's defeated army were in the common prison there some months later. Balfour (III, p. 341) records an order of the Estates for the execution of all surviving prisoners in November, 1645.

191. *Guthry*, p. 205.

192. Montrose's proclamation of a rendezvous at Dunkeld is among the *Breadalbane MSS* in *H.M. Register House*, Edinburgh. Wishart, pp. 147-8, 416.

193. *L.J.*, VII, p. 668.

194. Clarendon, Bk. IX, p. 122.

195. Walker, p. 124; *Clarendon State Papers*, II, pp. 199 seq.; *Cal. Clar. S.P.*, p. 200; *H.M.C., Ormonde MSS*, N.S., II, pp. 387-8; Clarendon, IX, 123; *The Earl of Glamorgan's Negotiations*, London, 1645 (*T.T.*, E. 328.9).

196. *H.M.C., Report VIII, Appendix*, p. 96; Warburton, III, pp. 194-5; Walker, pp. 145-6.

197. *B.M., Add. MSS*, 5461, *Sabran's Dispatches*, II, folios 398-9; *C.S.P.D.*, 1645-7, p. 190.

198. Clarendon, Bk. IX, 128; Eva Scott, *Rupert, Prince Palatine*, London, 1904, pp. 194-5.

199. Warburton, III, p. 195.

200. Walker, pp. 145-6.

201. Warburton, III, pp. 201-3.

202. Clarendon, Bk. IX, 129.

203. I follow Sir Edward Walker's account (pp. 146-8). The account in Richard Symonds (pp. 268-70) is taken very largely from a London pamphlet *The Bloodie Treaty* (*T.T.*, E. 311.27) and is annotated by Symonds himself as being inexact, though Gardiner (II, p. 374n) was of the opinion that it is substantially accurate. In it, the interchange about mutiny is much harsher:

King: By God, Digby is an honest man and they that say otherwise are traitors.

Gerrard: Then we must be all traitors.

King: You have spoke the words.

204. Walker, pp. 146-8; Symonds, pp. 269-70; *H.M.C., Ormonde MSS, New Series*, II, pp. 389-90. This last is a life of Bellasis by his secretary and tells the story from his angle with some interesting details.

205. *Cal. Clar. S.P.*, I. pp. 282ff; *A Great Victory Obtained by General Poyntz . . . at Sherborn in Yorkshire*, London, 1645 (*T.T.*, E. 305.14).

206. Bodleian Library, *Clarendon MSS*, Vol. 26, No. 2003; *Cal. Clar. S.P.*, I, pp. 283-4; *The Routing of the Lord Digby . . . at Carlisle Sands; A True Relation of the totall routing of the lord George Digby*. See also *The Earl of Glamorgan's Negotiations*, London, 1645 (*T.T.*, E. 308.7; E. 308.8; and E. 328.9).

207. *Major General Laugharne's letter . . . October 12; Two letters of Colonel Morgan relating the taking . . . of Monmouth* (*T.T.*, E. 307.14 and 15); See also E. 306.4; E. 307.7, 12 and 16; Phillips, *Civil War in Wales*, II, pp. 272-81.

208. Sprigge, pp. 143-4.

209. *C.S.P.D.*, 1645-7, pp. 212, 217.

210. Clarendon, Bk. IX, 133.

BOOK III: CHAPTER I

1. *C.J.*, IV, p. 199; W. A. Shaw, *Church of England*, Chapter IV.

2. *Nicholas Papers*, I, p. 68; Ketton Cremer, *Norfolk Gallery*, p. 109.

3. See L. E. Tanner, *Westminster School*, London, 1951, pp. 30-1.

4. **G. B.** Tatham. *The Puritans in Power*, pp. 59 seq., 204-5; Heylyn, *Aerius Redivivus*, pp. 55-6; Walker, *Sufferings of the Clergy* is the chief collective source for the expulsions. He based his work on much contemporary pamphlet and MS material; Matthews, *Walker Revised*, 1948, is a learned and very careful examination of the persecution with an attempt to arrive at a figure for the number of the extruded. The best known Puritan attack on the extruded Anglican clergy is J. White, *First Century of Scandalous Priests*, London, 1643; see also Shaw, especially Chapter IV.

5. *A Copy of a Remonstrance . . . by Thomas Goodwin, etc.*, London, 1645 (*T.T.*, E. 309.4); Baillie, II, p. 318.

6. *B.M., Add. MSS*, 5461, *Sabran's Dispatches*, II, folio 305.

7. Baillie, II, p. 185.

8. *Thomas Hawes, A Christian Relation of a Christian's Affliction*, London, 1646 (*T.T.*, E. 506.24).

9. Lilburne, *A Letter to Prynne;* Haller, *Liberty and Reformation*, p. 260.

10. See H. R. Plomer, *Secret Printing during the Civil War, The Library, New Series*, V, for an account of the clandestine presses with which Lilburne was involved.

11. For the Merchant Adventurers, see James, *Social Policy in the Interregnum*, pp. 149-50; Dietz, *Economic History*, p. 220.

12. Haller, *Liberty and Reformation*, pp. 267, 271, 274; Haller, *Tracts on Liberty*, III, pp. 257-307.

13. Haller, *Tracts on Liberty*, III, pp. 309-18; Haller, *Liberty and Reformation*, pp. 166ff.

14. *Ibid.*, pp. 282ff.

15. Haller, *Tracts on Liberty*, I, pp. 103-4.

16. Chapter XXXVIII of Gardiner's *Civil War* summarises these mainly useless plans and projects of the King.

17. Meikle, p. 129.

18. C. R. Boxer, *M. H. Tromp, Mariner's Mirror*, XL, pp. 46-7; see also M. G. de Boer, *Tromp en de Duinkerkers*, pp. 158ff.

19. *B.M., Add. MSS*, 5461, *Sabran's Dispatches*, II, folios 198f, 362f; for the treaty see Bigby, *Anglo-French Relations*, pp. 166-9.

20. *The Lord George Digby's Cabinet* (*T.T.*, E. 329.15), p. 40; *C.S.P. Ven.*, 1643-7, p. 198.

21. Aiazzi, *La Nunziatura in Irlanda di Monsignor Giovanni Battista Rinuccini*, Florence, 1844, pp. XLVIII-LI, LVIII-LXIX.

22. *Commentarius*, I, pp. 654, 680ff, 701f.

23. *Nunziatura*, p. 59; Bellings, pp. 293-7, 312-20.

24. *Nunziatura*, pp. 63-7; *Commentarius*, II, pp. 1-4.

25. *Nunziatura*, pp. 61, 68-9; *Commentarius*, II, p. 21; *C.S.P.I.*, 1633-47, p.p. 427-435.

26. *Nunziatura*, pp. 71-3; *Commentarius*, II, pp. 25-7.

27. *Commentarius*, II, p. 67; the letter was dated from Oxford in April, 1645. The text of the Glamorgan Treaty is given in *Commentarius*, II, pp. 557f.

28. *Commentarius*, II, pp. 86ff; *Nunziatura*, pp. 33, 76-8, 114.

29. *The Diplomatic Correspondence of Jean de Montreuil and the brothers de Belliévre*, 1645-1648, ed. J. G. Fotheringham, *Scottish History Society*, Edinburgh, 1898-9, I, pp. 1-3; see also Chéruel, *Lettres de Cardinal Mazarin*, Paris, 1872.

30. Baillie, II, p. 319; Meikle, pp. 141-2.

31. Balfour, III, pp. 317, 322; Baillie, II, pp. 301, 343.

32. Montreuil, I, pp. 9ff; *Thurloe State Papers*, I, pp. 71-2.

33. Baillie, II, p. 345.

34. Balfour, III, pp. 346, 352-3, 358-63; Guthry, p. 208; National Library of Scotland, Advocates Library, *MSS Memoirs of Richard Augustine Hay*, II, folio 388.

35. *Major General Poyntz's Letter*, London, 1645; *The Kingdom's Weekly Intelligencer*, 18-25 Nov. 1645 (*T.T.*, E. 309, 38 and 39).

36. Malbon, p. 189.

37. *Lancashire Civil War Tracts*, pp. 211-2.

38. *H.M.C., Portland MSS*, I, pp. 292-3; Sprigge, *Anglia Rediviva*, p. 144.

39. *H.M.C., Portland MSS*, I, p. 328; *Clarendon State Papers*, II, pp. 194-5.

40. Carte, *Letters*, I, pp. 102, 106.

41. *Cal. Clar. S.P.*, I, p. 281.

42. *A True Relation of a Great Victory*, London, 1645 (*T.T.*, E. 308.14); see also Phillips, *Civil War in Wales*.

43. R. H. Morris, *Siege of Chester*, p. 169; Phillips, *Civil War in Wales*, II, pp. 288-90; *C.S.P.D.*, 1645-7, p. 360. Lady Byron was sixteen years old and remained a famous beauty for many years; she is alleged to have been one of the mistresses of Charles II during the exile.

44. *Clarendon State Papers*, II, pp. 195-6; *Prince Rupert's Journal*, p. 740; Bodleian Library, *MSS, Clarendon Papers*, Vol. 26. No. 2043.

45. Josselin, *Diary*, p. 31.

46. Birch, *Memoirs*, pp. 29-30; *H.M.C., Portland MSS*, I, pp. 328-9; *A New Trick to take Towns* and *Several Letters from Colonel Morgan and Colonel Birch*, London, 1645 (*T.T.*, E. 314.12 and E. 313.17); Webb, *Civil War in Herefordshire*, II, pp. 251-4, 701ff gives *A New Trick* and Scudamore's defence of his conduct.

47. Walker, *Sufferings of the Clergy*, II, p. 34; Croft became Bishop of Hereford soon after the Restoration and was as fearless in criticism of the morals of Charles II, as he had been of the manners of the Puritan soldiers, and in much the same way. Burnet records: "He used much freedom with the King, but it was in the wrong place, not in private, but in the pulpit." A relief depicting his defiance of the Roundheads is on the restored West front of Hereford Cathedral.

48. For Colonel Washington's ferocious defence of Worcester, see *The Diary of Henry Townshend, Worcester History Society Publications*, I; the quotation occurs on p. 194.

49. *A Full Relation of the Desperate Design for Betraying Monmouth*, London, 1645 (*T.T.*, E. 308.19).

50. *H.M.C., Portland MSS*, I, pp. 320-1; *A True Relation of a Boy*, London, 1645 (*T.T.*, E. 311.12).

51. *B.M., Add. MSS*, 18981, *Prince Rupert's Correspondence*, folio 15.

52. *C.S.P.D.*, 1645-7, pp. 267-8.

53. The Oxford English Dictionary gives the earliest use of "highwayman" in 1649. James (Jemmy) Hinde has an article in the Dictionary of National Biography; a few more details are given in my article "Captain Hinde the Highwayman" reprinted in *Truth and Opinion*, London, 1961.

54. Carte, *Ormonde*, VI, pp. 328-9.

55. G. Albion, *Charles I and Rome*, Appendix X, p. 423.

56. *Clarendon State Papers*, II, p. 289; Clarendon, Bk. IX, 112.

57. *Clarendon State Papers*, II, pp. 196-7.

58. *C.S.P.D.*, 1645-7, p. 248; Rushworth, IV, i, p. 217.

59. *C.S.P.D.*, 1645-7, pp. 279-80; Rushworth, IV, i. p. 218.

60. J. Bruce, *Charles I in 1646*, Camden Society, London, 1856, p. 5; Montreuil, I, pp. 94-5.

61. Montreuil, I, pp. 66, 73, 96-9; *Clarendon State Papers*, II, pp. 209-10, 211-3; *H.M.C., Portland MSS*, I, pp. 323ff.

62. *L.J.*, VIII, p. 103.

63. *Lord George Digby's Cabinet*, p. 13. It has been argued that Ormonde really knew Glamorgan's plans throughout, but thought it wise to pretend ignorance. The chief evidence for this is the letter of recommendation (Birch, *Inquiry*, p. 62) which he

wrote to Lord Muskerry, in August, 1645, about Glamorgan. But the letter proves nothing beyond the fact that Ormonde, at the time, believed Glamorgan to be assisting him sincerely in making a treaty. Given the characters of the two men, it seems more probable that Glamorgan deceived Ormonde than that Ormonde knew what Glamorgan was about.

64. *Nunziatura*, p. 76; *Commentarius*, II, pp. 88-9.

65. Carte, *Ormonde*, VI, pp. 337-8; *Clarendon State Papers*, II, p. 346; T. Birch, *Inquiry*, p. 93; *The Earl of Glamorgan's Negotiations* (*T.T.*, E. 328.9) pp. 10, 33.

66. *C.J.*, IV, p. 409; Montreuil, pp. 114-5.

67. *L.J.*, VIII, pp. 123-4; Gardiner, III, p. 44.

68. *L.J.*, VIII, pp. 132-3.

69. Carte, *Ormonde*, V, p. 16; VI, pp. 347-9.

70. Dircks, p. 134.

71. *C.S.P.I.*, 1633-47, p. 426; Carte, *Ormonde*, VI, p. 553; Hynes, pp. 47-8; *Commentarius*, II, pp. 102-5.

72. *Nunziatura*, pp. 88-9.

73. *Ibid.*, pp. 96-7, 459; *Commentarius*, II, pp. 118ff.

74. *H.M.C.*, *Report VII, Appendix III*, p. 236.

75. *Cal. Clar. S.P.*, I, p. 304; *Clarendon State Papers*, II, p. 209; Carte, *Ormonde*, VI, p. 356.

76. *H.M.C.*, *Rawdon Papers*, II, p. 137; Morris, *Siege of Chester*, pp. 192-5.

77. Carte, *Ormonde*, VI, p. 356; *Clarendon State Papers*, II, p. 209.

78. Clarendon, Bk. IX, 107, 110, 133.

79. *Fairfax Correspondence*, III, p. 275.

80. Clarendon, Bk. IX, 134-5, 141; Carte, *Letters*, I, pp. 107, 109-10; *Cal. Clar. S.P.*, I, pp. 238-9.

81. Carte, *Letters*, I, pp. 137-8; *L.J.*, VIII, pp. 117, 121.

82. Peter, *God's Doing, Man's Duty*, p. 23.

83. *C.S.P.D.*, 1645-7, pp. 336-7; *L.J.*, VIII, pp. 123-4.

84. Clarendon, Bk. IX, 139, 142, 143; Carte, *Letters*, I, pp. 113, 116, 140-1; *Fairfax Correspondence*, III, p. 285.

85. Whitelocke, pp. 200-202; *Clarke Papers*, ed. C. H. Firth, *Camden Society*, London, 1891, I, p. 422; *The Earl of Glamorgan's Negotiations*, London, 1645 (*T.T.*, E. 328-8). For Hugh Peter's part in winning over the Cornish see Coate, pp. 206-9; Stearns, pp. 269ff.

86. Carte, *Letters*, I, pp. 117-8.

87. Sprigge, p. 205.

88. Carte, *Letters*, I, pp. 118f; *Fairfax Correspondence*, III, p. 287; Sprigge, pp. 209-17.

89. *Clarendon State Papers*, II, p. 228.

90. *Charles I in 1646*, pp. 14-16, 20.

91. *H.M.C.*, *Portland MSS*, I, pp. 351-2.

92. Dugdale, *Diary*, p. 84.

93. *H.M.C.*, *Report XIII, Ancaster MSS*, pp. 172-4.

94. *Clarendon State Papers*, II, pp. 226, 227.

95. *Charles I in 1646*, pp. 21, 22.

96. *C.J.*, IV, pp. 462-3.

97. *Ibid.*, p. 479.

98. Dircks, pp. 162-3.

99. *Charles I in 1646*, pp. 24-5.

100. Rushworth, VI, p. 140; *L.J.*, VIII, p. 231; Birch, *Memoirs*, pp. 34-5.

101. *Charles I in 1646*, pp. 28-9.

102. *Ibid.*, p. 28.

103. *L.J.*, VIII, pp. 248, 255-6; *C.J.*, IV, pp. 497, 498-9; *Acts and Ordinances*, I, pp. 841-2.

104. *Clarendon State Papers*, II, pp. 218-20.

105. *Charles I in 1646*, p. 31.

106. *Ibid.*, p. 37.

107. *Nunziatura*, p. 146; *B.M.*, *Harleian MSS*, 6988, folio 121, Charles I to Glamorgan, 6 April 1646.

108. Carte, *Ormonde*, VI, pp. 362-3.

109. *Charles I in 1646*, pp. 100-1; Napier, II, pp. 274-5.

110. Meikle, p. 170; *L.J.*, VIII, pp. 216-20, 258.

111. *C.J.*, IV, p. 507.

112. *C.J.*, IV, pp. 485, 506, 519-20.
113. *Cal. Clar. S.P.*, II, p. 311.
114. *Charles I in 1646*, p. 36; *H.M.C.*, *Portland MSS*, I, p. 376.
115. *Fairfax Correspondence*, III, p. 290; *C.S.P.D.*, 1645-7, pp. 416-7.
116. *Cal. Clar. S.P.*, II, p. 229; H. Cary, *Memorials of the Great Civil War*, London, 1842, I, pp. 45-6.
117. *Life and Works of Henry Mainwaring*, Navy Records Society, I, p. 313; Jean Chevalier, *Journal*, ed. Messervy, *Société Jersiaise*, St. Helier, 1914, pp. 286f.
118. *Memoirs of Lady Fanshawe*, London, 1907, p. 42; Chevalier, p. 328.
119. S. E. Hoskins, *Charles II in the Channel Islands*, London, 1854, I, p. 231.
120. Hoskins, I, pp. 273-5.
121. *A Late Victory obtained . . . near Farrington*, London, 1646 (*T.T.*, E. 330.21).
122. *Charles I in 1646*, pp. 36-7; Montreuil, I, pp. 178-80; *Cal. Clar. S.P.*, II, pp. 222-3.
123. Cary, *Memorials*, pp. 1-4; *Cal. Clar. S.P.*, II, p. 229; *A Narrative by John Ashburnham of his attendance on King Charles I*, London, 1830, I, pp. 78-9.
124. *Charles I in 1646*, pp. 37-8.
125. Abbott, I, p. 401.
126. Peter, *God's Doing, Man's Duty*, p. 24.
127. Meikle, p. 179; *C.J.*, IV, p. 527.
128. Rushworth, IV, I, p. 267.
129. *Ibid.*, pp. 268-9.
130. *Ibid.*, p. 268; Montreuil, II, p. 580; Meikle, p. 180-1; *C.J.*, IV, pp. 539-40.

BOOK III: CHAPTER II

1. Saintsbury, *Minor Poets of the Caroline Period*, Oxford, 1921, III, p. 54.
2. Cary, *Memorials*, I, p. 12.
3. *H.M.C.*, *Portland MSS*, I, pp. 371, 375, 383-4; Peck, *Desiderata Curiosa*, II, pp. 347f, 358-62; Peckard, *Life of Nicholas Ferrar*, Cambridge, 1797, p. 227.
4. Meikle, pp. 202-3.
5. *Ibid.*, p. 183; *H.M.C.*, *Portland MSS*, I, p. 378; Montreuil, p. 190.
6. Clarendon, Bk. X, 35; the full text, of which I give only a part, was II Samuel 19, 41-43.
7. Montreuil, I, pp. 190-1.
8. Montreuil, I, p. 199; *H.M.C.*, *Portland MSS*, I, pp. 369-75.
9. Montreuil, p. 197; Ashburnham, *Narrative*, I, pp. 85-5; *Charles I in 1646*, p. 39.
10. Rushworth, VI, pp. 274-5; *Evelyn*, ed. Bray, IV, p. 176; Whitelocke, p. 212; *L.J.*, VIII, 328, 329, 332.
11. Clarendon, Bk. IX, p. 161; *Charles I in 1646*, pp. 40-3.
12. Spottiswoode had surrendered to Lanark at Philiphaugh, but was denied the rights of a prisoner of war. Lanark does not appear to have entered any protest. Lanark's lamentable conduct is glossed over by Burnet in a more than usually disingenuous passage of his *Lives*.
13. Montreuil, I, pp. 199-200.
14. *H.M.C.*, *Report X, Appendix I*, p. 56; *Perfect Occurrences*, 16 Oct., 1646 (*T.T.*, E. 513.18).
15. Balfour, III, p. 319; Guthry, p. 214; Wishart, 166, 425-6.
16. *Britane's Distemper*, pp. 169 seq.; *Wardlaw MS*, p. 313; *New Spalding Club Miscellany*, II, p. 392; Napier, II, pp. 263-70, 272-3; Wishart, Chapter XX.
17. Blair, p. 101; *A Declaration against a late dangerous and seditious Band* (*T.T.*, E. 330.6); *Wardlaw MS*, Edinburgh, 1646, p. 315.
18. *Ibid.*, pp. 315-6.
19. References to his feelings of guilt about Strafford are frequent in the King's letters at this date.
20. Napier, II, p. 277; *Wardlaw MS*, p. 318.
21. *Charles I in 1646*, p. 49.
22. *Life of Mr. Robert Blair*, ed. M'Crie,

Woodrow Society, Edinburgh, 1848, p. 103.

23. *Charles I in 1646*, pp. 46-7.

24. Rushworth, VI, pp. 266-7, 272-5; *L.J.*, VIII, pp. 365-6; Meikle, p. 192.

25. Carte, *Ormonde*, VI, p. 392; Napier, II, pp. 280-1.

26. Rushworth, VI, pp. 275-6; *L.J.*, VIII, p. 374.

27. *Ibid.*, VI, pp. 399-401; *Nunziatura*, pp. 139, 186-9; *Commentarius*, II, pp. 247-8; Coonan, pp. 222-4, 225.

28. *C.S.P.I.*, 1633-47, pp. 477, 479.

29. Dugdale, *Diary*, p. 89.

30. Abbott, I, pp. 401, 416.

31. Rushworth, VI, pp. 280-5.

32. Rushworth, VI, pp. 309-17.

33. Burnet, *Lives*, p. 278; Meikle, pp. 188, 195.

34. Rushworth, VI, pp. 298-300.

35. *Charles I in 1646*, pp. 53-4; Ashburnham, II, p. 141.

36. *C.S.P.D.*, 1645-7, p. 458.

37. Dircks, p. 174.

38. Rushworth, VI, pp. 286-7.

39. Carte, *Ormonde*, VI, p. 370; Dircks, pp. 168-170; *Commentarius*, pp. 124, 158-61; *Nunziatura*, p. 129.

40. Carte, *Ormonde*, VI, pp. 371-2; Clarendon, Bk. X, 13, 14; Chevalier, p. 300.

41. Carte, *Ormonde*, VI, pp. 395; Cary, I, pp. 33, 77.

42. *C.S.P., Ven.*, 1643-7, p. 264; *Nunziatura*, p. 146; Ranke, *Englische Geschichte*, Berlin, 1859 seq., VIII, p. 173.

43. Clarendon, Bk. X, 43-4; Chevalier, pp. 336f; *Clarendon State Papers*, II, pp. 238-40.

44. Carte, *Ormonde*, VI, pp. 415-16; *C.S.P.I.*, 1633-47, p. 401.

45. *C.S.P.I.*, 1633-47, p. 485; *Nunziatura*, pp. 131, 151; *Commentarius*, II, pp. 300-18.

46. Burnet, pp. 279-80, 281; Guthry, p. 224.

47. Ranke, VIII, pp. 169-74.

48. Ranke, VIII, pp. 175-81.

49. *Clarendon State Papers*, II, pp. 242-3.

50. Whitelocke, p. 223.

51. Rushworth, VI, pp. 319, 20.

52. *L.J.*, VIII, p. 461; Baillie, II, pp. 386-91.

53. *Charles I in 1646*, pp. 56-7; Burnet, pp. 183-4.

54. *H.M.C.*, *Hamilton MSS*, p. 107.

55. Burnet, p. 283.

56. Baillie, II, pp. 383, 392.

57. Holles, *Memoirs*, London, 1699, pp. 4-5.

58. Brunton and Pennington, *Members of the Long Parliament*, pp. 24, 192-41.

59. *Ibid.*, pp. 24-9, 35.

60. Haller, *Liberty and Reformation*, p. 278; *C.J.*, IV, pp. 555-6; *L.J.*, VIII, p. 332.

61. *C.J.*, IV, p. 561; see also *The Humble Acknowledgment*, London, 1646 (*T.T.*, E. 339.12).

62. *C.J.*, IV, p. 569; Clarendon, Bk. X, 69.

63. Haller, *Liberty and Reformation*, pp. 263-5; M. A. Gibb, pp. 147-9; Lilburne, *Just Man's Justification*.

64. M. A. Gibb, p. 194.

65. Haller, *Liberty and Reformation*, pp. 284-5; Walwyn, *Pearl in a Dunghill*.

66. Mildmay, *Diary*, p. 113.

67. Malbon, pp. 207-10; *L.J.*, VIII, p. 401.

68. *Clark Papers*, I, p. 423; Haller, *Liberty and Reformation*, p. 256.

69. *C.S.P.I.*, 1633-47, p. 475.

70. G. Penn, *Memorials of Penn*, I, pp. 163ff; *Commentarius*, II, p. 270; see also *Nunziatura*, pp. 144-6.

71. *C.J.*, IV, pp. 631-2.

72. Baillie, II, p. 383; *Cal. Clar. S.P.*, I, p. 318.

73. John Wilkins the famous mathematician was protected by him.

74. Burnet, *Lives*, p. 283; *C.J.*, IV, p. 644; Abbott, I, p. 410.

75. Baillie, pp. 298, 368.

76. The authority for Henderson's last advice is *The Declaration of Mr. Alexander Henderson, made upon his death-bed* (*T.T.*, E. 443.1). This was published in London in May, 1648,

with an evident propaganda purpose and was condemned in the following August by the General Assembly of the Church of Scotland as a forgery. At the time of Henderson's death it was widely reported that he had been shaken and moved by the King's evident sincerity, a report fiercely contradicted by other Covenanting ministers including Baillie. On the evidence of the papers exchanged between Charles and Henderson at Newcastle, I am inclined to accept these rumours as basically true—the very vehemence of the denials suggests that the stories were near to the facts—and to believe that the death-bed declaration, though probably improved to suit the Royalist propaganda of 1648, is in general outline much what Henderson actually said. See also R. L. Orr, *Alexander Henderson*, London, 1919.

77. *Archaeologia Aeliana, New Series*, XXI, p. 124.
78. *Cal. Clar. S.P.*, II, July-August, 1646, *passim; Charles I in 1646*, p. 65.
79. Burnet, pp. 285-9.
80. *Mercurius Civicus*, Sept. 10-17, 1646 (*T.T.*, E. 354.12).
81. Carte, *Ormonde*, V, p. 17.
82. *Nunziatura*, pp. 145-6.
83. *Commentarius*, II, pp. 318f, 324f.
84. Carte, *Ormonde*, VI, p. 496; *Clarendon State Papers*, II, p. 252; *H.M.C., Egmont MSS*, I, I, p. 308; *Commentarius*, II, pp. 354, 364.
85. *C.S.P.I.*, 1633-47, pp. 497-8; *H.M.C., Egmont MSS*, I, I, p. 310; Dircks, pp. 175-7, 178-9; this devoted biographer of Glamorgan prints within a few pages of each other his hero's written oath to the Nuncio to cross the designs of Ormonde at every point, and his protestation of ignorance and innocence to Ormonde himself. His subsequent comment on Glamorgan's conduct is that, whoever else may have been

guilty of deceit in Ireland, Glamorgan was not. I know of few biographers who go quite so far as this in rejecting the evidence of their own researches.

86. *The Irish Papers containing Lord Digby's Letter*, London, 1646 (*T.T.*, E. 355.26).
87. Carte, *Ormonde*, VI, p. 497; *Nunziatura*, p. 161; *Commentarius*, I, pp. 283-4; see D. F. Cregan, *Daniel O'Neill*, in *Irish Historical Studies*, II, pp. 405-6 for the approaches made to Owen Roe on behalf of Ormonde.
88. *Nunziatura*, pp. 161-2.
89. *Ibid.*, p. 163.
90. Carte, *Ormonde*, VI, p. 449.
91. *Nunziatura*, pp. 114-5.
92. *Ibid.*, pp. 148-9.
93. *Ibid.*, pp. 162, 167.
94. Castlehaven, p. 113.
95. *C.S.P.I.*, 1633-47, p. 499.
96. Carte, *Ormonde*, VI, pp. 435-6.
97. Baillie, II, p. 401; *H.M.C., Hamilton MSS*, pp. 113-4.
98. Whitelocke, p. 233; *An Elegie upon the Earle of Essex Funerall*, London, 1646 (*T.T.*, E. 359.11); *L.J.*, VIII, p. 653.
99. *C.J.*, IV, pp. 493, 659.
100. See H. R. Plomer, *Secret Printing during the Civil War. The Library*, New Series, V; Frank, *Levellers*, p. 84; Haller, *Liberty and Reformation*, pp. 301-2; *Haller Tracts*, III, p. 353.
101. Haller, *Liberty and Reformation*, pp. 279-82; Overton, *Arrow against all Tyrants;* and *Commons Complaint*, in *Haller Tracts*, III.
102. Haller, *Liberty and Reformation*, pp. 268-9; Lilburne, *London's Liberty in Chains*, pp. 2-5.
103. *Dictionary of National Biography*.
104. *Clarendon State Papers*, II, p. 265; Burnet, pp. 381-386.
105. *Clarendon State Papers*, II, p. 267.
106. Baillie, II, p. 368; see also Argyll's defence at his trial in *State Trials*, pp. 1465-6.

107. Baillie, II, p. 385.
108. Meikle, pp. 203-4.
109. Meikle, p. 206.
110. *Ibid.*, pp. 207, 214.
111. *Ibid.*, pp. 207, 213, 215.
112. *Ibid.*, pp. 217-8; *C.J.*, IV, p. 672; Rushworth, IV, I, pp. 329-336.
113. *L.J.*, VIII, p. 515. *Acts and Ordinances*, I, pp. 907-8.
114. Meikle, p. 218.
115. Rushworth, IV, I, p. 329; Burnet, *Lives*, pp. 289-90.
116. *Britane's Distemper*, pp. 194-6; Rushworth, IV, I, p. 332.
117. Rutherford, *Testimony*, Lanark, 1739, p. 6.
118. *Clarendon State Papers*, II, pp. 271-3, 297; *Charles I in 1646*, pp. 91-2.
119. *C.S.P. Ven.*, 1643-7, p. 292; *Perfect Occurrences*, 23 Oct., 1646 (*T.T.*, E. 358.17); Gardiner, III, 170-1.
120. *Reliquiae Baxterianae*, ed. M. Sylvester, London, 1696, p. 56.
121. *A Perfect Diurnall*, 16-23 Nov., 1646 (*T.T.*, E. 513.25); *C.J.*, Nov. 16.
122. Rushworth, IV, I, pp. 388-9; Ludlow, I, pp. 144-5; *Reliquiae Baxterianae*, p. 57.
123. *Charles I in 1646*, pp. 77-81.
124. *H.M.C.*, *Hamilton MSS*, pp. 128, 131.
125. *Ibid.*, p. 134.
126. Burnet, *Lives*, pp. 302-3.
127. *Archaeologia Aeliana, New Series*, XXI, p. 133.
128. Chéruel, pp. 334-7.
129. *Clarendon State Papers*, II, p. 314; Montreuil, I, p. 319.
130. This was the defence he put forward at his trial in 1661. *State Trials*, pp. 1398, 1466.
131. Montreuil, I, p. 349.
132. Burnet, pp. 306-7; *Thurloe State Papers*, I, p. 74; Montreuil, I, p. 374.
133. Burnet, p. 307.
134. Rushworth, IV, I, p. 393.
135. *C.J.*, V, pp. 26-7.
136. Montreuil, pp. 347, 401; *Clarendon State Papers*, II, p. 324; for additional details see C. S. Terry, *Alexander Leslie*, pp. 428ff and Alex. Robertson, *Robert Moray*, Edinburgh, 1912.
137. *Records of Elgin*, II, p. 255.
138. Montreuil, I, p. 392.
139. Dalrymple, *Memorials*, I, p. 191.
140. Carte, *Ormonde*, V, pp. 18-19.
141. *H.M.C.*, *Egmont MSS*, I, p. 337; Carte, *Ormonde*, VI, pp. 441, 457-62; *C.S.P.I.*, 1633-47, pp. 544, 549.
142. *Commentarius*, II, pp. 416ff.
143. Ranke, VIII, p. 187.
144. *Archaeologia Aeliana*, XXI, p. 143 n.
145. Napier, II, pp. 300-1.
146. Whitelocke, p. 241.
147. Montreuil, I, pp. 438-9.
148. Nedham, *Digitus Dei*, London, 1649.
149. Blencowe, *Sydney Papers*, London, 1825, p. 4.
150. *C.J.*, V, p. 34; Abbott, pp. 420-1.
151. Haller, *Tracts*, II, p. 390-1; Haller, *Liberty and Reformation*, p. 280.
152. Argyll, *Maxims of State*, 1661, p. 169.
153. Peter, *God's Doing, Man's Duty*, p. 44.
154. Haller, *Tracts*, III.
155. Walwyn, *England's Lamentable Slaverie*, in Haller, *Tracts*, III.
156. Selden, *Table Talk*, p. 95.
157. Haller, *Tracts*, III, p. 269.

INDEX

INDEX

Aberdeen, taken by Montrose, 375-6

Abingdon, Rupert attacks, 404-5

Aboyne, Viscount, (James Gordon), 178, 186, 213, 282, 497

Accommodation Order, 367-8

Adwalton Moor, battle of, 224

Airlie, Earl of, (John Ogilvie), 97, 366, 480

Alford, battle of, 476-7

Alresford, battle of, 302-5

Alton, battle of, 281

Anne of Austria, Queen-regent of France, 268, 269, 520-1, 610

Antrim, Earl of, (Randall Macdonnell), 293, 318, 372; involved in Irish rising, 26, 75, 92-3; taken prisoner, 109, 240; at York, 213; offers troops to the King, 282-3, 291, 307, 316, 317, 351

Argyll, Marquis of, (Archibald Campbell), 64, 150, 478; character and policy, 94-6, 108-9, 313-14, 511, 560-1, 613; relations with the King, 65, 591, 602, 603, 608, 609; with the English, 250, 563, 567, 574; with Montrose, 240; lends money, 258; manifesto of, 287-8; quells the Gordon rising, 276, 314-7; prepares to suppress Irish invasion, 351, 363-4; operations against Montrose, 366-7, 376-7, 391, 394, 412-6, 479-81; in Ireland, 558

Army (Parliamentarian), discipline and organisation, 115, 120, 197-9,

211, 396; disorder and distress, 368-9, 383-4, 422; New Model formed, 399, 411, 418-20, 430, 432-4; discontent in, 438, 587-9, 606-7; reputation, 457, 473; Independents in, 513, 577, 579-80

Army (Royalist), discipline and organisation, 120-1, 203-8, 211; re-organisation (1644) 355-7, 381-2, 406-7; disorders of, 443, 499-500, 502-4, 531-2

Arundel Castle, besieged, 288-9

Arundel, Sir John, 170, 541, 564

Ashburnham, John, 450, 554-5, 557, 568, 572, 591

Ashburnham, William, 42

Ashley-Cooper, Anthony, 273, 372, 405

Assheton, Sir Ralph, 187, 203, 210

Astley, Sir Jacob (later Lord) 136, 205, 311, 530, 531, 544

Aston, Sir Arthur, 193, 194, 406

Aubigny, Lord, (George Stuart), 140; widow of, 218-9

Aubrey, John, 164

Auchinbreck (Duncan Campbell), 415-6

Audley, Mervyn, 474

Audley, Thomas, 166

Auldearn, battle of, 460-1

Baillie, Robert, letters quoted, 274-5, 297-8, 299, 344, 346-7, 361, 363,